EUROPE'S WONDERFUL LITTLE HOTELS AND INNS

EUROPE'S WONDERFUL LITTLE HOTELS AND INNS

FOURTH EDITION

edited by

HILARY RUBINSTEIN

illustrated by
Ray Evans

Congdon & Lattès   New York

Fourth Edition, copyright © 1982 by Hilary Rubinstein Books Ltd
Illustrations copyright © 1982 by Ray Evans
Maps copyright © 1982 by Consumers' Association

ISBN 0-86553-034-3
ISBN 0-312-92191-8 (St Martin's Press)

LIBRARY OF CONGRESS CATALOG CARD NO.: 81-71623

Rubinstein, Hilary
  Europe's wonderful little hotels & inns.

NY : Congdon & Lattès, Inc.
576 p.
8203   811202

Originally published in England as *The Good Hotel Guide 1982*
by Consumers' Association and Hodder & Stoughton

Published by Congdon & Lattès, Inc
Distributed by St Martin's Press
Published simultaneously in Canada by Thomas Nelson & Sons Ltd

Printed in the United States of America

First Printing

Contents

Acknowledgments

A Guide of this kind owes an immeasurable debt to its correspondents. We reply to every letter personally, but often feel apologetic that a generous set of reports, the fruit of much time and trouble, gets no more than a postcard acknowledgment. This page gives us an opportunity to express our perennial gratitude to all who write to us, whether they are simply endorsing an existing entry, or complaining that we had no business to include such a dump, or telling us of some new discovery which deserves to be a candidate the following year. Only those correspondents who are recommending or endorsing an entry get their names printed in the text, but there is a vast troop of writers who are not named but have helped to keep the Guide up to the mark.

Once again, Caroline Raphael has played an invaluable role throughout the year in ways large and small, and, most notably, in the thankless chore of checking every factual detail. Whatever the problem, she is resourceful, conscientious and unfailingly cheerful. She has been assisted during the busy season by Anne Abel Smith, Debbie Campbell and Uli Lloyd-Pack, who systematically assembled the nuts and bolts of each entry from the thousands of questionnaires, brochures, tariffs and menus which reach us in the course of our selection of entries and writing of copy; Anne Abel Smith also undertook the herculean task of typing the final draft.

Particular thanks are due to John Ardagh for help and advice in the preparation of the French section and to Derek Cooper for similar help with the Scottish. Others who have contributed with special generosity to individual sections include Michael Stevens, Anne Bolt, Charles Acton, Jeff Driver and D S Smith. We are also very grateful to Thea Brand for contributing this year's appendix.

Tourist Offices – with one or two dishonourable exceptions – have been extremely helpful in providing official hotel lists and dealing with awkward queries. The Editor would also like to thank *Holiday Which?* and *The Good Food Guide* for much valuable co-operation. The Guide is independently edited, but it has benefited greatly from advice from both these Consumers' Association publications.

Finally, a word of thanks to the Editor's family, who with cheerful patience have put up with the intrusion of so much hotel small-talk into their daily lives.

Introduction

For new readers

This is the fourth American edition of an annual guide to hotels in Britain and the continent of Western Europe that are of unusual character and quality. It is published in Britain (it's the fifth edition there) as *The Good Hotel Guide*. The entries are based on reports from readers who write to us when they come across a hotel which has given them out-of-the-ordinary satisfaction, and who also send us their comments, critical or appreciative, when they visit places already included in the Guide. Our task is to collate these reports, check and verify them, making inspections where necessary, and select those which we consider make the grade. No cash changes hands at any point: contributors are not rewarded for writing to us; hotels do not pay for their entries; the editor and his staff accept no free hospitality.

The Guide operates on the same principle as *The Good Food Guide,* but is independently owned and edited. We have no say in the hotels and restaurants chosen by our sibling publication, nor are they involved in our choices. But we are keen to share our correspondence where appropriate, and, unless asked not to, we will pass on to *The Good Food Guide* reports on any British hotel where the restaurant is an important feature. Hotels which are included in the 1982 *Good Food Guide* have the initials 'GFG' in brackets after the hotel's name.

The hotels in the book cover a wide range. People want different things from a hotel according to whether they are making a single night stop or spending a whole holiday in one place, whether they have young children with them, whether they are visiting a city or staying in the remote countryside, and according to their age and means. We make no claims of universal compatibility or comprehensiveness, but we hope that our descriptions will help you to find good hotels that suit your tastes, needs and purse. If an entry has misled you, we hope you will use one of the report forms at the back of the book, and tell us in order that we can do better next time; and we hope equally that, if you have found the Guide useful and a hotel has fulfilled your expectations, you will also write to us: endorsements and criticisms are both essential if the Guide is to achieve its purpose. A hotel is dropped unless we get positive feedback.

The first five years

In the Introduction to the first edition, we wrote:

> How do people find their good hotels? Brochures are an aid, but are often deceptive. Travel agents can sometimes be helpful if they specialize in particular localities, but they often only know at recent first-hand

a fraction of the hotels on their books. Michelin is an invaluable touring companion, especially to the gourmet, but all those conventional signs, useful though they are, can tell us almost nothing about the feel of a place. By far the most reliable way to choose a hotel is by word-of-mouth recommendation. This Guide, if it achieves its purpose, is the word-of-mouth made print.

It would be presumptuous to claim five years later that the Guide *has* achieved its purpose – we are conscious of many shortcomings and we particularly wish we had more budget-priced hotels to recommend in cities – but we are encouraged to think that we have been on the right lines from the growing number of people sending in reports, with an over-whelming preponderance of comments on existing entries being favourable. There has been a particularly large increase in our postbag this past year, perhaps due to our having introduced Freepost on our Report Forms last year. In consequence, this edition has 30% more entries than the 1981 Guide – there are nearly 700 entries this year compared with about 550 last year (our first edition contained a modest 305). The biggest single increase is in the French section, which now has more entries than England and Wales combined – a result in part of the favourable exchange rate, in part an indication of a shift in where people are taking their holidays, and in part a tribute to the flair shown by so many French hoteliers. We are also glad to say that the sections on Scandinavia and the Low Countries, which up till now have been woefully weak, are at last beginning to look less arbitrary and perfunctory. Northern Ireland, Finland, Hungary and Luxembourg are represented for the first time.

The inspection system which we inaugurated last year with the generous assistance of Consumers' Association has been extended. Inspections have been carried out in eight countries on the continent as well as in the United Kingdom and Ireland. We do not aim to visit every hotel in the Guide – a prohibitively expensive operation, and unnecessary in view of the extent of readers' feedback. But we do try to inspect hotels on which reports are ambivalent or inadequate.

The domestic entries have in fact grown little in the past two years, with the only significant increase, this year as last, being in Scotland. We don't consider the growth of Scottish entries an accident, but believe that the Scots often show in their hotels, as in other contexts, a particular grace in hospitality. In general, as perhaps one might expect, the warmly welcoming family-run hotel is more likely to be found away from the main tourist centres, with all their obvious temptations to exploit the seasonal invaders. Some of the most attractive hotels in the Guide are in the Hebrides.

We hope that the Guide, in the course of time, may help to improve the standards of domestic hotels as unquestionably *The Good Food Guide* has done for restaurants in its three decades of monitoring British restaurant cooking. We certainly do not expect any sudden changes for the better, but are encouraged by the large number of hotel owners who evidently care a great deal about being in the Guide and are sensitive to what we write about their shortcomings. Hotels up till now have been largely immune from critical attention. Only too often, the rapturous report of a hotel in a newspaper column derives from a journalistic freeload: few of us can write objectively about a hotel's shortcomings or even be aware of them when we have been the recipient of free hospitality.

Hard Times

In our 1981 Introduction, we spoke of an 'appallingly difficult' year for hotels. Inflation and recession have regrettably shown no signs of abating, and hotels almost everywhere in Europe, after many years of prosperity, have continued to face a decline in trade. Chain hotels, and those which belong to energetic marketing associations, are to some extent cushioned against depression, and hotels catering for package tours have enjoyed a modest boom in Spain and Greece. But the small independent hotel – like most in the Guide – is especially vulnerable to adverse trade winds. A few of the more choice but unconventional establishments in remote areas – including *Penlan Oleu* at Llanychaer, one of last year's Six of the Best – have closed their doors, and we fear there will be more closures again this year. We must repeat our 1981 warning always to check out the latest tariff at the time of booking, and even, perhaps, be prepared to find that the hotel of your choice has gone out of business.

A feature of our postbag this year has been the number of complaints from readers about lost deposits. More and more hotels are asking for deposits these days to minimize losses from 'no shows', but some of our correspondents have been surprised not to have had their money refunded if they have had to cancel their visit. We wish hotels would take more trouble than they normally do to spell out the conditions of a booking, but in general we think you should expect to lose your deposit if you cancel, irrespective of whether a hotel is full and could let the room to another party or not. The hotel that is empty needs the deposit most – never more so than in 1982. And you can always take out an insurance policy.

Another corollary of the present dismal economic climate is that, more than ever, the hotel of unusual quality needs all the support it can get. The line about not wanting to let on about your favourite hotel because, once it gets known, you will never get in again, has never cut much ice with the hotelier and now seems more threadbare than ever. If you are a satisfied customer, you will be doing yourself as well as the hotel a service by sending the Guide an account of your experiences.

Relais hotels

We referred above to marketing associations. There are many ways in which independent hotels can link themselves to others, nationally or internationally, to achieve promotional benefits such as the advertising of bargain breaks as well perhaps as to take advantage of bulk buying. Sometimes these groups are decidedly heterogeneous: we were surprised to find a *très soigné* country inn in the Ardennes belonging to an association which also contained a businessman's motel on the Coventry ring road. Others, like the self-explanatory *Relais de Silence* or the budget MinOtel group, have a useful unifying theme. But there is one association, French-based, but with constituents throughout the world, which has elevated itself to a unique position – the Relais et Châteaux hotels. So successful has been their PR that many people choose their holidays exclusively from the lavish Relais catalogue.

Relais hotels claim to display five Cs – character, courtesy, calm, comfort and cuisine. They are mostly small and in the country. They are exclusive in the sense that they black-ball candidates whom they consider are below their par, and a hotel pays a high price for membership. Since

9

their criteria are similar to the Guide's, they look like prima facie Guide material at the upper end of the market.

How much can you depend on a Relais hotel? Readers' reports, and our own observations, suggest that you can be sure that a Relais hotel will be well-maintained and sophisticated in its decor, and that it will be relatively or absolutely expensive, but that it would be rash to count on anything else. Some of the best hotels in the Guide are Relais, but there are many others which fall a long way short of qualifying. They can be models of courtesy to all-comers, but they can also be monsters of disdain to those they consider are inadequately heeled. Some have three-star kitchens; others serve meals which are disgraceful at their price. Once a hotel has been admitted to the association, no great efforts are made to ensure that standards are maintained, and hotels are rarely expelled. To sum up, a hotel is as good as it is, and a Relais logo on the notepaper or a Relais flag flying from a rooftop, should not, in itself, be regarded as an imprimatur of excellence.

Why are British hotels prices so high?
The British Tourist Authority will not thank us for returning to this abrasive topic since they took public issue with us last year over our reference to the high price of London hotels. We are glad to learn from a *Financial Times* report of July 1981 that London is no longer the most expensive city for hotels in the world – that dubious honour is now apparently shared amongst Barbados, Abu Dhabi, Paris, Chicago and New York – and from other reports that the average price of rooms in London has risen less than the increase in the Retail Price Index. These studies confirm our own impression that hotels are eager to make their prices more competitive as compared with, say, five years ago when there was an undoubted cashing in on a weak pound combined with a tourist boom. While applauding these efforts, we are bound to note that, simply based on the hotels in this Guide – admittedly by no means a cross-section of the whole hotel trade – prices of city hotels in Britain are still higher than those of comparable hotels in the Guide in continental cities. And the same in general is true of comparable country hotels too.

Why should this be so? Many factors are at play: doubtless the rate of British inflation and (until recently) a strong pound are much to blame. High land prices, especially in London, and soaring rates, have not helped. But one major reason why British hotel prices compare so unfavourably with French ones (the country most often quoted in comparison) must in part be the tradition in France of family-run establishments with all the economies that can be achieved when a whole family is involved. In France, and also in Italy, running a hotel is more like a profession; in England, it is usual to regard it as a business – as a way of making profit rather than an income. It would be simplistic to say that British hoteliers are greedier, but in general they are looking for a quicker profit in a shorter term.

For two people sharing a room, the disparity in prices between Britain and most of the rest of Europe is particularly striking because of the convention in this country of charging by the number of occupants rather than by the room. A hotel which changed to the continental practice might find that it significantly improved its trade, encouraging more couples or families to use hotels rather than camp or stay at home – in the

same way as Freddie Laker, by lowering transatlantic fares, has enfranch-
ised a new class of travellers to the United States. Meanwhile, this factor
alone makes hotel prices for some users so much steeper in Britain.

The cost of staff contributes to the high prices. There is a trend here,
which the Guide welcomes, towards more family-run enterprises, but it
will take a long time, we guess, for British people to overcome their
prejudice against 'service'. It is this antipathy – largely unknown in
France, Italy, Spain or Portugal – which accounts for the anomaly that, at
a time of exceptional unemployment, many hotels in Britain still have
staffing problems. Wages in the catering industry have traditionally been
low, but in fact have risen 75% in the past three years – and for the
minimum wages staff work a 40-hour week; staff are expected to work far
longer hours for less on the continent.

There are plenty of other explanations which can be offered to explain
or excuse our high hotel prices – the need to provide more indoor public
rooms than in Mediterranean countries because of our climate, for
instance. But VAT at 15% is clearly a major contributing factor. In our
Introduction last year, we deplored the custom in some hotels of quoting
prices exclusive of VAT so that, unless you read your small print
carefully, you will find your bill considerably higher than you expect. We
now learn that this practice has sometimes been a deliberate (though, in
our view, misguided) policy by a hotelier to draw attention to what he
feels is an unreasonable inflation of prices outside his control. We are glad
to learn that the Government now plan legislation to stop a practice which
has helped to give hotels here a poor reputation. But we do recognize the
case for reducing or not charging VAT for overseas visitors.

One final point: many British hotels these days, if they have empty beds,
are very willing to offer discounts, even for a single night. It is always
worth asking. . . .

Ripoffs and Seductions

Compilers of hotel guides are often staggered by the multifarious tech-
niques devised by rogue hoteliers for taking money off their customers.
Châteaux Ripoffs are found all over the world. And of course it isn't only
châteaux that rip you off; inns of inhospitality are also legion, as are the
ways in which any hotel can give too little and ask too much.

Fortunately, there are many hotels of a different kind, the sort celebrated in this Guide. Those of us who travel hopefully are waiting to be
seduced by a hotel's charm. And for every technique for screwing another
pound or dollar from the victim guest, one can catalogue ways in which a
visitor can be beguiled. They don't need to be fancy items like foam baths,
make-up removers, hair-dryers or complimentary glasses of sherry, and
they don't necessarily cost a lot of money: fresh flowers in a room or
making sure that a bedroom is heated adequately in advance of a guest's
arrival on a cold day are two simple ways of making a visitor welcome;
alas, we had a rash of complaints about poor heating in hotels in the
unseasonable summer of 1981 – and other examples of such short-sighted
meanness, like putting 25-watt bulbs in bedside lighting. Hotels which
remember special preferences from day to day or from visit to visit also
come in for special commendation; there is no lack of ways in which a
hotel which is trying can endear itself. And of course the most important
single beguilement is an unaffected cordiality on the part of the owner and

11

staff – on arrival and throughout one's stay. The word 'unaffected' is crucial. In France recently we came across a *patronne* who clearly prided herself on being a perfect hostess. For one night, it was amusing to watch her performance, but we should hate to have to endure a week of such self-conscious posturing. The gift of making one's guests feel welcome comes naturally to some and may be regarded as a kind of divine blessing; it is certainly not a trait that can be learned, and of course what works for one sort of person doesn't necessarily work for the next.

What it takes to be a hotelier is in fact the subject of the appendix written by Thea Brand of *Beaconside House* in Monkleigh, Devon, someone who had the nerve to open a hotel without previous experience. You don't need qualifications in catering or hotel management to run successfully a small hotel of character, but her piece reminds us of the many pitfalls and provocations of the profession.

America's Wonderful Little Hotels and Inns

The Guide is published in the United States and Canada under the title *Europe's Wonderful Little Hotels and Inns*. Its success in North America has led to a sister publication on American hotels based on the same principles. As with this Guide, the text is revised regularly. Readers with first-hand recent experience of good hotels in North America are urged to write to the American editor, Barbara Crossette, at 345 East 93rd Street, 25C, New York, NY 10028, USA. Report forms at the end of the book may be used, but regrettably Freepost is not available for transatlantic use.

A similar guide to the Caribbean is also being prepared. If you know of suitable candidates for travellers wishing to avoid the package-vacation resort hotels, please write with details to *Wonderful Little Hotels and Inns of the Caribbean* (including Bermuda, the Bahamas and Mexico's Yucatan Peninsula), also to Barbara Crossette at 345 East 93rd Street, 25C, New York, NY 10028.

HILARY RUBINSTEIN
London, December 1981

How to read the entries

As in previous editions, entries are in two parts – a citation, endorsed by one or several names, followed by relevant information about accommodation, amenities, location and tariffs.

We must emphasize once again that the length or brevity of an entry is not a reflection on the quality of a hotel. The size of an entry is determined in part by what we feel needs to be said to convey a hotel's special flavour and in part by the character and interest of the commendation. In general, country hotels get more space than city hotels because the atmosphere of the hotel matters more with the former and also because it is often helpful, when a hotel is in a relatively remote or little-known area, if the entry says something about the location.

The names at the end of a citation are of those who have nominated that hotel or endorsed the entry that appeared in a previous edition. Some entries are entirely or largely quoted from one report; if several names follow such an entry, we have distinguished the writer of the quoted material by putting that name first. We do not give the names of those who have sent us critical reports – though their contributions are every bit as important as the laudatory ones. .

The factual material also varies in length. Some hotels provide within their grounds a wide variety of facilities, others very little. But the paucity of information provided in some cases may derive from the fact that the hotel has failed to return our detailed questionnaire or send us a brochure. All hotels in the British Isles, except some Irish ones, have completed our form, but the same is not true for continental hotels, despite the fact that we send out our questionnaire in five languages, and repeat the operation for the recalcitrant a month later. Perhaps a quarter of the hotels in the second half have ignored our form or have returned it months later when the Guide has gone to press. In these instances, we have had to rely on the information available from national tourist offices. The fact that no lounge or bar is mentioned in an entry is not evidence that a hotel lacks public rooms or a licence – only that we can't be sure. The same applies to availability of parking, which we aim to mention in the case of town and city hotels. As to tariffs, in those cases where we have had no communication with a hotel, we have added a percentage increase on present tariffs according to informed views about the present and likely future trend of inflation in each country.

There is a limit to the amount of 'nuts and bolts' that can be given in any guide book, and we are against providing, as some other guide books do, a lot of potted information in complicated hard-to-decipher hieroglyphic form. The only shorthand we have used is 'B & B' for bed and breakfast and *'alc'* for *à la carte*; 'full *alc*' indicates a 3-course meal and a half bottle of wine, including service and taxes. For the first time this year we have employed the convention of a symbol (ᵭ) for the disabled.

There is one crucial point that must be emphasized with regard to the tariffs: their relative unreliability. We ask hotels, when they complete our questionnaire in the summer of one year, to make an informed guess as to their tariffs the following year. This year the task, never an easy one, has been harder than ever, and not only for hotels in the British Isles. We have done our best to bring some appearance of order out of this chaotic picture, but can only warn readers not to attach too much credence to the figures printed. In many cases prices may be steeper than those shown, though there may well be some hotels whose rates we have over-estimated. In all cases, we would urge readers to check at the time of booking and not to blame the hotel if our prices are wrong.

Terms are difficult enough to cope with at the best of times. A few hotels have a standard rate for all rooms regardless of season and length of stay, but most operate a highly complicated system which varies from low season to high (and some have a medium-high season as well), according to length of stay, whether there is a bathroom *en suite* and, in the case of most British hotels, whether a room is in single or double occupancy. And on top of all that, most British hotels operate bargain breaks of one kind or another, but rarely of the same kind. We try to give the essential information: what you may expect to pay for bed and breakfast either in a single room on your own or sharing a double room. When two figures are given, they indicate, unless otherwise stated, the range of prices per person for B & B, full board and so on. When a hotel has low and high season rates, the range shows the lowest price in the low season and the highest price in the high season. In the case of many hotels on the continent, particularly in France, we have given a rate for rooms, indicating the range between a single room (preferably with bath or shower) and the equivalent for a double room; but the B & B, pension and meals prices are still per person. But we do beg you to check your tariff with the hotel when you book, and if you are going for two days or more in the winter months, it would pay you to find out the exact terms of any special offers available. Sometimes these bargain terms are amazing value, but may call for some adjustment in your holiday plans in order to qualify.

We must end with our customary exhortation: we implore readers to tell us of any errors of omission or commission in both the descriptive and the information parts of the entries. And we should also like to know if there are points we ought to be covering. We hate it when we encounter people who say: 'We meant to write and tell you that your Guide would be so much better if . . .' We have made a great effort this year to improve our information under **Location**, especially with the more out-of-the-way places, but would be very grateful if readers would let us know of any cases where they have found our directions inadequate. If you have taken a wrong turning down some narrow Devon lane, don't just curse us, but please write, and we will do better next time. We recognize what an imposition it is to be asking readers to write us letters or complete report forms, but it is essential that people do let us know their views if the Guide is to meet consumer needs as well as it can.

Part One

ENGLAND
WALES
SCOTLAND
CHANNEL ISLANDS
NORTHERN IRELAND
REPUBLIC OF IRELAND

England

ABBERLEY, Nr Worcester   **Map 2**

The Elms   *Telephone:* Great Witley (029 921) 666

Both as a hotel, and as a restaurant, *The Elms* achieves a rare excellence. It has certain advantages, like a harmonious building – Queen Anne at its centre with two well-grafted modern wings – that is exceptionally grand and beautiful (the two by no means always going together). Of a piece with the house are the gardens and grounds, immaculately maintained and with a remarkable herb garden. Inside, Donald Crosthwaite, like all the best hoteliers, is constantly improving this or decorating that; one major work this past year has been the extension of the Regency Dining Room into a new garden room designed to give the impression of an Orangery. A lot of our readers have commented on the many little extra touches of generosity at *The Elms*: glasses of sherry to welcome one's arrival, home-made butter biscuits served with early-morning tea, fruit bowls in bedrooms renewed daily – not to mention trouser presses, after-shave lotion, Eau de Cologne, shampoo, hairdryer, bathrobes and other home-from-home goodies. Finally, we have been getting nothing but good reports of the cooking of the new head chef, Murdo McSween, formerly of *Walton's* (and, of interest to bookish people, a nephew twice over of the late Compton Mackenzie). In our entry last year, we quoted a reader's lament that a full English breakfast was no longer being served in the bedrooms. We are glad to hear that this crucial (for some) part of room service has now been restored – and that, thanks to the Scotsman in

17

the kitchens, porridge is once again on the breakfast menu. *(Katie Plowden, T E Brigden-Shaw, M Evans, T M Wilson, Derek Cooper, Richard Webb)*

Open: All year.
Rooms: 17 double, 3 single – all with bath, telephone, radio and colour TV. (Some rooms on ground floor.)
Facilities: 3 lounges, restaurant, sun terrace; 12 acres grounds with croquet lawn, tennis court, putting green; helicopter service to Birmingham airport.
Location: On the A443 Tenbury Wells road 10 miles NW of Worcester; 15 minutes' drive from junctions 5, 6 and 7 of the M5.
Restriction: No dogs in public rooms.
Credit cards: All major credit cards accepted.
Terms: B & B £23–28.50. Set meal: lunch £7.50; full *alc* lunch £9; dinner £12.50. Special meals for children.

ALFRISTON, Polegate, Sussex   **Map 2**

Deans Place Hotel   *Telephone:* Alfriston (0323) 870248

If we were in the business of awarding prizes for the most beguiling nomination of the year, we might well give it to the report below on the Brewsters' ivy-creepered 18th-century house by the river Cuckmere in the heart of the South Downs – and, incidentally, the only hotel in England, the proprietors believe, to have its own indoor bowling green.

'I am not sure this is good enough for the Guide, but when our batteries run down and we want to read and walk, not eat too much, not drive too far and generally "get away from it all" cheaply!! this is where we go. We found it years ago when our children were small. The Brewsters who own and run it had just bought it and were building it up. It was in the *Good Food Guide*. They let it drop out because they "could not be bothered". They had three small children and wanted a life of their own. Over the years they have built on rooms, added games rooms, outdoor swimming pool, a bowling alley (God knows why), given every room a private bathroom, and built a new dining room. It is sometimes not very warm in the lounge, sometimes not perhaps one hundred per cent clean. The staff has to be seen to be believed sometimes. For a long time they had Spanish staff, lots of them, but sadly most of them left to go back to Spain, more money there, leaving only a few. There are currently a couple of ex-sailors, and all sorts of odd bods. The food is English cooking, sometimes we suspect packets. It is good, plain and no nonsense. They will always give you cream and ice cream with it. Apple pies, apricot pies, roast joints. Fried fish. Excellent coffee. Some of the rooms are a lot more modern than others, all with a kettle and tea- and coffee-making facilities. Breakfast you help yourself to. It doesn't sound wonderful I know, and yet the hotel hardly ever has a room empty. It is a children's paradise. Masses to do and nobody cares what you do. Liberty Hall, they enjoy themselves. Old ladies come and visit and are not made to feel "out of it". No cocky waiters. School parents visit schools in the area. Adults like it, because again you do as you like. If you feel like tea go and make it or find someone, make your own booking almost. Drinks in the bar are cheap, very cheap, wine is very reasonable, while as for the rest of the prices, sometimes I feel it is cheaper than staying at home. It isn't wonderful, but it is somewhere that people enjoy going to, and return to, and that after all is what a good hotel is all about.' *(Heather Sharland)*

Open: All year, except end December–end January.
Rooms: 35 double, 11 single – all with bath, tea-making facilities and baby-listening.
Facilities: 2 lounges, dining room, games room, TV room; indoor bowling green, snooker, table tennis. 7 acres grounds with tennis court, outdoor swimming pool (heated in summer), croquet, putting. 3 miles from beach; golf, riding nearby. Glyndebourne 5 miles. Vegetarian meals provided. &.
Location: Heading for Eastbourne on the A22, take the right-hand turning for Seaford.
Restriction: 'Well-behaved' dogs allowed, but not in dining room.
Terms: B & B £9.50–12. Set meals: lunch £3.80; dinner £4.50. Reduced rates for children.

AMBLESIDE, Cumbria   Map 4

Rothay Manor Hotel [GFG]   *Telephone:* Ambleside (096 63) 3605
Rothay Bridge   *Telex:* 65294 Telecom G

'Probably the friendliest hotel I have ever stayed at. We enjoyed a wonderful Christmas in beautiful surroundings. Everything was laid on by Bronwen Nixon – nature rambles, party games, etc. The food is very good, but would be even better if simplified, with a lesser emphasis on cream and over-complicated vegetables. The wine list is excellent.' *(John Bennett)*

A characteristic tribute in more ways than one. *Rothay Manor* is a stylish Regency house near the head of Lake Windermere and within a few minutes' walk of the centre of Ambleside, but in a secluded position, with an attractive garden. It is very much a family affair: Bronwen Nixon is in charge of the kitchen, her son Stephen looks after the restaurant and the extensive wine list, and her son Nigel is the admin. man. The word 'friendly' or one of its synonyms appears frequently in our reports – about the Nixons and also about the young staff. The reference to nature rambles and suchlike over Christmas also makes a point: though *Rothay Manor* offers, in a superior form, a traditional kind of country-house hospitality (the waitresses, incidentally, are mob-capped and pinafored when waiting at meals), it is also a thoroughly go-ahead place, with lots of special events – wine tastings, Dickensian evenings, gourmet weekends and the like – taking place throughout the winter. Finally, there is the reference to food. The hotel has enjoyed for many years past a reputation for its excellent restaurant. Many of this year's crop of reports, though warmly endorsing last year's entry, have expressed some disappointment with one aspect or another of the cooking. We hope this is only a temporary falling-off from previous high standards. More reports would be welcome.

Open: All year except 3 January–26 February.
Rooms: 10 double, 2 single – all with bath, telephone and colour TV, 4 with radio.
Facilities: 2 lounges, 1 with bar, dining room. 1 acre gardens with croquet. Near the river Rothay. Steamer services, sailing and water-skiing nearby; also riding and golf.
Location: Lake Windermere ¼ mile; on the Langdale outskirts of Ambleside.
Restriction: No dogs in public rooms.
Credit cards: American Express, Diners.
Terms (service at guests' discretion): B & B £23–34; dinner, B & B £35–47. Set meals: lunch £4.50 (Sunday lunch £6.50); dinner £12. Children £7 per night B & B if sharing parents' room; special meals provided.

Wateredge Hotel   *Telephone:* Ambleside (096 63) 2332

The address is Ambleside, but the *Wateredge* is a mile from that bustling busy village. As its name suggests, it is right on the water at the northern tip of Lake Windermere, and most of its bedrooms look over the lakeside garden and down the length of the lake – a very pleasing prospect indeed. Don't confuse this hotel with its larger neighbour, the *Waterside*, which is on the main Windermere–Keswick road, whereas one of the pleasing aspects of *Wateredge* is that it is on a quiet byroad. It has been skilfully converted from two 17th-century fishermen's cottages, well grafted on to some modern extensions. There are several public rooms of differing sizes – enough to accommodate all the guests in comfort when the hotel is full. There is nothing flash about the *Wateredge*, and no special 'treats' in the bedrooms. But the cooking is ambitious without being pretentious or particularly pricey, and the helpings are generous alike for the full English breakfasts and the 5-course evening meal. There is a popular buffet lunch. Staff are friendly and efficient. *(HR; also Shirley Williams and others)*

Open: March–mid November.
Rooms: 15 double, 3 single–8 with bath, 2 with shower, all with baby-listening.
Facilities: Lounge, TV room, dining room. 1½ acres grounds with 200 ft lake frontage, private jetty, own sailing boat, fishing and safe bathing. Good centre for walkers and climbers.
Location: ½ mile from town; just off the A591 at Waterhead on Kendal–Keswick road.
Credit cards: Access/Euro/Mastercard.
Terms (no fixed service charge):   B & B £15.50–16.50; dinner, B & B £25.50–27; full board £29–31. Set meals: lunch £5; dinner £9.90. Reduced rates and special meals for children.

ASTON CLINTON, Buckinghamshire   **Map 2**

The Bell Inn   [GFG]   *Telephone:* Aylesbury (0296) 630252
                                              Telex: 826715

The Bell, at the foot of the Chilterns, has been an inn since 1650, and was once a staging post for the Duke of Buckingham from his seat at Stowe to his palace on the Mall. But the term 'inn' is quite inappropriate to today's elegant establishment. It has been owned and run by the Harris family since 1939. Michael and Patsy Harris aim to continue the gastronomic tradition of Michael's father, Gerard. One correspondent told us that *The Bell* had restored his faith in British catering. That tribute is fairly made. *The Bell* does not, in our view, offer haute cuisine – how could it really when serving up to 140 meals at a sitting? But the quality of the service and the ambience, and also perhaps the remarkable and reasonably-priced wine list, are what maintains the loyalty of *Bell*-lovers and justifies to them the high prices – £16.50, exclusive VAT (July 1981) for the obligatory 6-course set dinner served on Saturday nights (other meals *à la carte* only). On this matter of ambience, another reader wrote: '*The Bell* scores very highly on style and comfort. The building is basically old, and the original stone-flagged bar, with huge open fires, is a pleasant place to consider the menu. The dry sherry we ordered was exceptionally good, a happy reminder of the quality established by Gerard Harris. The large S-shaped dining room is modern, but furnished most tastefully in traditional style. The seating, table settings, lighting and atmosphere would be hard to fault. The service was both friendly and skilled. The maître d'hôtel has been at *The Bell* since 1960 – a good sign.' We should add that the accommodation – some in the old house and some across a minor road in a converted stable-block round a courtyard – is of a piece with the public rooms, extremely comfortable and full of thoughtful touches. *(Gerard and Helen Turner; also Curzon Couper, Raymond Harris)*

Open: All year.
Rooms: 21 double, 4 suites – all with bath, telephone, radio and colour TV. (7 rooms on ground floor.)
Facilities: Drawing room, bar, restaurant; conference facilities. 3 acres grounds at the foot of the Chiltern Hills.
Location: On the A41, 4 miles on the London side of Aylesbury.
Restriction: Dogs not allowed in public rooms.
Credit cards: Access/Euro, Barclay/Visa.
Terms (excluding VAT): B & B £19–32. Set meal: Saturday dinner £18.50; full *alc* about £18.

Note: Michael Harris tells us that the footnote in our last edition made him feel rather like a dog who bites the hand which feeds it. We are glad to say that he has now withdrawn his objection to our listing his hotel.

BARNSTAPLE, Devon   **Map 1**

Downrew House Hotel   *Telephone:* Barnstaple (0271) 2497
Bishops Tawton

Downrew is mostly a Queen Anne house (some parts older), with a lodge and a west wing. It's a few miles inland and 500 feet above Barnstaple near the tiny village of Bishops Tawton, on the southern slopes of Codden Hill. The nearest beaches are eight to ten miles away. It's been owned and run for the past 17 years by Desmond and Aleta Ainsworth, and has that settled feel which comes when a hotel has the good fortune to enjoy a long run in capable hands. No significant change this year, except – very much a sign of the times – all rooms have been given radio and colour TV.

Our last entry last year contained a sustained encomium, ending: 'Although the hotel is beautiful, it is not stuffy or pretentious, and the Ainsworths' welcome, though warm, is unaffected. Both have particularly sympathetic personalities and this comes across in every detail of the hotel – down to their caring for two superannuated donkeys who live in the orchard. Food and wine are excellent. For what is provided, the price is reasonable.' *(EG; also E G Caink, T J D Jeffrey, Thea Brand)*

Open: Mid March–early November and Christmas week. Restaurant closed to non-residents on Sundays; Monday–Saturday non-residents must book.
Rooms: 14 double, 4 suites – all with bath, radio and colour TV. 5 rooms in West Wing, 2 in Lodge. (2 rooms on ground floor.)
Facilities: Drawing room, 2 lounges with colour TV, bar, dining room, library, games room, solarium. 14 acres grounds with golf, croquet, tennis court, heated swimming pool. Free fishing within 1½ miles; beaches within 8–10 miles. &.
Location: Travelling to Barnstaple on the A361, turn left on to the A377 to

Exeter. After Bishops Tawton take the left fork off the A377 on to the Chittle-hampton road. Then 1¼ miles to *Downrew* on right.

Restriction: No dogs except in Lodge.

Terms (excluding VAT; no service charge): B & B £10–17; dinner, B & B £17.50–28. Set meal: dinner £9. Special autumn and spring breaks. Reduced rates and special meals for children.

BASLOW, Derbyshire   Map 2

Cavendish Hotel   *Telephone:* Baslow (024 688) 2311

There is no other hotel in the Guide whose entry gives us as much trouble. We left it out last year because, though the hotel had delighted some of its guests, the number of detailed criticisms made it impossible for us to write a recommendable entry. This year, the plusses have outweighed the minusses, but we should be glad of further reports. First on the plus side is the hotel's enviable location. Although on the A619, in the centre of Baslow village, all the rooms – both the public ones and the bedrooms – are on the opposite side to the road, overlooking Chatsworth Park – a noble vista. And these rooms, though they vary in size, are without exception elegantly furnished (some pieces are from Chatsworth House itself), warm and comfortable. The public rooms all have beautiful flower arrangements. Also on the plus side is the eagerness of Eric Marsh, who runs the *Cavendish*, to please. Whenever possible, he is on the spot to greet arriving guests, and, from our correspondence, it is clear that he cares greatly for the reputation of his hotel. We noted with interest a paragraph in his brochure inviting his guests to write to us with their comments. Eric Marsh's genial brother, Peter, is in charge of the bar and mixes excellent cocktails. In previous years, we have had complaints about lapses in the service, but not this year: two readers have in fact used the word 'faultless' about the staff. The Paxton Room Restaurant is another matter. The brochure speaks of 'its perfect view and its con-troversial menu of individually prepared dishes featuring home-made and local produce eaten from Wedgwood china and Sheffield plate'. We wouldn't quarrel with any of that, not least the word 'controversial': our readers have indeed differed about the quality and pretentions of the food – also about the prices which are 15% higher than they look because, as with the room tariff, they are quoted exclusive of VAT. (*J G Butlin, D and A Campbell, Richard Coopman, R Vickers, Henry Kingsley, Margaret Johnson*)

Open: All year.

Rooms: 13 double, 1 suite – all with bath, direct-dial telephone, radio, colour TV, tea-making facilities, refrigerated bar and baby-listening. (2 rooms on ground floor.)

Facilities: Lounge, bar, restaurant. 1 acre grounds, with golf practice (putting green and driving net); fishing in rivers Derwent and Wye. &.

Location: On the A619 Chesterfield–Bakewell road.

Restriction: Dogs by arrangement.

Credit cards: American Express, Barclay/Visa.

Terms (excluding VAT; no fixed service charge): Rooms £16.50–27.50 per person. Set meal: breakfast from £2.75; full *alc* from about £10. Special meals for children provided on request.

If you are thinking of writing reports on hotels for us, do it NOW!

BASSENTHWAITE LAKE, Cockermouth, Cumbria   Map 4

The Pheasant Inn   *Telephone:* Bassenthwaite Lake (059 681) 234

The address is mildly misleading. *The Pheasant* stands at the head of Bassenthwaite Lake, below Thwaite Forest, but does not in fact overlook the lake as there is a hill in between. It's an old-fashioned country inn, in the best sense of the term: it's 16th-century, offers real ale, and is full of old oak beams, chintzy pubbish furniture and the like. But it has good hotel virtues as well:

'We stayed for three nights in the *worst* April weekend ever recorded in the area I understand! Fortunately it couldn't have been cosier and nicer, and was very comfortable. Pleasant location off and *below* the A66 with wooded hills behind. A pretty garden (the blizzard stopped long enough for us to walk round it). Nice old building – long and low. Three exceptionally comfortable lounges with log fires. Real old traditional type bar with a lovely deep red womb-like ceiling – much patronized by well-heeled locals – very good bar snacks too! Excellent staff. The young waitresses neatly dressed; plenty of choice at meals nicely served. I unfortunately succumbed to 'flu and had trays brought up to me without sour faces and very quickly. It doesn't have telephones or TV in the bedrooms, or TV *anywhere*. But the latter to my mind is a positive advantage. Nice to get away from it, and anyway it stimulates conversation. I don't really require a bedside telephone and there are two closed-in ones downstairs. I have only two very minor "carps". Firstly, we never met the manager, and it's just one of the things I, personally, mind about. Not that we *needed* him. It was *most* efficiently run; everything went like clockwork – yet one didn't feel pressured about mealtimes etc. Secondly, it was really terribly cold, and the central heating didn't come on until 7.30 am so wasn't warm to dress to, even by 8.30. 6 am would have been more sensible, and perhaps switched off rather earlier at night. Otherwise it was everything we like. We hope to return soon – in better weather (and health).' *(Lady Elstub)*

Open: All year except Christmas Day.
Rooms: 13 double, 4 single – 11 with bath, 1 with shower. (3 rooms in annexe on ground floor.)
Facilities: 3 lounges, bar, dining room: facilities for private parties and small conferences. 15 acres grounds with 2 acres garden. ⓓ.
Location: 7 miles NW of Keswick just off the A66 (on the W side of Bassenthwaite Lake); parking for 80 cars.
Restriction: No dogs in bedrooms.
Terms: B & B £14.50–15; dinner, B & B £22.50–23; full board (winter only) £17–19. Set meals: lunch £4.80; dinner £8. Special winter rates. Reduced rates and special meals for children.

BATH, Avon   Map 2

The Priory Hotel   [GFG]   *Telephone:* Bath (0225) 331922
Western Road   *Telex:* 44612

Although *The Royal Crescent* (see below) must now be regarded as a serious rival to *The Priory* as the most elegant and comfortable place to stay for those taking the waters here, there are still plenty of supporters for John Donnithorne's establishment who would regard *The Priory* as one of the half-dozen most attractive city hotels in the country. The word 'flawless' appears like a refrain in our file. It's a large Gothic-style building, built in 1835 of mellow Bath stone a mile out of the town centre. One of its great attractions is its two peaceful acres of garden where you can take tea on the lawn under gigantic cedar trees. A heated swimming pool lurks discreetly behind flower beds. But the interior prospect is quite as pleasing as the outside: all the rooms are individually designed and maintained immaculately. One major change has taken place here this past year, however. After many years of service, the head chef, Robert Harrison, has left and his place been taken by Michael Collom. First reports are that the food is still very good, but not perhaps outstanding. More reports welcome.

Open: All year.
Rooms: 12 double, 3 single – 14 with bath, 1 with shower, all with telephone, radio and colour TV.
Facilities: Sitting room, lounge opening on to the garden, bar, restaurant. 2 acres garden with heated outdoor swimming pool.
Location: ¾ mile from town centre; ample parking.
Restrictions: No children under 10. No dogs.
Terms: B & B £30–34. Set meal: dinner £10.50; full *alc* £14.

BATH, Avon   **Map 2**

The Royal Crescent Hotel [GFG]   *Telephone: Bath (0225) 319090*
Royal Crescent   *Telex: 444251*

The Royal Crescent, only three years old and very much in the de luxe category, has been receiving a near-unanimous acclaim this past year. If only all our other popular tourist cities – Oxford or Cambridge, York or Brighton – could boast a hotel of this class and style! Its location, of course, at the very centre of the famous Crescent, Bath's shining architectural glory, is an incomparable asset. But the decor of both the public and the private rooms by Julie Hodgess, the choice of paintings and prints by Lord Crathorne, the altogether admirable restaurant under its chef, Raymond Duthie – everything in the place coheres. Perhaps its most remarkable achievement is that, despite the grandeur of the house, whether looking in or looking out, it maintains the feeling of a small, intimate and friendly establishment. *(J F Greenhough and others)*

Open: All year.
Rooms: 19 double, 4 single, 5 suites – all with telephone, radio and colour TV; baby-sitting by arrangement. (3 rooms on ground floor.)
Facilities: Lift, drawing room, cocktail lounge, restaurant. ½ acre grounds. &.
Location: 5 minutes' walk from town centre; parking for 7 cars.
Restriction: No dogs.
Credit cards: All major credit cards accepted.
Terms: B & B from £28. Set meal: lunch £8.50; full *alc* £17.05. Reduced rates for children.

> We asked hotels to estimate their 1982 tariffs some time before publication so the rates given here are not necessarily completely accurate. Please *always* check terms with hotels when making bookings.

BATH, Avon   Map 2

Somerset House   *Telephone:* Bath (0225) 66451
10 Dunsford Place, Bathwick Hill

We are always glad to hear of modest places to stay in cities as alternatives to the chic and glossy establishments. *Somerset House* is a small guest house in a listed Georgian terrace, ¾ mile from the Abbey and the Pump Room in a quiet residential area. It's a new venture on the part of Jean and Malcolm Seymour who formerly ran a restaurant in the Lake District. 'Our second very pleasant stay, in a room with a superb view of the city and the surrounding hills. The Seymours specialize in English traditional and regional dishes. During our four days, nothing came out of a tin. One evening we had leek soup with stilton, woodpigeon, followed by home-made black-currant liqueur ice cream – all for £4 per person. It's not licensed, but you can bring your own wine – no corkage charge. There's very good breakfast coffee. The main reason we returned to Somerset House was because of the very real consideration which the owners show to their guests. Although Mrs Seymour does not set out to cater for children, nothing was too much trouble for our boys of 2¾ years and 9 months.' *(Richard Firth; also Roger Smithells)*

Open: All year, except Christmas, New Year and annual holiday (usually October).
Rooms: 3 double (2 can be used as singles) – all with tea-making facilities and baby-listening, 1 with telephone.
Facilities: Lounge with TV, dining room. Small garden. 2 minutes from Kennet & Avon Canal – angling for temporary members of Bathampton Angling Club. 12 minutes from Abbey, Roman Baths, shops, etc.
Location: Bathwick Hill runs SE from A36 up to Claverton University and American Museum; plenty of kerbside parking.
Restrictions: Normally no children under 5. Small dogs allowed in bedrooms only.
Credit card: Diners.
Terms (hotel is not VAT rated): B & B £9–11; dinner, B & B £13–15.50. Set meal: dinner £4–4.50. Mid-week breaks: £24 per person any 2 nights (dinner, B & B Monday–Thursday). Special-interest weekends: £36.50–54 per person. Reduced rates for children sharing parents' room; special meals available.

BEANACRE, Melksham, Wiltshire   Map 2

Beechfield House Hotel [GFG]   *Telephone:* Melksham (0225) 703700

An inviting hotel in every aspect. Peter Crawford-Rolt, who previously ran a renowned restaurant with rooms in Steyning, opened the doors of this exceptionally well-preserved example of a small Victorian country house in the summer of 1979. Two years later, he shows every sign of establishing a hotel that combines punctilious attention to small details with a sympathetically intimate atmosphere. The house itself, for a start, has been restored with high fidelity: furnishings, including a splendid selection of brass bedsteads, mouldings, painted glass doors, are all of the kind that will delight the Victorian connoisseur – though it's not in the least spooky or 'Gothic' in the pejorative sense. There were eight bedrooms in 1981, and another eight are planned to be available in 1982 in the adjoining stable block. Although visiting eaters will normally outnumber the residents, both parties are well provided for in lounges and dining rooms. The cooking is of the order of excellence to be expected from the owner's reputation; there is an ambitious and expensive *à la carte* menu, but there are also – a refreshing change these days – very reasonable set menus which offer dishes almost equally ambitious as the *à la carte* ones, even if the ingredients lack the more *recherché* game and shellfish. Handsome grounds, with croquet and tennis – and a swimming pool coming shortly. *(HR)*

Open: All year. Restaurant closed for lunch on bank holidays.
Rooms: 16 double – all with bath, telephone, radio, colour TV, baby-listening. (8 rooms in annexe on ground floor.)
Facilities: Residents' lounge, bar, restaurant. 8 acres grounds with tennis, croquet, all-weather riding ring, stabling and paddock facilities with riding lessons available. Coarse fishing on the River Avon 300 yards away. &.
Location: On the A350 Melksham–Chippenham road, 2 miles N of Melksham.
Restriction: No dogs in public rooms.
Credit cards: All major credit cards accepted.
Terms (excluding 10% service charge): B & B £24–25. Set meal: lunch £5.50; dinner for 2 including wine £10; full *alc* £12. Special meals for children. Special winter breaks.

BIDEFORD, North Devon   **Map 1**

Yeoldon House   *Telephone:* Bideford (023 72) 4400/6618
Durrant Lane, Northam

Chris and Judi Fulford arrived in Yeoldon House in 1973, converting what had been a Victorian gentleman's residence into a smallish and stylish hotel. It has 2 acres of grounds overlooking the River Torridge, and lies 2 miles downstream from the pleasant old market town of Bideford; the same distance in the opposite direction leads one to the hard golden sands and championship golf course of Westward Ho!.

'The setting is delightful and peaceful, and there is a very pleasant atmosphere in the hotel. The accommodation is spacious and every detail correct – down to free sachets of shampoo, bubble bath and washing powder in the bathroom! The food deserves a mention because although sometimes variable in quality, it is always acceptable and extremely generously served. Just the thing after a day on the beach or a walk across the moors. I have never before seen a breakfast menu which ends "If you want more of anything please ask"! After-dinner coffee was delicious, and the breakfast coffee almost as good. Throughout our over-short stay, the proprietor frequently asked us whether everything was all right – the food, the room, the coffee, and took great pains to advise us on where to go to get the most out of our two days' stay. We really felt we could have complained if things were not perfect – but there was no need. Everything about this hotel is caring, generous and unstinting: such a welcome relief after the many expensive but penny-pinching hotels we've stayed in.' *(C Y Edwards)*

Open: All year, except 4 days over Christmas and 3 weeks in January and February.
Rooms: 9 double, 1 single – all with bath or shower, radio and colour TV; 1 four-poster bed; baby-listening if required.
Facilities: Sitting room, bar, restaurant. 2 acres grounds surrounded by fields and

river. At nearby Westward Ho! there are 2 miles of sandy beach with safe bathing and Malibu surfing; golf at the championship Westward Ho! course, and at Saunton; sailing on the estuary, sea and river; fishing, riding and pony-trekking; birdwatching.

Location: 2 miles downstream from Bideford.
Restriction: No dogs.
Credit cards: Access/Euro, American Express, Barclay/Visa, Diners.
Terms: B & B £16–22; dinner, B & B £16–30. Set meal: dinner £7–10; full *alc* £11. Bargain breaks and special gourmet weekends in winter. Reduced rates and special meals for children; babies and small children free.

BISHOPS TACHBROOK, Nr Leamington Spa, Warwickshire   Map 2

Mallory Court   [GFG]   *Telephone:* Leamington Spa (0926) 30214
Harbury Lane

In our entry last year for this superbly comfortable and gastronomically outstanding country house set amid immaculately maintained landscaped gardens, we offered one caveat. It was, we said, by far the most attractive place to stay within a 25-mile radius of the National Exhibition Centre outside Birmingham, but the consequence was that it was getting booked up years ahead by the trade-fair community. 'The feel of a hotel,' we wrote, 'where most people are spending company money rather than their own is necessarily different and less congenial than the other kind.' A correspondent, who uses *Mallory Court* regularly at Fair times and calls it 'the best hotel in England' replies to this charge: 'The reason we stay here is precisely to avoid the more unpleasant manifestations of expense-account visitors. Obviously, at the time we go, all the other guests are normally from the Trade Fair; but they tend to be from very small companies which are not lashing other people's money about. All the large hotels in Birmingham are quite unacceptable during the Trade Fairs and *Mallory Court*, in our experience over the last three years has not suffered.' We are glad to hear this, but would welcome further reports. Meanwhile, one other matter we complained about last year – inadequate hot water – is, we hope, being put right with a new boiler. (*B J Shawcross, N M Civval, Paul Henderson*)

Open: All year, except Christmas Day.
Rooms: 6 double, 1 single – 5 with bath, all with telephone, radio on request and colour TV.
Facilities: Lounge, drawing room, oak-panelled dining room, sun lounge. 10 acres grounds and landscaped gardens, water garden, rose garden, terraces; outdoor swimming pool, squash courts, croquet; golf 2 miles.
Location: 2 miles S of Leamington Spa off the A452.
Restrictions: No children under 14. No dogs.
Credit cards: All major credit cards accepted.
Terms (excluding service charge): B & B (continental) £25–28. Set meals: English breakfast £5; lunch £10.95; full *alc* £20.

> The length of an entry does not necessarily reflect the merit of a hotel. The more interesting the report or the more unusual or controversial the hotel, the longer the entry.

The Blakeney Hotel *Telephone:* Cley (0263) 740797

Built by the formidable Sir Henry Deterding of Shell fame in 1920, *The Blakeney* has a particularly agreeable site: it is a low rambling building right on one of the more picturesque of Norfolk harbours, looking out over flotillas of small craft to Blakeney Point and the sea. 'A well run friendly hotel in a delightful setting. There's a heated indoor pool and a large garden behind. Very comfortable spacious rooms, and pleasant helpful staff though sometimes the service is a little slow. There's a wide choice on a varied menu in the restaurant. Reasonable wines. Real ale in the bar. We will go again.' *(David R W Jervois)*

Open: All year.
Rooms: 37 double, 17 single, 2 suites – 36 with bath and TV, all with telephone, radio, tea-making facilities and baby-listening. 13 rooms in annexe. (Some rooms on ground floor.)
Facilities: 2 lounges, 4 bars, TV room, games room; heated indoor swimming pool, sauna. 6 acres garden with outdoor children's play area; safe bathing, fishing. ♿ .
Location: On the quay.
Restriction: No dogs in public rooms.
Credit cards: All major credit cards accepted.
Terms (no fixed service charge): B & B £15–26. Set meals: Sunday buffet lunch £2.50; dinner £7.50; full *alc* £9. Bargain breaks. Free accommodation for children under 12 sharing parents' room.

The Buckinghamshire Arms *Telephone:* Aylsham (026 373) 2133

'The countryside of central and north Norfolk is for the most part unexplored and grossly underrated. The 17th-century *Buckinghamshire Arms* lies quietly by the side of Blickling Hall, one of the National Trust's gems in Norfolk. (You can walk in the park for free, or pay to go round the Hall and formal gardens – well worth it.) It advertises itself as a hotel, but I'd call it an inn: the smell of beer somewhat permeates the bedroom corridors. The bars here are serious drinking places. There's the snug, where the owners and a group of local regulars hold court, and a larger saloon. The atmosphere is friendly after the character of a pleasant country pub. When the weather permits, there are tables in the courtyard and garden; and there's also a residents' lounge upstairs. The dining room is attractive, with lots of traditional fittings and candles on the tables. The lady-of-the-house takes orders, and the waiting is done very pleasantly and efficiently by a team of young girls. There's an excellent set-price menu, with lots of choices; main courses imaginative, and generous portions (*five* veg). Bedrooms are comfortable, though none has a bath. Hearty breakfast. I'd certainly recommend it to those who like to stay in a really friendly pub, with food well above average.' *(SL)*

Open: All year, except Christmas. Restaurant closed Sunday evening, Monday and Bank Holidays.
Rooms: 3 double – all with tea-making facilities.

Facilities: Lounge, 2 bars, restaurant. Small garden where food is served; stable accommodation 'for those arriving on horseback'. Close to lake fishing and Blickling Hall.
Location: 1 mile from Aylsham.
Terms (excluding service): B & B £14.40–18.50. Set meal: dinner £8.95; full *alc* £16.50. Special terms for full-board stays of 2 or more nights.

BLOCKLEY, Moreton-in-Marsh, Gloucestershire   Map 2

Lower Brook House [GFG]   *Telephone:* Blockley (0386) 700286

We are glad to welcome *Lower Brook House* back to the Guide after an interval following two changes of management. New owners, John and Mavis Price, installed themselves in September 1980, and serious eaters may like to know that John Price's parents ran the GFG-recommended *Three Shires* at Little Langdale. For readers unfamiliar with the name of Blockley, we should say that it is a small and delightful Cotswold village, on the way to nowhere in particular so that it is free from the ubiquitous tourism of neighbouring showplaces, such as Broadway and Chipping Campden. *Lower Brook House* is a cottagey kind of hotel, with cosy rather than spacious rooms, and a terraced garden leading down to a tiny stream from which it takes its name. Here is a first report since the new owners moved in:

'Mr and Mrs Price are doing a splendid job. The house is a delight, warm and spotlessly clean. Our private bathroom had a box containing bath-cap, bath-foam, sewing kit, shoe-shine, etc. Drinks by the log fire, before we launched into celery soup, an interesting starter made with peppers, partridge, delicious fresh vegetables, pears coated in chocolate and soufflé were delectable: we stayed two nights and ate as well the following evening. We also enjoyed the white "smokey" Three Choirs wine. Coffee and home-made mints and chocs to follow. Breakfast was splendid, with the usual eggs, bacon, etc, but with home-made croissants and whole strawberry jam to follow. The garden is a beautifully peaceful retreat.' *(Carol Daniel)*

Open: All year. Restaurant closed Monday lunch.
Rooms: 7 double, 1 single – 6 with bath, all with tea-making facilities; colour TV on request.
Facilities: Lounge, bar, restaurant. ½ acre garden.
Location: On edge of village; turn off the A44 2 miles N of Moreton-in-Marsh.
Restrictions: No children under 5. No dogs.
Credit cards: All major credit cards accepted.
Terms (service at guests' discretion): B & B £20–23.50; dinner, B & B £25–28.50; full *alc* £12.50. Winter breaks: mid November–mid March (dinner, B & B inc. VAT £24.50 per person per night in double room). Reduced rates for children sharing parents' room, and special meals.

Mary Mount Country House Hotel   *Telephone:* Borrowdale (059 684) 223
Telex: 64305 (AT LODORE)

A younger, smaller and more modest-priced sibling of Keswick's *Lodore Swiss Hotel* (q.v.) a few hundred yards down the road, with similarly spectacular views over Derwentwater and the Borrowdale Valley. The hotel has its own squash courts, but guests are also able to enjoy the extensive facilities of the larger establishment, including heated indoor and outdoor swimming pools, tennis court, hairdressing salon, massage and beauty treatments and so forth.

'A small hotel with an intimate atmosphere. Excellent *table d'hôte* menu (no *à la carte*), short but well-selected wine list. Rooms are comfortable, with TV and coffee/tea facilities. Lunchtimes a bit crowded as many travellers attracted by snack lunches. We've been three times with our young daughter, and intend to go again.' *(D P O'Neill)*

Open: All year, except 14–30 December.
Rooms: 15 – all with bath, colour TV and baby-listening, 6 with tea-making facilities. 6 rooms in annexe. (5 rooms on ground floor.)
Facilities: Lounge, residents' bar, dining room. 3 acre garden; heated swimming pool, squash and tennis available at the *Lodore Swiss* mid March–November; golf, pony-trekking, boating, fishing nearby. &.
Location: Overlooking Lake Derwentwater; 3 miles from Keswick.
Restriction: No dogs.
Terms (no fixed service charge):   B & B £18–23; dinner, B & B £24–28. Set meal: dinner £7.50. Bargain breaks (minimum 2 nights): 1 January–1 April. Reduced rates for children.

Seatoller House   *Telephone:* Borrowdale (059 684) 218

'We found Seatoller House *admirable* in atmosphere, in comfort and in the food,' writes a grateful visitor to this highly congenial guest-house at the foot of the Honister Pass. 'I have stayed in the Lake District for 50 years in every accommodation from climbers' huts to swank conference hotels, and found this the most satisfactory! For the walker it is ideal for position and amenities, and it is extraordinarily good value for money.' A characteristic tribute to the hospitality offered by ex-publisher Geoffrey Trevelyan and his wife Gillian. The house is 300 years old, and – of interest to social historians perhaps – has been in continuous use by the Trevelyan family as a fell-walking guest-house for more than a century. 'The unobtrusive Trevelyan personal touch and attention to detail is everywhere apparent,' writes another correspondent, who goes on, 'I was gratified to find no TV in the guest quarters. One was therefore mercifully spared the tyranny of television, in exchange for which the rich and varied personal library of the Trevelyans was placed at the disposal of guests.' *(Elliot Viney, R M Clarkson; also Sir Stuart Milner Barry, J M Cobb, W Ian Stewart)*

Open: Mid March–mid November.
Rooms: 8 double (2 rooms on ground floor.)

Facilities: 2 lounges, tea bar, picnic shop. Small conference facilities. 2 acres grounds.
Location: 8 miles from Keswick on the B5289. Regular bus service from Keswick.
Restriction: No children under 5.
Terms (service at guests' discretion): Dinner, B & B £14.50–16; weekly board £87–100. Reduced rates for children of 12 and under sharing parents' room (⅔ adult price).

Note: Sadly, as we go to press, we learn that the Trevelyans are giving up the active running of Seatoller, though the house will continue to be owned by a family trust. It is hoped that the new resident managers, David and Ann Pepper, will maintain Seatoller's traditional style of hospitality. Reports on the Pepper regime will be welcome.

BOWES MOOR, Nr Barnard Castle, Teesdale   Map 4

Bowes Moor Hotel   *Telephone:* Teesdale (0833) 28331

'The highest hotel in England' is a boast of *Bowes Moor*, 1,300 feet up on the A66, and roughly halfway between Scotch Corner (A1) and Penrith (M6). The hotel, a mainly 18th-century York stone building, is surrounded by the wild and lovely 12,500-acre Bowes Moor, and the Pennine Way passes close by. We like one line in the brochure: "Breakfast in bed is encouraged".

  'Run by an ex-TV critic of the *Daily Mail* who fled to the James Herriot country, the hotel successfully manages to be a roadhouse on the main cross-Pennine road, serving ale and coffee and pub lunches to the passing trade, and also to provide excellent food and wine and reasonable accommodation for the huntin', shootin', fishin' types who invade it every August 12. The hotel has its own fishing and rough shooting, the Bowes Moor lamb and grouse cannot be bettered, and Mark Johns is an entertaining host – so much so that guests occasionally complain at 3 am when Mark is still entertaining in front of his baronial fire.' *(MW)*

Open: 1 May–31 October.
Rooms: 9 double, 1 single; 4 bathrooms available.
Facilities: Reception/sitting area, bar, restaurant. Fishing, shooting and walking nearby; golf 8 miles. Convenient for visits to Lake District, Yorkshire Dales and Scotland.
Location: 4 miles W of Bowes on A66 main trunk road 20 miles W of Scotch Corner (A1); 25 miles E of Penrith (M6); 8 miles from Barnard Castle.
Restriction: No dogs.
Terms: B & B £10.50–25. Full *alc* from £6. Reduced rates for children in family rooms; special meals provided.

BRAMPTON, Cumbria   Map 4

Farlam Hall   [GFG]   *Telephone:* Hallbankgate (069 76) 234

A hearty vote of confidence in the comprehensively satisfactory hospitality offered by Mr and Mrs Quinion in their Border manor house, 17th-century in origin, four miles from Hadrian's Wall. Only complaints offered by grateful guests: that dinnertime deadlines are a bit on the rigid side, and that service at meals can at times be breathless. To set against these minor grumbles, here are a few of the compliments from this year's postbag: 'Warm and charming welcome . . . our room exceptionally appointed . . . Beds especially comfortable . . . All our meals were of outstanding quality.' 'An admirable place, and 15% cheaper than comparable alternatives. Excellent service, imaginative options at dinner.' 'Made to feel most welcome without going over the top.' 'Fully endorse entry: excellent dinner and breakfast with fine attention to detail.' *(John and Priscilla Gillett, Peter Brooke, Jessica Elliott, J and JW, A J Watt)*

Open: All year, except first two week November, Christmas, New Year and February; also closed Monday–Tuesday in November, December and January.
Rooms: 9 double, 2 single – 4 with bath, 2 with shower.
Facilities: 3 lounges, 1 with TV, bar, dining room seating about 50.
Location: On the A689 2½ miles SE of Brampton; Carlisle 9 miles W; Hadrian's Wall 4 miles. The hotel is on the A689, *not* in Farlam Village.
Credit cards: Access/Euro, American Express.
Terms (service at guests' discretion): B & B £16–19. Set meals: lunch (Sunday only) £7; dinner (Saturday) £10, (other days) £9.50.

BRIGHTON, East Sussex   Map 2

Granville Hotel   *Telephone:* Brighton (0273) 26722
125 Kings Road

Formerly a run-down guest-house, this 14-room bow-fronted sea-facing Regency hotel was extensively and enterprisingly restored three years ago by Audrey Simpson, who used to be a lecturer in Social Anthropology and Social Psychology, but has had a mid-life conversion to inn-keeping. However, she still claims to be doing work for her post-graduate studies with the help of her guests. She has certainly created a fashionably congenial atmosphere for her fieldwork, with the help of Laura Ashley (decorations) and Mary Quant (carpets); one room had a double bath, two have four-posters. The hotel is a family concern: Mrs Simpson's husband David gives assistance when he is not lecturing in politics, and her son-in-law, Wayne Spencer, is in charge of the kitchens at the hotel's basement restaurant, *Trogs*. About the latter, readers who like traditional menus had best be warned that *Trogs*' menu is unashamedly gimmicky. It is in the form of a theatre programme, with an 'Exotic Cocktail' as a Prologue (included in the price); then Scene One, with items like 'Scampi – lovingly wrapped in Bacon, finished off with Melted Cheese'. Among the dishes in Scene Two are 'Chicken on a Bed of Garlic – You stay away from Civilised Society after this one.' Scene Three includes 'Granville Swans. Our speciality Swans have already become famous, filled with whipped cream, fruit mmm – the "ignore the calories" sweet.' We have not yet had a chance to sample personally these concoctions, but, with one exception, both the rooms and the meals have gone down well with our readers. *(J French, Norman Voce)*

Open: All year, except Christmas. Restaurant closed Sunday.
Rooms: 12 double, 2 single – 1 with bath, 7 with shower, all with telephone, radio, colour TV, and baby-listening; 2 four-poster beds. (2 rooms on ground floor.)
Facilities: Lounge, bar, restaurant; patio in front of hotel. Fishing rods available on sea front. (*Note:* hotel is on 6 floors and has no lift.)
Location: Central; no private parking.
Restrictions: Children at management's discretion. No dogs.
Credit cards: All major credit cards accepted.

Terms (service at guests' discretion): Rooms £10.35–15 per person; B & B £13.35–18; dinner, B & B £18.35–23; full board £22.35–27. Set meals: lunch £4; dinner £5.50; full *alc* £11. Reduced rates out of season for 2-night stays. Reduced rates for children.

BRIXHAM, South Devon   Map 1

The Quayside Hotel   *Telephone:* Brixham (080 45) 55751
King Street

The most delightful aspect of *The Quayside* is its aspect: it is a conversion of five 17th- and 18th-century cottages overlooking the inner harbour of this small fishing village on the southern headland of Torbay. The rooms to go for are those in the front, even if you are woken at dawn by a cacophony of seagulls meeting the incoming fishing boats. The hotel has two bars – a small intimate one for residents and one in Edwardian style called the Ernie Lister, offering live entertainment several nights a week. The food is English traditional, with a good selection of locally caught fish *à la carte*. 'One of the most attractive hotels we have found in our wanderings, combining old-fashioned homeliness with modern comfort.' *(Mr and Mrs F K Godwin; also Alan Ross)*

Open: Early January–end November.
Rooms: 28 double, 4 single – 26 with bath, all with telephone, radio, colour TV, tea-making facilities and baby-listening. 2 rooms in annexe.
Facilities: Lounge, 2 bars, restaurant; live entertainment several times a week. Shingle beach and seawater swimming pool nearby; deep sea and mackerel fishing trips during season.
Location: 200 yards from town centre; ample parking.
Credit cards: All major credit cards accepted.
Terms: B & B £15.50–22. Set meal: dinner £6.50; full *alc* £12. Special bargain breaks. Reduced rates for children sharing parents' room; special meals provided.

BROAD CAMPDEN, Gloucestershire   Map 2

The Malt House   *Telephone:* Evesham (0386) 840295

Many owners of small country hotels would like their guests to feel that they were staying in a private country house even though paying for the privilege. Mrs Pat Robinson, whose *Malt House* is a conversion of three mellow Cotswold 17th-century cottages in an unspoilt hamlet a mile from Chipping Campden, is particularly keen to foster this atmosphere: her guests – the house can accommodate no more than eight – will often sit together round a large single table for the evening meal, though they can certainly opt for separate tables if they wish. And the price for dinner, bed and breakfast includes aperitif and wine as well as early morning and afternoon tea so that there is less than the usual settling of small bills at the end of a visit. 'An enchanting home . . . run with boundless energy and good cheer by Mrs Robinson who cooks stupendously with produce from her farm and garden. The atmosphere is happy and relaxed.' *(Roger Smithells)*

Open: All year, except 24, 25, 26 December.
Rooms: 3 double, 2 single; 3 bathrooms available.

Facilities: Drawing room, restaurant. 4 acres grounds with large gazebo and small brook. Spinning workshops held occasionally.
Location: Leave Chipping Campden by Sheep street, turn first left after garage on left into Broad Campden; *Malt House* second on left after the *Baker's Arms* pub; parking.
Restrictions: Children over 10 preferred. No dogs.
Terms: B & B £13; dinner, B & B (inc. early morning and afternoon tea, aperitifs and wine) £21. Set meal: dinner £8. Special weekend breaks available at 12% discount.

BROMPTON, Northallerton, North Yorkshire   Map 4

Manor House Hotel   *Telephone:* Northallerton (0609) 70501
19–20 Church View

A modest 17th-century manor house, with a number of weavers' cottages, provides 'a remarkably pleasant hotel' on the green of what is claimed to be Yorkshire's largest village, two miles from Northallerton. The North Yorkshire Moors, the Dales National Park, Brontë country and the great abbeys are all within easy range. The house has been attractively converted to provide 11 spacious bedrooms, all overlooking the green. The bar is popular with visitors and locals, and the restaurant, called *The Clacking Shuttles* after a forgotten best-selling novel of that name by a local authoress, is well spoken of. 'A hotel of great character and real friendliness.' *(Christopher Portway; also Roger Smithells)*

Open: All year.
Rooms: 10 double, 1 single – 8 with bath, 3 with shower, all with telephone, radio, colour TV, tea-making facilities and baby-listening.
Facilities: Lounge, 2 bars, restaurant, functions room. Small garden with unheated plunge pool.
Location: 2 miles from Northallerton on the A684; parking.
Restriction: No dogs in public rooms.
Credit cards: All major credit cards accepted.
Terms: B & B £14–20; dinner, B & B £22–28; full board £26–32. Set meals: lunch £3.50–5.50; dinner £8; full *alc* £11. Reduced rates and special meals for children.

BUDOCK Vean, Nr Falmouth, South Cornwall   Map 1

Budock Vean Hotel   *Telephone:* Mawnan Smith (0326) 250288

We had an entry for *Budock Vean* in the 1980 edition of the Guide, but left it out last year – not because we had had adverse reports on the place, but simply for lack of any feedback from our readers. We took the view that this substantial de-luxe hotel, converted from an 18th-century manor house but with modern extensions, with its 53 bedrooms, its 65 acres leading down to the Helford River, its 18-hole golf course, its indoor heated swimming pool with log fire and bar, its weekly dances – in effect, a Surrey country club dropped into the lush pastures of South Cornwall – was not what our readers cared about. We were clearly wrong, and began to stand corrected within a few weeks of the appearance of the 1981 edition. 'After a busy term at our school,' wrote one reader, 'nothing could be better than relaxation at *Budock Vean*, and we have booked for our twentieth visit in 1982. We would never find an adequate alternative.'

Another reader, who says that he stays at the hotel every two or three months, pulled out even more stops: 'Undoubtedly, it is by far the best hotel in the West Country. It is run by one of the most obliging, courteous and efficient staffs I have ever had the pleasure of meeting. The bedrooms are first-class and are quite unsurpassed by most British hotels. The food is quite superb as indeed is the wine list, and I can very definitely state that it is the best hotel that I have ever stayed in in Great Britain for the last ten years.' *(D F Quibell Smith, C L Turnbull; also B W Croft, F W Grant, A Furber Murphy)*

Open: March–January.
Rooms: 42 double, 10 single, 1 suite – all with bath and telephone; TV on request.
Facilities: Lift, 4 lounges (2 with TV), restaurant, games room, sun lounge; heated indoor pool. Weekly dance in restaurant and weekly disco in bar August/September. 65 acres grounds with gardens leading down to Helford River; golf course, private sandy tidal foreshore with sailing, windsurfing and fishing; horse riding and fly fishing nearby. &.
Location: 7 miles from Falmouth; take the A39 from Truro to Penryn Cross, then proceed to Mabe Bunrthouse, then to Mawnan Smith, and from Mawnan Smith to the hotel.
Restrictions: No children under 5. No dogs.
Credit cards: All major credit cards accepted.
Terms (service at guests' discretion): Dinner, B & B £27–32. Set meals: lunch £3; dinner £10.50. Off-season weekend rates. Reduced rates and special meals for children.

BURFORD, Oxfordshire   Map 2

The Bay Tree   [GFG]   *Telephone:* Burford (099 382) 3137
Sheep Street

This noble 16th-century house, just off Burford's luscious High Street, and worthy of its many fine Elizabethan neighbours, has for long been a source of contention among our correspondents. What is not in dispute is the lovely old-fashioned (in the best sense) character of the place – its oak-panelling, huge stone fireplaces, galleried stairs, many good pieces of antique furniture – not to mention its venerable sloping floors. But there have been many grumbles – notably, about the standards of the decor, amateur or stuffy service and the undependable quality of the meals – mixed in with expressions of gratification. Last year, we cut *The Bay Tree* out. We are reinserting it this year because the balance of reports have swung us the other way. We quote from two:

'We have recently returned to *The Bay Tree* for their remarkable value three-day winter bargain break. It was beautifully warm, food and service excellent with lovely old-fashioned, seldom seen, courtesies like hot-water bottles provided by the hotel in the beds, and the covers turned back, shoes cleaned overnight, lovely linen table napkins and linen sheets, attractive antique polished furniture and, when we had to leave at 6 am on our last morning, a delicious tray of rolls, flask of coffee, etc, left in our room the night before. The lounges are spacious and there are three with log fires lit in the mornings. My only small criticism is artificial flowers (as well as fresh ones which looked rather tired) but otherwise as good as ever and remarkable value.' *(Sue Riches)*

'The experience of this little inn is one we will remember always. There is definitely the feeling that you are returning to a place where the stress of the world is *not allowed*, and where you are sure to find an atmosphere of

35

quiet peaceful welcome. The older part of the inn is definitely the most charming as it is filled with the history of 400 years. The small bar has a cosy fireplace. The dining area overlooks the exquisite garden, and the view from our bedroom overlooked the garden and beyond into the Cotswolds. There are no telephones, no TV and no locks on the door. This lovely place is an escape from the 20th century.' *(Dr and Mrs James F Hood; also John and Priscilla Gillett, G Wilson, Ann Dally, T M Wilson)*

Open: All year.
Rooms: 15 double, 9 single – 17 with bath. 10 rooms in annexe.
Facilities: 4 lounges (3 with log fires), restaurant. 2–3 acres garden.
Location: In town centre; parking.
Restriction: No dogs in public rooms or garden.
Terms: B & B £13–18.50; full board (minimum 3 days) £18.50–23.50. Set meals: lunch £4 (Sunday £6); dinner £6. 3-day budget breaks available. Reduced rates for children.

BURY ST EDMUNDS, Suffolk   **Map 2**

The Angel [GFG]   *Telephone:* Bury St Edmunds (0284) 3926
Angel Hill   *Telex:* 81630 (Angel G)

The small market town of Bury St Edmunds with its many fine Georgian buildings, its little squares and old shop fronts, is a pleasure to visit in its own right as well as being a good touring centre for Cambridge, Newmarket and the many unspoilt villages of East Anglia. *The Angel*, patronized by Dickens (who immortalized it as the place where Sam Weller first encounters Job Trotter), is an ivy-covered series of linked buildings on the main square opposite the great abbey gate, one of the glories of the town. If you are allergic to noise, you should avoid the front, especially on market days. The hotel makes a lot of its Dickensian association: you can sleep in the room he actually occupied, Room 15, in a huge four-poster (one of several in the hotel) and downstairs there's a Charles Dickens Bar and a Pickwick Bar. One restaurant overlooks the abbey gate, and there is another in a cellar-like basement, with tables set under arches – possibly the abbey's charnel house, and now aptly called *The Angel Grillroom*. There's a somewhat conventional printed menu, but portions are generous and a reader described with pleasure 'beautifully tender rare roast beef carved from a huge joint kept warm under a colossal silver dome'. There's a good cold table, and the service is friendly.

As in previous years, there have been conflicting reports about the standard of upkeep, with more than one reader muttering about shabbiness, even while appreciating the place in other respects. In general, however, our impression of *The Angel* is that it is a superior example of professional innkeeping, with the owners, Mr and Mrs Gough, keeping a vigilant eye and maintaining a high morale among their staff. *(Alison Eldred, John Sidey, Miss M Cox)*

Open: All year.
Rooms: 27 double, 11 single, 5 suites – 35 with bath, 1 with shower, all with telephone, radio, colour TV and baby-listening.
Facilities: 2 lounges, 2 restaurants (one conventional, one in arched basement), 2 ballrooms, private dining room, Pickwick Bar, Main Bar.
Location: Town centre, facing Abbey Gardens; parking for 20 cars.
Restriction: Dogs allowed, but not in public rooms.

Credit cards: All major credit cards accepted.
Terms (no service charge): B & B £18.50–32. Full *alc* £13. Reduced rates for children.

CAMBRIDGE   Map 2

The Garden House Hotel   *Telephone:* Cambridge (0223) 63421
Granta Place (off Mill Lane)   *Telex:* 81463

Cambridge, like Oxford, is poorly served by hotels. Of the half-dozen establishments in the city, there is no question but that *The Garden House*, though a little more expensive than its competitors, is the most to be recommended. One of its attractions is its riverside garden along the waters of the Granta by the weir where it joins the Cam – a beautiful location, also dependably quiet. The hotel isn't strong on character, having been rebuilt in the Sixties after a fire, and there are those who don't much care for the decor. And the fact that it is a popular venue for city and university functions also deprives it of an intimate character. But in the past readers have appreciated a consistently high and friendly quality of service, and at least an adequate restaurant. It still scores on these grounds with some correspondents, but there has also been recently a vocal opposition reporting disappointing meals and patchy service. So this entry has to be a qualified one. Further reports would be welcome.

Open: 1 January–24 December.
Rooms: 55 double, 4 suites – all with bath, telephone, radio, colour TV and baby-listening. (7 rooms on ground floor.)
Facilities: Lifts, large lounge/cocktail bar overlooking gardens, restaurant, banqueting suites, some conference facilities; Saturday dinner-dances. 3 acres gardens and lawns reaching down to the river where tea and drinks can be taken; boating and fishing. ð .
Location: 5 minutes' walk from town centre; ample parking.
Restriction: No dogs.
Credit cards: Access/Euro, American Express, Barclay/Visa, Diners.
Terms (service at guests' discretion): B & B (continental) £21–36. Set meals: lunch £7.90; dinner from £7.50; full *alc* £13.50. Mini-breaks October–March. Reduced rates and special meals for children.

CHAGFORD, Devon   Map 1

Gidleigh Park Hotel   [GFG]   *Telephone:* Chagford (064 73) 2367 or 2225

Although less than 5 years old, *Gidleigh Park* must certainly rank as one of the dozen outstanding country hotels in England, not only for the superb quality of the cooking and the outstanding wine list – now 325 bins and, boasts Paul Henderson, the best selection of Californian wines in Europe – but also for the emphatically sybaritic comforts of the rooms: both the spacious and gracious public rooms and the equally generous bedrooms above. A consequence of this 'great luxury of space', as one reader put it, is that there has been a grumble or two about heating in the colder weather. Another cause of disaffection for some is that *Gidleigh* now serves an absolutely set meal changed daily – though there is a small *à la carte* selection if you prefer not to go the whole gourmet hog.

The success of Paul and Kay Henderson, a young American couple who

37

opened *Gidleigh Park* only after making a close study of the double and treble-starred Michelin establishments in France, is the greater in that their stockbroker Tudor hotel on the banks of the river Teign, a mile from the edge of Dartmoor, isn't easy of access. 'Keep heart, you are still en route to Gidleigh Park', is the encouraging sign after a couple of miles of winding lanes out of Chagford. But, to adopt a Michelin expression, the place merits not only a detour but also *vaut le voyage. (Richard Chinn, Padi Howard, Heather Sharland, R O Marshall, Hugh Johnson)*

Open: All year.
Rooms: 11 double – all with bath, telephone and colour TV.
Facilities: Front hall, large lounge, bar loggia, 2 dining rooms. 30 acres grounds and gardens with croquet lawn. North Teign river 50 yards in front of the house; 14 miles of trout, sea trout and salmon fishing. Golf, riding and walking nearby.
Location: Approach from Chagford, *not* Gidleigh. Take the M4 or M5, then the A30 to Whiddon Down. Then go to Chagford. From Chagford Square facing Webbers with Lloyds Bank on right, turn right into Mill Street. After 200 yards fork right and go downhill to Factory Crossroad. Go straight across into Holy Street and follow lane 1½ miles to end.
Restrictions: No children under 10. Dogs sometimes allowed.
Terms (excluding VAT): B & B £17.25–35. Set meal: dinner £11.25; full *alc* about £18. 4-day cooking courses, and wine-tasting weekends November–March.

CHAGFORD, Devon   **Map 1**

Thornworthy House   *Telephone:* Chagford (064 73) 3297

In terms of accommodation, Daphne and Graham Jackson's house is one of the smallest establishments in the Guide but, in terms of reader response, certainly one of the more popular. Hotel or guest-house? It really defies designation, but it is modest in price as well as in size, and a highly personal sort of place. Despite the address, it is 3 miles from Chagford, 1,200 feet up and on the very edge of Dartmoor – a position of exceptional tranquility. We had one long negative report – the single room was really very small, not everything worked and the cooking was a considerable disappointment. Most readers, however, have written appreciatively. Examples: 'We endorse everything. First-class unobtrusive attention. Very comfortable room: 9/10. Food *very* good: 9/10.' 'The Jacksons provide everything we look for in a hotel and avoid all that we deplore in many. One feels a guest of a particularly considerate host and hostess. The peace and quiet, the beauty of the surroundings and the excellent cooking are all outstanding. And we were delighted on our fourth visit to find that inclusion in the Guide has not led to any deterioration of standards.' 'A perfect retreat from urban civilization. It is possible to walk straight on to the moor from the hotel – and probably advisable as the lanes leading to it are narrow and circuitous and fraught with oncoming horses and traffic. We had an imaginatively furnished bedroom (in which it would have been easy to spend our whole stay), and the rest of the house was furnished in similar fashion. There is a comfortable lounge with a cosy wood-burning stove and a well-equipped games room. The food cooked by Mrs Jackson was excellent – exceptional were the mackerel caught by Mr Jackson and then smoked over oak chippings and the perfectly cooked grilled Devon trout. Beautifully cooked vegetables – all home grown, and an interesting wine list. After our first meal,

Mr Jackson noted that my husband had certain protein allergies and went to the trouble of adjusting dinner menus accordingly – which illustrates the caring attitude the Jacksons have towards their guests.' *(Mary-Jane and Simon Wilkins; also Dr and Mrs G N Evans, E W Emery and others)*

Open: March–end October.
Rooms: 3 double, 1 single – 2 with bath; additional 3 double bedrooms in barn cottage, mainly used for self-catering.
Facilities: 2 sitting rooms (1 with colour TV), dining room. 2 acres grounds with hard tennis court. Excellent walking, hill climbing and trout fishing, swimming in open-air pool at Chagford or, from the hardy, in moorland pools. No disturbing noises: 'Even the cows and sheep are quiet,' say the owners, 'and the only nightlife is conversation.'
Location: 3 miles from Chagford. From Chagford Square turn right into Mill Street. After 150 yards fork left at sign to Kestor Rock. At top of Waye Hill road curves to left. Immediately after, take right turn signposted to Thornworthy. From there on, follow signposts to Thornworthy, via Thorn and Yeo.
Restriction: Dogs discouraged, but accepted by arrangement.
Terms: B & B £11.75–12.50; dinner, B & B £17.50–18.25. Set meal: dinner from £6.75; full *alc* £8.50. Reduced rates for children under 10; special meals provided on request.

CHESTER, Cheshire   Map 2

The Grosvenor Hotel   *Telephone:* Chester (0244) 24024
Eastgate Street   *Telex:* 61240

A dignified mid-Victorian building, with lots of period features, near one of the gates of the old walled city amid Chester's special pride, the Rows. It belongs unquestionably to the 'grander' end of the hotel spectrum, and makes its living not just from the individual traveller but also from conferences, banqueting, coach parties and the like. But it is a first-rate hotel of its kind – and, a plus for wine-lovers, has an outstanding cellar to complement its restaurant. 'For me good service from a friendly well-trained staff is very important. This is what this outstanding hotel provides from the moment you arrive, and someone is quietly at your side to carry your suitcase. The bedrooms have all modern conveniences. There is an excellent dining room with the same efficient yet unobtrusive service as everywhere in this hotel. As for the wines, you get the Duke of Westminster's cellar selection or so it would appear. Go mad, just for once, but if you can, order the night before. Luxury without being too expensive.' *(George S Jonas)*

Open: All year.
Rooms: 60 double, 40 single, 6 suites – all with bath, telephone, radio, colour TV, mini-bar and baby-listening; 1 four-poster bed.
Facilities: Lifts, lounge, 2 bars, restaurant, ballroom, conference and banqueting facilities. & .
Location: Central; large NCP car park adjoins the hotel.
Restriction: No dogs.
Credit cards: All major credit cards accepted.
Terms (excluding service): Rooms £27–32.45 per person. Set meal: breakfast (continental) £2.85, (English) £4.10; full *alc* £11. Special mini-weekend tariff. Reduced rates and special meals for children.

Clinchs' Hotel   *Telephone:* Chichester (0243) 789915
Guildhall Street

Patrons of theatre festivals often look for a civilized bed-and-breakfast in preference to a long drive home or a flash motel. *Clinchs'* – so called because Daphne and Bill Clinch are the resident owners – is an elegant town house in a small quiet street adjoining Priory Park and no more than 300 yards from the Festival Theatre. You can park just behind the hotel. 'A delightful small hotel, serving the best English breakfast I have enjoyed in 60 years. The atmosphere is more that of a private home than a hotel, with a higher level of comfort than many private homes.' *(Christopher Calthrop)*

Open: All year. Restaurant closed Sunday.
Rooms: 5 double, 2 single – 5 with bath, 2 with shower, all with telephone, radio, colour TV and tea-making facilities.
Facilities: Lounge, restaurant.
Location: In town centre adjoining Priory Park; 300 yards from Festival Theatre; parking.
Restrictions: Not suited to children. No dogs.
Credit cards: Access/Euro/Mastercard, American Express, Barclay/Visa.
Terms: Rooms £15–22 per person; B & B £17–24. Set meals: lunch £7; dinner £11; full *alc* £13.50.

Note: Although recommended to us as a B & B, Clinchs' is in fact opening a restaurant after the Guide has gone to press. More reports welcome.

Kings Arms Hotel   [GFG]   *Telephone:* Evesham (0386) 840256

The *Kings Arms* is an awkward case. It certainly looks like a good hotel: it's an old building – part early 17th-century, part Georgian – looking out over Chipping Campden's enchanting Market Square, full of other noble Cotswold houses. It has lots of character inside too: great open fires, winding staircases, some good pieces of furniture, and an unusually good restaurant. But the accommodation has for many years been a source of complaint: 'As a good hotel, it's awful,' splutters one reader. 'The food, of course, is what you really go for, but how can you include in the Guide somewhere which in mid-winter doesn't have central heating in the bedrooms? We sat shivering in our coats for three hours before dinner on the first night. The hot-air blower didn't make much impact till Day Two. The room was prettily wall-papered, but badly furnished, and it was too cold to wash properly. The loo was down two flights of stairs. The ideal is to go for dinner . . . and then leave.'

Shortly after getting this diatribe, we received a totally different report: 'May I write a word in praise of the *Kings Arms*? We are a family of five plus an Airedale puppy, and were quite overwhelmed by the cordial welcome we received at this hotel. Dogs are not of course allowed in the public rooms, but no antagonism is shown towards them if they are well-behaved and kept in the bedroom. Our bitch was fussed over by the staff. And children are well-catered for too. Ours were offered a high tea of their own choice at a reasonable price. A camp bed was put up for one of them in our room – at a much reduced rate. So my wife and I were able to relax and enjoy ourselves in the comfortable bar with its two open fires and interesting antique furniture. We had dinner in the restaurant. The cooking showed skill and imagination, and service was friendly and informal. It's true that the floors creak, and that the number of bathrooms is limited, but this didn't worry us in the least. At the price charged, this is one of the best hotels I have been to.'

This last report is not an isolated endorsement: the *Kings Arms* has never lacked supporters – though perhaps fair weather ones? – as well as critics. We wish that Mr and Mrs Willmott, who are now the owners, would invest in full central heating and go in for some refurbishing in the bedrooms too. But on balance, and with appropriate warnings about woollies in the winter, we feel this entry should stay. *(John Huw Roberts; also K W Bogle, Mrs A A Kitrick, Sarah Litvinoff)*

Open: All year, except weekends only January–February.
Rooms: 11 double, 3 single – 2 with bath.
Facilities: Hall, sitting room, bar, dining room. 1 acre grounds. Local golf courses; horse racing locally during spring.
Location: In town centre, facing Market Square; parking for 50 cars.
Restrictions: No dogs in public rooms.
Credit cards: All major credit cards accepted.
Terms: B & B £15–19. Bar lunch from 60p; set meals: Sunday lunch £7.75; dinner £8.75–9.50 plus 10% service charge. Bargain break winter weekends £40 per person (2 nights). Reduced rates for children in cot or camp bed in parents' room; special meals provided.

CLANFIELD, Oxfordshire   **Map 2**

The Plough   *Telephone:* Clanfield (036 781) 222

The name is ridiculously misleading: no simple village pub, but a handsome 3-storey Elizabethan sub-manor-house, impeccably maintained inside and out, and combining a first-class highly sophisticated restaurant with half-a-dozen small but well-appointed bedrooms. The resident owners are Tony and Hedy Barnes, Hedy, who is German, being in charge of the kitchens. There is a long and enterprising menu, including items like Hedy's Special Sweet and Sour Starter and Hedy's Famous Cheesecakes which give a misleading impression of tweeness. An unusual feature of the restaurant is a special vegetarian menu. A special mention must also be made of the long and interesting wine list – part of what the Barnes inherited when they took over *The Plough* from Harry Norton on his move to *Rookery Hall* at Worleston (q.v.). Service is *comme il faut*.

Open: All year.
Rooms: 6 double – 1 with bath.
Facilities: Reception lounge, residents' lounge with TV, spacious lounge/bar, attractive restaurant. ½ acre garden.
Location: 20 miles W of Oxford on the B4449 between Standlake and Lechlade.
Restrictions: No children under 10. No dogs.
Terms (excluding 10% service charge): Rooms £11.50–21.50 per person; B & B £15–25. Full *alc* £12.

> Don't keep your favourite hotel to yourself. The Guide supports: it doesn't spoil.

41

Malvern View Hotel   [GFG]   *Telephone:* Bishops Cleeve (024 267) 2017

With no serious dissent, there has been once again a chorus of praise for the special quality of Paul and Mary Sparks' hospitality in their small Cotswold-stone house 750 feet up on the edge of Cleeve Common. One enthusiast was so carried away that she rang to let us know how impressed she had been by everything about the place – the consistently high standard of the meals, the spotless extremely comfortable rooms and, above all, by the welcome she had received. It's a rare hotel that succeeds in commanding such virtual unanimity of appreciation year after year, and perhaps rarer when that hotel is a restaurant with rooms – only seven bedrooms, but the restaurant can seat 42. But there has never been any suggestion of the residents being short-changed. *(Mrs A Litvin, J P Mackenzie, Eve Blumenau, Mrs M E Hartley, Vida Bingham and others)*

Open: All year, except 3 weeks at Christmas. Restaurant open to residents only for dinner on Sunday.
Rooms: 7 double – all with bath or shower and colour TV.
Facilities: Lounge, bar, restaurant. 1 acre garden leading on to Cleeve Common; excellent walks; golf nearby.
Location: On the A46 to Broadway, 4½ miles NE of Cheltenham.
Restrictions: No children under 6. No dogs.
Terms: B & B £15–20. Set meal: dinner £10.50. Special meals for children.

Bailiffscourt Hotel   *Telephone:* Littlehampton (090 64) 23511
Telex: 877072

We had an entry for this highly convincing, largely bogus medieval manor in an earlier edition, but left it out when the management of the time took exception to a mildly jokey reference to a keyhole which permitted our correspondent to see through to the bathroom next door. Since then, new owners have been making extensive renovations: we are sure that the voyeur's keyhole has been filled up. We offer below two views of the new improved *Bailiffscourt*:
   'In the early 1930s a British millionaire, the Hon. Walter Guinness, fell in love with Bailiffscourt. The 1,000-acre estate contained a derelict Norman chapel, a Georgian farmhouse, a moat and a 12th-century courthouse. Now, through the skills of renowned medieval domestic architect, Amyas Phillips, the spending of well over a million pounds on its reconstruction, the importation of such relics as a medieval two-light window from derelict Muchelny Abbey, a 15th-century barn door and 16th-century timber, it is one of the most unusual and peaceful hotels in Britain. Each of two subsequent owners have spent large sums on it, and its 19 bedrooms, plus bathrooms, could hardly be more appropriately or comfortably furnished. It is a happy hotel with many amenities and a fine restaurant, unusual and rare wines with a mark-up of £3 a bottle rather than the obnoxious 200% of many luxury hotels, and its grounds and swimming pool are only a few miles from Arundel Castle, Goodwood racecourse, and Chichester's famous cathedral and Festival Theatre. By

road it is 62 miles from Hyde Park Corner; I recommend it most warmly and enthusiastically.' *(Denis Morris)*

'I've known *Bailiffscourt* for twenty years, and it's always had a magic tranquillity. But the service has never quite lived up to the setting – until now. A new management has clearly put a lot of money and flair into this "monastery" by the shore, the staff are efficient, relaxed and friendly all at the same time, and the result is a combination of some of the romance of Thornbury Castle or Portmeirion, some of the elegance of *Maison Talbooth* and some of the freedom of being in your own home. As for accommodation, the B & B price covered a double room the size and shape of a Saxon church, with a four-poster bed, a log fire (real of course), remote-controlled TV, walk-in wardrobes, bathroom with twin Victoria baths, morning tea and papers, full English breakfasts served on beautiful china at any time up till lunch, the freedom to check out "when you feel like it, some time after lunch". Strongly recommended.' *(Jack Pizzey)*

Open: All year.
Rooms: 16 double, 3 single – all with bath, telephone and colour TV.
Facilities: 3 sitting rooms/lounges, TV room, restaurant; function/meeting rooms; table tennis and pool table. 20 acres grounds with tennis, heated swimming pool and riding stables; own path to beach.
Location: Near Arundel; turning to beach off the A259, 1 mile from Littlehampton on the Bognor Regis road.
Restrictions: No children under 10. Dogs by arrangement.
Credit cards: All major credit cards accepted.
Terms: B & B £22.50–35. Set meals: lunch from £5; dinner £11; full *alc* £13.50. Bargain mid-week winter breaks November–March inclusive.

COLYTON, Devon   **Map 1**

The Old Bakehouse   *Telephone:* Colyton (0297) 52518

Colyton is a village in rural south Devon, well away from the main roads though only three miles through country lanes to the beaches at Seaton Bay. *The Old Bakehouse* is 17th-century, with plenty of atmospheric oak beams, which has been agreeably converted into a restaurant (which seats 28) and rooms (seven). It is run by Susan Keen (who does the cooking) and Stephen Keen, her husband. They are a young, enterprising couple, and the food, which has won a high reputation far outside the locality, is French regional. There is no garden and only one real lounge, with another which doubles as a pre-prandial bar. The rooms, while simple, are pleasantly comfortable.

Open: 1 March–30 November.
Rooms: 6 double, 1 single – all with bath.
Facilities: 2 lounges (1 with bar), dining room. 2½ miles from the sea with sailing, safe bathing; riding, fishing, golf nearby.
Location: On the B3161, 2½ miles N of Seaton Bay. In Colyton follow Axminster signs.
Restriction: Dogs by arrangement.
Terms (excluding 10% service charge): B & B £16–17; dinner, B & B £22–25. Set meal: dinner £12.50. French regional dinner week-ends, and 4-day or week-end painting holidays available. Reduced rates for children.

STOP PRESS We have just heard that the Keens have left The Old Bakehouse; *the new owners are Mr and Mrs Giles. Reports, please.*

Treglos Hotel   *Telephone:* St Merryn (0841) 520727

'The *Treglos* is situated very close to Trevose Golf Club and within ¼ mile of the sea. There is superb walking along the Cornish Coastal Path. It is one of the few hotels that actually gives service and doesn't charge for it, gratuities being entirely at the customer's discretion. Early morning tea, breakfast, and indeed all meals can be served in your room if desired. Your shoes are cleaned and, wonder of wonders, your luggage is carried for you. The dining room organization and service is excellent, and nothing is too much trouble. Altogether the meals are satisfactory, though the cooking is not quite up to *Good Food Guide* standards. But it has a lot going for it as a place to stay.' *(BA; also Ian C Dewey)*

Open: 15 March–10 November.
Rooms: 33 double, 6 single, 3 suites – 42 with bath, all with telephone, radio and colour TV (1 suite on ground floor).
Facilities: Lift, 4 lounges, bar lounge, restaurant. 2 acres garden with croquet and heated swimming pool; sandy beach 300 yeards.
Location: Follow signs to St Merryn, then to Constantine Bay.
Restrictions: No children under 3 in restaurant. Dogs at owners' discretion.
Terms (excluding VAT and service):   Rooms £14.50–21; B & B £15.50–23; dinner, B & B £19.50–27. Set meals: lunch £4.95; dinner £6.95; full *alc* £15. Reduced rates for children sharing parents' room; special meals provided.

CRANBROOK, Kent   **Map 2**

Kennel Holt Hotel   *Telephone:* Cranbrook (0580) 712032

This small quiet well-bred Elizabethan beamed manor-house hotel in the Weald of Kent, with its attractive five-acre garden – only 50 miles from London, but secluded and peaceful – continues to please our readers. Mr and Mrs Fletcher are the resident owners of long standing, and the hotel has the settled air of knowing what it's about. Cooking is described as 'traditional English', and one reader felt the helpings were on the mean side. Another sent us this report:

'A quiet relaxed stay. An idyllic setting. Bedroom was spacious, clean and with adequate lighting. Breakfast and dinner was included in the price, but rather surprised that after-dinner coffee in the lounge was an extra. No choice of main dish at dinner – no disadvantage during our stay as all the main dishes were excellent. Joy to eat homegrown veg., local wine, and I suspect local-laid eggs. *[How does one tell these from the other sort? – Editor]* The home-made soups were excellent value, better than the alternative dish while the desserts were excellent. One could have as large a breakfast as one could eat. Plenty of space for guests to disperse after dinner – two lounges and a large hall. On a fine evening, there were the 5 acres to wander around! Very much a place to relax in, and the welcome and service were exceptionally good.' *(Martin W Stubbs; also H A Cohen)*

Open: All year except Christmas and the first 2 weeks in October.
Rooms: 5 double, 2 single – 7 bathrooms (4 *en suite*), all rooms with radio.
Facilities: 2 lounges (1 with colour TV), log fires, dining room. 5 acres grounds

with garden chairs and tea on the lawn. Riding school within 5 miles, golf course at Lamberhurst (5 miles) and Hawkhurst (6 miles); sea bathing 30 minutes by car; coarse fishing and some dry-fly trout reservoirs nearby.

Location: Turn off the A262 between Goudhurst and Cranbrook.

Restriction: Dogs 'if owners well-behaved'.

Terms (excluding VAT): Dinner, B & B single room £24, double room £48. Set meal: dinner about £6.75. No lunches.

CRANTOCK, Nr Newquay, Cornwall   Map 1

Crantock Bay Hotel   *Telephone:* Crantock (0637) 830 229

A jolly family hotel a mile outside the village of Crantock, in a beautiful and absolutely quiet position on the West Pentire headland, facing four-square on to the Atlantic: sandy and rocky beaches, caves and pools, easily accessible on both sides. Good surfing. Nothing fancy in the decor, and the food is traditional English fare. But it's the kind of place that tends to be habit-forming: lots of regulars.

'The position is perfect – main rooms all have superb wide views of the sea and adjacent headlands. Service couldn't be bettered. The proprietors, Mr and Mrs Eyles, and their children are real professionals in the best sense – welcome one by name and are attentive to detail at every moment. Spotlessly clean – all staff, local girls and women who are waitresses and cleaners, the gardener, handyman-barman, etc, are kindness itself. Food is plain and English, freshly cooked, varied and plenty of it. There is a lovely relaxed friendly atmosphere. Many guests have been before and know each other but newcomers like us are integrated and welcome. Children had an excellent "Smartie party" midweek and joined in bar billiards and table tennis competitions. They enjoyed the Rumpus room and garden games. It's a lovely coastline with a choice of accessible beaches, but the paths to them are steep and highish (only just possible for elderly and very young).' *(Sue Riches; also Mr and Mrs Steve Berson)*

Open: Easter–October.

Rooms: 19 double, 12 single – 14 with bath, most with sea views, all with radio, tea-making facilities and baby-listening. (1 room with bath on ground floor.)

Facilities: Lounge, TV room, games room, bar; dancing, slide shows, children's parties 2–3 nights a week. 4½ acres grounds with putting green, croquet, children's play area. Sea with sandy beach and safe bathing (lifeguard service) 200 yards from the hotel, reached through the grounds; tennis, riding, golf nearby.

Location: 1 mile from Crantock, 5 miles from Newquay.

Credit cards: Barclay/Visa.

Terms (excluding VAT; no charge for service): Dinner, B & B £10.50–16.50. Set meals: lunch from £1.50; dinner from £3.95. Bargain spring and autumn breaks. Children under 1, no charge; 1–5, 33% of adult charge; 6–12, 66% of adult charge; special meals provided.

DEDDINGTON, Oxfordshire   Map 2

The Holcombe Hotel   [GFG]   *Telephone:* Deddington (0869) 38274
High Street

Deddington is one of the charming little-known villages of the East Cotswolds on the A423 between Oxford and Banbury. 'A good country hotel hugs you when you go in, and that's precisely how you feel when you walk into *The Holcombe Hotel*. Deddington is an extremely pretty village, and the only hazard is traffic noise . . . so ask for a room furthest away from the main road. Prettily decorated rooms, and lovely public rooms create an atmosphere that you're somewhere special, and the restaurant is cosy and romantic. On Friday evenings they specialize in fondues . . . great fun if you want to unwind slowly, and you leave determined to come back.' *(Di Latham; also Carol Wright)*

Open: All year. Restaurant closed Sunday evening.
Rooms: 11 double, 1 single – 2 with bath, 1 with shower, all with baby-listening.
Facilities: TV lounge, bar, restaurant; facilities for meetings and seminars of up to 30 people.
Location: In village centre; parking.
Restriction: No dogs in public rooms.
Credit cards: All major credit cards accepted.
Terms: B & B £12.50–18.50; dinner, B & B open to negotiation. Set meals: lunch £5.50; dinner £9.50. Bargain breaks; craft courses. Reduced rates and special meals for children.

DEDHAM, Nr Colchester, Essex   **Map 2**

Maison Talbooth   [GFG]   *Telephone:* Colchester (0206) 322367
Stratford Road

On the face of it, it seems a crazy idea, if you want to make your mark as a successful hotelier/restauranteur, to maintain two separate establishments half a mile apart. And it certainly was not Gerald Milsom's original idea when he acquired the atmospheric half-timbered 16th-century building known now as the restaurant *Le Talbooth* beside the Stour. For some years, he kept everything under one roof, a restaurant with rooms, but demand for accommodation exceeding supply, he bought a large Victorian house on the other side of the A12, close to Dedham, and converted it into *Maison Talbooth*, with opulent bedrooms or suites, furnished with accessories like fresh fruit and flowers and remote-control colour TV which maximize the cossetting experience. Breakfast only is served in this latter establishment; other meals being taken at *Le Talbooth* – and, if you haven't a car, the hotel itself provides suitably grand transport. It doesn't sound an ideal arrangement – and for some *Maison Talbooth* is a little on the lush side. The fact that it works, and that our *Talbooth* file has been consistently filled with the perfume of bouquets, speaks eloquently for the skills of its resident owner in creating a harmoniously caring atmosphere in both parts of his enterprise, and also – a major factor in the enjoyment of one's visit – in providing in his restaurant an outstanding *table*. *(Patricia Roberts, D J Butterfield and others)*

Open: All year.
Rooms: 8 double, 1 single, 1 suite – 9 with bath, 1 with shower, all with telephone, radio, colour TV and baby-listening. (5 rooms on ground floor.)
Facilities: Large hall with french windows on to the garden, drawing room with open fire. The hotel stands in 2 acres of grounds, the restaurant in 3 acres on the banks of the river Stour; boating; seaside within half an hour by car.
Location: Off the A12 7 miles NE of Colchester at Stratford St Mary.
Restriction: No dogs.
Credit cards: All major credit cards accepted.
Terms (excluding 10% service charge): B & B (continental) £22.50–50. Set meals: English breakfast £2.50; Sunday lunch £8.50; full *alc* £16.

DROITWICH SPA, Worcestershire   Map 2

Château Impney   *Telephone:* Droitwich (0905) 774411
                                                        Telex: 336673

We had our first entry last year for this extraordinary 19th-century
mock-château, built for a wealthy Midlands engineer named John Corbett; it was a condition of marriage to a beautiful French governess with a
yen for the Palace of Versailles on which the *Château* is vaguely modelled.
The place, we are told, cost him every penny he had, and the lady soon
after left him for a local farmer. 'But,' says a recent visitor, 'his "folly" is
our gain, for it makes a sensational hotel situated in its huge grounds.'
This reader had come to *Château Impney* in a coach party, and was struck
by the fact that the hotel had mustered a welcome committee to meet the
coach at the front door: 'A French style of building, but down-to-earth
English friendliness and sincerity.' The hotel is different in scale from
most others in this Guide, and has extensive conference and banqueting
facilities, as well as catering for the charabanc trade. Whether it has any
place in the book is a moot point, but we were beguiled by P G
Wodehouse's fondness for the place (he wrote *Money for Nothing* here in
1927) and also by the original back-handed recommendation: 'Must go in
for its architecture alone. Rothschild's Waddesdon Manor in miniature. It
is an aesthetic pleasure to sleep here. Standards are high if a little plastic.
The restaurant is appallingly expensive, but they have a very pleasant
Carvery.' *(Lord Beaumont; also Christopher Portway)*

Open: All year, except 24, 25, 26, 27 December.
Rooms: 54 double, 12 single – 60 with bath, 6 with shower, all with telephone,
radio and colour TV; 24-hour room service. 39 rooms in annexe.
Facilities: Lift, lounge bar, 2 restaurants; conference, banqueting and exhibition
facilities; Saturday night dinner and dance. 70 acres parkland with tennis courts,
horse-riding, river and lakes.
Location: 25 minutes from Birmingham (leave M5 motorway at exit 5); 22 miles
from Stratford-upon-Avon and the Cotswolds.
Credit cards: Access, American Express, Barclay, Diners.
Terms: On application.

DULVERTON, Somerset   Map 1

Ashwick House   *Telephone:* Dulverton (0398) 23868

A promising new hotel venture, opened in the summer of 1980, 900 feet
up in a very secluded position on the edge of Exmoor. Here is a first
report:
  'A most comfortable bed, and a lot of other comforts in this isolated,
beautifully refurbished house, owned by recently-returned Rhodesians.
Superb views above Dulverton. Log fire and warm welcome. My wife
waxed about feminine colours and touches. All the little extras – complimentary sherry bottles, needle and pin cushions, bath foams, colour
TV/radio, dial telephone in each room. Two pillows each and super beds!
Really good central heating. Superb bathroom *en suite* – large *thick*
towels. Attractive dining room (chef ill so unfair to report on food). Has
to be best on Exmoor.' *(D H Bennett)*

Open: All year.
Rooms: 5 double, 1 single – all with bath, telephone, radio and TV.
Facilities: Library, lounge, hall/lounge, bar, restaurant. 5¾ acres grounds with croquet.
Location: From Dulverton take the B3223; continue uphill for 3 miles. Turn left at signpost to Ashwick Hotel. After ½ mile turn right at signpost; hotel is a few hundred yards down road.
Restrictions: No children under 10. No dogs in public rooms.
Terms (no fixed service charge): Rooms £10.75–14.75 per person; B & B £14–18; dinner, B & B £22–26; full *alc* £10.25. Bargain breaks. Reduced rates for children.

EAST GRINSTEAD, Sussex   Map 2

Gravetye Manor   [GFG]   *Telephone:* Sharpthorne (0342) 810567
                                                  Telex: 957239

Last year we chose this Elizabethan manor house, circa 1600, set in 30 acres of a celebrated English garden, as one of our 'Six of the Best', writing: 'In 1982, *Gravetye* celebrates the 25th anniversary of Peter Herbert's accession. The hotel is a vintage product. The fine Tudor house is set in magnificent grounds, maintained in the style to which they became accustomed when the great William Robinson lived there and created his famous and lovely garden. Everything about the place reflects the dedication of its owner to create a harmonious experience for his guests. The hotel deliberately eschews a swimming pool or a tennis court as likely to cause a breach of the peace. Of course you have to be prepared to pay the price for perfection.' No dissent from the above laudation, though it should have included a tribute to *Gravetye*'s fine chef, Michael Quinn.

Open: All year.
Rooms: 12 double, 2 single – 12 with bath, 2 with shower, all with telephone and colour TV.
Facilities: 2 sitting rooms, club members' bar, 2 restaurants (public and private dining room separate). 30 acres grounds and superbly planned and maintained pleasure gardens with croquet, clock golf; private trout fishing in nearby lake.
Location: 5 miles SW of Grinstead off the B2110 at West Hoathly sign. Glyndebourne opera 40 minutes' drive, Gatwick Airport 9 miles.
Restrictions: No children under 7. No dogs.
Terms (excluding VAT): Single rooms from £33, double rooms from £22 per person. Set meal: breakfast £3.30. Full *alc* about £24.

EAST PORTLEMOUTH, Nr Salcombe, Devon   Map 1

Gara Rock Hotel   *Telephone:* Salcombe (054 884) 2342

Set high on the cliffs overlooking the English Channel in a converted coastguard station, this unpretentious hotel has many families who return regularly because everything is planned for the enjoyment of both parents and children. An adventure playground in the shape of an Apache fort has recently been built. There is a secluded garden, swimming pool, tennis court, access down to the beach by a long path, also a games room, TV room and laundry. Almost all rooms enjoy a beautiful view over the sea. Entertainments are arranged for those who enjoy them. There is an early supper for younger children. Food is wholesome rather than gastronomic; the wines are relatively expensive. One recent visitor was saddened by the introduction of muzak in the public rooms; another complained that there was very little in the area except Salcombe, but devotees would claim that that is one of *Gara Rock's* chief attractions, and that it is one of the few places where they can 'get away from it all', even in August and peacefully enjoy the seaside life, the cliff walks and the lovely views. *(AC, Gill and Geoffrey Rowlands)*

Open: April–October.
Rooms: 53 double, 9 single – 21 with bath or shower, some with TV; baby-listening service; some self-catering flats.
Facilities: 3 lounges (separate TV room), weekly dances and regular entertainment in summer; laundry for use of guests. 5 acres grounds with heated swimming pool, tennis court, adventure playground and garden games; 2 acres vegetable gardens. Large beach with safe bathing; boating and fishing immediately below the hotel and 5 minutes away. 10-metre motor cruiser for charter; trips round Salcombe estuary organized in hotel boats.
Location: Take A38, then B3196 to Kingsbridge, then the road to Frogmore, East Portlemouth and Gara Rock, off the A379 between Kingsbridge and Dartmouth.
Credit cards: Access/Euro, American Express, Barclay/Visa, Diners.
Terms (excluding VAT): B & B £11.50–16.50; dinner, B & B £14.50–22.50. Set meals: lunch £2.75; dinner £6.50; full *alc* £8.75. Special 3-day breaks out of season. Reduced rates for children.

EASTWELL PARK, Ashford, Kent   **Map 2**

Eastwell Manor [GFG]   *Telephone:* Ashford (0233) 35751
                                                  Telex: 966281 EMANOR

Eastwell Manor opened with a splash early in 1980. It was evident that its young owner, Matthew Bates, was eager for his palatial home to become in a single bound one of the elect of country-house hotels. According to the glossies, he had spent an immodest fortune in bringing his 1920s reconstruction of an ancient manor up to the necessary standards of opulence, and another fortune in bringing at least 14 acres of the 3,000 acres of grounds into a similar spick-and-span condition of landscaped gardens. One reader, after making several stays at Eastwell, wrote to us:
    'Set in magnificent grounds and furnished impeccably, the rooms, both public and private are *superb*. Food is of excellent standard and service very friendly. Not cheap, but I believe the best all-round hotel in the United Kingdom.' *(H G Henry)*
    Another reader *had* reservations: he acknowledged the high degree of luxury, the meticulous attention to detail in the bedrooms, including a personal note of welcome with a bowl of fresh fruit (strawberries in February!), the large and generously furnished public rooms, superior silver plate tableware and cut crystal in the dining room, also the quality of the cooking. But he found the staff, though anxious to please, not working efficiently as a team, with slow service despite a dining room by no means full. In general, though this is always a tricky area, he felt the place didn't at the moment justify its very high prices. More views welcome.

Open: All year.
Rooms: 20 double – all with bath, direct-dial telephone, radio and colour TV.

49

Facilities: Lift, 2 halls, lounge, lounge bar, restaurant, snooker room; conference facilities. 14 acres garden in 3,000 acres estate; tennis. &.
Location: Off the A251, 3 miles from Ashford.
Restrictions: No children under 7. Dogs allowed only in kennels and grounds.
Credit cards: Access/Euro, American Express, Barclay/Visa.
Terms: B & B £25–38.50. Set meal: lunch from £9; full *alc* £15–18. Special bargain rates for 2-night stays; special winter rates.

EVERSHOT, Dorset   Map 1

Summer Lodge   *Telephone:* Evershot (093 583) 424

In our first entry for this hotel last year, we exposed the most flagrant case of collusion we had come across since we started editing this Guide. Four warm commendations for the hotel arrived out of the blue in one week from well-known public figures – and, strangely enough, these nominations were written on report forms 489, 493, 495 and 497. (Whatever happened, we wondered, to those scheduled to write on pages 491 and 499?) Despite the clear evidence of impropriety, the reports themselves were so clearly written *con amore* that, once we had satisfied ourselves as to the credentials of the hotel, we had no hesitation in including it. In the course of this year, many further reports have reached us, all equally unstinted in their enthusiasm for Nigel and Margaret Corbett's country house, formerly the dower-house of the Earl of Ilchester, deep in the heart of Thomas Hardy country. We give below one typical encomium, and interested readers may like to know that Nigel Corbett has now made a full confession; it turned out that he never did give anyone pages 491 and 499.

'We first visited *Summer Lodge* purely by chance last September and couldn't believe our luck. We had booked for one night and stayed five (our maximum possible) and we returned as soon as we could manage. It is the perfect place to stay – comfortable, attractive rooms, charming friendly service – Nigel recommended places to visit and things to do locally. There are beautiful flowers everywhere, lovely little posies in the bedrooms and on the dining tables, and the best food we've ever eaten in any hotel here, in Europe or the USA. There is no choice but that adds spice to one's anticipation. The ingredients are superb and every flavour is distinct – every meal was pure pleasure and we could detail them all (just ask us) from the slightly peppery sauce on a fantastic prawn cocktail (usually a dish we skip) with "proper" large prawns, chopped herbs on the courgettes and not one over-cooked vegetable, perfect *béarnaise* and *hollandaise*, tender well-flavoured Beef Wellington, rare and in lovely pastry, a fish pie full of surprises, a sharp fresh lemon/lime syllabub and so on and so on and always second helpings. We have never before felt enthusiastic enough about a hotel to write to you.' (*Dr and Mrs S R Montgomery; also A P Dean, L A E Ward, Gerard McCarten, D E Padfield, Elizabeth Price, Terence Lancaster*)

Open: 1 February–20 December.
Rooms: 7 double, 1 single – 6 with bath, 2 with shower, all with tea-making facilities.
Facilities: Large lounge, TV room, bar, dining room. 4 acres grounds with ping pong, tennis, croquet, badminton (heated swimming pool planned for 1982); stables. Golf, fishing; 15 miles from the sea and pebble beach; sandy beach at Weymouth 20 miles.
Location: 6 miles S of Yeovil.

Restrictions: No children under 8. Dogs by arrangement.
Credit cards: All major credit cards accepted.
Terms (excluding service): B & B £14.25–18.50; dinner, B & B £20–27.50. Set meal: dinner £10.35. Bargain 2-day breaks October–May. Reduced rates for children sharing parents' room.

FINDON, West Sussex   **Map 2**

Findon Manor Hotel   *Telephone:* Findon (090 671) 2269

Findon Manor, 55 miles from London, four miles north of Worthing, within easy reach of Chichester, Brighton, Glyndebourne and Goodwood, has a lot going for it. Findon is a pleasant village, famous for its racing stables, at the foot of the Sussex Downs and overlooked by Cissbury Ring. The *Manor*, dating from the 16th century but with 18th-century, Regency and late 19th-century contributions, has character and charm; the rooms are appropriately and agreeably furnished, if not quite well enough warmed on a very cold winter's day; and the food, not surprisingly for those who knew Adrian Bannister, the chef/proprietor, in his previous incarnation at *Bannister's Restaurant* in Brighton, is excellent. The hotel with everything? Almost, but not quite: at the moment, and it has only been going two or three years, it somewhat lacks warmth in the metaphorical as well as the literal sense. It may be that the restaurant will continue to be the dominant feature here, and that the hotel guests will feel cold-shouldered in consequence. But that would be a shame for those who like to sleep well where they have eaten well.

Open: All year.
Rooms: 5 double – 4 with bath, 1 with shower.
Facilities: 2 large lounges, 'Snooty Fox Bar', restaurant. 2 acres garden with croquet lawn. Close to racing, riding, walking, and flying; stabling by arrangement.
Location: 7 miles N of Worthing.
Terms (excluding VAT; service at guests' discretion): B & B £13.50; dinner, B & B £20.50. Full *alc* about £13.

FRENCHBEER, Nr Chagford, Devon   **Map 1**

Teignworthy   [GFG]   *Telephone:* Chagford (064 73) 3355

An admirable unanimity of appreciation for John and Gillian Newell's small south-facing hotel 1,000 feet above sea level but in a sheltered horseshoe of land and within walking distance of Dartmoor. It's a Lutyens-style building, built as a gentleman's residence by the same craftsman who built Lutyens' impressive Castle Drogo nearby, and was converted into a hotel at the end of the Seventies. Here are a few characteristic compliments: 'The smallness of the hotel allows for superb personal service, I definitely felt that I had been pampered. The views from the house are superb. I liked the absence of TV in the drawing room, but presence of a stereo record-player with a good selection of classical/jazz records.' 'All that the Guide claimed of it: welcoming, comfortable, fine location, very well appointed. I have seldom slept so well out of my own bed.' 'Delicate without pretentious service and food presentation, and the dinner was one of the best I've eaten in a hotel, like the very best home cooking.' 'This must rank as one of the best hotels I have visited

51

in recent years. Comfortable rooms, good service and excellent food. Altogether extremely good value for money.' Finally, a tribute (rarer than it should be) of a different kind: 'Quoted £20.50 a head including VAT. Bill absolutely on the nose. No messing about and the simplicity of presentation was much appreciated.' *(D S Kahn, Clive Booth, Carol Jackson, H F King, Phyllis Eames, W P Higman)*

Open: All year except January.
Rooms: 9 double – 8 with bath, 1 with shower, all with telephone, radio and TV.
Facilities: Drawing room with large log fire, small bar, dining room; some conference facilities; sauna and sunbed. 14 acres grounds, which include woodland, heathland and lawned garden; ¼ mile of the river Teign; fishing in the river at the bottom of the garden or in the Fernworthy reservoir; golf at Moretonhampstead; riding available. Dartmoor on the doorstep.
Location: 3½ miles SW of Chagford. Follow signs to Kestor Rock and Thornworthy.
Restrictions: No children under 14. No dogs.
Terms (no service charge, gratuities not expected): B & B £17.50–26; dinner, B & B £27.50–36. Set meals: Sunday lunch £8; dinner £12. (Bar lunches available.) Reductions for winter stays, 2 nights minimum.

GITTISHAM, Nr Honiton, Devon   **Map 1**

Combe House Hotel   *Telephone:* Honiton (0404) 2756

Most readers continue to appreciate the decidedly grand style of hospitality offered by John Boswell (a direct descendant of James) in his largely Elizabethan manor house in the heart of a 3,000-acre estate, a couple of miles off the A30. We did have one won't-go-again letter, however, from a visitor who had been given a poor room, felt the service lacked professionalism and minded, as she put it, 'paying a very large sum of money to sit on someone's ancestral furniture and be served by "nice" young people.' But the report below certainly represents the majority verdict on the charms of *Combe House*:

'This country manor-house hotel sits on a gentle slope of a valley set in a semi-wild garden with magnolias, firs and rhododendrons and a series of semi-overgrown, semi-cultivated walled kitchen gardens climbing the slope to bluebell woods. It is approached through a tiny thatched village, across cattle grids along a winding narrow road. The walks from the hotel are delightful. A large oak door topped by coat of arms leads into a high ceilinged dark panelled hall with open fire and deep, comfortable, pink and green floral furniture. In addition there are two prettily furnished drawing rooms, pink and green and gold being the dominant colours, one with an open fire, both with family portraits on the walls. There is a feeling of luxury and spaciousness even when the hotel is full of other guests (we were there at Easter) which enables you to experience the illusion of living in your own country house. Our bedroom was sumptuous, large, thickly carpeted and pink walled with oriental prints – though a double duvet would have been better than two single ones! Home-made biscuits still warm from the oven were replaced daily in a floral biscuit jar.

'Food over a four-day stay was nearly always of a high standard, though the vegetables were sometimes poor. As the proprietor said, his "source" for meat and fish is impeccable (though he did not reveal the secret of the supplier). Occasional lapses in standards probably arise from catering for the avocado pear/prawn cocktail brigade who come in for the occasional meal. Teas were particularly memorable, served from a help-yourself covered trolley and eaten in the drawing room or on the croquet lawn. The luxury 'pub' lunches, e.g. egg mayonnaise open sandwich, or *pâté* and lettuce, tomato, radish, lemon enabled me to enjoy dinner and the occasional tea. Reading a novel on a chaise longue on the croquet lawn overlooking the valley, or sitting at dinner in the pink dining room or the green dining room with black candles one can enjoy the surrounding hills, and Arab stallions, mares and foals (when in season) which wander freely from a local stud farm. The atmosphere is one of gentle, unhurried luxury, service is always readily and cheerfully available, never forced, and the employees appear to enjoy and know about their job.' *(Rosamund Keating; also R F Fernsby, Jeff Driver, Col. J Houghton Brown, J M French)*

Open: All year, except January and February.
Rooms: 13 double – 8 with bath, 3 with shower, all with colour TV.
Facilities: Large reception room, panelled log-fired drawing room, cocktail bar. 8 acres gardens in the 3,000-acre estate, with croquet. Trout fishing on the river Otter. Nearest beach Sidmouth 11 miles; sandy beach at Exmouth 16 miles; golf and riding nearby.
Location: 3 miles SW of Honiton.
Restrictions: No children under 10 in the dining room at night. No dogs in public rooms.
Credit cards: All major credit cards accepted.
Terms: B & B £21–50. Set meal: Sunday lunch £8. Full *alc* £15.50. Reduced rates for children sharing parents' room; special meals provided.

GRASMERE, Cumbria   Map 4

Michael's Nook [GFG]   *Telephone:* Grasmere (096 65) 496

Michael's Nook is a thoroughly idiosyncratic hotel. To some it is a natural for the Guide: rich in Victorian character, serving wonderful food in a lovely setting – it is just outside Grasmere in a beautiful garden, with views of hills and valley – its elegant rooms filled with antiques, *objets* and paintings worth looking at. 'One of the most comfortable and pleasant establishments in the whole of the United Kingdom,' writes one hyperbolic character. But it has another face: the owner, Reg Gifford, is much in evidence, and some find him a bit too autocratic for their tastes. Times for meals are set; you drink before dinner in the bar and take coffee afterwards in the drawing room. Mr Gifford knows exactly when you come in and out of the hotel as the front door is permanently locked. The reason given is that there are no locks on the bedroom doors, but it is disconcerting if it is raining, or if you have just gone out for a breath of air. And if your bedroom door has a tendency to burst open in a breeze there is no way you can lock or bolt it. Another problem derives from the popularity of the restaurant; the comfort of the residents suffers when the dining room is busy catering to non-residents. Recent visitors who spent two nights found their Saturday spoilt by a party who noisily dominated first the dining room and then the drawing room: they had no choice of when they ate, being obliged to join the second sitting at 9.15 by which time some of the food was past its best. The following day, when there was one session as only residents were dining, the food was far better, the service unhurried and the dining room peaceful. Despite reservations, this couple say they came away with happy memories – 'It was pricey, but we got a lot for our money,' and we reckon this would be a majority view. *(J C Rae, Heather Sharland, AC)*

Open: All year.

Rooms: 10 double – 9 with bath, 1 with shower, all with telephone, radio and colour TV. (1 room on ground floor.)

Facilities: Spacious hall with seating, drawing room, residents' and diners' bar, dining room. 3 acres grounds. Indoor heated swimming pool, sauna, solarium and games-room facilities available at the *Wordsworth Hotel*, 1 mile away, which is under the same ownership. ⅙.

Location: On outskirts of Grasmere; turn away from Grasmere village off the A591 Windermere–Keswick road up a narrow road by the side of the *Swan Hotel*.

Restrictions: No children under 12. No dogs in public rooms.

Terms (service at guests' discretion): Dinner, B & B £33–48. Set meals: lunch £11.50, dinner from £13.95. 10% discount for stay of 6 nights or more, except Bank Holiday periods.

Note: Mr Gifford has recently opened the Wordsworth Hotel *close by. It is larger and more conventional than* Michael's Nook, *and, since it makes a feature of its conference facilities, more business orientated. No reports on it yet, but guests at* Michael's Nook *have the free use of its heated indoor swimming pool, sauna and solarium.*

GRASMERE, Cumbria   Map 4

White Moss House [GFG]   *Telephone:* Grasmere (096 65) 295
Rydal Water

'A little like moving in with Mrs Tittlemouse,' was one reader's impression on arriving at *White Moss*. It is not just that the house – in fact three stone cottages knocked into one – is modest by hotel standards, but that some of the rooms (each with its tiny bathroom) are likely to be too cosy for some tastes, especially when they have to accommodate bulky trouser presses. In compensation, the bedrooms – spotlessly clean and gleaming like everything else here – are full of homely touches like sewing kits, books, magazines, guides to the area and *bric-à-brac*. And the atmosphere of caring and welcome extends to everything else – and especially to the restaurant which is a special reason for a visit here. Mrs Butterworth's cooking has been bruited abroad, and the hotel attracts a lot of outside custom. It's not at all a fancy menu, but depends on good use of local produce. There is no choice until you reach the dessert stage. Guests eat punctually at 8 pm; soft background music eases the constraint of conversation in the small dining room which seats 18 people at the most. Coffee is taken in the living room which has no television so you talk to your fellow guests or read the books that are scattered around.

The hotel itself has five bedrooms, and there are two more in a secluded cottage called Brockstone, five minutes' drive or an energetic walk up the fells from the main house. Brockstone has accommodation for two to four people and is only ever let as one booking. It also houses the only television set in the hotel. Visitors planning a stay of any length would be well advised to try to stay there as the main house is close to the busy A591 Windermere to Keswick road; the small garden in front of the hotel is separated from this only by a tall hedge and bedroom windows have had to be double-glazed to keep out the noise of traffic (though this does subside at night). *(AC)*

Open: Mid March–end October.

Rooms: 7 double – all with bath and radio. 2 rooms in cottage which also has TV.

Facilities: Lounge/hall, lounge, dining room. Garden.

Location: On the A591 just outside Grasmere in the direction of Ambleside.
Restrictions: No children under 15. No dogs.
Terms (service at guests' discretion): Dinner, B & B £33–35. Set meal: dinner £12.

GULVAL, Nr Penzance, Cornwall   Map 1

Trevaylor   *Telephone:* (0736) 2882

We continue to receive warm endorsements for Mrs Fleming's Georgian house in its ten acres of gardens, two miles outside Penzance and overlooking Mount's Bay. Here is a characteristic report:

'A delightful building in superb grounds with good views, ideally situated for exploring eastern Cornwall but well off the beaten track. We stayed in the newly converted coach house at the back, pleasantly and prettily decorated and pleasingly remote. The hotel itself had a comfortable lounge, games room and bar, with one or two lovely pieces of furniture, though it had a slightly spartan air in places, particularly the wood-panelled, bare-floored dining room where the sound of the sweet trolley arriving resembled the arrival of the 7.20 train from Penzance! We had a delightful welcome from the newly-resident godson of the proprietress who exhibited great tact and charm when attempting to arrange a taxi trip for two elderly, carless and slightly deaf ladies who wished to tour the area. We ate good-value country food, with enterprisingly cooked vegetables, all home-grown, and delicious sweets. There was a small but well-kept cheese board and a useful wine list. Breakfasts were excellent, with a fresh loaf of wholemeal bread set out each morning to supplement the toast. Perfectly cooked bacon and eggs and delicious home-made marmalade and honey. Very pleasant service. Highly recommended.' *(Simon and Mary-Jane Wilkins; also Edward Hibbert, Uli Lloyd Pack, David and Patricia Martin)*

Open: Easter–October.
Rooms: 5 double, 2 single – 4 with bath, 1 with shower.
Facilities: 2 lounges (1 with TV), large hall, small bar, dining room. 10 acres grounds and gardens with pretty woodland walks; vegetable garden and fruit trees. 1½ miles from sandy beach with safe bathing; fishing, riding, golf nearby.
Location: To reach Trevaylor from the A30, just before entering Penzance and after the speed-limit sign, turn right at the horse trough on to the B3311, signposted Nancledra, Zennor, St Ives. In just under half a mile, and before Gulval, turn left and after a few hundred yards turn right following signs for New Mill and Zennor. *Trevaylor* is on the left in just over half a mile.
Terms (no service charge): B & B £9–12. Set meals: Sunday lunch £4; dinner £6. Reduced rates for children sharing parents' room; special meals provided.

HAMBLETON, Oakham, Rutland, Leicestershire   Map 2

Hambleton Hall   [GFG]   *Telephone:* Oakham (0572) 56991
                                          Telex: 341995 Ref 207

'The setting is spectacular. Lovely gardens, and fields with fine trees, stretching away to the lake. Absolutely quiet – a great place to unwind. The decor is arguably the most pleasant of any English country hotel. Each room is individually furnished, and there isn't one that we wouldn't be happy to stay in. The food is absolutely first class – I don't think I've ever had a better meal in a new restaurant. The chef, Nicholas Gill, is young (early twenties), but he's had a year at Maxim's in Paris and is very creative. The treatment was imaginative, and presentation beautiful. The Harts are without doubt going to be superstars in the hotel business. Though not inexpensive (about £100 per couple per day to live well) we thought it very good value.' *(Paul Henderson)*

So ran our entry last year for this new star in the country-house hotel firmament – born July 1980. It's close to the centre of England in an area not much visited by tourists, but it's less than two hours from London by the A1(M), and there are any number of rewarding places to visit in the neighbourhood – Burghley House, Rockingham Castle and Belvoir Castle, to name but three. As for Hambleton Hall itself, it has a choice location, on a tongue of land that leads out from Oakham into the centre of Rutland Water, with fine views from the main windows of the lake scene. And having visited Hambleton ourselves last year, we would fully endorse last year's encomium – an outstanding hotel in all its aspects, not least in its open welcome to its guests. *(HR)*

Open: All year.
Rooms: 15 double – all with bath and shower, telephone, radio and colour TV.
Facilities: Lift, drawing room/bar, dining room; small conference facilities; private dining room. 20 acres grounds with tennis court; overlooking lake with trout fishing and sailing.
Restrictions: No children under 8. Dogs by arrangement.
Location: Off the A606 1 mile SE of Oakham.
Credit cards: All major credit cards accepted.
Terms: B & B (continental) £25–40; cooked breakfast £2.50 extra. Set meals: lunch £12.50; dinner £17.50.

HARROGATE, West Yorkshire　　　　　　　　　　　　　　　　**Map 4**

The Studley Hotel　[GFG]　　　　　　*Telephone:* Harrogate (0423) 60425
Swan Road　　　　　　　　　　　　　　　　　　　　　*Telex:* 57506

'Everything you say is correct. Entry should have "excellent value for money" in large type,' writes an exuberant reader, who goes on, 'We assumed that a mistake had been made in the attached account for dinner for two!!' Alas, since the bill was for £12.90, we feel pretty sure that the hotel had made an error on this occasion. But we repeat last year's entry, while warning readers that *The Studley* cannot always be expected to make mistakes in the customer's favour.

'If you have to visit the rather quaint Victorian town of Harrogate, this is a pleasant hotel in which to relax. It has been created from a terrace of stone town houses in the centre of town. Although it is quite an expensive establishment, the staff are young, helpful and refreshingly unstuffy. The bedrooms are comfortable, but light sleepers who want an early night should ask for a room away from the kitchen ventilation system! Nice touches are an electric trouser-press in the bedroom, a free morning newspaper and freshly squeezed orange at breakfast.

'Perhaps the major attraction of the hotel is the *Au Charbon de Bois* French restaurant (open to non-residents) which serves the most delicious French food. The service is friendly and efficient even on a busy evening. The portions are ample – so ample that neither of us could manage any of the delicious desserts, which is an unheard-of thing.' *(St John and Maybel Bates)*

Open: All year.
Rooms: 22 double, 17 single – all with bath, telephone, radio, colour TV and tea-making facilities.
Facilities: Lift, residents' lounge, restaurant. Small garden in front of hotel.
Location: 5 minutes' walk from town centre; car park and 6 lock-up garages.
Restrictions: No children under 7. Dogs allowed at the management's discretion.
Credit cards: All major credit cards accepted.
Terms (excluding service): B & B £19.25–30.50. Set meal: lunch £3.50; full *alc* £11.50. Bargain 'Mini-weekends' – Friday night to Sunday morning.

HASLEMERE, Surrey   **Map 2**

Lythe Hill Hotel   *Telephone:* Haslemere (0428) 51251
                                                          Telex: 858402

This well-heeled hotel is about a mile out of Haslemere on the road to Petworth, and has a quite exceptional situation – the Blackdown National Trust Woodland starts right from the hotel's own 14-acre grounds. It is in fact a strange hybrid: on one side of its courtyard is a luscious timbered 14th-century farmhouse with spacious rooms furnished with cherished antique furniture, known as the *Auberge de France*; the *Auberge* has a sophisticated *à la carte* French restaurant. Across the way is a 16th-century farmhouse, gutted and modernized and known as the *Entente Cordiale*; this modern wing has its own restaurant with a *table d'hôte* menu concentrating more on English dishes. To add to the international flavour, the *Entente Cordiale* has a glass-roofed room known as the Italian Garden. You pay your money – the same in either building – and you take your choice, or you can eat in one place and sleep in the other. One guest preferred the modern wing and thought the French restaurant a bit over-ambitious and pricey. Another, an American visitor, described the *Auberge* as a 'gastronomic feast'. We should be glad of further reports. *(Arnold Horwell, Louise L Becker)*

Open: All year.
Rooms: 23 double, 11 suites – 32 with bath, 2 with shower, all with telephone: colour TV in suites, others have mono; baby-listening. (14 rooms on ground floor.)
Facilities: Lounge, 2 bars, 2 restaurants, glass-roofed Italian Garden where dinner-dances are held on Saturday nights; sauna, boutique; games room with table tennis. 14 acres grounds with croquet lawn and hard tennis court, and lake with fishing. National Trust land adjoins for walking, golf, riding, polo and racing nearby.
Location: 1½ miles from Haslemere, on the Petworth road.
Restriction: Small dogs only, at management's discretion.
Credit cards: All major credit cards accepted.
Terms (excluding service): B & B (continental) £18.50–32. Set meals: English breakfast £3.50; lunch £5.50–8; dinner £7.50–10; full *alc* £11.50. Bargain break weekends October–May.

HAWKRIDGE, Nr Dulverton, Somerset   **Map 1**

Tarr Steps Hotel   *Telephone:* Winsford (064 385) 293

'One of the most beautifully situated hotels I have ever stayed in,' writes one recent visitor to this former Georgian rectory in the south-east corner of Exmoor, 'with superb views of beautiful woods, fields and hills.' *Tarr*

57

Steps stands in eight acres of what the brochure describes as 'slightly wild' gardens and grounds, 800 feet above sea level, overlooking the river Barle and its valley. Close by are the Steps which give the hotel its name, a cyclopean clapper bridge said to date from the Bronze Age. A lot of country pursuits are available from the hotel, and it is particularly popular with the fishing and riding fraternity as well as with keen Exmoor walkers.

In the spring of 1981, the owner of the hotel, Paul Hulme, retired to Suffolk, and Mr and Mrs Warner took over the management. We are not sure whether the fact that the Hulmes were taking steps to leave last year was responsible for some shortcomings, but – after several years of unstinted enthusiasm in our reports, we began to get a few complaints – weaknesses in the service and minor discourtesies on the part of the staff. The most recent report, while venting a number of disappointments, summed up: 'It *is* a lovely peaceful spot, it has a nice atmosphere and pleasant guests, and the management are trying hard.' But we should be glad of further reports. *(Michael V Salter, D H Bennett, R P Jervis, G Bond)*

Open: 21 March–end October.
Rooms: 12 double, 3 single – 6 with bath, 2 with shower. 3 rooms in annexe. (2 double rooms on ground floor.)
Facilities: Sitting room, bar (no TV), dining room. 7 acres grounds with garden and rough and clay pigeon shooting. 3½ miles of fishing (fly only – salmon and trout) on the river Barle (licences from the hotel); shooting over 500 acres of privately owned land; hunting – stag, foxes; riding and trekking from stables 2 miles from the hotel; stables and kennels for guests bringing their own horses or dogs. River bathing, 100 yards; sea bathing, ½ hour by car; fine walking and scenic drives over Exmoor. **&**.
Location: Off the B3223 between Dulverton and Exford.
Restriction: No dogs in hotel; welcome in grounds; kennels available.
Terms (excluding service): B & B £14.95; full board £23.90. Set meals: Sunday lunch £6.30; dinner £8.95. Reduced rates for children sharing parents' room; high teas provided.

HELFORD, Cornwall   **Map 1**

Riverside [GFG]   *Telephone:* Manaccan (032 623) 443

'*Riverside* is situated in the tiny and idyllically picturesque village of Helford, a tumbling muddle of whitewashed cottages clustered round and above a small creek winding into the Helford river. It is a mild and sheltered area of winding lanes and lush vegetation, in contrast with the austerities of the Lizard peninsula just to the south, and is ideally placed for exploring the wild and beautiful coastline of the extreme south-west with its beautiful coves and sandy beaches. The house itself is a very small and tasteful adaptation of two of the cottages, and it seems absolutely right that it is not called *Riverside Hotel* since the overwhelming impact is not of a hotel at all but of a welcoming home. Our bedroom was delightfully furnished and supremely comfortable and filled with vases of flowers, books and all the other little details which make one feel at home and which are all too often missing from hotels. It was obvious that someone had taken immense pains to anticipate anything that guests might possibly need during their stay. The private bathroom was of similar standard and similarly equipped, and the sitting room was as tasteful, attractive and comfortable as everything else. The food and wine need little comment. Suffice it to say that they fully lived up to the superb standard one would expect from someone with the reputation of George Perry-Smith and from a place which has for years received The *Good Food Guide's* highest accolades. The lasting impression is one of peace, friendliness, and good taste. After many years of experience of hotels we would unhesitatingly say that *Riverside* comes closest to our concept of the perfect hotel.' *(Norman Graham; also R O Marshall, Roger and Shelagh Utley)*

Open: March–October.
Rooms: 5 double – all with bath. 2 rooms in annexe.
Facilities: Residents' lounge, restaurant. 1 acre grounds on Helford creek off the Helford river and Falmouth bay, with beaches, sailing,and fishing.
Location: 12 miles from Helston off the B3293.
Restriction: No dogs.
Terms: B & B £17–20. Full *alc* £18.50. Reduced rates and special meals for children.

HEXWORTHY, Princetown, Yelverton, Devon   Map 1

The Forest Inn   *Telephone:* Poundsgate (03643) 211

'I hesitate to report on this place in case it becomes too well known and I cannot get in there should I need to in the future,' writes our correspondent about this simple inn in the heart of Dartmoor, and goes on to speak with gratitude about his evening meal – a crab 'fresher than fresh' with salad, followed by a 'superb treacle sponge with Devon cream in the same class as the treacle pudding at *Simpson's* in the Strand.' His bill (1981) for dinner (including a half-bottle of decent wine), bed and an 'excellent cooked breakfast with good coffee' came to a fraction over £18. The hotel has its own stretch of the West Dart for salmon and trout fishing, and also has its own horses stabled at the hotel. *(Douglas Jones)*

Open: All year.
Rooms: 13 double, 4 single – 4 with bath, all with tea-making facilities. 6 rooms in annexe.
Facilities: Lounge with TV, Salad Room (for light meals), restaurant, laundry. 12 acres grounds. Trout and salmon fishing in River Dart approx. 200 yards from hotel; riding with horses from hotel's own stables.
Location: On the outskirts of Ashburton, heading S on A38, turn right onto B3357. After Dartmeet (about 6 miles) look for left turn to Hexworthy.
Credit cards: All major credit cards accepted.
Terms (excluding VAT and service): B & B £8–9.50. Set meals: lunch £3; dinner £5; full *alc* from £7.50. Special 2-night breaks November–March (dinner, B & B plus 2 hours' horseriding £20). Reduced rates for children sharing parents' room; special meals provided.

HINTON CHARTERHOUSE, Nr Bath, Avon   Map 2

Homewood Park [GFG]   *Telephone:* Limpley Stoke (022 122) 2643

First reports on the Guide's youngest hotel, though probably restaurant with rooms would describe it better – opened December 1980:
    'Although Bath and its environs may be well endowed with good hotels there is plenty of room for *Homewood Park*. In a pleasant rural setting 5

miles outside Bath itself, the house is a friendly grey stone building of 18th- and 19th-century origin. Penny and Stephen Ross who own, manage and cook at *Homewood Park* previously played a similar role at *Popjoys Restaurant* in Bath itself. No fears about the cooking, which is excellent, French and inexpensive. The wine list also had knowledgeable selections and good value. The house has been thoroughly refurbished with fabrics and wallpapers from Osborne and Little and Designers Guild. My wife noticed old lace pillows (hand laundered) in the rooms and generally outstanding attention to detail. The result is homely, friendly and most attractive. It is in a price bracket firmly below the three most glamorous Bath hotels, *The Priory, The Royal Crescent*, and *Hunstrete House* at Chelwood (all q.v.). The genuineness and quality of the establishment puts it clearly above the also-rans of the hotel industry which previously may have been the only ones in the area you could afford!' *(Tim Hart)*

'At the moment, great value for money. Along with *Riverside* at Helford (q.v.), our favourite inexpensive bolt-hole.' *(Paul Henderson; also Roger Smithells)*

Open: All year, except 25 December–14 January.
Rooms: 8 double – all with bath, telephone, radio, and colour TV.
Facilities: Lounge, bar, public dining room, private dining room. 10 acres grounds adjoining Hinton Priory. Hotel overlooks Limpley Stoke valley. Tennis court in grounds and riding can be arranged with the stables next door.
Location: 6 miles S of Bath on the A36 Warminster road. Turn left after Pipehouse lane at sign for Freshford and Sharpstone.
Restriction: No dogs.
Credit cards: Access/Euro/Mastercard, Barclay/Visa.
Terms: B & B (continental) £20–27.50. Set meals: English breakfast £2.50; lunch £6.50; *full alc* £15. Special meals for children provided. Special off-peak breaks available.

HOPTON CASTLE, Nr Craven Arms, Shropshire   **Map 2**

Lower House Country Lodge   *Telephone:* Bucknell (054 74) 352

Once again, a rich shoal of compliments for Sally and John Dann's lovingly restored small black-and-white Tudor house in Welsh border country on the edge of the Clun Forest. There are only four bedrooms – none with bathrooms *en suite* but, as one guest put it, 'It's a small price to pay for such excellent service, atmosphere and superlative food.' Here is part of another tribute, from a couple who had just returned from their ninth visit: 'The standard of hospitality was, as always, of the highest. One of the great pleasures of visiting *Lower House* is to wander around or sit in the large and delightful garden, well-stocked with trees and old roses, and drink in the peaceful atmosphere. Another great pleasure, of a grosser nature, is Sally Dann's cooking – as always superb and imaginative. The dinner we were offered on our first night may be taken as an example: gravid lax with prawns, chervil and mustard sauce, fillets of venison (deliciously tender) with cashews and raisins, cauliflower with cheese sauce, buttered carrots, spring greens and game chips, then strawberry vacherin with ice cream and cheeses. There is no choice and no lunch is served – but neither is needed. You can have either the English or the continental breakfast – both are substantial and first class; one could mention specially the selection of home-made preserves. Sally Dann always takes note of a visitor's particular dietary requirements and John Dann guides one knowledgeably to the right wine to complement the wonderful food. They are both so kind and hospitable to their guests that leaving them and their beautiful home is always a real wrench.' *(Mr and Mrs Michael Sladen; also Patricia Roberts, Hazel Astley, Roger Smithells, Maggie Angeloglou, Angela Evans)*

Open: March–December.
Rooms: 4 double.
Facilities: 2 lounges, TV room, dining room. 2 acres grounds. Near wooded hills and Norman border castle of Hopton.
Location: 12 miles NW of Ludlow, 6 miles SW of Craven Arms via the B4368 and B4385 (sign to Hopton Castle just after Twitchen).
Restrictions: No children under 14. No dogs.
Terms: Rooms £12; B & B £15, dinner B & B £22.50. Set meal: dinner £7.50.

HORNS CROSS, Nr Bideford, Devon   Map 1

Foxdown Manor   [GFG]   *Telephone:* Horns Cross (023 75) 325

Belinda and Bruce Ross are now in their fourth year at this manor-house hotel (previously listed under Parkham) in its ten acres of woodland, about six miles west of Bideford, and once again our mail has been full of enthusiastic endorsers for their entry in the Guide. 'Friendly atmosphere, gourmet food, superb ambience and amenities,' writes one contributor – and that really sums it up. Belinda Ross, who used to edit the cookery pages of the American *Good Housekeeping*, is in charge of the kitchens and produces exceptional six-course dinners at far from exceptional prices. The nearest sandy beaches are about six miles away, but the hotel caters for many people's recreational needs within its grounds. A miniature golf course has been added this past year to the heated swimming pool, the Jaccuzzi pool, the tennis court, the clay pigeon trap and much else besides. *(Rosemary Goldsmith, Clive Bolton, Professor M E Streit, J G Fenwick, Mr and Mrs S V Bishop)*

Open: 1 April–1 November.
Rooms: 6 double, 1 single – 4 with bath, 2 with shower, all with colour TV and baby-listening; 6 2- and 3-bedroomed cottages sleeping 4–6 people, equipped for self-catering. (Some rooms on ground floor; one cottage designed for disabled.)
Facilities: Hall, 2 large lounges, bar, candle-lit dining room, games room; twice-weekly pianist. 10½ acres grounds with heated swimming pool and Jaccuzzi pool; tennis, miniature 18-hole golf course, sauna, solarium, clay pigeon shooting, croquet, putting, trout stream. Sea 1 mile; nearest sandy beach 6 miles, with good bathing and surfing; sub-aqua at Bideford. ف.
Location: Off the A39, 7 miles W of Bideford. Hotel turning is on left just outside Horns Cross.
Credit cards: Access/Euro, American Express, Barclay/Visa.
Terms (excluding VAT and service): B & B £10–16; dinner, B & B £17–23. Set meal: dinner £7 (£7.50 to non-residents). Reduced rates for children; special meals by arrangement.

> The terms indicate the range of prices in each hotel. Some have a low and high season, some do not. The lower price is likely to be for someone sharing a double room, and the higher price the maximum for a single occupant.

Worsley Arms Hotel   *Telephone:* Hovingham (065 382) 234

The *Worsley Arms* was once the coaching inn of this pleasant village, close to Ampleforth and Castle Howard, and noted for its cricket, and – wonder of wonders! – it still practises traditional virtues of inn-keeping like cleaning shoes left outside your bedroom door or turning down your bed at night while also serving meals which are a substantial cut above what can be expected from village inns. In our entry last year, we quoted a couple who called it 'one of the best hotels and best value for money that we have stayed in for some time – not highly sophisticated, but run by professionals in a quiet and efficient manner without familiarity.' A reader this year echoes the verdict: 'We found your comments accurate and were glad we went. A *very* comfortable well-run hotel. 10/10. Food, 6–7/10. Vegetables excellently and originally cooked, but main dishes somewhat lacking in flavour. Sweets totally excellent.' One word of warning: Hovingham is on a minor road, but there can be heavy traffic in the early morning. Light sleepers should ask for rooms at the back.

Open: All year, except 25, 26 December.
Rooms: 11 double, 3 single – all with bath.
Facilities: 3 lounges (1 with TV), cocktail bar, public bar, restaurant. ½ acre garden with croquet lawn.
Location: In Hovingham village, 18 miles NW of Malton and Castle Howard; Scarborough 26 miles E.
Credit cards: Access/Euro, Barclay/Visa.
Terms: B & B £14.50–18.50; dinner, B & B £18.50–26.50. Set meals: lunch £5; dinner £9.

Hunstrete House   *Telephone:* Compton Dando (076 18) 578
                                            Telex: 449540

Our file for *Hunstrete House* (located last year under Chelwood) makes heady reading. Quite simply, there is no other hotel in the Guide which elicits from its grateful readers such an intoxicating brew of superlatives. Last year we quoted from a number of tributes to this serenely handsome Georgian mansion set in 90 acres of gardens and pastures 8 miles SW of Bath. This year, we have contented ourselves with one extended report which can speak for all the other names given at the end of the entry. The only significant reservation among our correspondents refers to the food, which many find does not really match the perfection of the decor. No complaints, on the other hand about the wine list, distinguished both for its contents and the reasonableness of the mark-up.

'We arrived for dinner at *Hunstrete House* one golden July evening, and were so utterly beguiled by the beauty of the house, its decor and the garden, that we had booked a room for the following weekend even before we had seen the dinner menu. I entirely agree with last year's correspondent that this must be the best hotel in England (I am comparing it with *Gravetye Manor, Maison Talboth, The Bell Inn, The Priory*). It really is like staying in a large private house. The beneficial presence of the Dupays family ensures high standards of hospitality and thoughtfulness for one's comfort and well-being. The public rooms are furnished with impeccable taste – glazed chintzes in restful colours, Mrs Dupays' various collections of silhouettes, 18th-century needlework pictures, samplers, and, of course, her own exuberant paintings. Our room was in the annexe, a converted stable, and was light, airy and spacious with a splendid view over the Somerset countryside. The furnishings were as exquisite as in the public rooms. Each room is individually furnished. Antiques and paintings abound in every room, together with vases of freshly picked flowers.

'The Dupays family themselves went to enormous pains to make us as comfortable as possible. When I asked Mrs Dupays to recommend antique shops in the area, she not only listed her favourite ones and gave them an accurate star rating, but lent me her Antique Collector's Guide. The Dupays daughter, who helps very competently in the hotel, lent me her bathroom scales when I expressed anxiety over the aftermath of so much rich food. Which brings me to the subject of food. There is an unusually wide choice, and some variation each day. My very favourite meal was on our last night: *moules marinières* followed by *lobster cardinale* and then iced *Grand Marnier* soufflé. One caveat only: if you order tea, they automatically bring Earl Grey – deliciously refreshing at tea time but a shock to the system first thing in the mornings. I was told that if I wanted Indian tea I should ask for "Staff tea"! I long to return at the earliest opportunity.' *(Francesce Swann; also Patricia Roberts, Elizabeth Lambert Ortiz, Alison Stubbs, Mr and Mrs M Evans, T M Wilson, Adam Sisman, Lesley Goodden)*

Open: All year, except possibly few days early January.
Rooms: 15 double, 3 single, 2 suites – all with bath, telephone and colour TV. 6 rooms in annexe. (4 rooms on ground floor.)
Facilities: Drawing room, bar, dining room. 90 acres grounds and walled garden; outdoor heated swimming pool, hard tennis court, croquet lawn. &.
Location: On the A368 8 miles SW of Bath.
Restriction: No children under 9.
Credit cards: American Express, Barclay/Visa.
Terms (excluding VAT): B & B (continental) £27–40; English breakfast £2.50. Set meal: lunch (cold buffet) from £6.50; full *alc* £16. Special winter rates 1 November–31 March.

HUNTINGDON, Cambridgeshire   **Map 2**

The Old Bridge Hotel   [GFG]   *Telephone:* Huntingdon (0480) 52681
                                           Telex: 32706

Apart from the noise from passing traffic in the front rooms, *The Old Bridge* would seem like everyone's idea of a fine old market-town hotel: it is a handsome ivy-creepered Georgian building, with a garden running down to the river Ouse where the hotel has its own moorings. And the restaurant enjoys a serious reputation, for its food and also for its wine list. But we should welcome reports from recent visitors.

Open: All year, except Christmas Day and Boxing night.
Rooms: 11 double, 14 single, 1 suite – 12 with bath, all with telephone and colour TV.
Facilities: Main lounge, bar, restaurant; conference/banqueting facilities. 1 acre garden leading down to the river Ouse; private jetty.
Location: Near town centre; parking for 100 cars.
Restriction: No dogs in public rooms.

Credit cards: All major credit cards accepted.
Terms: B & B £16–18.50. Full *alc* £15–17. Special weekend breaks October–April. Reduced rates for children.

ILFRACOMBE, North Devon Map 1

Langleigh Country Hotel *Telephone:* Ilfracombe (0271) 62629
Broad Park Avenue

As a hotel, *Langleigh* is a newcomer – opened in 1980 by David Darlow, a BBC producer, and his wife Tessa. But the building itself has some pedigree, being in fact the oldest inhabited house in the town. It was built in 1570, but had an extensive facelift in the early 19th century, and is now essentially Regency. It has an attractive and secluded setting at the foot of a wooded valley, but is only a few minutes' walk from the town centre and Ilfracombe's sandy and rocky coves.

'A lovely old manor house, tucked away in a steep wooded valley. Horse-riders clop gently up the lane outside, and you fall asleep to the sound of a rushing stream. When we went, there was a mass of colour and fragrance from wallflowers, bluebells and rhododendrons. Nelson apparently slept here (the house belonged to two of his admirals), and I should think he would still feel at home: the floors slope, log fires crackle in the hearth, and jackdaws nest in the chimneys. Food, too, I should mention. No *à la carte*, only 3 main courses to choose from, but home-made bread, soups and pastry, fresh vegetables, some unusual herby cheeses, and wine at a price we could afford for a change. True, we could have done with a phone in the bedroom, but otherwise there was everything we needed . . . private bath, colour TV, a well-thought-out colour scheme, and a lovely view. An enchanting place and at a cost of £13 a day (May 1981), including dinner and VAT!' *(D L Munder; also John and Angela Terry)*

Open: All year, except Christmas week.
Rooms: 5 double, 1 single – 8 with bath, 2 with shower, all with intercom, radio, colour TV (at extra charge), tea-making facilities and baby-listening. Also 2 family cottages each with 2 bedrooms, living room and bathroom.
Facilities: Lounge, bar, dining room, 2 games rooms. 3 acres grounds. Badminton, solarium. Within walking distance of sandy and rocky coves in Ilfracombe. &.
Location: Off the A361 from Barnstaple, on the corner of Broad Park Avenue and Langleigh Road.
Restriction: No dogs in public rooms.
Terms: B & B £8–14; dinner, B & B £13–19. Family cottage £17–19. Children half-price if sharing parents' room; special meals provided.

IPSWICH, Suffolk Map 2

The Marlborough [GFG] *Telephone:* Ipswich (0473) 57677
73 Henley Road

An enterprising hotel, with a well-reputed restaurant, housed in a red-brick Victorian residence, a few minutes' walk from the town centre, opposite Christchurch Park. 'As a discerning traveller it is not often that I have reason to compliment a hotel management for their efficiency. However after a long and tiring motorway journey from Scotland, my wife and I were made most welcome at this well-appointed hotel and in spite of arriving at an inopportune time a full hot meal was served in our room. During our stay, nothing was too much trouble and our needs were attended to by a helpful and courteous staff.' *(R McSkimming)*

Open: All year, except Christmas night.
Rooms: 19 double, 4 single, 1 suite – 21 with bath, all with telephone, radio, colour TV and baby-listening.
Facilities: Lounge, bar, restaurant; function room. Small garden. 20 minutes by car from the sea at Felixstowe; convenient for exploring Constable country.
Location: 10 minutes' walk from town centre; 200 yards to the right from the A12 and Henley Road crossroads.
Restriction: No dogs in public rooms.
Credit cards: All major credit cards accepted.
Terms (no service charge): B & B £23–34. Set meal: dinner £7.60; full *alc* £13.50. Old English Weekends and 3-night breaks available at reduced rates. Reduced rates for children over 5 sharing parents' room. No charge for children under 5. Special meals by arrangement.

JERVAULX, Nr Ripon, North Yorkshire   **Map 4**

Jervaulx Hall   *Telephone:* Bedale (0677) 60235

The first entry for *Jervaulx Hall* appeared last year. John and Shirley Sharp had bought the Hall, which is in Wensleydale, on the edge of the Dales National Park, in 1979, and were new to the hotel business; but we stayed there ourselves at the turn of the year, and felt things promised well. The hotel is on the site of one of the famous Cistercian abbeys. Its ruins are less well-known than Fountains and Rievaulx, but nonetheless impressive. The *Hall* adjoins the ruins, separated only by a ha-ha, and enjoys the run of the substantial Abbey Park. Most of the building is early Victorian, with large comfortable public rooms, furnished with solid reassuring Victorian furniture. The bedrooms vary a good deal in size, and only a few so far have private bathrooms. But improvements are planned with regard to baths and basins. Shirley Sharp was taken ill last year, which put some strain on the hotel. We were particularly glad, therefore, to get the following report: 'We spent a delightful holiday at this very attractive place, and endorse your entry in the 1981 Guide. We found John and Shirley Sharp most welcoming and attentive. Shirley Sharp has had to take things gently, but it says a lot for her courage and that of her husband that they continue to run such a good service.' *(John W Dewis; also Peter R Copp)*

Open: 1 March–2 January.
Rooms: 8 double – 3 with bath, all with tea-making facilities and baby-listening. (1 room with bath on ground floor.)
Facilities: Residents' lounge, TV room, dining room. 8 acres garden with Abbey ruins; trout and grayling fishing available in nearby river Ure. .
Location: 12 miles N of Ripon on the A6108, between Masham and Middleham.
Credit cards: Access, Barclay.
Terms (no fixed service charge): Rooms £10–14 per person; B & B £12–16; dinner, B & B £18–22. Set meal: dinner £7.50. Reduced rates and special meals for children.

> Hotels were asked to estimate prices for 1982, but some hotels gave us only their 1981 prices. To avoid unpleasant shocks, always check tariff at time of booking.

Lodore Swiss Hotel   *Telephone:* Borrowdale (059 684) 285
                                                              Telex: 64305

The *Lodore Swiss* has a fine commanding presence on Derwentwater,
south of Keswick. It is called *Lodore* because the famous Lodore Falls are
within its 40 acres, and it is called *Swiss* because the Englands who have
owned and run it for more than thirty years are Swiss; they like to
introduce Swiss dishes on their menus and the way they run their hotel is
also in the Swiss tradition. By the standards of the Guide, it is, with 72
bedrooms, a substantial hotel and it also provides, after the fashion of big
and luxurious establishments, a whole range of exotic amenities – not just
heated indoor and outdoor swimming pools, saunas and solariums, but
hairdressing and massage salons, cathiodermie (a form of skin treatment), Slendertone and much else besides. On the question of size, Tony
England writes to us: 'We don't really consider ourselves a large hotel,
and we hope that a reasonable degree of intimacy is possible and
achieved. On the other hand we don't want to be any bigger and will not
increase in size as long as the family remains in full control.'
   The *Lodore Swiss* will not be to everyone's taste; to one contributor
indeed, it had 'the intimate charm of London Airport'. But it is clear from
our files that the hotel is greatly appreciated by others. The following
report speaks eloquently for the pro-*Lodore* faction:
   'Although the weather was awful for two of our three days we enjoyed
every minute of our stay. Considering its size the hotel is astonishingly
warm and friendly. It is most efficient. The food is excellent and the
service in the restaurant courteous and swift. Our bedroom was very
comfortable. Breakfast in bed every morning was a treat – my wife
particularly relishing a Muesli plus banana and cream dish, and I a swim in
the hotel pool just before. There was dancing two evenings out of three –
once with a good live band. We had saunas every afternoon and I had my
first massage ever. There was even ping-pong. It was really quite a
struggle to leave the hotel to go walking – even when it was not raining.'
*(Conrad Dehn QC; also Dr and Mrs T Heffernan, C N Georgano, C
Wingfield, John S Hunter)*

Open: Mid March–November.
Rooms: 60 double, 11 single, 1 suite – all with bath or shower, telephone, colour
TV and baby-listening.
Facilities: Lift, lounge, writing room, bar, dining room, ballroom; health and
beauty suite, sauna, exercise rooms, hairdressing salon, shop, indoor swimming
pool, children's nursery with resident nanny. Dancing every Saturday; disco twice
weekly during July and August. 40 acres grounds going down to Derwentwater and
the river Derwent; outdoor swimming pool, tennis court, children's playground.
Location: 3½ miles S of Keswick.
Restrictions: Children under 6 not allowed in dining room; special meals provided in nursery. No dogs.
Terms (excluding service):   B & B £25; full board (minimum 3 days) £36. Set
meals: lunch £6.50; dinner £8.50; full *alc* £11. Reduced rates and special meals for
children.

Deadlines: nominations for the 1983 edition should reach us not
later than 31 July 1982. Latest date for comments on existing
entries: 31 August 1982.

KILDWICK, Nr Keighley, West Yorkshire   Map 4

Kildwick Hall   *Telephone:* Cross Hills (0535) 32244

'Set high above the main road from Keighley to Skipton is this magnificent Jacobean manor house with later additions, including a superb dining room in Adam style. Antique furnishings and splendid decorations are all in character. It is family owned and run and the reception and service are exceptionally good. The food is imaginative and very well served and there is the stamp of quality and care about it. It makes a thoroughly civilized centre for touring the Yorkshire Dales.' *(Angela and David Stewart; also James Hill)*

Open: All year.
Rooms: 9 double, 3 single – 10 with bath, 2 with shower, all with telephone and colour TV; 2 four-poster beds.
Facilities: Main hall, lounge (including bar), dining room. 3 acres garden in own surrounding woodland. Ideal centre for the Yorkshire Moors and Dales.
Location: In Kildwick village. Take road between *The White Lion* and church, cross canal and turn left at top of hill.
Credit cards: All major credit cards accepted.
Terms: B & B £19–34; dinner, B & B £160–260 per week; full board £200–340 per week. Set meals: lunch £6.50; dinner £9.95; full *alc* £17.50. Special diets catered for by arrangement. Special weekly and off-peak rates available. Reduced rates for children sharing parents' room; special meals provided.

KINGHAM, Oxon   Map 2

The Mill   *Telephone:* Kingham (060 871) 255

This old mill house – the place itself is mentioned in records at intervals from the Domesday Book onwards – lies in open flat meadow land on the outskirts of Kingham village – not one of the more swinging Cotswold centres, but Stow-on-the-Wold and Chipping Norton are close at hand, and *The Mill* has the advantages of greater rurality. It has been owned and run for several years by John and Val Burnett, who have made many improvements, both in the garden and in the house. The rooms, though small, have been attractively furnished, with daintily flowered wallpapers and curtains to match; the beds have charming old-fashioned white bedspreads. There is a pleasant bar area with a huge roaring fire in the cool season and a lively atmosphere. Diners in the low-ceilinged dining room on the first floor are attended to by girls in flowery dresses and aprons. Opinions vary as to the quality of the food: some have been disappointed, others have much enjoyed their meals. Breakfasts and bar snacks have come in for compliments. The friendliness of the hosts – 'their quiet and effective helpfulness', as one writer described it – is mentioned by nearly all correspondents. *(Ian and Agatha Lewin, Mr and Mrs J Kavanagh, F E Brazier, W A Sedeloy)*

Open: All year.
Rooms: 9 double, 1 single, 2 family – 7 with bath, 3 with shower, all with tea-making facilities. 3 rooms in annexe. (1 room on ground floor.)
Facilities: Residents' lounge, TV lounge, dining room. 10 acres grounds with golf practice range and trout stream – fishing available. Horse-riding nearby. &.

67

Location: Mid-way between Stow-on-the-Wold and Chipping Norton on the B4450.
Restrictions: No children under 3. Dogs by prior arrangement only.
Credit cards: American Express, Barclay/Visa, Diners.
Terms (excluding 10% service charge): B & B £15–16.50; dinner, B & B £22.50–24. Set meals: lunch £5.25; dinner £7.50.

KINGSBRIDGE, Devon   Map 1

Buckland-Tout-Saints Hotel   *Telephone:* Kingsbridge (0548) 3055
Goveton

'The hotel is very much off the beaten track (car essential) in the beautiful South Hams region of South Devon, about 15 miles from Plymouth. The first impression is of utter peace, lovely grounds and views. Everything is spotless – woodwork polished, paint immaculate, silver gleaming. A good welcome from the owner when we arrived was continued throughout the visit, with careful service at every level from what seemed like happy staff, and enquiries for our comfort – such as offering an extra heater in the room (we arrived on a piercingly cold day) and so forth. We had a pretty bedroom, with a fresh pink-and-white colour scheme. The bathroom was carpeted, with a huge bath (much appreciated by 6-footers) and lashings of piping hot water at all hours. No room phone. Dinner was delicious (I had avocado mousse, a spicy tomato soup, roast duck and raspberry shortcake – there was a choice of at least 4 things at each course except the second). We chose a Pieroth wine from the lower end of their price range and it was excellent. Coffee and *petits fours* are included in the *table d'hôte*. The handsome Queen Anne house is pleasantly furnished with lots of deep, comfortable armchairs in the various sitting rooms, and much panelling. Altogether, a very soothing atmosphere and high standards all round.' *(EC; also Mr and Mrs R A Nisbet, Joshua Rozenberg)*

Open: 12 March–31 November.
Rooms: 13 double – 11 with bath, 2 with shower, 5 with colour TV.
Facilities: 2 lounges (1 with TV), cocktail bar, restaurant. 6 acres grounds with 9-hole putting green and croquet. 5 miles from the sea, bathing, fishing, sailing, riding and golf all nearby.
Location: 2½ miles NE of Kingsbridge off the A381, situated in 27 acres of parkland.
Credit cards: Access/Euro, American Express.
Terms: B & B £21.50–29.50; dinner, B & B £32–41. Set meal: dinner £11. Special terms for 2-day breaks, honeymoons, anniversary breaks. Reduced rates for children sharing parents' room; high tea at 6 pm.

KINTBURY, Nr Newbury, Berkshire   Map 2

Dundas Arms [GFG]   *Telephone:* Kintbury (048 85) 263

The *Dundas Arms*, in a quiet backwater, has long been appreciated by some urban dwellers as an admirable weekend battery-recharger. London is an hour-and-a-half's distance by the M4 which runs close by. It's a restaurant with rooms, located between the river Kennet and the Kennet and Avon canal (good canal walks). The rooms are in a stable-block, each with its patio, out of earshot of the restaurant, which is popular in terms of custom and serious in terms of its cooking. In our entry last year, we reported reservations about the upkeep of the place. We are glad to know that there has been a general overhaul this past year – all carpets repaired and so forth. 'The food was SUPERB – and worth the money. The bedrooms are splendidly comfortable, and the individual patio is a marvellous idea. We liked the general air of enthusiasm.' *(Rosemary Boyne; also Anne Voss-Bark)*

Open: All year, except Ascot week and Christmas week.
Rooms: 6 double – all with bath, 5 with telephone and colour TV. 1 room in annexe. (All rooms on ground floor.)
Facilities: Bar, restaurant. Kennet and Avon Canal alongside. ᕕ .
Location: In the Kennet Valley, S of the A4 and M4 5½ miles W of Newbury.
Restrictions: No children under 18 months. No dogs.
Credit cards: All major credit cards accepted.
Terms (excluding service):   B & B £14–24. Full *alc* (dinner) £11–14. Reduced rates for children sharing parents' room; special meals can be provided.

KIRKBY STEPHEN, Cumbria   Map 4

King's Arms Hotel   *Telephone:* Kirkby Stephen (0930) 71378
Market Street

'Just the sort of old posting inn I like to find in a small Cumbrian township: simple, friendly, its bar full of locals, and comfortable but not luxurious. I had no TV in my bedroom and had to go round the corner for a bath (the water was red-hot even during the early afternoon). My bed was extremely comfortable and there was lots of reading matter in the room and around the hotel. The restaurant provided a decent meal at a reasonable price, and my breakfast, though simple, was striking in that I was given a big hunk of butter and a full jar of Chivers' Olde English marmalade instead of the awful "plastic" stuff or a sliver of marmalade on a saucer. To my mind a most worthy hotel: just right for a walking or similar holiday.' *(Christopher Portway)*

Open: All year, except Christmas.
Rooms: 10 double, 1 single – 1 with bath.
Facilities: lounge, cocktail bar, TV room, dining room. ½ acre garden. Trout fishing in River Eden.
Location: In town centre; parking for 12 cars.
Credit cards: Access/Euro/Mastercard, American Express, Barclay/Visa.
Terms (excluding service):   Rooms £8–9; B & B £11–12; dinner, B & B £17.50. Set meals: lunch £4.50; dinner £7.50. 2-night 'Cumbria Break' (dinner B & B) £30, October–May (except bank holidays). Reduced rates and special meals for children.

LAMORNA COVE, Nr Penzance, Cornwall   Map 1

Lamorna Cove Hotel   *Telephone:* Mousehole (073 673) 411

'This remains a well-run, comfortable hotel,' comments a recent visitor, endorsing previous repots on facilities and service. We repeat last year's entry:
   This friendly family hotel lies close to the rugged toe of England; five

miles from the jolly bustle of Penzance and 10 from the grim razzle-dazzle of Land's End, but Lamorna Cove is a wholly peaceful haven, lying at the foot of a long leafy valley on the sheltered southern coast of the peninsula. The cove itself doesn't offer much in the way of sandy beaches – there's a bit at low tide – but you can go skin-diving or swim from the rocks; and the hotel has its own outdoor heated swimming pool. Sennen Cove, a wide, sandy and surfable beach on the north coast is about 10 miles by road. The hotel is an extensively modernized conversion of a number of old buildings, including a chapel and a former quarry-owner's home as well as recent extensions. It stands on one side of the cove in five acres of grounds with seaward views. The food, without being over-ambitious, gets high marks for quality and choice. Don't expect anything very chic in the furnishing, and some of the bedrooms are small with poor sound insulation. *(David Jervois, Brian and Margaret Aldiss and others)*

Open: February–31 November.
Rooms: 19 double, 2 single, 2 suites – 19 with bath, 4 with shower, 6 with telephone, all with radio, colour TV and baby-listening. 4 rooms in annexe.
Facilities: Lift, 4 lounges, bar, restaurant. Cottages for 4 and 5 in hotel grounds. 5½ acres garden in a wooded cleft leading down to the sea, 300 yards away; heated outdoor swimming pool.
Location: 6 miles S of Penzance.
Restriction: Dogs by special arrangement.
Credit cards: All major credit cards accepted.
Terms: B & B £12.50–22.50; dinner, B & B £17.50–27.95. Set meals: lunch £5.75; dinner £7.50; full *alc* £7.50. Winter breaks. Reduced rates for children sharing parents' room; special meals provided.

LASTINGHAM, North Yorkshire   Map 4

Lastingham Grange   *Telephone:* Lastingham (075 15) 345

The *Grange* is a well-kept, well-mannered small country house, stone-walled and creeper-covered, set round a courtyard in 10 acres of garden. It is within yards of superb walking country; the road peters out at the house and becomes a bridle path stretching across the moors to Rosedale. Over the years – and this year is no exception, readers have repeatedly appreciated the quiet comfort of the house and the 'nothing-too-much-trouble' caring attitude on the part of the resident owners, Major and Mrs Wood. The *Grange's* only weakness, according to one writer, is the absence of a bar. 'Drinks served at touch of a bell, but only keg beer. However, the village pub is near and has excellent beer and six types of single-malt whisky, and the walk up the hill from pub to hotel before dinner sharpens the appetite.' One other matter, it has to be said, crops up in our correspondence, even from some of the hotel's warmest admirers: a complaint that the cooking lacks distinction, and – a *cri de coeur* from a woman reader, 'They gave me a ladies' portion!' *(H Holden, Lady Elstub)*

Open: April–mid November.
Rooms: 11 double, 1 single – 9 with bath, all with radio and baby-listening.
Facilities: Large entrance hall-cum-reception, spacious lounge with log fire; sheltered terrace. 10 acres grounds with croquet, swings and slides. In the heart of the National Park, near moors and dales, 20 miles from the coast, riding, golf and swimming nearby.
Location: Off the A170 N of Kirkbymoorside. Turn N towards Appleton-le-Moors, between Pickering and Kirkbymoorside.
Restriction: No dogs.

Terms (no service charge): B & B £18–20; dinner, B & B £23.25–26.25; full board £27–30. Set meals: lunch £6.50; dinner £9.50. Reduced rates and special meals for children.

LAVENHAM, Suffolk   Map 2

The Swan   *Telephone:* Lavenham (0787) 247477
High Street

The Swan appeared in our 1980 edition and was omitted last year. It wasn't that we had anything against the hotel, but that we lacked fresh reports. It certainly has the appearance of a hotel of character: even by the standards of this old medieval weaving town, it is a remarkably handsome half-timbered building – a picture-postcard artist's model facade. Inside, too, there is no shortage of old-world features: great upright beams, uneven floors and vast fireplaces. The restaurant, formerly a Wool Hall, has a lofty timbered ceiling and a minstrel's gallery. In general the furnishings are in keeping with the house, and the modern conveniences tactfully introduced. It may be the fact that it is owned by Trust Houses Forte, and therefore lacks the personality which a resident owner can provide, which has prevented it winning support from our readers. But we were glad to get recently a special note of appreciation for the *Swan*'s service, and would be glad to hear how other visitors fare.

'I would endorse the comments in the 1980 edition, but would add a word about the staff. From the manager downwards, both in reception and in the dining room, they really work hard to make one's visit an extremely happy one – nothing seems too much trouble. If only all hotels were like this.' *(W L G Craig)*

Open: All year.
Rooms: 31 double, 10 single, 1 suite – all with bath, telephone, radio, colour TV, tea-making facilities and baby-listening. (9 rooms on ground floor.)
Facilities: 4 lounges, TV room, 2 bars, restaurant. Small garden.
Location: In village centre; most rooms overlook the garden; parking for 60 cars.
Restriction: No dogs in public rooms except bar.
Credit cards: All major credit cards accepted.
Terms: Rooms £17.50–27 per person; B & B £20.75–30.25; dinner, B & B £22.50–26.50; full board £29.50–33.50. Set meals: lunch £6; dinner £7.80; full *alc* £11.50. Weekend bargain breaks; special rates for 4-day visits. Reduced rates for children.

LEDBURY, Herefordshire   Map 2

Hope End Country House Hotel [GFG]   *Telephone:* Ledbury (0531) 3613

Hope End, once the home of Elizabeth Barrett Browning, made its first appearance in our Guide last year, with an encomium from a reader on its many civilized attributes. Some people might find the Hegartys' emphasis on organic foods (and a no-choice dinner menu) off-putting. One reader, while endorsing an entry, wailed: 'I was dying for something *bad* for me.' But most readers are warm in their praise. 'An inclusive price with no extras – very good value for perfection,' writes one correspondent, and here is how the hotel struck another reader:

'*Hope End* is tucked away in a gently sloping wooded valley and park of

71

forty acres near the Malvern Hills. It is a small country-house hotel with accommodation for only fourteen – ideal for a honeymoon couple or people wanting to get away from it all and simple rest a bit, or those, like myself who enjoy walking in the hills. The hotel itself is charming. It is owned by John and Patricia Hegarty who certainly go out of their way to make one's stay comfortable. The old house has been nicely converted and is furnished with many antiques and beautifully hand-woven fabrics. But probably the most enjoyable aspect of the place is the food which is really quite extraordinary. Much of it is grown in the acre walled garden, using the old-fashioned methods of compost and fertilizer; the eggs are all free-range from *Hope End*'s own chickens, and the estate is full of fruit-giving trees, the fruits of which go into some of the most delicious home-made desserts I have ever eaten. Breakfast includes home-baked fresh breads and rolls, fresh home-grown fruits and home-made yoghurt as well as the traditional fare.' *(Leslie Kenton; also Denise Coffey, Christine Rogers, Shirley and Alan Bailey)*

Open: March–November.
Rooms: 7 double – all with bath. 1 double with bath in annexe.
Facilities: 2 sitting rooms, dining room. 40 acres wooded parkland and nature reserve; 1 acre walled garden.
Location: 2 miles N of Ledbury, ¼ mile W of Wellington Heath.
Restrictions: No children under 14. No dogs.
Credit cards: Access/Euro, American Express, Barclay/Visa, Diners.
Terms: Dinner, B & B £28–30. Set meals: lunch (by arrangement only) £4; dinner £11.

LIFTON, Devon   **Map 1**

The Arundell Arms   *Telephone:* Lifton (056 684) 244

'Undoubtedly wins my accolade as one of my favourite hotels,' writes a keen supporter of *The Arundell Arms*, a much-creepered early 19-century stone building, originally a coaching inn on the A30 (but the five front rooms are sound-proofed). This correspondent, as will be clear from what follows, is a fisherman, and the hotel goes out of its way to attract fishing folk: it has 20 miles of its own water on the Tamar and four of its tributaries, a special beginner's course in fly fishing, trout-fishing weekends in the spring and so forth. But it also seeks to attract riding, shooting and golfing people too. Its restaurant serves simple English meals, appreciated by some but not all of our readers.

'The whole place has a most delightful atmosphere. We had a very warm welcome from the owner, Anne Voss-Bark, and our bedroom had all the things one would expect in one's own bedroom at home, including a nice posy of flowers from the garden. All the public rooms and bars were very comfortably furnished. Dinner was excellent, and served with a courtesy we have long forgotten about. Arrangements for packed lunches were first-class; we had a form to fill up the night before, so if you did not get what you liked it was your own fault. For the fishermen, they had turned a cock-fighting pit into a shop and the two gillies, Roy and David, were there every morning at 10 when you could buy, or hire, all types of equipment you could ever want, including clothing, waders, etc. The gillies also gave you the up-to-date news of the water on that day; they would also give you lessons on casting or fly-tying by arrangement. Being a dog-lover I was glad to see dogs in the lounge which is always a good way to make new friends, although they played hell with the After Eight Mints!' *(G R Appleyard)*

Open: All year, except 3 or 4 days at Christmas.
Rooms: 20 double, 7 single – 16 with bath, 5 with shower, all with radio, tea-making facilities and baby-listening. 4 rooms in annexe.
Facilities: Sitting room, TV room, 2 bars, restaurant; games room, skittle alley. Small terraced garden. Lake and river with salmon, trout and sea-trout fishing.
Restriction: No dogs in dining room.
Location: 3 miles E of Launceston on the A30.
Credit cards: Access/Euro/Mastercard, American Express, Barclay/Visa.
Terms: B & B £15–21; dinner, B & B £20.50–28. Set meal: dinner £8.75; full *alc* £11–12. Bargain breaks; sporting courses. Free accommodation for children under 16 sharing parents' room; special meals on request.

LINCOLN, Lincolnshire   **Map 2**

D'Isney Place Hotel   *Telephone:* Lincoln (0522) 38881
Eastgate

'A *must* for the GHG! A family-run establishment, 100 yards from the Cathedral, opened by Judy and David Payne two years ago; it was formerly a run-down Georgian building, but the hotel has lovely elegant rooms and beautiful furniture, fabrics, bedcovers, curtains, etc. No meals served except breakfast – brought to your bedside on Minton Bone china, cooked or continental – and no bar. But there's a good bar next door and Harvey's Restaurant close by. The friendliest and most satisfying place I've stayed in for a long time.' *(Christopher Portway)*

Open: All year.
Rooms: 11 double, 1 single, 1 suite – 11 with bath, 1 with shower, all with telephone, radio, colour TV, tea-making facilities and baby-listening. (6 rooms on ground floor.)
Facilities: Lounge. 1 acre garden with children's slide and swing. ⟁.
Location: 100 yards from Lincoln Cathedral; parking.
Credit cards: Access/Euro/Mastercard.
Terms (no service charge): B & B £13–19.50. Reduced rates and special meals for children.

LITTLE SINGLETON, Nr Poulton-Le-Fylde,
Blackpool, Lancashire   **Map 2**

Mains Hall   *Telephone:* Poulton-Le-Fylde (0253) 885130

'*Mains Hall* was hard to find at dusk, but worth the effort. Hidden up a little country lane off the A585, it overlooks the river Wyre ("England's least-known river," says Bob Owen, the proprietor), with trees and meadows and cows outside the breakfast window. This was particularly pleasant as I was there for a huge conference in the neon glories of Blackpool, only five miles and perhaps 10 minutes away, which is the nearest British equivalent to Las Vegas. The food at Mains Hall was also a delightful counterpoint to the chip buttys and mushy peas for which Blackpool is deservedly renowned. Bob and Beryl Owen took over the historic building in the spring of 1979, and have erased some of the more egregious errors of former owners, while restoring the structure as well as the character of the house in which the Heskeths lived in Elizabethan times and George IV, then Prince of Wales, courted Maria Fitzherbert, a virtuous widow, in the 18th century. My room, which was presumably George's in his day, was huge, sunny, beautifully appointed. My favourite room in the entire building is the wood-panelled entrance, whose carvings have never been subjected to modernization. The small, family-size lounge is a pleasant place to pass the time of day or evening with a host who obviously likes people, and a family who are clearly enjoying their new venture.' *(Nancy Foy)*

The above entry (slightly abbreviated) is taken from last year's Guide. Since then all rooms have been given their own baths or showers, and Nancy Foy's commendation has been endorsed: 'I was delighted with everything in this lovely old home. I, too, found it difficult to find at dusk, but well worth the slight detour from the M6. I received a warm welcome. Everything was exactly as ordered. I hope to call there soon again!' *(A Carson Clark)*

Open: All year.
Rooms: 5 double, 1 single – all with bath or shower and tea-making facilities.
Facilities: Hall with log fire, lounge bar, dining room; dogs allowed 'if well-behaved'. 4 acres grounds with croquet. Access to tidal river with birdwatching and fishing.
Location: 1½ miles from village, just off the A585.
Terms (no service charge): B & B £10.75–16.70. Set meal: dinner £5.75. Reduced rates for children sharing parents' room; special meals provided.

LONDON

Athenaeum Hotel   *Telephone:* (01) 499 3464
116 Piccadilly, W1   *Telex:* 261589 ATHOME

A prime position on Piccadilly overlooking Green Park (the hotel thoughtfully provides a jogging guide through the royal parks for their more active residents), hyper-elegant in its decor, a dependably good restaurant – the *Athenaeum* is everything one has a right to expect from a de-luxe capital hotel. That it is all that and something more owes a lot to its General Manager, Ron Jones, a hotelier of the old school, who sets the tone for his staff – described, by one recent visitor as 'most skilfully trained to appear effortlessly efficient and consistently genial'. *(PG)*

Open: All year.
Rooms: 81 double, 9 single, 22 suites – all with bath, shower, telephone, radio, colour TV, baby-listening and double-glazing.
Facilities: Lifts, lounge, cocktail bar, restaurant; conference facilities, facilities for private parties. &.
Location: Central; parking.
Restriction: Dogs only by arrangement.
Credit cards: All major credit cards accepted.
Terms: Rooms £43.50–72.50 per person. Set meals: breakfast £3.20–4.55; lunch £9.50; dinner £12.50; full *alc* about £19.60.

We would like to be able to recommend more hotels in the budget class in London. Nominations especially welcome.

LONDON

Basil Street Hotel
8 Basil Street, Knightsbridge, SW3

Telephone: (01) 581 3311
Telex: 28379

A newcomer to the Guide, but the *Basil* has had for several generations a faithful following both among overseas visitors and out-of-towners who want a quiet central location (Basil Street runs off Sloane Street and is five minutes from Harrods and Hyde Park) with the traditional virtues of hotel hospitality. There's nothing gimcrack or chrome about the *Basil*: it's a thoroughly well-bred kind of hostelry. 'It's a positive delight to stay here. 1) The staff are very efficient, and human without being subservient. 2) The decor and ambience are totally relaxing, with a variety of different public rooms and restaurants to cater for one's mood. The breakfast menu is very diverse and excellently presented. The prices are very reasonable for 19th-century accommodation and atmosphere in the 1980s. It's certainly my favourite hotel in London.' *(C Stuart-Menteth; also Leonard M Glushakow)*

Open: All year.
Rooms: 39 double, 62 single, 2 suites – 66 with bath, all with telephone, some with radio and TV.
Facilities: 2 lounges/writing rooms, TV room, coffee shop, wine bar, restaurant; limited nightlife daily in wine bar, except Sunday.
Location: Central; public car park nearby.
Restriction: No dogs in public rooms.
Credit cards: All major credit cards accepted.
Terms: Rooms £20–40. Set meals: breakfast (continental) £1.95; lunch £7.50; dinner £8.50; full *alc* £12.50. Special weekend rates. No charge for children sharing parents' room; special meals provided.

LONDON

Blakes
33 Roland Gardens, SW7

Telephone: (01) 370 6701
Telex: 8813500

Blakes is the hyper-elegant and pricey small hotel off the Fulham Road, much written about in smart magazines and hugely fashionable both in its decor and its guests. Our entry last year was written before we had had any reports on *Blakes'* new head chef, trained by Carrier and formerly at London's *Capital*. We were glad to receive the report below on the restaurant – not so happy about the mistake in booking. (Less happy, also, to note that on the hotel's attractive breakfast menu – £3 continental, £5 English, plus 15% service – fresh orange juice is an extra: 40p small, 70p large!)
   'It's something of a tragedy to have to begin a "rave review" of a hotel with a warning, but I think it's an unforgiveable error if you've booked a double room . . . and confirmed it in writing . . . to arrive at Reception to be told you asked for a single. As *Blakes* is everything you could wish in a hotel for a "special occasion" . . . like a honeymoon first night, a mistake like that is doubly disastrous. As it was, it says much for *Blakes'* instant charm that we accepted a tiny double room with relief. The decor is so exceptional that even its many appearances in glossy magazines don't do it justice, and the sense of being invited into someone's home is very strong

when each room is individually and exquisitely designed. But it's precisely because so much has been seen of Anouska Hempel's hotel that it's a bit vexing to end up in a room the size of a linen cupboard. Nevertheless it would have been worth sleeping on the step if that was the only way to eat in the restaurant. It's a gourmet's delight, as well as a visual joy . . . glittering mirrors and glass reflecting the white and black decor . . . attentive service by delightful staff, and an adventurous menu deliciously cooked, almost beyond compare in hotel circles. What's more . . . a lure to any true hotel-fancier, *Blakes* produced the best breakfast we have ever had. All in all then, and at a price, this blissful experience is to be highly recommended, but check your booking again . . . and again . . . to avoid the linen-cupboard and disappointment.' *(Diane Latham)*

Open: All year.
Rooms: 19 double, 10 single, 16 suites – all with bath, shower, telephone and colour TV.
Facilities: Lifts, bar, restaurant; sauna. &.
Location: Central; no private parking.
Restriction: No dogs.
Credit cards: All major credit cards accepted.
Terms: Rooms £36.25–50 per person. Breakfast from £3.50; full *alc* £19.

LONDON

The Connaught [GFG]
16 Carlos Place, W1

Telephone: (01) 499 7070

'The secret at *The Connaught* is detail. For example: the returning guest is routinely greeted by name at Reception after a year's absence. More surprising: one American, shown to his room by the young man in formal tie and striped trousers, commented that he had been given a different room this year. "Yes," said the hotel man, "we've given you one without an adjoining door." Only then did the guest remember that he had mentioned gently on his previous departure that one could hear conversation in the next room. The guest had forgotten; *The Connaught* had not. Another example: a woman arriving long after midnight from a dinner with a wine-spot on her dress asked for a lemon. The hall porter produced it together with cheerful advice on spot-removal in general. The rooms are, of course, immaculate, the paint perfect, the carpets unblemished. Two modern touches: dial phones have at last arrived, ending decades of friendly chat with the hotel telephonists, and the house staff now wear bleepers to speed them even more swiftly from task to task. The restaurant is said to be the best in London. Certainly our London guests are always delighted to dine at *this* hotel. One final touch – a Christmas card to the States from Paolo Zago, the nearly invisible hand which guides this unique establishment. Expensive, yes, but worth every p. of it. Long may it stand.' *(James H Silberman and Selma Shapiro; also Alan Williams and others)*

Open: All year.
Rooms: 105, including suites – all with bath, direct-dial telephone, and colour TV; 24-hour room service.
Facilities: Lounges, cocktail bar, grill/restaurant.
Location: Central; no private parking.

Restriction: No dogs.
Terms (excluding 15% service, 1981 prices): Rooms £42.50–55 single, £67.50–75 double, £126.50–148.50 suite. Set meal: breakfast (continental) £3.40; full *alc* about £25.

LONDON

Duke's Hotel
St James's Place, SW1

Telephone: (01) 491 4840/3090
Telex: 28283

Among the smaller of the half-dozen elegant hotels within a quarter-mile radius of Piccadilly, *Duke's* has a particularly quiet location, being in a cul-de-sac which is itself a cul-de-sac of St James's Street. Its regular guests, according to their brochure, include the kind of VIPs who want to avoid a barrage of photographers at the door. We are not sure how many of our readers belong to this category, but the hotel can safely be recommended for lesser mortals too. Its prices are high by comparison with comparable hotels in a central location in other capital cities, but not by central London standards. *(Shirley Museler, Mark Tarry, Sandy Scranton)*

Open: All year.
Rooms: 27 double, 15 single, 12 suites – all with bath, shower, telephone, radio and colour TV; tea-making facilities in suites; babysitting service.
Facilities: Lifts, lounge, bar, restaurant; banqueting and conference facilities. Courtyard.
Location: Central; off St James's Street, between Piccadilly and Pall Mall; 4 minutes' walk from Green Park station; parking facilities nearby.
Restriction: Dogs at manager's discretion.
Credit cards: All major credit cards accepted.
Terms: Single rooms £50, double £74–78; suites from £110 per night, depending on number of people. Set meals: breakfast (continental) £4, (English) £5.50; full *alc* £14. 25% discount for Friday/Saturday nights. Children using cot in parents' room additional £5; special meals on request.

LONDON

Durrants Hotel
George Street, W1

Telephone: (01) 935 8131
Telex: 894919 DURHOT G

This old-fashioned establishment (in the wholly complimentary sense) with a fine Regency facade, centrally placed (it's three blocks north of Oxford Street, just off Marylebone High Street, and a stroll away from the Wallace Collection in Manchester Square) continues to please those who are looking for that rare thing, a medium-priced city hotel of genuine character.

So ran the first paragraph of last year's entry. A reader comments: 'Super! It is everything you say, and a building of great character.' He goes on to mention the noise from George Street: 'like much of London (Mayfair even worse!) it goes to bed at 1 am and gets up at 7 am.' This correspondent enjoyed his Durrants' breakfast, but others, including some regulars, feel that the full English breakfast is a serious let-down in a hotel that is otherwise thoroughly satisfactory. *(Brian Croft, Sydney Downs, Richard Chinn, Jan Morris)*

77

Open: All year, but restaurant closed for lunch and dinner Christmas Day/ Boxing Day.
Rooms: 78 double, 26 single – 88 with bath or shower, all with telephone, radio and colour TV. (4 rooms on ground floor.)
Facilities: Lift, 2 lounges, breakfast room, dining room, conference and banqueting room.
Location: Central; no private parking.
Restriction: No dogs.
Credit card: Diners.
Terms: B & B £16–38. Set meals (excluding 10% service charge): lunch £8; dinner £10; full *alc* (excluding 10% service charge) £15.

LONDON

Ebury Court
26 Ebury Street, SW1

Telephone: (01) 730 8147

'I have enjoyed the *Ebury Court* frequently for nearly 30 years. It must surely be the best hotel in your Guide and deserves a Guide in itself.' Fortunate is a hotel that can attract such staunch support, but among the dozens of small hotels within range of Victoria, the *Ebury Court* is a special case, having been run with exceptional devotion by Mr and Mrs Topham for more than 40 years. Some of the rooms, admittedly, verge on the poky and we have had one report of a surly receptionist. But most of our readers who have stayed here warmly appreciate its personality. If readers know of more such hotels – in London or anywhere else – we should be glad to hear of them. *(G C Brown and others)*

Open: All year.
Rooms: 18 double, 19 single – 11 with bath, 1 with shower, all with telephone, radio and colour TV to hire.
Facilities: Lift, front hall, writing room with TV, club bar (visitors may become temporary members), restaurant; theatre suppers served.
Location: 3 minutes from Victoria Station; parking difficult.
Restriction: Dogs allowed, if small and well-behaved.
Terms (excluding service): B & B £17–23. Full *alc* lunch £8.50, dinner £9.50. Special meals for children.

LONDON

Elizabeth Hotel
37 Eccleston Square, SW1

Telephone: (01) 828 6812

We wish we had more budget hotels to recommend to our readers in central London as alternatives to the plusher but pricier establishments. The *Elizabeth*, a five-storey terrace house in the Belgravian style, is within walking distance of Victoria Station, but has an enviably quiet position overlooking a well-maintained square garden. It doesn't have a lift or a porter, so you must be prepared to carry your bags up steep stairs. Last year we printed a warm commendation of the *Elizabeth* from a New Zealander who had much appreciated the hotel's special tariffs for long stays (they also lower their prices when three or four people are sharing one of the larger rooms). This year, an Australian visitor writes: 'It is well kept, very clean and gives you a good English breakfast. I have used the hotel each time I have visited England for the past eight years and find it very reasonably priced and comfortable.' *(Mrs J Drabble; also Faye Evans White)*

Open: All year.
Rooms: 14 double, 10 single – 1 with bath, 6 with shower, all with internal telephone, some with colour TV.
Facilities: Lounge with colour TV, breakfast room. ½ acre garden with tennis court.
Location: Central; National Car Park for 400 cars nearby.
Restriction: No dogs.
Terms: B & B £13–16.50. Weekly terms off-season by arrangement. Reduced rates for children sharing parents' room.

LONDON

The Montcalm Hotel   *Telephone:* (01) 402 4288
Great Cumberland Place, W1   *Telex:* 28710

Previous editions of the Guide have contained long literary eulogies by Frederick Forsyth and Leslie Thomas on this smart elegant medium-priced (for London) hotel just behind Marble Arch. This year, correspondents have, for the most part, been equally appreciative if carrying less household names. One correspondent, however, had several complaints to make: he had asked for a quiet room and been given a noisy one, with the heating not working properly (it was a cold July), and other things had been faulty too. Another reader, a bachelor on his own had a different grouse: he felt that the bar and restaurant had treated him to the 'single guest syndrome' – a not unfamiliar complaint. These may be isolated cases. Other writers have paid tribute to the exceptionally fast, friendly and efficient reception and the excellent standards maintained in the rooms. We should be glad of further reports.

Open: All year.
Rooms: 72 double, 28 single, 15 suites – all with bath and shower, direct-dial telephone, radio and colour TV; baby-sitting available; 24-hour room service. (Some rooms on ground floor.)
Facilities: Lifts, lounge, penthouse suite, bar, *Restaurant 'La Varenne'* nightclub. All the amenities of a luxury hotel; services too: car hire, theatre tickets, tours of London, etc. ♿ .
Location: Central; car park opposite.
Restriction: Dogs at the management's discretion.
Credit cards: All major credit cards accepted.
Terms (excluding VAT and service): Rooms £27–46 per person; B & B £30.50–49.50. Full *alc* £13.50–15. Special meals for children.

LONDON

Number Sixteen   *Telephone:* (01) 589 5232
16 Sumner Place, SW7   *Telex:* 266638

An unusual sort of town-house establishment – and we wish there were more like them – offering exceptionally pleasant and well-equipped rooms in a non hotel-like environment. Clientele include the more sophisticated end of show-business – opera singers, choreographers, film

79

directors – some of whom will make this their base for weeks at a time. 'We have become connoisseurs of inexpensive London hotels in the last couple of years. This is our favourite. We've now stayed in five bedrooms, all very nice and individually decorated. Very nice sitting rooms, and a bar where you can help yourself. Pictures in public rooms are *very* good. Excellent location – close to South Kensington tube station, and parking available in the street. We feel at home there.' *(Paul Henderson)*

Open: All year.
Rooms: 20 double, 4 single – 11 with bath, 13 with shower, all with direct-dial telephone and colour TV on request.
Facilities: Reception, bar/lounge. Garden.
Location: Central; no private parking.
Restriction: Children over 12 preferred.
Credit cards: Access/Euro/Mastercard, American Express, Diners.
Terms (excluding service): B & B (continental) £16–26.

LONDON

The Portobello Hotel
22 Stanley Gardens, W11

Telephone: (01) 727 2777
Telex: 21789/25247

A six-floor Victorian terraced house, within strolling distance of the Portobello Road Market and Kensington Gardens: one of the few hotels in London with a distinctive character – palms and bits of Edwardiana, cane and wicker furniture, lots of satin cushions and beige upholstery – very much the creation of its owner, Tim Herring. Some of the rooms, rightly called cabins, will be too poky for some tastes: but even the smallest have a duvet-covered double bed, colour TV, tiny fridge, micro-bathroom and a shelf for the do-it-yourself breakfast, with croissants provided.

One correspondent this past year, while endorsing our entry and agreeing about the general panache and character of the hotel, felt that it wasn't quite what it had been – not just that the decor was looking a bit shabby, but that, though the food was good, the service had become erratic. More reports welcome.

Open: All year, except 24–29 December.
Rooms: 8 double, 8 single, 9 suites – 4 with bath, 21 with shower, all with telephone, radio, colour TV and drink-stocked fridge. (2 rooms on ground floor.)
Facilities: Lift, lounge, bar (open 24 hours a day to residents), restaurant. Access to communal gardens.
Location: Central; meter parking only.
Restriction: Dogs allowed at the proprietor's discretion.
Credit cards: Access/Euro, American Express.
Terms (excluding VAT): Single rooms £25–29, double £37–46. Full *alc* £11.

Do you know of a good hotel or country inn in the United States or Canada? Nominations please to our sibling publication, *America's Wonderful Little Hotels and Inns*, 345 East 93rd Street, 25C, New York, NY 10028.

LONDON

The Sandringham Hotel   *Telephone:* (01) 435 1569
3 Holford Road, Hampstead, NW3

A cheerful relaxed bed-and-breakfast hotel, the home of Maria and
Bertie Dreyer, in a Victorian house on the edge of Hampstead Heath.
Popular with American academics and their children. The Dreyers serve a
full English breakfast, it's quiet at night; and you can park on the
forecourt. *(A Harrison)*

Open: All year.
Rooms: 10 double, 4 single – 1 with bath.
Facilities: Lounge with TV, breakfast room. Small garden.
Location: 15 minutes from centre; parking on forecourt of hotel.
Restriction: No dogs.
Terms: B & B £9–11. Reduced weekly rate.

LOOE, Cornwall   Map 1

Klymiarven Hotel   *Telephone:* Looe (050 36) 2333
Barbican Hill, East Looe

Bruce and Daphne Henderson have been running this popular seaside
hotel for many years. Their house is a handsome one, formerly the Manor
House of East Looe, dating from about 1800. Looe is one of the more
picturesque resorts along the south coast of Cornwall, and gets uncon-
scionably crowded in the high season; but *Klymiarven*, five minutes' steep
walk from the centre of town, is well away from the milling throng and a
very pleasant place in which to relax, especially since it has its own heated
swimming pool in its three acres of grounds. The resident proprietors are
a warm and friendly couple, and many of their guests are faithful
followers, returning year after year. One correspondent felt that his
welcome had been a trifle over-effusive, but most of our contributors have
clearly enjoyed the enthusiastic hospitality of their hosts and the staff.
The quality of the meals is a slightly more debatable issue: 'super food',
according to one writer, but on the whole we feel this isn't a hotel for a
committed gourmet. *(Alan and Margaret Telford, Mrs J Angel, Pamela
Hill, Josephine Wrigley)*

Open: March–November; meals only at Christmas and New Year.
Rooms: 12 double, 1 single, 2 suites – 6 with bath, 2 with shower.
Facilities: Lounge, TV lounge, terrace bar, cellar bar with pool table, darts and
table tennis; pool tournaments and disco as required by visitors (but no disturbing
noise); recreation room. 3 acres grounds with heated swimming pool. 5 minutes
from sandy beaches with safe bathing.
Location: 5 minutes' walk from centre of East Looe; parking for 15–30 cars.
Approach via Barbican Road.
Terms (excluding 10% service charge): B & B £8.50–18.55; dinner, B & B
£13.50–23.50. Set meal: dinner (residents) £5.50, (non-residents) £7.50. No fixed
alc but special meals can be cooked by arrangement. Bargain breaks October and
March–April. Reduced rates and special meals for children.

Scale Hill Hotel　　　　　　　　*Telephone:* Lorton (090 085) 232

One of the more remote good hotels of the Lake District, *Scale Hill*, once a coaching inn, is in the Loweswater–Buttermere valley, near the National Trust land at Crummock Water. It's not a particularly sophisticated place: the public rooms have central heating (though one reader found the lounge a bit cold in June) and the bedrooms have electric fires. The set menus offer limited choice, and are not fancy in any way. But it's the sort of hotel which can inspire great devotion.

'*Scale Hill* is a special kind of hotel – a balance between luxury and simplicity is kept by Michael Thompson and his wife who are the thoughtful, efficient, good-humoured owners. It has a quality of life which appeals; one can walk or drive in a little known part of Cumbria, or just laze by the lake or in the garden, and then come in to masses of hot water, big towels and a spacious bedroom. Once changed, there is a friendly, well-stocked bar and an excellent dinner to look forward to. Food is always interesting, and generously served. Sunday night provides a good selection of salads. Sweets are served with masses of cream, and mints and fudge are available to eat with one's coffee. A comfortable, well-lit sitting room, piles of recent magazines and books, and usually some interesting people complete the evening. *Scale Hill* isn't just a hotel – it's a civilized way of life!' *(Chris and Dorothy Brining)*

Open:　27 March–7 November.
Rooms:　10 double, 3 single – 5 with bath, 1 with shower. (2 double rooms on ground floor.)
Facilities:　4 lounges, entrance hall, dining room. ½ acre grounds. Fine walking and climbing; fishing, swimming, golf, pony-trekking nearby. ♿ .
Location:　30 miles from the M6 at Penrith; 12 miles W of Keswick. Just off Lorton–Rosthwaite road.
Terms:　B & B £13.50–19; dinner, B & B £22–27.50. Set meals: lunch £5.50; dinner £9. Reduced prices for long stays and for children; self-catering flats in annexe.

The Feathers　　　　　　　　*Telephone:* Ludlow (0584) 2919/2718
　　　　　　　　　　　　　　　　Telex: 28905 Ref 685

One of the architectural glories of a town endowed with many beautiful buildings, *The Feathers* has been an inn since 1609. It is now the chief hotel of the town, thoroughly modernized and with all its bedrooms equipped with bathrooms *en suite*, but we are glad to say that it has lovingly preserved its period features. If one wanted to give a foreigner an impression of an Olde English inn (though of the grander sort), this would be a natural choice, and the hotel does in fact cater for a lot of coach parties as well as being a venue for conferences, banquets and the like. On the whole, we don't reckon to be a Guide to good coach-party hotels, but are glad to print the following unusual tribute: 'The one additional comment I have on this most comfortable establishment, with all mod cons and gleaming chrome facilities tucked sedately away amongst the old oak beams, is that coach parties – of which I was a member on this occasion – are treated by the management as human beings and not second-class citizens as is the practice of too many hotels. And my four-poster was a dream!' *(Christopher Portway)*

In our entry last year, we said that the hotel had been in the hands of the Edwards family for over a century. This was a mistake, for the present owner, Osmond Edwards, is no relation to previous Edwardses. But the important point remains that this is a personally-run hotel, not an impersonal member of a chain. In his letter to us, correcting this error, Osmond Edwards adds a p.s. which we pass on – make of it what you will: 'Our approach is unpretentious and maybe a bit unimaginative, perhaps as a reaction against the current "Lakeland" vogue of Barbara Cartland decor and fruit salad and firecrackers with everything!'

Open: All year.
Rooms: 29 double, 1 single, 1 suite – all with bath, radio, colour TV and tea-making facilities.
Facilities: 2 lounges, 2 bars, TV and writing room, stone and timbered restaurant with inglenook fireplace. Dances, private parties, wedding receptions catered for; conference facilities.
Location: In town centre; parking for 40 cars.
Restriction: No dogs.
Terms: B & B £21–27; dinner, B & B £29–36; full board £33–40. Set meals: lunch £4; dinner £9; full *alc* £10. Special rates 1 October–31 March (2 days dinner, B & B £48 per person). Reduced rates for children.

LUNDY, Bristol Channel, via Ilfracombe, North Devon　　　**Map 1**

Millcombe House　　　*Telephone:* Barnstaple (0271) 870870

For those who have never heard of Lundy Island, it rises 400 feet out of the sea in the Bristol Channel, with tremendous views of England, Wales and the Atlantic. It is just over three miles long by about half a mile wide, and the nearest practicable harbours are at Ilfracombe and Bideford, each about 24 miles away – further than England is from France. There is a sailing most days, though not normally on Mondays.

You will need to be fairly fit to stay at *Millcombe House*, the only hotel (or guest house) on the island, since it is set on a hill and there are no made-up roads or paths. Other creature comforts, basic for some, are also missing here: the hotel provides no TV or radio. 'We aim,' writes the hotel, 'to provide an atmosphere more of a house party than an ordinary hotel. Guests sit at one table, and talk is mainly about the island, its history and wildlife (over 425 different birds have been recorded here, as well as Grey Seals, Sika deer, Soay sheep and Lundy ponies). To stay at *Millcombe House* is a mixture of mild adventure – it is certainly unique in the hotel world – and being thoroughly spoiled. Our full board rate – there isn't any other – includes such things as early morning tea, afternoon tea and coffee after dinner, so once you have paid, you have no need to put your hands in your pockets again except for wines and spirits.' *(Ray and Beverley Williams)*

Open: Easter–mid October.
Rooms: 5 double, 2 single. 1,100 acres grounds. Sea ¼ mile with rock beach and safe bathing.
Restriction: Dogs not allowed to land on Lundy.
Terms (no service charge): Full board £15–27. Set meals: lunch £5; dinner £8. Reduced rates for children.

The Old Bell Hotel   *Telephone:* Malmesbury (066 62) 2346
Abbey Row

The old market town of Malmesbury – in fact the oldest borough in England – is fortunate to have as its chief hotel a venerable wisteria-clad hostelry like *The Old Bell*, once the inn of the famous Norman Abbey, which combines plenty of period character – the 12th-century castle is part of the fabric, and there's a medieval spiral staircase and a 13th-century window – with the other sort of features that make an attractive hotel in the 1980s. 'The most comfortable room we have ever enjoyed: 10/10,' writes one reader, who continued, 'Food: 9/10 except on Sunday evening when 6/10 (a superb weekday best end of lamb was this time tasteless and rather tough). Excellent carafe wine – Argentinian Franchette.' Another reader describes a weekend with three friends at an annual reunion: 'By general consent, it was the best hotel we've used for this event (this year was the tenth). The staff seemed really to enjoy what they were doing and from the manager down were unfailingly friendly and polite. Food good and plentiful.' *(D E Kimber)*

Open: All year except 10 days after Christmas. Restaurant closed Good Friday and bank holiday Mondays.
Rooms: 15 double, 3 single, 1 suite – 9 with bath, all with radio, TV (some colour) and baby-listening.
Facilities: Lounge, cocktail bar, public bar, large restaurant. 1 acre grounds with terraced garden leading to the river (fishing permits available).
Location: In town centre but quiet situation; parking for 25 cars.
Credit cards: All major credit cards accepted.
Terms (service at guests' discretion): B & B £14–27. Set meals: lunch £6; dinner £8. Special winter weekend rates (dinner, B & B £17.50, minimum 2 days). Reduced rates and special meals for children.

The Cottage in the Wood   *Telephone:* Malvern (068 45) 3487
Holywell Road

The Cottage in the Wood is an eyrie perched high on wooded slopes, with an eagle's eye view over the vast Severn valley and distant Cotswolds. It's a fairly grand cottage, being in fact a Georgian dower house, with additional bedrooms in a converted coach house, 200 yards from the main building. We had enthusiastic entries in earlier editions, but took the hotel out when it changed hands and lost character. Recent reports have been more encouraging, though still mixed. We offer one ambivalent report, and would be glad to hear from other visitors.

'When I first visited *The Cottage in the Wood* in 1976 it had great potential; dinner was carefully presented, prunes and china tea available for breakfast and great consideration given to guests. I was there in a thick December fog but could tell that the views would have been superb and I didn't mind that the place was slightly unkempt in the manner of a newly set-up home – unmatching chairs covered in matching fabric, that sort of thing. Then it got a bit of a reputation for its "Taste of England" cooking. An experimental lunch during a Malvern Festival revealed a complete

"House and Garden" face-lift and, being May, it also revealed a little terraced garden where you could sit in a sheltered private alcove with a Pimms and look over the fields. After the careless commercialism of Malvern's ———— *Hotel*, it was a treat. A request for a late bottle of wine and sandwiches in our room instead of dinner caused no surprise or difficulty (try it at the ————) and tea in the green and flowery lounge was delicious and restful. But, with my most recent visit, I felt things had changed – just a bit. It's as if *The Cottage in the Wood* has fluffed out its feathers in response to praise and has decided it knows what its guests want better than they do – rather like the sort of "secret" little hotel that caters almost exclusively for visiting Americans. Maybe I'm being unfair. The hotel is individually managed and maybe one is not always in tune with the individualism. On the whole, go to Malvern which is beautiful, stay in *The Cottage in the Wood* and make up your own mind.' *(Gillian Vincent)*

Open: All year, except 23–30 December.
Rooms: 17 double, 1 single – 17 with bath, all with telephone, radio, colour TV and baby-listening. 8 rooms in annexe with tea-making facilities. (4 double bedrooms on ground floor.)
Facilities: Lounge, bar, dining room, terrace with lovely view. 7 acres grounds with lawns and woodland; golf 1 mile away.
Location: 2 miles on the A449 travelling S to Ledbury, on right near Jet garage.
Restriction: No dogs.
Credit cards: Access/Euro/Mastercard, Barclay/Visa.
Terms: B & B (continental) £18–25. Set meals: full English breakfast £3; lunch £6; dinner £10; full *alc* £15. Bargain breaks. Reduced rates for children in winter; special meals provided.

MAWNAN SMITH, Nr Falmouth, Cornwall   **Map 1**

Meudon Hotel   *Telephone:* Falmouth (0326) 250541

Mawnan Smith lies in one of the most lush and sheltered corners of South Cornwall, between the Fal and Helford rivers. *Meudon*, at the head of a lovely valley leading down to its own private beach, is in a particularly choice part of it. It is an old Cornish mansion, a mellow stone building with massive granite pillars and mullioned windows, on to which has been grafted a stylish modern wing using local stone. A striking feature of the hotel is its 8½ acres of sub-tropical gardens, richly endowed with rare shrubs and plants, and believed to have been designed by Capability Brown – 'the loveliest garden imaginable' as one reader put it. As before, there has been consistent praise for the comfortable rooms, the admirable service and the pleasant atmosphere. Anyone wanting a restful break in beautiful surroundings could depend on finding it here. The only note of criticism in our files relates to the food – not quite as stylish as the ambience.

Open: All year, except January–mid February.
Rooms: 30 double, 8 single, 2 suites – 34 with bath, all with self-dial telephone, radio, colour TV, tea-making facilities and baby-listening. (18 rooms on ground floor.)
Facilities: 3 lounges, cocktail bar. 8½ acres of showplace sub-tropical gardens leading down to a private sea beach of sand and shingle with rock pools. Fresh and sea-water fishing including shark; sailing. Guests are full members of Falmouth's 18-hole golf club.

Location: Take the A39 from Truro to Falmouth for approx. 7 miles. At mini-roundabout drive straight across on to Helson road for about 1 mile until T junction. Turn right and immediately left on to Mabe/Mawnan Smith road. After 4 miles you reach Mawnan Smith: take left fork beside Red Lion Inn for 1 mile. *Meudon Hotel* is on right.
Restriction: No dogs in public rooms.
Credit cards: All major credit cards accepted.
Terms: B & B £13.20–44. Set meals: lunch £2.20–6.60; dinner £8.80. Off-season breaks. Reduced rates for children; special meals provided.

MIDDLE WALLOP, Stockbridge, Hampshire   Map 2

Fifehead Manor   *Telephone:* Wallop (026 478) 565/566

An unpretentious small manor house, dating in part from the 11th century, which once belonged to the Earl of Godwin, husband of Lady Godiva. It's close to the M3, about 1½ hours from London, and also within easy reach of Winchester and Salisbury. The house itself is quite close to the main road (A434), but backed by fields. The bedrooms in the main house are mostly spacious, light and comfortably furnished, with generous bathrooms; this upstairs part of the manor has the feel of a warm family house. The small, well-designed single rooms in the modern stable block annexe, each with a shower unit, have less character. The most attractive room in the house is the beamed dining room, cosy and candle-lit by night, and sparkling with polished brass and fresh flowers. The food is ambitious home cooking rather than *haute cuisine*, and not always, it would seem from our correspondence, uniformly successful – though the desserts have been warmly appreciated. The other public rooms on the ground floor – the bar and two sitting rooms – lack distinction and are a bit of a letdown. Despite some criticisms, reflected in this entry, most of our readers have enjoyed their visits to the *Manor* and appreciated the welcome of Mrs Leigh Taylor and the charming and hard-working youngsters from the local technical college who help her. *(Diana Johnson, Roger Smithells and others)*

Open: All year, except 24 November–11 January.
Rooms: 6 double, 6 single – 7 with bath, 5 with shower, all with telephone, mono TV and tea-making facilities; baby-listening can be arranged. 5 rooms in annexe.
Facilities: Lounge, bar/reception, conference room for up to 25 persons. 3 acres grounds with croquet and bowls. Fishing in the river Test 1 mile, riding 4 miles.
Location: On the A343 between Andover and Salisbury.
Credit cards: All major credit cards accepted.
Terms: B & B £18–23. Full *alc* £12.

MILTON ERNEST, Nr Bedford, Bedfordshire   Map 2

Milton Ernest Hall Hotel   [GFG]   *Telephone:* Oakley (023 02) 4111

Shortly before we went to press with the 1981 Guide, we learned with great regret of the death of Francis Harmar-Brown. In partnership with his wife Cynthia, he had undertaken the rescue of this dramatic example of Victorian Gothic – the only country house designed by William Butterfield, architect (among much else) of Keble College. *Milton Ernest Hall* is a natural for any Guide to hotels of unusual character: its amazing marble staircase, its striking but mad conservatory (it gets no sun after midday), its dovecote and huge high-ceilinged bedrooms – the place reeks of character whether you warm to the style or not. And the fact that the Harmar-Browns not only provided a distinctive setting for meals in the panelled dining room, but also cared a great deal about the quality of their cooking and had a formidable wine list too, only added to the attractions of a visit. We are delighted that Cynthia Harmar-Brown is maintaining the traditional hospitality of the house, and would be glad to hear from recent visitors.

Open: All year, except 25 and 26 December, and approx. 3 weeks late August/early September. Restaurant closed Sunday nights and all day Monday except for residents' breakfast.

Rooms: 6 double – 5 with bath, all with internal telephone and colour TV.

Facilities: Sitting room, conservatory and terrace, bar, 2 dining rooms. 6 acres grounds – the garden has a 100-yard frontage on the Great Ouse; croquet lawn, coarse fishing; garden centre.

Location: Off the A6, 4 miles N of Bideford.

Restriction: No dogs in public rooms.

Credit cards: Access/Euro, Barclay/Visa.

Terms: B & B £21. Full *alc* £14–15. Reduced rates for children using camp bed; some special meals provided.

MONKLEIGH, Nr Bideford, Devon   Map 1

Beaconside House   [GFG]   *Telephone:* Bideford (023 72) 77205

Andrew and Thea Brand – he a solicitor, she an advertising accounts director – deserted the metropolis and bought this elegant Victorian country house on a hillside near Bideford in 1978. We began to hear good accounts of their enterprise towards the end of the following year, and it appeared for the first time in the Guide last year, with a long eulogy from one writer, warmly endorsed by other correspondents. We have had a lot of letters about *Beaconside* since, all, without exception, complimentary. Amateurs at the hotel business the Brands may be, but they clearly have the knack, confirming our long-held view that, when it comes to running a good hotel, flair, enthusiasm and application count for far more than any apprenticeship at the Dorchester or diploma at a College of Catering. What people have liked about *Beaconside* can be summed up by one letter in our files: 'A very very pretty house and decor, splendid views high over the Torridge valley, charming bedrooms and comfortable beds, and delicious and imaginative food. Thea Brand is a very original cook, her ingredients from my experience absolutely top class, and they have their own vegetable and herb garden from which she makes her own judicious selection. Andrew is blessed in his cheese merchant, and has a good cellar and some fine malt whiskies, and they are both delightful company.'

Various changes since last year should be mentioned: observant readers may notice that the hotel now calls itself *Beaconside House*, because, says Thea Brand, *Beaconside* on its own summoned up visions of seaside landladies, like *Sunnyside* and *Braeside*. The garden, reported last year as tatty-ish, has been much improved with the dedicated help of a new gardener, though one reader comments: 'They are not over-tidied with carefully manicured lawns, and one may give advice, willingly listened to – gratifying!' Finally, the Brands are building their own quarters, so the over-exuberant house dogs referred to last year, will be less seen and heard. *(Margaret Burn, B and J Hill, Don and Maureen Montagu, F C Kluytmans, Christopher and Lindy Wright)*

Open: 5 March–28 December.
Rooms: 8 double, 1 single – 7 with bath, 2 with shower, all with colour TV and tea-making facilities.
Facilities: Drawing room, library (for residents only), bar/sitting room. 4 acres grounds with heated swimming pool and grass tennis court, swings and putting green. 5 miles from safe sandy beaches at Westward Ho! and Instow; concessionary rates for hotel guests at Westward Ho! golf course; riding at Westward Ho!; fishing nearby: trout and salmon on the Torridge, 5 miles away, trout and coarse fishing on local reservoirs and lakes; sea fishing by boat from Appledore, 5 miles.
Location: From Bideford take the A386 to Torrington for 2½ miles, turn right on to the A388 (marked to Holsworthy). *Beaconside House* is about ¾ mile uphill on the left.
Restriction: No dogs in house.
Terms: B & B £13–24; dinner, B & B £21.50–32.50. Set meal: dinner £9.50–10. Reduced rates for children in August; special meals by arrangement.

Note: For Thea Brand's own view of Beaconside House *see Appendix, page 481.*

NEW MILTON, Hampshire   **Map 2**

Chewton Glen Hotel   *Telephone:* Highcliffe (042 52) 5341
                                          Telex: 41456

A mixed press this last year for Martin Skan's unashamedly de-luxe hotel on the fringes of the New Forest – the most expensive English hotel in the Guide, we reckon, outside London. No one denies the brilliance of the hotel's young chef, Christian Deteil, who has earned well-justified awards in other Guides. And we have had no complaints about the standards of the service either. The hotel is immaculately maintained: the lawns are manicured, and everything that is polishable is highly polished and brightly gleaming. The trouble lies in part in the enthusiasm which Martin Skan brings to the marketing of his hotel, both here and in the States. There is always a danger, when the sales pitch is high, of the reality not matching the expectations. 'Nothing positive to complain about,' writes one reader, 'but a feeling that the place has expanded too far and thus become too large for effective and personal management – and too large for us to enjoy.' What size of hotel you like is a thoroughly subjective matter, but another cause of disappointment at *Chewton Glen* is the location: it is correctly described as on the fringes of the New Forest, but the forest certainly isn't on the hotel's doorsteps, but several miles to the north. Moreover, the grounds of 30 acres are much of them inaccessible. Hence another irritated guest: 'My husband and I stayed here after a wedding, and the first thing we tried to do to blow the cobwebs away was to go for a walk in the "acres of grounds". Impossible! There is nowhere to walk and we ended by walking down a very ordinary road in New Milton.' Finally, there is the contentious question of extras, particularly contentious when the prices are so steep anyway. Last year we referred to the hotel's charge of 70p if you wanted fresh rather than canned orange juice with your breakfast. Another visitor took umbrage, reasonably, we feel, at being charged £3.50 for eggs, bacon and sausage, since the hotel's price for bed and breakfast does not include the so-called full English breakfast.

Notwithstanding the above, we are clear that a lot of people thoroughly enjoy their stay at *Chewton Glen*, are attracted by the style and opulence of the place, couldn't care less if the New Forest is a few miles away since they will have cars (maybe chauffeurs too) to take them where they want to go, will be unaffected by the limitations of the grounds, very likely because they will be content to relax by the pool, and aren't the kind of people who count the pennies – or the extras. *Caveat emptor*, but also *quot homines*.

Open: All year.
Rooms: 39 double, 2 single, 7 suites – all with bath, telephone, radio and colour TV. 6 suites in annexe. (7 rooms on ground floor.)
Facilities: 1 large lounge, 2 small lounges, bar, dining room, shop, terrace. 30 acres grounds with croquet lawn, putting, swimming pool and tennis court. The sea is ½ mile away, with safe bathing from shingle beach; the New Forest spreads to the north. Fishing, riding, sailing close by; 12 golf courses within a radius of 20 miles.
Location: Do not follow New Milton signs. Take turning to Walkford and Highcliffe off the A35; go through Walkford to fork junction. Take left fork (A337 to Lymington). *Chewton Glen* is ¼ mile round corner to the left.
Restrictions: No children under 7. No dogs.
Credit cards: All major credit cards accepted.
Terms: B & B (continental) from about £31. Set meals: lunch from about £7.50; dinner from about £14.50; full *alc* from about £22. Special 3- and 5-day stays offered at reduced rates from 1 November–31 March excluding Christmas/New Year period.

NORTH TAWTON, Devon   **Map 1**

Nichols Nymet House   *Telephone:* North Tawton (083 782) 626

Of the hotels that made their first appearance in the Guide last year, none had had so many warm endorsements as *Nichols Nymet*, a pink-washed Georgian Manor House in the heart of Devon, 20 miles west of Exeter. All the correspondents named below write with similar unstinted enthusiasm about Denys and Christine Edgley's gift for turning their guests into friends, also about the quality of Christine Edgley's cooking. Here is a characteristic tribute: 'It is difficult to write critically about the Edgleys as they treated us as privileged friends and we were delightfully spoiled. If peace is an ingredient vital for one's holiday, *Nichols Nymet* provides this. The house has a graciousness that pervades all aspects.' *(Chris and Dorothy Brining; also E J Robertson, Rosemary Boyne, J V Armstrong, Peter Scrafton)*

Open: All year except two weeks in November and two weeks in February.
Rooms: 9 double, 1 single – 1 with bath.
Facilities: Residents' lounge with TV, lounge bar, dining room; 2 acres of grounds. Golf, riding, walking, fishing nearby.
Location: Small road N of the A3702 W of Crediton; lane marked to *Nichols Nymet* between village of Bow and turning to North Tawton.
Credit cards: Access/Euro, Barclay/Visa, Diners.
Terms: B & B £12.25–25.30; dinner B & B £18.75–32.30. Set meals: lunch £5.50; dinner £7; full *alc* £10. 3-day off-season breaks at reduced rates. Reduced rates for children under 13.

STOP PRESS We are particularly sad, in view of the above entry, to learn, as we go to press, that the Edgleys are selling Nichols Nymet. *No details yet available of new owners.*

Maid's Head   *Telephone:* Norwich (0603) 28821
Tombland   *Telex:* 975080

Not the most expensive hotel in Norwich, but the most atmospheric. It is situated between the Cathedral and Elm Hill, the old cobbled shopping street. It must be one of the oldest hotels in the country – parts date back 700 years; it has a covered courtyard, mullioned windows and one of those four-posters which Queen Elizabeth I may or may not have slept in. More to the 1981 point, several readers have commented on its noticeably courteous service.

So ran last year's report. A mixed postbag since. Some readers are enthusiastic – 'This famous hostelry is as delightful as ever,' also 'Most enjoyable: the staff really are quite outstanding' and 'Extraordinarily friendly and helpful staff – the porter would not accept a tip!' But there have been some harsh criticisms too – in particular, a long and detailed account of amateur service, characterless rooms and inferior meals. So it's a borderline case: it does have character, but also has some of the features of a superior commercial hotel. And we think that readers who care about their food will probably do better to eat at *Tatlers*, a hundred yards down the road. *(F Joan Heyman, Christopher Portway, John Sidwick, Joan M Marr)*

Open: All year.
Rooms: 46 double, 34 single, 2 suites – 64 with bath, 15 with shower, all with telephone, radio, colour TV and heated trouser presses.
Facilities: Lift, 3 large lounges, 2 bars, dining room; conference facilities; covered courtyard.
Location: Near town centre; parking for 100 cars.
Credit cards: Access/Euro, American Express, Barclay/Visa, Diners.
Terms: Rooms £17 per person; B & B £19–20; dinner, B & B £23.95. Set meals: English breakfast £3.20, lunch/dinner from £5; full *alc* £7.50. Bargain breaks throughout the year; special winter rates in November–March. Reduced rates and special meals for children.

PEVENSEY, Eastbourne, Sussex   **Map 2**

Priory Court Hotel   *Telephone:* Eastbourne (0323) 763150

In general we hear good accounts of this 16th-century timbered house which looks out over the Roman walls of Pevensey Castle. The hotel is on the A27, but double-glazing mitigates the rumbles. Our entry last year spoke about the 'lovely old building, immaculately kept, with flowers everywhere, decor and furniture in perfect accord'. This year's reports would endorse that – and also the very reasonable prices. In 1981 the bar was praised, but the restaurant was described as being a bit on the pretentious side. There has been a change in the menu in the interim, and the emphasis is now on traditional English food – enjoyed by one party, found somewhat uninspiring by another. More reports welcome. *(Tom Lea, G H Booth)*

Open: All year.
Rooms: 9 double – 4 with bath, all with TV. (1 room on ground floor.)

Facilities: Residents' lounge with colour TV, public lounges, dining room, William Room for private parties or meetings. 2 acres grounds. Safe sea bathing 1 mile; golf, riding, sailing, fishing nearby; walks across the Pevensey Marshes, noted for wide variety of birds.
Location: In village; parking for 38 cars.
Restrictions: No children under 12. No dogs.
Credit cards: Access/Euro, Barclay/Visa.
Terms (excluding 10% service charge): B & B from £10. Dinner B & B weekly from £95. Full *alc* £8–10. Bargain breaks: any 2 days £30 per person for dinner, B & B including VAT and service.

PILTON, Somerset   **Map 1**

The Long House   *Telephone:* Pilton (074 989) 283

One of those unassuming small hotels, offering a warm welcome and good simple food (though on a no-choice menu), which are a lot rarer than they should be. *The Long House*, a 17th-century building of character, is in a quiet and beautiful village halfway between Glastonbury and Shepton Mallet, and not on any well-trodden tourist path. It is owned and run by Paul Foss and Eric Swainsbury. Some of the rooms are on the modest side – and don't expect anything new-fangled like TV or a sauna. 'Mr Foss and his partner provide a magnificent service and most comfortable and pleasant rooms. Constant attention to detail without fuss – bed and bath linen particularly. The quality of cooking and table service is very high indeed.' *(H A Pierce; also W O Churchill)*

Open: All year.
Rooms: 6 double, 1 single – 4 with bath.
Facilities: Sitting room/bar, dining room. ½ acre garden.
Location: On S edge of village; parking for 10 cars.
Credit cards: Access/Euro, Barclay/Visa.
Terms: B & B £9.75–16.50; dinner, B & B £15.10–22.50. Set meal: dinner £6. Bargain breaks with 12½% discount for 3-night stays May–September, 2-night stays October–April. Weekly reductions available. Reduced rates for children sharing parents' room; special meals provided.

PORLOCK WEIR, Nr Porlock, Somerset   **Map 1**

West Porlock House   *Telephone:* Porlock (0643) 862492

Continued support from our readers for this spotless, beautifully furnished small Edwardian country house, enthusiastically run by Jo and Derek Page and a small local staff. The meals are described as fairly simple, but delicious and imaginatively conceived. It has an attractive situation in the Exmoor National Park, with views of the sea and the surrounding hills; bridle and footpaths lead up to the moor. The pebble beach of Porlock Bay is less than a mile down the road. A particular feature of West Porlock House is the 4-acre grounds, rich in magnolias, rhododendrons, azaleas and a lot of exotic plants, shrubs and trees imported from abroad. *(Geoffrey and Jenny Chater, WPH)*

Open: April–mid October.
Rooms: 7 double – 1 with bath, 1 with shower, all with tea-making facilities.

Facilities: Lounge, TV room, lounge/hall with bar, dining room. 4½ acres grounds with terrace, secluded lawns, woodland and fine display of exotic flowers, trees and shrubs; sheltered paddock for guests' own horses; abundance of wild life. Walking and riding in Exmoor National Park.
Location: 6½ miles W of Minehead, ¾ mile from Porlock Bay.
Restriction: No dogs in public rooms.
Credit cards: Barclay/Visa.
Terms (excluding VAT and service): B & B £11.75–13.75; dinner, B & B £18.75–20.75. Set meals: lunch from £2; dinner from £7. Reduced terms for stays of 7 days or more, and for children sharing parents' room; high tea for children.

ROMALDKIRK, Barnard Castle, Co Durham   Map 4

The Rose and Crown Hotel   [GFG]   *Telephone:* Teesdale (0833) 50213

'This is that mythical find, a genuine old country inn, full of fishermen and Dales folk swapping tall stories, the finest honest plain cooking outside a private house, excellent beer and comfortable, but not luxurious room. All the best ghost and fishing stories begin with a group of yarnsmen sitting round the fire in a place like this. On the banks of the Tees, in one of the finest of the Dales villages, and near High Force Waterfall and the Bowes Museum, it gets full in the grouse season, but is a pleasure all year round.' *(MW)*

Open: All year, except Christmas Day. Restaurant closed to non-residents Sunday evenings.
Rooms: 7 double, 4 single – 1 with bath, 2 with shower, 3 with colour TV, all with radio, baby-listening and tea-making facilities on request.
Facilities: 2 lounges (one with TV), 2 bars, 2 dining rooms; fishing, golf, sailing, pony trekking, shooting, etc, nearby. Barnard Castle 6 miles; Raby Castle and Bowes Castle within easy reach.
Location: 6 miles from Barnard Castle.
Restriction: No dogs in public rooms.
Credit cards: All major credit cards accepted.
Terms: B & B £10–14.50. Set meals: lunch £5.50; dinner £7.50. Special prices for 4-day stay (which must include a Sunday). Reduced rates and special meals for children.

ROWSLEY, Nr Matlock, Derbyshire   Map 2

The Peacock Hotel   *Telephone:* Darley Dale (062 983) 3518

Two unusually pleasant hotels lie on the borders of Chatsworth House – *The Cavendish* at Baslow (q.v.) to the north of the Park, and *The Peacock*, three or four miles to the south by the B6021 or, more agreeably, by foot along the banks of the Derwent. *The Cavendish* is the smarter of the two, serving more ambitious meals; *The Peacock*, a well-preserved 17th-century stone hostelry, which was formerly a dower house to Haddon Hall a mile up the road, is quite a bit cheaper, especially in the restaurant. It is owned by Embassy Hotels, a subsidiary of Allied Breweries, but is certainly more of a hotel than an inn. It's strong on creature comforts, has a lot of fine antique furniture in the public rooms, and an exceptionally beautiful garden bordering on the river Derwent on which the hotel has rights for two miles for brown trout and grayling, as well as seven miles for rainbow trout on the adjacent river Wye. The hotel naturally attracts a lot of fishing folk, but it is, of course, splendidly placed for walkers in the Peak National Park and for visitors to the indigestible number of noble houses to be seen in the district.

'Totally charming in the truest sense. There is a quiet elegance about the place which is immediately evident on arrival. The gardens are exquisitely kept, and are inviting and peaceful, as is the Derwent river walk directly to the side of the hotel. We arrived in time to have afternoon tea in the lovely sitting room and our excellent dinner that evening – we had trout caught in the local river – was in the cosy dining room which overlooks the gardens. Our room was *very* large and elegant in the old section. The total experience was one we shall never forget.' *(Dr and Mrs James F Hood; also Nigel and Clare Kemp)*

Warning: rooms facing the road, including those in the annexe, are noisy; the ones to go for are those in the rear overlooking the gardens.

Open: All year.
Rooms: 16 double, 4 single – 11 with bath, 4 with shower, 14 with radio, all with telephone and colour TV; tea-making facilities on request; 6 rooms in annexe.
Facilities: Lounge, residents' lounge with TV, restaurant, small private dining room; some conference facilities. Garden of ¾ acre on the river Derwent; fishing along a 2-mile reach for brown trout and grayling; private fishing for rainbow trout on the river Wye.
Location: 3 miles from Bakewell, near junction of A6 and A623; parking.
Restriction: No dogs in public rooms or unattended.
Credit cards: All major credit cards accepted.
Terms: B & B £16–40. Set meals (excluding service): lunch £6.50; dinner £10.50. Winter weekend breaks. Reduced rates and special meals for children.

RUSHLAKE GREEN, Heathfield, Sussex   **Map 2**

The Priory Country House Hotel   *Telephone:* Rushlake Green (0435) 830553

No shortage of bouquets for *The Priory* this year – literally so in the case of the reader who wrote appreciatively about the ubiquity of the flowers – 'huge clouds of cherry blossoms in the alcoves, magnolias on the table'. The same reporter was also chuffed at what she found by her bedside – not just biscuits and fresh fruit, but also books: 'I had Simenon, Saki, Colette in French, slender poetry and a couple of volumes on shooting and the countryside – something for all tastes.' Jane Dunn, who runs this re-formed and devotedly restored Augustinian priory in a thousand acres of Kent/Sussex countryside, is attentive to small details. Other caring personal touches noted by our correspondents include: Roger Gallet soap, huge soft towels, very fine cotton sheets, a hot-water bottle with cover in matching fabric to the curtains, home-made marmalade and jam and real honey at breakfast. The staff, though often untrained local girls, obviously contribute to the welcome of the place: 'Receptionist was pleased to see us (such a change from most hotels) and stood up as we stepped into the lounge. We were asked on departure if we had enjoyed our stay and thanked for coming (it is a long time since we were asked that).' And the food, too, comes in for its share of plaudits: 'Outstanding . . . Home produced and beautifully cooked, the sweets exceptionally good . . . Excellent, and everything served with love and care . . . The menus were masterpieces of imagination, and there wasn't an overcooked piece of meat or vegetable over three delicious dinners.'

But there have been some grumbles. One found the promised welcome somewhat lacking and poor breakfast service. He may have been on a bad day. Another complaint reported to us was from a reader whose plane had been delayed at Gatwick; he had phoned from the airport to ask for a cold meal to be left for him, but had felt that the plate that awaited him was very cold comfort indeed. He had to leave at 8 the next morning; the hotel offered neither an early call nor a breakfast at that hour. The hotel's reply is instructive and, we think, reasonable: 'We seek to provide the sort of comforts one expects if one goes to stay at a country house for a weekend or longer. We are not set up to provide late meals or early breakfasts or the sort of 24-hour service associated with hotels close to airports. In fact such a service would only upset our regular people who come here for peace and quiet.' We also appreciated a note at the end of our question-naire: 'We hope to maintain our room prices as last year unless there is a great increase in inflation.' *(Gillian Vincent, Peter Wilson, J Gazdak, Gordon Cole, Patricia Roberts, B M C Butting)*

Open: All year, except for 3 weeks at Christmas.
Rooms: 9 double, 1 single – all with bath and TV. 4 rooms in a converted oast house annexe.
Facilities: 2 drawing rooms, 2 dining rooms; small conference facilities, Glynde-bourne picnic facilities. 4 acres garden with croquet; 1,000 acres farmland with pheasant shooting and good walking. Brook fishing within 400 yards. Not far from the sea, the Weald, South Downs, Sissinghurst Castle, Glyndebourne, etc.
Location: About 15 miles N of Eastbourne. Turn S off the B2096 at Three Cups Corner which is 4½ miles from Heathfield, 8 miles from Battle.
Restrictions: No children under 9. Dogs by arrangement only.
Terms (no fixed service charge): B & B £16.25–22.50. Set meals: lunch £7.50; dinner £12.50.

RYALL, Whitchurch Canonicorum, Bridport, Dorset　　　　　**Map 1**

The Butts　　　　　　　　　　　　　*Telephone:* Chideock (029 789) 255

A newly-opened deeply rural hotel in one of the most lovely unspoilt parts of the South Coast. We ask on our questionnaire for any special features of a hotel that deserve mention in an entry, and record Mr Makinson's response: 'Every window enjoys wide far-reaching views without any road within sight or sound. True peace, seclusion, tranquil countryside, within easy reach of the sea.' Here is the first report:

'*The Butts* has been beautifully reconstructed from a bake-house and cottages *c* 1700. It is a country house in a secluded hamlet at the end of a "no through road", which turns at their gate into a bridle path. It stands on a hillside with lovely flowered gardens and lawns receiving sunshine all day. Every room is comfortable and tasteful and full of personal touches, with literature and flowers. The atmosphere is of a country house and the kindness and attention of our hosts never failed to amaze me. The food was gourmet standard, and I mean this as a regular buyer and user of the *Good Food Guide*. The four-course dinners served by candlelight were imaginatively prepared and always beautifully presented. In my experi-ence *The Butts* is somewhere to be valued, thought of with delight and revisited as soon as possible.

'I walked down a bridle track to the thatched cottages of Chideock, and along paths over fields to enjoy glorious views with wild life and flowers in profusion. About a mile from the sea I left the car on National Trust property and followed the lovely coastal paths to Golden Cap, the highest cliff on the south coast, and hunted for fossils at its base. We also visited various hillforts, each commanding splendid views and felt a peace and happiness, knowing that we were returning with pleasure to a hot or cool drink, hot baths or showers and a culinary experience, unhurried and relaxing. Mr and Mrs Makinson are two of the most delightful people one could ask to meet and their house is lovely. I am longing to return and so are my friends.' *(Shirley Donner; also Roger Smithells)*

Open: All year.
Rooms: 3 double, 1 single – 1 bathroom, 2 showers available.
Facilities: Drawing room with TV, dining room. 1 acre grounds. Sea within 2 miles farmland walk; riding, fishing, golf, tennis, squash nearby.
Location: Ryall signposted 1 mile W of Chideock on the A35.
Restrictions: No children under 17. Dogs permitted if kept in owners' car.
Terms: B & B £10; dinner, B & B £15. Set meal: dinner £5. (The hotel is not licensed to supply wines, so bring your own.) The hotel can be taken on an exclusive house party basis.

RYE, East Sussex   **Map 2**

Hope Anchor Hotel   *Telephone:* (079 73) 2216
Watchbell Street

Not an atmospheric old smuggler's inn like the *Mermaid*, which appeared in earlier editions of the Guide, but a house of character and worth nonetheless – a 17th-century red-brick building standing at the end of a narrow cobbled street and with a view over Romney Marshes to the sea. 'A fine situation, comfortable rooms, very good food, including nicely served breakfast. Roger Gallet soap in the bathroom – an example of their high standards. Worth asking for their special half-board rate.' *(Michael Schofield)*

Open: All year.
Rooms: 12 double, 2 single – 1 with shower, all with tea-making facilities and baby-listening.
Facilities: TV lounge, reception lounge, dining room. Sandy beach 3 miles.
Location: In town centre behind the main church; parking for 15 cars. Coming by car from Landgate, pass under Landgate Arch up hill to High Street. Take first left into East Street. Turn left by Flushing Inn into Church Square. Take first right into Watchbell Street. Hotel is at far end. Approaching from South Undercliffe, proceed up Mermaid Street to top and take 3 right turns.
Restriction: No dogs.
Credit cards: All major credit cards accepted.
Terms (excluding 10% service charge): B & B £13–14.70; dinner, B & B £19–21.15. Set meals: lunch £4.50; dinner £6.50; full *alc* £12–14. Reduced rates and special meals for children.

SALCOMBE, South Devon   **Map 1**

The Marine Hotel   *Telephone:* Salcombe (054 884) 2251
                                                           Telex: 45185

The Marine is Salcombe's smartest hotel, but it also has a long-standing reputation as a first-class hotel in a more than spit-and-polish sense. It is a personally owned place, with a keen staff, and enjoys a strong 'return trade'. There have been some changes this past year, however. The restaurant, with its superb dress-circle view over the bustling and cheerful harbour, is now only open in the evening; it has a new head chef, and offers three set price menus called respectively Dinner Menu (£9.75), Menu Cordon Bleu (£12.95) and Menu Épicurean (£14.95). (One reader considered the cooking well below the standards of the hotel in other departments – and the worse for being pretentious.) Breakfasts, lunches and light snacks are served in the Buttery. Terpischoreans will be sorry to learn that there is now only one dance a week, rather than three as previously. And the hotel has been moving with the times in other ways too. Here is how one long-standing enthusiast for *The Marine* reacts: 'As an arch conservative, I do not care for change, but these are quite comprehensible. The solarium has been completely redecorated, and now there is a lot less glass and a lot more furniture. It is still a very pleasant room, and the saving in heating must be enormous. Arrangements for breakfast and lunch have changed so that the dining room proper, with its wonderful view, is used for dinner only; the labour saving must be considerable. The service both upstairs and down remain quite faultless, and I have no hesitation in recommending this hotel strongly to those who can afford it. And there are no hidden extras.' *(Paul R Grotrian; also the Bishop of Edmonton and others)*

Open: 1 March–1 December.
Rooms: 41 double, 9 single, 1 suite – 51 with bath, all with telephone, radio and colour TV.
Facilities: Lift, lounge, bar, buttery, games room, conference rooms in off-season, solarium – all with panoramic views; dancing once a week in high season. Indoor and outdoor heated swimming pools; poolside bar. Garden of ½ acre with lawn; cliff railway from driveway to lawn level; hotel grounds lead to the water's edge, private launching and landing facilities. Sandy beach at Small's Cove across the estuary reached by local passenger ferry; fishing, tennis, golf and riding nearby. ♿ .
Restrictions: No children under 7. No dogs.
Location: Central; parking for 60 cars.
Credit cards: All major credit cards accepted.
Terms: B & B £23.75–39.75; dinner, B & B (minimum 3 nights) £33.75–44.75. Set meals: lunch (in Buttery) £5.25; dinner from £10.50; full *alc* about £16.95. Reduced terms for mid-week and one-week stays in autumn, spring and early summer. Family rates available in high and low seasons.

SEAVINGTON ST MARY, Nr Ilminster, Somerset Map 1

The Pheasant *Telephone:* South Petherton (0460) 40502

We had an entry in our 1980 edition for this small country hotel housed in a 17th-century farmhouse with adjoining cottages, but dropped it last year after a change of ownership. Under the previous regime, *The Pheasant* had had a long-standing reputation for its excellent restaurant. The hotel is now in the hands of Edmondo and Jacqueline Paolini, and the menu has acquired a definite Italianate bent. 'It fully lived up to my hopes. The atmosphere was peaceful and – in the most literal sense – charming. The bedroom, with bathroom *en suite*, was one of the most comfortable I have ever slept in. The bed and breakfast charge seemed very good value. I shall return with pleasure.' *(Peter Cornall)*

Open: All year, except Christmas, Boxing and New Year's Days.
Rooms: 8 double, 2 single, 2 suites – 10 with bath, all with telephone, radio, colour TV and tea-making facilities. 6 rooms in annexe. (4 rooms on ground floor.)
Facilities: Lounge, restaurant and bar with restricted licence (residents and those taking meals). 1 acre old-fashioned garden. &.
Location: 200 yards off the A303 between Ilchester and Ilminster; 3 miles from town centre; parking.
Restriction: No dogs.
Credit cards: All major credit cards accepted.
Terms: B & B £12.50–25. Full *alc* £12–15. Special meals for children.

SHIPDHAM, Nr Thetford, Norfolk   Map 2

Shipdham Place   *Telephone:* Dereham (0362) 820303
Church Close

We had our first entry last year for this 17th-century Rectory recently converted into a stylish country-house hotel. It is slap in the centre of Norfolk: despite the postal address, it is 20 miles north of Thetford and the same distance due west of Norwich. Justin de Blank, well-known in London as a purveyor of fine foods, and his wife Melanie, own and run it. Last year we called it a restaurant with rooms, and that's even more true since the restaurant can seat 30, and the hotel part has lost one of its rooms to staff and now has just four double bedrooms. But to give it that description does the extremely attractive residential part less than justice, and may also lead to disappointments on the culinary side. Briefly, our reports suggest that the kitchen, though aiming high, is uneven in the quality of its set dinners (five courses, with choice at the dessert stage only), and that the restaurant service sometimes falters. The hotel has a lot going for it – a remarkable wine list, for example, and uncommon taste in the furnishings. Good hotels are thin on the Norfolk ground: as headmasters say, we hope for a better report next term.

Open: Probably 2 January–21 December.
Rooms: 4 double – all with bath and telephone.
Facilities: 2 sitting rooms, dining room; conference facilities for up to 18 persons. 3 acres grounds.
Location: 5 miles SW of Dereham on the A1075.
Restrictions: No children under 12 except babies. Dogs at management's discretion.
Terms (excluding 10% service charge): B & B £17–30. Set meal: dinner £11.50–12.50.

SILCHESTER, Nr Reading, Berks   Map 2

Romans   *Telephone:* Silchester (0734) 700421

One of all too few recommendable country hotels within a 60-mile radius of London, *Romans* is an unassumingly pleasant small establishment, mock Tudor in the Lutyens style, roughly equidistant from the M3 (Exit 6) and the M4 (Exit 11). Perks for the guests include two hard tennis courts and a heated swimming pool (summer only), and the hotel has recently made a new residents' lounge opening on to the terrace. We have had favourable reports for the past two years and are glad to print this

latest endorsement: 'One is treated like an honoured guest in a private house. The chef is splendid and the service by local ladies is friendly and understanding. They make you feel that it is an honour for them to help you. The welcome was wonderful and it seemed that our departure was viewed with sorrow. We did not consider it dear: it was excellent value.'
(S W Burden)

Open: All year, except last 2 weeks of August, Christmas and bank holidays. Restaurant closed Saturday lunch and Sunday dinner (light meals available to residents).
Rooms: 18 double, 4 single – 22 with bath, all with radio and baby-listening. 12 rooms in annexe. (Some rooms on ground floor.)
Facilities: Lounge, TV room, small bar, restaurant bar, restaurant; conference facilities. 3 acres grounds with 2 hard tennis courts, heated swimming pool, putting green. Free fishing in the river Kennet nearby; golf courses and livery stables in the area. &.
Location: Between the M3 and M4; 14 miles from Reading.
Credit cards: American Express, Barclay/Visa, Diners.
Terms: B & B £20–30. Set meals: lunch £8; dinner £10 (£12 on Saturday). Reduced rates for children sharing parents' room; special meals provided.

SIX MILE BOTTOM, Newmarket, Suffolk   **Map 2**

Swynford Paddocks   *Telephone:* Six Mile Bottom (063 870) 234

This is the house where Byron's half-sister Augusta Leigh carried on her famous incestuous affair with the poet in 1813. One is glad to find that the hotel which now occupies the scene of this notorious episode should be so sumptuously maintained in its Georgian elegance. Ian Bryant, who also runs a 40-acre stud in the grounds, hasn't stinted in the upkeep. The gardens are immaculately pedicured, and the decor of the interior, which is delightfully light and spacious, are of a piece. There is a kind of largesse about the place: some of the bathrooms are as big as most people's bedrooms – and the baths and bath towels are also of noble proportions.

Because of its proximity to Newmarket, and also because of its owner's other interest, *Swynford Paddocks* has an obvious attraction to the racing fraternity and tends to get booked up well ahead at the time of the Newmarket races or the bloodstock sales. The hotel organizes parties to visit the stables, studs and the Jockey Club or to see the early-morning work on the Heath. But non-racing people would certainly find it a pleasant base for a visit to Cambridge or for touring the Fens. It could indeed, in our view, take its place in the top league of English country-house hotels. But at the moment, despite Ian Bryant's taste and generosity in the furnishing, it fails to meet the highest criteria on two counts. First, its restaurant, though in itself a delightful place in which to eat, and with an interesting wine list, serves meals which fall a long way short of the distinction of the setting. The other shortcoming of the house – a certain lack of warmth and character – may be harder to correct: if only Byron could take over as general manager for a season! *(HR)*

Open: All year, except 4–28 January.
Rooms: 8 double, 4 single – all with bath, telephone, radio, colour TV and tea-making facilities.
Facilities: Lounge, bar, restaurant; small conference room. Hotel is set in the 40-acre stud; hard tennis court, croquet, mini-golf, boules. Golf at Newmarket, riding nearby (there are no riding facilities at the stud).

Location: On the A1304, just off junction with the A11(M), 5 miles from Newmarket, 9 miles from Cambridge.
Restriction: Dogs at the management's discretion.
Credit cards: All major credit cards accepted.
Terms (excluding 10% service charge): B & B £24–33. Set meals: lunch/dinner £10.50; full *alc* £14. Special long weekend package available December–April.

SOUTH ZEAL, Okehampton, Devon   Map 1

Poltimore Guest House   *Telephone:* Sticklepath (083 784) 209

We are always glad to hear of modest alternatives to plush and pricey country house hotels. *Poltimore Guest House*, in the Dartmoor National Park, is an old thatched cottage on the side of a hill, with views of farmlands and woods. It is one of the few guest houses in the West Country to receive the British Tourist Authority's award for outstanding hospitality, service, food and value for money. 'Mr and Mrs Harbridge score on all points. Nothing pretentious here, but an instant sense of relaxed well-being. Central heating, a log-fire in the huge granite fireplace. Bedrooms are simple, spruce, strong on essentials – good bedside lights, somewhere to stand your case, razor point, sound plumbing. And Mrs Harbridge offers superlative home cooking – English dishes with a Devonshire accent.' *(Roger Smithells)*

Open: All year.
Rooms: 5 double, 2 single. 4 rooms in annexe.
Facilities: Lounge, TV lounge, dining room. 3 acres garden. Direct access to Dartmoor: horse riding, gaming, fishing.
Location: The hotel is near the *Rising Sun Inn*, 17 miles from Exeter along the A30 towards Okehampton. Coming from Exeter ignore the turning to South Zeal and continue along the A30 for another ¼ mile. Turn left when you see *Poltimore*'s black and white signpost.
Restrictions: No children under 7. No dogs in dining room.
Terms: B & B £9–9.25; dinner, B & B £13.50–14.50. Set meal: dinner £4.50. 10% reduction on above rates for minimum stay of 2 days. 70% reduction for children sharing parents' room.

STAMFORD, Lincolnshire   Map 2

The George of Stamford [GFG]   *Telephone:* Stamford (0780) 2101
                                                    Telex: 32578

'All that had been promised. Service at a level I have only experienced in much more expensive hotels (and not in many of those). We enjoyed an excellent dinner, with the most attentive wine service possible. The accommodation was spacious, clean and peaceful. Our bill was fair value.' A characteristic tribute from one of *The George*'s many satisfied customers. It is not a small hotel by the standards of this book, and it isn't, like most of the best hotels, run by a resident owner, but belongs to a small chain, Poste Hotels, who also own *The Old Bridge* at Huntingdon, *Bailiffscourt* at Climping and *The Haycock* at Wansford (all q.v.). But this traditional coaching inn in a particularly agreeable town, with its flower-tubbed courtyard and Monastery Garden, has the art of giving satisfaction in all departments. The hotel makes much, incidentally, of the man they call their 'biggest customer' – one Daniel Lambert, who weighed 52 stone 11 lb at his death in 1809. A painting of this mighty fellow hangs in the entrance, and is reproduced on the menus. Perhaps the hotel continues to pander to its trenchermen customers. Curiously, the only complaint in our *George* file this year was from someone who felt that his kebab had contained 'far, far too much food'. The writer continues: 'Often not a fault, but not what one expects in a kebab. Everything else perfect.' *(G Hay, Peter Brooke, E Fell, Diane Latham)*

Open: All year, except Christmas Day.
Rooms: 35 double, 10 single, 2 suites, 3 triple – 39 with bath, all with telephone and colour TV.
Facilities: Lounge, garden lounge, cocktail lounge and bars, restaurant, sun room; 5 function rooms. Grounds of ½ acre – Monastery Garden with gravel walks and sunken lawn. Golf 1 mile, fishing at Rutland Water 5 miles.
Location: In town centre (front rooms tend to be noisy); parking for 150 cars.
Restriction: No dogs in public rooms.
Credit cards: All major credit cards accepted.
Terms: B & B £17.50–28. Full *alc* £6.75–13.50. Reduced rates for children sharing parents' room; special meals provided. No charge for cats.

STORRINGTON, West Sussex   **Map 2**

Little Thakeham   *Telephone:* Storrington (090 66) 4416
Merrywood Lane

A welcome new arrival on the Sussex scene, *Little Thakeham* was opened by Timothy and Pauline Ratcliff early in 1980. It's on the South Downs, about ten miles north of the coast at Worthing. Here is a first report:
'It is in a class of its own: a superb Lutyens house only recently turned into a very exclusive hotel (only 7 rooms), set in a Gertrude Jekyll garden. What I found so attractive was the combination of stony grandeur with a very warm, informal atmosphere. Although it is in the luxury class, there was an ease about the place which was very pleasing. Downstairs are three great stone-walled rooms with vast fireplaces – but not dauntingly huge. Bar with immensely comfortable leather sofas, etc. Sitting room with carpet and furnishings more-or-less stone coloured, but with warm, flame coloured cushions (great flower arrangements complement the colours in each room, spotlighted). Third room is dining room – good silver and glass, candle-lit mainly. The windows are huge and look across uninterrupted countryside: in spring, a sea of pink appleblossom with woodland beyond. A feature of the garden is a very long stone and timber pergola stretching into the distance. The bedrooms are huge and luxurious (so are the bathrooms), with distinctive colour schemes. Even the Ladies is memorable for its French porcelain fittings, pretty curtains, etc. As to the food, not such unqualified praise. Two of the three courses were delectable but the steak I had was so tough as to be scarcely eatable. Extensive and interesting wine list, various price levels. The hotel is expensive, but far better value than some in its price bracket. If this were National Trust property, as well it might be, one would pay, maybe £1.50 merely to look at it, after all.' *(EG; also Nigel Buxton)*

Open: All year, except February and 24–31 December.
Rooms: 7 double – 6 with bath, 1 with shower, all with telephone, radio, colour TV and baby-listening. (1 room on ground floor.)
Facilities: Lounge, bar, restaurant. 6 acres formal garden. Heated swimming

pool, grass tennis court, croquet lawn. Riding, pony-trekking, golf available nearby. Within easy reach of Goodwood, Plumpton, Fontwell, Cowdray Park and Chichester Theatre.
Location: A24 to Worthing from London. About 1½ miles after Ashington village, turn right and follow lane for 1 mile. Turn right into Merrywood Lane. *Little Thakeham* is 400 yards on left.
Restriction: No dogs.
Credit cards: All major credit cards accepted.
Terms (excluding service): B & B £22.50–35. Full *alc* £15. Reduced rates and special meals for children.

STRATFORD-UPON-AVON, Warwickshire   Map 2

Shakespeare Hotel   *Telephone:* Stratford-upon-Avon (0789) 294 771
Chapel Street   *Telex:* 311181

For those who prefer a full-bodied hotel in Stratford, the *Shakespeare*, a 16th-century half-timbered and gabled building, looks the part and is in comfortable walking distance of the Theatre. The rooms are all fitted out with the trimmings to be expected of a Trust Houses Forte hotel. It's a popular place for conferences. 'A very pleasant place to stay. Our room was in the new extension, and had no atmosphere, but had a wonderful view of Shakespeare's garden at New Place, and was bright and cheerful. Dinner was conventional but good, and service was excellent.' *(Norma Gordon)*

Open: All year.
Rooms: 44 double, 21 single, 1 suite – all with bath, telephone, radio, colour TV, tea-making facilities and baby-listening.
Facilities: Lift, lounge, 2 bars, restaurant, ballroom; conference facilities. Small garden; boating and fishing on the river Avon.
Location: Central; private parking.
Credit cards: All major credit cards accepted.
Terms (applicable only to January–April 1982): Rooms: £27.50 (single), £39.50 (double). Set meals: breakfast (continental) £1.75, (English) £3.75; lunch £5.25; dinner £6.85; full *alc* approx £10. Bargain breaks: £24 per person per day (minimum 2 days). Children under 5 free of charge; 5–14 50% discount on meals, £1 charge if sharing parents' room; 14 and over £1 charge if sharing parents' room, otherwise 75%.

STRATFORD-UPON-AVON, Warwickshire   Map 2

Stratford House   *Telephone:* Stratford-upon-Avon (0789) 68288
Sheep Street

Last year, we singled out this bed-and-breakfast hotel, 100 yards from the Memorial Theatre, but with its bedrooms facing a quiet alley, as one of our own 'Six of the Best' hotels of the year: it fulfils, we believed, a long-felt need in Stratford for a more modest and personal alternative to the many conventional hotels in the town. *Stratford House* is the Georgian home of Peter Wade, who looks after his guests with scrupulous and generous attention to their needs.

There is always a danger, when an unassuming establishment gets this sort of limelight, that there will be a rash of reports from people who have

101

expected more than Mr Wade really offers. We did in fact get one such report: a visitor who hadn't appreciated that the bedrooms are small and simple in their furnishings (e.g. a formica dressing-table; we had mentioned antiques, but these are by the entrance and in the breakfast room). She also had not realized that *Stratford House* has no public rooms apart from the breakfast room. Her letter was written in disappointment rather than in anger: 'I feel a louse writing an unfavourable report when Peter Wade has just been making us feel very much at home, and, because of his attentiveness, we did enjoy our stay.' But she summed up: 'In favour were: the breakfast, swiftly and deliciously served, the flowers and china, tea-maker in bedroom, and above all the personal service, but we felt there was too much icing and not enough cake for our bill of £27 for the double room.'

This was an isolated letter, though we feel her points were worth making. But there have been many other reports of unalloyed gratitude: 'The most enchanting of all places we have visited recently.' 'We stayed here on our honeymoon, breakfast taken in our bedroom both mornings, everything in its place, atmosphere was fantastic, decor excellent. We could not fault it at all.' 'After a rash of tourist trap hotels, indifferent staff, and run of the mill food, it was refreshing to find *Stratford House* – a place to remember fondly.' *(Jose Romola Barbosa, George and Iris Wright, Ellen and Warren Trafton, P G Bourne, Melissa Cleland)*

Open: All year, except Christmas.
Rooms: 10 double – 8 with bath *en suite*, 1 4-bedded with private bathroom, all with colour TV and tea-making facilities; all available as singles if required. (1 room on ground floor.)
Facilities: Lounge, no bar but residential licence; some small conference facilities. Attractive walled courtyard. &.
Location: In town centre; no private parking but public car parks within a few hundred yards.
Restrictions: Not really suitable for children, though they are not excluded. Dogs allowed if small.
Credit cards: All major credit cards accepted.
Terms (excluding service):   B & B £14–24.50.

STURMINSTER NEWTON, Dorset   **Map 1**

Plumber Manor   [GFG]   *Telephone:* Sturminster Newton (0258) 72507

'It is more like staying in a country house than a hotel – no one asked us to sign a register, the rooms and furniture have that comfortable lived-in look, and nowhere, inside and out, is there any notice that says hotel.' There are many establishments converted from old houses that call themselves country-house hotels, but relatively few are chosen by their guests as deserving that distinction. The Prideaux-Brune's ancestral home – it has been lived in by the family since the early 17th century – is certainly of the elect. Other guests, first-timers, describe being treated by Richard P-B as long-standing friends. From all our correspondence, it is clear that Richard and Alison Prideaux-Brune, and Richard's brother Brian, who is in charge of the kitchens, have effortlessly mastered the art of hostmanship. They also serve 'outstanding' dinners: among items which have won particular praise this year have been asparagus 'Excellent – and every inch could be eaten'; 'smoked salmon rolls filled with avocado and cheese'; a *whole* lobster mayonnaise; lamb cutlets Shrewsbury served pink by request, and an overflowing sweet trolley 'the number of them making a diner feel guilty'. The restaurant where the gourmandizing takes place (Tuesday to Sunday, April–October, Tuesday to Saturday, November–March) does a lot of outside trade, so, with only six bedrooms, the owners choose to call *Plumber Manor* a restaurant with bedrooms. Occasionally, a noisy party of visitors can fracture the conversation of the residents, but in general the Prideaux-Brunes cope with the tidal flow in the restaurant with the same deftness that they bring to the rest of their activities. *(T F Morgan, T M Wilson, B M Newman)*

Open: All year, except first 2 weeks in November and all February. Restaurant closed Mondays, also Sundays November–March.
Rooms: 6 double – all with bath.
Facilities: Drawing room, bar, restaurant. 3 acres garden with a trout stream running through; 400-acre farm. Several golf courses, fishing on the river Stour, and riding nearby; coast 30 miles; within easy motoring range of Bath, Salisbury, Dorchester, Longleat, Stourhead, Wilton, etc.
Location: 2 miles SW of Sturminster Newton, on the Hazelbury–Bryan road, which is a southward turn off the A357 (about halfway between Sherborne and Blandford).
Restrictions: No children under 12. No dogs.
Terms: B & B £15–18. Set meal (service at guests' discretion): dinner £11.

TAUNTON, Somerset   **Map 1**

The Castle Hotel   [GFG]   *Telephone:* Taunton (0823) 72671
Castle Green   *Telex:* 46488

'Taunton's wisteria-clad *Castle* is a venerable institution,' was the opening line of our entry last year. Indeed it is: it still retains an atmospheric 12th-century Norman garden which dates from when there was a castle on the site, is rich in historical connections with Perkin Warbeck, Cromwell, Judge Jeffreys and the like, and has been a popular hostelry since the 17th century. Though it is large by the standards of the Guide, and one reader felt that the dining room and barn-like lounge were a bit gloomy, it is very far from being venerable or old-fashioned in its public posture. There is no hotel in the Guide which is so energetic in keeping us posted with its latest news of improvements and changes. Last year, we reported the arrival of a new chef from *Sharrow Bay* on Ullswater (q.v.). That gentleman has now departed, and we have had several letters to tell us of the new chef de cuisine, John Hornsby, 28, who comes from an equally distinguished stable (though that is hardly the word), having been executive sous chef at *The Dorchester* under the renowned Anton Mosimann. Christopher Chapman, the managing director, also tells us in December that plans are well advanced for the renovation and upgrading of the third floor rooms, and then in June that the said bedrooms are now completely refurbished. He promises to send us shortly detailed arrangements for their special Festival Weekends, with programmes on fine wines, music, theatre and heritage. We report this correspondence as evidence of the personal drive which has made *The Castle* a thoroughly successful hotel, constantly earning high marks from our readers for its dependable comfort and quality of service.

Open: All year.
Rooms: 25 double, 18 single, 1 suite – 40 with bath, all with telephone, radio, TV and baby-listening. (Road-facing rooms are double-glazed.)

Facilities: Lift, drawing room, 2 bars, restaurant, coffee shop; some rooms for functions and conferences. 1½ acres grounds with Norman moat, keep and square Norman well. &.
Location: Central; parking for 40 cars.
Restrictions: Dogs by arrangement.
Credit cards: All major credit cards accepted.
Terms: Rooms £25.50–33 per person. Set meals: breakfast £4.75 (English, £2.90 (continental); lunch £8.50; dinner £9.75; full *alc* £17. Reduced rates at weekends throughout the year and special weekend programmes of fine wines, music, theatre and heritage. Reduced rates for children at weekends only; special meals provided.

TEMPLE SOWERBY, Nr Penrith, Cumbria   Map 4

Temple Sowerby House   [GFG]   *Telephone:* Kirkby Thore (093 06) 578

We carried our first entry last year for this enterprising new hotel in a mostly Georgian residence on the A66 halfway between Penrith and Appleby (front rooms double-glazed), and are glad to have our initial good report endorsed by a recent visitor:

'*Temple Sowerby* is comfortable and cosy inside, and the walled garden will be magnificent when Joseph Armstrong and John Kennedy, who own the hotel, have completed all their plans for it. Joseph and John aren't too keen on having a proper bar, so have a little hatch in a small sitting room through which you can place your order. I must admit to preferring a proper bar where I can sit and drink, and order without feeling I am taking someone away from something, but they are obviously keen to run the place without too many staff. And that's really my only other quibble: we ate magnificently but with a starving 7-year-old in tow, we had to wait a long time, with Joseph doing all the cooking single-handed and only John and a friendly lady doing the serving to a full dining room. But I must say everyone was very nice to our son. The starters included a delicious fish cream with a lemony hollandaise, and melon, tomato and cucumber salad; the main courses were trout with almonds (beautifully cooked) and pork with walnut and raisin stuffing; the puddings were creme caramel, fresh half-pineapple with Kirsch, and chocolate roulade. We could hardly manage cheese and home-made biscuits, and the fudge that accompanied the coffee in the open-fired lounge had to be saved for the next day. I don't think that was at all bad for £9.50 per adult head (June 1981). The breakfast was wonderful, with *real* kippers, and much faster serving. Joseph and John are obviously dedicated to the place, will be improving both house and garden year by year, I feel sure, and deserve a lot of praise and encouragement.' *(Susan Fleming)*

Open: Early March–21 December.
Rooms: 10 double, 2 single – 10 with bath and radio; 2 four-poster beds. 4 rooms in the Coach House annexe. (2 rooms on ground floor.)
Facilities: 3 lounges, sun lounge, TV room; small conference facilities out of season. 2 acres walled Georgian garden. &.
Location: 6 miles from the M6 (Junction 40) on the A66 Penrith–Scotch Corner road, 6 miles NW of Appleby.
Restrictions: No children under 5. Dogs by arrangement.
Credit cards: Access/Euro, Barclay/Visa.
Terms (service optional): B & B £15–20; dinner B & B £25–30. Set meal: dinner £10.50.

TETBURY, Gloucestershire   **Map 2**

The Close   *Telephone:* Tetbury (0666) 52272
8 Long Street

One of the more luxurious Cotswold hotels, *The Close* is in the centre of this picturesque and prosperous old wool town. The bedrooms facing the large, well-tended wall garden are to be preferred. 'Welcoming 16th-century hotel, although the interior is unmistakably Georgian. Our bedroom was spacious and elegant, looking on to the walled garden. Thoughtful touches included a basket of fresh oranges, mineral water, hand cream, sewing kit, as well as shampoo, bath salts and plentiful tissues and cottonwool. Dinner in the Regency dining room was first-class: beautifully cooked vegetables – mange-tout, cauliflower, ratatouille and two kinds of potatoes. Breakfast included fresh orange juice, delicious local sausage and Wiltshire smoked bacon. The hotel is well situated for the Cotswolds and the magnificence of Westonbirt Arboretum. The staff were pleasant and courteous, the manager asking if we had enjoyed our meal every night. We will certainly return.' *(Mrs J H Noakes)*

Open: All year, except possibly New Year's Day.
Rooms: 10 double, 2 single, 2 suites – 10 with bath, 2 with shower, all with telephone, radio, colour TV, tea-making facilities and baby-listening. (Front bedrooms double-glazed, but may be slightly noisy.)
Facilities: Lounge, bar lounge, restaurant. Garden of ¼ acre with croquet and lily pond.
Location: From London, turn off the M4 at Junction 17 on to the A429 to Malmesbury and then take the B4014 to Tetbury. Hotel is central with parking for 24 cars.
Restriction: No dogs.
Credit cards: All major credit cards accepted.
Terms: B & B £16–29; dinner, B & B (minimum 2 nights) £26–36.50; full board £36.50–43. Set meals: lunch £6; dinner £11; full *alc* £14. £5 for children sharing parents' room.

THORVERTON, Exeter, Devon   **Map 1**

Berribridge House   *Telephone:* Exeter (0392) 860259

An unpretentiously agreeable small hotel half a mile outside the village on a quiet country lane converted from a terrace of thatched cottages dating from the 17th century, with those hallmarks of an old English country hotel – oak beams, log fires and suchlike. 'We stayed there for three nights – and it was like heaven. The owners welcomed us warmly, the rooms were beautifully decorated and furnished, and we much enjoyed the cooking. It's all very peaceful. The small garden in front is a mass of blooms and at the rear there is an acre of lawns and rock gardens. It's a wonderful find.' *(R J Harrison-Church)*

Open: All year.
Rooms: 6 double – 1 with shower; baby-listening by arrangement.
Facilities: Reception, lounge, TV lounge, bar. 1 acre grounds; golf with shooting nearby.

Location: Drive to top of village of Thorverton, take left fork, carry on for ⅔ mile on this country lane.

Restrictions: Children over 12 preferred, younger ones accepted by arrangement. No dogs in dining room.

Terms (no service charge): B & B £11–12. Full *alc* £5–9. Special rates for minimum 2–5 days' stay 1 October–30 June. £2.50 for children sharing parents' room; no charge if in cot; special meals provided.

TREBARWITH STRAND, Tintagel, North Cornwall   Map 1

The Old Millfloor   *Telephone:* Tintagel (084 04) 234

No hotel, but a tiny guest house – just three rooms – with a couple of self-catering chalet bungalows nearby. At £8 (the estimated price for B & B in 1982), it must rank among the cheapest entries in the book. 'Total silence and you are left in peace. Deep valley with millstream, dark peaceful house. Excellent cooking. One mile from beach – rocks, surf – and near cliff path. Take your own wine.' *(John Broadbent)*

Open: 15 March–15 December.

Rooms: 3 double with tea-making facilities on request; also 2 self-catering bungalows.

Facilities: Lounge. 14 acres grounds with stream and orchard. Sandy beach 10 minutes' walk.

Terms (no tax or service charge): B & B £8. Children under 12 half price; special meals on request.

TRESCO, Isles of Scilly, Cornwall   Map 1

The Island Hotel   *Telephone:* Scillonia (0720) 22883

The Island Hotel on Tresco has long been appreciated by those who want to get a bit further away from it all while still being looked after in a thoroughly civilized manner. Tresco itself is only two miles by a mile, and carless; *The Island Hotel* is fitted out with plenty of attractions of its own (see below), but some comments have been made both about the essentially English cooking – sometimes very good, but not consistently so – and also about the decor. The hotel, which belongs to the Prestige group, acquired new managers in January 1981, John and Wendy Pyatt, who tell us that they have been busy with redecorations and other small improvements. We should be glad to hear from other recent visitors, but meanwhile here is a tribute from one utterly gratified customer:

'There's no more magical place than Tresco in spring. My teenage son and I can't think of anywhere we'd rather be than feasting in the *Island Hotel*'s candle-lit dining room, and, through the windows, watching the gulls wheel and the sea crash. Afterwards my son recommends the discreetly distanced "games room" with its TV, ping-pong and Ceefax although I prefer a barefoot ramble to the hotel's private beach, burying my toes in Tresco's silver sand and inhaling the wonderful air which smells of wild flowers. No traffic, no streetlights, no Space Invaders – and a hotel whose friendly staff made us feel more important and cossetted than Prince Charles and Lady Di.' *(Mavis Campion)*

Open: March–mid October.

Rooms: 31 double, 5 single, 1 suite – all with telephone and baby-listening, most with colour TV; some rooms arranged in groups of 1 double and 1 single, sharing a bathroom. (3 rooms on ground floor.)

Facilities: Lounge, sun lounge, TV room, cocktail bar, dining room, games room for adults with table tennis and bar billiards, children's playroom, laundry facilities. 5 acres grounds with heated swimming pool, bowls, croquet and golf practice net; private beach with safe bathing; guests have use of motor sailing and rowing boats. &.

Location: There are boats and helicopters daily except Sundays from Penzance to St Mary's Airport, and Brymon Airways run a service to St Mary's from Exeter, Plymouth and Newquay. Island guests are met by launch from St Mary's. (Booking for flights is essential.)

Restriction: No dogs.

Credit cards: All major credit cards accepted.

Terms (no service charge): Dinner, B & B £27–56. Buffet lunch from £2.50; set meal: dinner £12. Tresco gardeners' holidays in spring and autumn. Reduced rates for children in bunk beds or cots; special meals provided.

ULLSWATER, Nr Penrith, Cumbria   Map 4

Howtown Hotel   *Telephone:* Pooley Bridge (085 36) 514

A long, low building among the peaks of the Eastern Fells, right on Ullswater and at the end of the eastern road from Pooley Bridge, *Howtown* has been owned for generations by the Baldry family, who farm the land around and use their own produce for cooking. Michael Baldry farms and runs the friendly bar, and Jacquie, his wife, does all the cooking.

'This hotel must be unique, the personality of the owners and their forebears being well and truly stamped upon it. From the moment you open the door, you realize that you are in someone's loved and cared-for home with its collections of china, glass, pewter, copper, paintings, flat irons. You name it, they collect it. There are a few fairly inflexible rules: no boots indoors; no tea in upstairs lounge (might get spilt on carpet); no dinner after 7.45; no breakfast before 9 am (although, when it comes, it's worth waiting for right down to the home-made marmalade and rolled butter pats). Mrs Baldry, who works like a Trojan, is a very good cook of the simple, old-fashioned English sort. At dinner home-made soups and *pâtés* and sometimes fresh salmon as starters. Two choices only for the main course and the result is that both are excellent. Delicious steak and kidney pie; ham with apricots and Cumberland sauce; fresh plaice; roasts of various sorts – all with home-grown veg. Chips unheard of. Nostalgic puddings: greengage pie; blackberry and apple crumble; bread and butter pudding – in fact the opposite of "sweets from the trolley". The salad and packed lunches are also excellent. The pretty girls who work around the place add a feeling of lightness and gaiety. The views from the windows are marvellous. Ten minutes' walk and you are in wild country. Fantastic value in my opinion. Can't think how they do it at the price.' *(Miranda Mackintosh; also Jean Stead)*

Open: 26 March–1 November.

Rooms: 13 double, 3 single; 2 cottages for renting. 4 rooms in annexe.

Facilities: 4 lounges, 2 bars, dining room. Garden of ½ acre. 300 yards from the lake with own private foreshore; yachting, boating, water skiing, fishing, walking, climbing.

Terms (no fixed service charge): B & B £9; dinner, B & B £13–15. Set meals: lunch £3.50; dinner £6.

Leeming on Ullswater Country House Hotel
Telephone: Pooley Bridge (085 36) 4444

On the opposite side of the lake from *Sharrow Bay* (see opposite), *Leeming on Ullswater* (which last year was indexed under Watermillock) could become something of a rival in terms of creature comforts to its well-known neighbour on the far shore. But judging from our reports, it is some way yet from *Sharrow Bay*'s class. The house itself was built in the Georgian style in the 1840s by a Midland industrialist. It became a small hotel in the de-luxe class in 1969. The Fitzpatricks took it over three years ago, have spent lavishly on the house itself and its large landscaped gardens which run down to the lake, and are full of enterprising schemes for attracting new custom, like a special Wordsworth Fortnight in daffodil time. One reader, while appreciating the special attractions of the public rooms and the grounds, and offering a special word of praise for the price range of the 300-bin wine list – 'from much cheaper than anyone could possibly expect at such a hotel to the very expensive for the wealthy connoisseur' – felt let down by the small not very well-appointed back room. Clearly rooms vary in size and character, and the ones overlooking the lake are to be preferred – though there is at present no price differential. The same reader was also disappointed with his continental breakfast, and asked why croissants should be reserved for Sundays only. Another reader complained of the unimaginative and, he felt, over-priced lunch buffet (cold, except for one hot dish of the day). We should welcome further reports, but would make it clear that not all our *Leeming* post was negative. Here is one correspondent who gave it an unqualified bill of endorsement:

'Not only is it a beautiful building splendidly furnished, not only is the food excellent, but, above all, the friendliness and helpfulness of the staff make any visit memorable. To give an example, my wife and I were without a car, and intended to go fell-walking. After exploring the fells on the near-side of Ullswater on one day, we wanted to get across to the far side on the next. There was no convenient ferry, but the manager drove us in his own car to precisely where we wanted to go at a time of our choosing. That was typical of the attitude of all the staff during our time there. My wife and I would also recommend the packed lunches which are imaginatively composed, and accompanied by small individual bottles of red or white Burgundy.' *(David Keene)*

Open: 19 March–3 January.
Rooms: 22 double, 2 single – 19 with bath, 3 with shower, 17 with radio, all with telephone. 7 rooms in cottages in the grounds. (2 rooms on ground floor.)
Facilities: Drawing room, Blue Sitting Room, library, bar, restaurant; occasional pianist or madrigal singers and dancing in the evening. 20 acres landscaped grounds with magnificent trees and views, lake frontage, jetty, swimming, sailing, fishing, croquet lawn. Fine walking and climbing country. Golf nearby; private shooting parties. &.
Location: W shore of Ullswater, on the A592 below Pooley Bridge.
Restrictions: No children under 8. No dogs in house.
Credit cards: All major credit cards accepted.
Terms (excluding 12% service):   B & B (continental) £25–35.75 (English breakfast £3 extra); full board £30–41.50. Set meals: lunch £5.75; dinner £11.60; full *alc* £14. Special winter breaks.

ULLSWATER, Cumbria   Map 4

Sharrow Bay Country House Hotel [GFG]
Telephone: Pooley Bridge (085 36) 301/483

For better for worse, *Sharrow Bay* has become an institution. Not the
largest, nor – though on the dear side – the most expensive hotel in the
Lake District, it is certainly, along with *Miller Howe* at Windermere
(q.v.), the most internationally known of lake hotels, and people are
constantly using it as a yardstick to measure the relative virtues of other
aspirant country-house hotels. For new readers, we should explain that
the hotel, a characteristic lakeland stone house but with Italianate overtones, lies on the eastern shore of Ullswater, with the lake lapping the
terrace wall and with a backdrop of woods and mountains. Most of the
accommodation is in the main house or in nearby cottages, though there
are also rooms, somewhat more spacious, at Bank House, a mile away
and higher up; breakfast only is served here, other meals being taken at
the hotel proper. All the rooms, even the smallest ones, are fitted out with
fridges, trouser presses and many other thoughtful extras. Regulars vary
as to which rooms they prefer. A reader this year felt a bit out of the fun of
things at Bank House, and also didn't really much fancy having to drive
back even a mile after the very good dinner. Others are glad of the extra
space and like to be away from the general hubbub. Mavis, Bank House's
housekeeper, comes in for special commendations. But it is the warmth of
welcome of Brian Sack and Francis Coulson, that and the remarkably rich
meals which Francis Coulson and his staff serve in the restaurant, which
are for most people what makes a visit to *Sharrow Bay* a memorable
experience. Perhaps the only reservation people have about the place
concerns these meals: a couple of dozen choices among the starters; then a
fish course, followed by a sorbet; seven or eight choices among the
entrées; the same number again of options among the sweets; and there is
still a trolley of cheese to follow, not to mention petit fours with the
coffee. 'Dining always reliable but a marathon,' writes a flabbergasted
reader. 'By the time one reaches the main course, one's appetite has been
nullified by the many substantial and rich preceding courses which are so
excellent that they cannot be refused. Fantastic soups and sweets. But
how do people cope with full board?' This reader is not the only one to ask
that question or to suggest that the hotel might offer an *à la carte* menu for
the faint-stomached. But capacities vary; undoubtedly many guests relish
these banquets, even twice a day. And because people cherish this place
as an institution, they would hate to see it change.

Open: 5 March–6 December.
Rooms: 22 double, 7 single, 2 suites – 17 with bath, 2 with shower, all with
telephone, radio, TV, some with tea-making facilities. 17 rooms in cottages and
Bank House. (7 rooms on ground floor.)
Facilities: 3 drawing rooms where drinks served as there is no separate bar,
elegant restaurant. 12 acres garden and woodlands; ½ mile of lake shore with
private jetty and boathouse; lake bathing (cold!) and fishing from the shore; boats
for hire nearby; steamer service in season across the lake; magnificent walking/
climbing country. &.
Location: On the E shore of Ullswater, 2 miles S of Pooley Bridge. M6 exit 40.
Restrictions: No children under 13. No dogs.
Terms: Dinner, B & B £37–55. Set meals: lunch from £14.50; dinner from £18.50.

Greenriggs Hotel   [GFG]   *Telephone:* Crosthwaite (044 88) 387

We carried a long and appreciative report on Frank and Christine Jackson's hotel last year, and offer a similarly enthusiastic one below:

'The hotel is developed from a former farm house with an annexe well converted from an old stables block. It is set at the foot of an escarpment some 3–4 miles west of Kendal in delightful countryside with peacefulness the keynote. There is a quiet sheltered garden, well "treed" with an ancient fig tree reputed to fruit every year. Inside the hotel there are four lounges, very comfortable and nicely furnished, one of which includes the bar. All are nicely decorated and as with the whole hotel spotlessly clean. Our bedroom was in the annexe and was of reasonable size, pleasantly furnished including very comfortable beds. The *en suite* bathroom was of good size and well equipped. We rated the food as very good indeed and continues to be worthy of inclusion in your sister publication. Dinners were always of a high standard. Wines were reasonably priced and ranged from low-priced Spanish to some reasonably costed château-bottled clarets. Wine and bar service was excellent. I have no hesitation in recommending *Greenriggs* to anyone desiring a quiet well-run hotel with the added bonus of good food at reasonable prices. There are, alas, all too few hotels of this type at the right price.' *(RCS; also Angela Evans, P Norris, Mrs William Hasker)*

Open: All year, except January.
Rooms: 14 double, 1 single – 9 with bath. 4 rooms in annexe.
Facilities: Residents' lounge, coffee lounge, cocktail bar, restaurant. 1½ acres grounds with croquet.
Location: 3 miles W of Kendal. M6 exit 36 or 37.
Terms (no service charge):   B & B £13–14; dinner, B & B £19–21. Set meal: dinner £9.50. Winter weekend breaks from November–March (dinner, B & B Friday/ Saturday and Sunday lunch £33–37 inclusive). Reduced rates and special meals for children.

WALLCROUCH, Wadhurst, East Sussex   **Map 2**

Spindlewood Hotel   [GFG]   *Telephone:* Ticehurst (0580) 200430

Considering the many attractions of the county – its historic castles, great houses and famous gardens – and its proximity to London and the sea, East Sussex has had disappointingly few entries in the Guide, which makes the opening of *Spindlewood* by a former Michelin inspector, Robert Fitzsimmons, particularly welcome. It's a late 19th-century house in five acres of gardens and woodland, 9 miles SE of Tunbridge Wells. The following extracts from reports give a good impression of the quality of the hospitality offered by the Fitzsimmons family, and augur well for the future.

'The new owner has refurnished the house to a very high standard throughout. He has a very gifted young chef and an old ex-market gardener growing all the fruit and vegetables in a walled garden. The grounds have been extensively improved – ponds cleared and ducks installed, stream and woodlands left natural, but elsewhere lawns planted surrounded by masses of rose bushes. All the rooms are big and there is lots of space. Every bedroom has big windows with views. There is total peace. And as to the food – it is quite exceptional.' 'All our meals at *Spindlewood* were highly pleasurable experiences, whether chosen from the *table d'hôte* or *à la carte* menus. My husband particularly enjoyed a starter of melon served with cream cheese and slices of ginger. My favourite was a lamb dish beautifully cooked with rosemary. We both thoroughly enjoyed the syllabub. We travel quite widely both here and on the continent, and we were both excited by every aspect of this hotel. We are already plotting our return.' 'A small hotel with a personal style. The impression is that the other guests are friends of long standing of the owner: not so, doubtless, but an indication of the attractive atmosphere. Ditto the welcome (at 8 pm in pouring rain) offered by two people who surged forward as the engine was turned off to help us in, carry cases, and be nice to the children. Next day a refreshing frankness: the senior Fitzimmons looked at the dried, still acceptable flowers in the dining room and wondered aloud why fresh ones – masses of them in the gardens – hadn't been introduced.' *(EG, Mrs B L Allsworth, AL)*

Open: All year. Restaurant closed to non-residents Sunday/Monday.
Rooms: 8 double, 2 single – 9 with bath, 1 with shower.
Facilities: Library lounge with TV, lounge bar, restaurant. 5 acres grounds with hard tennis court. Bewl Bridge Reservoir with trout fishing 3 miles.
Location: 2¼ miles SE of Wadhurst on the B2099.
Restriction: No dogs.
Credit cards: Access, Barclay/Visa, Diners.
Terms (no fixed service charge): B & B £12.50–16. Set meal: dinner £7; full *alc* £13.50. Bargain breaks October–March. Reduced rates for children.

WANSFORD, Nr Peterborough, Cambridgeshire   **Map 2**

Haycock Inn   *Telephone:* Stamford (0780) 782223

The *Haycock* is one of four hotels owned by a mini-group called Poste Hotels. Most of the entries in this Guide are run by resident owners, and in general we find that hotels belonging to a chain lack the character or flair which a caring proprietor on the spot can provide. We therefore salute the achievement of Poste Hotels in having all their four hotels in the Guide (the others are *The George* at Stamford and *The Old Bridge* at Huntingdon, both in the same area as the *Haycock*, and *Bailiffscourt* at Climping on the south coast). The *Haycock* is a true old inn, stone-built, dating back to 1632, rich in innish things like inglenook fireplaces as well as contemporary equipment like colour TV and trouser presses in the bedrooms. It also has quite a lot of history to boast of: no one has suggested that Queen Elizabeth slept here, but Mary Queen of Scots may have visited the place on her way to imprisonment at Fotheringhay in 1586, and Queen Victoria visited the inn in 1835 when she was Princess Alexandria Victoria. Honest English cooking. *(C J Rae)*

Open: All year, except Christmas Day.
Rooms: 18 double, 10 single, 2 suites – 15 with bath, 1 with shower, all with telephone, radio, colour TV and baby-listening; 1 four-poster bed. 7 rooms in annexe.
Facilities: 2 lounges, bar, restaurant; function rooms. 5 acres grounds; pétanque, fishing, cricket.
Location: Just off the junction where the A1 meets the A47.

Credit cards: All major credit cards accepted.
Terms: B & B £16–26.50. Bar meals from £4.50; full *alc* £12.50. Special weekend breaks October–April. Reduced rates and special meals for children.

WANTAGE, Oxfordshire   Map 2

The Bear   *Telephone:* Wantage (023 57) 66366
Market Square

Qualified praise only this past year for Wantage's old coaching inn in a corner of the picturesque market square, now smartened up with the three t's of a hotel that is keeping up with the times – telephones, TV and tea-making facilities in all the bedrooms. Improvements are still under way: at present only two of the bedrooms have baths *en suite*, but the Willmotts hope to add baths to several more in the course of the year, with stylish touches like brass bedsteads and stripped pine furniture. (Perhaps they will also provide stands for suitcases?) Service, it is generally agreed, is consistently friendly as well as efficient. But opinions do differ about the hotel's sophisticated, ambitious and fairly expensive menu. Not all the dishes are equally successful. *Bruins*, the hotel's wine bar in the courtyard, which also serves hot snacks, has been more generally approved of, but sadly this is no longer open in the evenings or on Sundays and Mondays. More reports welcome. *(Roger Smithells, A A Kitrick)*

Open: All year. Wine bar open Tuesday–Saturday 9 am–5 pm.
Rooms: 8 double, 10 single – 2 with bath, all with telephone, radio, mono TV and tea-making facilities.
Facilities: Drawing room, residents' lounge, bar, wine bar, restaurant; conference room; live folk music in wine bar at weekends. The hotel is built round a cobbled courtyard. 6 miles from river Thames, 2 miles from Berkshire Downs.
Location: In town centre.
Restriction: No dogs.
Credit cards: Access/Euro, Barclay/Visa.
Terms (no fixed service charge): B & B £14.25–22.50. Set meals: lunch £6.25; dinner £10.50–12. £5.75 extra for children sharing parents' room.

WAREHAM, Dorset   Map 1

The Priory Hotel   [GFG]   *Telephone:* Wareham (092 95) 2772
Church Green

We had our first entry for *The Priory* last year, one of the more ecstatic in the Guide: 'This lovely old building . . . incredibly quiet . . . two-acre garden delightful even in February . . . beautifully warm . . . furniture and decor outstanding . . . our bedroom a dream . . . relays of pleasant young staff most helpful and friendly . . . can't recommend too highly . . . children immaculately looked after.' We are glad to say that this year's crop of reports is in the same vein, with just one minor critical note, that the food, though always enjoyable, does not consistently maintain the highest standards. But in every other respect, *The Priory* continues to elicit superlatives: 'The nicest hotel we have ever stayed in . . . comfortable and attractive with lovely flowers . . . *all* the staff pleasant and helpful . . . English breakfast really good – the best bacon ever . . . very helpful with a 5-year-old's high tea. Lovely outlook.' 'This genuinely old priory converted to a very high standard indeed – difficult to fault the ambience, service and exceptional cleanliness.' *(Mary and Rodney Milne-Day, R F Morgan, Lady Elstub, AL)*

Open: All year.
Rooms: 9 double, 3 suites – 8 with bath, 4 with shower, all with telephone, radio and colour TV.
Facilities: Lounge, residents' lounge, bar, 2 dining rooms. 6 acres grounds with 2½ acres landscaped gardens – on river with bathing, fishing and sailing; shooting can be arranged.
Location: 150 yards from centre; parking.
Restriction: No dogs.
Credit cards: All major credit cards accepted.
Terms (excluding service): B & B £17.50–26. Set meals: lunch from £5.50; dinner (Monday–Friday) £9.50, (Saturday) £10.50; full *alc* £11.50. Winter weekend breaks 1 October–30 April except bank holidays. Reduced rates for children sharing parents' room.

WHIMPLE, Nr Exeter, Devon   **Map 1**

Woodhayes   *Telephone:* Whimple (0404) 822237

We had prepared an enthusiastic entry for Woodhayes, *a small Georgian hotel set among the cider apple orchards of East Devon, which for the past three years had been owned and run – much to the satisfaction of our readers – by David and Barbara Townsend. As we go to press, we learn that the Townsends have departed – apparently for the richer pastures of fudge manufacture. New owners are John Allan, a graduate of Grosvenor House, London, and more recently manager of a small country house hotel near Aberdeen, and Graham Hartley, until recently a hotel inspector for Michelin in Britain and on the continent, who will be in charge of the kitchens. Details below are of the Allan/Hartley regime. Reports welcome.*

Open: All year, except January; restaurant closed to non-residents Sunday and Monday.
Rooms: 5 double, 1 single – all with bath, telephone, radio and colour TV.
Facilities: Lounge, TV lounge, dining room. 1½ acres garden and 1½ acres paddock with lawns, aboretum, gazebo and kitchen garden. Horse-riding by arrangement. Fine views towards the sea at Budleigh Salterton and the river Exe estuary, westwards to Torbay, eastwards to Lyme Bay.
Location: On the edge of Whimple village, which is just N of the A30 Exeter–Honiton road, 9 miles E of Exeter.
Restriction: Dogs and children by arrangement.
Credit cards: Access, Barclay/Visa.
Terms: B & B £12–19. Set meal: dinner £7.50 (£8.50 to non-residents.) Guests staying 6 nights get a 7th free.

> We asked hotels to estimate their 1982 tariffs some time before publication so the rates given here are not necessarily completely accurate. Please *always* check terms with hotels when making bookings.

Whitwell Hall Country House Hotel
Telephone: Whitwell on the Hill (065 381) 551

An ivy-creepered Tudor Gothic mansion (circa 1835) of baronial grandeur in 18 acres of garden and woodland, with stupendous views over the
Vale of York. York is 12 miles to the south west, the Moors rise about the
same distance to the north and Scarborough lies 29 miles to the north east.
Whitwell Hall opened its doors as a hotel in the late Seventies, with
Commander and Mrs Peter Milner as the resident owners. They are keen
to provide a relaxed and personal style of hospitality. Rooms are lofty and
restful with flotillas of easy chairs in the log-fired drawing room. Staff
from the village give friendly informal service. Bicycles are available for
leisurely exploration of the countryside around. There are largish bedrooms in the main house, and smaller (and cheaper) ones, but with
showers only, in a converted stable-block 70 yards away. And – a nice
touch this – a chapel has been set aside for business meetings. *(Roger
Smithells)*

Open: All year.
Rooms: 18 double, 2 single – 10 with bath, 10 with shower, all with telephone,
radio, TV on request, and tea-making facilities. 9 rooms in annexe.
Facilities: Large entrance hall with bar, lounge, dining room. 18 acres grounds
with views over Vale of York. Tennis, croquet; bicycles provided; golf, shooting
and fishing nearby. ♧.
Location: 12 miles from York. Follow the A64 from York; hotel is signposted to
the left.
Restrictions: No children under 12.
Credit cards: All major credit cards accepted.
Terms (excluding 10% service charge): B & B £14.52–21.45; dinner, B & B
£24.64–32.45. Set meals: lunch £5.39; dinner £12.10. 2-day or weekend breaks
available.

WILLITON, Somerset   **Map 1**

The White House Hotel   [GFG]   *Telephone:* Williton (0984) 32306

Kay Smith's Georgian house is on the A39, and the one consistent
grumble that appears in our files is about the noise of passing lorries in the
rooms at the front. Poor sleepers would do better to ask for one of the
new, smaller and perhaps rather austere rooms in the annexe at the back.
On the whole, the quality of the meals is more dependable than the
accommodation, but the following may stand as a characteristic tribute to
the pleasures of a visit to *The White House*:
'The hotel is set in one of the few remaining uncommercialized areas of
the West country – excellent for spotting rare visiting bird species in the
Quantocks, walks among 17th-century gardens, and rock climbing among
the headlands, together with the more obvious delights of Exmoor itself
with its abounding trout rivers. *The White House* provided the ideal
retreat. The family-run hotel's outstanding features are the menu and
wine list. The food is meticulously prepared by the owners and offers a
tantalizing choice at each mealtime. The lounges are decorated to compliment the style of the house. Everything is spotlessly clean and polished.

We shall return again for the country atmosphere and the smell of those fresh-baked rolls wafting in through the windows of our pretty Laura Ashley bedroom suite.' *(Mrs D Slaughter; also Mary-Jane Wilkins, Alan Pratt, D E Fowler, Anne Boustred)*

Open: Mid May–end October.
Rooms: 13 double, 1 family – 4 with bath. (4 rooms in annexe on ground floor.)
Facilities: Lounge with TV, bar, dining room; small conference facilities. Sea 2 miles. &.
Location: On the A39 1½ miles SE of Watchet; in village centre; parking for 20 cars.
Restriction: Dogs by prior arrangement.
Terms (excluding service): Rooms £12–14.70 per person; B & B £14.50–17.20; dinner, B & B £22–24.70. Set meal: dinner £9.50. Reduced rates for children sharing parents' room; special meals on request.

WINDERMERE, Cumbria   Map 4

Miller Howe   [GFG]   *Telephone:* Windermere (096 62) 2536
Rayrigg Road

There are many good hoteliers in the Lake District, but we would put John Tovey, who last year celebrated his tenth birthday at *Miller Howe*, in the company of heavenly hosts. And if that sounds a little extravagant, it is, after all, in keeping with the exuberant style of this famous hotel and restaurant, and its highly innovative–romantic rather than classical–cuisine. This year, in place of our own description, we offer, with his permission, a view of *Miller Howe* by the *Observer*'s food correspondent, Paul Levy:

'*Miller Howe* is a first-rate stage setting. The hotel is perched on the edge of Lake Windermere; the view from my bedroom window was so perfectly arranged that I wondered whether the landscape itself might not be the result of artifice. It is true that the ambience is a little undisciplined for my taste. (I counted 12 ornaments, in addition to the vase of flowers and an oil lamp, on the tiny surface of my room's dressing table.) But all this, and the plumply over-furnished common rooms, are simply a backdrop to the drama of the food at *Miller Howe*. For dinner every evening Tovey serves a five-course meal. There is only one sitting, precisely at 8.30, and there is no choice – except for the dessert course, where the variety is such as to make mind and palate boggle together. After everyone is seated, the house lights go down, Lake Windermere glows richly, as if on cue, and a troupe of waiters appears with the first course. I have to admit that the appropriateness of music, an instrumental arrangement of "Keep the Home Fires Burning", was lost on me, and that the single red rhododendron blossom garnishing each plate did nothing for my appetite. But the food was stunning . . . [There follows a long course-by-course appreciation of the writer's dinner] His wine list is superb . . . There is no denying that Tovey and the hotel restaurant he has created are flamboyant, but not vulgar. After a spell in the Foreign Service, Tovey was an actor for a time; guests at *Miller Howe* are rarely allowed to forget it. But what fun the place is. Nobody could fail to enjoy himself there.'

Open: 12 March–mid December.
Rooms: 13 double – 11 with bath, 2 with shower, all with radio; TV available.
Facilities: 4 drawing rooms (drinks served here, as no separate bar), 2 dining

rooms, sun-lounge terrace; conferences possible out of season. 4 acres grounds with landscaped garden and views over Windermere and the skyline of high fells. Quick access to walking and climbing country; tennis nearby; easy access to Windermere with sailing and fishing and water sports; lake steamer service and cruises.

Location: On the A592 N of Bowness.
Restrictions: No children under 12.
Credit cards: American Express, Diners.
Terms (not including 12½% service charge): Dinner, B & B £38–55. Set meal: dinner £15. Cookery classes in off-season.

WITHERSLACK, Grange-over-Sands, Cumbria　　　　　　　**Map 4**

The Old Vicarage　[GFG]　　　*Telephone:* Witherslack (044 852) 381

'This little Georgian hotel is well worth a visit either en route to the Lakes or for those who wish to avoid the more touristy and crowded spots further north. It is situated in beautiful walking country south of Lake Windermere, and, though only 15 minutes from the M6, it is quiet and secluded, away from the heart of the village. Our welcome was friendly and unfussy. Mrs Brown and Mrs Reeve run the hotel informally as a joint family enterprise. The rooms are pleasantly furnished – William Morris-y curtains, Heals' lampshades, lots of pine and cane in the bedroom, ample reading light. The emphasis is on quality – a few rooms beautifully equipped and furnished; nothing flash, but first rate and imaginative. The food, too, was excellent. Home-made bread and rolls are a speciality. There is a five-course set menu dinner – no choice except at the dessert stage where a hot and a cold sweet are offered, and you can have both. We had elderflower and gooseberry crumble and a delicious gooey meringue, both irresistible. Breakfast was equally good, including home-made jam. The hotel has applied for a licence, but provide a small selection of wines for those who don't bring their own. Before dinner a carafe of dry sherry is provided for guests to help themselves. One criticism: the brochure speaks of 5 acres of grounds: this is a little misleading as much of it is vegetable garden and woodland, and the garden itself is quite small and rather ill-kept. Otherwise, though, it was difficult to find fault. The hotel is efficiently run with much thought and care. Very good value for money.' *(Anne Abel Smith; also Christopher Portway)*

Open: All year, except Christmas and Boxing Day.
Rooms: 7 double, 1 single – 3 with bath, 4 with shower, all with TV, tea-making facilities and baby-listening.
Facilities: Sitting room, coffee lounge, 3 dining rooms; musical evenings. Garden. Sea 4 miles, Lake Windermere 5 miles, river fishing 6 miles. Fell walking. Weekend cookery courses.
Location: Take exit 36 from the M6: follow route to Barrow-in-Furness. Turn off the A590 at Derby Arms into Witherslack; take first left to Witherslack Church.
Terms: B & B £12–15; dinner, B & B £19.50–22.50. Set meal: dinner £7.50 (£8.50 to non-residents). Reduced rates for children sharing parents' room; special meals provided.

If no one writes about a good hotel, it may get left out next year. WRITE NOW.

WIVELISCOMBE, Somerset   Map 1

Langley House   [GFG]   *Telephone:* Wiveliscombe (0984) 23318
Langley Marsh

Francis and Rosalind McCulloch moved to this mostly Georgian country house in an untouristy truly rural part of Somerset in the mid-Seventies. They were new to the hotel business, but, if our reports are anything to go by, their success shows once again that those who have the knack of running a good hotel show it straight away; those who haven't, we believe, never will. There have been some improvements in the accommodation this past year – there are now eight rooms instead of six, including one with a 'gorgeous' four-poster. But four-posters and bathrooms *en suite* are likely to be less important than the quality of the hospitality. Most correspondents pay tribute to the warmth of the welcome at *Langley House* and the excellence of the dinners – four courses Sunday to Thursday, and five-course gourmet dinners on Fridays and Saturdays. One reader complained, having expected lower charges because of the tariff we quoted last year. It is true that the McCullochs have raised their prices considerably in the interim, and another reader raised that tricky question about value for money. These reports excepted, our readers have felt prices reasonable – and, for what they received, were truly grateful. *(D J Little, Mrs J Hackett, Mrs D C McGirr, P A Harwood, G B Sweetman)*

Open: April–October. Restaurant open all year.
Rooms: 5 double, 3 single – 2 with bath, 2 with shower; 1 four-poster bed.
Facilities: Drawing room with small bar, lounge, sun room, beamed dining room, separate TV room; small conference facilities. 3 acres landscaped grounds, stabling for 8 horses; kitchen garden. The surrounding Brendon Hills border Exmoor; riding a few minutes' away; trout fishing 2 miles. Fine walking country.
Location: On the A361 between Taunton and Bampton.
Restrictions: No children under 7.
Terms (no fixed service charge):   B & B £13.60–16.83; dinner, B & B £22–25. Set meals: lunch £5.38; dinner £8.35. Special gourmet weekends. Reduced rates for children sharing parents' room; special meals provided.

WOOLVERTON, Nr Bath, Avon   Map 1

Woolverton House   *Telephone:* Frome (0373) 830415

This solidly comfortable early Victorian country house, close to (but out of earshot of) the A36 between Bath and Frome, has had the misfortune to suffer two changes of ownership within as many years, and the new proprietors have had to face comparison with the first lot of owners who had set exceptional standards of hospitality and gastronomy. John and Jean Fairfax-Ross took over early in 1981. Reports since have been encouraging: 'A friendly welcoming intelligent and helpful service, cooking above average, a decent breakfast with excellent local bread. Well decorated and very comfortable.' *(T M Wilson)* 'The Fairfax-Rosses are putting their stamp of taste and excellence on Woolverton House and are trying hard to regain the good name which the hotel used to enjoy. They certainly deserve to. We chose it for our first wedding anniversary and were delighted. Our room was enormous, with a huge bathroom, and very

117

attractively decorated. Breakfast was absolutely delicious and most generous. Dinner, too, was a great pleasure, with a reasonably-priced wine list. The service was consistently friendly and courteous, but not at all intrusive.' *(Martin and Carol Forster)*

Open: All year. Restaurant closed Sunday evenings, also Monday evenings to non-residents.
Rooms: 7 double, 1 single – all with bath, colour TV and tea-making facilities. 3 rooms in annexe.
Facilities: Lounge, bar, restaurant. 2 acres garden. &.
Location: Just off the A36, 10 miles S of Bath.
Restriction: Dogs at owners' discretion, in bedrooms only.
Credit cards: All major credit cards accepted.
Terms: B & B (continental) £14.50–24. Set meals: English breakfast £3; dinner £9.50. Bargain winter/spring breaks and special rates for 4 days or more. Reduced rates for children.

WORLESTON, Nr Nantwich, Cheshire   **Map 2**

Rookery Hall [GFG]   *Telephone:* Nantwich (0270) 626 866

Harry and Jean Norton made their gastronomic name in the Seventies when they ran with flair and showmanship *The Plough* at Clanfield (q.v.). They moved to Cheshire in 1979 to open *Rookery Hall*, which they describe with a characteristic absence of under-statement as 'The English Château'. Its prices are at the upper end of the scale, but, as the report below indicates, visitors to *Rookery Hall* have something to write home about.

'Deep in the heart of Cheshire's farming acres lies *Rookery Hall*, rebuilt early in the 19th century as the residence of a baron. The hotel, built in "Gothic Château" style, stands well back from a quiet road in 25 pastoral acres. There is a natural pool stocked with ornamental fowl, and a splendid fountain sets off the terrace. The public rooms are spacious, with beautiful plasterwork ceilings and chandeliers, and an Adam fireplace in the salon – but yet the scale is still that of a personal home rather than that of a hotel. The dining room is a gem, panelled in polished walnut and mahogany, reflecting the warm lighting and the blazing log fire; at one end a great mirror reflects the floor-length windows at the other. The wide, gracious panelled staircase leads to bedrooms named after the months of the year, and most are as elegant as the rooms below. Our double room was at the front, and not very inspiring (a corner bath did not compensate for lack of a shower!), but every possible thing for one's comfort was included: books on the bedside table, good and varied lighting: a bowl of fruit, television – even a "Welcome to *Rookery Hall* from Jean and Harry Norton" in the shape of a quarter-bottle of champagne!

'The dinner is a six-course affair. Jean Norton prepares a mainly English cuisine imaginatively and well – her fish mousses and her light-as-a-snowflake sorbets are particularly delicious. The impeccably cooked selection of fresh vegetables comes attractively presented as a separate dish so that the main course never appears overwhelmed or overwhelming: but the cheese board (on three separate visits) was disappointing: a dull and limited choice. The wine list is on the expensive side: a few are below £10, but most are considerably more costly – rising to £120 for a 1926 Château Talbot.

'The service everywhere we found to be outstanding – anticipatory, quiet and unobtrusive, never obsequious. We found our windscreens had been cleaned of ice while we had been having breakfast, for example. Finally, Harry Norton makes a most friendly host.' *(David and Angela Stewart; also Derek Cooper, G A and E J Watt)*

Open: All year, except 25 July–9 August and 24–30 December. Restaurant closed to non-residents on Sunday/Monday and bank holidays.
Rooms: 5 double, 2 single, 1 suite (with four-poster double bed) – all with bath, direct-dial telephone, radio and colour TV.
Facilities: 2 sitting rooms, 2 dining rooms. 28 acres garden and park with croquet, putting, hard tennis court, riverside and woodland walks, fishing.
Location: If possible avoid Nantwich town centre. *Rookery Hall* is 1½ miles along the B5074 towards Winsford. This road is off the B5073 (the 'Barony' – the Chester by-pass road around the town).
Restrictions: No children under 10. No dogs.
Credit cards: Access/Mastercard, American Express, Barclay/Visa, Diners, Carte Blanche.
Terms (service at guest's discretion): B & B £30.63–48.75; dinner, B & B £46.88–65. Set meals: lunch £7.75; dinner £16.25. Bargain breaks in and out of season.

YORK, Yorkshire   Map 4

Mount Royale Hotel   *Telephone:* York (0904) 56261

Many warm endorsements for Richard and Christine Oxtoby's Victorian Gothic hotel near the racecourse, a few minutes' walk from Micklegate and ¾ mile from the Minster, recently enlarged by the acquisition of the house next door. Its chief drawback is the noise of traffic in front rooms, made worse by there being traffic lights on a hill, though mitigated by double-glazing. One of its special attractions is its swimming pool – a rare bonus in a city hotel. Some typical compliments: 'In my view, undoubtedly the best hotel in or near York. The food is of a uniformly high standard. The older bedrooms are simply but attractively furnished, and the latest ones are quite luxurious.' 'One of the best hotels of its type that I have stayed at: delicious meals served by friendly staff.' 'First-rate in its food, both for quality, quantity and price. Add to that a welcome from owners and staff, and most comfortable furnishings in the public rooms. The bedroom and bathroom were less distinguished, but still quite adequate.' *(C B Simpson, D J J Parry, Patrick Harrison, Vicky and Brian Harrison)*

Open: Mid January–Christmas Eve. Dining room closed for lunch and for Sunday dinner.
Rooms: 20 double, 2 suites – all with bath, 2 with shower, all with telephone, radio, colour TV, baby-listening, tea-making facilities. (1 room on ground floor.)
Facilities: Residents' lounge, bar, bar lounge, dining room. 2 acres grounds with heated swimming pool.
Location: On A64 from Tadcaster (front rooms have double-glazed windows). Hotel is on right just before traffic lights at junction with Albemarle Road opposite sign to Harrogate (A59). Parking for 24 cars.
Credit cards: All major credit cards accepted.
Terms (excluding service): B & B single from £24.20, double from £15 per person. Set meal: dinner £9.50. 2-day breaks £44–48 per person. Reduced rates for children.

Report forms (Freepost in the UK) will be found at the end of the Guide.

Minffordd, Talyllyn

Wales

ABERDOVEY, Gwynedd   **Map 3**

Hotel Plas Penhelig   *Telephone:* Aberdovey (065 472) 676

A small Edwardian country house, recently converted for hotel use, in the village of Aberdovey, overlooking the Dovey estuary, in the Snowdonia National Park, with seven acres of garden and seven acres of parkland. 'The hotel has a most spectacular setting, and my room was extremely comfortable, spotlessly clean and well-furnished. The dining room is charming. There's a small wine list, but well put together and good value for money. For starters, I chose cucumber and cheese mousse – delightfully refreshing, and full of crunchy cucumber. The fillet of beef Wellington was cooked to perfection. Everything else I had during my two nights' stay was equally excellent, with a most interesting selection of sweets. Only the coffee could have been better. I feel the hotel is definitely worth an entry.' *(Donald Crosthwaite; also Harry Thorne, E H Cordeaux)*

Open: All year, except 1–17 November, 24–31 December.
Rooms: 11 double – 10 with bath, 1 with shower – all with telephone and TV on request.
Facilities: Lounge/hall, drawing room, bar, dining room. 7 acres grounds with garden, putting, croquet and tennis; flyfishing, sailing, golf, pony trekking and rock climbing nearby.
Location: 5 minutes' walk from town centre; overlooking the Dovey estuary; parking for 40 cars.

Restrictions: No children under 10. No dogs in bedrooms.
Credit cards: Access/Euro/Mastercard, American Express, Barclay/Visa.
Terms (no fixed service charge): B & B £13.50–17.50; dinner, B & B £20–27. Set meals: lunch £5.90; dinner £8.50. Bargain breaks.

ABERSOCH, Gwynedd   Map 3

Porth Tocyn Hotel [GFG]   *Telephone:* Abersoch (075 881) 2966

Porth Tocyn is a very model of a good country-house hotel. It has admittedly certain natural advantages on its side, like its position on its own headland overlooking Cardigan Bay. Although its address is Abersoch, it is in fact a good two miles from the village, reached through a maze of narrow lanes. It has its own heated swimming pool and tennis court, and is surrounded by its own 25-acre farm sloping down to the shore and golf links. But its site, its views and its amenities are simply added value: what makes the hotel 'work' is the striving for all-round excellence on the part of Barbara Fletcher-Brewer and her son Nick. Their 5-course dinners have long enjoyed an excellent reputation, but we were interested to learn that the hotel is now offering a lighter dinner within the menu for those on diets or who cannot manage the larger meal: we think many guests are oppressed at the size of meals offered to them, especially at hotels which confuse quantity with quality or who stress the former because the latter isn't really their forte. We also liked the sound of the lighter lunches which Mrs Fletcher-Brewer has introduced, concentrating on cold meats and fish salads served informally in their small dining room or out in the garden or round the pool. 'Admirably equipped for the energetic, *Porth Tocyn* is equally suitable for the idle who want to bask in the peaceful ambience of the Lleyn Peninsula,' write one couple who also speak appreciatively of sitting in a comfortable bed in a light and spacious room, taking in the uninterrupted panorama of Cardigan Bay and Snowdonia as a pleasure long held in memory. The same couple were struck that the Fletcher-Brewers didn't want to see their cheque card when it came to paying their bill. They felt that they had been admitted 'to an exclusive Eden uncontaminated by the misdemeanours of the outside world'. *(Kay and Norman Brangham)*

Open: January 2–end October and Christmas (weekends only January–Easter).
Rooms: 15 double, 2 single – 15 with bath; TV on request. (3 rooms on ground floor.)
Facilities: 2 lounges, TV room, library. Garden with tennis court and swimming pool, set within the hotel's 25-acre farm; 5 minutes' walk from sea; sailing, bathing, water skiing, fishing; golf and riding nearby. &.
Location: The hotel is about 2½ miles S of Abersoch. Drive through Abersoch, passing the Sarn Bach crossroads, bear left at the next fork, then turn left at the signpost for *Port Tocyn*, and follow the road to the very end.
Restrictions: Dogs at management's discretion and in bedrooms only.
Credit cards: Access/Euro, American Express, Diners.
Terms (excluding service): B & B £14.50–23; dinner, B & B £26.10–34.60; full board £31.10–39.60. Set meals: lunch £5; dinner £11.60. Reduced rates for children.

DO IT NOW! Send us a report on the hotel you are staying in.

BONTDDU, Nr Dolgellau, Gwynedd   **Map 3**

Bontddu Hall   *Telephone:* Bontddu (034 149) 661

A fairly choice example of the Victorian Gothic, imposing from the outside, but with friendly and efficient service within. It has an exceptional situation, looking out over well-landscaped gardens to the Mawddach estuary and the Cader Idris range of mountains; a large terrace provides an agreeable position from which to admire the view while fortifying oneself with drinks and bar snacks. The hotel has been owned and personally run for 35 years by Bill Hall and his wife – which may well be a record for the Guide.

Our entry for *Bontddu Hall* last year contained this tribute: 'A superb room overlooking an estuary of dramatic scenery, very well-appointed. Staff exceptionally welcoming; the dining room staffed by a bevy of nice looking pleasant and friendly girls who, if lacking in sophistication, compensated by charm and eagerness to make their guests feel welcome. The food was excellent, with specialities of local produce, and the prices reasonable.' *(Roger Kingsley)* A German television crew, who arrived at the hotel late one night, expecting a surly reception and finding the reverse, warmly endorsed all the above – not least the value for money. *(Robert Green and others)*

Open: All year, except Christmas and New Year (but closed Sunday November–April).
Rooms: 20 double, 2 single, 4 suites – 21 with bath, 5 with shower, all with telephone and colour TV. 8 rooms in annexe. (2 rooms on ground floor.)
Facilities: 2 lounges, cocktail bar, restaurant. Well-kept garden, private path to estuary. Beautiful walks to estuary or up the mountains behind. Quiet sandy beaches nearby, also trout, salmon and sea fishing, golf, pony-trekking.
Location: Just off the A496, E of Barmouth.
Restrictions: No children under 3. Dogs at management's discretion.
Credit cards: Access, Barclay/Visa.
Terms: Rooms £7.55–19.15 per person; B & B £10–21.60. Set meals: breakfast £2.45 (continental), £4.45 (English); lunch £2.95; dinner £10.50; full *alc* approx £14. No charge for children sharing parents' room.

CRICKHOWELL, Powys   **Map 3**

Gliffaes Country House Hotel   *Telephone:* Bwlch (0874) 730 371

Gliffaes is an Italianate country house with a campanile clock tower, 3½ miles from Crickhowell itself and half a mile from the A40. One of the pleasures of a visit is the grandeur and beauty of its 27 acres of parkland and garden – 'a miniature Kew'. And there are a lot of outside activities available in the vicinity: fishing, walking, tennis, putting, croquet, golf and riding to mention only a few. But our report last year on the inside scene was ambivalent, with reports of shabbiness in the maintenance and disappointment with the meals. Mrs Brabner, who, with her husband, has been running the hotel for the past 33 years, tells us that she has spent £18,000 on improvements since last year. On the matter of the food, she feels that some readers are judging her by the wrong standards because she was formerly listed in the *Good Food Guide*: she concentrates on traditional British cooking and reckons that a former entry in our sister

Guide did her and her guests a disservice. That sounds reasonable enough, though visitors should be warned that the serve-yourself buffet varies little from day to day and reappears at Sunday supper. Here, anyway, is our latest report from a loyal *Gliffaes*-ian:

'For our money *Gliffaes* continues to be a very good "buy" indeed for a pleasant, relaxing, "away-from-it-all" break – and never more so than this year, when we arrived on the day of the Blizzard (10 bonus points at least for a place which greets you after a traumatic wet and cold 2-hour drive with "you're in time for tea" – this at ten to six, with the habitual huge spread of sandwiches, scones, cakes, biscuits, etc., etc., all still available in the lounge with its blazing log fire). Other amenities (in addition to a view of the Usk) were adequate (though they might not suit the "telephone and television in every room brigade"!) with plenty of storage space and well-placed reading lights above the beds. Tea-making facilities are available in the room – and one can happily descend to a late breakfast without being in any way made to feel guilty by the dining-room staff, who cheerfully produce "cooked breakfast", in addition to the run-of-the-mill help-yourself items, at any time up to 10 am or so. Main meals are still enjoyably above-average. The lunch-time cold table is as good as ever. Dinners were, on the whole, as a correspondent of yours previously reported, "good rather than gourmet"; we detect a slight falling off from the standards achieved some years ago, but certainly never had a bad meal or even a dull one. Elastic meal-times are one of the joys of the place. No problem if one wants to dine at 9 pm. Public rooms unchanged. They certainly can't be described as shabby or run-down, even if we wouldn't always agree with the Brabners' taste in interior decoration. Some trouble is taken to see that the lounge and drawing room are gleaming and polished, with elegant flower arrangements.' *(J & JW; also Rev D S Yerburgh, Chris and Dorothy Brining)*

Open: Mid March–end December.
Rooms: 16 double, 5 single – 11 with bath.
Facilities: 2 large sitting rooms, sun room, bar with TV, dining room, billiards room. 27 acres grounds, including 5 acres garden, with hard tennis court, putting green, croquet lawn. Own 2½-mile stretch of the river Usk with salmon and brown trout; walks, bird-watching.
Location: 2½ miles W of Crickhowell, 1 mile N of the A40.
Restrictions: No dogs in hotel, kennels available.
Terms: B & B £11.80–18.80; full board £19.90–30.10. Set meals: lunch approx £5.40; dinner approx £7.50. Special weekly rates. Weekend and midweek bargain breaks. Reduced rates for children.

DOLGELLAU, Gwynedd   **Map 3**

Golden Lion Royal Hotel   *Telephone:* Dolgellau (0341) 422 579
Lion Street

'In the holiday areas of North Wales one tends to think that hotels that are open almost all the year are only for commercial travellers. Not so the *Golden Lion Royal*. This comfortable creeper-clad coaching inn, dating from Regency times, serves very decent food and excellent wines. We had a 1977 Gewurztraminer to accompany a sophisticated stuffed egg – this sounds dull, but it gave us a clue that the Chef "knew his onions". It was followed by roast duck – as good as one gets in French restaurants, and potatoes that had that French waxy quality but were not too hard, and served with melted butter. The bedrooms were clean with comfortable beds – not soft plastic ones. There are two bars, delightfully nostalgic with old red plush, and two lounges where coffee is served with open fires. There is also a rose garden where one can have drinks in warm weather. The service was very friendly. It is in a pedestrian precinct so there is no noise, and one can park one's car next to the hotel. I stayed here 20 years ago, when the owners had just taken over and, although greatly improved in most ways, it still retains an excellent homeliness.' *(CF Colt)*

Open: All year, except 21 December–2 January.
Rooms: 24 double, 2 suites – 13 with bath, all with internal telephone and tea-making facilities, most with colour TV. 4 rooms in annexe.
Facilities: 2 lounges, TV lounge, cocktail bar, public bar, coffee shop, large restaurant, shopping precinct. Grounds of ¼ acre with rose garden. Good centre for national park; safe bathing 9 miles; salmon and sea trout fishing; walking, climbing nearby.
Location: In pedestrian precinct in old town; parking next to hotel.
Credit cards: American Express, Barclay/Visa.
Terms (excluding VAT and service): B & B £13.50–19; dinner, B & B £19.50–25; full board £23.50–29. Set meals: lunch from £5.50; dinner from £7.50; full *alc* £9. Reduced rates for children.

EGLWYSFACH, Machynlleth, Powys   **Map 3**

Ynyshir Hall Country House [GFG]   *Telephone:* Glandyfi (065 474) 209
Hotel

John and Joyce Hughes continue to receive compliments from grateful guests at their 16th-century manor house set in a renowned 10-acre garden, surrounded by the famous Ynyshir Bird Reserve and close to the estuary of the river Dovey – a particularly agreeable part of Wales, and the Snowdonia National Park is only 8 miles away. Considerable refurbishing in the public rooms has taken place this past year, and the newly decorated dining room has been appreciated. From one report, it is clear that not all the bedrooms are in equally good nick; we hope that their turn for redecoration will come next year. The cooking of the chef, David Dressler, who is a vegetarian though the menus are not, has, for the most part, been warmly praised too. We offer one typical report:
    'We went there the weekend after Easter, and were looked after quite superbly. During our three-night stay – until the final evening – we were the *only* guests. All the same the attention we got was *beyond* the line of duty – even to both father and son donning dinner jackets on successive nights just to serve us in the bar. (We regretfully were only clean and tidy!) There was the feeling that the whole family were pulling together and absolutely dedicated to making one feel happy and cosseted. The dinner and breakfasts were a delight and I wish our appetites had been larger. I was amazed to see it so empty, but hope this is rare. They really deserve to succeed.' *(Lady Elstub; also A R Taylor, Barry and Margaret Caidan, TGP and others)*

Open: All year, except last 3 weeks in January.
Rooms: 8 double, 3 single – 6 with bath, 4 with shower.
Facilities: 2 drawing rooms, cocktail bar, dining room. 10 acres garden with flowering shrubs. 5 miles from sea with sandy beach.
Location: Just off the A487 6 miles S of Machynlleth.

Restrictions: No dogs in public rooms.
Credit cards: All major credit cards accepted.
Terms: Dinner, B & B £25–32.50. Set meals (excluding 10% service charge): lunch £6.95; dinner £10. Reduced rates for children.

LLANBERIS, Gwynedd Map 3

Gallt y Glyn Hotel   *Telephone:* Llanberis (028 682) 370

An unpretentiously sympathetic small hotel just outside Llanberis, and about ten minutes by car from Caernarvon. The prices are modest, and we are glad to know that Mr and Mrs Maslon-Jones do not propose to raise them for 1982. Since last year they have added a Buttery serving light snacks and an 'Alpine Dormitory' for 6 children. Two visitors who spent Christmas at *Gallt y Glyn* wrote independently. One said: 'Without doubt, the most friendly small hotel that my wife and I have ever visited.' The other wrote: 'It is, without doubt, the most friendly, hospitable, well-appointed and well-fed hotel I have ever visited.' Without knowing whether this belongs to the department of coincidence or not, it is clear from other reports that – though the hotel is not in the three-star class – the Maslen-Jones' informal hospitality, and their cooking, are continuing to give general satisfaction. *(John Boaden, A J Berrington, J K Van Denberg, Mr and P D Brown)*

Open: All year.
Rooms: 10 double (3 of which are family) – 3 with shower, all with radio and baby-listening.
Facilities: Buttery, TV lounge, bar lounge, dining room. 1 acre gardens.
Location: ½ mile out of Llanberis on the A4086 road to Caernarvon.
Restriction: No dogs.
Credit cards: All major credit cards accepted.
Terms (excluding service): B & B £11–13.50; dinner, B & B £15.50–18. Set meals: breakfast £2.25; lunch £4.65; dinner £6.25; full *alc* £10. Weekend and midweek bargain breaks. Dormitory £3, linen extra. Reduced rates for children.

LLANBERIS, Gwynedd Map 3

Glyn Peris   *Telephone:* Llanberis (028 682) 508

'When the *Gallt y Glyn* (above) is full, the proprietors refer you to Pat and Alec Turner's guest house, *Glyn Peris*, 100 yards along the A4086; Mrs Turner, in turn, will arrange your dinner reservations at the *Gallt y Glyn*. We felt that the combination of dinner at one and accommodation at the other was the best of all possible worlds. The Turners have spent recent years renovating a large, comfortable house "from the slate up". At present they have three enormous guest bedrooms (one with private shower), each with a big double bed and one or two single beds and beautifully furnished; shower rooms ditto. To say the house is spotless would be an under-statement. The Turners are hospitable: they are happy to go over sightseeing plans with you in their attractive sitting room and are delighted to have children as guests (they have two polite and sociable small boys). Breakfasts are large and very good. I would have no hesitation about recommending this gem of a guest house to anyone, especially in view of their very modest tariff.' *(Cate Duggar)*

Open: All year, except 1 week at Christmas.
Rooms: 3 family bedrooms – 1 with bathroom, the other 2 share bath. (5 more bedrooms in process of being renovated.)
Facilities: Breakfast room; small garden.
Location: 7 miles from Caernarvon; 1 mile from Llanberis.
Terms (no service charge): B & B £5.50–8. Reduced rates for children.

LLANGADOG, Dyfed   Map 3

Glansevin Hotel [GFG]   *Telephone:* Llangadog (055 03) 238

A three-storey Georgian mansion in the heart of rural South Wales, just off the A40. Like many other virtuous country-house hotels, it is furnished with austere good taste, with some lovely old furniture, cheerful log fires in winter – and, one benefit from its 18th-century origin, unusually large bedrooms, some with baths *en suite*. But the distinguishing feature of this hotel is its national character. Wil and Gwenda Rees are both bilingual, and make a feature of serving special Welsh dishes at meals, and memorably substantial Welsh teas. The most Welsh thing of all is the *Hwyrnos* or Welsh singing supper celebrated from Wednesdays to Saturdays in summer and on Fridays and Saturdays the rest of the year. *Cawn Cynhaeaf* or Harvest Stew is the chief item on the menu, with wholemeal bread, Caerphilly cheese and a Welsh apple pudding to follow, washed down, as they say, with beer or cider. Harp-playing, of course, but also clog-dancing and singing.

'The commercial basis of the enterprise no doubt is the *Hwyrnos*, a 19th-century entertainment of good cultural standard accompanied by simple food and drink; I have enjoyed it twice, but I write to commend the quiet comfort and excellent and soigné cooking of the (separate) eight-bedroomed hotel part. Wil, who is an Oxford graduate, and Gwenda who broadcasts, took up the business in order to bring up their children in a Welsh speaking area. I love the place. They have Loire wines which they fetch themselves annually.' *(H ap R; also J & JW and others)*

Open: All year, except Christmas, but advance booking advisable November–Easter.
Rooms: 8 double – 2 with bath, 2 with shower. No specific baby-listening service, but staff within earshot.
Facilities: Reception hall/lounge, bar/lounge, dining room. 4 acres grounds, partly wooded, with pleasant walks; children's play area; fishing, shooting. 'Rural silence may well disturb town dwellers,' say the proprietors; the nightlife – Welsh singing suppers – is in a separate wing.
Location: Just off the A40, halfway between Llandovery and Llandeilo. From the village square take the A4069 towards Llandovery (it passes between the Black Lion and the Mace foodstore.) In 100 yards branch right on to minor road to Myddfai. Carry on straight about 1½ miles. *Plas Glansevin* is on right.
Restriction: No dogs.
Credit cards: All major credit cards accepted.
Terms: B & B £13.25–19.25; dinner, B & B £21.50–30.50. Set meals: Sunday lunch £6.25; dinner £6.25–8.75; full *alc* £9. Special winter weekend rates. 50% reduction for children sharing parents' room.

'Full *alc*', unless otherwise stated, means a three-course dinner with half a bottle of house wine, service and taxes included.

Meadowsweet Hotel   [GFG]   *Telephone:* Llanrwst (0492) 640 732
Station Road

Until recently this Victorian terrace house on the outskirts of the market
town of Llanrwst overlooking the Conwy valley has been known chiefly as
an excellent restaurant, but recent major conversions by John and Joy
Evans have promoted it to hotel status. Here is a report from a keen
regular:
 'My fourth visit. Food as excellent as ever, and the addition of the new
bar for pre-meal drinks added to the pleasure. However, the extension to
the hotel and upgrading of all the rooms turns *Meadowsweet* into a quite
excellent all-round establishment. The accommodation is charming and
tasteful and clearly done with much thought for the comfort of the guests.
Good value for money.' *(Anthony Wallace)*

Open: All year. Restaurant only serves breakfast and dinner November–Easter,
except Christmas Day.
Rooms: 10 double – all with shower, telephone and mono TV.
Facilities: Bar lounge, residents' lounge, dining room. Salmon fishing, horse-
riding, golf within easy reach; 20 miles from North Wales coast.
Location: ½ mile from town centre; car park.
Restrictions: Dogs by prior arrangement only.
Credit cards: Access/Euro/Mastercard, American Express, Barclay/Visa.
Terms: B & B £10–15; dinner, B & B £18.50–24. Set meals: lunch £4.50; dinner
£9; full *alc* £11.50. Reduced rates and special meals for children.

Plas Maenan Hotel   *Telephone:* Dolgarrog (049 269) 232

'I have stayed at *Plas Maenan* several times, including when it was first
opened, and I could never understand why it wasn't raved about in *any*
guide. What more can you ask than a lovely house with breathtaking
views and unusual delicious Welsh cooking. It puts most English hotels to
shame.' *(Diane Latham)*
 In fairness to our competition, *Plas Maenan*, which first opened its
doors as 'The Welsh Hotel' in 1973, *does* appear in several other guides. It
has a choice position overlooking the Vale of Conwy and Snowdonia, and
its efforts are bent on providing visitors with a true taste of Wales. The
staff are largely bilingual, and the decor and cooking both have Welsh
ingredients. Not everyone, it needs to be said, is complimentary about the
cooking – some have found it unimaginative, with the desserts better than
starters and entrées. Harsh lighting in public rooms has also been commented on. The sound of harp and traditional singing are heard at regular
Noson Lawen or Welsh evenings held most weekends throughout the
year.

Open: All year.
Rooms: 14 double, 1 suite – all with bath, telephone, mono TV, tea-making
facilities and baby-listening.
Facilities: Lounge, 2 bars, restaurant and banqueting hall. 17 acres grounds; fine
views; excellent walking; fishing in the Conwy river. Bodnant Gardens (open to
public) 3 miles; Conwy Castle 8 miles. Nearest beach 10 miles.

Location: About half way between Betws-y-Coed and Conwy on the A470. 3½ miles from Llanrwst.
Restriction: No dogs.
Terms (no service charge):   B & B £13.85–17.85; dinner, B & B (2-day package) £14.75–18.75. Set meals: lunch from £3.75; dinner from £5.95; full *alc* £9. Special rates for off-season short stays and 7-night stays in high season. Free accommodation for children sharing parents' room.

LLANTHONY, Abergavenny, Gwent   Map 3

Abbey Hotel   *Telephone:* Crucorney (087 382) 487/559

'This is a rare and remarkable hotel, which offers excellent value. I unhesitatingly recommend it,' writes a correspondent, underlining this conclusion in red to press home the point. Having sampled for ourselves Susan and Lawrence Fancourt's romantic hospitality this past year, we unhesitatingly agree. This small unworldly hostelry – not really a hotel, nor a guest house, nor a restaurant with rooms, but *sui generis* – is part of the west range of a now mostly ruined 12th-century Augustinian priory in the wildly beautiful Black Mountains. There are just four bedrooms, reached by a Norman spiral staircase – 62 steps to the top and no lift – nor, for that matter, any H & C or central heating; from the top room, it's a long climb down to the shared bathroom and loo, but chamber pots (an almost vanished domestic convenience) are provided. Modest accommodation perhaps, but the prices (see below) are *exceptionally* modest by 1982 standards. And the meals, in contrast to the rooms, are anything but spartan. Susan Fancourt is American, but her cooking is excitingly eclectic, offering a number of Welsh specialities but also dishes from Morocco, Mexico, Portugal and Japan – and several vegetarian dishes too. In our entry last year, we mentioned that you may find yourselves with nylon sheets, and that early morning tea is not offered. Susan Fancourt replies: 'Your comment is quite fair, but tea is available if requested the night before. We set up a serve-yourself tea and coffee tray in the dining room. This is always available in the afternoon for residents FREE OF CHARGE. It is difficult for my husband to deliver pots of tea up the Norman spiral staircase in the morning because he is baking fresh bread from 6 am and it needs constant attention. We supply cotton sheets now for anyone staying two or more nights and always if people request them before they arrive. Thank you for continuing to place us in the Guide even though we are rather odd.' *(D J Penny, Maggie Angeloglou, HR and others)*

Open: Easter–end December. Restaurant closed Sunday and Monday night except bank holidays (bar snacks available).
Rooms: 4 double – no H & C, no central heating.
Facilities: Cellar bar, dining room. A place for tranquillity in fine walking country; hill-climbing in the Black Mountains and Brecon Beacons National Park; pony-trekking centres nearby.
Location: 12 miles N of Abergavenny, by the B4423 (off the A465), which follows the river Honddu.
Terms (excluding VAT and service):   B & B £7–8.50. Full *alc* £9.75. Reduced rates for children sharing parents' room (£4 added to room price).

> If you have difficulty in finding hotels because directions given in the Guide are inadequate, please help us to improve them.

Lake Vyrnwy Hotel   *Telephone:* Llanwddyn (069 173) 244

At first sight, *Lake Vyrnwy* seems like a thoroughly conventional kind of a hotel, but appearances are misleading. Its physical appearance is certainly conventional: it's a turn-of-the-century Tudor-style purpose-built hotel standing above the lake, which was created last century as a major reservoir for Liverpool. The hotel looks down the length of the lake on which it has trout fishing rights. What makes the hotel a rather rare species is the clear view of the owners, Mrs Moir and Colonel Sir John Baynes, as to the kind of hotel they want to run and their consistently successful efforts to maintain it as such. Their brochure says it all in three sentences: 'We try to run the hotel as much like a private house as we can. It aims at being a comfortable, old-fashioned sporting hotel and makes no concession to any modern image. The food is of the traditional country-house type, with the best possible ingredients used.' Many hotels would like to follow these guidelines; *Lake Vyrnwy* succeeds. And it should be added that the cooking here is consistently good of its kind, even though, as the brochure indicates, it rarely ventures beyond traditional English dishes. *Warning:* despite the postal address, the hotel is in Powys, some 40 miles west of Shrewsbury. *(HR)*

Open: 1 March–13 January.
Rooms: 16 double, 14 single, 1 suite – 11 with bath.
Facilities: Lift to first floor, drawing room, smoking lounge with TV, bar, bar billiards, nursery for small children's supper. 27 acres grounds with hard tennis court and games hut with ping pong. Trout fishing on Lake Vyrnwy, walking and bicycling. &.
Location: 10 miles W of Llanfyllin by the B4393, at the southern end of Lake Vyrnwy.
Restriction: Dogs in cars or kennels only, not in hotel.
Terms: B & B £11–20; full board £16–27. Set meals: lunch £4.50 (£6 on Sunday); dinner £7. Reduced rates for stays of over 4 days. Children under 10, half rate; children 10–16, two-thirds rate.

Hotel Portmeirion   *Telephone:* Penrhyndeudraeth (0766) 770228
                    Telex: 61467

This famous hotel, the architectural fantasy created by the late Clough Williams-Ellis on the edge of the estuary in Cardigan Bay, suffered a serious fire in the spring of 1981. The early Victorian main building, which contained the public rooms, restaurant and bar, and some of the accommodation, was completely gutted. Fortunately, none of the improbable Italianate cottages dotted round the estate – the buildings which made the hotel 'the sprightliest of modern English follies' (the words are Jan Morris's) – was damaged, and the hotel is still in business in a modified way despite the fairly major inconvenience that all their booking records and files have gone up in flames. Castell Deudraeth, recently opened as a conference centre, has been hastily refurbished as a restaurant and bar. At the time of going to press, no details of the accommodation and tariffs for 1982 are available.

ROBESTON WATHEN, Nr Haverfordwest, Pembrokeshire   **Map 3**

Robeston House   [GFG]   *Telephone:* Narberth (0834) 860 392

The Barretts have been at *Robeston House* for many years, and the style of their admirable restaurant and thoroughly comfortable small hotel (50 seats in the former, seven bedrooms in the latter – so they need to be put in that order) has a kind of mature assurance. 'The entire function of *Robeston House*,' runs a significant phrase in their brochure, 'is under the very personal supervision of the resident owners, Graham and Pamela Barrett.' We wish that all hotels could be under someone's very personal supervision. Since last year a heated swimming pool has been added to the amenities, and we are glad to know that the vagaries of the hot water system have been fixed. One small grouse among this year's crop of compliments which we pass on to the Barretts for their consideration: 'Although Access cards are accepted, there is a notice prominently displayed that they are unwelcome. They are so advantageous for visitors making a tour that I think Mr Barrett should make up his mind either to accept them (with their known disadvantages to him) or reject them.' *(G F Davies, TGP)*

Open: All year, except Christmas Day, Boxing Day and New Year's Day.
Rooms: 4 double, 2 single, 1 suite – 4 with bath, all with tea-making facilities and colour TV.
Facilities: Lounge, lounge/bar, dining room; heated swimming pool. 5 acres gardens; outdoor service when weather permits. Salmon and trout fishing, boating, golf, riding within easy reach. Sea within 8 miles to the S.
Location: On the A40 2 miles SW of Narberth and 8 miles E of Haverford West.
Restrictions: No children under 14. No dogs, but arrangements can be made for them at nearby kennels.
Credit cards: Access/Euro (reluctantly: owners prefer cheque or cash).
Terms (excluding 10% service charge):   B & B £15–21. Set meals: lunch £6.50; dinner £9; full *alc* about £12–13.

ST DAVID'S, Dyfed   **Map 3**

Warpool Court Hotel   [GFG]   *Telephone:* St David's (0437) 720300

A cheerful friendly hotel, humming with weekend activities even in the off-season, serving uncommonly good food (generous portions too) in a large early 19th-century house overlooking St Bride's Bay. It's on the edge of the cathedral city – village really – of St David's, and with a lot to offer the visitor – uncrowded roads, spectacular cliff walks (the Pembrokeshire coastal path is a stroll away from the hotel), empty beaches. It is wonderful country for the naturalist too: three famous offshore bird sanctuaries and carpets of wild flowers in the spring. For the historically minded, there are prehistoric remains, Celtic churches and Norman castles. For the sporting, there's golf, pony-trekking, sailing, fishing (the hotel has its own boat) and surfing.

'Commended as a family hotel, but this does not mean that children rule, merely that the relaxed and informal atmosphere adds to the comfort provided by very good service. Our room was spacious, light, airy and warm. The food was good on the whole, sometimes very good, though the coffee remained poor, especially at dinner; it was better at breakfast, a meal which yielded a wide choice, freshness and generous helpings. The gardens are pleasant, the heated swimming pool a great bonus, and the location, for dedicated coast walkers and sea-gazers, is superb.' *(Valerie and Harry Land)*

Open: All year, except January.
Rooms: 22 double, 3 single – all with bath or shower, radio, colour TV and baby-listening.
Facilities: 2 lounges, 2 bars, restaurant; conference room. 9 acres grounds with heated covered swimming pool; 6 beaches within 2 miles; excellent sailing; magnificent country and coastal scenery all around.
Location: Overlooking St Bride's Bay, 5 minutes from St David's.
Credit cards: Access, American Express.
Terms: B & B £17.10–19.50; dinner, B & B £23.35–26.35; full board £26.20–28.70. Set meal: dinner £8.30; full *alc* lunch £1.10–3.95; dinner £12.60. Large range of special-interest weekend and midweek bargain breaks. Children sharing parents' room: under 1, no charge; 1–4, £1 per day; 5 and over, 50%.

TALYLLYN, Tywyn, Gwynedd   Map 3

Minffordd Hotel   [GFG]   *Telephone:* Corris (065 473) 665

'*Minffordd* is a small family-run hotel, which is also our home,' writes Bernard Pickles of his former coaching inn at the foot of the Talyllyn pass, with the path to Cader Idris no more than 100 yards from the hotel door. 'We aim to provide a homely, friendly and relaxed atmosphere, with our personal care, plus the best of feshly prepared home cuisine. Every room is different and full of character, and furnished to a high standard.' Except for one couple, who complained of poor insulation to the room next door, and the misfortune to have the hotel's water supply apparently above their heads – it's extraordinary how often one seems to get that room! – our readers would entirely agree with this assessment. Here is how one enthusiast described her stay:

'A delight and well worthy of its idyllic setting. Bernard and Jess Pickles are excellent hosts. Little details such as maps and umbrellas offered without request or the special purchase of decaffeinated coffee for an insomniac guest show the *thought* that lies behind the gentle efficiency of this hotel. And the food's superb – no lunches, except packed lunches, but dinner's an occasion with delicious home-made cream soups, locally produced vegetables and imaginative sweets. The bar is restricted to diners and residents and in an emergency guests take charge. Such is the casual and trusting atmosphere! There's no newspaper delivery (the nearest village is five odd miles away), television, games room or disco, but the hotel's seclusion and lack of such facilities is its charm. Instead it affords peace, comfort and the warmest hospitality. Return visits are a must!' *(Anne Abel Smith; also Dr M G Budden, Dr Polly Hill, Julia de Waal, Angela Evans)*

Open: All year, but weekends only from November–February. Also closed New Year. Restaurant closed Sunday to non-residents.
Rooms: 6 double – all with shower. (1 room on ground floor.)
Facilities: Lounge, bar, dining room. Just over 2 acres of paddock with spectacular views of the Cader Idris southern escarpment; river at the bottom of the paddock. Situated at the foot of Talyllyn pass, ½ mile from Talyllyn lake; the peak

of Cader Idris rises from here, path to summit 100 yards away. Sea at Tywyn 12 miles; lake fishing by arrangement.

Location: Between Dolgellau (7 miles) and Machynlleth (9 miles) on the A487 at junction with the B4405.

Restrictions: No children under 3. No dogs.

Terms: B & B £14–16; dinner, B & B £17.50–24. Set meal: dinner £8. Reduced rates for stays over 5 days; 20% reduction March/April; bargain break weekends November–April. Winter midweek breaks, including 4-day courses for ladies (health and beauty, flower arranging, cookery, etc). Children 3–10, 50% discount; 10–14, 33⅓ discount.

THREE COCKS, Nr Brecon, Powys   Map 3

The Three Cocks [GFG]   *Telephone:* Glasbury (049 74) 215

This creepered 15th-century roadside inn, on the A438 between Brecon and Hay-on-Wye, has been a popular restaurant with rooms for some years past under several managements. The present owners, Barry and Jill Cole, have modernized the bedrooms (warning: front rooms are noisy), and continue to provide unusually ambitious and enterprising food, both for residents and for the gourmets of the neighbourhood. Their chief innovation has been the opening of their pub, the Old Barn Inn, opposite the hotel, serving bar snacks and light meals and also offering swings and climbing frames and trestle tables in the pub's large garden. 'A beautiful building, steeped in history, comfortable and clean. The staff are pleasant to children. The meals are thoughtfully and adventurously prepared, and the restaurant is spacious and romantic, with candlelight and a wall of leaded glass doors overlooking a peaceful garden.' *(Cate Duggar)*

Open: November–March. Restaurant closed lunch-time.

Rooms: 6 double, 1 single.

Facilities: Lounge with TV, public bar, restaurant-bar, restaurant. 7 acres grounds with outdoor playground; fine walking country; fishing and pony-trekking nearby.

Location: On the A438 between Hay-on-Wye (7 miles) and Brecon (12 miles).

Restrictions: No dogs in public rooms.

Credit cards: All major credit cards accepted.

Terms: B & B £11.50–13; dinner, B & B £21.45–22.95. Set meal: dinner £8.95. Reduced rates for children sharing parents' room.

WHITEBROOK, Nr Monmouth, Gwent   Map 3

The Crown   *Telephone:* Monmouth (0600) 860 254

We had an entry for *The Crown* in 1978 and 1979, when this cosy 17th-century inn in a steeply wooded valley a mile from the river Wye achieved fame – it was the only Michelin-starred restaurant in Wales – with Sonia Blech in charge of the kitchens. When the Blechs returned to London, the hotel was dropped from these pages. We are glad to welcome it back this year, with *The Crown* in the hands of the brothers Jackson. John Jackson is the maitre d'hôtel and sommelier, David Jackson the chef de cuisine, and they describe their establishment as a restaurant with rooms in the traditional French manner.

'A lovely pub remodelled charmingly as a ground floor bar and restaurant with rooms over. The food was out of this world, well-served in most elegant surroundings. They do an excellent two-day break in winter. Only fault: rooms, though well-fitted, are small.' *(S Burden)*

Open: All year, except 25–26 December.
Rooms: 7 double, 1 single – 6 with bath, 2 with shower, all with radio and baby-listening.
Facilities: Bar/lounge, restaurant. 2 acres grounds.
Location: Travel west on the M4, take the first exit after crossing Severn Bridge, follow signs for Monmouth (A466) through Tintern and Llandogo. At Bigsweir Bridge, bear left for Whitebrook. *The Crown* is 2 miles up a narrow country lane.
Credit cards: All major credit cards accepted.
Terms: B & B £14.25–20; dinner, B & B £25–30. Full *alc* £14. Winter breaks available October–April. Lecture/wine tasting weekends arranged during winter.

WOLFSCASTLE, Dyfed   Map 3

Wolfscastle Country Hotel   *Telephone:* Treffgarne (043 787) 225

Halfway between Haverfordwest and Fishguard, and thus very near the end of the long winding A40, Wolfscastle would be a good centre for touring the south-east corner of Wales if you didn't mind staying about eight miles inland from the coast. 'We aim at attracting, hopefully, everyone,' writes the resident director, Andrew Stirling, hopefully, 'but mainly people who have good eating and drinking in mind and possibly take advantage of our sporting facilities.' The latter refers to the hotel's two squash courts as well as a tennis court, which can be used free of charge by hotel guests. Andrew Stirling himself is a qualified coach who is always willing to play a guest in the absence of another partner. 'Quiet, despite main road, well-appointed, friendly, with good service. Food particularly good and house wine (Argentine red) smooth but of strength. In a week's tour of places, this was the best value for money – and incidentally the cheapest.' *(S W Burden)*

Open: All year, except 4 days at Christmas.
Rooms: 7 double, 2 single, 2 suites – 7 with bath, all with colour TV.
Facilities: Lounge, bar lounge, dining room. Garden, tennis court, 2 squash courts. Good area for windsurfing, riding, walking, bird watching, sailing, fishing and golf.
Location: Midway between Fishguard and Haverfordwest, just off the A40.
Credit cards: Access, Barclay/Visa.
Terms (excluding service): B & B £11.75–13.25; dinner, B & B £19.75–21.25. Full *alc* £11. 10% discount for stays of over 3 days or for parties of 4 or over. Prices negotiable for winter weekends. Squash coaching holidays several times a year. Reduced rates for children; special meals on request.

LATE (COURT) NEWS. As we go to press we learn that Rosanna Lloyd, the Hotel's head chef, is leaving to become the Prince and Princess of Wales's first cook-housekeeper.

Banchory Lodge, Banchory

Scotland

Summer Isles Hotel   [GFG]   *Telephone:* Achiltibuie (085 482) 282

One of the questions we ask in our questionnaire concerns facilities available in the vicinity. '24,000 acres of mountain behind the hotel,' was proprietor Robert Irvine's answer. The hotel is so keen to encourage walkers that it sets out a collection of tried and favourite walks, varying in length from three to 30 miles, beside every guest's bed – a pleasant contrast to many hotels, even in marvellous walking country, where a request from the reception desk for advice about a good walk or even a local map, will be met with a nil response. The brochure rubs home the point: 'Bring wellington boots and sensible shoes – and sunglasses, midge cream, cameras, paintboxes, binoculars, Thermos flasks and comfortable old clothes.' Not that walking is the only activity in this exceptionally remote and rugged part of Scotland. There's a shingle beach just by the crofts and empty bathing beaches two or three miles away. There's birdwatching, deer-stalking and climbing, and sea and brown trout fishing as well as sea angling. That might suggest that the hotel is essentially a spartan establishment dedicated to active pursuits only. Far from it. The surprising feature of the hotel is that it is as committed to fine cooking as it is to its beautiful wild landscape. It has its own smokehouse, and its menus are made up almost entirely of its own or locally produced products – free-range chickens, beef, pork venison, plus a variety of fish. One visitor this past year was disappointed with the cooking which he felt was over-priced for what was offered. Another had a different complaint: he felt the hotel favoured its Sassenach visitors over the Scottish ones. But these were minority reports. A more characteristic response: 'To maintain a really high standard of cooking in such a remote area, it is necessary for the owners of this delightful hotel to grow everything possible themselves and to bake all their own bread. This they do with a will. The accommodation is modern, the decor attractive, the service impeccable and the meals top-notch.' *(Mary W Lindsay)*

Open: Easter–8 October.
Rooms: 11 double, 3 single, 1 suite – 7 with bath.
Facilities: Lounge with bar, TV lounge, small cocktail bar. 24,000 acres mountain behind the hotel; shingle beach with boats nearby; bathing beaches 2 and 3 miles away. Walking, climbing, birdwatching, sea trout and brown trout fishing, sea angling.
Location: Take the A835 N of Ullapool for 10 miles, then turn left along single-track road skirting Lochs Lurgain, Badagyle and Oscaig; 15 miles later you reach Achiltibuie.
Restrictions: No children under 8. No dogs in public rooms.
Terms: B & B £13–22; dinner, B & B £26–35. Set meal: dinner £13. Reductions for stays of 6 nights or longer.

ARDNAMURCHAN, Argyll

Map 5

Glenborrodale Castle Hotel   *Telephone:* Glenborrodale (097 24) 266

We had an entry for this fairy-tale castle (a 19th-century fairy-tale, however) set in 150 acres on the shores of lake Sunart in the 1980 edition, but dropped it last year – not because of any adverse reports, but simply for lack of feedback. It is in fact on the westernmost tip of the British mainland – not on anyone's route to somewhere else. Shortly before we began to prepare the 1982 edition, we heard again from the reader who had first nominated the hotel; he was making a fresh tour of the Highlands and would report again. Here are his findings:

'I can only repeat most of what I originally wrote. The hotel is in excellent hands under Brian Rahilly, who has been here five years, and run by a very helpful staff – the waitresses and chambermaids being new, young, fresh, pretty, and if not expert at least sincere and unassuming. The hotel itself has all the facilities to make one's break restful and comfortable – tele, radios and tea-making facilities in the rooms, etc. The views are still "out of this world" on to lake Sunart and thereabouts, and we even saw some deer fleetingly in the hotel grounds. It's a great place for walking and comparatively cheap under the special terms of Trust Houses Forte. It is sad that we were nearly the only ones in residence in early May. The hotel has been having a rough time in the last two years. It will be frightful if such places fall by the wayside.' *(W R Needs)*

Open: March–November.
Rooms: 13 double, 5 single, 5 family – 2 with bath, all with telephone, radio, colour TV, tea-making facilities and baby-listening. 3 rooms in annexe.
Facilities: Lounge, cocktail bar, dining room. 150 acres grounds with putting green and croquet lawn. Boat hire nearby; fishing by arrangement.
Location: On the B8007 W of Salen.
Credit cards: All major credit cards accepted.
Terms: Rooms £14–21 per person; B & B £17.25–24.50; dinner, B & B £24–26. Special bargain breaks. Children £1 per night if sharing parents' room; 75% of full rate in room of their own; special meals provided.

ARDUAINE, by Oban, Argyll   Map 5

Loch Melfort Hotel   *Telephone:* Kimelford (085 22) 233

Just off the coast road between Oban (19 miles) and Lochgilphead, with
spectacular views south across to Jura and Scarba. What was originally a
characteristic lochside house has been converted into a small modern
hotel, with a motel-like extension of rooms with windows opening on to
balconies and patios. It has been owned and run for the past 15 years by
Jane and Colin Tindal; Colin Tindal is the Vice-Commodore of the
Highland Yacht Club, and the hotel is very popular with the sailing
fraternity who come ashore in the summer for drinks and meals. There is a
particularly attractive modern dining room with views over the loch; there
are loch Fyne kippers for breakfast and always some local seafood on
offer on their three-course set dinner menu. 'Jane and Colin Tindal are
excellent hoteliers and provide comfort and good food. An ideal hotel for
the family with sailing interests.' *(John Cooper; also Derek Cooper)*

Open: Easter–late October.
Rooms: 27 double, 1 single – 23 with bath. 20 rooms in annexe. (Some rooms on
ground floor.)
Facilities: Lounge, 2 bars, restaurant. 50 acres grounds on the loch. Yacht for
charter. &.
Location: 18 miles from Lochgilphead, 19 miles from Oban.
Credit cards: Access/Euro, American Express.
Terms (no fixed service charge):   B & B (continental) £15–20. Set meals: English
breakfast £2; dinner £10. Reduced rates for children sharing parents' room; special
meals provided.

AUCHENCAIRN, by Castle Douglas, Dumfries and Galloway   Map 5

Balcary Bay Hotel   *Telephone:* Auchencairn (055 664) 217

'A much modernized smuggler's house built right on (i.e. 20 feet from)
the Solway Firth. Everything shows the touch of a professional, but that
does not mean the hotel is impersonal. Everyone is very friendly and they
do their best to make sure the guests want for nothing. There is a
magnificent billiard table. But the scenery is really what makes this hotel
so special. It is at the very end of a road that leads nowhere and is
surrounded on three sides by hills and on the fourth by the sea. The
restaurant is good but could be much better. The general impression is
that the cook tries to do more things than he ought and the result is that
nothing is done as well as it could be. But the fish is good – a local
fisherman brings in whatever he can get every morning.' *(Michael Ridout)*

Open: 1 March–end November.
Rooms: 8 double, 2 single, 1 suite – 4 with bath, 1 with shower, all with telephone,
tea-making facilities and TV on request.
Facilities: Large oak-beamed lounge, smaller lounge with TV, cocktail bar, cellar
lounge bar, dining room, billiard room. 4 acres grounds. On Balcary Bay, rocky
beach with some sandy areas; boating trips arranged.
Location: Auchencairn is a small village off the A711 (Dalbeattie–Kirkcud-
bright). Hotel is 2 miles from village.
Restriction: No dogs in public rooms.

Credit cards: All major credit cards accepted.
Terms: B & B £15–22; dinner, B & B £22.50–29.50; full board £26.50–33.50. Set meal: dinner £8.50; full *alc* £12. Special winter rates November–March at 5% discount for stays longer than 3 days. Reduced rates and special meals for children.

BANCHORY, Kincardineshire   Map 5

Banchory Lodge Hotel   *Telephone:* Banchory (033 02) 2625

A well-bred Georgian building in a felicitous position, close to the confluence of the Dee and the Water of Feugh, and with fishing rights in the water directly opposite the hotel. It's naturally popular with the fishing fraternity, but there are also three good golf courses within easy reach, and magnificent walking and climbing to be had in the vicinity of Deeside. And the house itself, full of Victorian and Edwardian furniture and bric-a-brac lovingly collected over the years by the resident owners, Mr and Mrs Jaffrays, is a friendly place – with flower arrangements and open fires and other signs of welcome to guests. The food is commended – especially local products like Spey salmon, and good quality beef – and most particularly an enormous and celebrated Sunday evening cold buffet. *(Derek Wylie, DC)*

Open: February–mid December.
Rooms: 30 double, 3 single – 27 with bath, 1 with shower, 8 with TV, all with radio, tea-making facilities and baby-listening. 6 rooms with bath in annexe. (1 room on ground floor.)
Facilities: 2 large lounges (1 with colour TV) overlooking the river, bar, dining room. 12 acres grounds; salmon and trout fishing on the river Dee. Golf courses at Banchory, Aboyne and Ballater; tennis, putting, bowling at Banchory; Glenshee ski slopes an hour's drive west.
Location: On the A93 east of Aboyne.
Credit cards: American Express, Barclay/Visa.
Terms (excluding VAT): B & B £16.50–19.25; dinner, B & B £21.45–23.65; full board (minimum 3 nights) £24.75–27.50. Set meals: lunch £5; dinner £10.50. Reduced rates and special meals for children.

BEATTOCK, Moffat, Dumfriesshire   Map 5

Auchen Castle Hotel   *Telephone:* Beattock (068 33) 407
                                         Telex: 777205 Auchen

'I have stayed at this excellent hotel on five or more occasions in the last three years. The very high standard of courtesy, service and cuisine has been fully maintained. Although these visits have been widely spaced, I am always remembered and well looked after. The small wine list is carefully chosen and compliments the cooking.' *(R W Lloyd-Davies; also S Garman)*

    The hotel to which this commendation refers is a slightly stern-looking greystone mansion a mile out of Beattock, built in 1849 by the William Younger family. It has been a hotel only since the last war, and has an annexe built 15 years ago with rooms somewhat cheaper than in the main house. There are 17 acres of garden and grounds overlooking the upper Annandale, and the hotel has its own trout-stocked loch.

Open: All year, except 20 December–1 February.
Rooms: 20 double, 2 single, 3 suites – 12 with shower, all with radio, colour TV and baby-listening. 10 rooms in annexe.
Facilities: Lounge, TV lounge, bar, dining room; private party dining room/ conference room; Saturday dinner-dance October–March. 17 acres grounds with trout-stocked loch with boat. River Annan provides fishing for salmon, trout, sea trout. Golf, riding, tennis, sailing nearby.
Location: 1 mile N of Beattock village with signed access from the A74.
Credit cards: All major credit cards accepted.
Terms: B & B £7.90–20. Set meal: dinner £5.90 or £8. Special 'Border Breaks' and 'Dine, Dance and Stay-the-Night' rates. Reduced rates and special meals for children.

BRIDGE OF ORCHY, Argyll   Map 5

Inveroran Hotel   *Telephone:* Tyndrum (088 34) 220

Two tributes which between them catch the flavour of this modest in price but highly sympathetic old coaching inn set on the edge of Loch Tulla and surrounded by high hills – marvellous walking and climbing country (it is now on the West Highway Way, a very popular walk), not to mention fishing on river and loch, swimming in loch and burn or bird-watching. 'My wife and I, who want to enjoy the mountains and glens in peace and quiet, found this hotel just perfect for us. A gem! Such a joy to return after a day's outing on the mountains to welcoming fires in the two lounges, a big supper and adequate choice of drinks. We agree with Kate Fleming that it is the best hotel we have ever stayed in. We sincerely hope that Margaret Gravell will make no changes to her unique hotel. Her kindness and attention to our needs are a joy.' *(John and Priscilla Gillett)*
    'I needed a quiet place to recuperate, and this was an ideal choice. The food is ample and superb. Good Scottish meat, excellently cooked, wonderful home-made soups and inventive desserts made every dinner memorable. And at the price, their 5-course dinner must be one of the bargains of the Guide! It doesn't pretend to be a luxury hotel – no TV or telephones in the rooms (for which, personally, I am grateful), but in its own category I really couldn't fault it.' *(Carl A Grundy)*

Open: All year, except mid November–mid December and Christmas.
Rooms: 6 double, 2 single – all with tea-making facilities. (1 room on ground floor.)
Facilities: 2 lounges, bar, dining room. Spontaneous *ceilidhs* (Scottish song and dance). 1 acre garden. Safe bathing in the loch, boats for fishing; salmon and trout on the river Orchy, and several hill lochs; splendid scenery – fine walking and climbing country; skiing in winter nearby. ৬ .
Location: 3 miles from Bridge of Orchy (railway station).
Restriction: No children under 5.
Terms (excluding service): Dinner, B & B £13.50. Set meal: dinner £6.50. Reduced rates for children sharing parents' room; special meals provided.

In your own interest, do check latest tariffs with hotels when you make your bookings.

Ardfenaig House   *Telephone:* Fionnphort (06817) 210

'We stumbled on this little haven of civilized tranquillity on Mull by chance at the beginning of our holiday and only regretted that our budget prevented our abandoning our tour of the Islands and staying put! The house stands at the head of a small loch and is approached by a very long lane so the feeling of peace and remoteness is complete. The house is not distinguished architecturally, but is set in a delightful garden and inside is furnished and decorated with exquisite taste and lovely old furniture and paintings, obviously from the family homes of the two' owners, Robin Drummond-Hay and Ian Bowles. There are only five rooms for guests who share three bathrooms, and it all felt more like a house party than a hotel. We were reminded of childhood visits to grandparents, in an age before inflation had made such luxurious living impossible. Our bedroom was so beautifully and comfortably furnished (with a rocking chair and books too) that it was almost a wrench to go downstairs to the small bar and delightful drawing room (complete with grand piano, all possible magazines and newspapers).

'The whole ambience of luxury, good taste and charm was amply supported by the *wonderful* food. The partners take it in turns to cook the evening meal and obviously feel a friendly rivalry, though one feels that inventiveness would never militate against good eating. There was no choice at dinner (though we were asked if we had any strong dislikes or diet requirements) and none really was necessary. Breakfasts are alternately kippers or bacon and egg, though our plates overflowed with the almost extinct "English breakfast". This is the way people can no longer afford to live, except on a very large income or by opening their home. We've never before felt so thoroughly at home – it was almost decadent, though naturally in the very best taste.' *(Lt-Cdr and Mrs R Kirby Harris)*

Open: 1 May–1 October.
Rooms: 3 double, 2 single – all with tea-making facilities.
Facilities: Lounge, music room, dining room. 16 acres grounds sloping down to loch which has shingle beach, but plenty of sandy beaches nearby. Fishing; safe bathing.
Location: 3 miles from Bunessan on the Iona ferry road. The hotel's long drive is on the right.
Restrictions: No children under 13. No dogs in public rooms.
Terms (excluding VAT and 10% service charge): Dinner, B & B £21. Set meal: dinner £8.

Riverside Inn [GFG]   *Telephone:* Canonbie (054 15) 295

'An old fisherman's retreat on the banks of the Esk which has been considerably updated in traditional style representing a surprisingly sophisticated venture in such a quiet out-of-the-way place, the only intrusion being through traffic during peak hours. The atmosphere is one of comfortable lightness; there is a small lounge/foyer, a much larger split-level bar with pale wood and traditional furniture and a very pleasant dining room. Accommodation is limited to four pleasant double rooms with bathrooms. The policy for dinner is a small menu but considerable attention to detail. There were three starters, three main courses and three sweets. The cold fresh salmon salad had been beautifully prepared and the fish was probably the most succulent that I can remember. It was accompanied by a considerable number of hot fresh vegetables and the quantities were ample. Home-made apple and sultana pie to follow was also excellent. There is not much to do except walk by the river, which is extremely picturesque, so I recommend retiring to the attractive bar and sampling Real Ale or a tot from the range of malt whiskies. Breakfast was also good with quality coffee served.' *(R A Nisbet)*

Open: All year, except first two weeks in January. Restaurant closed Sunday evening, but 3-course meals available in lounge bar.
Rooms: 4 double – 3 with bath, all with radio, mono TV and tea-making facilities.
Facilities: Residents' lounge with TV, lounge bar, dining room. Garden. Park with children's play area and tennis courts nearby; fishing permits available from hotel. A good centre for visiting Hadrian's Wall.
Location: On the B6357 just E of the A7 Carlisle to Langholm road.
Restriction: No dogs.
Terms (no service charge): B & B £15.95–18.95. Bar lunch from £1.50; set meal: dinner £8.50; full *alc* £10. Special off-peak breaks. Reduced rates for children in low season only; special meals provided.

CRINAN, by Lochgilphead, Argyll   Map 5

Crinan Hotel   *Telephone:* Crinan (054 683) 235/242
                                                     Telex: 778817

A wonderful position for any hotel, the *Crinan* stands at the north end of the famous Crinan canal which joins loch Fyne to the Atlantic. Fishing boats chug out early in the morning towards the Western Isles, and there's a constant movement of yachts bound for the Inner and Outer Hebrides. The hotel is owned and run by Nicholas Ryan, who was trained at the *George V* in Paris, and whose two passions are sailing and seafood. The place suffered a serious fire in 1978, and only reopened, decorated and refurbished with the help of the Designers' Guild and Heal's, in early 1980. There's a veranda bar on the roof, looking seawards towards the mountains of Mull and the islands of Jura and Scarba – on a still day, it's said, you can hear the distant thunder of the Corrievrechan whirlpool. There's also, in addition to the main dining room on the ground floor, an expensive restaurant in the upper storey, *Lock 16*, specialising in seafood, which shares with the roof bar a spectacular outlook.

One correspondent found the only room available was one of the 'de luxe' ones, but reckoned it was well worth paying extra for an exceptionally lovely room and an incredible view from the huge picture window. Another visitor, while appreciating the well-decorated rooms, the pleasant outlook and the young and helpful staff, felt the place somewhat lacked character and that the food in the main dining room was expensive for what was served. His booking for *Lock 16* was cancelled as no seafood was available – and he gathered from others that this was not the first time this had happened. More reports welcome.

Open: 20 March–3 October.
Rooms: 20 double, 2 single – 20 with bath, 2 with shower, 9 with private balconies, all with telephone, radio and baby-listening.

141

Facilities: Lift, 2 lounges (1 with TV), cocktail bar, roof bar, dining room, roof-top restaurant – *Lock 16* – specializing in seafood; sauna. 1 acre grounds with well-kept garden on the loch side; fishing, sailing, water-skiing.

Location: NW of Lochgilphead by the A816, then take the A841 which skirts the Crinan canal, 9 miles long and flowing into the Sound of Jura.

Credit cards: Access/Euro, American Express, Diners, Visa.

Terms (service optional): Rooms £19–20.50 per person; B & B £20.50–22. Set meals: lunch £3.50; dinner in dining room £11.

DALRY, Castle-Douglas, Kirkcudbrightshire   Map 5

Milton Park Hotel   **Telephone:** Dalry (064 43) 286/202

'Scottish house of *circa* 1860, not beautiful but solid (doors well-made, etc). Large garden. Overlooks the waters of the Ken valley. Superb views of hills, moorland, etc. Pleasantly furnished in a rather old-fashioned manner. Our bedroom had attractive art nouveau furniture and splendid Maples beds, blankets slightly worn but gave impression of staying in a private house rather than a Hilton. The Graysons who run the hotel – he did bar, she cooking – extremely pleasant. Staff delightful and willing. Food simple but excellent; no lapses, but no attempts at elaborate sauces, etc. Coffee very good. Clean damask napkins at every meal. China new and pleasant – Royal Doulton for breakfast, Spode for dinner. Other guests included several amiable fishermen (great centre for fishing) plus north-country middle-aged and some young. Atmosphere remarkably pleasant. Marvellous valley for money compared with all other hotels we stayed at in Scotland.' *(Christina Bewley)*

Thus our entry in last year's Guide, endorsed by a more recent visitor who specially recommends the Graysons' breakfast and who also mentions that you are expected to be punctual for dinner at the sound of a gong. Mr and Mrs Grayson write to say that, though their address appeared correctly in the text, the hotel was inadvertently confused on the map with Dalry in Ayrshire, 60 miles further north. We are extremely sorry about this mistake. They go on to suggest that the entry could be improved in two other respects: 'Our customers are not solely made up of "north-country middle-aged" – they are very mixed!! And we do make *some* attempt at good sauces – not elaborate – but the statement is a little misleading; it may have been a reasonably simple menu on the occasion of Christina Bewley's visit.' Having looked at our entry again, we see no reason to change it. Nor perhaps do the Graysons, for their letter ends endearingly: 'Having re-read this letter, quite frankly it is entirely up to you what you put in the text – so long as the position on the map is correct!!' Fairly said.

Open: March–October. Also open over Christmas and New Year if sufficient demand.

Rooms: 15 double, 2 single.

Facilities: Residents' lounge, TV, bar lounge, 2 dining rooms. 4–5 acres extensive landscaped garden overlooking the waters of the Ken valley. Boats available for excellent fishing on 5 nearby lochs (brown trout, rainbow trout, pike and perch); river and sea fishing close by. Tennis court; golf 3 miles.

Location: NW of St John's town of Dalry, which is on the A713, near Earlston loch.

Restriction: No dogs in public rooms.

Terms (service optional): Rooms £8.50 per person; B & B £10.97; dinner, B & B £18.98. Set meal: dinner £8. Reduced rates and special meals for children.

142

DRUMNADROCHIT, Inverness-shire   Map 5

Polmaily House   *Telephone:* Drumnadrochit (045 62) 343

'Veronica Brown, who for the last 16 years has run this rambling Edwardian country house not far from loch Ness, has converted it with great skill and sensitivity. The low-ceilinged bedrooms have been decorated with flair so that they are both restful and interesting to the eye. They all have serene views of the wooded countryside. The house is beautifully furnished with skilfully arranged bygones – not too many but enough to give the feel that this is a home and not a hotel. One of the most remarkable rooms in the house is the drawing room which was the private chapel of the previous owners. Some of the religious murals have been left as a memento of the past. This room contains a grand piano and an 1832 table-top piano which like many of the other furnishings in the house is unique. Set in 22 acres, there is total seclusion and peace – a tennis court, decayed, for the energetic, a swimming pool, clay pigeon shooting and putting can be tackled. Miss Brown will also arrange fishing. The food here is excellent and uncomplicated, with imaginative six-course dinners. Small bar, good wine list, what more can one want? No wonder AA give it the Red Star accolade.' *(Derek Cooper)*

Open: Easter–end October.
Rooms: 9 – 5 with bath, all with telephone and radio.
Facilities: Drawing room, residents' lounge, bar, dining room, reading room. 22 acres garden with tennis, unheated swimming pool, putting, clay pigeon shooting; pony trekking and fishing nearby.
Location: 17 miles from Inverness W of Drumnadrochit on the road to Cannich.
Restrictions: No children under 8. Dogs at the management's discretion.
Credit cards: Access/Euro, American Express, Barclay/Visa.
Terms (excluding VAT; no service charge): B & B £12–14; dinner, B & B £21.50–23.50. Set meals: bar lunch £2; dinner £9.50.

DUNKELD, Perthshire   Map 5

The Atholl Arms Hotel   *Telephone:* Dunkeld (035 02) 219

A well-run traditional hotel in the centre of town (though village would be the more appropriate, despite Dunkeld's cathedral), overlooking the 5-arched bridge over the river Tay which Telford built in 1809.

'The view in autumn across the wide fast-flowing Tay towards Birnam Woods is quite superb. The hotel has a most attractive entrance hall which is always full of quiet activity. American sportsmen reading the newspapers before setting out in the morning for a day's shooting, people having morning coffee or afternoon tea. Yes, afternoon tea: "Would you like tea, Mr Ferrar?" (I had not spoken to him but the proprietor had learned my name). "Some scones?" he suggested and they turned out to be real melt-in-the-mouth quality. What else? "Full afternoon tea" or sandwiches. They prompted, and in a voice like Lady Bracknell because he was a little deaf, I ordered "cucumber sandwiches, nothing else, just scones and cucumber sandwiches". My wife rebuked me because cucumbers were out of season and very expensive, but nevertheless cucumber sandwiches, and very good ones, were produced, some with brown bread and some with white. At dinner the bar was a bit bare Scottish-style, so we

143

carried our sherry through to the hall. Dinner was a pleasant surprise. Friendly and efficient waitresses of mature years knew their job and had probably been with the hotel for some time: very much in character with the clean quiet atmosphere of the whole place: not out of date but undisturbed by life. The bedroom was a little small but nice enough, and the bathroom, though not *en suite*, was very handy. The baths had lovely big taps and were big enough to lie down in. (My son's single room was more spacious with armchair and gas fire.)' (*M L Ferrar*)

Open: All year.
Rooms: 18 double, 6 single, 1 triple (quiet rooms at back of house).
Facilities: Lounge, residents' lounge with TV, bar. Grounds of ½ acre on river bank, overlooking river Tay; fishing available in the area.
Location: In town centre; parking for 20 cars.
Restriction: No dogs in dining room.
Credit cards: All major credit cards accepted.
Terms: B & B £11; dinner, B & B £17; weekly B & B £70, weekly half board £105. Set meal: dinner £6 (no service charge). 2-day break: £30. Children under 12, ¾ price; children under 6, ½ price; children under 2, free; special meals on request.

DUROR, Appin, Argyll   **Map 5**

The Stewart Hotel   *Telephone:* Duror (063 174) 268
                                                        Telex: 778297

There has been a good deal of refurbishing since last year at David and Ailsa Assenti's personally run hotel on the southern shores of Loch Linnhe, and a major change in the style of cooking, with more enterprising menus than hitherto. The report below appreciates the new more cheerful decor and offers a qualified seal of approval of the fare.

'We stayed two nights here, over Easter, and can endorse the Guide's previous good report (apart from some reservations about the food – see below). The setting is beautiful and unspoilt (the view from our bedroom window, westwards over the blue water of Loch Linnhe and the stark Morvern mountains beyond, was as good as anything in Greece), and there are wonderful walks to be had in the hills just behind the hotel. The hotel, which faces west, gets the full benefit of any sun that's around (you can sit outside on a terrace above the delightfully lush garden, to read or have a drink). Inside, it has none of the musty baronial gloom of so many Scottish houses: it is cheerfully furnished, à la Habitat, with lots of red and orange (the dining room is yellow and green, cleverly spotlit – none of those ghastly overhead chandeliers). The lounge is much more welcoming than the usual morgue. The bedrooms, in the neatly-designed modern wing, are small but comfortable, and spotlessly clean.

'*Food.* Obviously a lot of care has gone into the planning of the sophisticated dinner menus: scallops and prawns in white wine – mushrooms in garlic butter – fruit salad vinaigrette – lemon sorbet *in between courses*. It was delicious to look at as well as to eat, but the portions were very small: perhaps there's a bit too much *minceur* in this cuisine? After a day walking in the open air, one longed for something more substantial (even some proper bread instead of Melba toast!). There was the same touch of parsimony (or perhaps just good Scots housekeeping?) about breakfast: the helpings of porridge were unnecessarily small, and the kippers tiny. Otherwise, we had no complaints. The young couple who run the place have a young family of their own, which helps create a relaxed atmosphere. In short, a pleasant family hotel in an exceptionally beautiful part of the British Isles.' *(Sally Sampson)*

Open: All year, except 1 November–10 February (possibly weekends only February/March).
Rooms: 26 double, 3 family suites – all with bath, radio, tea-making facilities, baby-listening and TV on request. (16 rooms on ground floor.)
Facilities: Lounge, TV room, bar, restaurant; packed lunches. Folk singing group most weekends. 15 acres woodlands and terraced garden with many rare shrubs and plants, which leads down to the river Duror at the bottom of the garden; hotel overlooks loch Linnhe; rock beach, safe bathing 2 miles; fishing available, also riding and pony-trekking; sailing, boating, hill walking, rock climbing; skiing.
Restriction: Dogs in bedroom only, at the management's discretion.
Location: On the A828 between Oban (30 miles south) and Fort William (17 miles north).
Credit cards: All major credit cards accepted.
Terms (service at guests' discretion): B & B £11–13.75; dinner, B & B £19.50–21.75 (2 nights minimum). Set meal: dinner from £6. Special autumn and spring rates. Reduced rates and special meals for children.

EDINBURGH   Map 5

The Albany Hotel   *Telephone:* Edinburgh (031) 556 0397/8
39 Albany Street   *Telegrams:* Albanyhotel

Patrick Maridor, who is Swiss, has been the resident owner of *The Albany* since 1975, but it recently doubled in size with the purchase of adjoining houses. It is a listed building dating from 1812, carefully restored: a pedigree example of Edinburgh Georgian. Reports this year have not been unanimously positive. A lot of small things seem to have been going wrong: no bedside lamp, a defective teamaker, a morning call overlooked, and, more than once, mention of poor service in the restaurant. But – with a warning not to expect too much – we think the following view catches the flavour:

'The service was extraordinarily pleasant though very slow, particularly at breakfast. But the rooms were comfortable and pleasantly decorated and, best of all, the staff were extremely friendly and nice to the children (four, small). They gave them a very good children's supper in the bar, chatted them up and generally went out of their way to make them feel wanted and grown up. They have the Swiss wine Dole in the dining room and the food was pretty good though one could have done with a little less of the Grand Hotels. But it's a very comfortable and welcoming place and much nicer than those great barns that Edinburgh specializes in (*The North British*, etc).' *(Tim Heald; also G Rebuck)*

Open: All year.
Rooms: 21 double – 15 with bath, 6 with shower, all with telephone, radio, colour TV, tea-making facilities and baby-listening. (6 rooms on ground floor.)
Facilities: Lounge, bar, restaurant; conference facilities. 250 square metres of garden.
Location: 5 minutes from town centre; car park nearby.
Restriction: Dogs allowed in bedroom and garden only.
Credit cards: All major credit cards accepted.
Terms: B & B £14–34. Full *alc* £12. Special winter breaks. Reduced rates and special meals for children.

Prestonfield House Hotel   *Telephone:* Edinburgh (031) 667 8000
Prestfield Road   *Telex:* 727396

A noble 17th-century house, two miles from the centre of the city, standing in splendid landscaped gardens, complete with strutting peacocks. The hotel prides itself on its elegant (and expensive) restaurant, and, with its four dining rooms and various other public spaces, is a popular house for functions of all kinds. The accommodation, though far from primitive, is not quite of the same order and it is clear that the restaurant business has priority here. Nevertheless . . .

'There can be few country-house hotels in Scotland so impeccably furnished as *Prestonfield*. In the hall a leather-bound inventory (dated 1933) lists what there used to be here; if anything the contents have been improved upon. There are fine oil paintings and superbly polished furniture in the dining rooms. An aura of history fills the rooms where, among others, James II, Boswell, Prince Charles Edward Stuart and Benjamin Franklin talked. We had here one of the finest lunches we have ever taken in Scotland – perfect soup and fish. If you can get in, this is the ideal hotel to lodge in for Festival visiting.' *(Derek and Janet Cooper)*

Open: All year.
Rooms: 5 double – 4 with shower, all with telephone and tea-making facilities; baby-sitting service available.
Facilities: 2 lounges, 2 bars, 4 dining rooms; conference facilities. 17 acres grounds. Golf adjoins; excellent walks nearby.
Location: 2 miles from city centre; airport 5 miles; parking for 200 cars.
Restriction: Dogs at management's discretion.
Credit cards: All major credit cards accepted.
Terms (no service charge): B & B £30 single, £41 double. Full *alc* £19.50. Reduced rates and special meals for children.

ERISKA, Ledaig, Connel, Argyll   **Map 5**

Isle of Eriska Hotel   [GFG]   *Telephone:* Ledaig (063 172) 371
                                    Telex: 727897 DOOCOT-E attn ERISKA

We always seem to be in trouble with our entry for this castellated Victorian magnate's Highland home on an islet linked by bridge to the mainland near Oban. No one seems to be willing to take a cool dispassionate view of the place: either they love it, warts and all, or are moved to rare outbursts of disparagement, incensed partly, we imagine, by second-class performance when paying first-class prices and also no doubt by over-enthusiasm on the part of those in favour. Here is a characteristic view from one who dotes:

'The style of our bedroom could not be called elegant, though attempts had been made, but the comfort was superb. The hospitality was nothing less than outstanding: the Rev Robin Buchanan Smith and all his staff seem to thoroughly *enjoy* their guests. This, I think, explains the house-party feel of the place – one feels *invited*. The owner himself describes his food as "simple" and if one acknowledges that in many ways this is true (the dishes are "uncontrived"), it is necessary to add that it approaches the Japanese ideal of simplicity. The ingredients and the respect with which they are prepared, combined and presented, are near perfection. I don't often rave this way, but we haven't often eaten so well (outside our own home!) *(Caroline D Hamburger)*

And now for an anti-dote: 'May I enter the wars of the Isle of Eriska on the side of the antis? First, the name: lovers of Mont St Michel or Mikonos should not get their hopes raised by the word "isle". Eriska is more accurately described as a low-slung, sprawling peninsula with a slim muddy neck. There is, to be sure, breath-taking scenery in every direction – none of it, alas, on Eriska. Service was fine, and the food was never less than good – but certainly never anything more. A hotel singled out for inclusion in your Guide – even a hotel charging Eriska's steep prices – need not, of course, offer a three-star restaurant into the bargain. But if it doesn't, it must have other compensating features. Our bedroom was tiny, with a tinier closet, no adequate reading chair, and bland modern furniture. Perhaps there were other rooms more elegant than the one I had – though it is hard to imagine the same taste which was satisfied with a gimcrack replica of an overnight hotel for harried businessmen magically producing better results elsewhere . . . The Buchanan Smiths have a fine old pile, an interesting setting and a pleasant junior staff. There are indications of effort – radios in the rooms, heather on the desk, hot-water bottles – but this effort must be directed to more important matters if they are to retain – regain rather – their reputation. They have got to get their act together.'

We would not have quoted this letter at such length if it was not amply supported by the testimony of others. But Caroline Hamburger is not alone in her enthusiasm. There simply is no consensus.

Open: Beginning April – end November.
Rooms: 18 double, 6 single, 2 suites – all with bath, telephone, radio and baby-listening. (2 rooms on ground floor; ramp into house for wheelchairs.)
Facilities: Hall, outer hall, drawing room, dining room, library. Private bridge to mainland; 270 acres grounds with formal garden, park and moorland; croquet, hard tennis court, bathing from shingle beach, sea fishing, anchorage, pony-trekking. Yacht with skipper for charter. &.
Location: 12 miles N of Oban, 4 miles W of the A828.
Restrictions: No children at dinner – high tea at 5.45 pm. Dogs at management's discretion.
Credit cards: American Express.
Terms (excluding VAT): Dinner, B & B £35–44; full board £205–240 per week. Set meals: lunch (cold table) £5; Sunday lunch £10.90; dinner £13. Reduced rates for stays of over 3 days out of season. Reduced rates and special meals for children.

FORT WILLIAM, Inverness-shire   **Map 5**

Inverlochy Castle   *Telephone:* Fort William (0397) 2177/8

In our entry last year for this emphatically grand (and appropriately expensive) Victorian castle on the lower slopes of Ben Nevis, we passed on a remark made by one disenchanted visitor that the place was feudal. But we also noted that 'those who like *Inverlochy* like it exceedingly – and some go overboard'. No hint of disenchantment in our postbag this year. We offer instead the view from one of the overboarders:

'Brilliant, outstanding and utterly memorable! It cost twice as much as ————, but price is almost irrelevant. We paid the same amount in petrol just to get up there and that *was* bad value. Anyone who says it is feudal is an inverted snob. It is quite simply on a different plane to almost anything else one experiences. Everest to a mountaineer, Glyndebourne to an opera lover, Taj Mahal to an architect. Admittedly, we had good weather, but we'd go again if it was surrounded in freezing fog! Only one odd out-of-place excrescence: canned music in the lounge! But a simple request and they turned it off. Service was I think the best I have encountered anywhere.' *(S C Whittle; also G Rebuck, Dr and Mrs T Heffernan)*

Open: 5 April–5 November.
Rooms: 10 double, 1 single, 2 suites – all with bath, telephone, colour TV and baby-listening; 24-hour room service.
Facilities: Great hall, drawing room, restaurant, billiards room, table-tennis room; facilities for small (25) conferences out of season. 50 acres grounds with all-weather tennis court; trout fishing on nearby private loch; several golf courses within easy driving distance; pony-trekking; chauffeur-driven limousines can be hired.
Location: Take turning to NW off the A82, 3½ miles N of Fort William. Guests met by arrangement at railway station or airport.
Restriction: No dogs.
Credit cards: American Express, Barclay/Visa.
Terms: B & B £45–65. Set meals: lunch £12; dinner £21. Children half price; special meals provided.

GIGHA, Isle of, Argyll　　　　　　　　　　　　　　　　　　**Map 5**

Gigha Hotel　　　　　　　　　　　*Telephone:* Gigha (058 35) 254

The little island of Gigha (pronounced Gee-ah, with the first G hard) is only 6 miles long by 1½ miles wide, and lies 3 miles off the Argyll peninsula. Thanks to the North Atlantic Drift, it enjoys a mild climate, and being largely flat, doesn't get as much rain as its hillier neighbours. Its chief glory is the ravishing 50-acre garden of Achamore House, created by the island's late owner, Sir James Horlick (he of the malted-milk nightcap). Garden lovers will make a pilgrimage to Gigha for the gardens alone, but the island, with an offshore population of about 200, also offers coves and caves and white sandy beaches. No one in his senses brings a car over, but you can hire bicycles. The *Gigha Hotel* is the old inn of the island, in its only village of Ardminish, looking out over the sound to the hills of Kintyre on the mainland. It was restored and substantially enlarged a few years ago, but it still retains its traditional facade with dormer windows and slate roof.

A recent correspondent, who visited the hotel largely because of our previous entry, which described it as 'a gem', writes: 'We found the hotel delightful, clean and friendly. The room had a lovely view over the bay. The food is simple but wholesome, and the home-made bread a pleasant start to the meal. Service was good and willing, and the wine list adequate. We hope to return next year.' *(R A Hood)*

Open: All year, except Christmas and New Year.
Rooms: 9 double – 3 with bath. 2 rooms in cottages.
Facilities: 2 lounges (1 with TV), public bar, restaurant; some conference facilities. ¼ acre garden. 300 yards from the sea with white sand and rocks and safe bathing; sea fishing arranged with local fishermen. Achamore Gardens (open April–September) 1 mile.

Location: A83 to Loch Fyne, through Tarbert; S for 17 miles to Tayinloan, and turn right for Gigha Ferry.
Restriction: Dogs allowed 'if well-behaved'.
Terms (service at guests' discretion):   B & B £13.50; dinner, B & B £22; full board (minimum 4 nights) £22. Set meals: lunch £4.50, dinner £8.50. Reduced rates and special meals for children.

GULLANE, East Lothian   Map 5

Greywalls Hotel   *Telephone:* Gullane (0620) 842144
Muirfield   *Telex:* PREHTL 727396 (Attention Greywalls)

A stylish rural alternative to staying in Edinburgh, especially for golfers. There's a tennis court and a croquet lawn at *Greywalls*, but the chief outdoor attraction of the hotel is the four acres of beautiful formal walled garden and the adjoining Muirfield golf course. The house itself is one of those thoroughly satisfactory Lutyens country houses, built at the turn of the century in a kind of quiet good taste that continues to be respected whatever the vagaries of architectural fashion. The furnishings are all of a piece with the house.

'It is rare to find a place where, from the time your luggage is put in your room until the moment you depart, you experience complete satisfaction and happiness. It is reassuring that such a place exists. *Greywalls* seems to "absorb" you rather than receive you. The public rooms are of the kind you find only as a rule in a private home. Log fires always burning brightly, comfort and quiet, good food. Bedrooms and bathrooms are equipped with all you could wish for. Books that you really want to read are at hand. Fresh fruit by your bedside. The house and garden were designed by the master hands of Lutyens and Gertrude Jekyll. The hotel staff are always available but unobtrusive. Fellow guests seem, in some strange way, to belong to this relaxed and happy place. To recall the time spent in this house is like a shaft of sun on a grey day!' *(Richard Webb)*

Open: Mid April–October.
Rooms: 16 double, 8 single – 19 with bath, all with telephone. 4 rooms in annexe. (Some rooms on ground floor.)
Facilities: 4 lounges, cocktail bar, restaurant; conference facilities. 4 acres formal walled garden with tennis and croquet. Sea and golf within easy reach. &.
Location: 19 miles E of Edinburgh; 1 mile inland from the sea.
Credit cards: Access/Euro, American Express, Barclay/Visa, Diners.
Terms (no service charge):   B & B £32. Set meals: lunch £5; dinner £10. Reduced rates for children and for stays of a week or more; special meals for children.

HARRIS, Isle of, Western Isles   Map 5

Scarista House Hotel   [GFG]   *Telephone:* Scarista (085 985) 238

'What a find. A former Georgian manse, done up by the young present owners, Andrew and Alison Johnson, overlooking a magnificent Atlantic beach. Delightful public rooms: an upstairs sitting room and downstairs a library with the owners' books available for browsing. Both these rooms, and the dining room, look over the Atlantic between the Toe of Harris and Taransay Island. Breakfasts very good. Dinners splendid; no choice of main course, but guests are asked if they have any dislikes, and alternatives are offered. A typical meal would have a rich soup; a fish course (sole in pastry, Sauce Aurore, and a plate of cold langoustines with a cream parsley sauce were two); main course – roast duck with damsons or lovely venison, with good vegetables. For Sunday dinner, we had a pot of duck liver *pâté* each to start, then a whole lobster (thermidor, but we were asked how we would like it); a whole pineapple stuffed with fruit, with lots of liqueur; then cheese – a choice of about 8 offered at each dinner; and finally more fruit. They are not allowed to sell alcoholic drinks, but happily serve what you take, without corkage, and with good service. The dining furniture is solid, and we dined off white linen, with linen napkins, changed daily, and by the light of candles in silver sconces. Warm though the house was, we had a fire lit in the library to take coffee by. Kettles and teapots in rooms, with choice of teas or coffee, plus biscuits. *Scarista* is outstanding. It's run by delightful people who take pride in their small hotel and in looking after their guests.' *(Michael Atkinson and Robert Holmes; also Iain Nicolson)*

Open: All year.
Rooms: 4 double – 2 with bath, all with tea-making facilities.
Facilities: Drawing room with peat fires (and central heating), well-stocked library, restaurant. 1 acre grounds. Access to miles of sandy beach; sea fishing, trout and salmon fishing.
Location: 15 miles SW of Tarbert on the A859, 50 miles from Stornoway. Regular ferries from Ullapool to Stornoway and Uig to Tarbert; daily flights to Stornoway from Glasgow and Inverness.
Restrictions: No children under 8. Dogs by special arrangement.
Terms (no fixed service charge): B & B £15–20. Set meal: dinner £10.

INVERSHIN, Lairg, Sutherland   **Map 5**

Invershin Hotel   *Telephone:* Invershin (054 982) 202

A family hotel – exceptionally modest in price – of no great pretensions architecturally, but facing the lovely Kyle of Sutherland. 'The value is incredible, particularly at a time when Scottish (as well as other grockle-orientated) shops and hotels are killing the golden egg by unjustifiable overcharging. [*Grockle or emmett*. Tourist, generally expected to offer no resistance when taken for a ride, e.g. 80p for vanilla ice cream wafer at Tower of London; £1.75 for stale haddock and chips at Melvich, both July 1980.] These 4-course plus coffee dinners, at £5 including VAT, consist of large, well prepared courses; in 10 evenings we were unable to find any fault with the way anything had been prepared, except that one portion of smoked mackerel was untypically small. Breakfasts were large, with a large choice. Frequently we felt no need for a midday meal, despite much walking. Major Hedley runs the hotel with his large and well-qualified family, all of whom like to make sure that no one is lacking adequate food, information, help of any kind. We noticed that passers-by could expect food and service at almost any time of day – and probably night as well. Background music is unobtrusive. Tables large, seating comfortable – but at very busy times, e.g. peak holiday time evenings, the lounge is too small for comfort and you must purchase midge repellent and sit outside unless you want to chat. Expect a certain amount of noise until about 11 pm, as the public bar is popular and busy; so are the road and adjoining railway. Our room had intercom, colour TV, carpeted private shower and lavatory; and do-it-yourself tea and coffee facilities, most welcome when coming and going at unscheduled times. It represented about the best value we have experienced anywhere in about 15 years.' *(W H Jarvis)*

Open: All year, except 1–4 January.
Rooms: 17 double, 7 single – 8 with bath, 8 with shower, 2 with telephone, all with radio, TV, tea-making facilities and baby-listening. 6 rooms in annexe. (Some rooms on ground floor.)
Facilities: 2 bars, 2 lounges. 25 acres grounds with riding by arrangement. The river Kyle is in front of the hotel with free fishing for hotel guests.
Location: Central; parking.
Restriction: No dogs in dining room.
Terms (no service charge): B & B £8.50–10; dinner, B & B £13.50–15. Set meals: lunch £3.50; dinner £5.50. Reduced rates and special meals for children.

ISLE ORNSAY, Skye   Map 5

Kinloch Lodge [GFG]   *Telephone:* Isle Ornsay (047 13) 214
                                          Telex: 75442 Donald G

A substantial postbag this year on Lord and Lady Macdonald's unstuffy hunting-lodge/hotel 100 yards from a sea loch – mostly very favourable, though two readers commented on somewhat poky rooms. Two other readers pay tribute to the *Lodge's* breakfast: porridge, figs with oranges, prunes, cereals; juices; eggs in various forms; excellent bacon; sausages; poached Mallaig kippers; baps, scones, toast, oatcakes, home-made marmalade, honey . . . Here is a typical report:
'The personal welcome on our arrival and eventual farewell at the end of our stay by Lord Macdonald and the friendly informal atmosphere, which pervades the whole of *Kinloch Lodge*, lived up to your recommendation – and more. My wife and I are delighted with this hotel, which is so ideal for those of us who want peace, no fuss and a centre for walking the mountains and glens and exploring the beauty of Skye. The set menu for dinner causes no problems of indecision! The food and cooking is absolutely fresh and of an exceptionally high standard. We will be returning to *Kinloch*.' *(John and Priscilla Gillett; also Derek Wylie, Michael Atkinson and Robert Holmes, Dr Peter Barham, June and Brodie Macdonald)*

Open: All year.
Rooms: 8 double, 2 single – 8 with bath. (Some rooms on ground floor.)
Facilities: Lounge, cocktail bar with TV, dining room. 40 acres grounds; 100 yards from the sea, safe sandy beach below the hotel at low water; fishing available on hotel's own freshwater lochs; splendid walking country. Daily flights from Glasgow to Skye. &.
Location: Off the A851 6 miles S of Broadford between Armadale ferry and Kyle of Lochalsh ferry.
Terms: B & B £15–21; dinner, B & B £22–30. Set meal: dinner £10.50. Reduced rates and special meals for children.

We asked hotels to estimate their 1982 tariffs some time before publication so the rates given here are not necessarily completely accurate. Please *always* check terms with hotels when making bookings.

KELSO, Roxburghshire — Map 5

Woodside Hotel
Edenside Road

Telephone: Kelso (057 32) 2152

From the outside, a fine upstanding four-square example of a small Georgian country house set in 4½ acres of grounds on the edge of Kelso – about ten minutes' walk to the centre of this agreeable Border town. Inside, though it is furnished with style and maintained immaculately, its character is slightly different, being animated by the warm Florentine personality of the resident owner, Marcello Becatelli. It's not just that Italian dishes appear on the menu, and the Frascati is recommended (as well as the MacAllan malt in the bar), but that the informal and sometimes erratic service – as when the dining staff have to be responsible for feeding the latest Becatelli infant as well as the guests – is, at least to one reader, endearingly reminiscent of one of those unpretentious *trattorie* where the life of the family spills unselfconsciously into the business. 'But,' says this reader in an admonitory vein, 'food in the *tratorria* sometimes arrives hotter and more promptly, and Signor Becatelli needs to beware lest charm and sentimental Italophilia fail to cancel out sloppy service, tired sweets and short cuts with the vegetables.' In general, however, people enjoy their stay at *Woodside*, whether in the house itself (slightly more expensive) or in a well-converted stable block – though the partitions here are said to be on the thin side. And the hotel evinced a particular expression of gratitude from a reader with an invalid mother. *(Aaron Goodstadt, Canon Peter Hawker, Mr and Mrs J Allan, Joan Marr, J & JW, Antony Dervillc)*

Open: All year.
Rooms: 10 double, 1 single – all with bath or shower, telephone, colour TV and baby-listening. 5 rooms in annexe. (Some rooms on ground floor.)
Facilities: Lounge, cocktail bar, dining room. 5 acres grounds with gardens and putting green. 10 minutes' walk from the river Tweed, rich in salmon and trout. Horse riding, golf; fishing and shooting facilities obtainable on request. ♿.
Location: 10 minutes from town centre; parking for 30 cars.
Restrictions: Dogs allowed, but only in public rooms and gardens.
Credit cards: American Express, Barclay/Visa, Diners.
Terms: B & B £11–19; dinner, B & B £17–27. Set meal: dinner £8.90; full *alc* £9.50. 15% discounts during off season. Reduced rates and special meals for children.

KILLIECRANKIE, by Pitlochry, Perthshire — Map 5

Killiecrankie Hotel

Telephone: Killiecrankie (079 684) 220

A friendly small hotel, formerly a dower house, at the northern entrance to the Pass of Killiecrankie just off the Great North Road (A9) – a convenient watering-hole, perhaps, for sportsmen travelling north for shooting and fishing.

'The hotel is situated in picturesque grounds, ideal for children (pets also made welcome), with good views of the surrounding countryside. The rooms were freshly decorated and spotlessly clean. The dining room is probably the main feature with large picture windows. The food was always piping hot and efficiently served offering a wide selection including traditional Scots fare and plenty of game and fish. If the dining room is closed, one can eat in the bar where lunches and bar suppers of an equally high standard are always available. The friendly approach of all the staff and the personal attention of the proprietors, Duncan and Jennifer Hattersley, was exceptional.' *(Dr Paul A Wilson; also Frank Colley)*

Open: Easter–mid October.
Rooms: 11 double, 1 single, 1 suite – 4 with bath, 6 with shower, all with baby-listening.
Facilities: Lounge with TV, cocktail bar, dining room. 6 acres gardens and woodlands with much wildlife at the northern entrance to the Pass of Killiecrankie. Putting green. District of Atholl is a natural beauty spot with rivers, lochs, moors and glens. Also of great archaeological interest. Golf, fishing, stalking and shooting, skiing, walking, mountaineering nearby. &.
Location: On the A9 Great North Road to Inverness. 3½ miles from Pitlochry.
Terms (service at guests' discretion): B & B £11.60–16.10; dinner, B & B £17.90–25.55. Set meal (excluding 10% service): dinner £7.70. Bar lunches available. The hotel hopes to initiate special weekend/week Nature Lovers courses in 1982. Reduced rates for children sharing parents' room; special meals provided.

KINGUSSIE, Inverness-shire   **Map 5**

The Osprey Hotel   [GFG]   *Telephone:* Kingussie (054 02) 510

A friendly informal family hotel in an agreeable Highland village, with all kinds of activities available in the region. Last year, we mentioned fishing, walking, golf, riding, skiing, climbing, pony trekking and canoeing – but Pauline Reeves, who runs *The Osprey* with her husband Duncan, tells us that we can add sailing, gliding and windsurfing to the list. Things which our readers like about this hotel include: the high quality of the food, especially their peat-smoked fish; their reasonably priced wine, served with uncommon care; their admirable packed lunches; and their welcome to young children. In a covering letter to us returning the questionnaire, Mr Reeves writes: 'Your Guide brings some of our nicest people to our door; and always one hears thoroughly complimentary remarks about the Guide and its effectiveness in locating good accommodation. You are obviously hitting the button.' While basking in the thought, we regret to say that we have had little news about *The Osprey* from our readers recently. Could some of those to whom we are hitting the button kindly reciprocate?

Open: 26 December–31 October.
Rooms: 7 double, 1 single, 1 family.
Facilities: Lounge, TV room, dining room. Small front garden with herbs and rockery. Most sports within easy reach: golf, salmon and trout fishing on the river Spey ¼ mile, loch fishing for trout 1 mile; wind-surfing; gliding at Glen Feshie nearby, sailing and canoeing 6 miles; all sports facilities at the Aviemore Centre 12 miles; fine country all around for birdwatching, walking and hill-climbing. Skiing in the Cairngorms, usually December–May, 30 minutes by car.
Location: Near the A9, about 10 miles SW of Aviemore and 200 yards from the village centre; parking for 10 cars.
Restriction: No dogs in public rooms.
Credit cards: Access, American Express, Barclay/Visa.
Terms (excluding service): B & B £9–11.25; dinner, B & B £16.50–18.50. Set meal: dinner £7.25; full *alc* £10. Reduced rates for children.

The Log Cabin Hotel   *Telephone:* Strathardle (025 081) 288

The Log Cabin, as you might expect, is a timber-frame bungalow made of Norwegian whole logs. The restaurant of the hotel is called the *Edelweiss* and there's a Tyrolean Bar (a former manager was Austrian). Despite these Continental elements, this is a thoroughly Scottish hotel, 900 feet up in the heather and forest pine. It's walking, climbing, riding, shooting and fishing country, with skiing in the winter. The hotel, which owns 1,500 acres of grounds, includes in its tariff the use of the hotel's own ponies, its own boat on the nearby loch, also its tennis court; stalking and shooting are extra. The cooking makes good use of local resources, including trout and salmon.

Our entry last year was confirmed by a recent visitor in the following qualified terms: 'Took my wife, my elder (grown-up) son and his girl-friend, for start of a week's fishing, walking, riding holiday in the Highlands. Booked in reliance on Guide. Reliance justified. Food very good – almost as good as *The Osprey* at Kingussie (q.v.) – but atmosphere would not suit everyone: the centre of the hotel is a vast under-furnished room, with a bar on one side, a pool table and a fruit machine and a bare wooden floor – no doubt designed for skiers, but less appropriate at other times of the year. In our party, the younger generation liked the place more than the older.' *(Conrad Dehn)*

Open: All year.
Room: 8 double, 1 single, 4 suites – 8 with bath, all with radio; colour TV available. (All rooms on ground floor.)
Facilities: Lounge, bar, restaurant; Saturday dinner dance, folk nights Wednesday and Friday in summer; simple laundry facilities available. 1,500 acres grounds with shooting, fishing, riding, stalking; heated swimming pool and all-weather tennis court. Excellent walking and climbing; skiing nearby.
Location: 1 mile off the A924, on the road to Pitlochry, 12 miles N; about an hour's drive from the M90 motorway.
Credit cards: All major credit cards accepted.
Terms (service at guests' discretion): B & B £12–16; dinner, B & B £17–19.50; full board £20–22.50. Set meals: lunch from £3; dinner £8. Special spring and winter weekends; special rates in high season for stays of 3 days or more. Reduced rates and special meals for children.

LEWIS, Isle of, by Stornoway, Western Isles   **Map 5**

Uig Lodge Hotel   *Telephone:* Timsgarry (085 05) 286

'Ugly, yes, not a tree in sight, but the beach it commands is breathtaking, and to wake up in the morning and look across this bare strand to where the far-off Atlantic breakers roll in is quite an experience,' was one sentence in our entry last year on this remote (34 miles from Stornoway) hunting and shooting lodge built by Sir James Matheson (of opium trade fame) over a century ago. The resident manager, Richard Davis, takes umbrage at these words: no other guest has ever called the *Lodge* ugly (it is, in fairness, typical of Scottish country house building of the period – austere would describe it better), and as for trees – 'there are several trees surrounding a small paddock within 50 yards and in full view of our front door, though of course lack of trees is a feature of the Hebridean landscape.' Our reporter last year, in praising fresh vegetables and 'perfect' roast mutton, had also regretted the use of Mother's Pride. We are glad to learn that the hotel has been making its own home-made bread since the start of the 1981 season. Could we hear from other visitors to this northern fastness? One warning: meals are taken communally, and fishing tends to be staple diet of conversational courses.

Open: 1 April–15 October.
Rooms: 9 double, 1 single, 1 family – 4 with bath, all with tea-making facilities and baby-listening by arrangement. (3 rooms on ground floor.)
Facilities: Hall/bar, lounge, dining room. 200 acres grounds – meadows, river shore, sea with sandy beach and safe bathing; private trout and salmon fishing nearby; birdwatching.
Location: On the W side of Isle of Lewis, due W of Stornoway.
Credit cards: All major credit cards accepted.
Terms (service at guests' discretion): Rooms £10–14; B & B £12–17; dinner, B & B £18.50–24. Set meals: lunch £4.75; dinner £9.25. Painting and art holidays in early summer with professional artist based at hotel. Reduced rates and special meals for children.

LOCHAWESIDE, by Taynuilt, Argyll   Map 5

Taychreggan Hotel [GFG]   *Telephone:* Kilchrenan (086 63) 211

An old coaching inn on loch Awe at what was once the main ferry point across the loch from Inverary to Oban. The ferry route has long since been closed, and the house, in 25 acres of its own grounds and right on the water's edge, enjoys an exceptionally peaceful and beautiful setting. The hotel has its own boats; there is a large picnic boat, complete with hamper, for exploring the islands of loch Awe. Fishing is obviously one activity hereabouts as well as walking, bird-watching and touring by car; but there's also good riding to be had, and some shooting.

The hotel owes a lot to the personalities of John Taylor and his Danish wife, Tove. The light modern interior is decidedly Scandinavian in design. The hotel serves no formal midday meal, but there is a variety of bar lunches available including always a Danish *koldt bord* and never, John Taylor tell us, 'fried food or "beasts in baskets".'

In our entry for *Taychreggan* last year, we quoted a report from a visitor who had been struck by the sympathetically vigilant eye of the management, which led to exceptional pride and enthusiasm on the part of the staff. The same correspondent has been back since, and reports again: 'It is often a disappointment to return to a hotel which has greatly impressed on a first visit. The fact that we liked *Taychreggan* as much as before is an indication of the hotel's particular virtue. It is consistent because it is well run by the owners. There has been a big change of staff since last year (inevitable perhaps with a seasonal operation), yet they were all as efficient as before, and as last year seemed imbued with the same enthusiasm and friendly helpfulness that seems to give the hotel such a pleasant atmosphere. As last year, we considered that the food was nicely cooked and served, and although *far* above the norm for Scottish hotels not quite of the *Good Food Guide* class.' (*Graeme Carmichael; also O W D Roberts, Antony Derville, Richard Webb*)

Don't keep your favourite hotel to yourself. The Guide supports: it doesn't spoil.

155

Open: 5 April–18 October.
Rooms: 18 double, 4 single – 10 with bath, 1 with shower, all with radio and baby-listening.
Facilities: 2 lounges, hall-lounge, TV lounge, all with log fires; bar overlooking courtyard, dining room. 25 acres grounds on the loch side, with fishing, bathing, boating. Riding, shooting, walking; fine scenery, gardens and historic sites within easy reach.
Location: Northern shore of Loch Awe, about 16 miles E of Oban by the A85, turning S just beyond Taynuilt to reach Loch Awe and the hotel.
Credit cards: All major credit cards accepted.
Terms (excluding 10% service charge): B & B £15–18; dinner, B & B £22–25. Set meals: buffet lunch £4.75; dinner £9. Reduced rates for children sharing parents' room: 50% if under 8 and taking high tea; 20% if over 8 and taking dinner.

LOCHGOILHEAD, Argyll   Map 5

Inverlounin House   [GFG]   *Telephone:* Lochgoilhead (030 13) 211

A very small highly individual hotel and restaurant (four bedrooms; seats 16) in the Argyll Forest Park, with marvellous Highland scenery; it's about half an hour by car to Inverary and Loch Fyne and just over an hour to Glasgow via the Rest and be Thankful pass and Loch Lomond. For the active visitor, there's plenty to offer: the hotel has its own boat on the loch which also has deep-water mooring; and there's walking, climbing, golf, riding or sailing at hand. Readers continue to appreciate the hospitality of Hugh and Anne Pitt, though one, who had much enjoyed his dinner and what he called 'the basics of breakfast', felt that he would have liked an alternative to the special hot dish, a rich fishcake called a Rutherglen Tram Stopper. Another guest of the Pitts had no reservations: 'The best recommendation is that we arrived to have lunch and decided to stay the night. A small and simple hotel located at the end of an atrocious road, but well worth the detour to get there. We were given superb friendly service with really original French-style cooking. I only hope the Pitts never get tempted to a large commercial enterprise. What they present at the moment is, I would think, almost unrivalled in the UK – very special food with very special attention.' *(P W D Roberts; also Michael Atkinson, Richard Webb)*

Open: All year, except March; closed for Thursday lunch.
Rooms: 4 double – 1 with bath. (1 room on ground floor.)
Facilities: Drawing room, dining room, covered terrace. 1½ acres formal gardens with summer house, badminton court, putting green, croquet. On the loch with own beach, own slipway, own moorings; safe bathing from sand and rock; fishing. &.
Location: 1½ miles from the village. Lochgoilhead lies about 6 miles S of the A83 Arrochar–Inverary road, along the B828 from Rest and be Thankful. It can also be reached along the B839 off the A815 Dunoon–Inverary road.
Restrictions: Children and dogs 'not encouraged'.
Terms (service at guests' discretion): B & B £13.50; dinner, B & B £21–24.50. Set meals: lunch £5–8; dinner £10.

> Deadlines: nominations for the 1983 edition should reach us not later than 31 July 1982. Latest date for comments on existing entries: 31 August 1982.

MOFFAT, Dumfriesshire   Map 5

Beechwood Country House Hotel   [GFG]   *Telephone:* Moffat (0683) 20210

In earlier editions of the Guide, we had an entry for another hotel in Moffat, architecturally grander than *Beechwood*, but with a restaurant that failed to match the quality of the building. *Beechwood* is an unassumingly pleasant old country house just outside the centre of Moffat, in 12 acres of beech trees overlooking the Annan valley, and it cares particularly for the reputation of its kitchen and its cellars. Sheila McIlwrick personally supervises the cooking, and her husband Keith oversees the front of house. 'This is my third visit to this small hotel situated on the hill above Moffat, with attractive views to the west and north over open country. On each occasion I have noticed the improvements Mr and Mrs McIlwrick have made to increase the comfort of their guests. Still to come over the next year are telephones in the bedrooms, the only one at present being in the outer hall which does not encourage long conversations in the winter! and radio/clock alarms. You receive a very warm welcome from the McIlwricks who will go out of their way to cater for your whims, and of course the food is excellent. The bedrooms are comfortably if a bit sparsely furnished.' *(J F Holman; also J Holmes)*

Open: All year.
Rooms: 6 double, 2 single – 3 with bath, 3 with shower, 6 with telephone, all with radio and tea-making facilities.
Facilities: 2 lounges (one with bar, one with colour TV), dining room. 1 acre garden. Fishing in river Annan; golf, tennis and riding nearby.
Location: Turn off the A701 at St Mary's church into Harthope Place. Then left and up track to *Beechwood*.
Restriction: No dogs.
Credit cards: All major credit cards accepted.
Terms (excluding service):   B & B £10.75–14.75. Set meal: dinner £7. Full *alc* about £8. Special terms for weekends in autumn 1982. 10% reduction for children; special meals provided.

NAIRN   Map 5

Clifton Hotel   [GFG]   *Telephone:* Nairn (0667) 53119
Viewfield Street

We had a particularly fruity entry last year for Gordon Macintyre's charmingly idiosyncratic house, which one reader had described as 'lavishly pink-taffeta Victorian slightly gone to seed'. 'I was *delighted*,' writes the proud owner, 'I love it.' He adds that he hopes before the next edition of the Guide appears to have added baths *en suite* to the last two rooms which have lacked that facility. We repeat the greater part of last year's entry, not indeed because it has given pleasure to the hotelier, but because we believe it gives a faithful picture of an agreeably characterful establishment.

'A hotel hand-crafted for lovers of theatre and the theatrical. With the Moray Firth as a backdrop, impresario Gordon Macintyre has filled his old family hotel with paintings, sculptures, bas reliefs, *objets trouvés*, long-gones, bygones, fargones, the indifferent nestling happily against the tasteful, the tasteless complementing the outrageous. Centrepiece of the whole establishment is the large sea-facing dining room with tables placed upon podiums of varying heights. You feel as you climb the steps to your own particular table that on some other night Macbeth may well have climbed up here or Hamlet's pa's ghost may have stalked these limelit battlements. Nor is this fancy. Mr Macintyre's principal preoccupation, apart from haunting salerooms and country house auctions from whence the house has been assembled, is the production of plays. The amateur cast is assembled from a 40-mile catchment area, the grand piano is rolled aside and drama happens. There are concerts and recitals too, and you may well find Maria de la Pau Tortelier playing the piano in the dining room while Papa Paul rehearses beside her. The food is elaborate and as ambitious as the theatrical productions. "Who does the cooking?" I inquired. "Forbes!" replied Mr Macintyre, and one could be forgiven for feeling that it might well be the mortal ghost of the immortal Sir John Forbes Robertson himself.' *(DC; also Emilie Jacobi, S C Whittle)*

Open: 1 March – end November.
Rooms: 17 double, 2 single – 14 with bath. (2 rooms on ground floor.)
Facilities: Large lounge, drawing room, TV room, bar, restaurant, writing room; plays, concerts, recitals October–May. 1 acre grounds. Fishing, shooting, riding available; beach, tennis courts, swimming pools 2 minutes away. 2 golf courses close by.
Location: 500 yards from town centre; parking for 20 cars.
Credit card: American Express.
Terms (excluding service): B & B £15–20.50. Full *alc* £10–12. Reduced rates for children sharing parents' room; special meals provided.

PEEBLES Map 5

Cringletie House Hotel [GFG] *Telephone:* Eddleston (072 13) 233

'For 12 years I have dreamed of going back to *Cringletie*. I found the reality better than the dream. This isn't some purple prose served up on a travel brochure, but a heartfelt expression of joy at finding the Maguires running this baronial house in peaceful grounds with even more expertise than their predecessors in the late 1960s. The house is not only peaceful, but the staff without exception are smiling and willing. The dinner menus are imaginatively planned and justify their price. There is a particularly well drawn-up wine list. The bar, too, is particularly well-stocked and the barman or Mr Maguire are only too ready to help a poor southerner explore the delights of malt whisky.' *(Peter Andrews)*
This warm tribute is to a noble example of Scottish baronial which stands in 28 acres of gardens and woodland close to the village of Eddleston, two miles north of Peebles on the Edinburgh road (A703). *Cringletie* has a distinguished pedigree: it was formerly the home of the Wolfe Murray family, and it was Colonel Alexander Murray from *Cringletie* who accepted the surrender of Quebec after General Wolfe had been killed. But it has been a renowned hotel for many years now.

Open: Mid March–December.
Rooms: 12 double, 4 single – 11 with bath, 1 with shower and WC.
Facilities: Lift, lounge, TV lounge, bar, dining room; occasional small conferences (8–15 people), central heating. 28 acres of gardens and woodlands with hard tennis court, croquet and putting. Golf and trout and salmon fishing nearby.
Location: Off the A703, 2 miles N of Peebles.

Restriction: No dogs in public rooms or unaccompanied in bedrooms.
Terms (service at guests' discretion): B & B £15–17.50; dinner, B & B £21.50–24.50 (£20–23 for minimum 5 nights). Set meals: lunch £6, dinner £10. £5 B & B for children sharing parents' room; high teas provided.

POOLEWE, Wester Ross   Map 5

Pool House Hotel   *Telephone:* Poolewe (044 586) 272

'Having gone to Poolewe to visit Inverewe Gardens we were attracted to the *Pool House Hotel* by its commanding position at the head of loch Ewe, and we were so charmed by the high standards of comfort and service and simply delectable food (at a very reasonable price) that we spent the remainder of our holiday there. Breakfasts were well-cooked (excellent porridge) and of the plentiful variety we had come to expect in Scotland – ideal for starting a day's walking in the beautiful surroundings. There was an agonizing choice again at dinner where local fresh salmon vied with venison in red wine or braised tongue with current sauce (delicious), all with home-grown vegetables and tasty starters and mouthwatering puddings. The hotel had recently changed hands, and had been redecorated the previous winter. There were pretty modern pastels in the bedrooms, and more conventional decor in the public rooms, which were comfortable though not luxurious. We were not keen on the shower unit in the corner of our bedroom (all the ones with private bath were occupied), but the breathtaking view from our main window was certainly an adequate compensation. The family did most things themselves and were very friendly, agreeable and courteous. The hotel has no pretensions to luxury (and was priced accordingly – a welcome change) and is simply a family hotel of the old type, but with such a pleasant and relaxing atmosphere (and good food!) that we were more than content to bask there for the last five days of our holiday.' *(Lt Cdr and Mrs R Kirby Harris)*

Open: 1 April–14 October.
Rooms: 10 double, 4 single – 3 with bath, 4 with shower; tea-making facilities on request.
Facilities: 2 lounges, TV room, 2 bars, dining room.
Location: ½ mile from Inverewe Gardens between Gairloch and Aultbea.
Restriction: No dogs in public rooms.
Credit cards: Barclay.
Terms: Rooms £10–20 per person; B & B £12–22; dinner, B & B (minimum 5 nights) £17.19; full board £17.19 for stays of 5 nights and over; bar lunches from £2.50; set meal: dinner £7.50. Reduced rates for children; special meals provided.

PORT APPIN, Argyll   Map 5

The Airds Hotel [GFG]   *Telephone:* Appin (063 173) 236

We continue to receive favourable reports like the one below on this old ferry inn overlooking Loch Linnhe, the island of Lismore and the mountains of Morvern: 'Our main regret was not being able to stay longer. This is a small comfortable hotel, spotlessly clean and very well decorated. The resident proprietors, Mr and Mrs Allen, are much in evidence, and obviously take a pride in their establishment. It is in peaceful surroundings with lovely views, and is an ideal centre for walking and boat excursions. The dinner menu featured Scottish dishes and was of a high standard not experienced in many more pretentious restaurants. The young staff are helpful and our stay altogether most enjoyable.' *(Derek W Beale; also Mrs Forsyth Lawson)*

Open: 5 April–31 October.
Rooms: 14 double, 2 single (2 rooms in annexe).
Facilities: 2 residents' lounges, cocktail lounge, public bar, dining room. Small garden. Near rock beach with safe bathing, fishing, boating, pony-trekking, forest walks.
Location: 2 miles off the A828, 25 miles from Fort William and from Oban.
Restriction: Dogs at owners' discretion.
Terms (no fixed service charge): B & B £11–16.50. Set meals: snack lunch £1.50; dinner £10. Reduced rates and special meals for children.

ROCKCLIFFE, by Dalbeattie, Dumfries and Galloway   Map 5

Baron's Craig Hotel   *Telephone:* Rockcliffe (055 663) 225

Galloway is one of the more neglected (i.e. unspoiled, not-yet-tourist-ridden) corners of Britain. It enjoys an exceptionally mild climate. Rockcliffe is a small village overlooking the mouth of Rough Firth as it opens out to the broad reaches of the Solway, and is surrounded by woods and heathered hills. *Baron's Craig*, as its name implies, is pure Scottish baronial, built a century ago of enduring granite. 'Its first appearance is slightly forbidding, but it is very comfortable inside. The manager is affable and considerate, the staff are friendly, the food is good (and I am fussy!) and there is a beautiful bay nearby.' *(R O Marshall; also Brian and Vicky Harrison)*

Open: 2 April–10 October.
Rooms: 19 double, 8 single – 20 with bath, all with radio and baby-listening. (5 rooms with bath on ground floor.)
Facilities: 2 lounges, 1 lounge bar, separate TV room. 11 acres wooded grounds and gardens with 9-hole putting course. 300 yards from safe, sandy beach.
Location: Rockcliffe is a small village off the A710 overlooking the mouth of Rough Firth.
Restriction: No dogs in public rooms.
Terms (no fixed service charge): B & B £17.60–27; dinner, B & B (minimum 3 days) £24.70–34. Set meals: breakfast £2.90; dinner £9; bar lunch from £2.50. Reduced rates and special meals for children.

ST ANDREWS, Fife   Map 5

Rufflets Hotel   *Telephone:* St Andrews (0334) 72594
Strathkinnes Low Road   *Telex:* 76687 SCOPEX G

Not the main hotel in St Andrews – the large modern *Old Course* beside the 17th fairway – but an agreeable family-run 1924 country house alternative, 1½ miles inland.
   'This is one of the most pleasant hotels we have stayed in, set in large beautifully kept grounds with a remarkable kitchen garden. Service is excellent. The food we had was consistently good, and not expensive by

today's standards. There seemed to be typical Scottish dishes on every menu – at lunch smokies and haggis with nips, and at dinner we had "Cubbie Claw" – a delicious sole dish which was on as a main course but available as a fish course at 50p extra. There was a sweet trolley but we chose to follow with Orkney and Inverness blue cheeses. There is a good wine list but the red house wine is undistinguished.' *(W Frankland)*

Open: Mid February–mid January.
Rooms: 22 – all with telephone and baby-listening. 3 rooms in annexe.
Facilities: Front hall, residents' lounge, lounge bar, TV room, restaurant. 10 acres grounds with putting, gardens with streams. 1 mile from beach; fishing, golfing, etc, can be arranged.
Location: On the B939 1 mile W of St Andrews.
Restriction: No dogs.
Credit cards: All major credit cards accepted.
Terms (no service charge): B & B £18–21; dinner, B & B £24–27. Set meals: lunch £3.75; dinner £7.50; full *alc* £12. Special Christmas and New Year packages with entertainment. Short winter breaks: dinner, B & B for 2 days from £35 per person 1 November–30 April. Children half price when sharing parents' room; special meals provided.

ST FILLANS, Perthshire   **Map 5**

The Four Seasons Hotel [GFG]   *Telephone:* St Fillans (076 485) 333

A well-designed modern hotel in an exceptional location, looking down the length of Loch Earn from the eastern shore. The hotel prides itself on its restaurant, also on a wide-ranging wine list. In addition to the accommodation in the main building, there are also six chalets on the hillside above, specially suitable for families. Sailing, waterskiing, golf, fishing, shooting, squash and tennis are all to be had in the immediate vicinity. 'A splendid position. Beautifully appointed bedroom and bathroom. Public rooms all very agreeably furnished. Staff pleasant and courteous.' *(J & A Hartley)*

Open: Easter–end October.
Rooms: 12 double – 11 with bath, 1 with shower, all with telephone, mono TV and baby-listening. Also 6 chalets in hotel grounds.
Facilities: Lounge, writing room, 2 bars, restaurant. Private jetty for use of guests with own boats. Waterskiing, sailing, golf, riding, fishing within easy reach.
Location: Just off the A85 W of Perth.
Credit cards: Access/Euro/Mastercard, American Express, Barclay/Visa.
Terms: B & B £20.50–25.50; dinner, B & B (minimum 3 nights) £26–33; full board £31–38. Set meals (excluding 10% service charge); lunch £6.30; dinner £8.90; full *alc* £12.70. Special rates for chalets if occupied by more than 2 people; high tea 5.45–6.30 pm.

SCOURIE, Badcall Bay, Sutherland   **Map 5**

Eddrachilles Hotel   *Telephone:* (0971) 2080

'Hotels – never mind good ones – are few and far between in this far North Western part of wildest Scotland. *Eddrachilles* has an unrivalled scenic position overlooking the island-studded Badcall Bay, and is ideally placed

161

for visiting the bird sanctuary of Handa Island. There are boats available for pottering around the hundreds of islets in the bay – and if it rains (it does) then the selection of malts in the bar will soon put on a glow! Mr and Mrs A Wood have created an impeccable haven of comfort: splendid and ample home cooking, a small but very well-chosen wine list and a cosy, well-stocked bar for after-dinner chats. My wife and I have stayed here twice now, and will return as long as we are able. The owners work very hard to maintain their own high standards: they are open all the year round and deserve to be fully booked every night of the year.' *(Brian and Arlette Singleton)*

Open: All year.
Rooms: 11 double, 2 single, 1 suite – 4 with bath, 10 with shower, all with radio, TV (8 mono, 2 colour), tea-making facilities and baby-listening.
Facilities: Lounge, lounge bar, public bar, 2 dining rooms. Hotel stands in its own 320-acre estate at the head of Badcall Bay with woodland paths. Brown trout fishing. Near to sea with rocky shore and boats, and to Handa Island bird sanctuary.
Location: Just off the A894 Kylestrome–Scourie road. The hotel is well signposted from the road.
Restriction: No dogs in public rooms.
Terms (no service charge): Rooms £10.75–15.40 per person; B & B £12.75–17.40. Set meal: dinner £4.75; full *alc* £9.70. Reduced rates available for stays of over 3 and 6 nights, and for children; special meals for children.

SEIL, by Oban, Argyll   Map 5

Dunmor House [GFG]   *Telephone:* Balvicar (085 23) 203

Commander and Mrs Campbell-Gibson have been running this gabled white hotel, part of a 1,000-acre farm, for over ten years. It's an isolated part of Scotland, but the island of Seil, four miles long by two miles wide, is joined to the mainland by Telford's Clachan bridge, and Oban, with all its island excursions, is only half an hour by car. But one of the pleasures of a stay at *Dunmor House* is its unspoiled beauty: you could go for a lazy do-nothing holiday or, if you felt like exercise, there are plenty of hills, cliffs and rocky beaches with breathtaking views over to the islands of the Inner Hebrides. Other pleasures are the uncommon quality of Mrs Campbell-Gibson's cooking and the friendly family and dog-loving (they even have a Dog's Visitor's Book!) atmosphere of the place. *(W R Needs, Derek Cooper, Antony Derville, George Mair, Mrs W E Hasker)*

Open: 3 May–15 October.
Rooms: 10 double, 1 single – 5 with bath, 4 with shower.
Facilities: Hall, lounge, TV room, dining room. The hotel stands in its own hill farm of 1,000 acres; near the sea with cliffs, rock and shingle beaches, safe bathing. Boat excursions to the islands; sea-fishing trips, trout fishing in lochs, very good walks; pony-trekking. Ideal for visiting Argyllshire gardens.
Location: 15 miles SW of Oban; ½ mile E of Easdale village.
Restriction: Children under 8 not allowed in dining room for dinner.
Terms (excluding service): B & B £12–16.50; dinner, B & B (minimum 7 days) £19.50–23.50. Set meal: dinner £8. Special meals for children.

Please write and confirm an entry when it is deserved. If you think that a hotel is not as good as we say, please write and tell us.

162

SELKIRK, Selkirkshire   **Map 5**

Philipburn House Hotel   *Telephone:* Selkirk (0750) 20747

A rare class of hotel this – one wholly geared to the needs of families with
young children – any amount of swings, chutes, Wendy houses, woodland
tree houses, games rooms, trampoline, etc in the 5 acres of grounds – but
which also succeeds in maintaining a high standard of cooking at dinner, a
meal which is strictly for adults except on special occasions. The house,
which is in the heart of Walter Scott country, four miles from Abbotsford,
dates from 1751. It is run by Jim Hill, a first-class chef, and his wife Anne.
For the active there is wonderful walking to be had in the surrounding
Border country, 200 miles of trout fishing, access to salmon rods, also
riding and pony-trekking.

'A very pleasing and satisfying place to stay: comfortable, casual,
attractive, relaxing. The grounds are delightful, even if you are not a
child. One could enjoy a holiday without leaving the grounds. The food is
excellent. Breakfast is quite an occasion, with its infinite variety – and so
substantial that one realizes why the midweek break terms don't include
lunch, for we didn't want any. Tea is a friendly affair with everyone sitting
round the lounge's excrutiatingly uncomfortable couches: it too is quite
substantial. At dinner, the soups and puddings were delicious. The main
course was the least enjoyable – mainly because there was too much, so
that one tired of it halfway through, and because it was too rich for my
appetite. It is a pity that hoteliers don't seem to realize that a huge heaped
platter of food, however good, is offputting at the outset; and, of course,
they could make a bigger profit or else charge less if they served less.
That apart, I warmly recommend the hotel and its cuisine.' *(W L Prentice)*

The Hills seem to have taken the hint. They are widening their 4-course
menus and also offering an *à la carte*. 'We find,' they say, 'that there are
fewer and fewer people interested in devouring meals of these proportions and in spending £10 unless it is a special occasion.' We welcome this
move – too many hotels in our experience invest in quantity because they
can't manage quality.

Open: All year, except January 3–30.
Rooms: 6 double, 1 single, 10 suites – 9 with bath, 1 with shower, all with radio,
colour TV, tea-making facilities and baby-listening. (Some ground-floor suites and
cottages overlooking the pool.)
Facilities: Lounge, coffee room, bar, all with log fires; restaurant, games room.
Saturday night folk singing and dinner-dances. 5 acres grounds and lawns with
heated swimming pool, badminton, children's play area, trampoline, tree houses,
etc. Riding, golf and excellent hill walking in the vicinity; fishing in nearby rivers
and lochs. &.
Location: ¾ mile W of Selkirk.
Restrictions: Children welcome but none under 15 at dinner; suppers and high
teas provided. No dogs.
Credit cards: Access, American Express, Diners.
Terms (excluding VAT and service): Dinner, B & B £15–27. Set meal: dinner (4
courses) £9.50; full *alc* (3 courses) £9.50. Special spring fishing, golfing, etc, breaks.
Reduced rates for children.

The length of an entry does not necessarily reflect the merit of a
hotel. The more interesting the report or the more unusual or
controversial the hotel, the longer the entry.

Skeabost House   [GFG]   *Telephone:* Skeabost Bridge (047 032) 202

A splendidly towered and crenellated Victorian mansion, with an impressive drive through banks of rhododendrons – a fine example of
Scottish baronial. From the tower you look across loch Snizort to the
Outer Hebrides. The river Snizort runs through the hotel's 12 acres of
grounds, and the hotel owns 8½ miles of fishing rights on both banks.
Most of the rooms are in the main house, but there is also accommodation
(slightly cheaper) in a bungalow close to the hotel.

In our entry last year, we quoted a reader, who, while fully endorsing
the hotel's inclusion in the Guide – she had had a spacious and comfortable room in the single-storey annexe, with a beautiful view of garden and
loch – had mentioned that she had found the resident owners, the
Macnabs and the Stuarts, a little too self-effacing. Another reader who
writes about the 'friendly house-party atmosphere and the excellent value
for money', rises staunchly to their defence: 'With our eighth visit
planned, we doubtless fall into the category of the "happy returners", and
as such are perhaps apt to view things a little differently from the first-time
writer. We have always found the management most helpful and ready to
assist when assistance is required. Ian Macnab extends a warm welcome in
the bar and John Stuart likewise in the dining room. Mrs Macnab of
necessity is most frequently out of sight in the kitchen, and the dishes
which delight us each mealtime are evidence of her skill and constant
supervision in that area.' *(Rosamund V Hebdon; also A W Palmer; Mrs C
J Robertson, W Ian Stewart)*

Open: Easter–October 17.
Rooms: 21 double, 6 single – 12 with bath, all with radio, tea-making facilities and
baby-listening. 5 rooms in annexe (some on ground floor).
Facilities: 3 lounges (1 with TV), cocktail bar, restaurant, snooker room. 12-acre
parkland; salmon and sea trout fishing on the river Snizort which runs through the
grounds (the hotel owns 8 miles on both banks), free to guests; there is a resident
angling coach. ㅤ.
Location: On the Dunvegan road, about 6 miles NW of Portree.
Restriction: No dogs in public rooms.
Terms: B & B £13.20–17.40; full board £138–184 per week. Buffet lunch from
£1.80; set meals: Sunday lunch £3.50; dinner from £7.50. Reduced rates for
children sharing parents' room; special meals provided.

SLEAT, Isle of Skye, Inverness-shire   **Map 5**

Hotel Eilean Iarman   *Telephone:* Isleornsay (047 13) 266
                                            Telex: 75252

There are several Welsh-speaking hotels in our book, but this is the first
with a wholly Gaelic-speaking staff and proprietor. It's an old-fashioned
Highland inn, with peat fires and hot-water bottles. There are electric fires
in the bedrooms and hot water, but no private bathrooms, so you will
need your dressing-gown. The hotel also disarmingly admits that the only
consistent thing about the weather in Skye is its unpredictability, so they
also recommend packing good books and warm jerseys. The hotel is on a
little fishing harbour looking over the Sound of Sleat to the waters of loch

Hourn and the mainland hills. 'A small friendly hotel in one of the prettiest of Highland villages. The menu is written in Gaelic (though many of the locals don't recognize some words, such as "Mèal Bhucan" for fresh melon), and the food is reasonably good, though the coffee is disappointing. Breakfast is large, leisurely and excellent. The hotel tends to be full in July and August – May and June are probably the best time to visit with the rhododendrons out.' *(Neil Mitchison)*

Last year's entry above is warmly endorsed by Nadine Gordimer who feels that 'reasonably good' does less than justice to the quality of the hotel meals.

Open: All year.
Rooms: 11 double, 2 single (5 rooms in annexe).
Facilities: Dining room, lounge, bar; occasional dancing; dogs allowed. Boat trips, fishing, shooting, stalking available.
Location: In peninsula of Sleat, at the south of Skye.
Terms (no service charge): B & B £12–17; full board £21–31. Set meals: lunch £5.50; dinner £9.00. Special winter rates.

SLIGACHAN, Skye   Map 5

The Sligachan Hotel   *Telephone:* Sligachan (047 852) 204

Sligachan has an honoured place in the annals of Scottish mountaineering. It is centrally placed for many of the best routes in the Cuillins, and some of the most famous 'firsts' are recorded in its visitors' book. It is an old, well-established hostelry, with a tradition of welcoming travellers and offering dependably good fare, above the regional norm. The quality of its 'bed', however, is not of the same standard as its 'board'. One reader this past year felt that the hotel, though thoroughly clean, was decidedly too spartan for his taste or for our Guide: he instanced a number of shortcomings – noisy old beds, worn carpets, sheets and towels unchanged for three days, wardrobe doors not closing. We suspect that the *Sligachan* has not moved with the times, and that accommodation which was wholly acceptable to the climbing fraternity – not the most fussy of customers when it comes to a bed instead of a bivouac – doesn't match the expectations of the new generation of tourists in Skye. But the hotel continues to give satisfaction to many. As another correspondent put it: 'It sustains its long-standing reputation and deserves inclusion in any Guide to prestigious hotels.' *(George Mair; also Brian and Arlette Singleton)*

Open: May–September.
Rooms: 15 double, 8 single – 9 with bath.
Facilities: 2 lounges, cocktail lounge, dining room. ½ acre grounds beside the river (fishing free to residents). Golf 3 miles; boats for hire on local lochs.
Location: Mallaig–Armadale ferry (Sligachan 30 miles); Kyle of Lochalsh–Kyleakin ferry (Sligachan 24 miles). Bus services from both ports to Sligachan.
Restrictions: No children under 8. No dogs in public rooms.
Terms: B & B £17.50–18; dinner, B & B £25–25.50 (4 nights and over). Set meal: dinner £8.50; full *alc* £7. Reduced rates for children.

Hotels were asked to estimate prices for 1982, but some hotels gave us only their 1981 prices. To avoid unpleasant shocks, always check tariff at time of booking.

The Heritage Hotel   *Telephone:* Stirling (0786) 3660
16 Allan Park

'In a country where average hotel standards appear to be abysmal, this place would seem to be an oasis and excellent value. It is run by Mr and Mrs Marquetty – he being French, she Scottish. It is a Georgian house situated in a quiet Georgian street very near to the castle. The rooms are tastefully decorated in a traditional style in such a way as to enhance the antique furniture and knick-knacks which are a feature of the place. Mrs Marquetty specializes in this side. The lounge/bar is an impressive through room and is more like that of a private dwelling than a hotel. The kitchens are run by Mr Marquetty, the chef de cuisine, and obviously have a French bias. The one disadvantage of *The Heritage* is that there are only four smallish bedrooms – so it is more of a restaurant with rooms than a hotel proper.' *(R A Nisbet)*

Open: All year, except Christmas and New Year.
Rooms: 4 double – all with bath.
Facilities: TV room, bar/lounge, dining room.
Location: Near town centre; parking for 12 cars.
Credit cards: Access, American Express.
Terms (excluding VAT and 10% service):   B & B £14. Set meals: lunch £4; dinner £8. Full *alc* £12. Reduced rates and special meals for children.

The Creggans Inn   [GFG]   *Telephone:* Strachur (036 986) 279
                                    Telex: 727396 att. Creggans

Two views of an old Highland inn on the shores of loch Fyne:
    'The minute you walk into *The Creggans Inn*, you can tell it has style. In the entrance hall there's a revolving stand of paperbacks. The eye expecting trash is astonished. Instead of *Saxpence in ma Sporran* by Hamish MacCouthie or *Tales of Crowdie* by Mave Boot there's a volume on Wittgenstein, not, as connoisseurs of the far west know, a philosopher whose views are of daily concern in the average hotel. But this is not the average hotel. In the first place, it is owned by that legendary figure Sir Fitzroy Maclean who 20 years ago took the inn and converted it into a comfortable hotel without destroying its character or, more importantly, depriving the village of its amenities. The public bar in the inn, hung with old photographs, warm and comfortable, could not possibly be mistaken, as most Highland public bars can, for a public lavatory. In the second place the hand of Veronica Maclean is everywhere to be seen. A noted author of cookery books she personally supervises the menus and tries wherever possible to bring the real taste of Argyll into the kitchen. There's loch Fyne fresh sea trout rolled in oatmeal, smoked mackerel from Mallaig, local baby scallops rolled in bread-crumbs and deep-fried, local salmon smoked over mountain bog myrtle, real Highland porridge which you are encouraged to eat out of a wooden bowl with a horn spoon and a delicacy created by the hotel's gardener and outdoor genius, Jimmy MacNab, which elevates that prince of fish, the herring, to the Upper House of gastronomy. The wine list and the malts at *The Creggans* are also

excellent. It is indeed a hotel to be commended.' *(Derek Cooper)*

'Staying here is a step back in time to a very well-run country house; service is courteous and efficient, the rooms pleasant and large; each window is a picture of loch Fyne, set in the great hills. All the meals are admirable – including the snacks served in the bar. I can think of no better centre for exploring Argyll which is as rich in history as it is in beauty.' *(Frances L Perry)*

Open: All year.
Rooms: 17 double, 5 single – 14 with bath, 2 with shower, all with telephone, radio, TV and baby-listening. (2 rooms on ground floor.)
Facilities: 2 lounges, sun lounge, TV room, restaurant; conference/party facilities. 6 acres grounds with woodland walk. Small beach by loch Fyne for bathing. Sea fishing in loch; trout and salmon fishing can be arranged. &.
Location: On the A815 Dunoon–Strachur road, on the edge of loch Fyne.
Credit cards: Access/Euro/Mastercard, American Express, Barclay/Visa.
Terms (excluding 10% service charge): B & B £16–20. Full *alc* £12. 10% discount on stays of 3 nights or more. Reduced rates and special meals for children.

TORRIDON, Western Ross   Map 5

Loch Torridon Hotel   *Telephone:* Torridon (044 587) 242

A beautifully sited Scottish baronial mansion, built by the first Earl of Lovelace in the mid 19th century, and now converted into a decidedly comfortable hotel by the resident owners, the fifth Earl and Countess. The hotel is set in 56 acres of woodland in the pre-glacial Torridonian mountains – marvellous for hill-walking and wildlife enthusiasts – and also has private fishing rights on the rivers Torridon and Balgy and several local lochs. 'A very pleasant atmosphere, with serene competent untroubled service. Good Scottish food, excellently cooked – fresh vegetables, local venison. A Scottish-sized breakfast that makes lunch unnecessary, though they do good packed lunches – asking what you want. Scenery of absolute beauty and rooms with views that keep one staring. I watched roe deer from my room in great comfort. Very hot water in a spacious bathroom. Library of many varied books. Come north for civilization.' *(Frances L Perry; also E H Plaut)*

Open: 1 May–mid October.
Rooms: 13 double, 6 single – 11 with bath, 12 with telephone; baby-sitting service.
Facilities: Lounge hall, drawing room, library, TV room, bar, restaurant. 56 acres woodland; fishing and yacht moorings available; gravel beach. &.
Location: On the edge of loch Torridon, S of Torridon.
Restriction: Dogs at the management's discretion.
Credit cards: All major credit cards accepted.
Terms (service at guests' discretion): B & B £12.10–15.90. Set meal: dinner £7.30; full *alc* £10. Special weekly rates. Reduced rates for children sharing parents' room; special meals provided.

Do you know of a good hotel or country inn in the United States or Canada? Nominations please to our sibling publication, *America's Wonderful Little Hotels and Inns*, 345 East 93rd Street, 25C, New York, NY 10028.

Uig Hotel   *Telephone:* Uig (047 042) 205

We had an enthusiastic entry last year for this old coaching inn on a hillside overlooking Uig bay and loch Snizort, with a modern annexe, Sobhraig House, in the grounds. The correspondent, a faithful returner over 20 years, particularly appreciated the diverse talents and characters of the four members of the Graham family who run it: 'A second home – save that all the chores are done for one.' Here are the impressions of another guest:

'When you arrive at *Uig Hotel*, you are immediately aware of the family atmosphere. You are introduced to your fellow guests before dinner and throughout your stay there is detailed consideration of your needs. The high standard of the meal and the priority of serving varied fresh home-grown produce rather than offering wide choice is appreciated. The well-equipped bedrooms are comfortable and attractive. The proprietors offer their fortunate guests the combined qualities of hotel and home. You can sail from Uig pier to the Outer Hebrides or encircle Skye's interesting northern peninsula by car or reach with ease Portree, Dunvegan and Sligachan. And from the hotel rooms you may quietly enjoy sunrise and sunset over Uig bay.' *(Margaret Widdowson; also R N Pepper)*

Open: Mid April–end September.
Rooms: 18 double, 6 single – 13 with bath, 11 with shower, all with tea-making facilities. 8 rooms in Sobhraig House. (4 rooms on ground floor.)
Facilities: 2 lounges, sun lounge, dining room. 2 acres grounds. Fishing for salmon and trout in river Hinnisdal; loch and sea fishing, walking, birdwatching, excursions to outer islands; car-hire arranged.
Location: NW corner of Skye overlooking Uig bay, reached by the A850 and the A856 from Kyleakin. Ferry services from Mallaig and Kyle of Lochalsh airport at Broadford, about 10 miles W of Kyleakin, with connections to Inverness and Glasgow.
Credit cards: All major credit cards accepted.
Terms (no service charge):   B & B £14–20; full board (weekly) £154–198.50. Snack lunch from £2.50; set meal: dinner £7.50–8.50. Reduced rates for children.

UPHALL, West Lothian   Map 5

Houstoun House   [GFG]   *Telephone:* Broxburn (0506) 853831
                                                       Telex: 727148

Houstoun House is a place of some breeding. For four centuries it was the Laird's house, and parts of it, including a fortified tower, date from the time of Mary, Queen of Scots. It has a rural setting, with its 18th-century garden surrounded by 26 acres of garden and woodland. It takes great pride in the quality of its restaurant, and has a distinguished wine list. It has a number of four-poster beds. The staff are 'cheerful and all smiles'. But it would be wrong to think of *Houstoun House* as just another country-house hotel. It openly sets out to attract two classes of custom: the business executive and the tourist, and it is particularly well-placed for the former being 13 miles from Edinburgh, 30 miles from Glasgow and 3 minutes from Scotland's main artery, the M8, which connects the two cities.

In pursuit of its targets, the hotel offers two types of accommodation: executive and traditional. The 12 executive rooms were all built in 1969 – highly mod-conned but conventional hotel rooms. The 17 traditional rooms are varied: some are small and cosy, some have 18th-century panelling, 9 have four-posters – the one in the tower is unusually large (popular with honeymooners) – and one room is completely furnished with Chinese lacquered pieces. 'Good welcome. Excellent room. The set menu was one of the best we have eaten.' *(G Rebuck)*

Open: All year, except 1–2 January.

Rooms: 23 double, 6 single – 26 with bath, 3 with shower, all with telephone, radio, colour TV and baby-listening. 2 rooms in annexe. (Some rooms on ground floor.)

Facilities: Lounge, bar, restaurant; small conference room (seating 20). Set in 26 acres garden and woodland; croquet.

Location: Off the A8/M8 1½ miles W of Broxburn.

Restriction: No dogs in restaurant.

Terms: B & B (continental) £21–34. Set meals: lunch £7.50; dinner £12. Reductions for stays of 4 days or longer and for children sharing parents' room. Reductions at lunch for children.

Aval du Creux, Sark

Channel Islands

HERM, via Guernsey Map 1

White House Hotel *Telephone:* Guernsey (0481) 22159 or Herm 83

'The hotel stands in the most perfect island I have ever clapped my eyes on. It is owned and run by Major Wood, the tenant of Herm, and quite plainly he has revelled in turning this old country house into a superb hotel with spacious dining rooms and lounges overlooking the sea. For island-lovers here is paradise.' *(Christopher Portway)*

We knew little of Herm when we received this commendation, but we learned more when we received a letter from the hotel's director, Andrew Forbes: 'Herm Island, which is 1½ miles long by 1 mile wide, has a population of 36 including children. There is a farm that produces and exports milk to Guernsey, a pub called The Mermaid, two beach cafés and 8 self-catering cottages. The island is leased from the States of Guernsey by Major Peter Wood, who also owns all the business on Herm, ensuring that no two businesses are in competition with each other. The hotel doesn't have a swimming pool: we don't need one as we have 1½ miles of magnificent sandy beach, including Shell Beach which has become famous for its rare shells. We don't have TV, because it would destroy the friendly atmosphere. The guests, even with small children, just don't want TV on Herm. We don't have Muzak, and we don't have clocks in the building. There are no cars or trains on Herm, and, unlike Sark, we haven't developed into a "hard sell" commercial island.'

We should be glad to hear from other visitors to this enchanted isle,

171

with its neat solution to the problems of competitive capitalism. But visitors should avoid August if they can: Herm gets about 2,000 trippers a day from Guernsey that month.

Open: April–November, Christmas/New Year period and weekends Friday–Monday in winter season.
Rooms: 22 double, 2 single, 10 suites – 31 with bath, all with radio, tea-making facilities and baby-listening. 20 rooms in annexe.
Facilities: 2 sea-facing lounges, 2 bars, 2 restaurants. 2 acres garden. Tennis, croquet, table-tennis available.
Location: Direct to Guernsey, then by high-speed launch to harbour where hotel porter will meet guests. (No cars on Herm.)
Credit cards: Barclay/Visa.
Terms (excluding service; no VAT payable in Channel Islands): Full board £20.50–27.50. Set meals: lunch £4.25; dinner £5. Full *alc* £6.50. Reduced rates for children; mid September–November and June children free of charge; special meals provided.

ST BRELADE, Jersey Map 1

Hotel l'Horizon *Telephone:* Jersey (0534) 43101
Telex: 4192281

In the old days, guests would have worn evening dress for dinner at a grand hotel like *L'Horizon*. It has very much the air of an ocean liner, though the outlook over St Brelade's bay is a good deal more rewarding than the Atlantic. Elaborate five or six-course dinners are served in the dining room, to the accompaniment of a band, playing both traditional Palm Court type music and livelier items for the younger set. There is an exceptional wine list, especially in the champagne section. The list of facilities below eloquently expresses the hotel's character. Not everyone's taste certainly, and perhaps more suited to the over 40s. But those who enjoy being spoilt in style in a distinctly opulent setting come back here year after year. 'Our fourth year here, and we support your entry. This hotel has a wonderful ambience – a rare commodity these days. The staff are the same – friendly but unobtrusive. Our small suite was a delight, with beautiful flowers from the manager to my wife.' *(B W Croft)*

Open: All year. Grill Room closed Monday.
Rooms: 75 double, 4 single, 1 quadruple, 7 suites – all with bath and shower, telephone, radio and colour TV; sea-facing rooms have balcony; baby-sitting by arrangement. (Some rooms on ground floor.)
Facilities: 2 lifts, 3 lounges, 3 cocktail bars, restaurant, grill room; 2 suites for conventions; terrace, enclosed sun-terrace; indoor heated swimming pool, sauna, solarium. Grounds with lawns, borders, rose garden, patio; hotel is directly on sandy beach with immediate safe bathing; scuba diving, water-skiing, fishing. Golf, riding nearby.
Location: On the beach, 6 miles W of St Helier.
Restriction: No dogs.
Credit cards: All major credit cards accepted.
Terms (excluding 10% service; no VAT payable in Channel Islands): B & B £16.50–26.50; dinner, B & B £23–33; full board £29–38.50. Set meal: dinner £8–9; full *alc* £10.50. Reduced rates and special meals for children.

If you are thinking of writing reports on hotels for us, do it NOW!

ST SAVIOUR, Jersey   Map 1

Longueville Manor Hotel   *Telephone:* Jersey (0534) 25501
                                                Telex: 4192306

Longueville Manor, 1½ miles inland from Jersey's capital, St Helier, and 2½ miles from the Royal Jersey Golf Course, has been for more than a quarter of a century the most sophisticated and attractive hotel on the island. In the last year, the hotel has created five new de-luxe suites, which will doubtless add to the general tone. It is a family affair; the owners, Neal Lewis and his wife, retired a few years ago and their daughter and son-in-law, Mr and Mrs Simon Dufty, are the present managers.

'My wife and I would like to endorse in every way the comments in your 1981 entry, including Pamela Vandyke Price's statement, "I can't wait to go back." The hotel is quite excellent in all respects; the owners and the managers and *all* members of the staff did all they could to make us feel comfortable throughout our stay. We took full board, and the meals were really outstanding with no necessity to change to *à la carte* on any occasion. And the new rooms are truly immaculate.' So ran one recent report. Another visitor, while concurring in the general view of the hotel's capacity to cosset ('A superbly run and truly elegant hotel. A place to be pampered indeed!') took a slightly less enthusiastic view of the restaurant side of things: 'A pity that the chef is not able fully to realize his ambitions on the *table d'hôte*. There is rather too much evidence of short cuts in the kitchen. But the breakfasts were magnificent!' *(C Ashley, W N Greenwood)*

Open: All year.
Rooms: 31 double, 5 single – 34 with bath, 2 with shower, all with telephone, radio and colour TV. (6 rooms on ground floor.)
Facilities: Hall lounge, bar/lounge, reading room, panelled dining room. 15 acres grounds with heated swimming pool, putting green, riding stables. Golf, bowls, squash, tennis within easy reach; coaches call by arrangement for island drives and other excursions. &.
Location: 1½ miles E of St Helier; ¾ mile from the sea; bus stop near main hotel gates.
Restrictions: No children under 7. No dogs in public rooms.
Credit cards: All major credit cards accepted.
Terms (no VAT payable in Channel Islands): B & B £28–33; dinner, B & B £37.50–42.50; full board £43.50–47.50. Set meals (excluding 10% service charge): lunch £6.25; dinner £9.50; full *alc* £12. Reduced rates for children sharing parents' room.

SARK, via Guernsey   Map 1

Aval du Creux Hotel [GFG]   *Telephone:* Sark (048 183) 2036

Some hotels can elicit from their grateful guests remarkable expressions of loyalty, and the *Aval du Creux* is a case in point. It is a well-modernized old farmhouse, which for some years past has been dispensing, under its chef/owner Peter Hauser, a particular warmth of hospitality and a notable distinction in the meals. 'Year Six (Year Seven booked already before leaving this year). I was not at all surprised this year to find that yet again Peter Hauser has sought to improve upon his previous year's performance

173

by the introduction of new dishes and additional niceties in the presentation and service of the food. The quality of service this year was the best yet, nothing was too much trouble, from the chef-patron down, to make sure that the guests derived the maximum pleasure from their meal and stay. As a result there was the usual compliment of guests seen removing the invisible flies from their eyes with handkerchiefs as they left on their homeward journey. For quality and value for money the *Aval du Creux* hotel, coupled with the name of Peter Hauser, is hard to surpass.' *(Ian Culley)*

Open: 1 May–1 October.
Rooms: 3 double, 2 single, 5 suites – all with shower.
Facilities: Lounge with TV, sun-lounge, bar (with zither music by request), dining room. 1 acre grounds.
Location: Just W of Creux harbour.
Restriction: No dogs.
Terms (no VAT payable in Channel Islands): Dinner, B & B £18; full board £20. Set meals: lunch £4; dinner £6.50; full *alc* £10. Reduced rates for children.

SARK, via Guernsey   **Map 1**

Dixcart Hotel   [GFG]   *Telephone:* (048 183) 2015

In our entry last year for the *Dixcart*, a pleasant early 19th-century stone-built and partly creepered building in the centre of the island – all parts easily accessible by foot, bicycle or horse-drawn carriage – we said that the food was one reason why people return here year after year, the vivacious character of the *patronne* Peggy Ravenshaw is undoubtedly another, and the very reasonable prices (and no VAT added) is a third. The report below is a characteristic tribute from a grateful guest:

'Our seventh consecutive annual visit proved as much a tonic and period of refreshments (literally and metaphorically) as ever! Peggy Ravenshaw is an incredible woman: she returned to Sark after a major operation the day we arrived and within hours was presiding in front of house and behind the scenes where she wore herself out in the kitchen over the August Bank Holiday! Great credit, too, to her loyal staff and to the fact that her regime flourishes. This particular weekend is always a "high spot" of the season, with many visitors rebooking the same rooms. It is like an annual family reunion. But the hotel's friendly atmosphere prevails at all seasons (we have been three times at Easter and four in the summer): much (all?) of the credit goes to Peggy Ravenshaw. Let us all hope she is restored to her full strength and vigour. Her spirit and determination is as evident as it ever was.' *(W N Greenwood)*

Open: Easter–October.
Rooms: 12 double, 6 single–7 with bath or shower. (8 rooms in wing and annexe.)
Facilities: 2 sitting rooms, lounge, library, bar, restaurant, forecourt. 9 acres grounds. 5 minutes' walk to sea with sandy beach and safe bathing; fishing from rock and sand; fine walks.
Restriction: No dogs in restaurant or bar.
Terms (excluding 10% service charge; no VAT payable in Channel Islands): Dinner, B & B £17–21.50; full board £19–23.50. Set meals: lunch £4.50; dinner £5.50. Full *alc* £8–9. Reduced rates for children.

If you think we have over-praised a hotel or done it an injustice, please let us know.

SARK, via Guernsey   **Map 1**

Hotel Petit Champ   [GFG]   *Telephone:* Sark (048 183) 2046

Petit Champ is in a secluded part of the island, well away from the day-trippers' track, but within half an hour's walk of any part of the island. Most of its rooms have superb views of the sea and the neighbouring islands of Guernsey, Herm and Jethou; there's a well-tended sheltered garden and, about 50 yards from the hotel, a solar-heated and spotlessly clean swimming pool built into a disused quarry – a fine sun-trap out of the wind. It has long enjoyed a reputation for the excellence of its restaurant.

' "Incapable of improvement" seemed the right comment for the visitors' book; Mr and Mrs Scott have succeeded in providing what for us is the ideal small hotel. The fresh cold lobster was certainly our best ever, and unusual dishes like corn fritters for breakfast, and tangerine ice-cream were delightful additions. The setting is idyllic, but of no interest to those who want colour TV, helicopters, conference facilities. There is, however, a wide selection of reading. And it isn't even very expensive. I confirm your report unequivocably.' *(Antony Fletcher)*

Open: Easter–October.
Rooms: 11 double, 3 single, 2 suites – 7 with bath, 4 with shower; tea-making facilities on request.
Facilities: 1 lounge, 3 sun-lounges, bar, 3 dining rooms, TV room. 1 acre garden with heated swimming pool.
Location: 30 minutes from Guernsey to Sark; then carriage to hotel, or lift by Island Transport to the top of the hill and a 20-minute walk.
Restrictions: No children under 8. No dogs.
Credit cards: Access/Euro, Barclay/Visa, Diners (but only for meals).
Terms (no VAT payable in Channel Islands):   Dinner, B & B £15.25–19; full board £16.25–20. Set meals: lunch from £2.75; dinner from £6.50; full *alc* £8. Reduced rates (⅓) for children sharing parents' room.

Northern Ireland

ANNADORN, Downpatrick, Co Down   **Map 6**

Nutgrove   *Telephone:* Seaforde (039 687) 275

Our first entry in Northern Ireland and a most attractive one despite the fact that *Nutgrove* is clearly not a hotel in the accepted sense of the term and both more idiosyncratic and also more sophisticated than the term 'guest house' implies. The description in the brochure tells a lot: '*Nutgrove* is an early Victorian Mill House, built about 1836, set in the heart of County Down. It is run by Christopher and Heather Cowdy – helped by Natasha, Jessica and Christopher-Robert – as a romantic revival of older-day living. The house now stands as it was built – original ceilings, fireplaces, door handles, shutter knobs. The family have been adamant that absolutely no changes should be made to the house at all. The dining room, which seats about 30 people, is open on Wednesdays, Thursdays, Fridays and Saturdays for dinner at 8.30 pm. If residents would like something to eat on the other evenings, a simple meal can be arranged. The menu, which changes every month, is very short, as everything is cooked that day by Heather Cowdy. 'We try to cook unusual food that requires, in some instances, lengthy preparation that perhaps one would not bother doing at home or more simple dishes that one might not have thought of.' To our questionnaire, the Cowdys appended the following note: 'Although a family atmosphere prevails here, we don't particularly welcome children under 10 as we furnish the house just as we would for ourselves and have quite a number of bits and pieces that are not suitable for small fingers. We don't have any notices or rules and are quite flexible about special diets, etc. The house is definitely rather quiet – no radio, no TV, no piped music and is up a narrow lane. Breakfast is taken on the large landing and we usually provide a log fire and newspapers on Sunday mornings. Most of our visitors come because we are slightly cut off from the outside world.' And here is the view of one grateful guest: 'A delightful blend of old-world grace and sophistication without pretension: delightfully and restfully unique.' *(Rosemary Metcalfe; also T R C Willis)*

Open: 1 April–30 November. Dining room closed to non-residents Sunday, Monday and Tuesday except by arrangement.
Rooms: 4 double – 2 with bath.
Facilities: Drawing room, breakfast room. Garden with stream. Golf, fishing, beaches nearby.
Location: From Seaforde village, turn into Seaforde road by the cottages. Take 2nd left and then 1st right.
Restrictions: No children under 10. No dogs in public rooms. Hotel has no licence so guests are asked to bring their own wines and spirits; no corkage charge.
Terms (no fixed service charge): B & B £9–14.50. Set meal: dinner £10.50. Special meals for children by arrangement.

DUNADRY, Templepatrick, Co Antrim   **Map 6**

Dunadry Inn   [GFG]   *Telephone:* Templepatrick (084 94) 32474
                                                    Telex: 747245

'The *Dunadry Inn* is in the country about 15 minutes from the airport; an old house with stables linked to it to form a long wing of bedrooms. A lovely arrival: a large entrance hall with polished floors and 'good' rugs, beams rescued, I understand, from an old water mill – and, most important of all, at 10.20 pm, a friendly and efficient welcome. The restaurant was closed, but in about 10 minutes a tray of excellent, hot, gamey soup, slightly plastic cheese, an apple and a good pot of coffee had been brought to my room. *Pace* Good Hotel Guide readers, I was delighted that there was a good colour TV in my room. Don't let the GHG outlaw television sets from hotel bedrooms. (We wouldn't dream of it. *Editor.*) The bedroom was spacious by modern hotel standards and sympathetically furnished – it was at the far end of the wing, overlooking a small courtyard – and the bathroom excellent. All the downstairs areas and rooms are huge – and the dining room one of the biggest, looking out over the river surrounded by lush foliage. The breakfast was "good hotel" (butter and marmalade in horrid packs) but the poached eggs had been done in water properly, and the toast was fresh. Altogether a hotel which combines the best of the old and the new, very well-run, convenient and in a pleasant setting. But do we have to pay £31 (July 1981) to stay a night and eat a breakfast in such an establishment? It was certainly streets better than other places I've stayed at at similar prices, though, and gave a superb first impression of Northern Ireland.' *(Elizabeth Stanton)*

Open: All year.
Rooms: 46 double, 31 single, 8 suites – 57 with bath, 20 with shower, all with telephone, radio, colour TV and baby-listening. 2 rooms in an annexe.
Facilities: Reception lounge, restaurant, ballroom; dinner dance every Saturday. 6 acres garden; river with trout fishing. &.
Location: 3 miles from Antrim; 13 miles from Belfast.

Restriction: No dogs in public rooms.
Terms: B & B £25–34; dinner, B & B £34.50–43.50. Set meals: lunch £4.50; dinner £9.50; full *alc* £14.50. Weekend breaks. Special meals for children on request.

Cashel Palace, Cashel

Republic of Ireland

CASHEL, Co Tipperary   **Map 6**

Cashel Palace Hotel   [GFG]   *Telephone:* Tipperary (062) 61411
(code only applicable within Ireland)
Telex: 26938

A magnificent 18th-century episcopal palace – built in 1730 for Archbishop Bolton by Sir Edward Lovett Pearce (the architect of the old Parliament House in Dublin, now the Bank of Ireland), with a noble red-brick Queen Anne facade and a garden bordering on the Rock of Cashel, also a fine picture collection – promises to become a fine example of a 20th-century country-house hotel. The palace was recently bought by Patsy and Declan Ryan – he was trained by the Troisgros brothers in Roanne and won culinary honours at *Arbutus Lodge* in Cork (q.v.). Declan is said to have taken half the *Arbutus'* legendary cellars with him. 'As a hotel and restaurant, Declan and Patsy's *Palace* should have a splendid future.' *(Charles Acton; also AF)*

Open: All year.
Rooms: 18 double, 2 single, 3 suites – all with bath, 3 with TV, all with bath, telephone and radio. (1 suite on ground floor.)
Facilities: Hall/drawing room, TV room, bar, 2 dining rooms; occasional music in bar. 20 acres grounds with walled garden. Fishing on the river Suir 3 miles; golf and hunting nearby.
Location: Off Cashel's main street; car park.
Terms (excluding service):   B & B IR£16.50–27. Set meal: dinner IR£13.50. Special weekend breaks.

Cashel House   *Telephone:* Cashel (Co Galway) 9; or Clifden 252
                                            Telex: 8812 C.H.H.E.I.

This handsome white-painted mid 19th-century house stands at the head
of Cashel Bay in a specially beautiful and cared for 50-acre estate. It was
converted to a hotel in 1968 by Dermot and Kay McEvilly, and almost at
once hit the world headlines as the hotel chosen by De Gaulle as his
away-from-it-all holiday on his resignation. Nothing comparably exciting
has happened in *Cashel House* since; the chief news in 1981 is that the
hotel has increased its accommodation by adding 8 new suites. A reader
last year was quoted as saying that in 30 years of experiencing hotels all
over Europe, he had never had better service (all Irish) and seldom better
food. 'For my money, more beautiful than Kerry and much less polluted
by tourism – modestly priced too.' Readers this year have in general
agreed, though with some continued reservations about the food. (*A
Woods, AF, Brian Moore*)

Open: 1 March–30 November.
Rooms: 20 double, 2 single, 9 suites – 30 with bath. (8 rooms on ground floor.)
Facilities: 2 lounges, dining room. 50 acres gardens with flowering shrubs and
woodland walks; hard tennis court; small sandy beach private to residents; grounds
lead to Cashel Hill. Many other beaches within easy reach; golf, lake and river
fishing, birdwatching, riding, deep-sea fishing. &.
Restrictions: No children under 5. No dogs in public rooms.
Credit cards: Access/Euro, Barclay/Visa.
Terms (excluding 12½% service):   B & B IR£12.50–19.50; dinner, B & B
IR£22.50–29.95. Set meal: dinner IR£10.50; full *alc* IR£12.

Arbutus Lodge Hotel   [GFG]   *Telephone:* Cork (021) 501237
Montenotte   From UK dial 0002 instead of 021
                                            Telex: 75079

One of the more famous hotels in Ireland, renôwned alike for the
reputation of its restaurant and for the comforts of the house. *Arbutus
Lodge* is owned by Sean Ryan, hitherto in partnership with both his sons,
Declan and Michael, but Declan, with his wife Patsy, have recently
started their own hotel, the *Cashel Palace* in Cashel (q.v.). Michael, with
his wife Catherine, remains at *Arbutus Lodge*. A significant fact for
gourmets about the Ryans is that they received their training as chefs at
the Troisgros brothers' famous restaurant at Roanne (three stars in
Michelin, and authors of *La Nouvelle Cuisine*). The Ryans say that they
would like to make in Ireland a restaurant worthy of three stars, though
neither reckon they have yet done so. However, as one of our nominators
writes: 'We are not regular diners in French three-star places, and the
Arbutus will do for us.' Another calls the *Arbutus*' cooking 'possibly the
best in Ireland'.
    As for the *Lodge*, it is a merchant's house, circa 1802, built on the north
scarp of the river Lee in one of the fashionable suburbs of Cork,
Montenotte, 15 minutes' walk or 5 minutes' drive from the city centre.
There are fine views over the city, especially at night. One of the features

of the hotel is its splendid terraced garden, with many fine trees including *Arbutus unedo* from which it gets its name. Another is a notable collection of modern paintings. The entrance floor has a large and comfortable bar, a residents' lounge and the restaurant, with its large bay window and reassuringly solid Victorian appearance – starched white table-cloths, good china and glasses, flowers, candles, etc. Bedrooms are on the upper floor, and there are reception rooms for weddings and suchlike on the lower floor: disco noises will sometimes percolate to the public rooms, but not to the bedrooms, which are thoughtfully equipped with good-quality furniture and the usual range of mod cons. Everything about the place reflects the caring hand of the owners – not least the service. As one regular patron puts it: 'I have never known anything but discreet, efficient, smiling, friendly but not "familiar" service from the entire staff, all of whom have a pride in the place and a desire that the customers should really enjoy themselves.' *(Thomas Annesley, Ann and Sydney Carpenter)*

Open: All year, except Christmas. Restaurant closed Sunday but bar food available.
Rooms: 12 double, 8 single – 16 with bath, 4 with shower, all with telephone, radio and colour TV.
Facilities: Lounge, bar, restaurant. Small garden with patio for eating out in summer.
Location: 5 minutes by car from town centre; parking.
Restriction: No dogs.
Credit cards: All major credit cards accepted.
Terms: B & B IR£22.25–30. Set meals: lunch IR£10.90; dinner IR£13.90; full *alc* IR£17.

GLENCAR, Co Kerry **Map 6**

Glencar Hotel *Telephone:* Glencar 102/113

A very quiet and secluded old-fashioned country hotel in 350 acres, 25 miles west of Killarney near the centre of the Ring of Kerry. The hotel owns extensive fishing rights in neighbouring rivers, and is much patronized by fishing people; there are three golf courses in the vicinity; but it would also make a scenically magnificent base for touring the wild and lovely country around. The food is described as good English (Irish). One recent visitor, who was not able to stay, felt the place was in need of some refurbishing. We should be glad to hear from other guests.

Open: 1 February–1 October.
Rooms: 19 double, 11 single – 15 with bath. (Some on ground floor.)
Facilities: Lounge, TV lounge, bar, restaurant, games room. 350 acres of grounds with tennis court and free trout fishing; salmon fishing available 17 January–12 October; beaches nearby; golf, deep-sea fishing; riding and trekking available. &.
Location: Killarney ½ hour; Shannon 2 hours; Cork 2½ hours; Dublin 4 hours; Rosslare 4¼ hours.
Credit card: American Express.
Terms (excluding 10% service charge): B & B IR£14–17; dinner, B & B IR£19–22. Set meal: dinner IR£10. Reduced rates for children.

Marlfield House   *Telephone:* Gorey (055) 21124
                                        (Code only applicable within Ireland)

Mary Bowe, the owner, herself converted this noble three-storey Regency house, formerly the dower house of the Courtown estate, into a peaceful country-house hotel. The comforts of the house, its position – a mile from the sea with sandy beaches, close to a golf course and with plenty of the beauty spots of Co Wicklow and the south-east within easy touring distance, not to mention the cooking which is taken seriously here and has a substantial non-resident following (strong emphasis on locally caught fish, home-grown vegetables and fresh herbs) – all are reasons why people return here regularly. One reader this past year commented on the overcrowding in the public rooms when the restaurant was at its full stretch, and slow service, also a few blemishes in the cooking. But this was an isolated complaint; for the most part, visitors to *Marlfield* have warmly appreciated the quality of the meals, the friendly but not over-effusive service, and the presence of a caring owner.

Open: 14 February–14 December.
Rooms: 11 double – 10 with bath, 1 with shower, all with telephone.
Facilities: Lounge, TV room, restaurant. 36 acres woodland with river, duck pond, pheasantry; shooting available. Sandy beaches with safe bathing and fishing 1 mile; golf club nearby. ዼ .
Location: On the Gorey Courtown road, 55 miles from Dublin, 28 miles from Wexford.
Restrictions: No children under 6. No dogs.
Terms (service at guests' discretion):   B & B IR£15.20–19.80; dinner, B & B IR£27.20–32.80. Set meal: dinner IR£12–13; full *alc* IR£15. Bargain weekend breaks September–April.

Newpark Hotel   *Telephone:* Kilkenny (056) 22122
Castlecomer Road   (Code only applicable within Ireland)
                                                           Telex: 28080

'In the middle of Ireland, there are not many places of real comfort. This would be the best hotel to stay within a radius of 50 miles. Kilkenny is a lovely medieval/18th-century town in a rich agricultural countryside. The *Newpark* is about a quarter-mile outside – small, modern and comfortable. It does have conference rooms, but they are well separated from the rest of the hotel so residents are not inconvenienced. Service is unobtrusive and friendly. The owner, Bobby Kerr, claims that he knows nothing about gastronomy, but he does provide a pleasant table, though helpings tend to be massive, and occasionally a little over-elaborate. Although it is a modern hotel, it does have a certain atmosphere, perhaps because Bobby Kerr really cares about it – remember the old farming proverb, "the farmer's boot is the best manure"?' *(TA)*

Open: All year.
Rooms: 45 – most with bath or shower, all with telephone and TV.
Facilities: Restaurant; conference facilities. Garden; tennis court.

Location: 30 miles from Waterford on the N77; parking.
Credit cards: All major credit cards accepted.
Terms (excluding service): Rooms IR£16.50–28.60. Set meals: breakfast IR£4; lunch/dinner IR£5.50–11.

KILLARNEY, Co Kerry   Map 6

Aghadoe Heights
                                       Telephone: Killarney (064) 31766
                                       (Code only applicable within Ireland)
                                       Telex: 26942

'In spite of all the hoo-ha, Killarney is almost unbelievably beautiful outside the scruffy market-cum-tourist town. *Aghadoe Heights* is a modern hotel overlooking the lakes just over three miles outside the town (car recommended). Half the bedrooms (and the dining room) have a view over the lakes and mountains that no possible travel brochure could excel. W B Yeats wrote that it was not the green land of Ireland that was so wonderful, but the clouds and skies over it. I have spent whole mornings after breakfast just lying in bed looking at the changing colours and sky patterns on lakes and mountains. There is a little too much muzak in the public area, and the food in the restaurant is international and willing rather than gastronomic. The proprietor, Louis O'Hara, has ties with France, whence come many professional people to play golf, enjoy the superb scenery – and the peace.' *(Thomas Annesley)*

Open: All year except 18 December–20 January.
Rooms: 46 – most with bath, all with telephone and TV.
Facilities: Lounge, restaurant; conference facilities. Garden; tennis court.
Location: 3 miles from town centre; parking.
Credit cards: All major credit cards accepted.
Terms (excluding service): Rooms IR£18.50–34; full board IR£33–37.50. Set meals: breakfast IR£4; lunch/dinner IR£5.50–10.50.

LETTERFRACK, Connemara, Co Galway   Map 6

Rosleague Manor Hotel [GFG]   *Telephone:* Moyard 7

'This hotel, a Georgian house with a modern bedroom wing, is situated among the scenic grandeur of Connemara, with an exquisite view across Ballynakill bay. It is 2 miles from the Connemara National Park. The public rooms are comfortable, and there is an air of tranquillity about the place. It is spotlessly clean and well-run by Patrick and Anne Foyle, who are brother and sister. The food is superb; one night we had a sea trout caught that day by the chef himself. We look forward to another visit.' *(Noel and Evelyn Cowper)*

Open: Easter–November.
Rooms: 15 double, 2 single, 1 suite – 16 with bath, all with baby-listening.
Facilities: 2 lounges, bar, dining room. 40 acres grounds with paths to sea through woods. Fly fishing tuition by hotel chef; good local sea trout, salmon, etc. Sauna.

If you have difficulty in finding hotels because directions given in the Guide are inadequate, please help us to improve them.

Location: 7 miles from Clifden.
Restrictions: Dogs, if small, by arrangement, but not in public rooms.
Credit card: Visa.
Terms (excluding 10% service charge): Rooms IR£11–13 per person; B & B IR£14–16; dinner, B & B IR£22–25. Set meal: dinner IR£9.50; full *alc* IR£10. Reduced rates and special meals for children.

MALLOW, Co Cork   Map 6

Longueville House   [GFG]   *Telephone:* Mallow (022) 27156
                                    (Code only applicable within Ireland)

In what was probably the longest quoted report in the 1981 edition, a reader praised the O'Callaghans' splendid Georgian mansion in a 500-acre estate overlooking the Blackwater river in the following terms: 'The kind of establishment to which I should be pleased to contribute even if never privileged to stay there. It seems to me to epitomize a way of life which, regrettably, both in Ireland and England, must fast be disappearing . . . A keynote of this place is care and concern, hard work and determination: despite its extremely high standards, it gives itself no false airs . . . The public rooms are of classic pattern, well suited to the elegance of the house . . . Our bedroom reflected the care and taste of the conversion . . . The noise from other visitors is the most minimal of any hotel I know. The country surroundings are of deep silence at night broken only by morning calls . . . The timing and manner of service at meals is worth a special mention . . . The naturalness of the procedure is totally akin to the country surroundings. We consider it inexpensive for the quality of the experience.'

Fulsome certainly. Over-pitched? If our postbag is an indicator, not at all. 'Mr Downs's tribute in the '81 Guide is remarkable, but I do not disagree with it,' writes one reader. 'The food at dinner was certainly the best I have encountered in Ireland,' writes a second. 'A wonderful and memorable place,' writes a third. A fourth writes: 'Every bit as good as previous reports have indicated and probably better, even to the extent that the bar is no longer furnished in plastic. Atmospherically, this is without doubt the most pleasant hotel at which my wife and I have ever stayed. All is so personal: we were known by name to *all* the staff within minutes of arrival and their one concern appeared to be our comfort and enjoyment; without unwanted intrusion, Jane O'Callaghan's cheery presence was felt throughout – one cannot imagine how she finds the time to chat and laugh with guests, and, at the same time, organize the delights that pour forth from her kitchen.' *(Sydney Downs, A C F Armstrong, D T White, Andrew H Latham)*

Open: Easter–mid October.
Rooms: 14 double, 4 single – 15 with bath, 3 with shower. 3 rooms in annexe.
Facilities: Drawing room, TV room, cocktail bar, President's dining room, library, conservatory; billiards, table tennis, darts. Situated in 500 acres wooded estate, with garden and 5 miles of salmon and trout fishing on the river Blackwater which flows through the estate. Riding nearby and free golf on the Mallow course. &.
Location: 4 miles W of Mallow on the Killarney road.
Restrictions: No children under 10. No dogs.
Terms: Rooms IR£13 per person; B & B IR£17. Set meal: dinner IR£13.

MARLFIELD, Clonmel, Co Tipperary   Map 6

Inislounaght Country House   *Telephone:* (052) 22847
(Code only applicable within Ireland)

A characteristically Irish thoroughbred Georgian house standing in large grounds, with gardens and wooded walks. The house is owned by the Reilly family, who grow their own fruit and vegetables. Fly fishing for trout is available on the river Suir, which is a field away from the house. 'A beautiful quiet country house of distinction. Breakfast included home-made marmalade – the acid test of a first-rate establishment.' *(Brian Scott-McCarthy)*

Open: 1 April–15 October.
Rooms: 6 double, 1 single – 5 with bath, 1 with shower.
Facilities: 2 lounges, dining room. 15 acres grounds with gardens and croquet lawns. Fishing and golf available nearby. Waterford Glass Factory, Kilkenny Design Centre within reach – also Rock of Cashel, Cahir Castle, Mitchelstown Caves.
Location: 1 mile W of Clonmel, in village of Marlfield; parking.
Terms (excluding 10% service): B & B IR£15. Set meal: dinner IR£10. Reduced rates for stays of 3 or more days and off-season weekend breaks. 10% reduction for children under 10; special meals provided.

OUGHTERARD, Co Galway   Map 6

Currarevagh House [GFG]   *Telephone:* Galway (091) 82313
(Code only applicable within Ireland)

'Quite the highlight of my tour,' writes a correspondent, reporting on no less than five Irish entries. 'The atmosphere really is more relaxed and country-house like than at any other hotel I have been in. Everything fits together here – the setting, the hospitality of the Hodgsons, the friendli-ness of the other guests.' *Currarevagh House*, the highlight in question, is a mid-Victorian house on the banks of Lough Corrib with 150 acres of its own grounds. It has been the Hodgson family home for five generations, and June and Harry Hodgson have been running it as a personal unstuffy hotel for many years. It's the kind of place where second helpings are offered at meals, and where shoes left outside the door are polished overnight. Its decor is traditional too – big peat fires, lots of Edwardian furniture, capacious beds with heavy linen sheets, and splendid bathroom fittings. The only change since last year is the installation of six further bath/shower rooms – 'outstandingly adapted,' writes a correspondent, 'from existing public bathrooms with ceiling mouldings carefully match-ed, everything in keeping.' *(A T W Liddell, Val Watson)*

Open: Easter–early October.
Rooms: 11 double, 5 single – 11 with bath and shower. 4 rooms in annexe.
Facilities: 2 sitting rooms, TV room. 150 acres park and woodland; 100 yards from Lough Corrib, 2 miles of foreshore belonging to the hotel; trout fishing, grilse in June/July; the hotel owns several boats. The lough is unpolluted and safe for bathing; much other fishing in the vicinity. Sporting rights over 5,000 acres moors near the house for grouse, woodcock and snipe in season; golf and riding nearby.
&.

Location: 4 miles NW of Oughterard on lake shore road; Galway 20 miles.

Restrictions: 'Children are tolerated but not encouraged. Consequently parents wanting to bring children will have an agreed reduced rate only if children share parents' room. No listening service or games.' Dogs by arrangement.

Terms (excluding 10% service charge):   Rooms IR£11.10 per person; B & B IR£14.85; dinner, B & B IR£23–24.35; full board IR£25.80–30.55. Set meals: lunch IR£4.80; dinner IR£9.50; full *alc* IR£8. Reduced rates for children by advance agreement, if children share parents' room; special meals 'if absolutely necessary'.

RIVERSTOWN, Co Sligo   Map 6

Coopershill Farmhouse   *Telephone:* Sligo (071) 75108
                                        (Code only applicable within Ireland)

Coopershill is in no sense a hotel, but a farm guest house – one of a group of such establishments (details from the Irish Tourist Board) which are inspected regularly and maintain standards. We repeat the previous entry, endorsed by a recent visitor – except in respect of the food, which he found disappointing:

'An enchanted and enchanting piece of country: to the south stretch the dramatic Bricklieve Mountains and vast peat bogs; to the north is Sligo and the sea; and a few miles farther north again is Drumcliff, where the poet Yeats is buried, the scene glowered over by the ship-shaped mass of Benbulben, its mountain profile visible for miles around. Designated a farmhouse, *Coopershill* is, in fact, a spacious Georgian building four-square, solid, beautifully furnished and run by charming people at amazingly cheap prices. There is a wine licence and the food is excellent farmhouse fare. Except for the lure of the surrounding sights, which it would be criminal to miss, there is enough going on around the farm to keep you there for the duration.' *(Diana Petry; also D T White)*

Open: Easter–30 September.

Rooms: 5 double, 1 suite – 1 with bath; most rooms with four-poster beds.

Facilities: Drawing room, dining room, playroom for children with TV, piano, record-player, table tennis, etc. Large garden within 500 acres of farmland; ponies for riding, also a donkey and cart. A river runs through the grounds, with fishing for pike and perch; trout fishing nearby; sandy beach at Sligo, also golf.

Location: 2 miles from Riverstown; on road from Dublin to Sligo, take second right turn towards Riverstown, by shop. After about 1 mile, by black post and rail fence, turn left; turn right by ruined lodge, cross stone bridge and two cattle grids.

Terms: B & B IR£10; dinner, B & B IR£80 per week. Set meal: dinner IR£8. 25% discount for children.

SCHULL, Co Cork   Map 6

Ard na Greine Inn   *Telephone:* Schull (028) 28181
                                        (Code only applicable within Ireland)

This pink-washed country inn, formerly an 18th-century farmhouse, is a mile from the fishing and sailing village of Schull in the far south-west corner of Ireland, facing Fastnet Rock lighthouse, and with bleak mount Gabriel as an impressive backdrop. It changed hands in 1980. Here is a first report of the hotel since Frank and Rhona O'Sullivan took over: 'A charming inn and Mrs O'Sullivan is an artist in the kitchen. The lamb, with a fresh delicate mint sauce and the brill baked in a savoury olive and caper sauce were superb. A hot carrot soup was served the following evening, savoured with a pinch of nutmeg – delicious! Mr O'Sullivan went out of his way to do our booking for us. Had we not been in search of better weather, we would have extended our visit.' *(Mr and Mrs J E Brown; also Mrs J Aulb)*

Open: Easter–end September.
Rooms: 9 double, 1 suite – all with bath and tea-making facilities.
Facilities: Lounge, residents' lounge, bar, restaurant. Garden with children's playground; coarse and sea fishing, sailing. &.
Location: 1 mile from Schull.
Credit cards: American Express, Diners.
Terms (excluding 10% service charge): B & B IR£13.75–22.50. Set meal: dinner IR£10.50.

SHANAGARRY, Co Cork   **Map 6**

Ballymaloe House   [GFG]   *Telephone:* Midleton (021) 62531
                                          (from Britain dial 0002 instead of 021)

'*Ballymaloe* may not be everyone's idea of a dream hotel,' we said in our entry last year, 'but it is clear from our files that it is very much to the taste of our readers. It won't appeal, we suppose, to those who are looking for a hotel sort of hotel. As Myrtle Allen, owner and presiding genius, puts it: "*Ballymaloe* is registered as a Grade A hotel. In reality, it is a warm and comfortable old family home, with the family still in it, children and grandchildren come and go, guests become friends." '

The question of what sort of establishment *Ballymaloe* is unexpectedly reached the leader page of the London *Times* in the summer of 1981. A paragraph in their Diary reported that the Irish Tourist Board had refused at the last moment to assist in the promotion of *The Ballymaloe Cookbook* because the publishers had inadvertently described it as a hotel when that isn't how the Irish Tourist Board classified it. The question, so far as we are concerned, is of strictly academic interest; *Ballymaloe* certainly suits our book.

The house itself is mainly 17th-century, though there's still a 14th-century keep. It's in the middle of a 400-acre farm, 20 miles east of Cork. The sea is 2½ miles away and there are plenty of lovely walks in the vicinity, but there is also a lot going on within the grounds of the house, including a swimming pool, a tennis court and a nine-hole golf course. Fifteen of the rooms are in the main house; others are in the Old Coachyard, the Gate Lodge and a 16th-century Gatehouse.

No indication of any fall in Myrtle Allen's high standards. Telephones have been introduced in the bedrooms, and a slight improvement is reported in the very 'bush' golf course. The food is as excellent as ever, and the service quick and reliable. The only serious complaint once again derives from the popularity of *Ballymaloe*'s restaurant with non-residents, and the consequent over-crowding of the one large drawing room at mealtimes (it's strictly private except during restaurant hours). One suggestion from an addicted Ballymaloean, which we hasten to pass on, is that a door could be fitted to the small room off the passage leading to the kitchen, which would serve the needs of non-drinkers and those who do not wish to drink before dinner. *(A C F Armstrong and others)*

189

Open: All year, except 24–26 December.

Rooms: 23 double, 3 single – 17 with bath, 3 with shower, all with telephone and baby-listening. 9 rooms in annexe. (4 ground floor rooms with bathrooms suitable for wheelchairs in annexe.)

Facilities: 3 sitting rooms (1 with TV), restaurant, playroom. 400-acre farm and grounds with tennis court, swimming pool, 9-hole golf course, trout pond, children's play area. Horses and ponies available for guests. Sea 2½ miles, with safe sandy beaches; sea and river fishing by arrangement. The Shanagarry pottery is a mile down the road, with Mr Pearse's pots (cheaper than in the shops) and his son's glass. Irish craft shop in the grounds, selling tweeds, woollens, pictures, also fresh produce. ᗷ .

Location: 20 miles E of Cork.

Restriction: No dogs in bedrooms.

Terms (excluding 10% service charge): B & B (continental) IR£11–19, (English) IR£12.70–21; full board IR£28.20–38.75. Set meals: lunch IR£5.75; dinner IR£12; full *alc* buffet lunch approx. IR£8.25; dinner approx. IR£14.50. November–February 10% off all stays of 3 nights or more. Reduced rates for children; special children's tea approx. IR£2.40.

Part Two

AUSTRIA
BELGIUM
DENMARK
FINLAND
FRANCE
GERMANY
GREECE
HOLLAND
HUNGARY
ITALY
LUXEMBOURG
MALTA (including Gozo)
NORWAY
PORTUGAL
SPAIN (including Andorra, the Balearics
and the Canaries)
SWEDEN
SWITZERLAND (including Liechtenstein)
YUGOSLAVIA

Gasthof Deim zum Goldenen Hirschen, Freistadt

Austria

BEZAU, 649M Vorarlberg   **Map 12**

Hotel Gams   *Telephone:* (05514) 2220
                                                 Telex: 59144

'The Vorarlberg, Austria's most westerly province, carries at least its fair share of tourist traffic. But even in the height of summer it is possible to escape the buzz of the cars around Lake Constance and take refuge in the Bregenz Forest, where cattle and not combustion engines provide most of the sound. Bezau is literally the end of the line. A tiny train drawn three times a week by a steam engine chugs up from Bregenz through the hills. Beyond Bezau, the mountains take over: the Klein Walserthal, the other side of the range, is a part of Austria accessible only from Germany.

'The *Hotel Gams* looks like an old coaching inn that might have had songs composed by Robert Stolz. Petunias cascade down from the balconies; the public rooms are numerous; the mountains provide the view. I'm not sure that I like my outlook broken by tennis courts and swimming pool, but some people cannot resist keeping fit on holiday. The more sensible will discuss the cellar with the owner and if they show themselves sufficiently informed, they will soon find themselves sharing a bottle with him, but not one from the Vorarlberg itself which is now reduced to two vineyards, both of them indifferent. Ask for a room with a balcony and take your breakfast with a gulp of the Bregenzer Wald air.' *(John Higgins; also Gitta Sereny, B W Ribbons)*

193

Open: All year.
Rooms: 65 beds – 16 rooms with bath, 11 with shower, some with balcony.
Facilities: Lift, lounge, dining room; sauna, swimming pool, tennis courts.
Location: 37 km NW of Lech.
Terms: B & B 250–430 Sch; full board 410–600 Sch.

DRASSBURG, A 7021, Burgenland   Map 12

Hotel Schloss Drassburg   *Telephone:* (02686) 2220

'I cannot recommend this hotel too strongly. It is close to the Hungarian border and was once the summer residence of the Esterhazys; the present owner is the fifth generation of the family that succeeded them. There are 25 acres of grounds laid out by Le Nôtre of Versailles fame, though naturally only the gardens round the house can be kept up to his original standard. The service is remarkably cheerful and helpful. The staff have some English, but if there is any difficulty, the owner has fluent if picturesque English. The food – including venison, pheasant and river fish – is the best I have ever tasted in any hotel, and I've known them in 21 countries. You won't find any condiments on the table, and you won't need them. There are swimming pools, indoor and out, and tennis courts, and you can also ride on Hungarian horses from the castle's stables or take trips in horse-drawn carriages.' *(T M Wilson)*

Open: 1 April–30 November.
Rooms: 25 double, 11 single, 1 suite – 22 with bath, 8 with shower; radio and TV on request. (Some rooms on ground floor.)
Facilities: Large hall with fireplace, salon, glassed-in veranda; baroque dining room; conference facilities; indoor swimming pool. 25 acres of grounds with swimming pool, sauna, tennis courts, ice-skating rink, riding course. English spoken.
Location: 11 km from Eisenstadt; private landing strip 6 km; bus connections from all directions; guests can be met at Wiener Neustadt railway station; Swechat airport is about 1 hour away.
Credit cards: American Express, Diners.
Terms: B & B 470–560 Sch; dinner, B & B 590–680 Sch. Set meals: lunch/dinner 260 Sch.

DÜRNSTEIN, A 3601 Lower Austria   Map 12

Richard Löwenherz   *Telephone:* (02711) 222

Dürnstein is on the northern bank of a particularly luscious stretch of the Danube, about 50 miles east of Vienna. The whole area, known as the Wachau, is steeped in the history of central Europe from the Stone and Roman ages onwards. Richard the Lionheart was imprisoned in the town in 1192 – hence the name of the hotel. Many of the finest buildings of the Austrian Baroque are close at hand. 'You find this entirely delightful hotel at the end of a narrow side street in this romantic village. The main road now passes beneath the village in a tunnel, so all is quiet. The hotel is built on the site of an old abbey and incorporates some of the old buildings; there are flower-filled gardens and a shady bar-terrace on top of a cliff looking across one of the most beautiful stretches of the Danube.

Comfortable rooms, good food and wine from the hotel's own vineyard.'
(William Goodhart)

Open: Mid March–31 October.
Rooms: 34 double, 4 single, all with bath and telephone.
Facilities: Hall, TV room, dining room. Large garden with heated swimming pool. English spoken.
Location: 15 minutes' drive from the nearest large town; parking.
Terms: B & B 425–700 Sch; dinner, B & B 605–850 Sch. Set meals: lunch/dinner 150–180 Sch; full *alc* 250 Sch.

DÜRNSTEIN, A 3601, Lower Austria   **Map 12**

Schloss Dürnstein   *Telephone:* (02711) 212
3601 Dürnstein/Donau   *Telex:* 071147

Schloss Dürnstein was built in 1630. The Emperor Leopold I, escaping from the Turks during the Siege of Vienna in 1683, took refuge here. For centuries it belonged to one of the great aristocratic houses before being reincarnated as a luxurious hotel about 50 years ago by the Thiery family who still own and run it. Lovely antique furniture is in evidence both in the public and in the bedrooms, most of which have a spectacular Danube view. The restaurant terrace is a specially agreeable place to eat – for the view as well as for the fine cooking. Some of the wine comes from the castle's own vineyards. 'Expensive but highly elegant and with a very good restaurant.' *(HC and Elsa Robbins Landon)*

Open: 25 March–5 November.
Rooms: 31 double, 4 single, 2 suites – 35 with bath, 2 with shower, all with telephone, radio and baby-listening; colour TV on request. (Some rooms on ground floor.)
Facilities: Lift, salon, TV room, writing room, bar; restaurant unit includes rooms of all sizes – catering for conferences, weddings and other occasions. Terrace overlooking the Danube for fine-weather refreshments. Large heated swimming pool, sauna, solarium. English spoken. &.
Credit cards: All major credit cards accepted.
Terms: B & B single 580–680 Sch, double 395–550 Sch per person; dinner, B & B 575–860 Sch. Set meals: lunch 175 Sch; dinner 195 Sch; full *alc* 400 Sch. Reduced rates for stays of more than 5 days in July. No charge per children under 6 sharing parents' room; special meals available.

FAAK-AM-SEE, A 9583, Carinthia   **Map 12**

Hotel Insel   *Telephone:* (04254) 2145

'A charming anachronism: the *Insel* sits at the edge of an island, half-a-mile by a quarter-mile, which, apart from the hotel, contains a superb old-fashioned bathing establishment, some tennis courts, and a dense wood. The island itself sits in the middle of the small Faaker See, said to be the warmest of the Carinthian lakes. The mainland is reached by a gently purring motorboat (1925 model) driven by a naval person with peaked cap. The food is superb, the service efficient and cheerful; shoes left outside the room-door are back early next morning, cleaned and polished – an anachronism indeed. The whole is presided over by Herr and Frau Bartosch, who personify Austrian charm at its best. This is the second time we have been at the *Insel*, and we will come again.' *(Rudolf and Hanna Strauss)*

Open: Easter–mid October.
Rooms: 81 beds, in rooms and suites – most rooms with bath or shower.
Facilities: Salon, bar, restaurant. Garden with private beach; tennis.
Terms: B & B 350–900 Sch; dinner, B & B 450–870 Sch; full board 520–1,000 Sch.

FREISTADT, A 4240 Upper Austria   Map 12

Gasthof Deim zum Goldenen Hirschen   *Telephone:* (079 42) 2258
Böhmergasse 8

'Dropping in at hotels recommended by scruffy youths lounging in small town market squares is not always a rewarding experience, but the merest glimpse of the flower-bedecked facade of the *Gasthof Deim* positively compels the weary traveller through the medieval gateway, passageways and tiny courts, on and into the gay warmth and welcome of the life within. Everything afterwards is but a dream – a dream of (princesses in) canopied (but firm and comfortable) beds, of ancient walls and arched roofs (ceiling is too dull a word), of foaming (locally brewed) beer pots, of superb Upper Austrian (lighter than Viennese) cuisine and wine, of happy laughing girls in simple local costume gaily serving one's simplest and one's most awkward requests. Antique furniture and etchings, rural artefacts and discrete hyper-efficient modern plumbing, also a beautiful garden. An absolute gem in a peaceful late Gothic and early Baroque walled town set in the soft loveliness of Upper Austria with summer and winter sports and relaxations for all – cultural, athletic or merely hedonistic. Ideal for refugees from Socialist reality escaping down the E14 from Prague or even from tourists in Festival-struck Salzburg. Cheap too. They speak enough English to entrance but not enough to encourage linguistic sloth. Best of all I shall remember the gentle strains of the local chamber orchestra drifting across from the castle into our bedroom and, of course, the hot raspberries and whipped cream to round off a memorable meal. Ah, bliss indeed!' *(T J Wiseman)*

Open: All year, except November.
Rooms: 23 double, 4 single – 10 with bath, 5 with shower, most with telephone.
Facilities: Salon, TV room, breakfast room, restaurant. Garden. Tennis, swimming, riding, winter sports nearby. English spoken.
Location: Central; parking.
Credit card: Diners.
Terms: B & B 130–250 Sch; dinner, B & B 300 Sch; full board 320 Sch. Set meals: lunch/dinner 80–100 Sch; full *alc* 160 Sch. Reduced rates for children.

We asked hotels to estimate their 1982 tariffs. Not all hotels in Part Two replied, so that prices in Part Two are more approximate in some cases than those in Part One.

FUSCHL-AM-SEE, A 5322 Hof bei Salzburg   **Map 12**

Hotel Schloss Fuschl   *Telephone:* (062 29) 253
                                                    Telex: 633454

A former 15th-century hunting lodge of the Salzburg prince-archbishops, and now a distinctly regal but wholly lay establishment. It overlooks lake Fuschl, with the mountains as an awesome backdrop; Salzburg and its festival are 20 km along the road.

'You may well think this too posh for the Guide, though it's in no sense a "grand hotel" but more like an Austrian equivalent of *Miller Howe* on Windermere (q.v.). It's an old country house, beautifully situated at the edge of the lake; romantic, luxurious (and expensive). Despite its being the ex-home of von Ribbentrop, and the present haunt of rich German industrialists and richer American widows, it's superb – the height of unostentatious luxury. Some rooms are in the main building facing the lake, but even better are the chalets in the garden. One lunches or dines overlooking the lake, and at dinner there are spectacular summer sunsets. The food is Austrian international at its best. The lake, which one can walk around in two hours, is a dream – and quite unspoiled. There's swimming both indoors and in the lake. If I had all the money in the world, I think I would squander half of it on a couple of weeks staying here during the Salzburg Festival.' *(Charles Osborne)*

Open: Mid April–mid October.
Rooms: 50 double, 13 single – 57 with bath, all with telephone and radio, 12 with TV.
Facilities: Salon, bar, 2 restaurants; conference room, 4 banqueting rooms, shop; indoor swimming pool, sauna. Gardens with access to the lake and beach; fishing, sailing, boating, 9-hole golf course, tennis courts, riding, cycling. English spoken.
Location: 15 km from Salzburg.
Credit cards: All major credit cards accepted.
Terms: B & B 700–1,400 Sch; dinner, B & B 1,000–1,700 Sch; full board 1,300–2,000 Sch. Set meals: lunch/dinner 300 Sch; full *alc* 340 Sch. Free accommodation for children under 14 sharing parents' room.

FUSCHL-AM-SEE, A 5330 Salzburg   **Map 12**

Seewinkel Hotel   *Telephone:* (062 26) 344

'Herr and Frau Ferstl make one very welcome in their beautiful, new hotel, situated at the end of the village in a quiet spot beside lake Fuschl. Although only recently erected, the hotel is built in the traditional style with splendid wood and wrought-ironwork. All the rooms have bath and toilet as well as balconies, the majority of which are overlooking the lake. There are chairs and a table on the balconies. There is also a television lounge. A small private beach connects the hotel with the lake. Only breakfast is served, but Frau Ferstl allows guests to leave food in her fridge which is useful if you take picnics or have snack meals on your balcony. There are several hotels in Fuschl where you can get an excellent meal. Being less than 15 miles from Salzburg, Fuschl is an ideal place to explore that city and at the same time to enjoy a quiet stay in the beautiful countryside.' *(Mr and Mrs P E Roland; endorsed by J Dixey)*

197

Open: All year.
Rooms: 19 double, 3 single, 3 triple – all with bath or shower and balcony, most with lake view.
Facilities: Lounge/hall, TV lounge. Garden with playground, private beach. Mini-golf, boating, sailing, riding, tennis, swimming, walking, cycling, winter sports.
Location: 15 km from Salzburg on the edge of the village; garage parking.
Terms: B & B 165–280 Sch.

GMUNDEN, A 4810, Salzkammergut   Map 12

Schlosshotel Freisitz Roith   *Telephone:* (076 12) 4905
Traunstreinstrasse 87

Gmunden is a colourful small resort town on the Traunsee in the Salzkammergut, with one of the best-equipped lake beaches on the north slopes of the Alps. The *Freisitz Roith* is a traditional balconied turn-of-the-century hotel, a few minutes from the centre of Gmunden at the foot of the Traunstein, and with panoramic views across the Traunsee. In addition to the restaurant, there is an attractive terraced café and a vaulted bar. 'The building seems quite old, but the rooms and bathrooms have been modernized with care and were entirely suitable to our needs. The views were beautiful. Our reception was cordial, there was help with our luggage, and our host was agreeably attentive and helpful on the two evenings of our visit. The food was very good and well-presented. We shall return.' *(J Dixey)*

Open: All year.
Rooms: 19 double, 7 single – 19 with bath, 7 with shower, all with telephone.
Facilities: Lift, lounges, TV room, bar, restaurant, café. Private beach. English spoken.
Location: SW of Linz on the N145; on E bank of Traunsee.
Credit cards: American Express.
Terms: B & B 310–370 Sch; dinner, B & B 400–460 Sch; full board 490–550 Sch. Set meals: lunch 100 Sch; dinner 120 Sch; full *alc* 200 Sch.

HEILIGENBLUT, am Grossglockner, A 9844 Carinthia   Map 12

Hotel Senger   *Telephone:* (048 24) 2215

'The Grossglocknerstrasse is surely one of the most spectacular mountain highways in Europe. Far too many people just drive over it, and go on to the Carinthian lakes, to Italy or Yugoslavia. But skiers who want to get off the most beaten tracks in Austria, and summer walkers – serious climbers too, who collect their 3,000-metre peaks – know that Heiligenblut, at the Carinthian end of the Grossglocknerstrasse is ideal, beautiful, adventurous territory. The very lucky ones amongst them already know that, just above the village, there also happens to be one of those rare family hotels that offer comfort, excellent food, and the kind of personal attention that makes everyone feel relaxed and good-humoured. At any time, more than half the guests in the *Haus Senger* are people who have come again and again, sometimes twice a year in winter and summer. It looks like a typical, large mountain chalet – in fact it's an old one with a new house skilfully added. Most of the rooms have balconies – two of them have large terraces – and almost all have either showers or baths. There is a sauna in the basement. The telephones have the direct-dialling system normally found only in luxury hotels. The food is so copious that almost everyone opts for breakfast and dinner, and skips lunch – though the cook bakes fresh cheesecakes, and Sachertorte and Apfelstrudel almost every day, and there is always the temptation to try it still warm from the oven for afternoon coffee after a day out on the mountains.

'But the hotel's greatest asset is the Senger family. Rosie Senger, vivacious, good-looking, keeps a sharp eye on all that goes on, and generates warmth and charm around her. Her husband, Hans, a former Austrian Olympic skier, runs a souvenir shop in the village; but is much travelled, and offers expert advice on the local climbing and skiing. Peter, the cook, Elizabeth and Waldtraut and Jeanette, the three waitresses, are always friendly, helpful and willing. They are happy to work there; and guests are happy to meet them. This is not just Austrian *Gemütlichkeit* – it's a place that you are always sad to leave, and where you know that you will return.' *(Hella Pick)*

Open: June–September; December–April.
Rooms: 20 double, 6 single, 2 suites – 4 with bath, 11 with shower, 2 with terrace, most with balcony, all with telephone.
Facilities: Salon, bar, TV room, restaurant; sauna, table tennis. Garden. Walking and winter sports.
Location: On the 107 N of Lienz; 10 minutes from centre. Parking.
Terms: Rooms with breakfast 200–280 Sch; dinner, B & B 310–400 Sch. Set meal: dinner 130 Sch; full *alc* 150 Sch. Reduced rates for children sharing parents' room; special meals provided.

KITZBÜHEL, 6370 Tyrol   **Map 12**

Hotel Pension Erika   *Telephone:* (053 56) 4885
                                                             Telex: 051264

'The description of our hotel is exceptionally good,' writes Uschi Schorer in returning our questionnaire. 'We have even had a number of guests who came because of your Guide. We would not have thought that so many people would have read your little book and followed up its recommendations. All the reader/guests have been delighted with our house and Kitzbühel.' While appreciating the modest compliment, we wish we could have heard ourselves from some of these guests. Reports welcome. In the meantime, we repeat last year's entry.

'My wife and I have travelled extensively in Europe, and our favourite hotel of all time is the *Hotel Pension Erika*. Run by a young couple of extraordinary energy, good cheer and talent, this hotel is well-located – a short walk either to the narrow streets of the old town, or to the Kitzbühlerhorn ski lifts. The old house, situated within a pleasant garden, has been tastefully modernized. Each room is different. The food is infallibly delicious and generous. Plan on gaining a few pounds! But the best thing about the *Erika* is the owners. Uschi and Benedikt Schorer treat each visitor as a welcome guest and friend. They know the mountains well, can plan a hike for any capability, and frequently join their guests for a walk. Activities such as entertainment by local music students playing antique instruments and singing, scavenger hunts, an outing to a 400-year-old farmhouse/museum for smoked ham, games evenings, ski movies, etc, delight young and old. Our highest recommendation.' *(Richard and Anne Selph)*

Open: All year, except part of April and all November.
Rooms: 36 double, 2 single – all with bath and telephone; colour TV on request.
Facilities: Large hall, sitting room with TV, games room, indoor swimming pool, sauna, solarium. Garden. Games evenings, films, barbecues. English spoken.
Location: 5 minutes from town centre and cable car; ample parking facilities.
Credit cards: American Express, Diners.
Terms: Dinner, B & B 300–600 Sch; full board 330–630 Sch. Set meals: lunch/dinner 80 Sch. Full *alc* 150 Sch. Reduced rates for children sharing parents' room: 50% discount up to 7 years; 30% 7–12 years; special meals on request.

LANS, Nr Innsbruck, A 6072 Tyrol   **Map 12**

Gasthof 'Zur Traube'   *Telephone:* (052 22) 77.2.61

A characteristic Austrian Gasthof, decidedly Tyrolean both in its furnishings and its style of cooking, dating from the 14th century, is in the centre of the village of Lans, which is in the hills to the south of Innsbruck, about 20 minutes' distance by car. The hotel has been in the hands of the Raitmayr family for fifteen generations! 'Absolute fantastic scenery, both in summer and winter. The friendliness of Herr Raitmayr and his staff is typically Tyrolean, and I recommend the local dishes on the menu.' *(P R Cockman)*

Open: 1 May–10 October, 20 December–15 March.
Rooms: 23 double, 7 single – 2 with bath, 11 with shower.
Facilities: Hall with TV, dining room. Occasional Tyrolean evenings with local band. 10 minutes from lake with safe bathing; golf, tennis, riding, winter sports nearby.
Location: 10 minutes' drive from Innsbruck. In village centre; parking.
Terms: B & B 180–270 Sch; dinner, B & B 270–340 Sch; full board 330–390 Sch. Set meals: lunch 100 Sch; dinner 120 Sch. Reduced rates for children sharing parents' room: 50% discount 2–6 years; 30% 6–10 years; special meals on request.

SALZBURG, A 5020   **Map 12**

Hotel Elefant   *Telephone:* (062 22) 43.3.97/43.4.09
H Sigmund-Haffnergasse 4   *Telex:* 63 2725

Continued expressions of satisfaction about this reasonably-priced (even in mid-Festival), central (in the middle of the old town and about three minutes' walk from the Opera House and concert halls), old (there's a beam on the third floor with 1259 carved on it, though the house has been renovated over the centuries) and friendly hotel. Breakfast is served in a charming Beidermeierish dining room. One reader this year complained that the hotel would not serve him a drink after 11 pm; but there are plenty of places to drink in the locality after hours. One warning: the hotel is in a pedestrian precinct, and not too easy to find. It is a 5-minute walk from a large underground car park. Warning: even pedestrian precincts can be noisy. *(J C Nicholson Belwell, Ian and Agathe Lewin)*

Open: All year. Restaurant closed Tuesday.
Rooms: 24 double, 16 single – 13 with bath, 25 with shower, all with telephone and radio.

Facilities: Lift, hall with bar, cellar bar, lounge, breakfast room, dining room. English spoken. &.
Location: Central, but located in pedestrian precinct; 5 minutes from municipal parking. Drive along Hauptstrasse, follow Rudolfstai, go round Mozart-Platz and Alter Markt.
Credit cards: All major credit cards accepted.
Terms: B & B single 280–350 Sch, double 480–600 Sch. Set meals: lunch/dinner 100–120 Sch. Reduced rates for children under 10 sharing parents' room; special menus.

SALZBURG, A 5020   Map 12

Hotel Markus Sittikus   *Telephone:* (062 22) 71.1.21
Markus Sittikus Str 20

'A delight from the moment we arrived when a thoughtful maid scooped up all my heavy baggage and carried it upstairs. We had a lovely room, with a polished floor, a cosy corner with a table and two upholstered chairs, and even a small balcony. The reasonable price included a small WC as well. The beds were the most comfortable imaginable. Breakfast (the only meal provided) was served in our room on Bavarian chinaware with real (not packaged) jam, and the butter carefully curled.' *(Marjorie Den-Bleyker)*

Open: All year.
Rooms: 23 double, 17 single – 11 with bath, 19 with shower, all with telephone and colour TV.
Facilities: Lift, hall, TV room, breakfast room. English spoken. &.
Credit cards: Access/Euro/Mastercard, American Express, Barclay/Visa.
Terms: B & B 250–460 Sch.

STEINACH, 1048M Tyrol   Map 12

Hotel Weisses Rössl   *Telephone:* (052 72) 6206

'We have stayed several times at this hotel on the Austrian side of the Brenner Pass and have always found a ready welcome and a comfortable room. We expect that it would be equally good for a longer stay in summer or winter by those pursuing more active pastimes such as skiing. There is nightly dancing in the Rosskeller, which we did not sample, but it is insulated from the bedrooms by being below the restaurants. Notices on the bedroom floors ask for quiet and we were not disturbed. The food was good. The restaurant at the front of the building was more intimate than the main large and rather crowded hotel dining room, and no more costly – at least to those not on *pension* terms.

'The *Weisses Rössl* is on the narrow main street through the town, opposite the church and there is no forecourt. However, the motorway over the Brenner (on which there is a toll to pay) keeps much fast traffic outside the town. Steinach itself is an attractive little alpine resort with pleasant walks in the neighbourhood in the summer.' *(Charles Baker)*

Open: 20 December–20 October.
Rooms: 34 double, 10 single – 13 with bath, 27 with shower and *sitzbad*, some with radio, all with telephone; TV on request.

Facilities: Lift, 2 bars, hotel dining room, smaller intimate restaurant; indoor swimming pool, sauna. Mountain climbing, good walks, winter sports.
Location: Central, but not much noise at night; garage.
Terms: B & B 270–300 Sch; full board 400–460 Sch. Set meals: 85–116 Sch; full *alc* 149 Sch.

VIENNA, A 1010 — Map 12

Pension Elite — *Telephone:* (0222) 63.25.18
Wipplingerstrasse 32

'Our favourite hotel in Europe. This A-class pension is on the third floor of a centrally located office building near the Graben. Our room (with bath) was very reasonable, and authentically furnished even to the goose-down filled red satin quilts. There is a charming breakfast room and lounge and – most important – the staff are very friendly and helpful. Breakfasts featured excellent coffee and wonderful rolls.' *(Martin and Deborah Zehr)*

Open: All year.
Rooms: 26 – 10 with bath, 12 with shower.
Facilities: Lift, lounge, breakfast room.
Location: Central.
Terms: B & B 360–440 Sch.

VIENNA, A 1015 — Map 12

Hotel Europa — *Telephone:* (0222) 52.15.94
Neuer Markt 3 — *Telex:* 112292 hoeuw a

In contrast to the ornate baroque of the *Sacher*, the *Imperial* and many other of the traditional Viennese grand hotels, the *Europa* is spanking modern – but carried out with quiet panache. Its entrance is in the Neue Markt, with its fine Donnerbrunner fountain; its back faces the smart shops of Kärntnerstrasse, halfway between the Opera and St Stephen's Cathedral. Everything about the *Europa* works superbly well – not excepting the quality of its restaurant and coffee house. *(HR; also Hella Pick)*

Open: All year.
Rooms: 90 double, 10 single – all with shower, telephone, radio, mini-bar and air-conditioning; TV on request.
Facilities: Hall, café, restaurant; conference facilities. English spoken. &.
Location: Central; garage parking.
Credit cards: All major credit cards accepted.
Terms: B & B 710–900 Sch; dinner, B & B 840–960 Sch. Set meals: lunch/dinner 200 Sch. Children under 12 accepted free of charge.

Do you know of a good hotel or country inn in the United States or Canada? Nominations please to our sibling publication, *America's Wonderful Little Hotels and Inns*, 345 East 93rd Street, 25C, New York, NY 10028.

Hotel Kaiserin Elisabeth   *Telephone:* (0222) 52.26.26
Weihburggasse 3   *Telex:* 112422

A thoroughly traditional Viennese hotel – perhaps a little on the genteel
side – on the edge of the pedestrianized Kärntnerstrasse and within a few
yards of St Stephen's Cathedral; the entire Inner City is within a few
minutes' walk. The public rooms, though large and comfortable, face
inwards – not a major drawback, however, if one is out all day sightseeing. Rooms vary in size and price. Few of the single rooms have private
bathrooms, and some rooms are a little claustrophobic. But the *Kaiserin
Elisabeth* has many loyal followers:
  'Although it has only been a hotel for seventy years or so, it is a historic
house and Liszt was among its visitors. While discreetly modernized, it is
still a really Viennese hotel, much patronized by those whom one used to
term the Viennese "gentry" – as well as a few fortunate foreigners. It is
utterly quiet. There is a warm welcome and great courtesy; no restaurant,
but a fine breakfast served on fine porcelain. Prices are very reasonable
for these days.' *(E George Maddocks)*

Open: All year.
Rooms: 51 double, 21 single, 2 suites – 59 with bath, all with telephone and
air-conditioning.
Facilities: Lift, hall, salon, breakfast room. English spoken. ᪣ .
Location: Central, near St Stephen's Cathedral; public parking nearby.
Terms: B & B 550–700 Sch.

Pension Nossek   *Telephone:* (0222) 52.45.91
Graben 17

'An old-fashioned quiet establishment which feels as though it has hardly
changed since the '30s. It is at one end of one of the most fashionable
streets in Vienna – now a pedestrian precinct: five minutes' walk to the
cathedral and the Kärntnerstrasse, about 12–15 minutes to the Opera. It
occupies the top floors of an old building of which the bottom floors house
offices. Access is by a lift running up through the old stone staircase.
Guests are given a large bunch of keys; one for the heavy outside door to
the building, one to their floor, and one to their room. Our room was large
and light (all the rooms are high) simply furnished with good cupboards
and lights, wash basin, and a rather basic but effective shower unit in the
lobby. And the price was remarkably cheap by current Austrian standards.' *(Nigel Gosling)*

Open: All year.
Rooms: 22 double, 4 single, 3 suites – 1 with bath, 6 with shower, 24 with
telephone.
Facilities: Lift, breakfast room, reading room. ᪣ .
Location: Central; underground car park.
Terms: B & B 180–270 Sch. Reduced rates for children.

Hotel im Palais Schwarzenberg   *Telephone:* (0222) 78.45.15
Schwarzenbergplatz 9   *Telex:* 136124

Some people like to be in the very centre of things when staying in a
glamorous cosmopolitan city like Vienna. The *Palais Schwarzenberg*
doesn't quite qualify on that count: it is 15 minutes' walk to the Opera and
the main shopping area, but it has formidable compensations. It is
discreet, quiet, impeccably elegant in all its furnishings, and it is housed in
one wing of the very grand and handsome palace which the Schwarzen-
bergs have lived in since the early 18th century; it was bombed during the
war, but has been faithfully reconstructed. Most of the rooms are in fact in
what was once the servants' quarters and stables, but there is nothing
menial in its present incarnation. Antique furniture and original oil
paintings abound, and quality is apparent in every aspect, not least in the
restaurant which is one of the best in Vienna. An additional pleasure for
the guests is the 20-acre park of the Palace. It must also be recorded that
the Editor and his family (travelling incognito of course) were delayed in
sitting down for dinner, owing to a misunderstanding, till 11.15 pm. A
meal of exceptional delicacy was served with relaxed sangfroid and
civility. It was certainly not a deliberate test of the hotel's service, but the
Palais Schwarzenberg passed with full marks. *(HR and others)*

Open: All year.
Rooms: 36 double, 3 single, 3 suites (1 with kitchenette) – all with bath,
telephone, radio; TV on request. (Some rooms on ground floor.)
Facilities: Lift, hall, bar, restaurant with terrace; conference facilities. 18 acres
private park with tennis courts, swimming pool and sauna. English spoken. &.
Location: Central, but very quiet; unlimited parking.
Credit cards: All major credit cards accepted.
Terms: B & B 675–1,400 Sch. Full *alc* approx 600 Sch. Special meals for children
on request.

Hotel Sacher   *Telephone:* (0222) 52.55.75
Philharmonikerstrasse 4   *Telex:* 01/12520

'At the height of Imperial grandeur in this most baroque of all cities, the
Hotel Sacher became the premier hostelry of the Austro–Hungarian
Empire. It maintains its position inside Vienna's Ring opposite the Opera
House. Go here to be pampered de luxe, and remember to sample the
sybaritic *Sacher Torte* from the original pastry kitchen – which taste quite
different from the exported examples.' *(George Herzog)*

Open: All year.
Rooms: 83 double, 38 single, 3 suites – 115 with bath, 3 with shower, all with
telephone, radio and colour TV.
Facilities: Lobby, lift, Blue Bar, Red Bar, Marble Room, café, restaurants with
piano and sometimes zither music; conference and banqueting facilities. &.
Location: Off the Ringstrasse, behind the Opera.
Terms: B & B 825–1,100 Sch. Set meals: lunch 600 Sch; dinner 660 Sch. Special
meals for children on request.

Pension Suzanne   *Telephone:* (0222) 52.74.15
Walfischgasse 4

Probably the first hotel in the Guide that has its rooms above a sex-shop. Don't be put off! The Walfischgasse is no sleazy Soho alley, but a respectable thoroughfare, 100 yards from the Opera House and the start of the pedestrianized Kärntnerstrasse. Like other Viennese pensions, the entrance is unimpressive: the bedrooms are on the second and third floors, some facing the street (double-glazing) and some a parking lot in the rear. No public rooms: breakfasts are served in your own bedroom. What distinguishes the *Suzanne* is its agreeable Viennese furnishings – no ticky-tacky stuff, but handsome beds, chairs and tables, fine mirrors, decent pictures – that, and friendly efficiency on the part of the English-speaking staff. *(HR)*

Open: All year.
Rooms: 43 beds – 18 double rooms with bath, 5 with shower.
Facilities: Lift. English spoken.
Location: Central.
Terms: B & B 270–350 Sch.

WINDISCHGARSTEN, A 4580 Upper Austria   **Map 12**

Hotel-Pension Schwarzes-Rössl   *Telephone:* (075 62) 311

The pleasant village of Windischgarsten in the Teichl valley makes a good centre for a spring or autumn walking holiday as well as for winter sports. The *Schwarzes-Rössl* is in the centre of the village. Thick walls and double-glazing, however, prevent noise from becoming a major nuisance. The hotel, which dates from the early 15th century, has all the virtues of an old family inn. Its rooms are larger and more characterful than in many modern hotels, the beds more spacious, the bed linen better quality. Bedroom lighting adequate (just). And the Baumschlagers are an exceptionally warm and hospitable couple; Frau Baumschlager speaks good English. Don't expect any special chic in the cooking, though there are plenty of local dishes and the helpings cater for Upper Austrian-sized appetites. But you can count on a spotlessly clean, very *gemütlich* inn, and an admirable centre for an inexpensive family holiday. 'Altogether one of our best holidays and most certainly the best value.' *(Robert Barratt)*

Open: All year, except November. Restaurant closed Monday out of season.
Rooms: 17 double, 5 single, 2 suites – 14 with bath, 2 with shower. 12 rooms in annexe.
Facilities: Reading room, TV/playroom for children, restaurants. Entertainment (zither and concertina playing, etc.) can be arranged on request. Indoor and outdoor games for children. 2½ acres garden 200 metres away, with tennis court. Mountains, skiing, fishing, alpine flowers, swimming pool nearby. English spoken.
Location: Central; parking.
Terms: B & B 200–230 Sch; dinner, B & B 250–270 Sch; full board 270–290 Sch. Set meals: lunch/dinner 75–100 Sch; full *alc* 150–200 Sch. 50% reduction for children up to 6 years; 25% reduction for children 6–10 years; special meals provided.

Le Sanglier des Ardennes, Durbuy

Belgium

BRUGES, 8000   Map 8

Hôtel Duc de Bourgogne   *Telephone:* (050) 33.20.38
Huidenvettersplein 12

'I have stayed at this enchanting hotel several times, and its charm and
comfort remain consistent. It is situated at the junction of two canals – you
look out across the water to delightful Renaissance buildings all round,
over banks of scarlet geraniums at the right time of year, and the dining
room fits into the canals like the prow of a ship. Quiet except for the bells
of the Carillon (but this is silent at night). The food is some of the best I
have ever eaten – but start saving up now! Table number five is the most
desirable, right in the window – you have to book it months ahead.' *(Mrs
R B Richards)*

Open: All year, except January and July. Restaurant closed Monday.
Rooms: 8 double, 1 single – all with bath and telephone.
Facilities: Salon, dining room. English spoken.
Location: Central. Make for Grand Place after Philipsstockstraat by the Place du
Bourg, where you park – from there 2 minutes' walk.
Credit cards: All major credit cards accepted.
Terms: B & B 825–1,050 Bfrs. Set meals: lunch/dinner 1,700 Bfrs. Special meals
for children on request.

L'Hôtel Amigo   *Telephone:* (02) 511 5910
1–2 rue de l'Amigo   *Telex:* 21618

Medium-priced (by capital city prices) and medium-sized, the *Amigo* is the first choice in Brussels for many visiting diplomats and marketeers. It's a post-war construction of a Belgian builder, who is also responsible for two other recommended *Amigo* hotels in Verviers and Masnuy-Saint-Jean – all possessing similar virtues of good design inside and out. There's no special chic about the Brussels *Amigo*, and the restaurant is wholesome rather than enterprising. There are far more exciting meals to be had in dozens of places within strolling distance of the hotel, and one of the best restaurants in the city, the *Maison du Cygne*, is fifty yards up the street. What commends the *Amigo* is its dependable efficiency and welcome, and its close proximity to one of the supreme joys of Brussels, the *Grand Place*. It is the only hotel of 'class' close to the square. *(HR; also Graham W Greene, Peter Allsop)*

Open: All year.
Rooms: 157 double, 26 single, 11 suites – 173 with bath, 10 with shower, all with telephone, radio and colour TV; baby-listening on request.
Facilities: Lift, various salons, TV room, restaurant. English spoken.
Location: Central, behind the Grand Place; garage.
Credit cards: All major credit cards accepted.
Terms: B & B 1,800–3,700 Bfrs. Set meals: lunch/dinner 690 Bfrs. Children accepted free of charge if under 12 years; special meals available.

DURBUY, 5480 Luxembourg   **Map 8**

Hôtel Sanglier des Ardennes   *Telephone:* (086) 21.10.88
Au Vieux Durbuy   *Telephone:* (086) 21.20.23

'The little village of Durbuy was given the title of town in 1331, and now calls itself the smallest town in the world. It is in the beautiful sheltered valley of the river Ourthe, and is a centre for walks along the river and in the unspoilt forest of the Ardennes. The vast car park in the village square could probably take a charabanc for every inhabitant, but they come and go in daytime; at night Durbuy is calmness itself. Nevertheless, choose to go before the high season – May is green and lovely, autumn sees the Ardennes clothed in red and golden splendour.

'The main hotel for a gastronomic treat is the *Sanglier des Ardennes*. Only the brave or starving would tackle the six-course *menu gastronomique*, but any smaller meal taken in the dining room overlooking the tumbling Ourthe and the flowering lilacs on its bank in the spring, is still a pleasure. The hotel specializes in good regional dishes such as river crayfish (not in May and June) and games from the forest. *Sanglier* is wild boar. The table service is impeccable, white linen cloths and napkins. The *Hôtel Au Vieux Durbuy* (same owners) is used as an annexe when the *Sanglier* is full and is much preferred for a quiet night as the tables in front of the *Sanglier* can contain noisy parties who rev up their sports cars on leaving. Opt for rooms overlooking the river and with views to the medieval witch-hatted castle. *Au Vieux Durbuy* provides excellent accommodation, breakfast is served in the room, and luxurious bathrooms to every bedroom. The rousing trumpet call at 8 am is the local fishmonger announcing his wares.' *(Valerie Ferguson)*

Open: All year, except 1 January–10 February. Restaurant closed Thursday, except holidays.
Rooms: 36 double – 13 with bath, all with telephone. 14 rooms in annexe.
Facilities: Salon, TV room, 2 restaurants; 2 banqueting/conference rooms; terrace on the river, boating. English spoken.
Location: 45 km S of Liège.
Credit cards: All major credit cards accepted.
Terms: Rooms 450–980 Bfrs per person. Set meals: breakfast 150 Bfrs; lunch/dinner 895–1,300 Bfrs per person. *Weekends gastronomiques* and *Soirées évasions* – special terms. Reduced rates for children under 10; special meals provided.

GENT, 9000 East Flanders   **Map 8**

Hôtel St Jorishof   *Telephone:* (091) 23.67.91
Cour St Georges
Botermarkt 1

'Described in its brochure as "the oldest hotel in Europe", though really more a restaurant with rooms. But those rooms have been modernized so that they have not lost their period flavour. The hotel had only rooms without bath left, but we were comfortable with lots of towels and enough space. The restaurant offered enormous amounts of food – cooked richly and well. Around the corner is a noisy city with lots of cafés and bars and things to see. We were just by the Cathedral of Saint Bavon with van Eyck's "Mystic Lamb" and – while we were there – Maestro Abbado rehearsing the LSO!' *(Bishop of Edmonton)*

Open: All year, except 20 December–1 January. Restaurant closed Sunday and public holidays.
Rooms: 73 – 44 with bath, all with telephone, TV and baby-sitting.
Facilities: Lift, bar, restaurant; conference facilities. &.
Location: Central; garage and car park.
Terms: B & B 700–1,460 Bfrs. Set meals: lunch/dinner 715 Bfrs.

ITTRE, 1460 Brabant   **Map 8**

Le Relais du Marquis   *Telephone:* (067) 64.71.71
Rue de la Planchette 10

'Ittre is a small village 20 miles S of Brussels strung out along a narrow winding country lane. It is very quiet and the gentle hills are lovely. *Le Relais du Marquis* is more than just a hotel: it is also a centre for the local people. It has an indoor swimming pool, a sauna, a solarium and various table games. Everyone was extraordinarily pleasant and very patient with our broken French; there was no hustle or fuss. It was good, too, to be told that as residents we could have the "menu pension" which was highly recommended and much cheaper, told in a way that was friendly and quite without condescension. The food *was* excellent too, and the rooms were delightful. However that is not what we remember so much as things like the leisurely swim in the company of two or three local schoolchildren;

and the attitude of all the staff which contributed to a sense of peace and well-being. And all at a cost that would have got us something very scruffy indeed in the city itself.' *(Alwyn Eades)*

Open: All year, except July. Restaurant closed Sunday.
Rooms: 32 double – 18 with bath, 14 with shower, all with telephone and radio. (4 rooms on ground floor.)
Facilities: 2 TV rooms, bar, tavern, restaurant; conference facilities; indoor heated swimming pool, sauna, solarium, billiards, table tennis. Horse riding, sailing, waterskiing, fishing nearby. &.
Location: 32 km from Brussels and 12 km from Nivelles. Take Wauthier–Braine or Haut–Ittre exits off the E10 Paris motorway. Hotel is in centre of Ittre village and has 2 garages and a car park.
Terms: Rooms 375–650 Bfrs per person; B & B 475–750 Bfrs; full board 1,560–1,930 Bfrs. Set meals: breakfast 100 Bfrs, lunch 500 Bfrs, dinner 570 Bfrs; full *alc* 750 Bfrs. Special meals for children.

KORTRIJK (Courtrai), 8500 West Flanders   **Map 8**

Hôtel Damier   *Telephone:* (056) 22.15.47
Grote Markt 41

'An old coaching inn on the market square, but my enormous room at the back was totally quiet. The bar, alongside the arched entrance, is a lively spot, much frequented by local businessmen. The huge inside lounge is comfortable and peaceful. The dining room opens off it, and whilst at first sight, it looks fairly ordinary, the food (not expensive) more than makes up for lack of pretty decor, and the place is always packed.' *(Tony Morris)*

Open: All year.
Rooms: 30 double, 18 single, 2 suites – 20 with bath, all with telephone.
Facilities: Lift, hall, TV room, café-bar, restaurant; conference facilities. &.
Location: In town centre; parking opposite.
Terms (excluding VAT): Rooms 650–750 Bfrs per person. Set meals: breakfast 150 Bfrs; lunch 650–930 Bfrs; dinner 930 Bfrs; full *alc* 1,000 Bfrs. Reduced rates and special meals for children.

NOIREFONTAINE, 6831 Luxembourg Belge   **Map 8**

Le Moulin Hideux   *Telephone:* (061) 46.70.15

One of the higher pleasures of the practising hedonist is to enjoy a supremely good dinner and then be able to retire to a bedroom which is in every way as sympathetic as the meal. Perfection on both scores is not so easily found: often the double- or treble-starred restaurants have no rooms, or if they provide accommodation, it isn't quite as exquisite as the cuisine. It is the rare achievement of Monsieur and Madame Lahire, a young couple but both descended from a line of hoteliers, to score equally on both counts. *Le Moulin Hideux*, a venerably creepered 18th-century mill in a secluded corner of the Ardennes forest just north of the French border near Sedan, has only thirteen rooms, but this is a true hotel not just a restaurant with rooms. Unassumingly impeccable elegance is the keynote. You would need a strong constitution, if you were to make a protracted stay here and engage yourself nightly on the wonderful *table d'hôte* (1,750 Bfrs in 1981), but the hotel is much patronized by active ramblers who presumably are able to walk off during the day the gastronomic exercises of the night before. *(HR)*

Open: Mid March–mid December. Restaurant closed Wednesday.
Rooms: 11 double, 2 suites – all with bath, 1 with shower, all with telephone and mono TV.
Facilities: Sitting room, loggia, restaurant; tennis court; golf 40 km, riding 10 km. Fine walking country. English spoken. &.
Location: 22 km N of Sedan, 4 km N of Bouillon.
Credit card: American Express.
Terms (excluding 16% tax): B & B 2,000 Bfrs; full board 4,000 Bfrs. Set meals: lunch/dinner 1,800 Bfrs.

OOSTKAMP, 8020 Map 8

Château des Brides *Telephone:* (050) 82.20.01
Breidels 1 *Telex:* 81.412 (aero)

'Very little can be found to put in the "minus column" for the *Château des Brides*. The multilingual amiability and helpfulness of the owners, together with a faint air of amateurism, creates a relaxed and familial atmosphere. Our suite (the "Versailles") was mildly surreal – worn at the edges (but marvellously comfortable beds), an outrageously chinois sitting room and huge Edwardian bathroom, all three rooms with superb views over the park. On chilly spring days, heating can be temperamental. The breakfast room (no other meals – the only visible staff being the owners' daughter and an aged gardener) has an air of faded elegance and provides a delicious if basic foundation for the day's gastronomic delights. An oasis of tranquillity with formal gardens, ponds and innumerable rabbits, ten minutes' drive from Bruges.' *(Don and Di Harley)*

Open: All year.
Rooms: 11 – 6 with bath.
Facilities: Entrance hall, salon, breakfast room; conference facilities. Large garden and woods. English spoken.
Location: 7 km from Bruges; 25 km from the exit Oostkamp on the Ostend–Brussels motorway.
Credit cards: All major credit cards accepted.
Terms: B & B 800–2,100 Bfrs.

ROCHEHAUT SUR SEMOIS, 6849 Map 8

Hostellerie Un Balcon En Forêt *Telephone:* (061) 46.65.30

An exceptionally thrilling panorama over the Ardennes forest and a wide bend of the lovely Semois river is without question the chief attraction of the *Balcon*. The hotel uses the view to its best advantage, both in the split-level public rooms and in the bedrooms, most of which have their own private balconies with rather uncomfortable easy chairs. The furnishings are a bit fake rustic with French provincial overtones (e.g. florid chintzes and wallpaper), and the restaurant, despite offering gastronomic weekends, has no special claim to distinction. But the hotel has a

211

thoroughly friendly air, owing much to the welcome of the owners Beatrice and Jacques Duruisseau. *(HR; also Frances Howell)*

Open: All year, except December and January when they open only at weekends. Restaurant closed midday on Wednesday.
Rooms: 14 – all with bath and telephone; TV on request.
Facilities: Sitting room, restaurant, terrace; indoor swimming pool. English spoken.
Location: 26 km N of Sedan. Hotel is 300 metres outside Rochehaut on the Alle road opposite Frahan viewpoint.
Credit cards: American Express, Euro.
Terms: B & B 1,000–1,700 Bfrs; dinner, B & B from 1,600 Bfrs. Set meals: lunch 485–600 Bfrs; dinner 600–1,200 Bfrs. Reduced rates for children.

RONSE, 9681 Maarkedal   **Map 8**

Hostellerie Shamrock   *Telephone:* (055) 21.55.29
Ommegangstraat 148, Nukerke

'A *Relais de Campagne* hotel, conveniently situated about 10 miles from the E3 autoroute, 35 miles from Brussels in the "foothills of the Flemish Ardennes" (i.e. not quite flat!). This is a beautifully furnished small country house, not particularly old, but very Belgian in appearance. Standing in its own grounds, it is extremely peaceful, both inside and out. Main attraction is the restaurant, serving set-price (expensive!) beautifully prepared meals. There are only a few rooms, immaculately kept, with enormous bathrooms. Robes, slippers, etc., all provided, and the owner's family run the hotel with obvious pride. An oasis of calm and quality.' *(Pat and Jeremy Temple)*

Open: All year, except Sunday evening, Monday, the last 2 weeks in August and 15 January–14 February.
Rooms: 5 double, 1 single – 5 with bath, 1 with shower, all with telephone and radio.
Facilities: Salon, bar, restaurant. Shady gardens of 5 acres. Swimming pool and tennis 4 km; golf 15 km; fine walking country.
Location: Ronse 4 km.
Terms: B & B 900–1,200 Bfrs. Set meals: lunch/dinner 800–1,500 Bfrs; full *alc* 1,100 Bfrs.

SART-CUSTINNE, 6871 Namur   **Map 8**

Hostellerie Moulin de Boiron   *Telephone:* (061) 58.87.60

'The *Hostellerie Moulin de Boiron*, which opened in 1978, is a deceptively simple-looking farmhouse and mill, almost totally isolated on the edge of a small lake, a few kilometres from the small slate-grey town of Gedinne, in the south-east corner of the Belgian Ardennes, on the road to Rienne – hardly a major highway, but in a calm agricultural area, away from the main Ardennes forest. It would be an ideal base from which to explore the more hilly area to the south, the valley of the winding, tumbling Semois, or the Belgian château country to the north towards Dinant. The proprietor and chef, Jean Lemaire, has rebuilt the ancient mill to provide eight

very spacious comfortable bedrooms, simply but attractively furnished in light pine and each with a bathroom or shower. The bar and lounge overlook the lake and boats are available to give gentle exercise, desultory fishing or quiet contemplation on the reflective water. The dining room is Monsieur Lemaire's pride and joy, the culmination of his long professional training, so the food is well-organized and seriously good.'
(Valerie Ferguson)

Open: All year, except 20 December–30 January. Restaurant closed Thursday.
Rooms: 8 double, 1 single – all with bath or shower. (Some rooms on ground floor.)
Facilities: Lounge, bar, dining room; conference room. 100 acres grounds bordering a lake with sailing, waterskiing, fishing. English spoken. &.
Location: 20 km from Beauraing and from Bouillon.
Credit cards: American Express, Diners.
Terms (excluding 16% service): B & B 840–1,350 Bfrs; dinner, B & B 1,450 Bfrs; full board 1,750 Bfrs. Set meals: lunch 495 Bfrs; dinner 900–1,100 Bfrs; full *alc* 900 Bfrs. Special meals for children.

Hotel D'Angleterre, Copenhagen

Denmark

BRAMMING, Nr Esbjerg, Jutland 6740　　　　　　　　　**Map 7**

Bramming Hovedgård　　　　　　　　　*Telephone:* (05) 17.33.25

'During a business trip to South Jutland I stayed at this hotel (13 miles east of the port of Esbjerg) for two periods of five days. I travelled many miles by car each day so that I could return to its calm and congenial atmosphere in the evenings. It is a medieval manor house run by the Lord and Lady of the Manor who personally take part in cooking and serving meals, which are cooked to a high standard, and agreeably served. The dining room and lounge in the manor house itself are spacious and dignified and contain many objects of artistic interest. The guest apartments, each quaintly named after some well-known personality, are in the adjoining buildings. Six of them have their own lounge and can be regarded as separate flats or cottages.' *(L A Clark; warmly endorsed by Tony Morris)*

Open: All year.
Rooms: 15 – all with bath or shower.
Facilities: 2 lounges (1 with TV), dining room. 10 acres grounds with a small river nearby; riding facilities (the hotel has its own tackle room); swimming 1 km; fishing (for bream and roach) on the river Holstead (free to guests) and on the nearby Sneum and King's river (small charge).
Location: 13 miles E of Esbjerg.
Terms: Rooms 105–275 Dkr; full board 204 Dkr.

Hotel d'Angleterre   *Telephone:* (01) 12.00.95
Kongens Nytorv 34   *Telex:* 15877

Big old-fashioned city hotels are not to everyone's taste, and some have
found the *d'Angleterre*'s pomp and circumstance a bit excessive, and the
service on the cool side. To others, as to the correspondent below, it
represents an ideal of hotel grandeur.

'The *d'Angleterre* is very much a national institution and keeps up the
old style very effectively. Its vast lobby is likely to be filled by Japanese
visitors or Arab millionaires, but a humble tourist gets equally polite
service. The hotel has the necessary ballrooms and reception rooms, and
you may find yourself peeking at an array of dinner jackets and evening
gowns. The hotel's grand restaurant, *La Reine Pédauque*, has a *table
d'hôte* with all you can drink, which is a bargain, given the high cost of
alcohol in Copenhagen. A block-long terrace café overlooking the
Kongens Nytorv, with its lovely park, complements the picture. Unfortunately, the hotel's bistro, the *Krinsen*, is now closed. The hotel is close to
the harbour, the royal palace, the state theatre and the famous department store, Magazin du Nord, all at the end (or start) of the famous
walking street, Strøget. As to rooms, the *d'Angleterre* is well-equipped
but not inspiring, with furniture from a period before Danish furniture
stood for good design. Still, each room has all it needs and usually a lovely
view. Service is impeccable; one's exquisitely light Danish pastries come
up in a few minutes, along with a handsome, full service, including a very
large pot of coffee.' *(André Schiffrin)*

Open: All year.
Rooms: 89 double, 42 single, 13 suites – all with bath, 4 with shower, all with
telephone, radio and TV; baby-listening can be arranged.
Facilities: 3 lifts, salon, bar, terrace bar, restaurant, coffee shop, pâtisserie;
dinner dances; conference and banqueting facilities; gift shop. English spoken.
Location: Central; car park for 150 cars nearby.
Credit cards: All major credit cards accepted.
Terms: B & B 500–700 Dkr. Set meals: lunch/dinner 125 Dkr; full *alc* 210 Dkr.
Reduced rates for children.

FREDENSBORG, 3480 Seeland   **Map 7**

Store Kro   *Telephone:* (03) 28.00.47
Slotsgade 6

Store Kro is close to Fredensborg Castle, the Queen's spring and autumn
residence. It was built by Frederik IV in 1723 at the same time as he was
putting up his royal palace next door. He was in fact, we are told, the first
innkeeper here, and one of the original buildings is still in use as an
annexe. The main building, however, is much more modern, and is
constantly being extended. The modest inn is now quite a grand sort of
hotel, but still retains an intimate atmosphere. 'Run like the *Priory* in
Bath (q.v.), but on a larger scale. Proprietor is an internationally known
restaurateur. The hotel caters for the overflow from the Royal Palace, but
you can dine quietly not aware that there is a party of 100 also dining. The

rooms are individually furnished. The cuisine is superb.' *(C R E Gillett; also John Rowlands)*

Open: All year.
Rooms: 15 double, 31 single, 3 suites – all with bath and baby-listening. 16 rooms in annexe.
Facilities: Lift, lounges, dining room; banqueting rooms, conference facilities. Riding and tennis nearby; near Esrum lake with fishing and bathing; sea at Hornbaek 15 km.
Location: 9 km NE of Hillerød. Hotel is in centre of Fredensborg; parking for 20 cars.
Credit cards: All major credit cards accepted.
Terms: B & B 240–310 Dkr; dinner, B & B 330–375 Dkr; full board 385–435 Dkr. Set meals: lunch 99 or 160 Dkr; dinner 123 Dkr.

RIBE, 6760 Jutland **Map 7**

Hotel Dagmar *Telephone:* (05) 42.00.33
Torvet 1

Once the nation's capital, Ribe is one of Denmark's oldest and best preserved towns. It's on the windy west coast of Jutland, in typically flat Danish countryside. The town itself has great charm, with its 800-year-old cathedral, its cobbled narrow streets and many listed buildings. In the spring, you can see the celebrated storks' nests on the rooftops. The *Dagmar* is in the central square. It was built in 1581, and is well in keeping with the rest of the town. The public rooms are of various shapes and sizes, rather ornately gilded in places, mostly old-fashioned and full of character, with low ceilings and chintzy armchairs. Some bedrooms are in the atmospheric old part, but there is also a new wing with thickly carpeted, net-curtained comfortable rooms with modern bathrooms. There are two restaurants – a posh one, with a considerable reputation for its cooking, and a livelier cheaper one in a cellar. 'Olde-worlde in the nicest sense (i.e. genuine), with the management equally so.' *(Tony Morris)*

Open: All year.
Rooms: 35 double, 7 single – 20 with bath or shower, all with telephone and radio.
Facilities: 2 salons (1 with TV), 2 restaurants; fishing, riding, swimming pool nearby.
Location: Central.
Terms: Rooms 160–350 Dkr.

VEJLE, 7100 **Map 7**

Munkebjerg Hotel *Telephone:* (05) 82.75.00
Telex: Munken 61103

'Four miles by free hotel bus to the town of Vejle, *Munkebjerg* is a large hotel in lovely beechwoods above the Vejle fjord. Outwardly it is a bit impersonal, but the personal care and attention shown by the staff puts it in the intimate class. Bedrooms are standard comfortable but a bit small, and the public rooms are spacious and airy with large areas of exposed brickwork and open hearths. But what makes this hotel special is its isolation, its facilities and the fact that it is almost entirely self-sufficient. It has its own farm, own butcher, baker, smokerie and vegetable garden. Outside there are special trails for walking in the woods, horses, bikes, tennis, boats on the fjord and a good golf course nearby. You can walk down to the fjord below in about fifteen minutes. It's a splendid hide-away for those who want to relax, eat well and exercise, and a good base from which to explore a very lovely part of Denmark.' *(Susan Grossman)*

So ran (in part) an earlier entry for *Munkebjerg*, subsequently omitted for lack of feedback. A recent visitor reports: 'We stayed over Easter when they have a special offer which is extremely good value. The food was very good. There is much more staff than one has become used to when staying in Danish hotels, all willing and capable. The rooms (there are also suites) were small but adequate. The wine list looked extremely impressive – a very unusual list of old vintages for those with that sort of money. But the really important point about the hotel is the service and, certainly if one gets a special offer, the excellent (well, almost: the peas the first night were perfect, the beans the next terrible) value for money in the restaurant. If one has to pay the full price it is better than the norm in Danish provincial hotels. There is dancing in the cellar bar at times, but teenagers won't like it, as the music is rather trad. Small children seem to be very welcome. To sum it up: if anybody can afford to spend a holiday in Denmark, this is a very good hotel situated near-perfectly for touring Jutland.' *(Dr and Mrs W N Brown)*

Open: 5 January–20 December.
Rooms: 108 double, 16 single, 2 suites – 62 with bath, 62 with shower, all with telephone and radio; baby-sitting can be arranged.
Facilities: Lounge, TV room, restaurant, nightclub open nightly except Sunday; billiard room; sauna, solarium; bicycles; 18-hole golf course 1 km. English spoken.
Location: 6 km from town centre; limited parking facilities. To reach hotel drive along the S side of the Vejle fjord.
Credit cards: All major credit cards accepted.
Terms: B & B 206.25–253 Dkr; dinner, B & B 242–308 Dkr; full board 321–357.50 Dkr. Set meals: lunch approx. 77 Dkr; dinner approx. 105 Dkr. Reduced weekend full board rates: 363 Dkr. 50% reduction for children under 12 sharing parents' room; special meals provided.

Hotel Kalastajatorppa, Helsinki

Finland

Kalastajatorppa
Kalastajatorpantie 1, Fiskatorpsvågen

Telephone: 90-488 011
Telex: 121571

'Whilst basically I am against huge modern hotels, this one is something else again. At the water's edge, it is a long low complex. A restaurant is separate from the hotel. The whole place (which is totally away from other habitation, although only a mile or two from Helsinki centre) has an air of opulent spaciousness, and the service is impeccable. Very quiet. All mod cons in abundance. And the prices are very reasonable.' *(Tony Morris; also Michael J Fitzpatrick)*

Open: All year.
Rooms: 157 double, 78 single – all with bath or shower, radio and telephone.
Facilities: Lift, bar, café, restaurant; conference facilities; hairdresser; night club; keep-fit room, swimming pool, sauna; beach 15 m; tennis, boating, fishing, winter sports nearby.
Location: 1 mile from town centre; garage parking.
Terms: Single 220–320 FM, double 300–395 FM.

If you have kept brochures for foreign hotels, please enclose them with your reports.

L'Auberge du Vieux Fox, Fox-Amphoux

France

Hostellerie des Trois Mousquetaires　　　　　*Telephone:* (21) 39.01.11

This small late 19th-century château is about halfway between Calais and Arras and only 13 km from Lillers where the Paris autoroute to the Channel Ports currently ends, but it continues to be popular with our readers not just because of its convenience as a night-stop. The rooms are thoroughly comfortable, and full of little extras. There is a lounge for coffee after dinner, also a garden, well-kept (at least by French standards), with a small playground for children. As anticipated last year, the 'leading girl' in the first-class team of energetic young women who wait and do the housework has married the son of the house, Philippe Vernet, who is also the chef. He is said to have put on weight – 'always a good sign'. Everyone speaks enthusiastically of the food, and the reasonable prices both for board and lodging. *(Robert Pascoe, Bruce I Nathan, Angela and David Stewart, A S C Hobrow, John and Jill Dick, P R Harrison)*

Open: All year, except 15 January–15 February; closed Sunday evening and all day Monday.
Rooms: 8 double – 6 with bath, 2 with shower – all with telephone and TV.
Facilities: Salon, TV lounge, 2 restaurants. 7 acres garden with lawns leading to a river. English spoken.

Location: Between Calais and Arras, 2 km from centre of Aire on the Arras side; private parking; 60 km from the sea.
Terms (excluding 15% service charge): Rooms 55–160 frs. Set meals: breakfast 15 frs; lunch/dinner 45–100 frs. Special meals for children.

AIRVAULT, 79600 Deux-Sevres   Map 8

Auberge du Vieux Relais   *Telephone:* (49) 64.70.31

Airvault is within easy reach both of Poitiers and the Loire valley châteaux. The *Auberge* is an old coaching inn in the quiet centre of the town which has a magnificent Romanesque church. It's a simple sort of place, with nowhere except the bar and a courtyard to sit in the evenings; the aurally sensitive should be warned that there is intermittent piped music in the former and the courtyard has in one corner a mini-aviary with vociferous canaries and budgerigars. Good selection of wines, including some interesting local Vendée wines, and the menus are excellent value. 'We were delighted with this hotel as a good night-stop. Very friendly welcome, and good food; and the fact that the lavatory was actually *in* the bedroom, masked only by a curtain, was irrelevant compared with the pleasantly old-fashioned furniture and the rose on the breakfast tray.' *(Jessica Mann; also Carol O'Brien and Philippa Harrison)*

Open: All year, except 1–16 October and 1 week in February. Closed Monday.
Rooms: 9 double, 3 single – 3 with bath, 4 with shower.
Facilities: TV room, bar, restaurant; courtyard and garden; river and swimming pool nearby; fishing and hunting. English spoken.
Location: Just off the N138 about halfway between Saumur and Niort – about 30 km from either. In the town centre near the church. Parking.
Terms: Rooms 50–120 frs; full board 100–130 frs. Set meals: breakfast 12 frs; lunch/dinner 40, 52, 90, 140 frs; full *alc* 90 frs.

AIX-EN-OTHE, 10160 Aube   Map 8

Auberge de la Scierie   *Telephone:* (25) 46.71.26

'In the heart of the Othe region, 31 km from Troyes, near the lovely old cathedral towns of Sens and Auxerre, and about 400 km from Calais or Boulogne. The inn is in attractive grounds with a river containing delectable trout: for those who are animal-orientated there are ducks, geese, peacocks, a donkey and two dogs. We have been there four times now, and always receive a warm welcome and a drink. One of the waiters speaks a little English, but all the staff are most helpful. The rooms are in chalets in the garden, round a small unheated swimming pool: light and airy, and prettily decorated with flowery paper. There is an attractive rustic bar with lots of wooden beams, horse brasses, woodcutters' tools, sheepskins, bellows, etc. The dining room reflects the same mood: tables are well-spaced, and have attractive linen, cutlery and glasses. The wine list is good apart from a very limited choice of white wines, which is surprising being near Chablis. The food is excellent with very generous portions. We have enjoyed excellent *jambon cru*; *pâté*; huge Ogen melon which overflowed with port; trout; black pudding which is a speciality; quails, sweetbreads. There is an immense cheese board. Puddings are

more adventurous than usual in France. We thoroughly recommend it.
(Padi Howard; also Warren Bagust)

Open: All year, except Monday evening and Tuesday in low season. Restaurant
closed Monday evening and Tuesday.
Rooms: 10 double – 6 with bath, 4 with shower, 3 with mono TV, all with
telephone and radio. (5 rooms on ground floor in chalets.)
Facilities: Salon, TV room, bar, restaurant. Garden and river; unheated swim-
ming pool. English spoken. ♿ .
Location: On the RN374 between Troyes and Sens, 2 km S of Aix-en-Othe.
Parking.
Credit cards: American Express, Diners.
Terms: Rooms 140 frs; full board 170 frs. Set meals: breakfast 20 frs; lunch/
dinner 98–130 frs; full *alc* 150 frs. Special meals for children.

ALBI, 81000 Tarn   **Map 8**

Hostellerie Saint-Antoine   *Telephone:* (63) 54.04.04
                                                       Telex: 520850 MAPALBI

Not far from Albi's glory – its stunning red-brick cathedral – and only a
stone's throw further to the Toulouse-Lautrec museum, this former
convent, with its rooms built round a lovely inner garden, now dispenses
far from monastic hospitality (extensive renovations in 1964 and 1972) to
modern Albigensian pilgrims. It is spotless and elegant and full of fine
furniture and pictures. The restaurant is *renommé*. Prices, both for the
rooms and for the meals, reasonable compared with other hotels of a
similar class in the vicinity. *(R S Ryder)*

Open: All year.
Rooms: 44 double, 12 single – 40 with bath, 16 with shower and WC, all with
telephone and TV.
Facilities: Lift, salon, TV room, bar, restaurant; conference room. Delightful
inner garden; open-air swimming pool. Tennis court 3 km.
Location: Situated in large park in the centre of Albi; very quiet; parking.
Terms: Rooms 160–340 frs; dinner, B & B 210–350 frs; full board 290–430 frs. Set
meals: breakfast 20 frs; lunch/dinner 100 frs; full *alc* 140 frs. 50% reductions for
children.

ANNOT, 04240 Alpes de Haute-Provence   **Map 9**

Grand Hôtel Grac   **Telephone:** (92) 83.20.02
Place des Platanes

'This is an old country inn with real character – simple, mind you, but we
personally don't mind that. It's in the shady main square of a very pretty
little town in a relatively unknown corner of inland Provence, but we
found much of interest nearby – Alps and gorges, and the amazing walled
medieval village of Entrevaux. The *Hotel Grac* is furnished in the local
style, and has a garden with swings which our small daughter enjoyed.
The Provençal food is really super, copious and amazing value – where in
England would you get a five-course lunch for less than £4 (1981),
consisting of mixed hors d'oeuvres, coq au vin, salad, cheeses, and a *délice*

au Grand Marnier? No wonder the dining room seemed always packed out with locals and tourists.' *(John and Ludmila Berry)*

Open: 1 April–30 October.
Rooms: 30 – 12 with shower.
Facilities: Restaurant. Garden.
Location: NW of Vence on the D908; parking.
Terms: Rooms 45–75 frs; full board 100–110 frs. Set meals: breakfast 11.50 frs; lunch/dinner 30–95 frs.

ANTIBES, 06600 Alpes-Maritimes, Provence   **Map 9**

Hôtel Caméo   *Telephone:* (93) 34.24.17
Place Nationale

A family-run hotel in a small square in the Old Town, about 150 yards from the Picasso museum and the ramparts. No garden, but there's a good sandy public beach about 1 km away.

'Very French, very noisy, and very good of its type. Giscard d'Estaing would never stay here, but Hemingway would probably have done so. It is not strong on public rooms other than the bar, so would not suit TV addicts or those wanting Earl Grey tea served in a chintzy-furnished lounge. Busy restaurant packed with locals (excellent choice on set menu). Meals can be taken outside on the *Place*. My wife and I were the only English staying in the hotel except for a party who arrived at the weekend for the Monaco Grand Prix. The barman is the only person with a knowledge of English, so one's French improves. The bar is a cameo from Simenon without Maigret: lots of pastis and Gauloises, and an almost endless card game. Very reasonable terms. Ask for what Madame called a "chambre luxe". These are roomy, clean, with modern bathrooms attached. The cheaper rooms have showers, some sited on the balconies overlooking the *Place*! They would be considered luxurious by anyone who has been through Dartmouth or the average English public school.' *(J K Gunn)*

Open: All year, except 5 January–5 February. Restaurant closed Tuesday in winter.
Rooms: 10 double – 9 with bath or shower, all with telephone.
Facilities: Lounge, bar/restaurant with air-conditioning, terrace; conference facilities.
Location: Old part of Antibes, 5 minutes from bus station; airport bus from Cannes to Nice airport stops here; parking.
Terms: Rooms 80–155 frs; full board 176–200 frs. Set meals: breakfast 22 frs; lunch/dinner 57–110 frs.

ARDRES, 62610 Pas de Calais   **Map 8**

Grand Hôtel Clément   *Telephone:* (21) 35.40.66
                                                 Telex: 130886 F

'Having noticed in your book that this hotel lost its Michelin star, I can only say GIVE IT BACK!!!' In fact, this unassuming small hotel, 17 km from Calais, lost its single Michelin star more than five years ago, but the loss still rankles with motorcades of Britishers for whom the *Grand*

Clément is the invariable first or last stop. Not every one is equally enchanted and there is another faction which feels that the hotel has been spoiled by its popularity with Britishers. Our own view is somewhere between these extremes: the rooms have no special distinction and some are on the poky side, but Paul and Monique Coolen do offer a warm welcome to their guests, Paul Coolen, whether he is in the Michelin class or not, is a wholly respect-worthy cook and the hotel, a member of the *Relais du Silence*, is a pleasantly quiet haven after a long drive. *(HR, T Brigden Shaw and others)*

Open: All year, except 15 January–15 February. Closed Sunday evening and Monday midday out of season.
Rooms: 17 double, 1 single – 12 with bath, 4 with shower, all with direct-dial telephone.
Facilities: Salon, bar, 2 dining rooms; conference facilities in winter. Garden with swings, terrace; ping pong. 1 km from lake. English spoken.
Location: 17 km from Calais on the N43 to St Omer and Lillers, whence autoroute to Paris.
Credit cards: Access/Euro/Mastercard, Barclay/Visa.
Terms: Rooms 120–200 frs. Set meals: breakfast 18 frs; lunch/dinner 100–200 frs. Special meals for children.

ARDRES, 62610 Pas de Calais   **Map 8**

Le Relais   *Telephone:* (21) 35.42.00
Telex: 130886 F

Recommended as a slightly cheaper alternative to the often crowded *Grand Clément*, in a quiet situation with a particularly pleasant garden, and first-class French home cooking, though if you are thinking of more than a night's stay you need to be warned that the menus do not change from day to day. 'A worthwhile stop. The dining room is attractive French olde-worlde, phoney but tasteful. The service was good, and the food excellent in quantity and quality. We chose from three attractive fixed-price menus with no apparent cost penalty. Good, reasonably-priced house Beaujolais.' *(John M Sidwick; also A H H Stow)*

Open: All year, except January. Restaurant closed Friday or Saturday evening November/December.
Rooms: 11 double – 3 with bath, 8 with shower, all with telephone.
Facilities: Bar/restaurant; party/conference facilities. Garden. English spoken.
Location: Central; parking.
Credit cards: Access/Euro/Mastercard, American Express, Barclay/Visa.
Terms: Rooms 100–165 frs. Set meals: breakfast 14 frs; lunch/dinner 45 and 75 frs; full *alc* 85 frs.

ARLES, 13200 Bouches-du-Rhône, Provence   **Map 9**

Hôtel d'Arlatan   *Telephone:* (90) 96.36.75
26 rue du Sauvage   *Telex:* S I Arles 440096

The ancestral home of the Counts of Arlatan and Beaumont, dating from the 15th century, just below Arles' Roman forum, described by one enthusiastic traveller as 'A true hotel of character in a fascinating city' and by another as 'One of the loveliest hotels I have ever visited . . . One passes through an arched gateway into a courtyard with a lone palm rising from the centre . . . a cool place to sit and sip on a hot day. The interiors are done with great taste and care, with lovely antiques and fabrics. The service is excellent, and the owner and all the staff are charming and helpful. Breakfast only served.' *(Tom Congdon, Janet Leipris, Marilee Thompson Duer)*

Open: All year.
Rooms: 41 double – 37 with bath or shower, all with telephone.
Facilities: Reading room and library, Louis XIII lounge with TV; conference room. Garden with courtyard patio decked with trees and shrubs for outdoor refreshments.
Location: Central, near the river; garage parking.
Credit cards: American Express, Diners.
Terms: Rooms 110–250 frs. Set meals: breakfast 17 frs.

ARPAILLARGUES, 30700 Uzès, Provence   Map 9

Château d'Arpaillargues   *Telephone:* (66) 22.14.48
    Telex: 490730

'I really should not recommend this. Next year there may be *tout le monde.*' Our correspondent need not be too troubled: the château, also known, confusingly, as the *Hotel d'Agoult*, already appears as a three-turreted red establishment in Michelin and as "Hôtel Très Confortable" in Gault-Millau. This converted 18th-century château, with an annexe converted from an old barn, lies about 3 km west of the lovely town of Uzès – well-placed for the Pont du Gard, Nîmes and Avignon, the Cevennes and the Camargue. It was once the home of Liszt's friend Marie d'Agoult. It is maintained impeccably, with cool and spacious rooms furnished with antiques. On fine days meals are served on a beautiful terrace overlooking an attractive garden. *(Antony Vestrey)*

Open: 15 March–15 October. Restaurant closed Wednesday.
Rooms: 27 – all with bath or shower and telephone. Some rooms in annexe.
Facilities: Salons, restaurant, terrace; conference facilities. Garden, tennis court, swimming pool. &.
Location: 3 km W of Uzès; parking.
Credit cards: Barclay/Visa, Euro.
Terms: Rooms 220–420 frs; full board 355–415 frs. Set meals: breakfast 24 frs; lunch/dinner 105–120 frs.

ASTAFFORT, 47220 Lot-et-Garonne   Map 8

Hôtel de la Tour   *Telephone:* (58) 67.11.96

'For those travellers seeking the peace and quiet of the French country-side, there can be nowhere quite like Monsieur and Madame Wenger's *Hôtel de la Tour*. It is in a class of its own, and is as yet quite unspoiled. The hotel is set in secluded tree-filled grounds in quiet hills just outside the village of Astaffort, which is between the Armagnac country and the Garonne, 16 km south of Agon on the N21, and about 48 km north-west of Toulouse. We were welcomed by Madame Wenger, who speaks good

English, not as customers but as guests. Setting foot inside the hall, we felt as if we were stepping back in time as we found ourselves surrounded by wood-panelled walls on which hung family paintings. The rooms are large and comfortable, and it was a pleasure to eat in the Wengers' stylish dining room. The cuisine was superb: French home cooking at its best. Although only a stopping point for us, we stayed an extra day and look forward to returning.' *(Jane Williams and Nigel Sabin)*

Open: April–October.
Rooms: 9 double – all with bath and telephone.
Facilities: Large hall, 2 dining rooms.
Location: At Astaffort, after the bridge, take left turn, D114 route de Cuq.
Terms: Rooms 90–110 frs; full board 130 frs. Set meals: breakfast 15 frs; lunch/dinner 55–80 frs; full *alc* 60 frs.

AUBENAS, 07200 Ardèche, Massif Central   Map 8

Hôtel La Pinède   *Telephone:* (75) 35.25.88
Route de Camping

La Pinède occupies an exceptionally agreeable position about a mile outside and above Aubenas on the river Ardèche. It is in the wild and beautiful department of the Ardèche, in the south-east of the Massif Central and within fairly easy reach of Le Puy, the Cevennes and the lower Rhône valley. It overlooks the town, and has a large garden full of flowers and trees. There's an outdoor shaded terrace for drinks. Service is good, the food excellent and the prices moderate. But not, according to one recent visitor, the place for those with very young children. *(M Hardwick, Jim and Olga Lloyd)*

Open: All year, except 1 November–1 January. Restaurant closed Monday.
Rooms: 30 double, 2 single – 26 with bath, 4 with shower, all with telephone. 12 rooms in annexe.
Facilities: Restaurant, outdoor terrace. Large woodland garden; tennis court. ᗉ .
Location: Aubenas 1.6 km; Montelimar 43 km SE; car park.
Credit cards: Euro, Barclay/Visa.
Terms: Rooms 90–170 frs. Set meals: breakfast 12 frs; lunch/dinner 48–75 frs; full *alc* 85–90 frs. Reduced rates for children according to age.

AVALLON, 89200 Yonne, Burgundy   Map 8

Hostellerie du Moulin des Ruats   *Telephone:* (86) 34.07.14
Vallée du Cousin

'I suspect this is a better investment than a stay at the *Poste* in nearby Avallon. It is a very special hotel in an idyllic green valley two miles west of Avallon in the direction of Vézelay. One can be lulled to sleep by the murmurs of a brook running under this hotel which was once a mill. One can also enjoy a superb bottle of wine from nearby Chablis while sitting in the grounds of the hotel. The rooms are fairly small and not overly elegant but are eminently comfortable. The food I thought outstanding: once rated one-star by Michelin, I can only imagine the star was lost because of a management change. And a lost star may be a boon: someone is trying *very* hard to regain it. The restaurant was packed and the patrons obviously included many locals, a high recommendation. Friendly and welcoming in a low-key way.' *(Caroline D Hamburger; also J M Dennis, Angela and David Stewart)*

Open: 1 March–31 October.
Rooms: 21 – 13 with bath, all with telephone.
Facilities: Restaurant.
Location: 3 km W of Avallon in the direction of Vézelay; parking.
Credit cards: American Express, Barclay/Visa, Euro.
Terms: Rooms 90–210 frs. Set meal: breakfast 22 frs; full *alc* 110–175 frs.

AVALLON, 89200 Yonne, Burgundy   **Map 8**

Hostellerie de la Poste   *Telephone:* (86) 34.06.12
13 place Vauban

'As we drove into the cobbled courtyard, two smartly uniformed porters came out to greet us and take our luggage. We were escorted to our room by a porter and a chambermaid (who looked and was dressed like a chambermaid) who hung up our coats, arranged our bags and put out the pillows. All this was done in so natural and pleasant a fashion that one almost forgot that this sort of service is not an everyday event. And it was the same smiling, helpful and practical approach without any sign of servility that we appreciated so much whether it was at the reception, in the room or in the restaurant. The fact that the *patron*, René Hure, seems to be everywhere at once all the time, and without ever moving much faster than a snail, must surely account for the warm and professional atmosphere felt throughout this hotel. For the rest, the hotel is well-maintained and furnished, beautifully warm and well-lit, and has a superb restaurant. The food was everything one expected and more. Search as I did, my only cavil (and how petty can one get?) was the oversweetness of the commercially produced jams served with the breakfast. If only they'd been home-made!

'If you are going to run a hotel to the highest of standards in which the cost of employing a large and professional staff must be a major expense then it cannot be cheap. The prices at *La Poste* are elevated but justified. It is expensive. But if your rich friends say: "If you're near Avallon you must stay at . . .", no one is forcing you to take their advice. In fact a cheaper alternative could be *Le Relais Fleurie* just 4 km up the road where you can eat for 60–100 frs and get a double room for about 125 frs. But don't expect it to be in the same class as *La Poste*.' *(Geoffrey Sharp)*

Open: All year, except end November–beginning January.
Rooms: 17 double, 3 single, 5 suites – 22 with bath, 2 with shower, all with telephone.
Facilities: Lounge, bar, restaurant. Small garden.
Location: In town centre; parking.
Credit cards: American Express, Barclay/Visa, Diners.
Terms (excluding 15% service charge): Rooms 170–300 frs; dinner, B & B 420–500 frs. Set meals: breakfast 28–30 frs; lunch 150–200 frs; dinner 200 frs; full *alc* 275 frcs. Special meals for children.

Report forms (Freepost in the UK) will be found at the end of the Guide.

AVALLON, 89200 Yonne, Burgundy   Map 8

Le Moulin des Templiers   *Telephone:* (86) 34.10.80
Vallée du Cousin

'This ancient watermill has been very attractively converted into a thoroughly comfortable and peaceful hotel on a narrow strip of land between the small road and the river. The gardens stretch along the river, and there is a beautiful terrace at the water's edge where breakfast is served. The hotel serves no other meals, but Avallon with its Michelin stars is only 5 km or so away, while Pontaubert, a quiet little town with at least two decent restaurants, is just down the road. Within easy reach of the N6 and A6 and only 15 km from Vézelay, *Le Moulin* is ideal for an overnight stop and would make an excellent base for local exploration. Reception and service were friendly and efficient. Recommended without qualification.'
(Warren Bagust)

Open: 15 March–2 November.
Rooms: 14 – most with shower, all with telephone.
Facilities: No restaurant. Breakfast terrace. Garden, river.
Location: 3 km W of Avallon in the direction of Vézelay; parking.
Terms: Rooms 85–135 frs. Set meal: breakfast 14 frs.

AVIGNON, 84000 Vaucluse, Provence   Map 9

Hôtel d'Europe   *Telephone:* (90) 82.66.92
12 Place Crillon   *Telex:* 431965

'A splendid building dating back to 1588. It has been a hotel since 1799. Cool, spacious and elegant. Beautifully decorated rooms with Nobilis wallpapers and well-appointed. The furniture scattered about on the stairs and in the public rooms would make an antique dealer salivate, as would the period mirrors and collections of china. You sat in the courtyard under the plane trees. During the day the pigeons watch you from the trees and can be a menace. The hotel is unobtrusively well-run and the staff speak American. It could not be better placed: just inside the walls, close to the Rhône, the Palais des Papes and the Pont of dancing fame, easy of access for those coming from Nîmes and the west as it is close to the bridge to Villeneuve. Despite being inside the city walls it is quiet at night. Food in the *Vieille Fontaine* restaurant is excellent. Service could be better. Wines well-chosen. The Côtes du Rhône are best value. There is a fine white Châteauneuf de Pape. Relaxed luxury at four star level.'
(Antony Vestrey)

Open: All year. Restaurant closed 1 January–8 February and midday 1 October–30 April.
Rooms: 50 double, 9 single, 6 suites – 53 with bath 13 with shower and telephone.
Facilities: Lift, 2 salons, restaurant; conference facilities. Courtyard. English spoken.
Location: Central; no parking facilities.
Terms: Rooms (single) 265 frs, (double) 310–400 frs. Set meals: breakfast 25 frs; dinner 78 frs.

In your own interest, do check latest tariffs with hotels when you make your bookings.

Hôtel de l'Île Rousse   *Telephone:* (94) 29.46.86
Bvd Louis-Lumière   *Telex:* 400372

Bandol, 50 km east of Marseille, is a busy, bustling small resort town with lots of boats in its harbour, popular with the French throughout the year and with foreigners as well. There is plenty going on around the beach area: waterskiing, regattas, sand sports, and a casino and dancing. Offshore (seven minutes by boat) is the island of Bendor, with zoological gardens, exhibitions of local and other wines and spirits, and a sailing and riding school. Something for everyone, in fact, which accounts for the popularity of the resort in high season; best months, when it is quieter, are May and June. The *l'Île Rousse* is the de-luxe hotel of the place – modern, with its own large heated swimming pool, and with exceptionally well-furnished and attractive tile-floored rooms. It lies on a narrow street, somewhat above the town, which is backed by wooded hills, and has its own small cove and beach – a distinct advantage. Choose rooms facing the cove, if possible, say some: the ones looking on to the little street can be noisy. Others prefer the street side, even without the lovely view, because of the noise of trains on the other side of the bay. *(Martin Gilbert)*

Open: All year.
Rooms: 53 double, 2 suites – all with bath, telephone, radio, colour TV and air-conditioning.
Facilities: Lift, large lounge overlooking the beach, TV room, bar, night club; 4 conference rooms. Heated swimming pool; solarium; direct access to private sandy beach and safe bathing. Tennis courts, riding, sailing, casino nearby. English spoken.
Location: 5 minutes from town centre; parking.
Credit cards: All major credit cards accepted.
Terms: Rooms 255–600 frs; full board 260–270 frs per person added to room price. Set meals: breakfast 30 frs; lunch/dinner 120 frs; full *alc* 150–200 frs. Extra bed for child in parents' room 70 frs; special meals for children.

Hostellerie de la Clé d'Or   *Telephone:* (6) 066.40.96
73 Grande-Rue

Barbizon, much frequented by Millet, Théodore Rousseau and other 19th-century painters, is in the heart of the forest of Fontainebleau, 10 km from the town of Fontainebleau and about half an hour's drive from Paris. The *Clé d'Or* is the oldest inn in the village, and is known in the area for its food as well as its pleasant service. Spacious rooms all open on to a small garden with geraniums, an atmosphere which reminded one reader of some of Mexico's more personable village hotels. The furniture is agree-ably old, the plumbing – most of the time! – agreeably modern. *(P R Harrison, Nancy Foy)*

Open: 18 December–15 November. Closed Sunday evening and Monday.
Rooms: 12 double, 1 single – 7 with bath and WC, 6 with shower and WC. (8 ground-floor rooms in annexe.)

Facilities: Salon, bar, restaurant; rooms for receptions, banquets, etc.; interior patio. Garden. English spoken. ⚭ .
Location: Central, just off the D64; parking.
Credit cards: Access/Euro/Mastercard, American Express, Barclay/Visa.
Terms: Rooms 120–165 frs. Set meals: breakfast 20 frs; lunch/dinner 100–120 frs; full *alc* 180 frs. Special meals for children.

BARFLEUR, 50760 Manche, Normandy   Map 8

Hôtel Moderne   *Telephone:* (33) 54.00.16
Place Général-de-Gaulle

'Barfleur is a fishing port 27 km east of Cherbourg. Situated 100 metres from the charming small port, the *Hotel Moderne*, built in the first decade of this century, is an architecturally attractive small hotel which has obviously been in the hands of one family. No sea views from rooms, but bedrooms tastefully and simply furnished and very reasonably priced (mine was 40 frs – 1981). Food excellent and equally reasonable (Réserve de la Maison recommended as good cheap red wine) and decor of dining room exceptionally pleasant and traditional – no French equivalents of horse-brasses. Service slow but courteous. One of the quietest and most likeable small hotels I know in France.' *(James Michie)*

Open: All year.
Rooms: 20 – 2 with bath.
Facilities: Restaurant. ⚭ .
Location: Central; parking.
Terms: Rooms 40–45 frs; full board 120–145 frs. Set meals: breakfast 9 frs; lunch/dinner 35–80 frs.

BAR-SUR-AUBE, 10200 Aube   Map 8

Hôtel du Commerce   *Telephone:* (25) 27.08.76
38 rue Nationale

'Bar-sur-Aube itself is one of those unexpected but delightful small French towns. It is near the upper Marne valley, halfway between Champagne and Burgundy. It is also where Madame de la Motte, of the famous "missing necklace" case, had her house. All the centre is lined with old, picturesque houses; there is a mill race. Right in the middle of the main road is the *Hôtel du Commerce*, with its courtyard, where you can park your car for the night. Bedrooms are splendidly over-decorated; bathrooms excellent; and the dining room delightful in the worst possible French taste. The restaurant regularly earns one rosette and is indeed very good. Altogether it is an admirable first night-stop on the way out; or last night-stop on the way back to Calais, 400 km to the north-east. Service is efficient and helpful.' *(Martyn Goff)*

Open: All year, except January and Sunday evening and Monday 1 October–30 May.
Rooms: 15 double, 3 apartments – 8 with bath, 4 with shower, all with telephone and colour TV.
Facilities: Salon, TV room, restaurant. English spoken.

Location: In town centre; parking.
Credit card: Euro.
Terms: Rooms 70–180 frs. Set meals: breakfast 18 frs, lunch/dinner 80–113 frs; full *alc* 200 frs.

LES BAUX-DE-PROVENCE, 13520 Maussane,
Bouches-du-Rhône, Provence **Map 9**

Oustau de Baumanière *Telephone:* (90) 97.33.07
Telex: 420 203

The ruined village and castle of Les Baux, on a high spur of the Alpilles, has become one of the show places of Provence. Formerly the seat of an ancient and powerful feudal house, it has had a long, romantic, often bloodthirsty history. The original dynasty died out in the 15th century, it fell into the hands of Protestants, and Richelieu had the castle and ramparts – 'the eagle's nest' he called it – demolished in 1632. Now it is a ghost city, and coachloads from Arles and Avignon daily pick their way across the grey jagged rocks of bauxite (hence the name) and through the spooky remains of medieval grandeur.

You can stay, if you wish, in the old town, but the connoisseurs of high living will make for the *Baumanière*, one of the great restaurants of France. The *Baumanière* should, properly speaking, be called a restaurant with some rooms, in view of the extensive non-residential trade, and is so designated by Michelin which gives it their top five red knives-and-forks and three star treatment. The Queen and Prince Philip dined here on their last State visit to France in 1972 – it's that sort of place. It is also one of the few top restaurants in France still to stick rigorously to classic cuisine and to eschew the modish *nouvelle cuisine*. One reader this year enjoyed his stay, but found the food disappointingly uneven. He had to send back one dish. On the other hand, unlike in many restaurants, especially perhaps of the smarter variety, the maître d'hôtel – and indeed the whole of the staff – could not have been more helpful and accommodating. He summed up: 'A very nice place to stay, but at these prices one tends to look for absolute perfection, and at least in the food department it was not always there.' Another reader was totally enchanted: 'SUPERB! Lived up to our expectations, particularly dinner. Excellent wine list with many local specialities very reasonably priced. Very comfortable room with four-poster, not quite as lavishly furnished as it could be. Well-equipped bathroom, etc. Good breakfast and friendly, efficient staff. And our car had been washed and polished when we came to leave the next morning!' *(Pat and Jeremy Temple, James Burt)*

Open: All year, except February.
Rooms: 15 double, 11 suites – all with bath, telephone, TV and air-conditioning. 16 rooms in 3 annexes. (10 rooms on ground floor.)
Facilities: Salon, arcaded restaurant. Garden, swimming pool, tennis courts, riding stables. English spoken. &.
Location: 19 km SW of Arles; 60 km NW of Marseilles.
Credit cards: All major credit cards accepted.
Terms: Rooms 220–300 frs. Set meal: breakfast 40 frs; full *alc* 330 frs.

In the case of many continental hotels, especially French ones, we have adopted the local habit of quoting a price for the room whether it is occupied by one or more persons. Rates for B & B, half board, etc., are per person unless otherwise stated.

BAYEUX, 14400 Calvados, Normandy   Map 8

Lion d'Or   *Telephone:* (31) 92.06.90
71 rue St Jean

Few visitors are likely to be unimpressed by Bayeux itself, one of the most fascinating old towns in Normandy, and by its famous Tapestry. Nearby are the Normandy invasion beaches and notably the D-day museum at Arromanches, well worth a visit.

Last year we were obliged to give an ambivalent entry for this well-established Michelin-starred *Relais de Silence* hotel. Opinions varied widely as to the decor of the rooms, the service, and the quality and pricing in the restaurant. Regrettably our postbag this year has been as mixed as ever. Some readers have been delighted with the place, have found the service anything but cool or rude and their rooms, recently redecorated, immaculate. 'No English visitor could possibly regard this as anything but a bargain' was one comment. But there have also been continued grumbles about this or that. Further reports would be welcome.

Open: 20 January–20 December.
Rooms: 32– 24 with bath or shower, all with telephone.
Facilities: Large dining room. Garden.
Location: Central; parking.
Credit cards: Barclay/Visa.
Terms: Rooms 90–180 frs; full board 180–280 frs. Set meals: breakfast 16.50 frs; lunch/dinner 60–137 frs.

BAZAS, 33430 Gironde, Aquitaine   Map 8

Relais de Fompeyre   *Telephone:* (56) 25.04.60
Route Mont-de-Marsan

On the eastern fringe of the huge Landes forest, just outside the small town of Bazas, 58 km south-east of Bordeaux and close to the Sauternes country. Would make a good overnight stop on the way to or from the Pyrenees. The *Relais de Fompeyre* is a very reasonably-priced three-star hotel. 'We hadn't booked; there were four of us, and there was room only for two. But the manager and his staff were exceedingly helpful and found a folding double bed. The children enjoyed the pool. The gardens were pleasant, the room comfortable and quiet, the surroundings tranquil. But the main reason for including the *Relais de Fompeyre* is its restaurant. We had a superlative meal, served with great friendliness and intelligence, and the wines were excellent.' *(James Price)*

Two recent visitors agree – one whole-heartedly, and the other with the warning that, despite its large garden, you will need ear-plugs if you sleep with your window open as lorries grind all night up the long hill of the main road outside. *(B J Woolf, Angela and David Stewart)*

Open: All year, except November and Monday 1 December–15 March. Restaurant closed Sunday 1 December–15 March.
Rooms: 31 plus 4 suites – some with bath or shower.
Facilities: Lift, restaurant, covered terrace for meals and refreshments; some

conference facilities. Large park and garden. 2 swimming pools (1 for children), tennis court.
Location: About 35 miles S of Bordeaux on the D932; parking.
Credit cards: American Express, Barclay/Visa.
Terms: Rooms 90–150 frs; full board 165–253 frs. Set meals: breakfast 16.50 frs; lunch/dinner 77–165 frs.

BEAULIEU-SUR-MER, 06310 Alpes-Maritimes, Provence   **Map 9**

Le Métropole   *Telephone:* (93) 01.00.08
15 Boulevard Mar. Leclerc   *Telex:* 470304

'For once a luxury hotel of the old style that has not been over-modernized but simply kept in immaculate order. It is in no way pretentious. Set back from the road, overlooking the sea and Cap Ferrat and Italy, surrounded by a pretty garden and terrace, *Le Métropole* enjoys absolute quiet except for the occasional speed boat or the more relaxing "chug-chug" of a tiny fishing boat. It is right on the beach (shingle and concrete like all this part of the coast). For swimming and sunning you can choose between the pleasant pool or a generous concrete area below with direct access to the sea. In either case, once installed, your table, chairs, towels, etc., will all be laid out for you in the same spot each day. Bar service in both these areas. Use of swimming facilities at modest fee. Compared to some prices on private beaches in this part of the world it can be considered *un cadeau*. Lovely restaurant on a large terrace outside the dining room. Sitting under the enormous white awning and enjoying the stunning view while contemplating the sensible menu gives genuine pleasure. Food and service excellent and you are never hurried. From the five-course menus, *grilled scampi with rouille, tranche de gigot aux herbes* and a *coupé* composed of vanilla ice cream with *crème anglaise* and a chocolate sauce were a few of the highlights. No credit cards accepted. No "direct dial" phones, but obviously "English Spoken". Air-conditioning. Particularly good-value out-of-season terms.' *(Geoffrey Sharp)*

Open: All year, except 1 November–20 December.
Rooms: 50 – all with bath or shower and telephone.
Facilities: Lift, bar, terrace restaurant, dining room, air-conditioning. Garden with terrace, swimming pool, private beach. English spoken.
Location: 10 km from Nice on the N559; parking.
Terms: Rooms 270–900 frs. Set meals: breakfast 33 frs; lunch/dinner 185 frs.

BEAUNE, 21200 Côte-d'Or, Burgundy   **Map 8**

Hôtel Le Cep   *Telephone:* (80) 22.35.48
27 rue Maufoux

'The *Hôtel Le Cep* is a charming old house just a few minutes' walk from the centre of this pleasant little town, the capital of the Burgundy wine region where the famous wine auctions, banquets and festivities take place every November. Parking is available in a large private garage to the rear. The entrance hall, which also serves as a lounge is welcoming, beautifully furnished with antiques and offers a most civilized atmosphere in which to sip one's pre-prandial drinks. It is impossible to forget that one is in Burgundy since the bedrooms, again comfortably furnished in antique style (but most have pretty, modern bathrooms), are named after the wines of the regions. At breakfast, really fresh orange juice followed by Earl Grey tea were bonuses. The proprietor is most friendly, and while he speaks no English, staff are at hand in Reception who do.' *(Rosamund V Hebdon)*

Open: February–November.
Rooms: 21–20 with bath or shower.
Facilities: Reception lounge; conference facilities. English spoken.
Location: In town centre; garage parking.
Credit cards: American Express, Diners.
Terms: Rooms 140–330 frs. Set meals: breakfast 20 frs.

BELFORT, 90000 Jura   **Map 8**

Hostellerie du Château Servin   *Telephone:* (84) 21.41.85
9 rue General Négrier
7 rue Heim

Belfort, 65 km west of Basle, is one of the main routes from Paris to Switzerland. Well worth a visit is the famous statue of the Lion of Belfort, at the foot of the Vauban castle. This huge monument was erected to commemorate the heroism of the Belfort garrison in fighting off the Prussians in 1870.

'Weary from long hours on the French motorways, we sought a good meal and a quiet, restful night: we could hardly have improved upon the Hostellerie. A 19th-century town house in its garden, surrounded by high walls and tall wrought-iron gates: inside, a slightly cluttered Victorian reception hall, not very well lit: but the dining room was beautiful, with walls and curtains elegantly draped in tawny velvet, lamps and a flower arrangement on every table, and the food all that one believes the French are capable of, with a devotion to detail and presentation that clearly showed why this restaurant bore two rosettes from the Michelin Guide. There are only ten rooms, and the family are clearly involved at every stage (we glimpsed at least four generations having their own meal at one long table in another room, as we arrived). We occupied the Louis XV room, charmingly furnished in period style with deep rose velvet, and the most comfortable bed and utter quiet that we had met for a long time. As one would expect, not cheap – but we felt fair value for money. Definitely a place we would plan to fit into our next touring holiday!' *(Angela and David Stewart)*

Open: All year, except August and Wednesday.
Rooms: 10 – all with bath or shower and telephone.
Facilities: Reception, dining room, air-conditioning; conference facilities. Garden.
Location: Hotel has two entrances (see above) 50 m E of Faubourg de Montbeliard; parking.
Credit cards: American Express, Diners.
Terms: Rooms 209–308 frs; Set meals: lunch/dinner 99–242 frs.

Deadlines: nominations for the 1983 edition should reach us not later than 31 July 1982. Latest date for comments on existing entries: 31 August 1982.

Hôtel Bonnet   *Telephone:* (53) 29.50.01

Madame Bonnet, known to several generations of *Bonnet*-fans, died, aged 90, two years ago. We are glad to know that her daughter admirably maintains the traditions of the house.

'Most attractively situated on a bend of the lovely Dordogne river below a village which winds up to the château, which is open to the public. A wide staircase leads up to the entrance beneath the terrace which is attractively arranged with tables and umbrellas. The welcome was friendly; in fact all the staff were most charming and helpful. The bedroom was small but attractively furnished. The bathroom shone with care and cleanliness. We chose the cheaper of the two *prix-fixe* menus and this was a six-course meal of large proportions and very good, particularly the *tourtière de poulet aux salsifis* – chicken in a delicious sauce with salsify on a flaky pastry base. Beynac is lovely in itself, but is also a good base to visit Sarlat, Domme, Les Eyzies, Rocamadour, the Lot and the Tarn. The *Bonnet* would provide a peaceful holiday in delightful surroundings at very moderate cost – definitely to be recommended.' *(Ray and Angela Evans; also A G Don)*

Open: 1 April–15 October.
Rooms: 20 double, 2 single – 17 with bath, 3 with shower, all with telephone.
Facilities: Salon, bar, restaurant, creeper-covered terrace for meals above the river. 2 gardens. The hotel overlooks the Dordogne, with beach and bathing nearby; also boating, canoeing and fishing. English spoken. ♿.
Location: 9 km W of Sarlat.
Terms: Rooms 70–150 frs; dinner, B & B 155–170 frs; full board 185–200 frs. Set meals: breakfast 18 frs; lunch/dinner 65–120 frs.

Auberge des Templiers   *Telephone:* (38) 31.80.01
                   Telex: 780998

'An old posting house on the N7 about 1½ hours drive south from Paris, luxuriously renovated and with about 20 rooms and apartments scattered around the grounds at the rear in various (new) buildings. Our room, with an enormous bathroom, was like a small bungalow. Beautifully furnished and spotlessly clean. The restaurant boasts two Michelin rosettes and the cooking, classical French, was excellent. Breakfast can be taken in the room or the lounge bar in the main building. There is an outdoor swimming pool and tennis courts and in summer the gardens would be most attractive. A good base for the upper Loire, though very expensive. Owners and staff most welcoming and friendly.' *(Pat and Jeremy Temple)*

Open: All year, except mid January–mid February.
Rooms: 27 – all with bath or shower, telephone and TV.
Facilities: Lounge bar, restaurant; conference facilities. Garden; swimming pool; tennis court. ♿.
Location: On the N7, 37 km S of Paris and 69 km E of Orléans.
Credit cards: Barclay/Visa, Diners.
Terms: Rooms 230–430 frs, suites 460–660 frs. Set meals: breakfast 27 frs; lunch/dinner 165–240 frs.

BIOT, Alpes Maritimes, Provence   Map 9

Café des Arcades   *Telephone:* (93) 65.01.04
16 Place des Arcades

'Here's a real oddity for you – but *il vaut le detour*, as they say. It's in a small arcaded square in the old hill-village of Biot, just inland from Antibes: the superb Fernand Léger museum is just down the road. This "café" *is* in part just that: a noisy café where the villagers drink, chatter and play chess. But it's also rather more: a 15th-century inn of great character, *and* believe it or not, an art gallery. This is due to its *patron*, André Brothier, an engaging, bohemian type, who lines the inn's dining room with Braques and Miros and is a friend of Vasarely and his son Yvaral, painters whom I happen to adore. The bedrooms are too, too olde worlde, but the plumbing, happily, is not. The inn has a hyper-relaxed ambience which may not suit all tastes, and it can be trying to have loud pop music resounding from the café while you eat your *tian provençal* or *tripes niçoises*. Nonetheless, at least for a day or two's visit, this eccentric and endearing place is exhilarating fun.' *(Jenny Towndrow)*

Open: All year, except November; restaurant closed Sunday evening and Monday.
Rooms: 10 double – 5 with bath, 5 with shower, all with internal telephone.
Facilities: Restaurant, art gallery. Beaches nearby.
Location: 8 km from Antibes.
Terms: Rooms 100–130 frs. Set meals: breakfast 12 frs; lunch/dinner 75 frs plus 10% service; *alc* 90 frs (excluding wine).

BLOIS, 41000 Loir-et-Cher, Loire Valley   Map 8

Hostellerie de la Loire   *Telephone:* (54) 74.26.60
8 rue du Maréchal-de-Lattre-de-Tassigny

'On the Quay overlooking the Loire close to the bridge – front rooms will be noisy – a basic inn with fairly cheap bedrooms, perfectly all right for an overnight stay and its restaurant is excellent. Pleasant informal staff: on holidays they are given to handing you the front-door key and telling you you won't see any of them until next day . . . it's all yours. Engaging!' *(Charles Osborne)*

Open: All year, except 15 January–15 February. Restaurant closed Sunday.
Rooms: 17 double – 8 with bath, all with telephone.
Facilities: Bar, restaurant. English spoken.
Location: On the quay near old port; 100 m from town centre; parking.
Credit cards: American Express, Diners.
Terms: Rooms 60–180 frs; dinner, B & B 110–150 frs. Set meals: breakfast 13 frs; lunch/dinner 60, 90 and 140 frs; full *alc* 150 frs.

Please write and confirm an entry when it is deserved. If you think that a hotel is not as good as we say, please write and tell us.

BONIFACIO, 20169, Corsica Map 9

Hôtel les Voyageurs *Telephone:* (95) 73.00.46
Quai Comparetti

Bonifacio, at the southern foot of Corsica is an exceptionally attractive small resort even though you need a car to reach good beaches. The medieval citadel and old town, which has no hotels, is on a high promontory, overlooking the harbour, now a popular marina. The quayside is ringed by fish restaurants, some with accommodation, as well as chandlers and boutiques. It is the most exciting place to stay in Bonifacio if you enjoy a ringside view of marina-life and don't mind the racket of late-night revellers and early-morning garbage vans. *Les Voyageurs* is a modest inn, offering simple accommodation, friendly service and excellent meals at reasonable prices. *(D F Johnson)*

Open: All year.
Rooms: 7 double, 3 single – 7 with shower.
Facilities: Restaurant. Rock beach nearby, sandy beach 6 km.
Location: Central, on the quay. It is possible to park opposite the hotel.
Terms: Rooms 80 frs; dinner, B & B 130 frs. Set meals: breakfast 15 frs; lunch/dinner 40 frs; full *alc* 70 frs.

LE BOURGET-DU-LAC, Nr Chambéry, 73370 Savoie Map 8

Hôtel Ombremont *Telephone:* (79) 25.00.23

Formerly an important Savoie port for steamers travelling up the Rhône from Lyon, Bourget-du-Lac is now simply a large village, with an attractive *plage* and a fine Carolingian church. The *Ombremont*, a mile or so north of Bourget itself via the N504, has a specially attractive location, with views over lake and mountains. 'Our room smallish but very comfortable and well-appointed. Bath and toilet *en suite*. Superb views. Country-home style, like *Sharrow Bay* at Ullswater (q.v.), but without the antiques. Gardens well cared for, reaching down gradually to the swimming pool and the lake, about 100 feet below. Very friendly, English-speaking proprietors. Food superb – gourmet menus available. Large terrace for eating open air in summer. Very quiet, well off the main road.' *(Dr D M C Ainscow)*

Open: 1 April–30 September.
Rooms: 20 – 18 with bath, all with telephone.
Facilities: Salon, restaurant. Garden leading down to lake, with swimming pool. English spoken. &.
Location: 2 km N of Le Bourget on the N504.
Credit card: American Express.
Terms: Rooms 120–275 frs; full board 320–350 frs. Set meals: breakfast 22 frs; lunch/dinner 90–220 frs.

If you know a good hotel that is not in the Guide, tell us. WRITE NOW. Freepost (UK only) forms are at the back of the Guide.

BRANTÔME, 24310 Dordogne   Map 8

Auberge du Soir   *Telephone:* (53) 05.82.93
5 rue Georges Saumande

Brantóme, one of the most beautiful small towns in the south-west of France, is on an island site on the river Dronne, 27 km north of Périgueux. Its chief glory is the imposing Benedictine abbey, with an exquisite 11th-century belfry. Gourmets may like to know that it boasts a Michelin-starred hotel and a Michelin-starred restaurant with rooms, with another starred restaurant with rooms no more than 5 km away. The *Auberge du Soir* is not, gastronomically speaking, in the stellar class. On the other hand, its prices are far from astronomical . . .

'A small and enchanting hotel in a quiet alleyway which welcomes hordes of British, French and others to cosy, chintz-papered bedrooms and extremely good food. An old, creaky building, full of low ceilings and comfort, in a lovely village which is worth more than just an overnight stop. Even in March we were lucky to get a room so it would be wise to book in advance. A cheerful chef who likes to cook other things than the interminable and limited local dishes!' *(Hugh and Anne Pitt)*

Open: All year, except Monday October–March and January.
Rooms: 8 double – 1 with bath, 7 with shower.
Facilities: 2 dining rooms, TV room. Small garden. Close to river; tennis and swimming. English spoken.
Location: 27 km N of Périgueux.
Terms: Rooms 75 frs; full board 110–130 frs. Set meals: breakfast 12 frs; lunch/dinner 38–115 (excluding service); full *alc* 120 frs. Reduced rates for children under 5.

BRINON-SUR-SAULDRE, 18450 Cher   Map 8

Auberge La Solognote   *Telephone:* (48) 58.50.29
Grande Rue

Brinon is a small pleasant village a few miles east of the N20 between Bourges and Orléans. It is in the heart of the strange haunting forests and marshlands of the Sologne, i.e. at the centre of the Alain Fournier country, near to his birthplace at La Chapelle d'Angillon and to the château which inspired him to write *Le Grand Meaulnes*. The inn is close to the centre, but we had a peaceful night, with practically no traffic noise. Modest bedroom, clean and comfy. Bar-cum-seating area adjacent to small shingle patio, with tubs and pots of flowers and umbrellas. Attractive dining room in country style: tiled floor, pottery plates and local artists' pictures on the walls; thick damask table linen and flowers on each table. Monsieur and Madame were very welcoming (they helped us make several phone calls to England about our journey home through the French fishermen's blockade of the French ports). Good food. We had the second most expensive menu. The *mousseline d'homard* was really memorable with chunks of lobster in it – we had succulent steaks and a dish of fried aubergines and cheesy potato cakes, and for dessert *tarte aux fraises du bois* – locally picked. The overall impression was of efficient, professional, friendly, caring people. They have very few English visitors, perhaps as they are a bit off the beaten track; but the inn is really worth a visit for a comfortable quiet night en route north or south.' *(Maureen A Montague)*

Open: All year, except February, 1–15 June, 1–15 September, Tuesday evening and Wednesday 1 October–1 July.
Rooms: 13 double – 6 with bath, 4 with shower, all with telephone. (2 rooms on ground floor.)
Facilities: Salon, bar, patio. Tennis 200 metres. English spoken. ﾎ.
Credit cards: Access/Euro/Mastercard.
Terms: Rooms 65–125 frs per person; B & B 80–140 frs; full board 140–160 frs. Set meals: breakfast 15 frs; lunch/dinner 40, 65, 100 and 150 frs; full *alc* 130–160 frs.

BRIOUDE, 43100 Haute Loire, Auvergne   Map 8

Hôtel de la Poste et Champanne   *Telephone:* (71) 50.14.62
1 Boulevard Docteur-Devins and
Avenue Paul Chambriand

Brioude, about halfway between Clermont-Ferrand and Le Puy, is an ideal centre for touring the Massif Central. It is a medieval town of narrow streets, and is most famous for its 11th- and 12th-century romanesque basilica of Saint-Julian. The *Poste et Champanne* is a family hotel presided over by Madame Albertine Barge, and assisted by her granddaughter. It is in two parts: the restaurant, with a bar, is in an old house on the main road, and serves magnificent and very reasonable food; it caters for a lot of local groups and also for coach tours, though these are accommodated in a separate dining room. Residents stay in an entirely modern and noise-free annexe in a garden 50 yards behind the main building. *(M W Hardwick)*

Last year's entry, quoted above, is endorsed by a recent visitor who stayed a week at the *Poste*, and found it an admirable centre for an Auvergne holiday. 'We were very well treated. Our rooms in the annexe were comfortable, the food was plentiful and good, and the terms most reasonable.' *(E H Plaut)*

Open: All year.
Rooms: 20 – 10 with bath, all with telephone. 10 rooms in annexe.
Facilities: 2 salons (1 with TV in annexe), 2 dining rooms (1 for conferences and seminars). Small garden. 1 km from river Allier with swimming and boating. English spoken.
Location: On the N102, 70 km from Clermont-Ferrand, 61 km from Le Puy; in town centre; parking.
Terms: Rooms 50–100 frs; dinner, B & B 75–100 frs; full board 90–120 frs. Set meals: breakfast 10 frs; lunch/dinner 40–65 frs.

CABRERETS 46330 Lot   Map 8

La Pescalerie   *Telephone:* (65) 31.22.55

Cabrerets is a picturesque village with two castles in the valley of the river Célé, close to the lovely valley of the Lot. It is near local beauty spots such as St Cirq-Lapopie; Cahors is 35 km to the west.

'This quiet and very special hotel is run with true charm and kindness. It opened only in June 1980, after four years of restoration, an 18th-century

240

Quercy country house, decorated with the most exquisite and restrained taste. There is a large semi-formal garden which stretches away to the wooded banks of the Lot where jays call and kingfishers arrow through the shadows. Our meal was good but disappointingly unambitious. There is no lift, and the beautiful wooden staircase is rather steep for the less youthful. But the luxury of the bedrooms was almost sinful, the elegance of breakfast on the terrace under a huge magnolia tree, with oleanders in bloom, was unforgettable.' *(Don and Maureen Montague)*

Open: 1 April–15 November.
Rooms: 10 double – all with bath, telephone and colour TV.
Facilities: Lounge, TV, bar, dining room. Garden running to the river with swimming, fishing, boating. English spoken.
Location: 35 km from Cahors; on the departmental road No. 19 towards Figeac, 2.5 km after Cabrerets.
Credit cards: All major credit cards accepted.
Terms: Rooms 210–380 frs; B & B 240–410 frs. Set meals: lunch/dinner 110 and 140 frs; full *alc* 220 frs. Reduced rates and special meals for children.

CAGNES-SUR-MER, Haut-de-Cagnes, 06800 Alpes-Maritimes   Map 9

Le Cagnard   *Telephone:* (93) 20.73.21 and 20.73.22
Rue du Pontin-Long

'An oasis of medieval tranquillity amid the urban sprawl of Cagnes! Highly romantic,' was how one visitor summed up his impression of this small exceedingly *soigné* hotel converted from several old houses on the ramparts of what is, itself, along with St Paul and Vence, one of the more sophisticated hill villages of the region. Rooms vary in size and comfort – some are small suites – but the conversions have been cunningly done to harmonize new with old, while also offering such mod cons as a small fridge. You eat either on the terrace – stunning views over the village to the Med. just west of Nice airport – or in what was once the guardroom of the Château Grimaldi. Monsieur and Madame Barel, the owners for more than 20 years, are constantly engaged in improvements: the new chef with new kitchens has made substantial changes in the menu, with some *nouvelle cuisine* touches.

'Everything here is *haute*,' we said last year, 'the cuisine as well as the position; the decor is the height of elegance; not surprisingly, the prices are steep as well. (And one visitor reported a disagreeable *hauteur* on the part of one or two members of the staff.)' No further haughtinesses have been reported to us, we are glad to say, though one visitor felt the service a bit lackadaisical. *(Pat and Jeremy Temple, James Burt)*

Warning: the hotel is approached by two narrow tortuous alleys. Allow at least 15 minutes getting in and out by car at busy times. And if you don't have a Mini, it's safer to arrive by foot.

Open: All year. Restaurant closed 1 November–15 December.
Rooms: 10 double, 2 single, 7 suites – 18 with bath, 1 with shower, all with telephone; mono TV in suites. (Suites in annexe.)
Facilities: Lift, salon/bar, elegant restaurant. Terrace and flower garden. Fishing, tennis, riding, swimming 2 km; golf within 6 km. English spoken.
Location: 2 km from Cagnes-sur-Mer, 9 km from Vence, 3 km from Nice airport; parking can be difficult in high season.

Credit cards: American Express, Barclay/Visa, Diners.
Terms: Rooms 80–250 frs per person. Set meals: lunch/dinner 170 frs; full *alc* 190 frs.

CAHORS, 46000 Lot

Map 8

Terminus
5 avenue Ch-de-Freycinet

Telephone: (65) 35.24.50

The old town of Cahors stands proudly above the river Lot – it is the capital of the Lot department – between the Dordogne and Toulouse.

'100 metres across from the station, this is an old, beautifully furnished hotel with palatial rooms and a very helpful husband-and-wife team who are pleased to see you and will do all they can to help. No restaurant, only breakfast served. A delightful place to stay in a delightful town and a marvellous centre from which to explore lovely countryside. Ask the Patron's advice – he knows every place worth seeing.' *(Hugh and Anne Pitt)*

Open: All year.
Rooms: 31 – 26 with bath or shower, all with telephone.
Facilities: Lift, breakfast room. &.
Location: In town centre; parking.
Terms: Rooms 95–175 frs. Set meal: breakfast 15 frs.

CALAIS, 62100 Pas-de-Calais

Map 8

Hôtel Meurice
5 rue E-Roche

Telephone: (21) 34.57.03

'Big, old mid-town hotel, rebuilt in original style after war damage. Quiet and very spacious, with huge rooms (some smaller ones in an annexe) comfortably furnished with antiques and neo-antiques. An excellent breakfast, with *fresh* orange juice, is served in a neatly converted corridor. A pleasant stop before or after a Dover–Calais crossing. If you have a few hours to fill in, the city museum is opposite the hotel and Cap Blanc (Beachy Head plus-plus-plus) is just down the coast road in the direction of Boulogne.' *(Frank and Joan Harrison)*

Open: All year.
Rooms: 40 – all with bath or shower, telephone and TV. Some rooms in annexe.
Facilities: Lift, breakfast area. Garden.
Location: In town centre; garage parking.
Credit cards: American Express, Diners.
Terms: Rooms 80–160 frs. Set meal: breakfast 13 frs.

We asked hotels to estimate their 1982 tariffs. Not all hotels in Part Two replied, so that prices in Part Two are more approximate in some cases than those in Part One.

CÉAUX, 50220 Ducey, Manche, Normandy   Map 8

Au P'tit Quinquin

Telephone: (33) 58.13.46

'A very modest but pleasant hotel for an overnight stop en route to Cherbourg from Brittany or south-west France. It's in a quiet village, 3 km from Pontanbault. We had the most expensive menu at 60 frs (1980): it was superb, quite the best meal of our entire holiday. Monsieur Barbier, the owner, does the cooking, and drives to Granville to buy the fish straight off the trawlers. We had tender little *crevettes au naturel* then *praires farcies*, served in their shells with parsley and garlic butter. For main course we chose *sole meunière* and were each given two small plump fish – creamy and succulent. One astonishing note: the sheets on our beds were linen and hemstitched by hand – and dazzling white: we saw line on line hanging to dry in the orchard.' *(A S Kyrle Pope)*

Open: 4 April–5 October. Restaurant closed Tuesday 1 April–30 June.
Rooms: 16 – all with bath or shower and telephone.
Facilities: Restaurant.
Location: 11 km SE of Avranches, 4 km from Pontanbault on the D43; parking.
Terms: Rooms 55–105 frs. Set meals: breakfast 10 frs; lunch/dinner 30–100 frs.

CHABEUIL, 26120 Drôme   Map 8

Relais du Soleil
Route Romans

Telephone: (75) 59.01.81

'One of the most agreeably direct routes into Provence by the Rhône valley is the uncrowded road (D538) which climbs out of Vienne, runs parallel to the RN7 but hugs the feet of the Dauphine range to finish up at Cavaillon. The *Relais du Soleil* is a good overnight stopping-place. It is about a mile north of the small town of Chabeuil on the Romans-sur-Isère road. Set back in its grounds, which are the car park, this is one of the modern *Logis de France*. Steps lead up to glass doors, picture windows, potted palms, spacious entrance hall, a broad and marbled stairway. In its functional way it is handsome. There are bedrooms with bathroom or shower which are well-designed, quiet and comfortable. Large sliding windows (complete with blinds and curtains) look out on the distant and dramatic flank of the Vivarais hills, with the flat and rural immensity of the Rhône valley in between. Reception may be somewhat offhand (but is that anything new in France?), but the three-course dinner is sound and not expensive, and the house wine is smooth and reasonably priced.' *(Norman Brangham; endorsed, with reservations about the food, by Dr Michael Matthews)*

Open: All year, except February and Monday.
Rooms: 21 double – most with bath or shower, all with telephone. (4 rooms on ground floor.)
Facilities: Lounge with TV, restaurant. Garden with bowls, children's games. &.
Location: 1 km from town centre; 10 km from the Vercors; 15 km from the Ardèche; garages and car park.
Credit cards: All major credit cards accepted.
Terms: Rooms 80–140 frs. Set meals: breakfast 20 frs; lunch 65 frs; dinner from 100 frs. Weekly rates available.

Hôtel Lameloise   *Telephone:* (85) 87.08.85
36 Place d'Armes

Chagny is a village halfway between Beaune and Chalons-sur-Saône, in Burgundy wine-growing country. 'The main attraction here is the restaurant, three stars in Michelin, and it is probably more suited for one night than a long stay. Chagny itself is not very interesting, but the surrounding Burgundy countryside has many places to explore, and it is a convenient staging-post between Paris and the Riviera. The hotel is very comfortable, with large well-equipped rooms and bathrooms, fresh flowers and bowls of sweets. Needless to say, the food is superb (more or less *nouvelle cuisine*) though expensive. Breakfasts, too, are of an excellent standard.' *(Pat and Jeremy Temple)*

Open: All year, except 30 November–17 December, Thursday midday and Wednesday.
Rooms: 32 – 23 with bath or shower, all with telephone and TV.
Facilities: Restaurant.
Location: Central; parking.
Credit card: Barclay/Visa.
Terms: Rooms 125–275 frs. Set meal: breakfast 22 frs; *alc* 165–210 frs (excluding wine).

Hôtel de l'Écho et de l'Abbaye   *Telephone:* (71) 00.00.45

'This small Auvergnat town, high up in the Massif Central, 41 km north-west of Le Puy, is picturesquely dominated by the vast, mainly 14th-century abbey, with its superb series of Flemish tapestries (binoculars recommended). The little hotel is pleasantly situated in an open space by the side of the abbey buildings. It is run by very agreeable people, and the food is good, though with a rather limited repertoire so it might seem monotonous if you were to stay a week or more.' *(DPW)*

Open: 1 February–5 November.
Rooms: 11 – 5 with bath, 4 with shower, all with telephone.
Facilities: Salon, TV room, dining room. Situated in abbey grounds and very quiet. Forest walks, bathing, skiing in winter. English spoken.
Location: La Chaise-Dieu is 41 km NW of Le Puy. Hotel is off the road; ask for directions near the abbey.
Credit cards: American Express, Barclay/Visa.
Terms: Rooms (single) from 100 frs, (double) from 130 frs; full board 140–180 frs. Set meals: breakfast 13 frs; lunch/dinner 40–100 frs. Reduced rates and special meals for children.

We asked hotels to estimate their 1982 tariffs some time before publication so the rates given here are not necessarily completely accurate. Please *always* check terms with hotels when making bookings.

CHAMBORD, 41 Loir-et-Cher, Loire Valley   Map 8

Hôtel du Grand Saint-Michel

Telephone: (54) 46.31.31
Telex: 41250 Bracieux

'Though short on quaintness the *Saint-Michel* is clean, comfortable and bright, and the rooms are adequately furnished, although the walls seemed a trifle thin. But the chief recommendation is the hotel's situation. It is within strolling distance of the Château de Chambord with its 365 pinnacles, 440 rooms and 50 staircases. After dinner in the summer you can saunter over to the *son et lumière*, and before breakfast you can drive out to see the wild boar, deer and dogs of Chambord forest feeding. The hotel itself keeps a good table, specializing in regional food and wine; the service is good, and the portions extremely generous.' *(Paul Vaughan)*

Open: All year, except 15 November–23 December. Restaurant closed Monday evening and Tuesday 1 October–1 April.
Rooms: 40 – 12 with bath, 8 with shower, all with telephone.
Facilities: Restaurant; conference facilities; terrace, grounds with tennis court.
Location: Just S of the Loire valley, 18 km from Blois; opposite the château; parking.
Credit card: Barclay/Visa.
Terms: Rooms: 80–250 frs. Set meals: breakfast 16 frs; lunch/dinner 65 frs; full *alc* 120–150 frs.

CHAMPILLON, Nr Épernay, 51160 Ay, Marne, Champagne   Map 8

Hôtel Royal Champagne

Telephone: (26) 51.25.06
Telex: 830906 F2

Standing 6 km out of Epernay on the Reims road, this 18th-century coaching inn has a grand restaurant on the main road, but also offers in its grounds sophisticated accommodation in chalet bungalows, each room having its own veranda overlooking the famous vineyards of the area. About the restaurant, no complaints: one reader speaks with awe about his *Menu de Champagne*, where every course has been created to be enhanced by the champagne with which it is served – 'a memorable effect'. Other readers, too, reach for their superlatives: 'Perfection', 'Superb', 'Deserves two rosettes in Michelin', 'Wonderful wine list' and so forth. But about the rooms, there is no clear consensus: some found their accommodation 'extremely comfortable – ideal for honeymooners' and 'charming'. But, as last year, there have also been grumbles about the state of repair – bathrooms in need of maintenance, an unfixed door-handle, a slight odour of drains. One reader mentioned that he had a very pleasant newly decorated room, and it may be that the management are in the process of putting their house in the same admirable order as their restaurant. More reports welcome. *(Janet Leipris, Raymond Harris, Angela and David Stewart, John Bennett, M Cookson)*

Open: All year.
Rooms: 14 double – 12 with bath, 2 with shower, all with telephone, radio and private veranda. (All rooms on ground floor.)
Facilities: Salon, TV room, bar, restaurant. Park and garden. Tennis, riding in the forest, swimming pool and golf in vicinity. English spoken. &.

245

Location: Near the N51 between Rheims and Épernay.
Credit cards: American Express, Diners, Barclay/Visa.
Terms: Rooms 200–300 frs. Set meal: breakfast 20 frs; full *alc* 200 frs.

CHÂTEAUNEUF-EN-AUXOIS, 21320 Pouilly-en-Auxois, Côte d'Or, Burgundy

Map 8

Hostellerie du Château

Telephone: (80) 33.00.23

Châteauneuf is a Burgundy hill village of old fortified farms dating from the 14th and 15th centuries, which can be seen from the A6 autoroute between Beaune and Avallon, about 15 minutes from the Pouilly exit. Next to the château is the *Hostellerie* – a very simple country hotel, well-modernized from an old building, still with flagged stairs down to a sitting room.

'A most unusual place. The village, at the end of a long lane apparently leading nowhere, is picturesque to a degree. The *Hostellerie* is very small, and the dining room, and many of the bedrooms, would be found too cramped for a long stay. All rooms have hot and cold water, but provision of WCs would be inadequate when the hotel is full. The cooking is really first-class, reaching an extraordinarily high standard for a place of obviously limited resources; it has clearly a considerable local reputation. The wine list includes an impressive array of vintage burgundies, both red and white.' *(C T Bailhache; also G C Brown)*

Open: Easter–November. Closed Monday evening and Tuesday out of season.
Rooms: 11 double – 4 with bath, 7 with shower, all with telephone.
Facilities: Sitting room, restaurant, banqueting room. Small garden with games for children; sailing on reservoir 3 km. A little English spoken.
Location: 7 km from Pouilly-en-Auxois. *Note:* Although the château is visible to the east of the motorway, one must go *west* from the Pouilly exit, along the road to Arnay-le-Duc; there is a signpost to Châteauneuf after a short distance.
Credit cards: All major credit cards accepted.
Terms: Rooms 72–165 frs. Set meals: breakfast 15.50 frs; lunch/dinner 82–165 frs. Special meals for children by arrangement.

CHÂTEAUNEUF-LES-BAINS, 63390 St Gervais d'Auvergne, Puy-de-Dôme

Map 8

Hôtel du Château

Telephone: (73) 86.67.01

'A good example of the unpretentious friendly type of French country inn. Mod-cons a little lacking by today's standards but good food and excellent value for money. Châteauneuf-les-Bains is a tiny, charmingly derelict spa set in the narrow, wooded valley of the Sioule, 49 km north-west of Clermont-Ferrand and well away from any heavily-trodden tourist tracks.' *(William Goodhart)*

Open: 1 May–30 September.
Rooms: 35 double, 3 single – 21 with bath, 9 with shower. 18 rooms in annexe.
Facilities: Reception, salon, bar, restaurant. Garden with tennis court and play area for children. Near river with bathing and fishing.
Location: On the D109, off the N143 between Riom and Montlucon.
Credit card: Barclay/Visa.

Terms: Rooms 45–100 frs; full board 70–140 frs. Set meals: breakfast 12 frs; lunch/dinner 35–65 frs; full *alc* 90 frs. Reduced rates for children sharing parents' room; special meals on request.

CHÂTEAUNEUF-SUR-SARTHE, 49330 Maine et Loire   Map 8

La Sarthe   *Telephone:* (41) 42.11.30

'A friendly family hotel, beautifully situated beside the river Sarthe. It is idyllically peaceful, but within easy driving distance of Angers, the Monastery of Solesmes and many Loire château. There is a terrace on the river bank for lunches and drinks, and a dining room overlooking the river. It is extremely clean and comfortable. My wife and I have been coming here for the past 18 years, and its cuisine justifies its inclusion in Michelin.' (*Norman Swallow*)

Open: All year, except October and first week in March. Restaurant closed Friday and Sunday evenings and Monday in winter.
Rooms: 7 double, 2 suites – 2 with bath.
Facilities: Bar, rustic dining room overlooking river; terrace overlooking river. Public swimming pool 100 m; tennis courts 200 m. English spoken.
Location: 31 km north of Angers.
Terms: Rooms 55–110 frs. Set meals: breakfast 12 frs; lunch/dinner 40, 60 and 100 frs; full *alc* 90 frs.

CHÂTEAU-RENAULT, 37110 Indre et Loire, Loire Valley   Map 8

L'Écu de France   *Telephone:* (47) 56.50.72
37 Place J Jaurès

'Situated on the large market square, this old inn has been modernized without losing character. The host, Monsieur Julien, was solicitous for his guests' welfare. Our spacious room was quiet except when late-night motor-bike yobboes used the deserted square for a race-track. There is a good restaurant – just missing "gastronomique" standards, but very enjoyable. The town, halfway between Blois and Tours, is convenient for visiting châteaux in the Loire valley. The ruined château was floodlit in the evening with lovely music, and there is an interesting tannery museum – all free!' (*Janet Foulsham*)

Open: All year, except Christmas, Monday midday and Sunday evening September–June.
Rooms: 6 double, 6 single – 6 with bath, 2 with shower, all with telephone.
Facilities: Lounge, TV room. Swimming pool 500 m; walks in the forest. English spoken.
Location: Central; parking.
Credit cards: All major credit cards accepted.
Terms: Rooms 105–180 frs. Set meals: breakfast 12 frs; lunch/dinner 50 and 100 frs. Special meals for children.

In the case of many continental hotels, especially French ones, we have adopted the local habit of quoting a price for the room whether it is occupied by one or more persons. Rates for B & B, half board, etc., are per person unless otherwise stated.

Hostellerie du Château

Telephone: (54) 46.98.04

'A village inn (1930-ish, timber and concrete) on a fairly busy road, rather closed in by surrounding houses and very much part of the village, but with a swimming pool and small garden, at the foot of the gorgeous château where Catherine de Medici lived and practised necromancy. The Bonnigals, who run the *Hostellerie*, bought magnificent antiques from the château when its furniture was sold in 1937. Attractive bedrooms, luxuriously fabric-covered walls for the most part, well-equipped bathroom to each; those on the first floor are rather more splendid, and quieter because they overlook the Loire, than those on the second floor facing the road. Exquisite food, attentive service. A good base for exploring the neighbouring châteaux.' *(Sheila Kitzinger; also David Wooff, R S Ryder)*

Open: 15 March–15 November. Restaurant closed Tuesday.
Rooms: 20 – all with bath or shower and telephone.
Facilities: Lounge, separate TV room, bar, restaurant, banqueting hall, cocktail room. Terrace and garden with swimming pool; fishing and boating on the Loire.
Location: Between Blois and Amboise on the N751; parking.
Terms: Rooms 150–330 frs. Set meals: breakfast 22 frs; lunch/dinner 105–135 frs.

CHAUMONT-SUR-THARONNE, 41600 Loir-et-Cher   Map 8

La Croix Blanche
5 place Mottu

Telephone: (54) 88.55.12

Chaumont-sur-Tharonne is deep in the Sologne, a strange flat region of wide forests and little marshy lakes. *La Croix Blanche* is a well-modernized creeper-covered old building in the central square, with a flowered courtyard where you can eat or drink in sunny weather. A convent in the days of Charlemagne, it has been the village inn for the last 300 years, with a distinguished, exclusively feminine gastronomic tradition for the past two centuries. Gisèle Crouzier, Vice-President of the *Association des Restauratrices Cuisinières*, has been in charge of the kitchens for the past 35 years. 'Comfortable beds were good for sleeping off the *fabulous* meal. Guests walk through a large kitchen, all oak beams, scrubbed tables and gleaming pottery tiles, to the dining room. Madame Crouzier is one of the best cooks in France and a very original one. (Books which include some of her recipes are set out on a sideboard in the breakfast room; and she has high accolades in French hotel guides.) The service was friendly and professional, with the family very much in charge of a skilled staff. Well worth the detour, south from the Loire.' *(Sheila and Uwe Kitzinger)*

Open: 20 February–8 January.
Rooms: 11 double, 4 single, 1 suite – 9 with bath, 6 with shower, all with telephone. 10 rooms in annexe. (5 rooms on ground floor.)
Facilities: Hall, salon, 3 restaurants. Courtyard for refreshments; garden with ping pong and boules. Handy for Loire châteaux. English spoken.   .
Location: Midway between Romorantin and Orléans (Orléans 34 km) S of La Ferté St-Aubin by the D922.

Credit cards: American Express, Diners.
Terms: Rooms 100–300 frs; dinner, B & B 187–280 frs; full board 287–380 frs. Set meals: breakfast 18 frs; lunch/dinner 100–240 frs; full *alc* 250 frs. Reduced rates and special meals for children.

CHEFFES, 49330 Châteauneuf-sur-Sarthe — Map 8

Château de Teildras
Telephone: (41) 42.61.08
Telex: 720910 Public Angers F

'The Comte de Bernard du Breuil inherited this 17th-century château, with its 60-acre park (24 km north of Angers and within easy reach of some of the Loire châteaux) some eight years ago, at the same time as he retired from the French Navy. He decided that the only way to preserve his family estate was to turn it into a small hotel. The process of conversion has been slow, but has been meticulously executed, with everything done to the very highest standard. The Comtesse cooks, cuisine minceur: *vraiment formidable*. Two charming daughters variously serve and help with everything. The Comte produces the wine, including their own home-cultivated house *blanc*, which is delicious. Comfortable, quiet, unhurried, the best of family atmospheres. What more could one ask? We revelled in it.' *(Timothy Benn)*

Open: 15 February–15 November. Restaurants closed Tuesday lunchtime.
Rooms: 11 double, 1 suite – all with bath and telephone; TV on request.
Facilities: 2 salons, 2 restaurants. Wooded park, river within 500 metres; fishing, riding.
Location: 24 km N of Angers; parking.
Credit cards: All major credit cards accepted.
Terms: Rooms 240–440 frs; full board 425–485 frs. Set meals: breakfast 26 frs; *alc* 135–175 frs (excluding wine).

CHENEHUTTE-LES-TUFFEAUX, 49350 Gennes, Maine-et-Loire — Map 8

Hostellerie du Prieuré
Telephone: (41) 50.15.31

This famous hostelry which, in its former incarnation as a priory, dates back to the 12th century, has an awesome position on a bluff overlooking the Loire. It's one of the *Relais Châteaux*, and, as you would expect, luxurious in all its appointments; both the grand public salons and the bedrooms are furnished in high style. There is an unusually large heated swimming pool in the grounds, and 60 acres of private wooded park. The restaurant of the *Prieuré*, which has now recovered the Michelin rosette it lost in 1979, is as elevated as its location – and its prices.
One visitor this past year registered a slight disappointment: the food was as excellent as he had expected, but the service had been on the cool side; although some of the rooms are in the château itself, others are in bungalows in the grounds – a long walk through a garden which, he felt, could have done with some attention. Another reader, though not without a few reservations, was more positive: 'We booked one night and stayed three. A lovely modern room the first night, spotlessly clean with everything in luxury you could think of – bath robes, bath oil, perfumed

soap. The second and third nights we had a smaller older room in a turret overlooking the Loire. We really felt that we were defending it. The bathroom, well that was loo and wash-basin in one cupboard, and nip out and into another cupboard for bathing! Not quite so luxurious, but beautifully furnished. A lovely terrace for drinks, and a beautiful salon in which you dared hardly breathe. Why are French lounges like this? The meal was very very fine indeed.' *(Heather Sharland; also Raymond Harris)*

Open: All year, except 5 January–1 March.
Rooms: 35 double, 1 suite – 34 with bath, 2 with shower, all with telephone; baby-sitting by arrangement. 15 rooms in bungalows in the grounds. (Some rooms on ground floor.)
Facilities: 2 salons, bar, dining room. 60 acres grounds with heated swimming pool, mini-golf and tennis courts. English spoken. &.
Location: Overlooking the Loire; 7 km W of Saumur off the D751.
Credit card: American Express.
Terms (excluding 15% service charge): B & B 164–304 frs; dinner, B & B 289–429 frs; full board 359–499 frs. Set meals: breakfast 24 frs; lunch/dinner 90, 140 and 185 frs; full *alc* 240 frs. Reduced rates for children; special meals on request.

CHINON, 37500 Indre-et-Loire, Loire Valley　　　　　　　　**Map 8**

Hôtel Diderot　　　　　　　　　　　　　　*Telephone:* (47) 93.18.87
7 rue Diderot

Near the Loire valley in a lovely old town where Joan of Arc first met the Dauphin, sustained chorus of appreciation once again for this modest-priced but highly sympathetic bed-and-breakfast hotel, run by a Cypriot couple, whose age has been the subject of controversy in recent editions. We don't normally identify the occupation of our correspondents but, in view of its content, should explain that the tribute below, typical of the many we have had, is from the Arts Council's Literature Director:

'The couple who run this charming and friendly little inn have been described both as "young" and "elderly". These are relative terms: to the youthfully 54-year-old Charles Osborne, the Kazamias couple seemed to be a not very young pair, in their forties. The hotel looks a dump from the front, but the rooms are large, cheerfully light and clean, and mine had a fine modern bathroom. You get your own front-door key, which is useful, and there is plenty of space to park in the backyard. Be careful not to run over the proprietors' kids, and be grateful for the seemingly endless number of jars of home-made *confitures* (including elderberry and rhubarb, apricot and myrtle) which will be offered you at breakfast. Incredibly cheap. You could stay here happily for weeks writing your novel on your Arts Council grant. Minimum of fuss: they make you welcome and then leave you alone.' *(Charles Osborne; also Alan Cooke, Mrs R B Richards, B J Woolf)*

Open: All year, except 15 February–31 March.
Rooms: 20 double – 10 with bath, 10 with shower. (3 rooms on ground floor.)
Facilities: Salon with TV, breakfast room; limited conference facilities. 400 square metres gardens and courtyard. English spoken. &.
Location: On the N751, 48 km from Tours; central; private parking.
Credit cards: Access/Euro/Mastercard, Barclay/Visa.
Terms: Rooms 70–140 frs; B & B 82–87 frs.

250

CLUNY, 71250 Saône-et-Loire, Burgundy — Map 8

Hôtel de Bourgogne
Place Abbaye

Telephone: (85) 59.00.58

'Cluny in Burgundy was once one of the most powerful influences in Europe; its abbey, now almost totally destroyed, was the largest church in Christendom until the building of St Peter's Rome. Now it is a delightful medieval town of narrow streets and rose red tiles, well worth a short detour off the Autoroute du Soleil, not least to experience the special charm of Monsieur Gosse's well-run hotel. An inn since the 18th century (Lamartine frequently stayed here), it overlooks the main square. Furnished throughout elegantly, but never excessively, the *Hôtel de Bourgogne* provides a welcome haven after a long drive.

'Most of the bedrooms look out either to the green surrounding hills or the towers of the abbey buildings; they are all papered on walls and ceilings, with intricate designs, and many have spotless private bathrooms. The dining room, with bold black-and-white tiled floor, and a wide fireplace at the far end, provides many pleasures. Our *feuilleté de coquelet* was delicious and light, a difficult choice from a long *à la carte* menu; the cheeseboard is large, even by French standards, and the "chariot" groans with peaches and nectarines in wine, *crème caramel* of prodigious size, and *millefeuilles.* Sadly (as so often in good French hotels, especially in Burgundy) even the cheapest wine, an unexciting Mercurey, is horribly expensive. It is hard to believe anyone would object to taped Scarlatti and Mozart with breakfast in the Bar Classique, of which the owner is very proud. Monsieur Gosse's slightly anxious solicitude and the personal attention he and his wife give to small details is what makes this a very special hotel. It also makes it wise to reserve a room well in advance for it is usually full.' *(Bryan Stevens; also Anthony Price, IM)*

Open: 10 February–15 November, except Tuesday and Wednesday midday.
Rooms: 18 double – 13 with bath or shower, all with telephone.
Facilities: Salon with TV, bar, restaurant. Courtyard.
Location: On the N79, 19 km from Mâcon. Hotel is opposite the Abbey; garage parking.
Credit cards: American Express, Barclay/Visa.
Terms: Rooms 60–195 frs. Set meals: breakfast 17 frs; lunch/dinner 90–165 frs.

CLUNY, 71250 Saône-et-Loire, Burgundy — Map 8

Hôtel Moderne
Pont de l'Etang

Telephone: (85) 59.05.65

'Much less attractive externally than the *Bourgogne*, and in a less central position being on the river a kilometre out of town, everything else at the *Moderne* makes it the only place to stay. Not all the bedrooms are well-decorated, but one can always enjoy the pretty terrace over the river, and the staff make a special effort to be welcoming and helpful. Prices are very reasonable. It no longer has a Michelin star because of a change of ownership, but every effort is being made to regain it. The prices of the dinner menus are exceptionally low – our 60 franc dinner with choices (1980) was *memorably* better than at our 2-star restaurant later in the trip. The best chocolate gâteau I've ever eaten.' *(Caroline Hamburger)*

Open: All year, except 15 November–30 November and 1 February–10 March. Restaurant closed Sunday evening and Monday 15 September–15 June.
Rooms: 12 double, 3 single – 7 with bath, 1 with shower, all with telephone.
Facilities: Dining room for 40–60; banqueting room for up to 90. English spoken.
Location: 1 km from centre in the direction of Mâcon; parking for 6 cars.
Credit card: Barclay/Visa.
Terms: Rooms 50–140 frs. Set meals: breakfast 13 frs; lunch/dinner 55, 65, 110 and 140 frs; full *alc* 120 frs.

COLROY-LA-ROCHE, 67420 Saales, Bas-Rhin, Alsace   Map 8

Hostellerie La Cheneaudière   *Telephone:* (88) 97.61.64

'A great location, in the midst of flowery Alsatian villages; breathing the mountain air was a treat. Despite the hairpin curves that must be negotiated, the descent to the valley doesn't take long, and one can easily manage a day trip to Riquewihr and Kaysersberg. *Extraordinary* comfort in the new part of the hotel. I felt a bit guilty staying in a rather Holiday Inn ambience instead of in a place with more "character", but we did thoroughly enjoy it. The rooms in the old part of the hotel might have more flavour, but the view from *my* part of the hotel was splendid. The menu is very limited, poor in the way of starters (all outrageously expensive), but we enjoyed the best venison we have ever eaten, and the desserts are superior.' *(Caroline D Hamburger)*

Open: All year, except January and February.
Rooms: 23 double, 1 suite – 21 with bath, 3 with shower, all with telephone.
Facilities: Salon, restaurant. Garden. English spoken. .
Location: 62 km SW of Strasbourg on the N420; parking.
Credit card: American Express.
Terms: Rooms 240–350 frs. Set meals: breakfast 30 frs; dinner 180 frs; full *alc* 200–220 frs. Reduced rates for children.

CONQUES, 12 Aveyron, Massif Central   Map 8

Hôtel Sainte-Foy   *Telephone:* (65) 69.84.03

Conques is roughly equidistant from Figeac and Rodez and a good place to stop if you are driving from the Dordogne to the Tarn gorges. Medieval historians know it as one of the famous staging points on the pilgrimage to Santiago de Compostela. Amazingly, this small village on a wooded hillside, 3 km from the main road, with its slate-roofed houses and cobbled streets surrounding a massive and awesome abbey church, has retained the air of a sacred place and is wholly of the Middle Ages. The abbey is famous above all for the masterly Romanesque stone-carving on the west doorway and for its very rich gold and silver treasure. The *Sainte-Foy*, the only hotel, is called after the martyred girl whose weird gold relic is still to be seen in the abbey museum. It's a fine medieval house, facing the great abbey, with a shaded courtyard in the rear, and with handsome old furniture in the public rooms. The hotel has enjoyed for many years a well-merited Michelin rating for good meals at a modest price (dinner only). The service is exceptionally friendly, with the staff putting themselves out to accommodate families who want to share rooms or menus. It isn't a place for an extended stay, but Conques itself is so remarkable, especially in the evening when the abbey is floodlit and the daytime sightseers have departed, that it is well worth a special visit and a night-stop. Among readers who have written to us this past year about the *Sainte-Foy*, one felt that we hadn't praised the place enough: it was one of their best night stops in their tour of France. Another, just as enthusiastic – 'a very delightful hotel in a splendid place' – offered a warning to light sleepers: two sets of church clocks tell the time (varying by a minute or two) at half-hourly intervals throughout the night. *(Peter Fraenkel, Angela and David Stewart, John Hills)*

Open: 15 March–5 November.
Rooms: 18 double, 2 single – 12 with bath, 8 with shower, all with telephone.
Facilities: 2 reading rooms, TV room, dining room; small patio. English spoken.
Location: Off the D601 and not far from the N662 between Figeac (54 km) and Rodez (37 km). Hotel is central, opposite cathedral; garage and car park.
Terms: Rooms 80–200 frs; B & B 84–118 frs; half board 140–180 frs. Set meal: dinner 55 frs; full *alc* 80 frs.

CORDON, Nr Sallanches, 74700 Haute-Savoie   **Map 8**

Hôtel des Roches Fleuries   *Telephone:* (50) 58.06.71

'*Roches Fleuries* has a grandstand view of the permanently snow-covered Mont-Blanc and its neighbouring peaks. It is a sight you will never forget; especially if you watch the snow turn pink in the sunset as you take your *apéritif* on your balcony and later see the full moon come up over the ridge while you are having a splendid dinner. The hotel, Alpine in style, is attractive, quiet and very comfortable. Food and service are excellent. There are spacious terraces and then fields between this and neighbouring hotels. There is a separate chalet bar in the garden. An ideal base for a walking or skiing holiday. Sallanches, 4 km away on the road to Chamonix, has one of the very best markets we have seen.' *(Warren Bagust)*

Open: All year, except 10 October–20 December.
Rooms: 29 – 25 with bath or shower, all with telephone, some with balcony.
Facilities: bars, restaurant, terraces; conference facilities. Garden.
Location: 4 km from Sallanches on the D113; parking.
Terms: Rooms 125–145 frs; full board 160–190 frs. Set meals: breakfast 19 frs; lunch/dinner 65–90 frs.

COTIGNAC, 83850 Var   **Map 9**

Hostellerie Lou Calen   *Telephone:* (94) 04.60.40

Cotignac is a genial village nestling in the hills of the Haut Var. It calls itself *Village des Artisans, Le Saint Tropez du Haut Var*, which is stretching things a lot, but arts and crafts abound in the region, and the local craft shop does have a superior display. *Lou Calen* (the Provençal name means 'place of the oil lamp') is *the* hotel – an admirable family-run establishment. Rooms are simply but pleasantly furnished, with modern plumbing. You eat well on a beautiful terrace facing a wide view. There is a large swimming pool. Nothing outstanding, but everything as it should be – including a warm welcome. Only minor drawback: though the hotel faces sideways to the road, there is some traffic noise – revving and gear-changing at night. P.S. Don't miss the château at Entrecasteaux, 8 km away: a wonderful reconstruction by the Scottish artist/diplomat, Ian Garvie-Munn. *(HR)*

Open: 15 March–3 November. Restaurant closed Tuesday/Wednesday/Thursday and midday, except June–September.
Rooms: 13 – most with bath and TV.
Facilities: Salon, bar, restaurant, terrace. Garden with swimming pool. Tennis 1 km.
Location: On Route des Gorges du Verdon. For Cotignac take exit Brignoles or Le Luc – Toulon off the N7.
Terms: Rooms 140–200 frs; half board (obligatory for stays of 2 days or more) 160–185 frs; full board 215–255 frs. Set meals: breakfast 17 frs; lunch/dinner 65–145 frs.

COURRY, 30500 St-Ambroix, Gard **Map 8**

Auberge Croquembouche *Telephone:* (66) 24.13.30

'Returning from Spain to Calais via the autoroute, we decided to "cut the corner" at Montpellier as a respite from the hectic rush. In doing so we arrived at the D904 north of St-Ambroix in the eastern foothills of the Cevennes. It was in the proverbial middle of nowhere when we suddenly saw a sign pointing down a narrow lane indicating the *Auberge Croquembouche*. We decided to investigate and came upon a true haven for the weary traveller. A smiling welcome from Madame Labrosse, who spoke good English, and invited us into her delightful Auberge which had been converted by her husband from a ruin. The public rooms are small, interconnecting and cellar-like, whilst the bedrooms, all complete with bathrooms, are of the highest standard. Outside is a small swimming pool and plenty of ground for the children to tire themselves out in. However the best treat was still to come when we went down to dinner. The cooking, which is done by the Labrosses' son, is superb. A *terrine de poissons à la menthe fraîche* was followed by *grenadin de veau à l'estragon*, delightful pats of cheese from the local village and fresh fruit. An ideal place to rest for the night when travelling to or returning from the Mediterranean resorts.' *(Ann and Michael Lisamer)*

Open: All year, except February.
Rooms: 5 double plus 1 suite for 4 people – all with bath.
Facilities: Reception, salon, bar, restaurant. Garden with swimming pool. English spoken.
Location: Off the D904 from Alès to Aubenas, 6 km N of St-Ambroix.
Credit cards: American Express, Euro, Diners, Barclay/Visa.
Terms: Rooms 150–250 frs. Set meals: breakfast 16.50 frs; lunch/dinner 55 frs. 30% reduction for children under 7.

The terms indicate the range of prices in each hotel. Some have a low and high season, some do not. The lower price is likely to be for someone sharing a double room, and the higher price the maximum for a single occupant.

LA CROIX-VALMER, 83420 Var, Provence   Map 9

Parc Hôtel   *Telephone:* (94) 79.64.04
Avenue Georges Sellier

La Croix-Valmer is an inland village of no particular charm, 6 km from the beach at Cavalaire-sur-Mer, and near the attractive Côte d'Azur villages of Ramatuelle and Gassin. The *Parc Hôtel* is on the outskirts of the village, set back from the road, behind formal gardens and tall palms. It's an imposing-looking building, like a former stately home, with terraces and an elegant cream-coloured facade. You get a marvellous view down to the sea and the islands of Porquerolles.

'A very pleasant base for a holiday in the area, yet avoiding the expensive razzmatazz of the coast. The hotel occupies what must have been a grand château, and is at the beginning of the scenic route to St Tropez via Ramatuelle. It stands in attractive and spacious gardens with beautiful views of the sea and the Hyères islands from the front windows. Inside all is cool and spacious with lofty ceilings, chandeliers, patterned marble floors and spotlessly clean. It is all so large and airy that one is unaware of anyone else staying there and it would be a good place to hide away and write a book for example. There is a lift. The bedrooms were quite large, pleasantly furnished and comfortable and the bathrooms excellent. There is a bar but no restaurant. The staff were pleasant and helpful and breakfast was served in the bar or on the terrace. One personal niggle – why in a hotel of this type is one given wrapped butter pats and tiny wrapped portions of jam?' *(Ray and Angela Evans)*

The above report was fully confirmed by another reader. His only complaint: lukewarm coffee at breakfast, and soft butter . . .

Open: 15 April–15 October.
Rooms: 24 double, 1 single, 8 suites – 14 with bath, 19 with shower, all with telephone.
Facilities: Lift, 2 salons (1 with TV), bar. Attractive grounds and terrace; beaches nearby with sailing and underwater fishing.
Location: 500 metres from town centre; parking; off the N559 Toulon–Nice road on the D93, travelling E.
Credit card: Diners.
Terms: Rooms 90–220 frs. Set meal: breakfast 17–18 frs. Reduced rates out of season.

DIEPPE, 76200 Seine-Maritime, Normandy   Map 8

Hôtel de L'Univers   *Telephone:* (35) 84.12.55
10 Boulevard de Verdun   *Telex:* 770741

The *Univers*, facing Dieppe's elegant esplanade, has many British devotees, who make it a regular night-stop on their way to or from the south, or who come over specially from Newhaven for a weekend break. It is a middle-class hotel with old-fashioned virtues, run by professionals who know their business. Food, furnishings, service have all been appreciated, with only an occasional dissenting note. *(Heather Sharland, Jeff Driver, Raymond Harris)*

Open: 30 January–15 December.
Rooms: 30 – 28 with bath or shower, all with telephone and TV.

255

Facilities: Lift, restaurant; conference facilities. ᵭ .
Location: Central; parking.
Credit cards: All major credit cards accepted.
Terms: Rooms 130–240 frs; full board 215–275 frs. Set meals: breakfast 20 frs; lunch/dinner 65–95 frs.

DIJON, 21000 Côte d'Or, Burgundy   **Map 8**

Le Chapeau Rouge   *Telephone:* (80) 30.28.10
5 rue Michelet   *Telex:* 350535F

A lovely old-fashioned town hotel, a stone's throw from the famous cathedral – and (important for gourmets) the only hotel in the city with a Michelin star. It's a noisy street: back rooms, though possibly darker and less comfortable, are quieter, though front ones have double-glazing. Warning: parking can be devilish! 'The restaurant is the most elegant and tastefully furnished and lit that I have ever encountered, and the food fine, even by Burgundy standards, and matches the restaurant's ambience. All sights in the beautiful old town are within easy walking distance. The museum is not to be missed.' *(Arnold Horwell)*

Open: All year, except 20 December–4 January and Wednesday from December–Easter.
Rooms: 26 double, 7 single – all with bath, radio, TV, air-conditioning and refrigerated mini-bar.
Facilities: Lift, hall, salon, bar, elegant restaurant; conference facilities. English spoken. ᵭ .
Location: Central; parking for 15 cars.
Credit cards: All major credit cards accepted.
Terms: B & B 125–200 frs; dinner, B & B 235–310 frs. Set meals: breakfast 21 frs; lunch/dinner 100 frs. Reduced rates and special meals for children.

DIJON, 21000 Côte-d'Or, Burgundy   **Map 8**

Hôtel du Nord   *Telephone:* (80) 30.55.20
Place Darcy

'We were thwarted in our attempts to locate *Le Chapeau Rouge* by Dijon's one-way traffic system, which I can only describe as a Gallic puzzle, and we came upon the *Hôtel du Nord* quite by chance. The hotel is centrally placed for exploring the city. Sadly it has no private parking but you can park in the *Place*. The furnishings are traditional. We had a spacious bedroom with nice solid old furniture, heavy brocade bedspread and curtains and a large adjoining bathroom with ample clean towels. The candlelit dining room is especially inviting. The walls are panelled and the ceiling beamed. Windows on two sides overlook the *Place Darcy*. Service was efficient and most courteous and we were offered a good choice of dishes with Burgundian specialities very much in evidence. We ate extremely well in a very pleasant atmosphere and were sorry that our schedule restricted us to only one overnight stop.' *(Rosamund Hebdon)*

Open: 14 January–23 December.
Rooms: 26 double, 2 suites – 16 with bath, 10 with shower, all with telephone.
Facilities: TV room, bar, restaurant, banqueting room. English spoken.

256

FRANCE

Location: Central; parking in square.
Credit cards: All major credit cards accepted.
Terms: B & B 49–84 frs; full board 104–139 frs. Set meals: lunch/dinner 70–100 frs; full *alc* 95 frs. Reduced rates for children; special meals on request.

DOLANCOURT, Nr Bar-sur-Aube, 10200 Aube   Map 8

Moulin du Landion   *Telephone:* (25) 26.12.17

'A converted mill – the dining room with picture windows is built around the mill stream – in absolutely quiet countryside. The rooms are modern, plain and of good size – a blessing for people who find cramped conditions tiring, and very reasonably priced. The kitchen provides good food, the cellar stocks wines of a fair range, also not unreasonably priced. The staff are pleasant and helpful – for example, I wanted a vegetarian meal for dinner, and there was no difficulty about adapting the menu and no extra charge. An excellent place from which to explore the little-known and most interesting southern part of Champagne, completely restful, with none of the strident "attractions" that spoil many otherwise pleasant hotels. Recommended for the lover of peace and quiet plus unostentatious comfort.' *(Pamela Vandyke Price)*

This encomium to the tranquillity of the *Moulin du Landion* has come in for two contradictory comments. One reader was dismayed to discover that the main Paris–Basle railway line was behind some trees, but little more than 100 metres from her bedroom. Another writer, who found it was the only hotel he had stayed in during a fortnight in France where the water was hot at all times, and who also found the food very good indeed and beautifully presented, agreed whole-heartedly with the final sentence of last year's entry. Everything was as lovely and peaceful as our entry had led him to expect . . . *(A H H Stow; also M H Smye)*

Open: All year, except 1 December–5 January.
Rooms: 16 – all with bath and telephone.
Facilities: Salon, dining room. Garden. English spoken.
Location: 9 km from Bar-sur-Aube, on the N19 between Troyes (52 km) and Chaumont (42 km).
Credit cards: Access/Euro/Mastercard, Barclay/Visa, Diners.
Terms: Rooms (single) 115 frs, (double) 140 frs; full board 225–265 frs. Set meals: breakfast 15 frs; lunch/dinner 72–135 frs; full *alc* 120–150 frs. Reduced rates out of season.

DOL-DE-BRETAGNE, 35120 Ille-et-Vilaine, Brittany   Map 8

Logis de la Bresche d'Arthur   *Telephone:* (99) 48.01.44
36 Boulevard Deminiac

Dol-de-Bretagne, roughly half way between St Malo and Mont-St Michel is a most attractive town, full of fine medieval houses and an imposing cathedral. The 8th-century tidal wave which turned Mont-St Michel into an island, swept up to Dol-de-Bretagne; it is surrounded by fertile marshland, and is sometimes called the Capital of the Marshes.

'The rooms of the *Bresche d'Arthur* are a little spartan, but more than compensated for by a wonderful variety of food – a very wide choice all most thoroughly prepared. The receptionist is a young female who tries to

257

be snooty – but don't let her! The proprietor is young and very helpful. Parking is easy, and, despite traffic, the hotel is quiet. It is a useful staging-post to the morning boat from St Malo, 24 km to the north-west.' *(S W Burden)*

Open: All year, except 1 November–1 December.
Rooms: 25 – 19 with bath, all with telephone. (3 rooms on ground floor.)
Facilities: Salon/bar, restaurant; conference facilities. Garden. 6 km from sea. English spoken. &.
Location: Between St Malo and Mont-St Michel on the N176; hotel is central; underground garage.
Credit cards: All major credit cards accepted.
Terms: Rooms 85–138 frs; dinner, B & B 120–145 frs; full board 170–200 frs. Set meals: breakfast 16 frs; lunch/dinner 42–125 frs; full *alc* 75 frs. Reduced rates and special meals for children.

DOMME, 24250 Dordogne   **Map 8**

Hôtel l'Esplanade   *Telephone:* (53) 28.31.41

'Domme, overlooking the Dordogne valley, is tastefully restored, in the tradition of Viollet-le-Duc, a stone tribute to the determined orthodoxy of French fine art tradition, and it is full of expensive antique shops and *foie gras*. The caves, to which one may descend by lift in the covered market square, are not very interesting, since no local Abbé Breuil had time to colour them prehistorically, but they are cool on a hot day. The countryside around is varied, hilly, and there is swimming not far away in the river or in a *piscine municipale*. (Such places, by the way, are nearly always clean and agreeable in small French towns.)

'Monsieur and Madame Gillard (he the chef, she the front-of-house manager) have refurbished this hotel which always enjoyed a superb view but could not, until their arrival, be viewed as superb. The *Esplanade* has become a testimony to their energy and expertise. The rooms are individually decorated in a variety of floral wallpapers in the best tradition of the French country hotel, but they also have private baths or showers. Monsieur Gillard's dishes deserve stellar acknowledgment: the *mousseline de brochet* is particularly delicious. His table can be recommended not only for the skill he brings to it, but also for the size of the dishes in which that skill is revealed. Monsieur Gillard is a generous man as well as a resourceful cook. The dining room is large and airy, and the hotel stands at the peak of a town on a peak.' *(Frederic and Beetle Raphael)*

Open: All year. Restaurant closed Wednesday November and February.
Rooms: 14 double – all with bath and telephone.
Facilities: Salon with TV, 2 dining rooms; terrace with panoramic views. English spoken.
Location: 1 km S of the Dordogne; Sarlat 12 km, Gourdon 26 km.
Terms: Rooms 120–180 frs; full board 190–220 frs. Set meals: breakfast 15 frs; lunch/dinner 70–155 frs; full *alc* approx 120–200 frs.

If no one writes about a good hotel, it may get left out next year. WRITE NOW.

EUGÉNIE-LES-BAINS, 40320 Landes, Aquitaine   Map 8

Les Prés d'Eugénie   *Telephone:* (58) 58.19.01
Telex: 420 470F

'Michel Guerard's restaurant at Eugénie, 53 km north of Pau, is world-famous for the *nouvelle cuisine* in its most pure form: dishes which are at once gastronomically delicious and low on calories. Ancillary to the restaurant is an excellent hotel, a thermal establishment and, paradoxically, a health farm where guests pay to reduce on diets devised by a three-star chef. The casual visitor who has practised consistent self-denial in order to minimize the effects of advancing years and a liking for good food and drink can feel comforted as he looks around him on the sun terraces or by the pool at those who have been rather less disciplined – some enjoying an obscenely topless tanning session. The rooms are individually furnished in lavish French bad taste, the bathrooms are large and well-equipped with double basins. A rare sign of a really well-run hotel – while we were at dinner the chambermaid who came in to turn down the beds also cleaned the bathroom, tidied up the usual jumble of toilet articles left scattered about and renewed all the towels. The receptionists, waiters and chambermaids were all *very* pleasant and relaxed; one could sense a genuine enjoyment of their work. Needless to say the food is impeccable, its presentation theatrical and the prices are commensurately high.' *(David Wooff)*

Open: 1 April–31 October.
Rooms: 33 double, 3 suites – 22 with bath, 11 with shower, 20 with colour TV, 13 with mono TV, all with telephone and radio.
Facilities: Salon, smoking and billiard room, TV room, gallery, dining rooms. Beauty salon, sauna. 2 tennis courts, bowls, unheated swimming pool. Garden and river. Golf 25 km. English spoken.
Location: Off the D944 St-Sever–Aubagnan. 50 km from Pau.
Credit card: American Express.
Terms: Rooms 488–563 frs, suites 605 frs. Set meals: breakfast 40 frs; lunch/dinner 240 and 290 frs. Reduced rates for children under 11.

LES EYZIES-DE-TAYAC, 24620 Dordogne   Map 8

Hôtel du Centenaire   *Telephone:* (53) 06.97.18

The *Centenaire* is a modern hotel facing a busy crossroads, though the hotel assures us that the traffic is *'très faible la nuit'*. It has long had a distinguished gastronomic tradition, but both its kitchens and its restaurant underwent a major overhaul in 1980 and 1981, as a result of which it last year was awarded for the first time a second Michelin rosette.

'The *Centenaire* might easily seem just the kind of characterless and over-priced place to avoid. It is certainly somewhat expensive (though not by the standards of routine English hotels), but it is not to be missed, especially if food is part of your idea of a good holiday. (If it isn't, what point is there in going to the Dordogne?) The *Centenaire* is not one of a chain with a cost-conscious accountant at the head of the table; it remains a family affair, now in the hands of the younger generation, with a brilliant *nouveau cuisinier* in the kitchen and his charming, elegant brother-in-law in charge of the front-of-house. The dining room is somewhat formal in style, but the cooking deserves a proud frame. Pretentiousness is wholly absent.

'Les Eyzies is dominated by the steep cliffs which are riddled with the most astonishing concatenation of prehistoric caves in Europe. The call of culture can thus be answered honourably, and variously, between meals and, if desired, swims in the rivers (dangerous) or the reliable *piscines municipales* of the region. Les Eyzies is not, perhaps, the prettiest place in the department, but beauties abound in all directions. The *Centenaire* is unashamedly a *bourgeois* hotel; its suitability for family holidays may be questionable, but its courtesies and delights are beyond criticism.' *(Frederic and Beetle Raphael; also R S Ryder)*

Open: 15 March–15 November.
Rooms: 21 double, 6 single, 3 suites – all with bath or shower and telephone. 10 rooms in annexe. (5 rooms on ground floor.)
Facilities: Lounges, bar, restaurant. Garden, terraces. English spoken. &.
Location: 20 km from Sarlat on the D47; 45 km from Périgueux.
Credit cards: All major credit cards accepted.
Terms: Rooms 150–190 frs; B & B 102–170 frs. Set meals: lunch/dinner 100–250 frs; full *alc* 250 frs.

LES EYZIES-DE-TAYAC, 24620 Dordogne   **Map 8**

Hôtel du Centre   *Telephone:* (53) 06.97.13

A modest-priced alternative to the posher *Centenaire* (above) and *Cro-Magnon* (below). As its name suggests, it is in the centre of this seasonally busy village, near the river, but in a quiet location. It has an open-plan reception lounge, and two restaurants, one more formal than the other, which earns a Michelin accolade for a reasonably priced meal. Bedrooms vary in size and may be a bit tatty. Recommended for its five-course menus and excellent value for money. The hotel has new proprietors, M. and Mme Brun – he the chef, she front of house. Further reports welcome.

Open: February–end November.
Rooms: 16 double, 2 suites – all with bath and telephone.
Facilities: Reception-cum-lounge, 2 restaurants, covered terrace. English spoken.
Location: Central; parking.
Credit card: Barclay/Visa.
Terms: Rooms 100–160 frs; dinner, B & B 145 frs; full board 165 frs. Set meals: breakfast 13 frs; dinner 55, 65, 80 and 140 frs; full *alc* 70 frs. Special meals for children.

LES EYZIES-DE-TAYAC, 24620 Dordogne   **Map 8**

Hôtel Cro-Magnon   *Telephone:* (53) 06.97.06

The *Cro-Magnon*, though it shares with the *Centenaire* above the distinction of having one of the two best *tables* in town, is in other respects quite dissimilar. It's a creeper-covered, much-mansarded building, on the outskirts of the town, away from the tourist hubbub and with a delightful garden and swimming pool. It has a special atmosphere because of its association with the discoverer of the prehistoric sites nearby. The founder was a pre-historian of the late 19th century, who first identified Cro-Magnon man, and the hotel, which has a rather formal elegant decor, contains rooms with the artefacts he dug up on display, and is itself cut into the side of a rock shelter. 'An outstandingly pleasant, comfortable and well-furnished hotel, with memorably good food. We wholly endorse your recommendation.' *(Jessica Mann)*

Open: 1 April–10 October.
Rooms: 25 double, 3 suites – 25 with bath, 2 with shower, all with telephone. (1 room on ground floor.)
Facilities: 2 lounges, 2 dining rooms. 5 acres parkland with heated swimming pool; river at the foot of the grounds. English spoken. &.
Location: 600 m from town centre; garage and parking facilities.
Credit cards: All major credit cards accepted.
Terms: Rooms 130–300 frs; dinner, B & B 169–270 frs; full board 198–300 frs. Set meals: breakfast 19 frs; lunch/dinner 70–185 frs; full *alc* 120–200 frs.

FÈRE-EN-TARDENOIS, 02130 Aisne   **Map 8**

Hostellerie du Château   *Telephone:* (23) 82.21.13
                                                Telex: 830.906 Code 900

An emphatically luxurious hostelry, renowned for its cuisine. This grand part-Renaissance, part-19th-century manor 45 km west of Reims is in a substantial park which is itself in the seclusion of the forest. 'We picked a perfect day to visit the *Hostellerie du Château*. It was so hot that we had iced Perrier and lemon on the attractive terrace before being taken up to see several rooms. The room we decided on was quite large and covered with typical French flower design silk wall hangings. Beautiful linen and bedspreads; dainty chairs, bedside tables; a writing desk with writing paper and envelopes; a fridge filled with just about every drink one could desire; some fresh fruit, a knife and napkins. The bathroom was huge and well-fitted, including, joy of joys, a hairdrier. The windows opened on to a superb view of the grounds, and in the early morning we watched rabbits playing on the lawns. The service was very formal, but quite faultless. We had drinks on the terrace before dinner while we studied the simply enormous menu and an equally vast wine list. We finally decided on the tasting menu, which enabled us to try minute portions of three different fish courses: lobster mousse, *goujons* of sole and asparagus and *lotte* poached in wine wrapped in lettuce. All delicate and exquisitely presented. This was followed by a delicious sorbet of marc, and then a very uninteresting rabbit. Excellent cheeseboard. The desserts were masterly; any thoughts of calories must be discarded. The dining room was delightful with elegant furnishings and superb linen and tableware. The hotel was full of nice touches – a silver card with mints wishing us a good night, and a similar card on the breakfast tray wishing us a safe journey.' *(Padi Howard; also Raymond Harris)*

Open: All year, except January/February.
Rooms: 20 double, 7 suites – all with bath or shower and telephone; some with frigo-bar. (5 rooms on ground floor.)
Facilities: Salons, TV, restaurant; some conference facilities. Large park and formal gardens within surrounding forest, with tennis court. Fishing, riding 5 km; golf 40 km. &.
Location: 3 km N of Fère-en-Tardenois. Take the D967 and the Route Forestière.
Credit cards: American Express, Barclay/Visa.
Terms: Rooms 205–400 frs. Set meals: breakfast 28 frs; lunch/dinner 155–285 frs.

Hôtel-Restaurant au Moulin   *Telephone:* (6) 431.67.89
6 rue du Moulin

An enchanting 13th-century mill, beautifully converted in a picturesque
country village, 25 km south-east of Fontainebleau and 10 km from
Montereau-Faut-Yonne by the D120. A restaurant with rooms, but
correspondents in the past have appreciated both features with equal
enthusiasm, with one reader, quoted last year, describing her dinner as 'a
gastronomic experience, three hours long and cost more than the room!'
(Janet McWhorter)
    'Only a visit or a set of photographs can do this place justice. Rushing
water can be seen and heard from the delightful lounge featuring some of
the mill-wheels and pulleys. The restaurant also overlooks the same
rushing torrent. Our bedroom was overlooking and on top of the lock
gates. The resident cat wakes you in the morning by scratching at the
door. It's not too hard to spend more on food than on sleep. Our room
only cost 160 frs plus breakfast for two (June, 1981). Unfortunately we did
not find dinner to be "a gastronomic experience" – only average. But
everything else made up for it. We would certainly go again.' *(Peter
Marshall)*

Open: All year, except 11 December–11 January, 14–24 September; also Sunday
evening and Monday, except July and August.
Rooms: 10 double – all with bath.
Facilities: Lift; lounge, bar, beamed restaurant. Garden with riverside terrace.
Location: 20 km E of A6 motorway; 10km SW of Montereau: about 85 km S of
Paris.
Credit cards: Diners, Barclay/Visa.
Terms: B & B 100–150 frs/full board 260–300 frs. Set meals: lunch/dinner 70–95
frs; full *alc* 130–160 frs.

Hôtel Aigle Noir   *Telephone:* (6) 422.32.65
27 Place Napoléon Bonaparte   *Telex:* 600080

'We found it almost impossible to criticize – everything here was excellent, and they could not have been more helpful and pleasant. Maybe the
colour of the dining room walls were a little bright and unromantic, but
that is a matter of taste.' The hotel that gets this handsome accolade is the
grandest place to stay in Fontainebleau, in the centre, facing the gardens
of Napoleon's favourite palace. 'Ambiance Napoléonique' was how an
earlier visitor had summed up the experience. The hotel combines classic
Empire decor with all the latest mod cons – glass-fibre sound-proofing,
mini-bars, direct-dial telephones *et al*. But it also remains a family hotel,
run by Monsieur Duvauchelle and his two sons, Richard and Bertrand.
(Mr and Mrs R G Ewen, Raymond Harris, Dr D M C Ainscow)

Open: All year.
Rooms: 20 double, 6 single, 4 suites – 28 with bath, 2 with shower, all with
direct-dial telephone, radio, TV, mini-bar and double-glazing.

Facilities: Lift, hall, lounge, bar, dining room; banqueting and conference facilities. Garden for meals and refreshments in fine weather. Golf 1 km, tennis and swimming nearby. English spoken. &.
Location: Facing the Palace gardens; garage.
Credit cards: All major credit cards accepted.
Terms: B & B 168–357 frs. Set meals: lunch/dinner 120–165 frs; full *alc* 170 frs.

FONTAINEBLEAU, 77300 Seine-et-Marne, Île-de-France   Map 8

Legris et Parc   *Telephone:* (6) 422.24.24
36 rue Parc

'A welcome and unexpected find after a long slog up the Autoroute du Sud. It exudes style as befits its 1659 ownership by Louis d'Oyer, Marquis de Cavoye, a favourite of Louis XIV and friend of Racine. Large bedrooms; plenty of towels in well-appointed bathroom. Furnished in keeping with the general fabric of the building, backing on to the elegant railings of the Palais de Fontainebleau Park. A fine dining room looks out over a formal garden in the French style, with flowers and shrubs planted for spring and summer colour. Friendly and discreet service, comfortable public rooms. No traffic noise.' *(Kay and Arthur Woods)*

Open: All year, except 20 December–1 February.
Rooms: 24 – most with bath or shower and telephone.
Facilities: Salons, restaurant; conference facilities. Garden.
Location: Adjoining Palace grounds, W of Avenue des Cascades.
Credit cards: Barclay/Visa, Euro.
Terms: Rooms 125–190 frs; full board 190–250 frs. Set meals: breakfast 16.50 frs; lunch/dinner 65–130 frs.

FONTVIEILLE, 13990 Bouches-du-Rhône, Provence   Map 9

Auberge La Regalido   *Telephone:* (90) 97.70.17
Rue Frédéric-Mistral

'Olives used to be pressed in this old *moulin à huile* now converted, with two adjacent houses, into a gracious *auberge* in the foothills of the Alpilles in Provence, north-east of Arles. There are only 11 bedrooms, but each, named for a plant (mine was *genévrier* – juniper), has great individual charm. The *Auberge* is run by the Michel family. Madame Michel's hand is evident in the decor of the rooms and bathrooms, which are extremely comfortable, in the pretty garden, and in the flowers which grace all the rooms. Monsieur Michel *père*, himself a fine cook, now supervises the Auberge, while his son does the cooking in the restaurant, which has a well-deserved Michelin star. The food is memorable, and I particularly enjoyed two of the house specialities, *gratin de moules aux épinards*, and the *pièce d'agneau en casserole et à l'aîl*. I am not a lover of desserts but found the parfaits and sorbets exceptionally good. The greatest talent of the Michels, however, is to have created so warmly welcoming an atmosphere.' *(Elisabeth Lambert Ortiz)*

Open: 15 January–30 November. Restaurant closed Monday, and Tuesday midday (except holidays).
Rooms: 11 double – 10 with bath, 1 with shower, all with telephone.

Facilities: Large reception room, 3 small salons (1 with TV), restaurant. Garden. Sea 35 km.
Location: Arles 8 km W; Avignon 30 km N. Parking.
Credit cards: All major credit cards accepted.
Terms: Rooms 220–400 frs; full board 350–440 frs. Set meals: breakfast 30 frs; lunch/dinner 135–190 frs.

FOX-AMPHOUX, 83126 Var, Provence   Map 9

L'Auberge du Vieux Fox   *Telephone:* (94) 80.71.69

Our entries in previous editions for this highly personal small inn have been – despite references to amateurism – decidedly mouth-watering. Here, for instance, is part of last year's encomium:

'The village looked charming as one drove towards it – a typical Provençal perched village within easy reach of such Provençal splendours as the Verdon gorges and the abbey of St-Maximin. The hotel was formerly the schoolhouse. The present owners came five years ago on a visit from Paris, he an interior decorator and she an economics graduate, and, she said, in 48 hours had totally changed the direction of their lives. The young owners had no experience so learnt by trial and error, he the chef and she the manager and waitress. A feeling of amateurism still pervades, but this is charming and rather like dining with a friend who is a gifted cook but can't quite synchronize it all perfectly. The lovely bubbly *patronne* served and chatted to everyone present (perhaps that is how the soup and coffee were not hot). The dining room was charmingly furnished, the bedrooms were very comfortable and exceptionally attractive, each having a special colour scheme. For us this hotel was a real find and we cannot wait to go back.'

The trouble with the more seductive descriptions in the Guide is that they can easily lead to dangerous inflation of the anticipatory glands – and subsequent disappointment. Several correspondents this year have felt that the previous nominator had been seeing the *Auberge* through rose-tinted spectacles, and had been insufficiently sensitive to the absence of professionalism in the food and the shabbiness of some of the rooms. No one disputes the loveliness of the setting, but not everyone has been equally charmed by the management. More reports welcome. *(Angela and Ray Evans, Geoffrey Tate, W Ian Stewart)*

Open: 1 April–15 November. Restaurant closed for lunch April/May/June, October/November, Tuesday, Wednesday and Thursday.
Rooms: 9 double, 1 single – 6 with bath, 4 with shower, all with telephone.
Facilities: Lounge, TV room, 2 dining rooms. Terrace. Garden. Hunting and fishing nearby.
Location: The hilltop hamlet of Fox-Amphoux is just off the Barjols–Salernes road; about 30 km N of the A8 Autoroute; 65 km from the coast at St-Raphaël.
Terms: Rooms 105–190 frs. Set meals: breakfast 17 frs; lunch/dinner 78 frs; full *alc* 120 frs.

'Full *alc*', unless otherwise stated, means a three-course dinner with half a bottle of house wine, service and taxes included.

GIVRY, 71640 Saône-et-Loire, Burgundy   Map 8

Hôtel de la Halle   *Telephone:* (85) 44.32.45

On a minor road about 5 miles east of Chalon-sur-Saône on the A6 autoroute, this modest small hotel is in the centre of a pleasant Burgundy village, facing the old market hall (no longer in use) on the other side of the square. It is itself a venerable building with a fine spiral staircase. The hotel's restaurant, warmly recommended, is much used by locals. Christian Renard, the *patron*, is also the chef, and learned his trade on an Atlantic liner. Warning: front rooms are distinctly noisy. *(E Scott)*

Open: All year. Closed Monday.
Rooms: 10 – 2 with bath, 4 with shower.
Facilities: Salon, restaurant. Garden. Swimming pools 5 and 8 km away, also swimming in nearby river; walks in woods and vineyards. English spoken.
Location: On a minor road (D981) between Chagny and Cluny.
Credit cards: Access, American Express.
Terms: Rooms 70–115 frs. Set meals: breakfast 12 frs; lunch/dinner 55–185 frs.

GOUMOIS, 25470 Trevillers, Doubs   Map 8

Hôtel Taillard   *Telephone:* (81) 44.20.75

'We have been going to the *Taillard* en route to Switzerland for several years now. It has a simply beautiful situation at the northern end of the Jura, overlooking the river Doubs where it separates France and Switzerland. It must be a fisherman's and walker's paradise. There are only 18 rooms; the ones overlooking the valley are particularly attractive – some with small balconies on which one can have evening drinks or breakfast. The rooms are all papered with lovely flowery French wallpapers, and have good cupboard and drawer space, comfortable beds and usually excellent lightning. Bathrooms vary considerably, and some are the little sitting-only type. A few of the more expensive rooms have a minibar, and the prices are not greedy. The Taillard family have owned the hotel for more than a century and cater mainly for people wanting peace, quiet and good food. The staff are friendly and helpful. The dining room is most attractive, overlooking the valley; there are usually enormous vases of flowers, and the meals cater for hearty appetites (healthy as opposed to cardiac hearty). Specialities include *jambon de montagne, caquelon de morilles à la crème* and *truite belle goumoise*. We have sampled all the dishes and can thoroughly recommend them. The wine list is very comprehensive, with an excellent choice at varying prices, including some lesser known Jura wines not often found elsewhere.' *(Padi Howard)*

Open: 15 February–15 November. Closed Thursday October, February and March.
Rooms: 16 double, 2 suites – 15 with bath, 2 with shower, all with telephone. Some with mini-bar. (2 rooms on ground floor.)
Facilities: Salon, TV room, bar, 2 dining rooms, terrace; river, fishing; riding and winter sports nearby. English spoken.
Location: 50 km from Montbeliard, 18 km from Maiche on the D437A and D437B. Leave autoroute A36 at Montbeliard Sud or Besançon exits.

Credit card: Diners.
Terms: Rooms 85–160 frs; full board 125–160 frs. Set meals: breakfast 15 frs; lunch/dinner 75, 100, 130 and 170 frs; full *alc* 120 frs. Reduced rates and special meals for children.

GOUPILLIÈRES, 14210 Evrecy   Map 8

Auberge du Pont de Brie   *Telephone:* (31) 79.37.84
Halte de Grimbosq E

'This is the heart of the Suisse-Normande – by a wide river, and surrounded by nature at her most profuse. It is in the Michelin under Thury-Harcourt but is 8 km up the valley, and its red rocking chair is more than justified. We were there before the hay was cut and the blossom was still out – quite delicious. The *Auberge* is quite modern so that the bedrooms have luxurious bathrooms, pretty tiles to the ceiling and gleaming fittings. One tip: two bedrooms open on to a large safe balcony – one room with twin beds, the other has a double, so they would make an ideal base for a family holiday. Wonderfully cheap. The food was excellent. We hope very much to go back for longer.' *(Elizabeth Stanton)*

Open: All year, except 17 August–2 September, 1–15 February, and Wednesday.
Rooms: 6 – most with bath.
Facilities: Restaurant. Garden.
Location: 42 km from Caen off the D562 on the D171, 8 km from Thury-Harcourt.
Terms: Rooms 52–60 frs; full board 120 frs. Set meals: breakfast 13 frs; lunch/dinner 40–90 frs.

LA GRAVE, 05320 Hautes-Alpes   Map 8

Hôtel La Meijette   *Telephone:* (76) 80.05.34

La Meijette, 5,000 feet up, is on the N91 Grenoble–Briançon road where it runs above the Romanche torrent on a ledge which just allows a few houses and a car park. The *Restaurant Panoramique*, beautifully constructed in wood, has been cantilevered out over the Romanche and has spectacular views, also shared by the bedrooms, over the Upper Romanche valley and the high snow mountains – La Meije rises almost to another 9,000 feet only 5 km away. One reader, who has been coming to *La Meijette* since 1967, recommends it as a splendid centre for mountain walks of every standard. Another writes:
'This is as near a perfect hotel for us as any we know – for its combination of setting, unostentatious comfort, very good, homely food, friendly family and possibly the best area for wild flowers known to us (our holidays tend to revolve around this interest). There are some older *Chambres Grand Confort*, but most of the bedrooms are now (1979) chalet-type and very comfortable. There is a five-course meal each evening and there is a different menu on a two-week cycle. It is run by a delightful family, the Juge family – father, mother and three daughters. Father and mother are behind the scenes cooking and organizing, the eldest daughter, who speaks good English, runs the hotel and the second daughter runs the restaurant with fascinating efficiency and friendliness. We have watched this hotel improve its rooms and its restaurant since

1973, but its friendly welcome has remained the same. Though it is possible to eat *à la carte*, most people are on *demi-pension* and have the set menu. The time to go for mountain flowers is between mid June and mid July – the millions (yes millions) of narcissus and violas are expected to be at their best about the end of June. There are endless possibilities for the plant hunter in every direction.' *(A H H Stow; also Alison Chesshyre)*

Open: 15 February–15 October. Restaurant closed Monday.
Rooms: 18 – 15 with bath or shower and telephone.
Facilities: Restaurant. English spoken.
Location: On the N91 Grenoble–Briançon road.
Terms: Rooms 45–250 frs. Set meals: breakfast 14.50 frs; lunch/dinner 55–66 frs.

GRIMAUD, 83360 Var, Provence   Map 9

Hostellerie du Coteau Fleuri   *Telephone:* (94) 43.20.17

A charming small hotel, 3 km from Port Grimaud, beautifully situated in one of those characteristic Provençal *villages perchés*, full of old stone houses and tiny alleys, surrounded by vineyards and with views down to the distant coast. The *Coteau Fleuri* is a cool, comfortable house, with tiled floors, an open hearth and plenty of flowers around. The bedrooms are modern with pretty furnishings and Provençal prints. There's a small bar, with a terrace that leads on to the delightful rambling garden slope. The dining room has a wonderful view overlooking the countryside, and the food is warmly recommended, including thick hot chocolate and croissants for breakfast.

Open: All year, except November and Christmas. Restaurant closed November–March.
Rooms: 14 double – 9 with bath, 5 with shower, all with telephone.
Facilities: Salon with TV and piano, bar, restaurant. Terrace. Small garden with fine views. Beach 5 km. English spoken.
Location: 3 km from Port Grimaud; 10 km from St-Tropez.
Terms: Rooms 160–260 frs; dinner, B & B from 260 frs. Set meals: breakfast 13 frs; dinner 50–65 frs; full *alc* 110 frs.

GUIDEL, 56520 Morbihan, Brittany   Map 8

La Châtaigneraie   *Telephone:* (97) 65.99.93
Route Saint Maurice

There are hotels that appeal by the warmth of their hospitality, and the conviviality that welcome generates among the guests. *La Châtaignevaie* scores in precisely an opposite way. It offers, for those with a taste for it, a kind of absolute in luxurious privacy. The hotel itself is a modern purpose-built manor-house hotel in secluded grounds, about 2 km from the small resort town of Guidel, and 5 km from one end of a spectacular 16-km stretch of sandy beach, in the direction of Lorient. Lots of campers and caravan sites in the area, but plenty of beach for all.

La Châtaigneraie serves no meals except for a lavish breakfast, and fellow guests are hardly seen or heard. The rooms, small but hyper-elegant, are thickly carpeted on all six surfaces – the walls and ceiling in velvet. By each bed is a console (also cloaked in velvet) which provides controls for the large TV (no need to get out of bed to change the channel), radio and clock; there is also a panel of buttons to avoid your having to shout out to the waiter with your breakfast *'Entrez'*, *'Attendez'*, or *'Occupé'* as the case may be. It would make a perfect hotel for a honeymoon, though in the wrong company *La Châtaigneraie* could well seem like a prison of padded cells. *(HR, H K Wilford)*

Open: All year.
Rooms: 10 double – all with bath, telephone, TV and radio.
Facilities: Breakfast room. Garden. 5 km from beach.
Location: On the D162, 10 km from Lorient, 12 km from Quimperlé. Hotel is 1 km from Guidel on the road to Clohors and Carnoët.
Credit cards: Barclay/Visa, Diners.
Terms: Rooms 230 frs. Set meals: breakfast 20 frs.

HAM, 80400 Somme, Picardy   Map 8

Hôtel de France   *Telephone:* (22) 21.00.22
5 pl. Hôtel-de-Ville

Ham, between Compiègne and St-Quentin, is not the most attractive of towns, but the *France* is a useful night stop about two hours' drive from the Channel ports; it is near the main road, but with ample garaging and undisturbed by traffic noise. Our double room with private bathroom was comfortable, pretty and good value for money. The dining room is attractively decorated, with crisp table linen, gleaming cutlery and glassware and is the venue for locals enjoying family dinner parties. The food here rates a deserved Michelin rosette. The hotel is family-run and the service willing and friendly.' *(Rosamund V Hebdon)*

Open: All year, except August, February school holidays, Sunday evening and Monday.
Rooms: 14 double, 2 single – 6 with bath, 8 with shower, all with telephone.
Facilities: Restaurant. English spoken.
Location: In town centre; parking.
Credit cards: American Express, Barclay/Visa, Diners.
Terms: Rooms 60–130 frs. Set meals: breakfast 12 frs; lunch/dinner 60, 100 and 180 frs; full *alc* 130 frs.

HENNEBONT, 56700 Morbihan, Brittany   Map 8

Château de Locguénolé   *Telephone:* (97) 76.29.04
                                                Telex: 740853 Inflor 145

On the south coast of Brittany, near Lorient, and 45 km west of Vannes. 'A graceful mansion situated in acres and acres of its own woodland, with a meadow, some three or four hundred yards square, stretching from the front of the house to the banks of the river Blovet which, at this point, must be getting on for half a mile wide. On a warm, sunny afternoon, such as it was when I was there, it must be one of the most restful places on earth, with only the birds stamping about in the trees or the occasional fly on booster-jets to disturb the tranquillity. Most of the furniture in the public rooms, and some of the bedroom furniture too, is well over a hundred years old (I had an Empire *escritoire* in my room) as are the prints and pictures that adorn the walls. I start to have reservations, however, when this passion for antique furnishings extends to stair carpets. When new, the plain, scarlet carpet must have glowed like a coal against the dark wood of the stairs; today, it is fifty per cent soiled scarlet and fifty per cent hessian backing that shows and, to me at any rate, it gives the impression of threadbare *haute couture* and darned stockings.

'The glory of the *Château de Locguénolé*, however, radiates with unmistakable brilliance from its cuisine. As often seems to be the case in France, hoteliers share their hopes, ambitions, loves and labours in the ratio of about 80/20 between cuisine and accommodation. Not that the accommodation is inferior, far from it: but the food, its preparation and presentation, is proud, caring and truly magnificent. The château is both hotel and restaurant; the latter, justifiably, very popular and well worth its two Michelin stars. Indeed, at meal times, although the dining-room staff are very efficient and perfectly capable, everyone seems to gravitate towards the dining room, receptionists desert switchboards, and seek to share with the kitchen in its finest hours. Some might think it expensive. Personally, for the setting, the square miles of private quiet, the (rather genteel) charm – perhaps a little frayed in places – but, above all, for the deference and imagination which they extend towards the wholesome ingredients of a good meal, I am happy to pay the price.' *(Jeff Driver)*

Open: 1 March–1 December. Restaurant closed Monday, except July.–August.
Rooms: 34 double – all with telephone. 12 rooms in annexe. (10 rooms on ground floor.)
Facilities: 5 salons, bar, 3 dining rooms, TV room; banqueting room, conference facilities. 250 acres park; unheated swimming pool. Tennis 3 km, golf 20 km. On river; 9 km from beaches. Riding and disco nearby. English spoken.
Location: 3 km from Hennebont. Take the D781 and travel S for 4 km; sign to hotel is on right. On the highway from Vannes, Auray, Nantes and Rennes use the exit Port Louis.
Credit cards: Access/Euro/Mastercard, American Express, Diners.
Terms: Rooms 175–380 frs; dinner, B & B 240–350 frs; full board 350–480 frs. Set meals: breakfast 18 frs; lunch/dinner 127–132 frs. Bargain riding and sailing breaks; special business tariffs. Reduced rates and special meals for children.

HÉRICOURT-EN-CAUX, 76560 Doudeville, Seine Maritime, Normandy, 8   Map 8

Auberge de la Durdent   *Telephone:* (35) 96.42.44

'Héricourt is a small peaceful Norman village 10 km north of Yvetot. The inn stands at the edge of the village – a stream runs behind and through the inn, with a glass panel in the dining room floor. The accommodation is reached by a footbridge over the stream; it is thus away from the road and very quiet. There are 15 rooms, all at ground-level and all very pleasantly furnished. The ample *petit déjeuner* had the most delicious bread I have tasted in France. Service was cheerful and friendly – in fact the whole atmosphere was one of easy-going friendliness. The village is some 50 km from Rouen, and provides a quiet haven of rest after a day exploring the city.' *(D R Stevens)*

Open: All year, except 10–30 October, 10–28 February.
Rooms: 15 – all with bath. (All rooms on ground floor.)
Facilities: Restaurant. Garden with terrace for outdoor meals, and river. English spoken. &

Location: 10 km N of Yvetot; 50 km from Rouen.
Terms: Rooms 85 frs; dinner, B & B 110 frs; full board 140 frs. Set meals: breakfast 10 frs, lunch/dinner 42–85 frs.

HONFLEUR, 14600 Calvados, Normandy   Map 8

Hôtel du Dauphin   *Telephone:* (31) 89.15.53
10 place Pierre Berthelot

On the *place* of the medieval wooden church of St-Catherine, with a view down the narrow streets to the highly picturesque harbour, the *Dauphin*'s special charm derives from its sympathetic conversion of a number of old town houses. It has a *salon de thé* for breakfast, but does not provide any other meal. However, Honfleur is well provided with restaurants, and a walk back to the hotel after dinner is a pleasure in itself. *(David Machin)*

Open: All year, except 3 January–18 February.
Rooms: 29 double – 27 with bath, 2 with shower, all with telephone. (1 room on ground floor.)
Facilities: *Salon de thé*, bar with TV. &.
Location: Central, near St. Catherines' church.
Terms: Rooms 110–160 frs. Set meal: breakfast 14 frs.

LES HOUCHES, 74310 Haute-Savoie   Map 8

Le Bellevarde   *Telephone:* (50) 54.41.85
Telex: 385000 OFITOUR

'An all-season 2-star hotel 7 km from Chamonix and the Mont Blanc tunnel, an easy one-hour drive from Geneva. Large, well-furnished, south-facing bedrooms with wide balconies offering splendid views of the Aiguille du Midi. There is a big dining room, tastefully furnished in rustic style with an open log fire. Recent renovation has stopped short of a lift (the bedrooms are on the second and third floors) and a residents' sitting room. These are planned for. The sitting accommodation and bar space, though full of character and of characters (local), are inadequate. The food, cooked by the owner, is excellent and varied, and English guests who sampled the "menu gastronomique" spoke highly of it. The main distinguishing feature of this hotel is the kindness and imaginative care lavished on the guests by Monsieur and Madame Paillou. My husband had an accident which kept him in Chamonix hospital for a few days and the Paillous did all they could think of to make things easy for us. The village is attractive, with an unusually efficient Tourist Bureau, and the skiing facilities are excellent, though we heard much criticism of the Ski School. There is a short chair lift at the side of the hotel and the ski bus passes the door.' *(Barbara Blake)*

Open: 1 June–20 September, 15 December–20 April.
Rooms: 25 doubles and triples, 3 suites – all with bath, telephone, balcony, TV on request.
Facilities: Salon, bar, restaurant, games room. Winter sports. English spoken.
Location: Central; parking.
Credit card: American Express.

270

Terms: Rooms 80–140 frs; dinner, B & B 120–140 frs; full board 140–155 frs. Set meals: breakfast 12 frs; lunch/dinner 30–90 frs; full *alc* 60 frs. Reduced rates for children and for groups.

ITTERSWILLER, 67140 Bas Rhin, Alsace Map 8

Hôtel Arnold *Telephone:* (88) 85.50.58
98 route du Vin

'This small modern hotel is at the end of a typical village on the Alsace *route du vin*, windows looking on to a panorama of vineyards. They have no restaurant in the hotel, which makes it wonderfully quiet. Almost opposite, in the village street, they have their own *Weinstube* or restaurant, a bar, and a small shop stocking excellent local souvenirs. The restaurant is "Alsace rustic" in style, many regional dishes are on the menu, the wine and liqueur lists are long. Hotel clients use the restaurant as they wish. The staff are friendly and pleasant, and the Alsatians find the place very popular, which is in itself a tribute.' *(Pamela Vandyke Price)*

Open: All year, except 29 June–10 July. Restaurant closed Sunday evening out of season, and Monday.
Rooms: 27 – 15 with bath, 12 with shower, all with telephone, radio and colour or mono TV, most with balconies.
Facilities: Hall, salon, breakfast room; some conference facilities; restaurant, bar and shop opposite. Garden; river nearby. &.
Location: On the N425, 40 km SW of Strasbourg; parking.
Terms: Rooms 115–285 frs. Set meals: breakfast 17.50 frs; lunch/dinner 38–176 frs.

JOUÉ-LES-TOURS, 37300 Indre-et-Loire, Loire Valley Map 8

Hôtel du Château de Beaulieu *Telephone:* (47) 28.52.19
Route de l'Épan

Jean-Pierre Lozay and his wife, who is Scottish, have thoroughly modernized this quintessential 18th-century château on the outskirts of Tours – an appropriate base for a holiday in the Loire. There are seven acres of formal gardens ('a mini-Versailles'), and, inside, an elegant wide staircase, large rooms furnished in style, and well-decorated bedrooms overlooking the park. One couple, who enjoyed their visit, registered disappointment with the cooking. To another – 'It completely lived up to our expectations.' *(Joy and Lenny Alcock)*

Open: All year.
Rooms: 16 double, 1 single – 9 with bath, 7 with shower, all with telephone. (3 rooms on ground floor in annexe.)
Facilities: 2 sitting rooms (1 with TV), 2 dining rooms; conference room. Large garden with ping pong and boules. Tennis, swimming and mini-golf nearby; riding, fishing, golf, sailing a few km away. English spoken. &.
Location: 4 km from Tours by the D86 and D207.
Terms: Rooms 80–320 frs. Set meals: breakfast 20 frs; lunch/dinner 100, 125 and 200 frs; full *alc* 120–150 frs. Full and half board rates for 2 people staying more than 3 days. Reduced rates and special meals for children.

Hotel les Ramparts   *Telephone:* (89) 47.12.12

'A recently built hotel in the quiet surburban outskirts of one of the more beautiful Alsatian wine villages. The rooms (all with bathroom) are excellently equipped, complete with tiny balcony looking out towards the encircling vineyards. It is extremely efficient and completely impersonal. Not for those requiring atmosphere, but a *haven of comfort* after a long day. No restaurant, but plenty of eating places near. At weekends and in holiday months booking is essential in all of this area.' *(E Newall)*

The above entry, from last year's edition, has been endorsed by recent visitors. One reader, however, complained about the 'continuous sonorities of the plumbing'. Another wrote to recommend the *Auberge du Tonneau d'Or* (closed Monday evening and Tuesday) for excellent Alsace meals at remarkably low prices. *(B W Ribbons; also J Dixey)*

Open: All year.
Rooms: 23 double – all with bath, telephone, radio, mini-bar and balcony, 14 with black and white TV. (12 rooms on ground floor.)
Facilities: Salon, bar, breakfast room. Located in centre of vineyard, near the forest. (Small park in front of hotel.) Tennis and swimming pool 1 km. English spoken. ᕍ .
Location: 200 m from town centre; parking. Kaysersberg is 11 km from Colmar.
Credit card: American Express.
Terms: Rooms 70–80 frs per person. Set meal: breakfast 14 frs.

Hôtel du Midi   *Telephone:* (75) 06.41.50
Place Seignobos

'A small town near the Rhône valley, 40 km west of Valence on the road to Le Puy. It's a much more attractive town than its description in the Green Michelin would suggest. The hotel is pretty, and is in the market square. Its restaurant, called *Barattero*, deserves its star in Michelin, but the hotel is also extremely comfortable and friendly. We had a lovely room overlooking an inner courtyard. Breakfast was served precisely at the time suggested, and the coffee was heated as at home.' *(Conrad Dehn)*

Open: 1 March–15 December. Restaurant closed Sunday night and Monday lunch.
Rooms: 18 double, 4 single – 12 with bath, 3 with shower, all with telephone. (1 room on ground floor.)
Facilities: Salon, 2 restaurants. Garden. ᕍ .
Location: Central; parking.
Credit card: Barclay/Visa.
Terms: Rooms 65–120 frs; full board 150–220 frs. Set meals: breakfast 18 frs; lunch/dinner 120–200 frs. Reduced rates for children.

Hotels were asked to estimate prices for 1982, but some hotels gave us only their 1981 prices. To avoid unpleasant shocks, always check tariff at time of booking.

LANGRES, 52200 Haute-Marne   Map 8

Grand Hôtel de l'Europe   *Telephone:* (25) 85.10.88
23 rue Diderot

'An excellent *étape* on the way either to Switzerland or the French Alps,' writes a reader endorsing last year's entry for this pleasant and modest-priced hotel, one of the few two-turreted establishments in Michelin also to win a red R for a meal offering specially good value – most hotels with a red R are in the cheaper one-gable class. And Langres is well worth a visit on its own account – largely 17th- and 18th-century in its architecture, it is steeped in earlier history and is surrounded by 5 km of ramparts. The main road bypasses the town, which is therefore quiet at night. *(Daphne Pagnamenta, Alison Chesshyre, A H H Stow)*

Open: 1 November–30 September, first week in May and Sunday night 1 October–1 June. Restaurant closed Sunday night and Monday lunch.
Rooms: 26 double, 1 single, 1 suite – 8 with bath, 17 with shower and WC, all with telephone. 9 rooms in annexe.
Facilities: Salons, bar, 2 restaurants. Garden. English spoken.
Location: Between Chaumont (35 km) and Dijon (66 km); railway station 3 km. Central; parking.
Credit cards: Access/Euro/Mastercard, American Express, Barclay/Visa.
Terms: Rooms 50–95 frs per person. Set meals: breakfast 11 frs; lunch/dinner 35–85 frs.

LAON, 02000 Aisne, Picardy   Map 8

Hôtel de la Bannière de France   *Telephone:* (23) 23.21.44
11 rue F Roosevelt

A millenium ago, give or take a few years, Laon was the capital of France. It was not until 987 AD that Hugues Capet, elected King, decided to move his court to Paris. There is not much left in Laon of that distant era, but it is a highly atmospheric town with splendid 13th-century ramparts, on a ridge commanding an immense plain, and the old part is full of fine houses in narrow streets clustering around a magnificent 12th-century cathedral. Reims and Compiègne are both fairly near. *La Bannière de France* stands aloft in the old town in a narrow one-way street (some readers have found the front rooms noisy). The hotel has its own garage or you can park free in a parking area nearby with a vast view over the town walls towards the plain below. The hotel continues to be popular with those looking for a first or last night stop from the Channel ports, about 3½ hours' drive. Bedrooms are simple, clean and comfortable, with good lighting. High standards of food and service are maintained in the dining room, and, for those with ferries to catch, they serve breakfast from 7 am. Prices are reasonable. *(Rosamund V Hebdon, B W Ribbons, Daphne Pagnamenta)*

Open: All year, except 20 December–10 January.
Rooms: 14 double, 4 single – 5 with bath, 7 with shower, all with telephone.
Facilities: Small bar, 2 dining rooms; banqueting room. English spoken.
Location: Central; hotel has garage (small payment); free car park nearby.
Credit cards: All major credit cards accepted.
Terms: Rooms 50–175 frs. Set meals: breakfast 14 frs; lunch/dinner 50–78 frs; full *alc* 125 frs.

LECHIAGAT, 29115 Guilvinec, Finistère

Map 8

Hôtel du Port

Telephone: (98) 58.10.10

This village is on the coast of south-west Brittany, in the charming Bigouden country where Breton folk traditions survive most strongly. Quimper is 30 km away. 'The *Hôtel du Port* is really a large French pub, with a big dining room and *chambres*. I have stayed here two years running, and it grows on you. Food is normally excellent and copious – especially the *plateau des fruits de mer*, which is colossal and a speciality. However, when it is the chef's night off, things may slip. The hotel looks out over the harbour basin but is quiet.' *(S W Burden)*

Open: All year, except 22 December–6 January.
Rooms: 31 – most with bath or shower, all with TV and telephone.
Facilities: Restaurant.
Location: 1 km from Guilvinec.
Credit cards: Barclay/Visa, Diners, Euro.
Terms: Rooms 75–130 frs; full board 155–190 frs. Set meals: breakfast 13 frs; lunch/dinner 55–200 frs.

LEVENS, 06 Alpes-Mar, Provence

Map 9

La Vigneraie
Rue Saint-Blaise

Telephone: (93) 91.70.46

'It is hard to believe that the bustle of Nice is a mere fifteen miles away, when you settle into this quiet and very pretty little family-run hotel, just outside the hill-village of Levens. We found it a good centre for exploring the beautiful Alpine country to the north. The bedrooms are simple but comfortable and amazingly cheap – a mere 60 frs for two in 1981. I can't think how they do it. The Bastiens, a local couple, are charming hosts, and we had a happy time, though young people might find the place a little *too* quiet; it seems to attract mainly the old. The Provençal cooking is rather good, and on fine days you eat out in an idyllic creeper-covered patio. We should have liked a little more choice on the menu.' *(Anthony Day)*

Open: All year, except October/November.
Rooms: 20 – 10 with bath or shower, all with telephone.
Facilities: Restaurant. Garden, patio.
Location: 23 km from Nice on the D19; parking.
Terms: Rooms 45–65 frs; full board 100–120 frs. Set meals: breakfast 8 frs; lunch/dinner 30–55 frs.

LUMBRES, 62380 Pas de Calais

Map 8

Auberge du Moulin de Mombreux

Telephone: (21) 39.62.44

'A very pretty converted millhouse, 40 km south-east of Calais. Plenty of flowers and lovely garden furniture. The sort of place where your spirits rise as you drive in. Spotlessly clean. You can sit in the front and listen to the noise of the mill race. Really a restaurant with six rooms, all with

private bathrooms, all named after flowers. Very small, not luxurious, but very French and very pretty. We had *Nasturtian*, and overlooked the flower gardens where the chickens industriously scratched about among the flowers. Also cockle-oodle-dooed at about 4 am. Pleasant people. Star in the Michelin. Good food but I don't think meriting a star. Wines far too expensive. We enjoyed it though, as it was a pretty place.'
(Heather Sharland; also, some with more enthusiasm for the food but some with reservations (also about the service) – *Dr D M C Ainscow, Warren Bagust, Robert Pascoe, Norman Braugham)*

Open: 1 February–20 December. Closed Sunday evening and Monday.
Rooms: 6 double – 4 with bath, all with telephone.
Facilities: Salon, bar, restaurant. Garden, leading to river with fishing. Tennis and swimming nearby. English spoken.
Location: 2 km from Lumbres; between the RN42 from Boulogne to St-Omer and the D202 Nielles–Lumbres.
Credit card: Diners.
Terms (excluding 15% service charge): Rooms 100 frs. Set meals: breakfast 10 frs; lunch/dinner 50, 100 and 150 frs; full *alc* 140 frs.

MARTIN-ÉGLISE, 76370 Neuville Les Dieppe, Normandy   Map 8

Auberge du Clos Normand   *Telephone:* (35) 82.71.01

Six km from Dieppe: an ideal first or last night's stop, but also an easy place to go for a weekend in France without the bother of taking the car. And the point about this restaurant with rooms is that, while very close to a Channel port, it is extremely French and very much abroad. The bedrooms are in a separate rather dilapidated building, perhaps once a stables or a hayloft, with a romantic garden which has a pavilion for eating out in summer, and a stream; it's very quiet except for farmyard noises, emanating from the farm which lies just across the stream. 'There is something Chekhovian about the place,' wrote Susan Campbell, who first recommended the *Clos Normand*; 'it is slightly decrepit, but has great charm and is not expensive.' Not all our correspondents have been equally ravished by the Chekhovian charm. Some of the rooms are decidedly modest, and dinner (*à la carte* only) is obligatory. The food is typically Norman: lashings of cream, butter and calvados and no nonsense about *nouvelle cuisine*. Here is how the place struck one visitor who *was* enchanted:

'Six of us went for Bank Holiday weekend, including two small children. The rooms are in an old barn, each with a little balcony and creeper growing up the outside of the building – so very pretty. All our rooms were pleasantly furnished and the beds *really* comfortable. The food – well, it really was lovely. Perhaps the atmosphere contributed a lot to this feeling. The wife takes the orders, fetches the drinks and serves the tables, while the husband-cum-chef does all the cooking at the end of the long room, in full view of everyone. We were asked questions – would the children like one or two chops etc. – which makes one feel as if each order is cooked for that particular person. Coffee is made in those rather ancient machines and tastes marvellous! Altogether one feels one has discovered a place that has not been hit by tourism and still remains enchanting and rural. It's a magic place for a weekend away.' *(T Brigden-Shaw; also P and EC)*

Open: March–mid November, except Monday evening and Tuesday.
Rooms: 7 double, 1 single – 3 with bath, 1 with shower, 3 with basin and bidet, in

separate building in the garden.

Facilities: Lounge, restaurant. Garden with large lawn and stream flowing at the bottom; pavilion for outdoor summer meals. Function ballroom below bedroom annexe.

Location: 6 km from Dieppe; off the D1 to Neufchatel.

Terms: Double rooms 70–130 frs. Set meal: breakfast 13 frs; full *alc* 88–150 frs.

MERCUREY, 71640 Givry, Saône-et-Loire, Burgundy   Map 8

Hôtellerie du Val d'Or   *Telephone:* (85) 47.13.70

'A restaurant with rooms in a very good location for touring Burgundy vineyards. Our bedroom, though tiny, had obviously been recently redecorated, and whoever was responsible had excellent taste. The restaurant, rated one star by Michelin, is a cosy room with a fireplace, and the proprietors were much in evidence during the meal, showing great concern that we enjoyed it. Out of the ten hotels we visited on our holiday this was the only one to offer an outstanding soup (most offered none at all – no profit in it?), an important plus to a soup-lover like me. My *coq au vin*, unfortunately, was ordinary (not bad, just not special), but a replacement was offered. My husband's Charolais beef was excellent.' *(Caroline D Hamburger)*

Open: All year, except 31 August–19 September. Closed Sunday evening in low season, and Monday, except public holidays.

Rooms: 12 – 6 with bath, 5 with shower, 6 with colour TV, all with telephone.

Facilities: Reception, 2 salons, bar, restaurant. Garden. English spoken.

Location: 13 km from Chalon-sur-Saône. Leave the autoroute at the Chalon exit and take the D978 Autun–Nevers road, then a turning to the right to Mercurey.

Credit card: Barclay/Visa.

Terms: Rooms 70–170 frs. Set meals: breakfast 18 frs; lunch/dinner 65, 95 and 165 frs; full *alc* 126 frs.

MEXIMIEUX, 01800 Ain   Map 8

Hôtel Claude Lutz   *Telephone:* (74) 61.06.78
17 rue de Lyon

'A town just west of the Jura foothills, on the old main road from Lyon to Geneva. 'Anyone going near this hotel who enjoys *superb* food should visit it. My wife had *fricassée de la volaille de bresse à la crème*, and considered it a "most superior dish". I had sliced breast of duck, and it was really beautiful. It is seldom that we use these adjectives – the only occasion on this holiday. The hotel is in need of redecoration, and the restaurant might be considered drab, but the reception and service were most friendly and welcoming – particularly creditable as there was a large wedding reception in the hotel the night we dined. We stayed here because we wanted to visit the bird sanctuary at Villars-les-Dombes (France's Slimbridge). It was sad to see all the eagles caged (though they are obviously well-looked after for they are in splendid condition), but the large *étang* has a huge range of free duck and geese. There must be many of your readers who would enjoy the combination of the *Parc Ornithologique* and the *Claude Lutz*.' *(A H H Stow)*

Open: All year, except Sunday evening and Monday 17 October–9 November.
Rooms: 17 double – 5 with bath, 10 with shower, all with telephone.
Facilities: TV room, bar, restaurant; conference facilities. Garden. English spoken.
Location: 36 km NE of Lyon on the N84. In village centre; private parking. There could be some noise from the autoroute.
Terms: Rooms 80 frs; dinner, B & B 185–200 frs. Set meals: breakfast 15 frs; lunch/dinner 50–140 frs; full *alc* 190 frs.

MEYRARGUES, 13650 Bouches-du-Rhône, Provence   Map 9

Château de Meyrargues   *Telephone:* (42) 57.50.32

'Most beautiful Provençal château perched on high hill above Meyrargues, north of Aix-en-Provence. Very old, very peaceful, very attractive. We found it through the Michelin Guide, and it is a "three red knife and fork" restaurant, though it also has 15 bedrooms. Unfortunately, we were there on a Sunday evening, when the restaurant was closed, but judging by the number of French people still recovering from lunch I would guess the food is good! Our bedroom was charming and the bathroom had an interesting Gothic-shaped loo and bidet. It was expensive but worth it for the decor and view and peace. (*Lady Elstub*)

Last year's entry has been warmly endorsed by *Barbara Anderson* and *Dr J. E. M. Whitehead*, though a third reader complained of inadequate hot water and disappointing food. More reports welcome.

Open: All year, except 1 December–31 January. Restaurant closed Sunday night and Monday, except July–August.
Rooms: 15 double – 13 with bath, 2 with shower.
Facilities: Salon, bar, dining room; conference facilities; courtyard. 12 acres grounds with terrace and park. By the river Durance; 45 minutes from the sea by autoroute. English spoken.
Location: 15 km from Aix-en-Provence; 47 km from Marseilles.
Credit cards: American Express, Diners.
Terms: Rooms 180–285 frs; full board 250–285 frs per person. Set meals: breakfast 15 frs; lunch/dinner 90 frs; full *alc* 130 frs. Reductions for stays of over 3 days. Reduced rates and special meals for children.

MEYRONNE, Nr Souillac, 46200 Lot   Map 8

Hôtel La Terrasse   *Telephone:* (65) 32.21.60

A modest and very cheap but highly *sympathique* hotel housed in an old monastery above the Dordogne river, run by three hard-working ladies. The food is excellent, accommodation on the basic side. 'One of the secret sanctuaries in our life, and should never have been revealed to the tourist world. Is nothing sacred?' was an anguished cry from a reader last year. This year, once again, we have had grateful letters from those who have benefitted from the generosity of our correspondents. As we have said before, highly individual establishments like this one need all the encouragement they can get: they thrive on recommendations and die from neglect.

We think the report below, from a visitor in April, catches the character of *La Terrasse* pretty well: 'We started badly, cold and tired, and wanted above all else a soothing hot bath, which of course there wasn't. A

277

dribbling shower and handkerchief towel didn't help, nor did the cold lino. But the warmth of the welcome more than compensated. Log fires were lit and free drinks offered. Our first three courses for dinner by the fire were vegetable soup, *pâté de fois gras truffé*, and surprisingly a pink grapefruit. For one awful moment we thought this must be starters, meat and dessert, but no, along came in bewildering succession: *jambon cru, veau aux champignons, haricots verts*, cheese and oranges flambéed in rum. This with a litre of wine and coffee accounted (1980) for 35 frs on our bill! The room was another 35 frs for two! I had admired the first *muguets du bois* (lilies of the valley) on the tables. When we left, they were wrapped up and left in the car. The breakfast bread *was* very stale, but the *muguets* came fresher than ever at the Hilton. Perhaps April was too early. We loved every minute of our three days there, but it would have been pleasant to have sat on that terrace overlooking the Dordogne, and to have been a bit warmer in bed (extra blankets hastily provided when discomfort discovered). Next time we shall go later and for longer.'
(Patricia Fenn; also Michael and Eileen Wilkes, David Holbrook)

Open: 1 March–1 December.
Rooms: 10 double. 6 in annexe.
Facilities: Dining room; also meals on terrace overlooking the Dordogne. Small garden.
Location: Between Souillac and Rocamadour, 12 km from Souillac.
Restriction: No children under 4.
Credit card: American Express.
Terms: Rooms 40–45 frs; dinner, B & B 65–75 frs; full board 80–90 frs. Set meals: breakfast 9 frs; lunch/dinner 40–60 frs; Full *alc* 45 frs. Reduced rates for children.

MIONNAY, 01 Ain, near Lyon   Map 8

Alain Chapel   *Telephone:* (7) 891.82.02

Alain Chapel was chosen *'premier cuisinier'* of France in 1980, and Gault-Millau awarded his cooking their *meilleur repas de l'année* in 1981. His restaurant, in an otherwise undistinguished village, has long carried Michelin's three rosettes, as well as four red knives and forks. He is a great innovator, and changes his menu regularly according to the season and what is available in the market. His is a light imaginative style of cooking – *nouvelle cuisine*-ish. Some, no doubt, would vote him the greatest chef in the world, though how any judge could survive such arbitration is difficult to imagine. But *Alain Chapel* also has 13 bedrooms – in the best of good taste, though, for one reader, *much* too expensive, and lacking certain contemporary refinements such as a mini-bar and a television set. On the question of food, there is no equivocation: 'The best food I have ever eaten – with *crise de foie* to match, the next day.' *(Paul Levy; endorsed by the Editor, with no reservations, no complaints, no* crise de foie*)*

Open: All year, except January. Restaurant closed for lunch Monday/Tuesday.
Rooms: 13 double – all with bath and telephone.
Facilities: Restaurant, private dining rooms. Garden. Swimming pool nearby. English spoken.
Location: 18 km N of Lyon on N83. Coming from Paris on the autoroute A6 take first exit after Villefranche and take the D51 S.
Credit cards: American Express, Diners.
Terms: Rooms 275 frs. Set meals: breakfast 41 frs; lunch/dinner 200 and 275 frs; full *alc* (excluding service) 315 frs. Reduced rates and special meals for children.

MIRABEL-AUX-BARONNIES, 26110 Nyons, Drôme, Provence   Map 9

Hôtel Le Mirabeau   *Telephone:* (75) 27.11.47

A village in the extreme north-west of Provence, 9 km from Vaison-la-Romaine, with its medieval streets and nearby Roman remains. 'A small 18th-century Provençal mansion, the last building in Mirabel on the Nyons road, this hotel embodies the best characteristics of a modest Provençal *logis de France*. Restaurant, bedrooms and staircase, all have the ample solid proportions that make old bourgeois houses such a delight. The large, low-ceilinged bedrooms have traditional red hexagonal tiles on the floor, old furniture, bedcovers and tablecloths that glow richly and welcomingly. The restaurant is spacious, dim and panelled. On bright, hot days, the cool half light is a welcome relief. Menus usually contain a regional speciality. It is agreeable food, interesting, well-served at tables set spaciously apart, and the wine list is adequate; Madame Corbet supervises with swift competence. *Le Mirabeau* is inseparable from its surroundings. It is a place for peace and quiet. There is nothing much to do after dark. Mirabel is not one of the most attractive villages of the region. But there are walks, especially along the track to Les Pilles, through the olive groves, and across rough *garrigue* country.' *(Norman Brangham)*

A recent visitor endorses our original report, quoted above, but recommends a visit either of one night or at least three to take advantage of *en pension* terms. On their second evening, a Sunday, she was only offered the more expensive menu, and the food struck her as tired, being re-heated from a large lunch-time *carte*; all the other guests were getting a better *pension* meal. *(Alison Chesshyre)*

Open: All year, except 5 January–15 February and restaurant closed Tuesdays.
Rooms: 8 double – 6 with shower.
Facilities: Restaurant. Garden.
Location: Nyons 7 km; Orange 36 km SW. Parking.
Credit card: Barclay/Visa.
Terms: Rooms 40–105 frs; full board 110–140 frs. Set meals: breakfast 11 frs; lunch/dinner 35–85 frs.

MOLINES-EN-QUEYRAS, 05390 Hautes-Alpes   **Map 8**

Hôtel L'Équipe   *Telephone:* (92) 45.83.20
Route St-Veran

'A Belgian couple were at the hotel for the 18th time, and they said that they never tired of the walks around this hotel at nearly 6,000 feet where the tourist brochures claim over 2,000 different flowers. Awful weather prevented our appreciation of this, but the friendly reception and the simple, wholesome food – with more than a touch of flair – greatly pleased us. A new annexe was just being completed when we were there. We intend to go back for the weather really was exceptional, and we thoroughly enjoyed the pleasant restaurant and the food (menus – 1981 – at 35, 52 and 78 frs). The interesting village, St-Veran, is nearby, at over 6,500 feet claiming to be the highest village in Europe and a narrow, rough road runs into Italy via Col Agnel.' *(A H H Stow)*

279

Open: 8 June–12 September, 15 December–25 April. Restaurant closed Wednesday to non-residents.
Rooms: 14 double, 1 single – 10 with bath, 2 with shower, all with telephone. 7 rooms in annexe.
Facilities: TV room, bar, restaurant; fondue party with dancing once a week. Good walks in area and winter sports.
Location: 1 km from the village of Molines on the road to St-Veran.
Terms: Rooms 86–146 frs; dinner, B & B 100–150 frs; full board 135–185 frs. Set meals: breakfast 16 frs; lunch/dinner 35–75 frs; full *alc* 65 frs. Reduced rates and special meals for children.

MONTBAZON, 37250 Veigne, Indre-et-Loire Map 8

Château d'Artigny *Telephone:* (47) 26.24.24
Telex: 750900

For those who like their hotels grand in the old style, the *Château d'Artigny* would be an obvious place to recommend as a base for touring the châteaux of the Loire. It is 13 km from Tours. It looks like a peerless 18th-century château itself, but appearances deceive; it was in fact built in the 18th-century style just before the First World War by the famous parfumier, François Coty. He didn't spare much in the way of expenses; there is a huge staircase in polished limestone, an imposing gallery, a brass-inlaid marble floor in the dining room, delicate wood-carving in the library and so on. There are plenty of trimmings outside too: swimming pool, tennis, 50 acres of wooded walks. Chamber music concerts are held in the autumn and winter. 'Elegant, expensive but well worth it. Everything you would want for the high-life including a restaurant which is much admired by Michelin and, more to the point in my opinion, Gault-Millau.' *(Charles Osborne)*

Open: 9 January–28 November.
Rooms: 47 double, 4 single, 4 suites – most with bath, all with telephone; baby-sitting facilities. 20 rooms in 3 annexes.
Facilities: 3 salons, TV room, bar, 2 dining rooms; conference facilities. Large garden with 2 tennis courts, heated swimming pool, ping pong; fishing, riding, rowing; golf 12 km away.
Location: Leave the N10 at Montbazon, 10 km S of Tours. At Montbazon turn right on the D17 towards Azay-le-Rideau. 2 km on left is private road leading to Château.
Credit card: Barclay/Visa.
Terms (excluding service): Rooms 160–500 frs; suites 580–770 frs; full board 350–700 frs. Set meals: breakfast 30 frs; lunch/dinner 120–250 frs.

MONTBAZON-EN-TOURAINE, 37250 Indre-et-Loire Map 8

La Domaine de la Tortinière *Telephone:* (47) 26.00.19
Telex: BOY 750806 162Y

Our previous entry for this quintessential Second Empire château, with a 37-acre park, overlooking the valley of the Indre and centrally placed in château country, recorded a devotion to satisfying a guest's every whim that went well beyond the normal call of a patronne's duty. A reader had expressed a wish to see the Loire valley from the air . . . by balloon.

Madame Olivereau-Capron, had risen (metaphorically) to the occasion! No such amazing tribute from our latest report, but still an agreeably warm appreciation: 'A marvellous château with a wonderful view despite modern structures in the valley. The staff were the best we found on our 10-day trip, and the dinner was out of this world – a gastronomic treat, and with excellent local wine. My parents had a turret room, well worth asking for. The *large* bathroom was an added luxury.' *(Marilee Thompson Duer)*

Open: 15 February–15 November. Restaurant closed Sunday evening and Monday out of season.
Rooms: 14 double, 7 suites – 20 with bath, 1 with shower, all with telephone, 3 with colour TV; baby-sitting on request. (3 rooms on ground floor.)
Facilities: Salon, 2 dining rooms; conference facilities. 100 acres grounds bordering on the river Indre with fishing, boating, swimming pool.
Location: Tours 13 km; Azay-le-Rideau 26 km; Chenonceaux 34 km; Loches 40 km.
Credit cards: American Express, Diners.
Terms: Rooms 230–495 frs. Set meals: breakfast 27.50 frs; full *alc* 125–165 frs.

MONTE CARLO, Principality of Monaco   Map 9

Monte Carlo Beach Hôtel   *Telephone:* (93) 78.21.40
St-Roman, 06190 Roquebrune-Cap-Martin   in UK ring (01) 491 7431
in USA ring (800) 221 4708

The address of this hotel may look confusing, for in fact it is just inside France, in the commune of Roquebrune. But in all other ways it really belongs to Monaco: it is at the eastern end of Monte Carlo Beach, and its owners are the mighty Société des Bains de Mers, the Monegasque State giant that seems to own nearly everything in the tiny Principality. So we list it under Monte Carlo.

'This delightful place is much smaller than the other luxury hotels in Monte Carlo and in many ways is pleasanter for a true seaside holiday, in this brash city of skyscrapers and big business. The hotel stands quietly on its own at the end of a beach (imported sand), and is right next to a lido and beach club which is free to hotel guests – we could walk from our bedroom in swimming-clothes to go bathing. The lido has a heated swimming pool and a massage-parlour; it will teach you waterskiing, and will even look after your children all day if you wish. We were delighted with our bedroom, newly-decorated in pale green, supremely comfortable, and with a wide balcony facing the sea. I think the other bedrooms are much the same. Service was most attentive. My husband was here on business, so the bill was taken care of: it was pretty high, but I suppose it was value for money, by plutocratic Monte Carlo standards. The hotel and the lido have three restaurants. We chose *Le Rivage*, which is right on the beach: everyone was bronzed and near-naked, and at the next table was the American Negress singing-star from the Casino's cabaret. The food, mainly fish, was nothing special, but the setting was certainly glamorous.' *(Jenny Towndrow)*

Open: 1 April–17 October.
Rooms: 46 – all with direct-dial telephone, air-conditioning, TV and mini-bar.
Facilities: Lift, 3 restaurants. Adjacent lido and beach club with heated swimming pool, massage, waterskiing, screened-off sun-terrace for nudist (if desired) sun-bathing; tennis and golf nearby.
Location: At E end of Monte Carlo beach, about 1 mile NE of Casino.

Credit cards: All major credit cards accepted.
Terms: Rooms 400–550 frs, suites 900–1,100 frs. No *pension* terms. All restaurant meals *à la carte*, about 100–200 frs.

MONTICELLO, 20220 l'Île Rousse, Corsica   Map 9

Hôtel A Pastorella   *Telephone:* (95) 60.05.65

'Monticello is a medieval clump of dwellings that sits on a hill 600 feet above the port and beaches of Île-Rousse. The *Hôtel A Pastorella* is Corsican, not imitation-French. It was built about 20 years ago, so the walls are thin and it can be a bit noisy, but it is clean, bright and happy. The food is plentiful and surprisingly cheap, usually beginning with a real soup, moving on to something small and interesting like something stuffed with something else, then perhaps a plate of *charcuterie*, followed by a bit of meat, cheeses and fruit. The hotel is run by the Martini family – papa used to be a shepherd – and the meats come from a butcher in the family who lives up in the mountains. In other words, an unpretentious, very friendly, clean hotel with valleys and seas in front of you, the mountains behind, and good family food to keep you going.' *(Frank Muir; also Sean and Eithne Scallon)*

Open: All year, except November. Restaurant closed Sunday 1 October–1 March.
Rooms: 14 – some with shower.
Facilities: Bar, restaurant. Garden.
Location: Île-Rousse 3 km.
Rooms: 75–120 frs; full board 140–165 frs. Set meals: breakfast 13 frs; lunch/dinner 50–65 frs.

MONTPELLIER, 34000 Hérault, Languedoc   Map 9

Demeure des Brousses   *Telephone:* (67) 65.77.66
Route de Vauguières

We had a slightly cautious entry last year for this 18th-century Languedocian country house in a park of 25,000 square metres. It had been extensively renovated in the Sixties, but recent visitors had felt that it was no longer quite so spick and span, and they minded the slight constant hum of the nearby motorway, particularly noticeable in the bedrooms facing the front. (It's just off the A9 autoroute, 3 km from Montpellier in one direction, 6 km from the beaches in the other.) Our entry ended: 'But it has the elegant trimmings of a fine old house, the owners are courteous and the public rooms and grounds are spacious and relaxing.'

A report this year is much more positive: 'From the moment we arrived, we felt as though someone had turned the clock back 50 years. What a pleasure it was – faded opulence maybe, but we enjoyed the whole scene. Donkey sitting outside front door, walking round the grounds, a horse strolling outside our bedroom window at the back. A lovely place to unwind quietly, away from the rush of life. Our room for 180 frs for two, plus 32 frs for breakfast (May 1981) was excellent value. The hotel's restaurant, *Le Mas*, is run as a separate business. We had an excellent set meal at a cost of 90 frs, and good local wine at 35 frs a bottle. And when we stayed again on our way back from Spain, it was every bit as good.' *(Peter Marshall)*

Open: 1 April–31 October. Restaurant closed Sunday evening, Monday evening and all February.
Rooms: 20 double, 1 suite – 18 with bath, 2 with shower, all with telephone. (2 rooms on ground floor.)
Facilities: Hall, 2 salons (1 with TV), restaurant adjoining. Park with orangery. 5 km from sandy beach with safe bathing, sailing and watersports; riding, tennis, bowling 10 minutes away. English spoken.
Location: 3 km E of centre of Montpellier, off the A9. Leave the A9 at exit Montpellier Est. Go towards Fréjorgues. After 1 km, at crossing, go towards Boirargues, after 80 m go towards Montpellier for about 1 km.
Credit cards: American Express, Diners.
Terms: B & B 110–220 frs; full *alc* at *Le Mas* 115–165 frs (excluding wine).

MONTREUIL, 62170 Pas-de-Calais   **Map 8**

Château de Montreuil   *Telephone:* (21) 06.00.11
Chaussée Capucins

'Civilized overnight stopping places are few and far between in the Pas-de-Calais. The *Château de Montreuil* combines a peaceful location, comfort and style, an excellent restaurant, with easy access to the ferries at Boulogne and Calais. We usually start and end our holidays here. The hotel appears excitingly French on the outward journey and comfortingly English on the return. It is a large old house set in extensive and pretty gardens, tucked away on a quiet road close to the ruined citadel in Montreuil. The rooms are all different and furnished in a variety of styles. Some are smaller and situated in an annexe in the garden. The rooms have polished tiled floors with rugs – some have panelled walls and fireplaces – one even has plaster monkeys as a wall decoration over the bed. The large bathrooms in the main house with baths set in mirrored alcoves have a faded Thirties glitter. The restaurant has a number of well-tried specialities such as *loup de mer en croûte* and lobster omelette, although it does have occasional lapses surprising in a French restaurant which has maintained its Michelin star over a number of years. The charming daughter of the owner speaks fluent English although she will patiently collaborate in one's efforts at French conversation. In good weather drinks and snacks can be taken in the garden; there is a swimming pool but this is only used when the weather is appropriate (not very often in this area). It's not easy to find a vacant room here in the summer if one arrives without booking well ahead. All in all, an individualistic and excellently run hotel in a casual sort of way.' *(David Wooff)*

Open: 1 March–20 November, except Sunday evening and Monday in winter.
Rooms: 14. Some rooms in annexe.
Facilities: Salon, restaurant; conference facilities. Garden with swimming pool. English spoken.
Location: 38 km S of Boulogne on the N1; parking.
Credit cards: American Express, Diners.
Terms: Rooms (including breakfast) 220–330 frs; full *alc* 150–225 frs.

> If you are thinking of writing reports on hotels for us, do it NOW!

Hôtel La Mère Poulard   *Telephone:* (33) 60.14.01

Mont-St-Michel, that spectacular outcrop of pyramidal granite rising out of the sea at high tide – at once a fortress, a town and one of the great Benedictine monasteries of France – is inevitably a mecca for pilgrims, both religious and lay. A visit is rewarding even if made in the company of a milling throng, but there is a lot to be said for an overnight stay: you can appreciate the aura of the place when the crowds have left in the evening and the amazing abbey can be visited early the following morning before the crowds arrive. *La Mère Poulard* is *the* hotel of the town, facing you as soon as you pass through the rampart gates. It isn't the only hotel (the *Mouton Blanc* has been recommended to us as a decent cheaper alternative), but *Mère Poulard* is the place with character and tradition, and also with a renowned restaurant. 'Very comfortable, well-run, excellent food in a stunningly romantic position. Warmly recommended.' *(William Goodhart; also Angela and David Stewart)*

Open: 1 April–1 October.
Rooms: 24 double, 3 triple – 14 with bath, 8 with shower, all with telephone.
Facilities: Salon, restaurant, omelette room. English spoken.
Location: 54 km from Dinan.
Restriction: No dogs in restaurant.
Credit cards: American Express, Diners.
Terms: Dinner, B & B 203–335 frs. Set meals: lunch/dinner 110–240 frs.

Hôtel du Tribunal   *Telephone:* (33) 25.04.77
6 place du Palais

The Perche area of Normandy is quite distinctive: an undulating land-scape of wooded hills and wide green valleys, full of charming villages. The manor houses of the district have their own character too, being in effect small castles, complete with watch-towers and turrets. Mortagne-au-Perche, still partly fortified, is the former capital, with a fine flamboyant Gothic church. The *Hôtel du Tribunal* is an old-fashioned inn on the site of the old law courts. 'Room delightful, and atmosphere, on a bitterly cold July day, cheering with log fires in bar and dining room. Dinner was excellent; fish beautifully done with proper *beurre noir*, good cheeseboard and delectable *tarte aux poires*.' *(E Davies)*

Open: All year, except 2 middle weeks in January. Also closed Sunday evening and Monday.
Rooms: 15 double, 1 suite – 8 with bath, 1 with shower, all with telephone. (1 room on ground floor.)
Facilities: Salon with fireplace, dining room. Gardens. English spoken. &.
Location: In centre of old fortified town; parking for 60 cars. Mortagne is on the D391 at the junction with the D398, 17 km N of Bellême.
Terms: Rooms 50–100 frs; dinner, B & B 90 frs (minimum 3 days). Set meals: breakfast 10 frs; lunch/dinner 40–90 frs.

MOYE, 74150 Rumilly, Haute Savoie   Map 8

Relais du Clergeon   *Telephone:* (50) 01.23.80

Sustained expressions of appreciation for the hospitality offered by the brother and sister Chal in this unpretentious stone-built hotel in the Savoy mountain hamlet of Moye, reached by a winding lane from Rumilly, a little way north of Aix-les-Bains. It overlooks a vast valley towards the Montagne du Gros Foug. 'We are going back next year for a much longer stay,' writes one visitor. 'Our charming bedroom in the new annexe, which had a private bath and WC, had one wall a picture window, with a door to a private balcony commanding beautiful views over the valley and the Col du Clergeon. We were received with extreme friendliness, and invited to try local specialities such as *fera* fish, which was not on the menu. Absolutely delicious!' Another writes: 'The view of the beautiful valley from this hotel has been under-estimated in your previous reports. It is breathtaking – and apart from the odd traffic on the road side of the hotel, the sounds are cowbells, dogs barking and the odd tractor. Service *very* helpful and pleasant. Food not terribly exciting, but *pommes savoyardes*, fresh strawberry mousse and raspberry tartlets were delicious. Local wines from Seyssel and Chauvague were good and reasonable. Beds really wide and comfortable; very strong rough country sheets and wool blankets – give a real "Heidi" feel.' *(Joy and Lenny Alcock, C Jackson; also B W Ribbons, Patricia Solomon)*

Open: All year, except January and 2 weeks at the beginning of September. Restaurant closed Monday.
Rooms: 21 double (2 pairs of communicating rooms), 1 single – 9 with bath, 6 with shower. (4 rooms on ground floor.)
Facilities: Hall, salon, TV room, bar, breakfast room, dining room. Garden with children's play area and boules. Peaceful country; walks, tennis, swimming nearby. English spoken. &.
Location: Access from autoroute A41 at Alby-sur-Cheran; 4 km from Rumilly by the D231.
Terms: Rooms 68–160 frs; full board (minimum 3 days) 128–180 frs. Set meals: breakfast 12 frs; lunch/dinner 38–100 frs; full *alc* 70 frs.

MUROL, 63790 Puy-de-Dôme, Auvergne   Map 8

Hôtel du Parc   *Telephone:* (73) 88.60.08

'Strongly recommended for a holiday in the Auvergne, the *Hôtel du Parc* is a family-run hotel – father (the cook), mother (in reception), son (does the accounts, supervises drinks, etc.), and daughter-in-law (housekeeping). As well as being a good centre for touring (a car is a must), it is also the centre of an attractive village complete with floodlit castle. However, the main attraction is the comfort – several lounges all with easy chairs, even a small library; and a garden with a swimming pool and tennis court.

'The *pension* food was quite excellent (and seemed better than what we saw of the *à la carte*) – we even had lobster one day. The only weakness was their soups. An ideal hotel for the middle-aged and onwards – 80% of the clientele were French and in that age bracket, including some quite elderly folk, a sprinkling of Belgians and one German family. Altogether the best French hotel we have stayed in, very well managed – we booked for three days and stayed 12, despite bad weather.' *(Elizabeth Pelkie)*

Open: Easter–end September. Open for groups and conferences in winter.
Rooms: 38 double, 2 single, 5 suites – 40 with bath, 2 with shower, all with telephone. 5 rooms in annexe.
Facilities: Lounge, reading room, TV lounge, restaurant. Large garden with children's play area, tennis and heated swimming pool; terrace for sun-bathing, meals or refreshments. Close to Lac Chambon, with beach, swimming and boating; winter sports. Some English spoken.
Location: In village centre; parking. Murol is 37 km SW of Clermont-Ferrand.
Terms: Rooms 70–165 frs; full board 140–165 frs. Set meals: breakfast 12 frs; lunch/dinner 45–65 frs; full *alc* 60 frs. Bargain rates on request. Reduced rates for children.

NAJAC, 12270 Aveyron, Massif Central Map 8

Hôtel Restaurant Belle-Rive *Telephone:* (65) 65.74.20

Najac, though it is in an off-the-beaten track region of France, affords a good overnight stop if one is motoring down from the valley of the Lot towards Albi (48 km south) and Spain. It is a beautiful medieval village on the river Aveyron, with a fairy-tale medieval castle high up on a hill overlooking the river. *La Belle-Rive* has a choice traffic-free position by the bridge; it is a friendly family hotel, run by Louis Mazières, and especially popular for the quality and reasonable price of its meals. In a letter to us, Monsieur Mazières challenges a remark we quoted last year about everyone going to bed at 9 am: not so, he claims – his guests are likely to be around till the hotel closes at 11.30 pm watching television or in the bar. He goes on: 'What is essential to mention is the situation of our establishment. It is surrounded by verdant green on the banks of the river, a very tranquil environment, swimming pool reserved exclusively for our guests, a large shaded terrace opposite the château which is illuminated at night. Meals are served on the terrace, highly recommended for a restful stay.' Our readers agree. Good reports continue to reach us about the *Belle-Rive*. 'A very peaceful place and it can't be surpassed for value.' *(Richard Whiting)*

Open: 15 March–15 October.
Rooms: 39 double – 29 with shower and WC, 8 with shower only, all with telephone.
Facilities: 2 salons (1 with TV), 3 dining rooms, bar. Shady terrace with view of castle and river. Garden with swimming pool, tennis, ping pong, boules, children's play area. Bathing, fishing and boating in the river. English spoken. &.
Location: 2 km from the centre of Najac; very quiet. At top of Najac take road to Parisot.
Credit card: American Express.
Terms: Rooms 58–110 frs; full board 110–145 frs. Set meals: breakfast 11 frs; lunch/dinner 45–90 frs; full *alc* 100 frs.

The length of an entry does not necessarily reflect the merit of a hotel. The more interesting the report or the more unusual or controversial the hotel, the longer the entry.

NANTUA, 01130 Ain
Map 8

Hôtel de France
44 rue du Dr-Mercier
Telephone: (74) 76.50.55

The considerable charm of Nantua, at the eastern end of a beautiful lake, with tree-lined promenades, beflowered gardens and lovely views of the Jura hills, has been flawed, until recently, by the heavy traffic of Euro-lorries. The family-owned *Hôtel de France* – not the largest or smartest hotel in the town, but the one with the best restaurant – *is* on the main road, but traffic is no longer a major nuisance and front rooms have double glazing.

'Excellent. The rooms were all one could wish for and the double glazing ensured a peaceful night's sleep. Breakfast was good, with limitless coffee. But all paled into obscurity when remembering the dinner. With the menu, we were told that every dish was a speciality of the house – and what specialities! There were only three of us so we can hardly report on the extensive *haute cuisine* menu: but what we had was French cooking at its best. The artichokes and the terrine were superb. We had to have *quenelles*, and cannot imagine them better. The sweets and the cheeseboard were excellent. And the wine list ranged from our splendid and reasonably priced *vin de la maison* to wines about which we have only read. We rated it excellent value for money.' *(John M Sidwick)*

Open: 20 December–31 October, except Christmas and New Year. Closed Friday, except during school holidays.
Rooms: 15 double, 4 single – all with bath and telephone, 11 with colour TV.
Facilities: Salon, bar, restaurant. Garden; lake close by. English spoken.
Location: 50 m from town centre; garage.
Credit cards: Barclay/Visa, Diners.
Terms: Rooms 120–210 frs; dinner, B & B 216–246 frs. Set meals: breakfast 16 frs; lunch/dinner 80 frs; full *alc* 160 frs. Reduced rates and special meals for children.

NARBONNE, 11100 Aude, Languedoc
Map 8

Hôtel La Résidence
6 rue de la Mer
Telephone: (68) 32.19.41
Telex: 500428

'In the heart of this ancient Roman city, three minutes' walk from its famous palace and cathedral, *La Résidence* is a most unusual little hotel, ornately decorated and furnished in an old-fashioned style that some might find a little *too* precious. But the comfort is exceptional and prices not too high. No restaurant; but you can eat very well at the *Alsace* and *Floride* restaurants, both near the station.' *(John Ardagh)*

Open: All year, except 5 January–5 February.
Rooms: 26 double – 16 with bath, 10 with shower, all with telephone.
Facilities: 2 lounges (1 with TV). Breakfast only served.
Location: Central; parking.
Terms: Rooms 140–200 frs per person. Set meal: breakfast 20 frs.

> If you think we have over-praised a hotel or done it an injustice, please let us know.

Le Gourmet Lorrain   *Telephone:* (93) 84.90.78
7 avenue Santa Fior

One reader this past year commented on a prevailing tattiness at this
cheerful and lively modern hotel/*pension* or rural inn or restaurant with
rooms a mile or so inland from the sea in a small street off the Avenue
Borriglione, so we were glad to be told by Monsieur Leloup (he from
Lorrain and a genuine prize-winning gourmet – hence the name of the
establishment) that he is planning a major overhaul of his furnishings in
the winter of 1981. The quality of the cooking is one reason for staying
here, and the remarkable wine list is a second; the place is much
patronized by discerning locals. One reader also commented on the
friendly family party spirit that animated the place. The facilities offered
in the bedrooms may be an additional draw. All the rooms are fitted with
radio, telephone, TV and alarm clock, but you may also find a bedside
switch for opening and closing window-shutters. And now the Leloups, an
enterprising young couple, are offering a bonus: video films (French only
at the moment) are available on demand, free of charge in the bedrooms.
A first – at least in our book.

Open: All year. Restaurant closed Sunday night and all October.
Rooms: 15 double – 5 with bath, all with air-conditioning, telephone, radio and
mono TV.
Facilities: Salon with TV, bar/terrace, restaurant; some conference facilities;
roof solarium, children's swimming pool, ping pong; beach 3 km. English spoken.
Location: 2 km from centre of town; free parking. From autoroute take exit Nice
Nord, then Avenue du Roy, turn right on Avenue Borriglione.
Credit card: American Express.
Terms: Rooms 110–160 frs; dinner, B & B 110–140 frs per person; full board
120–160 frs. Set meals: breakfast 12 frs; lunch/dinner 50–150 frs (excluding 15%
service charge); full *alc* 150 frs.

La Pérouse   *Telephone:* (93) 80.34.63
11 Quai Rauba-Capeu   *Telex:* 461 411

'I have been coming to Nice for thirty years, and though I like the place, I
find nearly all the hotels are utilitarian bores – except for a luxury palace
like the *Negresco*, which I can't afford. So what a delight to come across
this medium (well, upper-medium) priced hotel that has some character
and, above all, a superb setting. It is perched half way up the castle rock,
at the east end of the promenade, and from our bedroom balcony we had a
stunning view of the town and the Baie des Anges. Our room had a
kitchenette, too, which is useful, as the hotel has no restaurant (but they
serve you a light lunch by the heated swimming pool in summer). The
hotel is modern, but not cold or impersonal: they even have a pretty patio
with lemon trees where you can take breakfast or a drink. The staff are
very friendly.' *(Anthony Hildesley)*

Open: All year.
Rooms: 58 double, 4 single, 3 suites – 56 with bath, 9 with shower, all with

telephone and colour TV, some with cooking facilities.
Facilities: Lift, lounge, bar, snack bar (open in summer); conference facilities. Garden with patio and heated swimming pool, sauna; beach 20 yards. English spoken.
Location: Central, at E end of Promenade des Anglais, by the Château.
Credit cards: American Express, Barclay/Visa, Diners.
Terms: Rooms 140–300 frs; B & B 150–310 frs.

PARIS   Map 8

Hôtel de l'Abbaye St-Germain   *Telephone:* (1) 544.38.11
10 rue Cassette, 75006, 6e

A delightfully restored 18th-century residence tucked between St-Germain-des-Prés and Montparnasse, furnished and decorated with simple elegance. Wide windows open on to a lovely little flagged courtyard with palms, pot plants and flowers, where breakfast or refreshments can be taken at ease (no other meals served). It belongs to the Relais du Silence, and the quietness of its central position, as well as its reasonable prices, have made it highly popular. Early booking essential. *(André Schiffrin and others)*

Open: All year.
Rooms: 45 double – 38 with bath, 7 with shower, all with telephone. Baby-sitting by arrangement. (Some rooms on ground floor.)
Facilities: Lift; 2 salons (1 with TV), bar, breakfast room; interior courtyard/garden for fine-weather breakfast and refreshments. English spoken. &.
Location: Central, near St-Sulpice Church; parking.
Terms: Rooms with breakfast 290–400 frs.

PARIS   Map 8

Hôtel des Deux Îles   *Telephone:* (1) 326.13.35
59 rue St-Louis-en-l'Île, 75004, 4e

'A tiny, very prettily designed hotel in the middle of the Île St-Louis (so no lovely views of the Seine). Not perhaps a place to stay on business – the bedrooms are small and there is no restaurant – but a delightful base for a weekend in Paris or whatever. Our bedroom was charming, furnished with Provençal fabrics; its smallness was amply compensated for by the generous bathroom – apparently this is a deliberate policy of the designer, who believes in sleeping in the bedrooms and having room to move round in the bathrooms – which was equally attractively decorated, this time with Portuguese blue and white tiles. It should be added that the bed was both large and comfortable. Breakfast, which included freshly-squeezed orange juice, was delicious and prettily served in blue and white china. A most agreeable contrast to the mass-production feeling in the design of larger hotels.' *(Sophie Macindoe)*
    Our original entry above has met with 'heartfelt agreement' from a recent visitor. 'Hotel, bed and bathroom just as described, but the very attractive cellar bar should also be mentioned – and the flower-filled glass-sided central well opening out on to the hall. Excellent value for such a central position.' *(Dr and Mrs P H Tattersall)*

Open: All year.
Rooms: 17 – 18 with bath, 9 with shower, all with telephone, TV on request.
Facilities: Lift, reception hall; bar-library. No restaurant. &.
Location: Central; no parking facilities.
Terms: Rooms 195–295 frs. Set meal: breakfast 16.50 frs.

PARIS   Map 8

Hôtel d'Isly   *Telephone:* (1) 326.64.41
29 rue Jacob, 75006, 6e

'This small, quiet hotel lies between the Boulevard St-Germain and the
Seine and is convenient for such diverse features of Parisian cultural life as
the Musée de Cluny and the *Deux-Magots*, and easy to get to by public
transport. The rooms, most of which have private bathrooms, are
pleasantly decorated in floral wallpapers with matching curtains, the beds
are comfortable, the rooms clean. The management is unusually helpful
about making telephone calls, taking accurate messages, calling taxis and
generally giving advice. There is no dining room or bar, but breakfast and
simple snacks – sandwiches, etc. – and beverages can be ordered in a small
lounge off the main hall. There's nothing particularly special about it, but
it has quiet merit and is not ruinously expensive.' *(Caroline Hobhouse;
endorsed by Sydney Downs, Ena Towndrow)*

Open: All year.
Rooms: 36 – most with bath or shower and telephone.
Facilities: Lift, hall, small lounge for breakfast and snacks. No restaurant.
Location: In Latin Quarter; parking.
Terms: Rooms 135–260 frs. Set meals: breakfast 13 frs.

PARIS   Map 8

Hôtel Lancaster   *Telephone:* (1) 359.90.43
7 rue de Berri, 75008, 8e   *Telex:* Loyne 640991F
                                    Reservations: in UK ring (01) 568 6841
                                                in USA ring (800) 223 55 81

One of the more exclusive of Paris hotels: just off the Champs Elysées and
close to the Arc de Triomphe. 67 rooms, and a staff of 82 to attend to their
occupants. It is owned by the Savoy group who also own London's
Connaught (q.v.) – and might be called a Paris equivalent, though without
the latter's gastronomic distinction. Antique furniture, fine paintings, a
profusion of flowers, the best quality linen sheets – changed daily of
course. Very quiet for a city hotel: you can listen, we are told, to the birds
singing while having a glass of champagne in the flowered courtyard. The
management tell us that they would always try to accommodate any
request that a client might have – a challenging thought . . . *(H C
Beddington and others)*

Open: All year. Restaurant closed Saturday and Sunday night.
Rooms: 25 double, 21 single, 11 suites – all with bath and telephone; radio or TV
on request; baby-sitting by arrangement; some air-conditioning.
Facilities: Lift, several salons where drinks are served, small bar; facilities for

private dinner parties and small functions. Delightful garden patio which many rooms overlook, used for meals in fine weather. English spoken. &.
Location: Central but quiet, off Champs Elysées and near Arc de Triomphe; parking.
Credit cards: Access/Euro/Mastercard, American Express.
Terms (excluding 15% service charge): Rooms (single) from 500 frs, (double) from 800 frs. Set meals: breakfast 35 frs; lunch/dinner 100 frs; full *alc* 165–175 frs. Special reductions July/August, and winter weekends.

PARIS   Map 8

Hôtel Lenox   *Telephone:* (1) 296.10.95
9 rue de l'Université, 75007, 7e

'Rosy table lamps and oriental rugs welcome guests into the little marble foyer of this bed-and-breakfast hotel a stone's throw from the river on the left bank. Rooms are simply furnished but with great style – our room had walls the colour of Colette's 'pale mauve of hot chocolate' and the furniture was a good quality light cane. The hotel is run with great care: bath towels are big and fluffy and breakfast china is sparkling white. There is a mirrored bar on the ground floor where you can relax among the plants and eat a *croque monsieur* or drink a glass of champagne (the barman popped some fresh popcorn for us in case we were peckish and seemed able to cope with a variety of cocktails for a group of beautifully-dressed Parisians in the other corner). The receptionist was most efficient and helpful and happily stowed a gâteau for us in her refrigerator against our departure. The rooms are a little small but, if you don't mind that, *Hotel Lenox* is a very comfortable and pleasing place to stay in Paris.' *(Gillian Vincent)*

Open: All year.
Rooms: 34 – all with bath or shower, telephone and TV.
Facilities: Lift, bar; no restaurant. &.
Location: Central; no parking facilities.
Terms: Rooms 170–280 frs. Set meal: breakfast 15.50 frs.

PARIS   Map 8

Hôtel Lord Byron   *Telephone:* (1) 359.89.98
5 rue Châteaubriand, 8e   *Telex:* 250302 Publi Bti Paris

A quiet hotel close to the Champs Elysées, and with recently modernized well-appointed rooms (mostly on the small side) with views of the Eiffel Tower through tall traditional windows. No restaurant, but excellent *café complet*. One correspondent tells us of his surprised pleasure, having been given only one pillow and having improvised a second from a blanket in the wardrobe, finding the next night that he had been given another pillow without having had to ask for it. Everything about the place pleased him – 'I shall never use any other, either on business or pleasure'. *(D R Stevens; also Marillee Thompson Duer, Nancy Foy)*

Open: All year.
Rooms: 15 double, 1 single, 10 suites – 23 with bath, 3 with shower, all with telephone and TV.

Facilities: Lift, 2 salons, breakfast room. Garden. English spoken.
Location: Central, near Champs Elysées; garage 500 m.
Terms: Rooms 245 frs, suites 320 frs. Set meal: breakfast 16 frs. Extra bed for child in parents' room 80 frs.

PARIS Map 8

Hôtel Relais Christine *Telephone:* (1) 326.71.81
3 rue Christine, 75006, 6e *Telex:* 202606 F

'A newly converted hotel, once a 16th-century abbey, on the left bank, situated half way between the river and the Boulevard St-Germain, a few moments' stroll from the lively food markets and shops of the rue de Buci and St-Germain-des-Prés. The rooms are set round a most attractive courtyard. Breakfast is in the converted chapel in the basement (there is no restaurant). Plus points are that all rooms have bathrooms/WC, colour television and mini-fridge; and there is a car park in the basement. Best of all it is extremely peaceful and quiet; there is very little traffic in the area.' *(Pat and Jeremy Temple)*

Open: All year.
Rooms: 51 – 47 with bath, 4 with shower, all with telephone, radio, colour TV and mini-bar.
Facilities: Lift, 14th-century breakfast room; conference room for 20; patio.
Location: Central; private parking within hotel.
Credit cards: American Express, Diners, Barclay/Visa.
Terms: Rooms 400–700 frs. Set meal: breakfast 30 frs. Out-of-season reductions.

PARIS Map 8

La Résidence du Bois *Telephone:* (1) 500.50.59
16 rue Chalgrin, 75116, 16e

A highly exclusive small *de luxe* hotel a few hundred yards from the Étoile but in a quiet position, and with an enchanting garden. The hotel does not reckon to serve more than breakfasts, but will produce light meals if asked. It's a Third Empire mansion and the rooms, both the bedrooms and the salons, are exquisitely furnished with period pieces.

Open: All year.
Rooms: 16 double, 1 single, 3 suites – 16 with bath, 4 with shower, all with telephone and colour TV. English spoken.
Facilities: 2 salons, bar. No restaurant, but simple meals served to residents on request. Beautiful garden full of trees and flowers for fine-weather refreshments.
Location: Central; parking nearby.
Terms: Rooms including breakfast (single) 345–385 frs, (double) 470–600 frs.

We would like to be able to recommend more hotels in the budget class in Paris. Nominations especially welcome.

PARIS Map 8

Hôtel Roblin *Telephone:* (1) 265.57.00
6 rue Chauveau-Lagarde, 75008, 8e *Telex:* 64014

Last year we offered two contrasting pictures of this midtown, medium-priced, middle-class establishment – 'Bored reception, shabby carpet and paintwork, poor breakfast, poky bathroom' on the one hand, and 'High-ceilinged, quiet, even atmospheric – everything the Romantic English could hope for' on the other. Reports this year don't greatly alter the picture. A lot of people like the *fin de siècle* decor, and the high, handsome scale of the place – 'a cultural experience' – though the better rooms at the front are likely to be noisy in this narrow one-way street off the north-east corner of the Place de la Madeleine. The public rooms on the ground floor are agreeably intimate in scale and furnishing. The adjoining restaurant, the *Mazagran*, is reported 'first-rate'. *(David Ballard; AL)*

Open: All year. Restaurant closed Saturday, Sunday and all August.
Rooms: 45 double, 16 single, 4 suites – 60 with bath, all with telephone.
Facilities: Lift, 2 salons (1 with TV), bar, restaurant. English spoken. &.
Location: Central; parking nearby.
Credit cards: American Express, Diners.
Terms: Rooms including breakfast (single), 250–280 frs, (double), 265–385 frs.
Set meal: lunch 100 frs; full *alc* 150 frs.

PARIS Map 8

Hôtel Scandinavia *Telephone:* (1) 329.67.20
27 rue de Tournon, 75006, 6e

On the lovely street which runs from the Boulevard St-Germain down to the Luxembourg Palace and its attractive gardens. This exceptionally sympathetic hotel is a recently converted and modernized 17th-century building. Bedrooms are agreeably decorated and furnished simply but with a few really good antique pieces. There is a pleasant lounge; no restaurant – only breakfast served in your room. Not expensive for this part of Paris, but hard to get into. *(H C Beddington, Thomas Neurath)*

Open: All year, except August.
Rooms: 22 – all with bath and telephone.
Facilities: Large salon; no restaurant.
Location: Central; no parking facilities.
Terms: Rooms 190–275 frs. Set meal: breakfast 15 frs.

PAU, 64000 Pyrénées-Atlantique, Aquitaine Map 8

Central *Telephone:* (59) 27.72.75
15 rue Léon-Daran

'A small and comfortable hotel (without restaurant) in this historic, busy and enjoyable town with its boring château. Although very near the centre, it is surprisingly quiet with comfortable rooms at a reasonable rate. Not surprisingly it gets very full, even out of season, so booking is a good idea. It is also literally "just around the corner" from *Pierre* – one of the best restaurants in this part of France.' *(Hugh and Anne Pitt)*

Open: All year.
Rooms: 22 double, 5 single – 5 with bath, 12 with shower, all with telephone.
Facilities: Salon/bar with TV, breakfast room; casino and park nearby. English spoken.
Location: Central; no special parking facilities.
Terms: Rooms 65–145 frs. Set meal: breakfast 12 frs.

PEILLON, 06440 L'Escarène, Alpes-Mar, Provence   Map 9

Auberge de la Madone   *Telephone:* (93) 91.91.17

'Only ten or so miles from Nice, yet you seem in the middle of nowhere. This civilized auberge is just outside one of the most attractive hill-villages in the area, and has super views of the valley and hills. What we liked best of all is that the young owners, the Millos, manage to create a family atmosphere, without overdoing it. The chef's high-spirited kid sister does the waiting. The food is quite varied, and includes some oddities such as a kind of chilled *bouillabaisse*. The place seems to attract the nicest kind of Parisian – cultured, but not snooty – and we made several French friends during our stay. If you want a really quiet room, ask for one at the back.' *(Anthony Day)*

Open: 15 December–15 October. Restaurant closed Wednesday.
Rooms: 19 double, 5 suites – 15 with bath, 4 with shower, 2 with TV, all with telephone.
Facilities: 2 salons, TV room, dining room; conference facilities. Garden; sea 20 km. English spoken. &.
Location: 19 km NE of Nice on the D21.
Terms: Rooms 100–220 frs, suites 220 frs; full board 125–230 frs. Set meals: breakfast 16 frs; lunch/dinner 80–100 frs; full *alc* 140 frs. Reductions for children according to age.

PÉROUGES, 01800 Meximieux, Ain   Map 8

Ostellerie du Vieux Pérouges   *Telephone:* (74) 61.00.88

'A hotel and Michelin-starred restaurant converted from several 13th-century buildings in the beautiful medieval village of Pérouges, 36 km from Lyon on the route to Geneva. The village is splendidly preserved and, although it obviously attracts many tourists, it is a historic monument and has not been commercialized in the usual sense at all. All traffic is banned unless visiting the hotel, or a resident in the village. Monsieur Thibaut who owns the hotel is also the mayor and owns a considerable part of the village as well. The hotel forms one side of the village square, dominated by an enormous tree, several hundred years old. Hotel rooms are in several different houses around the square or in an adjoining manor. Ours, "Chevalier", was enormous. Furnishings were all antiques, with a half tester bed. The modern tiled bathroom was beautifully equipped and as large as many hotel bedrooms. The *Ostellerie* itself serves meals, drinks and coffee virtually all day. A very pleasant sparkling wine, grown locally, Bugey, is their house wine, and the food is excellent. Perhaps not a place for a long stay, but extremely pleasant and interesting for a couple of days.' *(Pat and Jeremy Temple)*

Last year's entry has been heartily endorsed by recent visitors who describe Pérouges as 'the most beautifully preserved village we have ever visited – and don't miss a visit to the wine vaults'. *(Jill and John Dick)*

Open: All year.
Rooms: 22 double, 3 single – all with bath and telephone.
Facilities: Lounge, dining room. Gardens. English spoken. &.
Location: In the town square; parking available. For Pérouges take the N84 from Lyon to Geneva; turn off on the D4 at Meximieux.
Terms (excluding 15% service charge): Rooms 190–350 frs. Set meals: breakfast 22 frs; lunch/dinner 80–180 frs; full *alc* 150 frs.

LA PLAINE-SUR-MER, 44770 Loire-Atlantique   Map 8

Hôtel Anne de Bretagne   *Telephone:* (40) 21.54.72
au Port de Gravette

'A modern hotel facing the rocky shore and setting sun, 3 km out of La Plaine-sur-Mer. Very clean and comfortable. Lots of activity in the seaweed-covered rock pools as the tide goes out and local people search for shellfish. Eight miles from the picturesque port of Pornic and beaches of the Jade Coast on the south side of the Loire estuary. Very professional cooking and service combine to provide an excellent meal in the attractively furnished restaurant, overlooking the sea. Beware 30 frs toll on the St-Nazaire bridge on the way to/from La Baule and Brittany!' *(R J Harborne)*

Open: All year.
Rooms: 26 – all with bath or shower and telephone.
Facilities: Restaurant; conference facilities. &.
Location: 3 km from La Plaine-sur-Mer; 8 km from Pornic; parking.
Terms: Rooms 90–140 frs; full board 110–190 frs. Set meals: breakfast 12 frs; lunch/dinner 45–125 frs.

PLÉHÉDEL, 22290 Lanvollon, Côtes du Nord, Brittany   Map 8

Château Hôtel de Coatguelen   *Telephone:* (96) 22.31.24

In north Brittany, 7 km from the sea, near to good beaches and to interesting old Breton towns such as Tréguier. 'This is a genuine 19th-century château, near an older and bigger one still being restored, both owned by the Marquis de Boisgelin (Boisgelin is the gallicized version of the Breton Coatguelen – Coat = Wood and Kelen = holly – so Hollywood). He is constantly about, but does not impose himself! The hotel is all repro – beautifully done. It must have cost a fortune to restore. We had the Bridal Suite in the tower and it was most comfortable and attractive. The food was excellent. The hotel opened in the spring of 1981, and is run by Madame de Morchoven, a really sweet person. One hopes she will not be let down by being too trusting. The welcome could not be better. Work is still in progress. There is lovely country about. It is a mistake to go to the town of Pléhédel – we made a Tony Lumpkin journey to get there. The château is 2.5 km south-west of the village of Pléhédel on the main Lanvollon to Paimpol road.' *(H ap R)*

Open: All year, except 5 January–1 March. Restaurant closed Tuesday.
Rooms: 11 double, 2 suites for 3, 1 suite for 4 people – 13 with bath, 3 with shower, all with telephone.
Facilities: Living room with TV, salon/bar, children's dining room and playroom; conference room. Garden, swimming pool, tennis, children's play area, 3 horses (fishing, shooting and 9-hole golf course planned for 1982); beach 7 km, sailing and sea fishing 10 km. English spoken.
Location: On the D7 between Lanvollon and Paimpol.
Credit cards: Access/Euro/Mastercard, Diners.
Terms: B & B 145–250 frs. Set meals: lunch 110 frs; dinner 120 frs; full *alc* 155 frs. Special rates for 5 days minimum. Reduced rates for children.

PLÉVEN, 22130 Plancöet, Côtes-du-Nord, Brittany   **Map 8**

Le Manoir de Vaumadeuc   **Telephone:** (96) 84.46.15

The Vicomtesse de Pontbriand personally converted this elegant 15th-century manor house into a small highly personal hotel. It lies in a substantial park in the forest of Hunaudaye, 18 km from the sea on the road from Dinan to Lamballe, in northern Brittany.

'This place made an overpowering impression on us. The interiors particularly are stunning; the colours of the furnishings are most beautiful. The food is ordinary though good, and much overpriced were it not that the cost of restoring and maintaining the place so wonderfully must be met somehow. The same applies to the wine prices. The service shows very good training by someone, and is most efficient and charming. The *Manoir* is, as we realized, a hymn of praise to the past by (evidently) a most capable person of great taste and energy who has spared no pains or expense. There are many fine old pieces of furniture. But the seven great fire-places are modern reproductions made to look ancient – likewise many of the exposed beams. The total effect, however, is unbeatable.' *(H ap R)*

Open: April–November.
Rooms: 9 double – 7 with bath, 1 with tea-making facilities, all with telephone. 2 rooms in pavilions in the garden.
Facilities: Lounge, dining room. Park with small lake. Golf, tennis, angling, boating, sailing available.
Location: 18 km from the sea, on the road from Dinan to Lamballe (through the forest of Hunaudaye).
Credit cards: Access/Euro/Mastercard, Barclay/Visa.
Terms (excluding 15% service charge): Dinner, B & B 205–275 frs; full board 290–360 frs. Set meals: breakfast 20 frs; lunch/dinner 130 frs.

In the case of many continental hotels, especially French ones, we have adopted the local habit of quoting a price for the room whether it is occupied by one or more persons. Rates for B & B, half board, etc., are per person unless otherwise stated.

POLIGNY, 39800 Jura   Map 8

Hostellerie des Monts-de-Vaux   *Telephone:* (84) 37.12.50

'Despite the fact that the hotel is decorated in excruciatingly bad taste, this was a perfect location in the Jura, 5 km east of Poligny (a lovely under-rated town), and near Arbois and the *Route du Vin*, the magnificent *Route des Sapins*, and the *Régions des Lacs*, with its waterfall. The view from the hotel is also spectacular, and one wakens to the sound of cowbells which adorn all the chubby cows of the area, known for their Comté cheese. We felt the need at this point of our holiday for a *simple* meal, and, unlike some hotels, the *Monts-de-Vaux* could oblige. We enjoyed melon, trout stuffed with rosemary and good raspberry sorbet.' *(Caroline Hamburger)*

Open: All year, except 1 November–31 December. Hotel and restaurant closed from midday Tuesday to Wednesday 18.00 hrs.
Rooms: 7 double, 1 single, 2 suites – all with bath and telephone.
Facilities: Salon, restaurant. Large garden. English spoken.
Location: 5 km from Poligny in the direction of Geneva.
Terms: Dinner, B & B 250–400 frs; full *alc* 150 frs.

PONT-AUDEMER, 27500 Eure, Normandy   Map 8

Auberge du Vieux Puits   *Telephone:* (32) 41.01.48
6 rue Notre-Dame de Paris   *Telex:* 27500 PONT-AUDEMER

'This hotel – mentioned by Flaubert in *Madame Bovary* – is on the unpromising-looking main ring road leading south from the Pont de Tancarville, making it very easy to find. From outside it is hard to imagine how calm and attractive it will be: an enchanting group of 17th-century beamed Norman houses around a courtyard centred on a magnificent weeping willow. Both bedrooms and public rooms are small, comfortable, and nicely decorated without being in the slightest chi-chi. Fresh flowers, painting on the wall, and a good smell of wood smoke. Staff friendly and helpful (quite happy to put our cheese in their fridge overnight), though not prepared to organize a 7 am breakfast. But full marks for posting back to England, very promptly and unsolicited, a pair of trousers left behind in the bedroom. The food is imaginative and excellent – high-class French cuisine, and good value for money, though the set menu unusually represented no saving over choosing *à la carte*. They suggested a refreshing *champagne/framboise kir* as aperitif in the leafy garden. For dinner, the trout Bovary, the Calvados sorbet (served between the first and second courses) and the *crêpes flambées* were all unusually delicious. The town is in a deep valley only one hour (48 km) from Le Havre – an ideal place for a first or a last night in France or as a base from which to explore Normandy.' *(Carol O'Brien and Philippa Harrison; also Gordon Hammond)*

Open: All year, except 20 December–20 January and 29 June–9 July. Closed every week Monday evening to Wednesday morning.
Rooms: 6 double, 2 single – 5 with shower, 2 of these also with WC.
Facilities: 2 small salons, 2 restaurants, decorated with antique furniture, china, etc. Small garden. English spoken.

Location: 300 m from town centre, but quiet as all rooms overlook garden. Parking.
Restriction: No young children.
Credit card: Barclay/Visa.
Terms: Rooms 70–140 frs. Set meal: breakfast 16 frs.

PORTICCIO, 20000 Ajaccio, Corsica   Map 9

Hôtel Le Maquis

Telephone: (95) 25.05.55
Telex: 460597

We continue to receive good reports of this chic and quite expensive small hotel 16 km south of Ajaccio. 'An outstanding hotel, immediately across the bay from Ajaccio. It's an old Mediterranean manor with its own sandy beach. The hotel is beautifully furnished. The charming hostess who owns and runs it with her son and daughter has had the place for 20 years. The family is French from northern France, and most of their guests are educated French who return year after year. Excellent food.' *(Curtis and Sally Wilmot-Allistone; also Uwe Kitzinger)*

Open: April–October approx.
Rooms: 28 double – all with bath or shower, some with terrace, some in a cluster of curly-roofed cottages adjoining the main building.
Facilities: Lounge, bar, dining room, all arched and beamed; roof-terrace with wonderful sea views; trees and shrubs surround the house. Private sandy beach with sun beds and sun umbrellas.
Location: 15 km S of Ajaccio; 12 km from airport. Parking.
Credit cards: American Express, Diners.
Terms: B & B approx 200 frs per person. *Alc* approx 130 frs (excluding wine).

PRATS-DE-MOLLO-LA-PRESTE, 66230 Pyrénées-Orientales   Map 8

Hôtel des Touristes

Telephone: (68) 39.72.12

The hotel lies just outside the picturesque medieval spa town of Prats-de-Mollo, close to the Spanish border and with plenty of rewarding excursions to be made by foot in the hills of the Pyrenees and by car to Collioure on the Mediterranean coast (55 km away), or to Céret with its art gallery, or into Spain. 'The hotel is charming, the prices are modest, the food is simple but good, and the family who run the place are delightful and do their best to help in every way.' *(Neville and Alison Chesshyre)*

Open: 1 April–22 October.
Rooms: 40 double, 4 single – 15 with bath, all with telephone; baby-sitting by arrangement. 16 rooms in annexe.
Facilities: 2 salons (1 with TV), bar, beamed restaurant, arcaded covered terrace. 2½ acres grounds divided into 2 gardens and parking area; ping pong, boules; tennis, miniature golf, heated swimming pool nearby. 8 km from thermal station. English spoken.
Location: Eastern Pyrenees, 14 km from the Spanish border; Perpignan 60 km.
Credit cards: Access/Euro/Mastercard, American Express.
Terms (excluding service): Rooms 70–138 frs. Set meals: breakfast 12 frs; lunch/dinner 46–96 frs; full *alc* 100 frs. Discounts for full board for stays of over 3 nights. Reduced rates for children; special meals if required.

QUENZA, 20122 Corsica — Map 9

Hôtel Sole e Monti — *Telephone:* (95) 79.91.11

An immaculate small modern hotel on the outskirts of the village with balconied bedrooms offering stunning views of the awe-inspiring *Aiguilles* mountain. The food is honest robust Corsican fare. As for Quenza, it is a village of simple charm – a popular base for cross-country skiing in winter and for mountain walking in summer. What earns the hotel its entry is the dedicated solicitude of its proprietor, Félicien Balesi, a man of character and a true hotelier. He tells us that among many English visitors who have enjoyed his hospitality are Margaret Thatcher and Denis Healey. *(HR)*

Open: 15 May–15 October.
Rooms: 20 – all with shower.
Facilities: Salon, bar, dining room; discotheque. Near river; fishing, hunting. English spoken.
Location: On the D420, 14 km from Aullene towards Zonza; 40 km from the sea via winding mountain roads.
Credit cards: Access/Euro/Mastercard. American Express, Barclay/Visa,
Terms: Rooms 125 frs; dinner, B & B 180–200 frs. Set meals: breakfast 20 frs; lunch/dinner 55 frs; full *alc* 80–100 frs. Reduced rates for children under 5..

QUIBERON, 56170 Morbihan, Brittany — Map 8

Hôtel des Druides — *Telephone:* (97) 50.14.74
6 rue de Port-Maria

The highly popular south Breton resort of Quiberon is on the southern tip of the 15-km-long Quiberon peninsula – once an island and now joined to the mainland by a narrow isthmus – famous for its huge, curving sandy beach on the eastern side and for the Côte Sauvage on the ocean-facing coast.

'Quiberon will be too much of a seaside resort for some, but the sun and the sand suited us admirably. The *Druides* is modern and unpretentious, but very clean, comfortable and friendly. The cooking is of a high standard. Specialities include *homard à l'Amoricaine* and *bar grillé au fenouil*. The hotel makes a point of varying its menus for its *pensionnaires*. Its packed lunches *en panier* are really baskets of food not a packet of sandwiches. The hotel is run by three ladies: Madame Carn, the proprietor, who has run the place sine 1964, her daughter Agnès, whom she hopes will keep it on after her retirement, and Madame Villière. Their influence is to be seen everywhere; the service of meals, to take one example, proceeds with tremendous teamwork and smoothness. All three ladies read and speak reasonable English.' *(Sydney Downs)*

Open: 1 April–30 September.
Rooms: 29 double, 1 single – 14 with bath and WC, 12 with shower and WC, all with telephone.
Facilities: Lift, reception hall, small TV room, 2 restaurants; conference facilities. Garden; 20 m from sandy beach with safe bathing, fishing, boating. English spoken. &.
Location: Central; parking.
Terms: Rooms 70–86 frs; full board 140–200 frs. Set meals: breakfast 14 frs; lunch/dinner 48–85 frs.

Hôtel Chez Pierre   *Telephone:* (98) 06.81.06

A friendly unpretentious seaside hotel in south-west Brittany, a few yards
from a stretch of unspoilt beach. It has been owned and run by the Guillou
family for many years; Monsieur Guillou is the chef, and his local fish
dishes are strongly recommended. Since last year, a pleasant garden and
terrace area have been added as well as a salon and a bar, and the rooms
have been upgraded, but prices are still amazingly reasonable.
'Altogether a most attractive small hotel, serving for 46 frs (June 1981) a
dish of crab and langoustines as a starter, an excellent sole and a
mouth-watering *vacherin*. Thoroughly recommended.' *(H David Segat)*

Open: 4 April–3 May, 15 May–29 September. Restaurant closed Wednesday
July/August except in the week of 16–23 August.
Rooms: 21 – most with bath or shower, all with telephone.
Facilities: Salon, bar, restaurant; conference facilities; terrace. Garden. Beach
nearby.
Location: 12 km from Pont-Aven.
Terms: Rooms 90–165 frs; full board 135–170 frs. Set meals: breakfast 12 frs;
lunch/dinner 50–95 frs.

RAMATUELLE, 83350 Var, Provence   **Map 9**

Hôtel Le Baou   *Telephone:* (94) 79.20.48

Even at the height of the summer, the charming, friendly little village of
Ramatuelle, in the hills behind St-Tropez, retains its dignity and character, in contrast to the fairground atmosphere of the former jet-set
playground a few miles below. *Le Baou* is an ultra-modern hotel – very
small but with the highest standards. Each of the rooms has a private patio
overlooking the vineyards and the sea. Breakfast is served in the rooms;
other meals (on which reports would be welcome) can be taken on the
rooftop with breathtaking views all round. 'Not cheap, but worth it for the
comfort and the glorious view.' *(Anthony and Sally Sampson)*

Open: 14 March–5 November.
Rooms: 16 double – all with bath, patio, telephone and air-conditioning.
Facilities: Rooftop restaurant. Garden, swimming pool. ♿ .
Location: St-Tropez 5 km; parking.
Credit cards: American Express, Diners.
Terms: Rooms 250–385 frs. Set meals: breakfast 22 frs; lunch/dinner 130 frs.

ROANNE, 42300 Loire   **Map 8**

Hôtel des Frères Troisgros   *Telephone:* (77) 71.66.97
Pl. Gare

The three-starred *Troisgros* is categorized by Michelin as a restaurant
with rooms, but it calls itself a hotel and has 18 bedrooms. The brothers
Troisgros are of course, along with Guérard, Alain Chapel and Vergé, the

leading propagators of the so-called *nouvelle cuisine*. The *Observer*'s food correspondent sends us these notes from what he calls a Christmas binge: 'Excellent big rooms decorated in amazing tastelessness in great contrast to the visual sensitivity of the Troisgros in the presentation of food. But thoroughly comfortable and good value although expensive. And of course one of the best restaurants in the world.' *(Paul Levy)*

Open: All year, except January and Tuesday.
Rooms: 18 – all with bath or shower, telephone and TV.
Facilities: Restaurant. ໄ .
Location: 86 km NW of Lyon on the N7; parking.
Credit cards: American Express, Diners.
Terms: Rooms 200–385 frs. Set meals: breakfast 20 frs; lunch/dinner 220–310 frs.

LA ROCHELLE, 17000 Charente-Maritime   **Map 8**

Hôtel Les Brises   *Telephone:* (46) 34.89.37
Chemin de la Digue de Richelieu

Two eloquent recommendations for this modern hotel in a prime position overlooking the estuary and outer harbour of the town. 'Bed and break-fast only, but what luxury – and the best breakfast I have ever had in France. The hotel is right on the sea-front, with a vast terrace on which one can sun oneself over a drink, and two luxurious lounges where one can get coffee or tea. A very warm welcome. Not cheap, but really excellent value for money. Private underground garage. Utterly quiet, with a park between the hotel and the road.' *(E George Maddocks)*
'Staggering view, charmingly furnished room, with a balcony, and several welcome *petits soins*, including finding that our car's windows had been cleaned in the morning. Three red turrets and red rocking-chair in Michelin well deserved.' *(Jessica Mann)*

Open: All year, except 5 December–15 January.
Rooms: 41 double, 5 single – 39 with bath, 7 with shower, all with telephone.
Facilities: Salon, TV room/library, restaurant, bar; terrace; panoramic views over Îles d'Aix, d'Oléron et Ré. English spoken.
Location: On sea front 1½ km from town centre, close to the Parc F Delmas; underground garage and car park.
Credit cards: Barclay/Visa.
Terms: Rooms 260–300 frs (including breakfast).

LA ROCHELLE, 17000 Charente-Maritime   **Map 8**

Hôtel de France et d'Angleterre   *Telephone:* (46) 41.34.66
22 rue Gargoulleau   *Telex:* 790717 Fratel Rochl

'In my view, La Rochelle is the most attractive town in France – a kind of maritime Bruges, with echoes too of Dubrovnik and the less absurd aspects of St-Tropez. The narrow streets of this ancient fishing port have been beautifully paved and closed to motor traffic, and all summer the town is splendidly animated, especially during the avant-garde arts festiv-al in July. The *France et Angleterre* is a hotel worthy of La Rochelle – high praise. The hotel has been gracefully modernized, and is set round a small flowery garden. Staff are well above the French average for amiability.

The hotel's distinguished restaurant, the *Richelieu*, wins acclaim for the more-or-less *nouvelle cuisine* of its patron-chef, Richard Coutanceau, a disciple of Michel Guérard, and other leaders of this movement. Personally, I am one of those who find this modish style of cooking a little over-refined and pretentious, when set beside the more robust tastes of classic cuisine. Nonetheless, I admired the chef's *aiguillettes de bar frais* as well as the town's local delicacy, *mouclade* (mussels in a spicy sauce).' *(John Ardagh)*

'Off the beaten tourist track, but an outstanding find. Modern, but not too modern, highly comfortable, efficient and very friendly service, and very good value. A bustling market nearby, the stunning *Café de la Paix* round the corner, and close to the shops and cathedral. John Ardagh catches the charm exactly.' *(Brian MacArthur)*

Open: All year. *Le Richelieu* restaurant closed Sunday and 10–31 December.
Rooms: 74 double, 2 single – 36 with bath, 29 with shower, all with telephone, radio, 36 with mono TV. (Some rooms in 2 annexes.)
Facilities: Lift, salon, TV room, breakfast room, restaurant; conference facilities. Interior garden for refreshments or meals.
Location: Central; parking in adjacent rue du Minage.
Credit cards: All major credit cards accepted.
Terms: Rooms 148–224 frs. Set meals: breakfast 17 frs; lunch/dinner in the *Richelieu* about 120 frs.

ROLLEBOISE, 78 Yvelines, Île-de-France Map 8

Château de la Corniche *Telephone:* (3) 093.21.24
Telex: 695544

'Rolleboise is 69 km north-west of Paris and about four hours' easy driving from Calais or two from Dieppe. The Monet museum at Giverny, 12 km distance, is a special draw. Its splendid *Château de la Corniche*, built by King Leopold II of Belgium, is perched high above the Seine. Front rooms have a marvellous view of the countryside and the river; the barges provide an almost non-stop show as they go through a nearby lock. Bedrooms and public rooms are luxuriously comfortable. Service was faultless during our two-day stay. By French standards expensive, which means that you pay about the same as you would in a smart English country hotel, but get something about five times as good. Recommended unconditionally.' *(Warren Bagust)*

Open: All year, except 25 January–6 March. Closed Sunday evening and Monday 1 September–30 April.
Rooms: 23 double, 3 single, 1 suite – 21 with bath, 6 with shower, 11 with mono TV, all with telephone and radio. 6 rooms in annexe.
Facilities: Lift, salon, TV room, games room, 2 bars, restaurant, disco; conference room. 4 acres park with heated swimming pool, tennis court; sailing and surfing 8 km away. Claude Monet museum at Giverny 12 km.
Location: 3 km from Bonnières exit off the Autoroute de Normandie (A13) between Paris and Rouen, or turn off the RN13.
Credit cards: Access/Euro/Mastercard, Barclay/Visa, Diners.
Terms: Rooms 150–280 frs; B & B 142–192 frs; full board 336–420 frs. Set meals: breakfast 22 frs; lunch/dinner 110–120 frs; full *alc* 200 frs.

DO IT NOW! Send us a report on the hotel you are staying in.

ROQUEBRUNE-CAP-MARTIN, 06190 Alpes-Mar, Provence   Map 9

Hotel Vistaëro   *Telephone:* (93) 35.01.50
Rte de la Gde Corniche   *Telex:* 461021

'Seen from below, it's hard to believe that this glamorous luxury hotel is not about to fall into the sea, so vertiginously is it built out from the cliff-top, beside the Grande Corniche, a thousand feet directly above Monte Carlo. Alike from the bedroom balconies, from the bar with its big picture windows, and from the outdoor dining-terrace, the views of this spectacular coast are enough to put you off your hot croissants, champagne cocktails or *jambonnette de caneton aux figues*. The hotel is owned by the German hi-fi firm, Grundig – good for them – and has a young half-American manager, Mr Boone, who is most cordial, as are all his staff. We enjoyed the ultra-modern decor, both in the bedrooms and the public rooms – marble floors, ornamental indoor pool, and all that. The heated swimming pool below the hotel is fine, but it's a bit of a climb, coming back. We paid through the nose at this place, but felt it was worth it – and it's a good excursion centre too. The hill-village of Roquebrune, right next door, is one of the most attractive we've come across in Provence.' *(Peter and Sarah Abbott)*

Open: 10 February–15 November.
Rooms: 22 double, 2 single, 2 suites – all with bath or shower, direct-dial telephone, colour TV and mini-bar; some with balconies.
Facilities: Lift, 2 salons, bar, dining-terrace, restaurant; conference and banqueting facilities; heated swimming pool. Garden. Beaches and water sports 4 km. English spoken.
Location: 5 km from Monte Carlo on the D2564. Leave Autoroute A8 at exit La Turbie–Monaco.
Credit cards: All major credit cards accepted.
Terms: B & B 207–382 frs; dinner, B & B 347–522 frs; full board 379–662 frs. Set meals: lunch/dinner 190 frs.

ROUEN, 76000 Seine-Maritime, Normandy   Map 8

La Cathédrale   *Telephone:* (35) 71.57.95
12 rue St-Romain

There are plenty of smart hotels in Rouen, but *La Cathédrale* is the place for those who appreciate old-world atmosphere and courtesy. It's centrally placed in the old town, on a cobbled pedestrian alleyway that runs alongside the cathedral block. It looks as though it has survived from the age of coaching, with a great pair of wooden doors giving on to a charming flowered courtyard. The back rooms are modern and rather characterless, but marvellously quiet. The front rooms are well-proportioned and graciously furnished but distinctly noisy at night if you open the double glazed windows. *La Cathédrale* serves no meals except breakfast, but that's scarcely a hardship in a city as richly endowed with good restaurants as Rouen. *(HR; also Tony Morris)*

Open: All year.
Rooms: 26 – 7 with bath, 14 with shower, all with telephone.

Facilities: Hall. Flower-filled courtyard. English spoken.
Location: Central; no special parking facilities.
Terms: Rooms (single) 95–135 frs, (double) 125–165 frs. Set meal: breakfast 12 frs.

STE-ANNE-LA-PALUD, 29137 Plonévez-Porzay, S. Finistère, Brittany

Map 8

Hôtel de la Plage   *Telephone:* (98) 92.50.12

In western Brittany, close to the picturesque old town of Locronan and the busy fishing port of Douarnenez. Ste-Anne has one of the most famous of Breton *pardons* (religious processions) held on the last Sunday in August. 'A lovely place set at the edge of a beach with hills behind and with only a tiny village nearby. No great distance though from main centres by car: Quimper is only 25 km away. The bar has a splendid view of the Bay of Douarnenez, so does much of the dining room and many of the 28 bedrooms. As well as the wide sandy beach there is a heated swimming pool and the gardens are lovely. The building is attractive, white with steep-pitched slate roof, and the rooms are very comfortable indeed and tastefully decorated. Madame Lecoz presides over the hotel with great charm and equal efficiency. The food is wonderful, especially for lovers of fish and shellfish, as there is an abundance of oysters and *palourdes* (clams) and magnificent *plateaux de fruits de mer* dominated by an impressive crab. There are such splendid dishes as *lotte au poivre vert* (anglerfish with green peppercorns) and bass with sorrel. Meats and poultry are fine too and so are the desserts, but it was the fish and shellfish I enjoyed. I also enjoyed the ambience, the peaceful view of the wide bay and great stretch of yellow sand as the tide retreated.' *(Elisabeth Lambert Ortiz, endorsed (with reservations about the set menu) Margaret Sheaf)*

Open: 1 April–30 September.
Rooms: 28 double – all with bath and telephone. (4 ground floor rooms in annexe.)
Facilities: Lift, bar, restaurant. Garden with heated swimming pool. English spoken.
Location: 16 km from Douarnenez; 25 km from Quimper.
Credit cards: Barclay/Visa,Diners.
Terms: Dinner, B & B 380–430 frs; full board 420–480 frs. Set meals: breakfast 22 frs; lunch 110 frs (Sundays and public holidays 150–200 frs); full *alc* 180–200 frs. Reduced rates for children.

ST-BENOIT, 86000 Poitiers, Vienne

Map 8

À l'Orée des Bois   *Telephone:* (49) 57.11.44
Route de Ligugé

About 4 km south of the old cathedral and university city of Poitiers: don't miss Poitiers' church of Notre-Dame de la Grande with its romanesque facade. 'This was the pleasantest hotel in our two-week tour and you have nowhere in the area yet, so . . . Main trouble is *finding* it. When you get there, you'll be welcomed by the young management and extremely well fed (we had *salade niçoise, moules mouclade*, pork with prunes, then cheese – all for 35 frs [1980]). I pointed out an error in the bill (in our favour, for a change!) and was presented to their nine-day old daughter by way of explanation!' *(Alan Cooke)*

Open: All year.
Rooms: 15 – 6 with bath or shower.
Facilities: Restaurant.
Location: Leave Poitiers by the N10 to the S (Angoulême direction), then 2 km from the town centre turn left along the D4 and go through the suburb of Naintré. The inn is just beyond Naintré on the left after a dual carriageway.
Terms: Rooms 35–70 frs.

ST-CYPRIEN, 24220 Dordogne   Map 8

Hotel l'Abbaye   *Telephone:* (53) 29.20.48

'A most comfortable three-star hotel in an attractive village very centrally situated for touring the Dordogne. The food and service are excellent, the wines most reasonably priced. Madame Schaler who runs the hotel with her husband is very friendly and speaks excellent English. The hotel is well-appointed and has a swimming pool. Half *pension* is very good value.' *(Richard O Whiting)*

Open: 15 March–5 November.
Rooms: 17 double, 3 single – 8 with bath, 12 with shower, all with telephone. 5 rooms in annexe. (2 rooms on ground floor.)
Facilities: TV room, restaurant. Garden, terrace, heated swimming pool. English spoken. ᪲ .
Location: 200 metres from town centre on the N703 towards Les Eyzies, 9 km from Beynac, 19 km from Sarlat; parking.
Credit cards: American Express, Diners.
Terms: Rooms 105–250 frs; B & B 119–139 frs; dinner, B & B 155–180 frs; full board 195–220 frs. Set meals: lunch/dinner 40, 80 and 155 frs; full *alc* 85 frs.

ST-ÉTIENNE-LES-ORGUES, 04230 Alpes de Haute Provence   Map 9

Hôtel St Clair   *Telephone:* (92) 76.07.09

'St Étienne-les-Orgues sprawls at the foot of the southern flank of the long hump of the Montagne de Lure. This is a less frequented corner of Provence, though favoured by walkers, geologists and naturalists. The *Hôtel St Clair* is 2 km out of St Etienne, standing solid on a knoll. Surrounding its gardens are wide expanses of landscape with a backcloth of distant hills. The hotel is a simple, modern, spotlessly clean, fairly large, honest *logis de France*. Taps and fittings gleam and work. The thirty rooms are spacious, if simply and adequately furnished. The bar is tiny, but the list of drinks is long, interesting and modestly priced. What an excellent dinner there was for 40 frs! [1980] *Pâté* with prunes and *crudités*; a splendid salmon-trout with pine kernels, creamed spinach and succulent pommes frites; cheese; ice-cream; and a house-wine which is Beaujolais red, white or rose. Unpretentious, good value.' *(A N Brangham)*

Open: All year.
Rooms: 27 double – 9 with shower. (1 room on ground floor.)

305

Facilities: Salon, bar, restaurant. Garden with swings; terraces. English spoken. ⅋ .

Location: 2 km out of St Étienne. Coming on road from Forcalquier, turn left at entrance to St Étienne. Parking.

Terms: Rooms 65–100 frs; full board 110–170 frs. Set meals: breakfast 11 frs; lunch/dinner 45, 70 and 90 frs. Reduced rates for children sharing parents' room.

ST-JACUT-DE-LA-MER, 22750 Côtes du Nord, Brittany   Map 8

Le Vieux Moulin   *Telephone:* (96) 27.71.02

'*Le Vieux Moulin* is frequented mainly by French bourgeois families of three generations holidaying together, small children of four applying the same intent concentration as their grandparents to the serious business of eating – lunch (five courses) is the highlight (specially good *moules*, mackerel, *colin*, roast beef and an excellent house wine); supper much simpler for those *en pension*. Madam Papin presides over the dining room, Monsieur Papin over the kitchen. Very good value for a quiet holiday in an old-fashioned atmosphere, rooms adequate, all looking out on to the garden and there is an annexe by the beach. St-Jacut-de-la-Mer, a fishing village, where the locals gather shellfish at low tide, is almost an island, and apart from windsurfing, swimming from the numerous sandy coves, or walking along the headland and the beaches, there is blissfully nothing to do except relax. We paid 110 frs each for full *pension* (August 1980).' *(Michael and Sasha Young)*

Open: March–October.

Rooms: 26 – 7 with bath, all with telephone.

Facilities: Restaurant, terrace. Garden; beach.

Location: 26 km from St Malo; parking.

Terms: Rooms 60–115 frs; full board 120–165 frs. Set meals: breakfast 10 frs; lunch/dinner 30–80 frs.

ST-JEAN-DU-BRUEL, 12230 La Cavalerie, Aveyron, Massif Central   Map 8

Hôtel du Midi   *Telephone:* (65) 66.62.04

The *Midi* has had a facelift this past winter, with a new salon and bar, and more rooms given the baths *en suite* treatment. All rooms now have telephones. Its official category has been changed from one star to two, but prices continue to be very reasonable. 'Recommended in *The Observer* in the Sixties, and still outstanding value, St-Jean is on the river Doubie, roughly equidistant from Millau and Lodève, and an excellent centre for walking holidays in the Cevennes or for visiting the Gorges du Tarn. The hotel has a good atmosphere, rooms well-decorated and adequately furnished. The dining room overlooking the river is very attractive, and the food first-class and very reasonably priced. The owners take an evident pride in the place and a friendly interest in their guests. In spring the outlook over the river is marvellously green and peaceful; nightingales vie with the sound of the river at night. The only disturbance is caused by the village dogs who suffer a short *crise de nerfs* when the church bell rings on Sunday mornings. A very attractive and agreeable small hotel.' *(J A F Somerville)*

Open: 15 March–15 November.
Rooms: 16 double, 2 single – 11 with bath, all with telephone.
Facilities: Lounge, TV room, dining room; situated on the banks of the river Doubie. English spoken.
Location: SE of Millau (45 km) off the D7.
Terms: Rooms 45–53 frs per person; B & B 55.50–63.50 frs; full board 105–132 frs. Set meals: breakfast 10.50 frs; lunch/dinner 38–90 frs; full *alc* 70 frs. Reduced rates for children.

ST-JEANNET, 06640 Alpes-Mar, Provence   Map 9

Auberge d'Antoine   *Telephone:* (93) 59.50.06
Place Sainte-Barbe

'The old hill-village of St-Jeannet, near Vence, is in a splendid part of the Nice hinterland, with fine views towards the coast and a great tooth-like rock looming up behind (good for rock-climbing, I'm told, though we funked it ourselves). Chez *Antoine* is the kind of down-to-earth French inn that we like, a bit noisy, but full of jollity, and dominated by its rotund and extrovert young owner, Antoine Plutino. He talks good English, having been chef at the Burford Bridge Hotel, in Surrey. He also adores modern paintings, hangs them all over his inn, has many artist friends, and will talk you into the night about e.g. the rival merits of Matisse and Chagall. What's more, he does the cooking himself, rather well, and inventively – he's proud of his 'creations' such as *filets de volaille à la ciboulette* and *sole aux oranges*. The bedrooms are OK, but don't expect *grand luxe*.' *(John and Ludmila Berry)*

Open: All year, except Monday and Janyuary.
Rooms: 9.
Facilities: Restaurant, function room, terrace. Garden. English spoken.
Location: 8 km from Vence.
Terms: Rooms 60–70 frs; dinner, B & B 90–110 frs. Set meals: breakfast 11 frs; lunch/dinner 55 and 82 frs.

ST-JEAN-CAP-FERRAT, 06290 Alpes-Mar, Provence   Map 9

Voile d'Or   *Telephone:* (93) 01.13.13
Port de St Jean   *Telex:* 470317

'A very beautiful, modernized luxury hotel, built on a low promontory right beside the harbour, on the edge of the fishing village of St-Jean. We had a very pretty and spacious bedroom, with views of the sea, and we were equally delighted by the rest of the hotel – the pastel-shaded decor, the idyllic garden-terrace where you can eat or take a drink, and the two swimming pools. One is down by the rocks, and they serve lunch there (as well as indoors) so you don't have to come back in and change. The atmosphere is informal, though chic. And the food is outstanding: they prepare local fish in delicious and unusual ways. We also enjoyed exploring beautiful Cap-Ferrat with its pinewoods, its charming zoo and the Rothschild museum. The only snag is the lack of sandy beaches on this part of the coast – but that's hardly the hotel's fault.' *(Peter and Sarah Abbott)*

Open: 1 February–30 October.
Rooms: 44 double, 6 single, 1 suite – 50 with bath, all with telephone, TV and baby-sitting on request.
Facilities: Lift, TV room, restaurant, air-conditioning; conference facilities. Garden with terrace; 2 heated swimming pools. English spoken. ᕻ.
Location: 10 km from Nice; 1½ km from town centre, by the harbour; parking.
Terms: Rooms 240–825 frs; full board 530–770 frs. Set meals (excluding service): lunch 155 frs; dinner 200 frs; full *alc* 330 frs.

ST-LATTIER, 38160 Saint-Marcellin, Isère   Map 8

Le Lièvre Amoureux et sa Cheneraie   *Telephone:* (76) 36.50.67

St-Lattier is a small village halfway between St-Marcellin and Romans-sur-Isère on the N92, not far from the National Park of the Vercors with its winter and summer resorts. Grenoble is 70 km away and Valence 32. 'A "restaurant with rooms", or delightful country hotel by any other name. Michelin over-rates the cooking but the ambience of the surrounding maize fields, the proximity of the level crossing (reminding one of the presence of industry on which all the indulgence is based) and the al fresco dining makes up for such marginal disappointments. There are fine views of the foothills of the Vercors mountains. An open-air wedding reception with dancing enlivened our evening meal and entranced the children even if it diminished sleep. However, the staff were solicitous the next day. As ever, rooms cheap, food inexpensive.' *(J M Dennis)*

Open: All year, except Monday and January (but open bank holidays).
Rooms: 9 double, 2 suites – all with bath or shower and telephone; TV in suites.
Facilities: Restaurant, air-conditioning. Garden and terrace.
Location: Halfway between St-Marcellin and Romans-sur-Isère on the N92.
Credit cards: American Express, Diners.
Terms: Rooms 190 frs; suites 420 frs. Set meals: breakfast 24 frs; lunch/dinner 110–200 frs.

ST-PAUL-DE-VENCE, 06570 Alpes-Mar, Provence   Map 9

La Colombe d'Or   *Telephone:* (93) 32.80.02
    Telex: 970 607 F

A *très très chic* small hotel in one of the showplace hill-towns behind Nice, but by no means your usual sort of de-luxe establishment. For one thing, the place is a modest treasure house of modern art – paintings and sketches by, among others, Picasso, Braque, Matisse, Calder and Miro, many given to the former owner in payment by artists who have stayed here, are accommodated in a beautiful old house, along with many fine pieces of old furniture. A less modest treasure house of modern art, the Fondation Maeght, the finest collection of its kind in the South of France, is only a mile away. Each room has a distinctive character – some with original beams, others all in white stucco with window-seats overlooking gardens. Many have lovely terraces and outsize bathrooms. There is a splendid large flowered veranda where lunch is served; dinner is taken indoors in a large sophisticated rustic dining room. There is a swimming pool set in the midst of cypress trees. But the place isn't going to suit everyone. Service is emphatically casual, and not everything is maintained in 100% working order. One reader summed up the experience as follows: 'If you appreciate this sort of place, it's splendid and worth every penny. But (a) if you want quiet in the mornings (traffic starts at 7 am) (b) a spick-and-span, spotlessly clean bedroom with adequate accommodation for suitcases (c) formal dining and (d) polished service, this isn't the place. But it deserves its entry in the Guide: it is unique, quite unlike any other luxury hotel I have ever visited.' *(IM; also John Hills and others)*

Open: All year, except 5 November–20 December.
Rooms: 16 double, 8 suites – all with bath, telephone, radio and colour TV; many with terrace. (1 room on ground floor.)
Facilities: Salon, restaurant, terrace for lunch or refreshments, sauna. Garden with swimming pool. 10 km from the sea. English spoken.
Location: 10 km from Nice.
Credit cards: American Express, Diners.
Terms (excluding 15% service charge): B & B 280–400 frs; dinner, B & B 400–580 frs (suite 60 frs extra). Full *alc* 160 frs.

ST-PONS-DE-THOMIÈRES, 34220 Hérault, Languedoc   Map 8

Château de Ponderach   *Telephone:* (67) 97.02.57

'A superb château set in lovely gardens, and a splendid resting place after a long and tiring day. It is in the Haut Languedoc Nature Reserve. St-Pons, a pleasant town with an interesting 12th-century church, lies at the foot of the Montagne Noire and is within easy driving distance of Carcassone, Narbonne and the Languedoc centres. Our room was at the top of the old building up an old stone staircase, and beautifully furnished and equipped. Like most of the hotels in the *Relais et Châteaux* association, it was expensive, particularly the *à la carte*, where our cheese cost us 45 francs each (1980). Our main complaint was a *saumon truite* which turned out to be an ordinary rainbow trout. Such a shame to spoil such a superb place which has been the owners' family home for some 300 years.' *(Angela and David Stewart)*

Open: Easter–15 October.
Rooms: 11 – 9 with bath, all with telephone.
Facilities: 2 sitting rooms (1 with TV), restaurant. Large garden where you can eat in good weather. Small lake nearby. English spoken.
Location: 52 km N of Narbonne on N112.
Credit cards: American Express, Diners.
Terms: Rooms 150–235 frs; dinner, B & B 95 frs added to room rate. Set meal: breakfast 23 frs. Reduced rates for children.

ST-SERVAN, 35400 St-Malo, Ille-et-Vilaine, Brittany   Map 8

Le Valmarin   *Telephone:* (99) 81.94.76
7 rue Jean XXIII

'St-Servan, south of St-Malo's harbour, is not easy to find, but this hotel is worth the effort. It is an 18th-century country house in an attractive garden. Rooms were beautifully decorated (ours in white, green and gold). There is no restaurant at *Le Valmarin*, but the amiable owner booked a table for us at the excellent *La Métairie du Beauregard* some 5 km away.' *(H ap R)*

Open: All year.
Rooms: 5 double, 5 single – all with bath, telephone and radio.
Facilities: Salon/bar. Sizeable garden. 100 m from safe sandy beach. English spoken.
Location: 100 m from town centre near the Port Solidor; parking in garden.
Credit card: American Express.
Terms: Rooms 210–290 frs; breakfast 20 frs.

ST-TROPEZ, 83990 Var, Provence   Map 9

Le Mas de Chastelas   *Telephone:* (94) 56.09.11

'If you must go to St-Tropez – and to be honest it can be delightful in May, June and late September – here, at last, is the sort of hotel that this unique resort deserves. Converted from a 17th-century *mas* (though really more a *bastide*) it is two miles out of the town just off the road leading up to Gassin. It is simple yet elegant, sophisticated yet unpretentious. The owners, Dominique and Gérard Racine, are very much in evidence. The furnishings are mostly in pine and the walls plainly distempered. There are flowers in the bedrooms and all have bathrooms *en suite*. The luxury of having your towels changed, bed re-made and room tidied whilst at dinner, plus direct-dial phones, makes this a very superior hotel, and miles away from the trendy smart circuit. It is very quiet. There is a small dining room (or you can eat out on the terrace) with very refined cooking – a buffet at lunch, and an *à la carte* menu in the evening; the breakfasts are excellent. You can sit outside in the sun or shade round the heated pool or in the charming garden. Tennis courts are nearby.' *(Geoffrey Sharp)*

The above description of *Le Mas de Chastelas*, taken from last year's edition, has been enthusiastically endorsed by recent visitors: 'A superb place to stay. Owners and staff very helpful. Furnishings, polished tile floors, pine furniture, immaculate bathroom, all added up to a maximum of satisfaction. The place felt right and we felt right in the place. We wish we could have stayed longer.' *(Peter Marshall; also A Fraser)*

Note: Monsieur Gérard Racine, who writes in faultless English, tells us that he hopes in 1982 to have ready ten new large suites, and a second swimming pool reserved for children.

Open: Easter–end September.
Rooms: 20 double, 10 suites – 27 with bath, 3 with shower, all with telephone; TV in the suites.
Facilities: Lounge, TV room, bar, restaurant. Gardens with 4 tennis courts, 2 swimming pools, Jacuzzi, ping pong and boules. Beach close by. English spoken.
Location: 3 km from St-Tropez, just off the Gassin road to the E.
Credit cards: American Express, Diners.
Terms: Rooms 320–550 frs. Set meals: breakfast 30 frs; lunch 100 frs; full *alc* 160 frs.

Do you know of a good hotel or country inn in the United States or Canada? Nominations please to our sibling publication, *America's Wonderful Little Hotels and Inns*, 345 East 93rd Street, 25C, New York, NY 10028.

ST-VAAST-LA-HOUGUE, 50550 Manche, Normandy   Map 8

Hôtel de France et des Fuchsias   *Telephone:* (33) 54.42.26
Rue Maréchal Foch

St-Vaast-La-Hougue is an attractive fishing port, 30 km east of Cherbourg on the Cotentin peninsula. It crops up several times in the history of cross-Channel invasion: Edward III landed his troops here before the battle of Crécy; Louis XIV assembled a fleet in its harbour to help James II regain his throne; and it was also in the forefront of the fighting during the Normandy landings of 1944. *France et des Fuchsias* is the main hotel, an unpretentiously pleasant family-run establishment which would make an ideal holiday centre for anyone wishing to explore western Normandy, or an overnight stop for tourists coming from Cherbourg.

We had a report recently of a poor meal and of a dress ruined by stains from the fuchsias which covered the tables and chairs. Beware before you sit! But another reader offers a more favourable view: 'A delightful place. Charming room, freshly decorated and very comfortable. Excellent dinner – especially the *raie au beurre noire* and the veal sweetbreads, though the still frozen profiteroles rather chilled one's appreciation! A very attractive hotel we thought. The fuchsias hanging in crimson tresses from overhead wires above the tables in the conservatory/dining room and trained up the walls and round the windows of the front of the hotel – most romantic! Not as cheap as we had expected, but still cheap compared to English hotels and excellent value.' *(A S Kyrle Pope)*

Open: All year, except January and Monday October–May (but open school holidays).
Rooms: 12 double, 4 single – 9 with bath, 4 with shower, all with telephone.
Facilities: Hall, salons, bar, 2 dining rooms. Flowery garden for meals and refreshments. 300 m from beach; sailing, tennis. English spoken.
Location: 30 km E of Cherbourg. Hotel is central; parking.
Credit card: Diners.
Terms: Rooms 70–150 frs; full board 130–170 frs. Set meals: breakfast 18 frs; lunch/dinner 60–160 frs; full *alc* 110 frs. 50% reduction for children under 7.

SALON-DE-PROVENCE, 13300 Bouches-du-Rhône   Map 9

Abbaye de Sainte-Croix   *Telephone:* (90) 56.24.55
Route du Val de Cuech   *Telex:* STECROI 401247

'This venerable 12th-century abbey, two miles out of Salon on a private road, is perched on a flower-filled platform commanding the flatlands of Roman Provence – Aix, Arles and Avignon are each some 40 km away. Luxury now abounds in a careful restoration after 200 years of neglect. Double rooms, all with baths, lead off many separate staircases and passages: our children's room, happily arranged to be opposite our own, had its own tiny stone balcony (once for prayer reading?) overlooking the cloister. The *menu d'enfants*, quite right and ample for them (salami, lamb chops, yogurt and a choice from the *chariot de pâtisseries*), was an appetite-whetting sight for the splendid main menu to come: home-smoked fish of many kinds, steak in blueberry sauce, pork in a wild mushroom sauce, a battery of cheeses, that same chariot of puddings. The monks must have toiled up here, and then cultivated their own garden for

311

food and drink: today the traveller works off his sumptuous meals by swims, walks and rides in the hills behind the abbey or by tennis at the nearby club.' *(AL)*

Open: All year, except 15 December–15 January. Restaurant closed Monday midday.
Rooms: 22 double – 18 with bath, 2 with shower, all with telephone. (3 rooms on ground floor.)
Facilities: Salon, bar, 2 dining rooms, room for receptions, covered terrace. Wooded grounds and garden with swimming pool and boules. Riding 3 km, sea 25 km. &.
Location: 3 km NE of Salon, off the D16; sign in Salon after exit from the autoroute. Parking.
Credit cards: American Express, Barclay/Visa, Diners.
Terms: Rooms 270–430 frs; full board 400–690 frs. Set meals: breakfast 28.75 frs; lunch/dinner 100–165 frs; full *alc* 150–180 frs.

SÉGURET, Vaison-la-Romaine, 84110 Vaucluse, Provence　　　**Map 9**

La Table du Comtat　　　　　　　　　　　　　*Telephone:* (90) 36.91.49

'*La Table du Comtat* is a "rosette" restaurant with rooms, high above the tiny village of Séguret – which is south-west of Vaison-la-Romaine, and within half an hour of the "Orange" autoroute exit. It is as far as you can go up a very windy lane. The setting is outstanding – a 100 ft drop just below the windows – with the Rhône valley sweeping away into the distance, and a nice little mountain to the left, and cliff-like rocks up behind. The food was pricey – as one would expect with a "rosette": 75 frs [1981] for the cheapest menu, so nondescript they obviously considered it quite beneath them. The next was 110 frs – the most we paid this year – and felt we *had* to! I can visualize a "Bateman" cartoon: "The British couple who *dared* to choose the 75 frs dinner!" Our bedroom happened to be the one featured in the brochure, which looks very grand, but was actually quite small and simple, apart from the sexy bit of drapery behind the bed! The bathroom small – but adequate, and a *most* comfortable bed – the best we had out of four hotels. A better-than-usual breakfast with *fresh* orange juice, lashings of hot water, plates! and a large slab of butter for a change (at 14 frs). The service was quite good in a dour sort of way, only "Madame" herself smiled at us occasionally. I think really the "residents" are just a less important side-line. The restaurant is what matters here. Nevertheless, a good one-night stop, in a very pleasant area (Mont Ventoux so near) with beautiful drives and walks.' *(Lady Elstub)*

So ran last year's entry. Recent visitors have commented on the fact that the set menus rarely change and have queried whether *La Table's table* quite justifies its Michelin star. But, as one recent guest puts it, 'There is about the hotel and its environment a compelling charm which overrides critical scruples'. *(Norman Brangham)*

Open: All year, except mid January–end February. Restaurant closed Tuesday evening and Wednesday (except July and August).
Rooms: 9 double – all with bath and telephone.
Facilities: Lounge, dining room; unheated swimming pool.
Location: 9 km SW of Vaison-la-Romaine just off the D977; parking.
Credit cards: Access/Euro/Mastercard.
Terms: Rooms 150–230 frs. Set meals: breakfast 18 frs; lunch/dinner 80–120 frs; full *alc* 160 frs.

SEILLANS, 83440 Var, Provence   Map 9

Hôtel des Deux Rocs   *Telephone:* (94) 76.05.33

'A real find. Seillans is a Saracen town way up in the hills of Var, a good hour from St-Tropez or Port Grimaud. The *Deux Rocs* is a beautiful old house, charmingly decorated in a chic Provençal style by the owner, a beautiful 40-ish ex-biochemist from Paris, Madame Hirsch, who lives in a little tower beside it. The rooms all have little bathrooms and are decorated each in an utterly different way – grand toile de Jouey, little Boussac prints. Very quiet and the terrace outside, which is a sort of public squat with a fountain and huge oak tree, has little white tables where you can have lunch in the summer. It's been written up by *Gourmet* (US) and the food is delectable.' *(Diana Weir)*

So ran our entry last year. One recent visitor agreed with every word of it: 'A lovely inn. The welcome could not have been warmer, the food was absolutely delicious and our room was better decorated than any other we had come across in France.' Another guest of *Deux Rocs* did have reservations, however, finding the dinners a long way short of *Gourmet* standard, and service in the restaurant also faulty. An isolated bad experience? We should be glad to hear from others. *(James Burt, Lady Elstub)*

Open: 1 April–1 November. Restaurant closed Tuesday out of season.
Rooms: 15 double – 6 with bath, 9 with shower and WC, all with telephone.
Facilities: 2 salons (1 with TV), bar, dining room. Near sea and lake of St-Cassien.
Location: Grasse 31 km; St-Raphaël 41 km.
Terms: Rooms 120–210 frs; full board 200–270 frs. Set meals: breakfast 14 frs; lunch/dinner 50–135 frs.

SEILLANS, 83440 Var, Provence   Map 9

Hôtel de France   *Telephone:* (94) 76.06.10

One recent visitor to this family-run hotel in Seillans' old quarter found it comfortable, clean and good value, but a little lacking in warmth and character. Another guest, who tells us that she spent an idyllic honeymoon here, also commented on functional and undistinguished furnishings in the bedrooms which are housed in a modern annexe. No reservations, however, about the hotel's restaurant, called *Clariond*, which is the name of the resident owner.

'The restaurant has a fine reputation and, for the whole of our stay, the food was absolutely delicious and beautifully presented. We were delighted to find that the dining room, which was in the old part of the hotel, was a large, airy room decorated with a profusion of plants and flowers and had the most spectacular views to the south over the Provençal hills. It also overlooked the swimming pool which had been built in what must have been the old courtyard twenty feet below. Despite our disappointment over our room, which was on the ground floor and rather overshadowed by a large hedge outside the window, we had a lovely week and would certainly want to stay there again.' *(Teresa Kennard)*

Open: All year, except 3 weeks in January. Restaurant closed Wednesday in low season.
Rooms: 26 – 13 with bath, 13 with shower, all with telephone.
Facilities: Salon (with TV), restaurant. Garden with swimming pool. English spoken.
Location: Grasse 31 km; St-Raphaël 41 km.
Terms: Rooms 80–240 frs; dinner, B & B 200–300 frs; full board 280–380 frs. Set meals: breakfast 25 frs; lunch/dinner 85 frs.

SEPT-SAULX, 51400 Mourmelon-le-Grand, Marne, Champagne   Map 8

Hôtel du Cheval Blanc   *Telephone:* (26) 61.60.27

'Anyone who contemplates staying in the Reims area should make a real effort to stay here unless they actually like noisy towns,' writes a reader who goes on to call this old coaching inn in a rural location 'wholly civilized . . . and extraordinary value by British hotel standards.' The hotel is in fact a member of the *Relais du Silence* association, and has been known for many years past by gastronomes looking for a useful first or last night-stop when travelling through northern France. It has usually been reckoned as four hours from Calais, though the new motorway from Calais to Laon when completed will certainly bring the attractions of the *Cheval Blanc* closer. One reader this year was not overly impressed – problems with the loo, slow service at breakfast and 'the stream running through the garden was not an olfactory success'. But this was an isolated complaint: most readers continue to find the hotel – and Robert Lefevre's cooking – very much to their liking. *(D J I Garstin, J Dixey, Caroline Hamburger)*

Open: All year, except 1 month from mid January–mid February.
Rooms: 20 double, 2 suites – 12 with bath, 10 with shower, all with telephone and TV. (Some rooms on ground floor.)
Facilities: Reading room with colour TV, restaurant, 2 function rooms, billiard room. Hotel is situated in large park bordered by the river Vesle; tennis, mini-golf, table tennis, volley ball, fishing. English spoken.
Location: 20 km E of Reims, on the D37 off the N44 in the direction of Châlons.
Credit cards: American Express, Barclay/Visa, Diners, Euro.
Terms (excluding 15% service charge): Rooms 90–130 frs. Set meals: breakfast 17 frs; lunch/dinner 110 and 180 frs; full *alc* 170 frs.

SERRE-CHEVALIER, 05240 Hautes-Alpes   Map 8

La Vieille Ferme   *Telephone:* (92) 24.02.79
Villeneuve La Salle

'Serre-Chevalier, 6 km west of Briançon, is the collective name, taken from a nearby summit, given to three old hamlets. The whole complex is notable for the great friendliness of the inhabitants and many of their guests. Essentially it is a family resort, with little night life, where people go to ski in winter and to take part in various other pursuits in summer. By no means can it be said to be smartly elegant, but the French do seem to have a natural flair nonetheless. *La Vieille Ferme* has considerable rustic charm. It is a 17th-century house that a group of Parisians got together to save some ten years ago. The proprietor and manager did most of the modernization with his own hands, and with help from members of his family and friends. Most nights in the winter he is a *rôtisseur* and his *rôtisserie* is usually full. He is helped, in most of his endeavours, by his delightful wife, and by a young, friendly and competent staff that don't seem to change much over the years. Nights in the hotel are perfectly quiet. It is located on the fringe of the old part of Villeneuve, and is approached steeply on foot uphill from the main street. By car there is a 2 km detour. The place largely caters for those in pursuit of active leisure, but those who by reason of youth, old age or choice wish to spectate from the sidelines are by no means excluded. All is done with considerable *éclat*, much good taste, great comfort and delicious food – and yet remains delightfully *in*formal. *(H C Beddington)*

Open: 1 December–1 May and 15 June–15 September.
Rooms: 23 double, 7 suites – 17 with bath, 11 with shower, all with telephone.
Facilities: Salon, games room with TV, bar, restaurant, *rôtisserie*, terrace. Tennis in summer, winter sports; covered swimming pool nearby.
Location: 6 km W of Briançon off the R91. Hotel is in centre of Serre-Chevalier with private parking. Coming by car in bad weather telephone the hotel from the Lombard area halfway between Lyon and Grenoble to check if the col du Lautaret is closed; alternative route is the tunnel of Fréjus.
Terms: B & B 95–230 frs. Set meals: lunch/dinner 60, 82 and 100 frs; full *alc* 70 frs. Special rates for tennis and skiing holidays. No charge for children under 4 sharing parents' room; 10% reduction for children between 4 and 10.

SERRES, 05700 Hautes-Alpes   **Map 8**

Hôtel Fifi Moulin   *Telephone:* (92) 67.00.01
Route de Nyons

'Never retrace your steps, they say. We did and were glad to have done so. In 1966 our bedroom had been dainty with a chintzy and cosy intimacy. This time, it was more austere but comfortable enough. Moreover, a rarity in France: a room with its own WC, and without the bathroom or shower that usually has to accompany it. The hotel is larger now, and improved by a spacious lounge and patio which, the September evening we were there, looked on to the hills of the Hautes-Alpes in a serene sunset light. A young, energetic couple have run the *Fifi Moulin* for the last five years. Fourteen years ago, its restaurant had a Michelin star, and the meal was not very interesting. Now, it has the far more reliable Michelin red R ("Good food at moderate prices"), and deserves it. The sweet trolley is really pretty spectacular. The breakfast tray is a yesteryear sight, for there is a good, honest square of butter, honey and apricot jam in open dishes, and the coffee tasted as it should. And my log-book reminds me that the *Fifi Moulin* gave us one of our least expensive nights on the road in 1980.' *(A N Brangham)*

'Unostentatious comfort, a good welcome, excellent food, quiet rooms – and at under £20 per night for dinner, bed and breakfast [1981], a real bargain stop.' *(A H H Stow)*

Open: February–November, except Thursday October–June.
Rooms: 25 – all with bath or shower and telephone.
Facilities: Lounge, restaurant, patio. ₺ .
Location: 64 km from Nyons on the N75.
Credit cards: American Express, Diners, Euro.
Terms: Rooms 65–100 frs; full board 135–160 frs. Set meals: breakfast 12 frs; lunch/dinner 45–80 frs.

Hôtel des Étrangers   *Telephone:* (93) 04.00.09
7 boulevard de Verdun

'The hinterland behind Menton is surprisingly little known, and the charming old town of Sospel makes an ideal centre for exploring its delights – for example, the hill-village of Saorge, clinging to the side of a cliff, and the Vallée des Merveilles, where a rocky lunar landscape is covered with prehistoric graffiti. The patron/chef of the *Hôtel des Étrangers*, Jean-Pierre Domérégo, will tell you all about this, and more, for he has written a book about Sospel and adores his region. Having worked in the US and Bermuda, he is both anglophone and americo-anglophile. With great gusto he runs an unpretentious but comfortable little family hotel, and does all the cooking, rather well. His special dishes even include a bouillabaissse made of local trout. The hotel receives regular English package-tours, of the discreet, up-market kind: the guests we talked to were all pleased with their stay, as we were too.' *(Anthony Day)*

Open: All year, except 1 December–20 January.
Rooms: 33 double, 2 single – 14 with bath, 13 with shower, all with telephone. 7 rooms in annexe.
Facilities: Lift, salon, TV room, 3 restaurants; conference facilities; riverside pergola. English spoken.
Location: 22 km from Menton on the D2204; parking.
Credit cards: Euro/Mastercard.
Terms: Rooms 60–150 frs; full board 120–180 frs. Set meals: breakfast 15 frs; lunch/dinner 45–80 frs; full *alc* 130 frs. Reduced rates for children.

Auberge de Tavel   *Telephone:* (66) 50.03.41

'The *Auberge de Tavel* stands at the edge of the famous little wine-village, facing open, unspectacular country in the direction of Rochefort-du-Gard. The atmosphere tempts the lingerer. The hotel is not cheap by my standards, but its discreet quality dispels anxiety over such delightful extravagance. Eleven bedrooms are furnished with functional simplicity but with an agreeable hint of cosy luxury. A bar looks out on a small garden and pool; a few steps lead into a lounge at the entrance to the restaurant, which is elegant and high-ceilinged. The restaurant's tables are set well-apart, and menus have touch of distinction. The centre-table is loaded with *hors d'oeuvres* of subtly prepared *crudités, pâtés* and meats; they could make a complete meal on their own. Tavel wines, of course, head the wine list. During our stay, we never strayed from them. Never has Tavel tasted so elegant and tingling to the tongue.

'The village, surrounded by holm-oak woods, is a hub from which to radiate to Avignon and the glories of northern Vaucluse; to the Alpilles and the Montagnettes; to the Camargue, Crau and Languedoc coast; to Nîmes, the ever-admirable Pont du Gard and the *garrigues*. Little roads straggle away from Tavel. Even the A9 autoroute which misses the village by a whisker is raised on a hillock to be inaudible and invisible from the *Auberge de Tavel*.' *(Norman Brangham)*

Open: All year, except mid January–end February. Restaurant closed Monday 1 October–31 March.
Rooms: 11 double – 6 with bath, 5 with shower, all with telephone.
Facilities: Lounge, bar, restaurant. Small garden with swimming pool. English spoken.
Location: Avignon 14 km SE; Orange 20 km N. 200 m from village centre; parking.
Credit cards: American Express, Barclay/Visa, Diners.
Terms: Rooms 155–200 frs. Set meals: breakfast 18 frs; lunch/dinner 75–130 frs; full *alc* 215 frs. Reduced rates and special meals for children.

TONNERRE, 89700 Yonne, Burgundy — Map 8

L'Abbaye Saint Michel

Telephone: (86) 55.05.99

Tonnerre lies in a valley in the extreme north of Burgundy, quite close to Auxerre with its cathedral and Chablis with its white wines. The château of Tanlay, 8 km from Tonnerre, is worth visiting too.

As we anticipated last year, the restaurant of this 13th-century Benedictine abbey, converted into a thoroughly comfortable hotel, has been given its well-merited Michelin star, and has also won a *toque rouge* from Gault-Millau for its fine *nouvelle cuisine*.

'Apart from the clever use of plate glass in the reception area the exterior has the appearance of a lovingly restored Burgundian farmhouse on a rather grand scale. Ivy clings to the walls, the white shuttered windows are scattered at random along the length of the building and the slate roof is in perfect condition. The situation is ideal – just out of the town on the slope of a gentle hill; it has an attractive view looking back towards Tonnerre and the église St-Pierre and the valley of the Armançon. It is blissfully quiet. Inside the rooms are nicely appointed, though as to their decoration I would have preferred to have seen more of the cleverly hidden beams and less of the rather heavy French fabric. There is a particularly attractive suite over the entrance with original stone floor and traces of original paintings on the wall. The restaurant is half underground and in the evening had a warm and welcoming ambience. Maybe it would be less inviting at midday. The food veers towards *nouvelle cuisine* and was excellent. There is an extensive wine list. The hotel is not cheap – but for what it offers it is not over-priced.' *(Geoffrey Sharp)*

Open: All year, except 20 December–31 January and Monday October–April.
Rooms: 7 doubles, 3 suites – all with bath, telephone, radio and TV.
Facilities: Reception, drawing room, bar, restaurant, terrace. Garden with tennis court, children's games, boules; river nearby. English spoken.
Location: Between the church and the post office in Tonnerre; parking.
Credit cards: American Express, Barclay/Visa, Diners.
Terms: Rooms 300–440 frs. Set meals: breakfast 30 frs; lunch/dinner 150 frs; full *alc* 200 frs.

We asked hotels to estimate their 1982 tariffs. Not all hotels in Part Two replied, so that prices in Part Two are more approximate in some cases than those in Part One.

Hôtel La Saône   *Telephone:* (85) 51.03.38
Rive gauche

Tournus, roughly half way between Chalon and Mâcon, and on the river Saône, makes an admirable breather or night stop for those beating down the A6. Its special glory is the abbey church of St-Philibert, older even than Cluny, and one of the best-preserved Romanesque churches in France. But the town is full of fine old medieval houses in cobbled streets. 'The *Hôtel La Saône*, on the *rive gauche*, is in the "plain but adequate" class in Michelin: it's badly sign-posted, but once there it's really pleasant if very simple. No rooms with baths, but a sympathetic management and very cheap. The restaurant overlooks the river, and has menus at 45 frs (recommended in red in Michelin for good value) and 75 frs [1981]. We had the former, and it proved perfectly adequate and enough for two! There's an attractive garden front and back. An ideal stopping-off place, especially for families with children who need to let off steam.' *(Uli Lloyd Pack)*

Open: February–November. Restaurant open 1 March–29 October, except Thursday.
Rooms: 12 – some with shower.
Facilities: Restaurant. Garden.
Location: On the A6 between Chalon and Mâcon; on the left bank of the river Saône; parking.
Terms: Rooms 40–70 frs. Set meals: breakfast 8.50 frs; lunch/dinner 50–80 frs.

Hôtel Balzac   *Telephone:* (47) 05.40.87
47 rue de la Scellerie

'In a city crammed with hotels often of dubious quality, we found this bed-and-breakfast hotel modestly priced for the high standard of comfort offered. Welcome from the Breton owner idiosyncratic but helpful – the breakfast provided was superb and he was utterly reliable about phone calls, messages etc. The hall provides comfortable seats and tables where you can meet guests – a boon in France. We recommend it.' *(E Davis)*

Open: All year.
Rooms: 12 – all with bath or shower and telephone.
Facilities: Breakfast room.
Location: Central; no parking facilities.
Credit cards: All major credit cards accepted.
Terms: Rooms 60–155 frs. Set meal: breakfast 12 frs.

Deadlines: nominations for the 1983 edition should reach us not later than 31 July 1982. Latest date for comments on existing entries: 31 August 1982.

TOURTOUR, 83690 Var   Map 9

La Bastide de Tourtour   *Telephone:* (94) 70.57.30

Tourtour is an attractive 'village in the sky' as it picturesquely describes itself, 2,100 feet up, and situated between Aups to the north west and Draguignan to the south-east, in central Provence. A good centre for the Gorges du Verdon, Lac le Croix and many lovely drives in all directions, and very pretty in the immediate vicinity. *La Bastide* was custom-built with Rothschild money in the Sixties: rooms are exceptionally large and well-designed with beautiful toile for wall-paper and handsome chairs. Nothing obtrusive – not even (unusually) TV. One wall of the bedroom is a picture window, opening out on to a private terrace. As befits a luxury hotel, there's a big swimming pool and tennis court, and the hotel also enjoys a rosetted restaurant. What earns *La Bastide* a place in the Guide, however, is not just its sumptuous fixtures and fittings, but its warm *acceuil* – by no means always found in expensive hideouts. *(HR)*

Open: 26 February–12 November. Restaurant closed Tuesday out of season.
Rooms: 24 double, 2 single, all with bath, WC and telephone. (Some on ground floor.)
Facilities: Lift, bar, salon, TV room, dining room; conference and banqueting facilities. Garden with heated swimming pool and tennis court. ᴅ.
Location: 500 m from Tourtour on Draguignan road; 20 km NW of Draguignan; parking.
Credit cards: American Express, Barclay/Visa.
Terms: Rooms 220–300 frs. Set meals: breakfast 30 frs; lunch/dinner 130–180 frs; full *alc* 170 frs.

TOURTOUR, 83690 Var, Provence   Map 9

Petite Auberge   *Telephone:* (94) 70.57.16

'The *Petite Auberge* (a *Relais du Silence*) looks a small rather unremarkable purpose-built hotel – but it has enough to recommend it to encourage us to return for a second year running. It is built on the steep pine-covered slopes a mile below the village, with magnificent views for miles across undulating country, with the Massif des Maures in the far distance. Quite isolated, with olive groves just beyond the perimeter. Rather a windy spot, perhaps a little bleak – but the service and the welcome really compensate, we thought. The staff work like demons, and are so pleasant. It is spotlessly clean with comfortable bedrooms. This time we had the "grande suite" (the only room left) with 1 double and 2 single beds, but were charged only for the double. Solid rustic-style furniture. Adventurous wall fabrics (though I wasn't *entirely* sold on this year's Jacobean pattern in ultramarine and mustard!). Lovely bathroom. All bedrooms have access to the terrace *without* going through the lobby, which is sensible if one is using the swimming pool. I'm afraid the bedside lamps were only 40 watt, but that didn't worry us; we've learnt that typical French "meanness" and always carry our own! The food was good and far too generous, so the second night we settled for *à la carte*, and it worked out cheaper. Breakfast – which they *prefer* you to have in your room – arrived almost before we had put the phone down – with, of all things, piping-hot *cups*, quite an idea! The worst one can say about this little hotel is that it certainly isn't glamorous. But if you want good, friendly service, gorgeous views, and complete tranquillity – this is it.' *(Lady Elstub)*

Open: December–October, except Wednesday.
Rooms: 15 – all with bath or shower and telephone.
Facilities: Restaurant, terrace; swimming pool. ᵹ .
Location: 1.5 km out of Tourtour on the D77.
Terms: Rooms 140 frs; full board 185–260 frs. Set meals: breakfast 15.50 frs; lunch/dinner 70 frs.

TRELLY, 50660 Quettreville-sur-Sienne, Manche, Normandy   Map 8

Hôtel de la Verte Campagne   *Telephone:* (33) 47.65.33

Right in the middle of nowhere, this old 18th-century Normandy farmhouse, converted into a small country restaurant with rooms, makes an ideal first stop from Cherbourg, 80 km to the north, along the Normandy coast on the western side of the Cotentin peninsula. It is not far from Coutances, with its haunting Gothic cathedral, and the popular little resort of Granville (warmly recommended for its Saturday market) is an easy drive south. The former (English) proprietor died a few years ago, but his widow, Madame Meredith, seeks to maintain the tradition and character of this country hotel. With some reservations recently about the food, the hotel has continued to meet with warm approval from our readers: 'The rooms are charming, all different. The tiny single one is delicately sprigged, the next one is done tastefully in red-and-white checked gingham with exposed beams and ancient wardrobe. There is another one that has an added shower which is a bit of a failure, because the shower seems to ruin the proportions. All the rooms are amazingly well-equipped (for France) with Nina Ricci soap in tiny shell-shaped case. It's one of the few cheapish French hotels I've stayed in where the bathrooms and loos don't smell "French", and where one feels as comfortable as in one's own. Roses climb up the walls and in at the bedroom windows. More roses in the small paddock. The salons are traditional country-house elegant with beams, wood fires, deep chairs. The fish is outstandingly fresh and good. Rich and savoury *pâté*, decent cheeses, special apple tart flamed in old calvados. Sensible limited menus. Wine list OK, *cidre fermier* splendid and not expensive.' 'Charming spot! Rooms clean and comfortable. Owner delightful. Madame Meredith presided over the kitchen on the chef's night off with superb expertise (though she frowns on guests who feed her dogs at table).' 'Particularly nice. Lovely food, and outstandingly good bathroom.' *(AH, Bill and Betty St Leger Moore, Janet McWhorter)*

Open: All year, except 15 November–5 December. Restaurant closed Monday.
Rooms: 5 double, 3 suites – 5 with bath, all with telephone. (1 room on ground floor.)
Facilities: 2 salons, bar, restaurant. Rose garden and paddock. ᵹ .
Location: At the hamlet of Chevalier. Nearest beach Coutances 12 km; Granville 23 km S. Parking.
Terms: Rooms 85–200 frs; full board 120 frs. Set meal: breakfast 15 frs; full *alc* 110 frs (excluding wine).

> Don't keep your favourite hotel to yourself. The Guide supports: it doesn't spoil.

VAISON-LA-ROMAINE, 84110 Vaucluse, Provence Map 9

Le Beffroi *Telephone:* (90) 36.04.71
Rue de l'Evêché

Vaison-la-Romaine is a charming small market town in the heart of the Rhône wine country, conveniently near the A7 autoroute, 27 kilometres from Orange. If you don't have a car, there is an adequate bus service from either Avignon or Orange, but no railway connection. There are considerable Roman remains, carefully tended, in the present city on the plain. Above it, high up in the old town, is a medieval castle and a cluster of old houses in terrifyingly steep and narrow streets. Here is *Le Beffroi*, an authentic old-fashioned rambling provincial French hotel. 'Monumental carved wooden armoire, terracotta flagged floor with Turkish rug in the bedroom; outside the shuttered windows, water tinkling from a mossy fountain. An elegant little salon adjoining a restaurant so full of happy diners that, as latecomers, we could not get in. Breakfast on a gravelled terrace with trees and flowerbeds, overlooking the town below.' So writes one correspondent. Another, who stayed longer at *Le Beffroi*, spoke enthusiastically about the meals, eaten in fine weather on the terrace, and also about the remarkably cheap prices. Don't be put off by twee names on the bedrooms, he warns: his, it seems, was called 'Le Cosy'. *(R B Chapman, Navin Sullivan)*

Open: 1 March–15 November. Restaurant closed all day Monday and Tuesday midday.
Rooms: 18 double, 3 single, 1 suite – 5 with bath, 10 with shower, all with telephone. (1 room on ground floor.)
Facilities: Salon, restaurant, function room. Garden, terrace. English spoken. &.
Location: 20 km from Orange, E of the RN7. Hotel is in the upper part of the town; parking.
Credit cards: American Express, Diners, Euro, Visa.
Terms: Rooms 50–185 frs; full board 192–330 frs. Set meals: breakfast 14–16 frs; lunch/dinner 70–110 frs; full *alc* 150 frs.

VAL D'ISÈRE, 73150 Savoie Map 8

Hôtel Le Kern *Telephone:* (79) 06.06.06

Not one of the larger hotels in Val d'Isère, and not one of the more pricey ones either. *Le Kern* is in the centre of town, but not on the main road, and has a regular following among professional people – doctors, lawyers, journalists. 'Monsieur and Madame Jeanbin do much to make their guests feel at home. Madame Jeanbin is herself responsible for the restaurant (called *La Grange*), at one end of which is an attractive bar. Downstairs, there is a small but comfortably furnished salon. The bedrooms are simply furnished, but service is good. The friendly atmosphere of the hotel, which is up a small alley, so quiet, the excellence of the food (no *en pension* rates – and dinner is always *à la carte*), and the efforts of the owners to ensure that their guests were well looked after, made it a very attractive place to stay in this expensive and crowded ski resort.' *(Anthony Wingate; warmly endorsed by H N Hall)*

Open: December–May.
Rooms: 18 – all with bath or shower and telephone.
Facilities: Salon, bar, restaurant.
Location: In town centre.
Terms: Rooms 85–160 frs.

VALENÇAY, 36600 Indre Map 8

Le Lion d'Or *Telephone:* (54) 00.00.87
Place du Marché

'Valençay is a good first night stop for those going south west, about 230
miles from Dieppe and 300 from Boulogne; it is 48 km south of the Loire.
Hardly bigger than a village but with a classical Renaissance château. The
inn is old, set round a courtyard virtually roofed in by a wisteria. Rooms
comfortable, large, unpretentious with plenty of hot water in a quite good
bathroom. Dinner as usual in France these days good value. Service not
bad: one waitress managed to serve four courses and coffee to a nearly full
dining room in one and a half hours. Wine list undistinguished, but
reliable if you avoid vin rouge de Valençay (we grow better reds in
England than this).' *(Kay and Arthur Woods)*

Open: All year. Restaurant closed January/February and Monday.
Rooms: 10 double, 2 single, 3 suites – 7 with bath, 2 with shower, all with
telephone. (All rooms on ground floor.)
Facilities: 2 salons, restaurant; conference facilities. English spoken. ◔.
Location: Central; Valençay is on the D956 from Blois, 40 km N of Châteauroux.
Parking.
Credit cards: American Express, Diners.
Terms: Rooms 50–75 frs; full board 95–135 frs. Set meals: breakfast 15 frs;
lunch/dinner 33–95 frs; full *alc* 100 frs.

VENCE, 06140 Alpes-Mar, Provence Map 9

Hôtel Diana *Telephone:* (93) 58.28.56
Avenue des Poilus

Not to be missed in Vence is Matisse's lovely Chapel of the Rosary; also
the cathedral. A correspondent also recommends, as the *Diana* only
serves breakfast, two good medium-priced restaurants in the centre of
town, *La Farigoule* and *Les Portiques*. 'An elegant and efficient small
hotel near the centre of Vence. The rooms, all with private bathrooms,
although small are beautifully designed and furnished. Ours (and I think
many of the others) had a small *cuisinette*. The hotel serves only breakfast,
a generous continental breakfast of croissants and brioches and plenty of
really hot coffee, accompanied by a copy of *Le Figaro*. There is a pleasant
bar and we found the service impeccable. Adequate garaging for all
guests.' *(Winston and Irene Moses)*

Open: All year.
Rooms: 23 double – all with bath, telephone; some with cooking facilities.
Facilities: Lift, TV room, library, bar. Garden. English spoken.
Location: 12 km from the beach; 200 metres from town centre; garage.
Credit cards: All major credit cards accepted.
Terms: Rooms 130–150 frs. Set meal: breakfast 15 frs.

VERNET-LES-BAINS, 66500 Pyrénées Orientales   **Map 8**

Hôtel des Deux Lions et Restaurant Le Thalassa   *Telephone:* (68) 05.55.42

Vernet is in the foothills of the eastern Pyrenees. A 2 km drive to the south and then a steep 30-minute climb on foot, brings you to the romantic Abbey of St-Martin-de-Canigou, lost in the lovely wooded hills. Today it is much used for Catholic retreats. Also strongly recommended is the Abbey of St-Michel-de-Cuza, near Prades, north-east of Vernet. 'A jolly, family hotel/restaurant at the entrance to this enchanting mountain village spa where Kipling once lived and helped found the Anglican Church of St George. It was also popular with Trollope. Nothing is too much trouble and the food very good indeed, imaginative and fresh. Garden and terrace for sunny days, big log fire in dining room in winter, etc. Rooms cosy, simple and clean. Good cheap wine list. A great find.' *(Hugh and Anne Pitt)*

Open: All year, except 15 November–10 December.
Rooms: 15 – 4 with bath, 9 with shower.
Facilities: Salon, TV room, restaurant, terrace, solarium. Garden (meals outdoors in fine weather). Swimming pool, riding, skiing, tennis nearby. English spoken.
Location: 40 km from Perpignan off the N116.
Credit card: Barclay/Visa.
Terms: Rooms 80–100 frs. Set meal: breakfast 10 frs. Special rate for stay of 10 days for Good Hotel Guide readers.

VERNEUIL-SUR-AVRE, 27130 Eure, Normandy   **Map 8**

Hostellerie du Clos   *Telephone:* (32) 32.21.81
98 rue de la Ferté-Vidame

'The hotel is a two-coloured brick château-type building (unusual, but charming) located in its own grounds (well-trimmed but not much) on the edge of this interesting old Norman town. It's on one of the best routes from Rouen to Chartres, 85 km south of the former and 56 km north-west of the latter. Our room was moderate in size but crammed full of furniture: two large stuffed chairs and a largish table (for serving breakfast), a desk (no writing paper) and a dresser with a colour telly. The room was attractively decorated, with everything sort of going together. We got a little box of chocolates with the room. The bathroom was almost as large as the bedroom, with lots of extras. The hotel was quiet, but there was a bit of noise from the N12. The best bit was dinner: delicious. Some of the best dishes include a terrine of langoustine, a breast of duck with a cider vinegar sauce (my mouth is watering thinking about it), a fillet of beef with pistachio sauce, delicate little potato pancakes and a strawberry mousse with raspberry sauce. The wine list included some bargains (relative); a very cheap Sancerre was delightful. Service was excellent. The proprietors were friendly and the bill was reasonable.' *(J Gazdak)*

Open: 15 January–15 December. Closed Monday, except public holidays.
Rooms: 9 double, 2 suites – 7 with bath, 4 with shower, all with telephone and TV. 14 rooms in annexe. (Some rooms on ground floor.)
Facilities: Salon, 2 dining rooms. Garden. English spoken.

323

Location: In town centre, just off the N12; parking.
Credit cards: American Express, Barclay/Visa, Diners.
Terms: Double rooms 250–350 frs; dinner, B & B 300–350 frs. Set meals:
breakfast 12.50 frs; lunch/dinner 100 frs.

VÉZAC, 24220 St-Cyprien, Dordogne   **Map 8**

Rochecourbe Manoir-Hôtel   *Telephone:* (53) 29.50.79

'Surpassed our expectations. The peace and tranquillity of its country
setting and the comfort of the rooms and bathrooms were superb. A spiral
staircase in the tower leads from the peaceful garden (reclining chairs for
drinks before and after dinner) to the large dining room, and then up
again to the seven bedrooms. From our room we looked across the valley
to the château at Beynac, and the loudest noise was the bleating of sheep
and singing of birds. Dinner is not provided in the evening, but their *petite
carte de soir* consisted of food ordered to our desire – *pâté*, omelette,
salad, salmon mayonnaise, cheese, fresh strawberries, etc. We cannot
speak too highly of the comfort and kindness provided by Monsieur and
Madame Roger.' *(Dr and Mrs P H Tattersall)*

Open: 1 April–5 November.
Rooms: 5 double, 1 single, 1 suite – 6 with bath, 1 with shower, all with telephone.
Facilities: TV room, dining room. Garden. 2 km from river; riding and swim-
ming nearby; excursions to châteaux, museums, caves, etc.
Location: 8 km from Sarlat. On the D5 between Sarlat and Beynac (Michelin
map No. 75).
Restriction: No children under 2.
Credit card: Diners.
Terms: Rooms 100–120 frs. Set meal: breakfast 20 frs; full *alc* 80 frs.

VÉZELAY, 89450 Yonne, Burgundy   **Map 8**

Poste et Lion d'Or   *Telephone:* (86) 33.21.23
Place du Champ-de-Foire   *Telex:* 800949

The small hill town of Vézelay, 50 km south of Auxerre, is one of the most
rewarding night stops for those driving up or down the A6. The medieval
town itself, faithfully conserved, is a pleasure in itself, but the supreme
glory of Vézelay is its basilica of Sainte-Madeleine, once one of the great
pilgrimage churches of France, and still a place for lay pilgrims in cars and
coaches, a splendidly airy Romanesque building, with a wealth of magnificent stone carvings. The *Poste et Lion d'Or* is the chief hotel of the town,
with something of the atmosphere of a large handsome country house, at
the foot of the hill leading to the cathedral. Bedrooms, which are
furnished to a high standard, look out over the countryside; the beds,
according to one visitor, had the best linen sheets she had ever slept in.
Rich classic Burgundian food is elegantly served in a charming dining
room. 'Completely agree with your 1981 entry. Good beds and linen.
Excellent food and service. Beautiful location. Only drawback: thin
bedroom walls, however typically French they may be.' *(T Crone; also
Daphne Pagnamenta, Navin Sullivan and others)*

Open: 18 April–2 November.
Rooms: 42 doubles, 5 suites – most with bath, all with telephone.
Facilities: Restaurant. Conference facilities. Garden.
Location: 13 km from Avallon; 50 km S of Auxerre; parking.
Terms: Rooms 160–320 frs, suites 420 frs. Set meals: breakfast 19 frs; lunch/dinner 100–190 frs.

VILLANDRY, 37300 Joué les Tours, Indre et Loire   Map 8

Le Cheval Rouge   *Telephone:* (47) 50.02.07

'Hotel on roadside 100 yards from Château Villandry (with the famous 16th-century formal gardens), in a very small village. Not much in village, but there's a road opposite the hotel leading (half a mile) to a quiet stretch of the Loire. Pleasant "pottering spot". Do not expect a rapturous welcome from Madame – she only smiled when we praised the place on leaving. However, she runs an efficient, small, modern country hotel with pleasant entrance lounge and clean bedrooms. The restaurant was *the feature*. It was spacious, air-conditioned and very clean. The food was "gastronomique" – even on the cheapest menu; it was superbly cooked and presented. This hotel was well worth an overnight stop – or would make a good base for visiting other châteaux in the Loire valley.' *(Janet Foulsham)*

Open: All year, except January/February and Monday out of season.
Rooms: 20 – all with bath or shower and telephone.
Facilities: Lounge, restaurant, air-conditioning; conference facilities. Garden.
Location: 10 km from Azay-le-Rideau; 20 km from Tours; parking.
Credit card: Barclay/Visa.
Terms: Rooms 80–175 frs; full board 170–265 frs. Set meals: breakfast 15.50 frs; lunch/dinner 60–145 frs.

VILLEFRANCHE-SUR-MER, 06230 Alpes-Mar, Provence   Map 9

Hôtel Welcome   *Telephone:* (93) 55.27.27
1 Quai Courbet   *Telex:* 470281F

Villefranche is a delightful, animated and fairly unspoilt fishing-port and seaport, despite being so near Nice and Monte Carlo. The *Welcome* is right on the harbour, and directly opposite the little fisherman's chapel so charmingly decorated by Cocteau. 'A pleasant, simple hotel belonging to the Mapotel chain who run it well. All rooms have sea views and bathrooms and most have balconies. As the hotel faces east these get the breakfast time sun. The hotel overlooks the *Rade* and there is the constant spectacle of the comings and goings of boats big and small. Good breakfasts. Auto-dialling phones (though they keep the necessary codes a big secret). Restaurant, called *St-Pierre*, on the quay level is pleasant. A rather boring bar with a narrow balcony on the floor. above. Slight noise at night from distant trains and a few over-revved motorbikes on the quay.' *(Geoffrey Sharp)*

Open: All year except 1 November–20 December.
Rooms: 32 – 28 with bath or shower, all with telephone.

Facilities: Lift, bar, restaurant; conference facilities; terrace. Beach and water sports nearby. English spoken.
Location: On the quay, near the port follow signs for Chapelle Cocteau; garage for 2 cars only.
Credit cards: All major credit cards accepted.
Terms: Rooms 140–310 frs; dinner, B & B 225–385 frs; full board 280–445 frs. Set meals: breakfast 18 frs; lunch/dinner 80–145 frs; full *alc* 110 frs.

VILLERS-COTTERÊTS, 02600 Aisne   Map 8

Hôtel Le Régent   *Telephone:* (23) 96.01.46
26 rue Général-Mangin

Villers-Cotterêts was once the natural stopping-place for travellers going north from Paris, for example to Reims or Belgium. Although a small town, it had 32 inns in the late 18th and early 19th centuries, many of them beautiful buildings with a dignified facade, a central entrance for horses and coaches and an inner courtyard. Most of the buildings are still there, but only one is used for its original purpose. The *Hôtel Le Régent* was operational from 1575 to 1864, but was used thereafter as stables until a certain Madame Peytavin restored it and reopened it in 1970. 'She showed great courage,' the hotel tells us, 'in giving back to this dwelling-place all its lustre and comfort. We must render homage to Mrs Peytavin for her dare, her perseverance, her good taste in decoration, leading to a successful result. Her work is really great and wonderful. So, we can't do more than *applaud* her strongly.'

We repeat last year's entry, applauded strongly by a recent visitor to whom the hotel had shown, she felt, exceptional courtesy. She had phoned to say that she was unavoidably detained and would be arriving very late: the hotel not only left a key out for her by the front door but also had kept supper for her.

'The *Hôtel Le Régent* is just the place for people who would like to stay in comfort and at very reasonable expense in a quiet country town, yet be within 50 miles of Paris. Villers-Cotterêts is where Alexandre Dumas *père* was born. The dozen or so rooms in the hotel are named after him and his relations. They are spacious, elegantly furnished and quiet – once the mild bustle of the market town has died down in the evening. There is comfortable sitting space within; and the courtyard is charming. Breakfast is served in the rooms, but other meals (and drinks – *Le Régent* is "dry") are taken at the *Hôtel de Commerce* on the other side of the road, which is under the same amiable management. Guests in both establishments are made to feel thoroughly welcome.' *(Alan and Jane Davidson; also Maggie Pearlstine)*

Open: All year, except 1–15 February. Restaurant closed 15 January–15 February.
Rooms: 13 double, 2 single, 1 suite – 8 with bath, 8 with shower, 10 with TV, all with telephone and radio. (3 rooms on ground floor.)
Facilities: Hall, lounge-cum-smoking room; some conference facilities. Large garden and courtyard. English spoken. ♿.
Location: Paris 70 km SW; Meaux 42 km S; Soissons 23 km NE. Hotel is central near church and château, and has garages.
Credit cards: Barclay/Visa, Diners.
Terms: Rooms 75–190 frs; B & B 87–107 frs; full board 180–200 frs. Set meals: lunch/dinner 48, 62 and 80 frs; full *alc* 63 frs. Reduced rates for children.

VONNAS, 01540 Ain	Map 8

La Mère Blanc
Telephone: (74) 50.00.10
Telex: 380776

'Vonnas is a small quiet *village fleuri* roughly half way between Mâcon and Bourg-en-Bresse, in an area of picturesque old villages and lakes in pleasant countryside. Although *La Mère Blanc* is classified by Michelin as a two-starred restaurant with rooms,* we feel it deserves an entry as a hotel as all the services are there. The rooms are extremely comfortable, almost all with their own bathrooms, overlooking the river Veyle. There is a swimming pool, gardens and several terraces. Obviously the hotel is secondary to the superb restaurant of Georges Blanc, who also owns vineyards, sells his own bottled wine in the hotel and in an adjoining boutique and writes cookery books. He himself advises on the choice of meal and wines before you are led through the immaculate kitchens (bigger than most restaurants) into the dining room, also beautifully furnished. The whole atmosphere is friendly, warm and welcoming, without the pretentions sometimes associated with the "grand chefs de France". Not cheap, but an excellent stopping place between Paris and the south, only 15 minutes from the A6 Autoroute.' *(Pat and Jeremy Temple)*

Open: All year, except January. Restaurant closed all day Wednesday and Thursday until 16.00 hrs.
Rooms: 23 double, 2 single, 4 suites – 20 with bath, 3 with shower, all with telephone and colour TV.
Facilities: Lift, salon, bar, dining room, terraces; on the river Veyle. 2½ acres grounds with garden, heated swimming pool and tennis court. English spoken. &.
Location: 19 km E of Mâcon, 24 km W of Bourg-en-Bresse.
Credit cards: American Express, Barclay/Visa, Diners.
Terms: Rooms 120–520 frs. Set meals: breakfast 30 frs; lunch/dinner 150–300 frs.

LA VOULTE-SUR-RHONE, 07800 Ardèche	Map 8

Hôtel de la Vallée
Quai Anatole France
Telephone: (75) 62.41.10

We continue to get mostly appreciative comments on this modern hotel in a pleasant position on the outskirts of La Voulte (19 km S of Valence), facing the river though there is a road in between. 'Don't be put off,' writes a reader, 'by the fact that the main road runs past. Although my bedroom was in the front, there was little or no noise from the road.' Not everyone agrees. Insomniacs beware! And there have been recent criticisms about declining standards in the restaurant and the upkeep of the house. Other readers, however, pay tribute to the agreeable decor, the welcome of the young resident owners, the excellent food – and the exceptional value for money. More reports welcome. *(C T Bailhache)*

Open: All year. Restaurant closed Saturday.
Rooms: 14 double, 3 single – 6 with bath, 4 with shower, all with telephone.

---

* *Note:* Since this report was written, *La Mère Blanc* has been reclassified by Michelin as a 3-starred, 4 red-turreted hotel.

Facilities: Salon, dining room, terrace.
Location: Leave the A7 at Valence-Sud exit, then take the N86 going S towards Nîmes. Hotel is on outskirts of La Voulte and has garage.
Credit cards: Barclay/Visa, Euro.
Terms: Rooms 65–140 frs; full board 120–140 frs. Set meals: breakfast 11 frs, lunch/dinner 35–70 frs.

Hotel Drei Könige, Bernkastel-Kues

Germany

ASCHHEIM, Nr Munich 8011   **Map 10**

Hotel-Gasthof zur Post   *Telephone:* (089) 903.20.27
Ismaningerstrasse 11

About 13 km east of Munich and 2.5 km from Munich airport. 'Very new and of an artistic standard I have not experienced anywhere. The rooms are more like elegant suites than ordinary hotel rooms, so cleverly are they constructed, furnished and subdivided. The decor, furnishing and carpeting belong to a super-luxury flat as one sees it in modern films rather than in normal life. The breakfast room is, in itself, a showpiece and like a modern museum, though the other dining room is of the local Bavarian cosy type. There is plenty of choice on the menu, and the service is not confined to unwilling acceptance of orders, but expanded to advice and explanation. The only drawback is the absence of a comfortable lounge, yet the individual rooms are so lavishly appointed that, even if a sitting room were provided, hardly anyone would prefer it to the rooms. Altogether, an unexpected gem – and very reasonably priced.' *(P G Bourne)*

Recent visitors, endorsing the above entry in all respects, mention one extra drawback: the hotel will take no credit cards, only currency. *(Michael and Eileen Wilkes)*

Open: All year, except Christmas–mid January.
Rooms: 20 double, 30 single – 18 with bath, 22 with shower, most with telephone.
Facilities: TV room, dining and breakfast rooms.
Terms: Rooms 30–59 DM. *Alc* 13–37 DM (excluding wine).

Gartenhotel Heusser   *Telephone:* (06322) 8491
Seebacherstrasse 50   *Telex:* 4/54889

'Bad Dürkheim, a spa with the character of an English market town, is on
the famous Weinstrasse, a few kms south of the motorway leading from
France via Saarbrucken to the German motorway at the Worms, Ludwig-
shafen, Mannheim junction. The *Gartenhotel Heusser* calls itself "an oasis
of calm and peace", and is really just that. About half a mile from the
town centre (towards Seebach), the *Heusser* consists of several buildings,
surrounded by a wonderful garden, and is bordered on one side by a large
vineyard. The hotel has a pleasant open-air pool and a splendid very large
indoor pool, kept crystal clear and clean; bathing-caps and rubber shoes,
both required, are all provided free, also a hair-drier. Service is a model of
efficiency. Breakfast is a vast self-service buffet in a room overlooking the
flower garden. The hotel has no restaurant at present *(but see note below)*;
however, in about 10 minutes' walk or two minutes' drive you can reach a
gemütlich restaurant in the tiny village of Seebach with the peculiar name
of *Käsbüro* (cheese-office).' *(P G Bourne)*

Open: All year, except 20 December–20 January.
Rooms: 85 double – all with bath, shower and telephone.
Facilities: Lift, hall with bar, lounge, 3 TV rooms, breakfast room; conference
facilities; terrace. Garden, heated indoor and outdoor pools, sauna, solarium. &.
Location: 1 km from town centre towards Seebach. Garages and large car park.
Coming by the B271 from Neustadt, turn left at Amtsplatz.
Terms: B & B 47–65 DM. The hotel will start to serve meals in 1982: prices not
yet known. Reduced rates for children under 10.

Mönchs Posthotel   *Telephone:* (07083) 2002
Doblerstrasse 2   *Telex:* 07245123

'A traditional old posting house in an attractive little Black Forest spa
town, really a village. Very peaceful, surrounded by forests with a small
river running through its gardens into the village part across the road
where one can taste the spa water, warm or cold (actually rather nasty!).
Everywhere there are flowers; baskets of geraniums in all colours cascad-
ing down every house and wall. The welcome was extremely friendly and
the room excellent. Deep pile carpet everywhere, beautifully fitted
bathroom with bathrobe, slippers, bath essence, shower hat, etc., immaculately clean and very comfortable. The beds all have duvets which
we find a real pleasure. There is a dining room which appeared to be for
guests *en pension* but we ate in the adjoining restaurant, *Klosterschänke*,
very popular locally as well, which was excellent. It has a well-deserved
Michelin star. Breakfast was lavish, part chosen from a central buffet,
part served. The gardens had a swimming pool, bar area for summer
months and, everywhere, flowers.' *(Pat and Jeremy Temple)*

Open: All year.
Rooms: 30 double, 20 single, 10 suites – 35 with bath, 15 with shower, all with
telephone and colour TV.

Facilities: Hall, salon, TV room, bar, restaurant, breakfast terrace. Garden with heated swimming pool. 9-hole golf course close by. English spoken.
Location: Central; parking.
Credit card: American Express.
Terms: Rooms 60–90 DM per person; B & B 70–102 DM. Set meals: breakfast 12 DM; lunch 30 DM; dinner 38 DM; full *alc* 65 DM. Reduced rates for groups out of season, and for children; special meals for children.

BAMBERG, 8600 Bayern Map 10

Hotel Garni Alt Bamberg *Telephone:* (0951) 26.66.7
Habergasse 11

Bamberg is one of the showplace medieval towns of southern Germany, as atmospheric as Rothenburg and Dinkelsbühl, but less commercialized than either. There are many larger and posher hotels than the *Alt Bamberg* but this would be a natural choice if you were seeking the *echt* Bamberg experience. The rooms are pleasant and airy and look out on to a winding old narrow street, full of other houses of the same period. There is very little noise, though you are only a short distance from the high Domplatz, with the town's beautiful cathedral, its world-famous Reiter sculpture and its elegant Residenz. *(Louise Linn)*

Open: All year. Restaurant closed 1–15 August.
Rooms: 9 double, 11 single, 1 suite – 5 with bath, 8 with shower, 21 with telephone.
Facilities: Breakfast room which serves as living room, with TV. English spoken.
Location: Central, near Grüner Markt; look for Elefantenhaus when trying to find it.
Terms: B & B 35–80 DM; full board 60–105 DM. Set meals: lunch 12.50 DM; supper 10.50 DM. Full *alc* 25 DM.

BAYREUTH 8580 Bayern Map 10

Bayerischer Hof *Telephone:* (0921) 23.06.1
Bahnhofstrasse 14 *Telex:* 642737

'The *Bayerischer Hof* has probably the best facilities of the hotels available in this famous little town in northern Bavaria, formerly Franconia. The staff are always courteous and helpful. I have stayed there in the summer, and in the depths of snowy winter; and have enjoyed comfortable, elegant rooms, an excellent heated indoor swimming pool, and luncheon and dinner menus which include plenty of local dishes. Franconian wine occupies a fairly large section of the wine list, and justifiably so. The hotel is in the centre of the town and one minute's walk from Bayreuth railway station, but the trains are never heard. During the *Wagnerfest* the hotel is likely to be full of visiting notables, but at other times the town resumes its normal quiet rhythm, with music in the old churches and the baroque opera house, its new University, and its surrounding countryside of rolling hills, low mountains and forest slopes and slumbering villages.' *(John Spencer)*

Open: All year. Restaurant closed Sunday out of season.
Room: 62 – most with bath or shower, all with telephone and TV.

Facilities: Lift, Hans Sachs Room, Spanish-style cellar restaurant, roof-garden restaurant, conference room. Indoor swimming pool, sauna. Garden with sun-terrace and small swimming pool. English spoken.
Location: Central, near station; garage.
Credit cards: Access/Euro/Mastercard, American Express, Diners.
Terms: B & B 40–98 DM. Set meals: lunch/dinner 16–27 DM; full *alc* from 35 DM. Reduced rates for children: 30% reduction when sharing parents' room; 10% in own room; special meals provided.

BERLIN 15   Map 10

Hotel Am Zoo   *Telephone:* (030) 88.30.91
Kurfürstendamm 25   *Telex:* 0183835 zooho d

'It's not often one can find a hotel slap in the middle of a famous kind of street-life where one can also get some sleep. We asked for a courtyard or well-facing room. I don't know how much rest one would get in the front rooms; I imagine the penance for a free perpetual circus outside the windows would be a very high noise level. But the courtyard-facing room we got was large, high-ceilinged, airy and quiet. We could surge along the Kurfürstendamm among the buskers and street-café eaters and then duck back to the tranquillity whenever we felt tired. We were within a block or two of theatres, the good bookshops and the station at which one takes the Underground for East Berlin, the obligatory one-day pass that enables one to go and see the Berliner Ensemble. The hotel staff – all English-speaking – were outstandingly helpful. Not a "charming" hotel; but an extremely comfortable and convenient place to stay when what one wants is to experience the honest vulgar centre of the city.' *(Nadine Gordimer; also Professor O Pick)*

Open: All year.
Rooms: 52 double, 89 single, 2 suites – 115 with bath, 20 with shower, 35 with TV, all with telephone and radio.
Facilities: Lift, salon, TV room, bar, dining room (hotel guests only), 2 conference rooms; courtyard. English spoken.
Location: In city centre; parking.
Credit cards: All major credit cards accepted.
Terms: B & B 80–108 DM; full board 40 DM added to B & B price. Full *alc* 30 DM. Reduced rates for children under 7.

BERNKASTEL-KUES, 5550 Rheinland-Pfalz   Map 10

Hotel Drei Könige   *Telephone:* (06531) 2327
1 Bahnhofstrasse

'An old-established and spacious hotel alongside the river Mosel on the Kues side of town, with most of the bedrooms offering excellent views of Bernkastel and its castle and vineyards. The ground floor has been let to a clothing store, and the *Drei Könige* operates as a *hotel garni* – bed and breakfast only – on the upper floors. The rooms are well-furnished and spacious, and they serve an ample breakfast. There were many good restaurants nearby. Prices were very reasonable.' *(Bruce I Nathan)*

Open: All year, except 6 January–March.

Rooms: 36 double, 6 single – 9 with bath, 14 with shower, 22 with telephone, 2 with TV, 23 with radio.
Facilities: Lift, TV room, lounge, bar, breakfast room; wine cellar with dancing each weekend. Garden. English spoken.
Location: 200 m from town centre, on the Mosel; parking.
Credit card: Euro.
Terms: B & B 55–58 DM (single), 90–110 DM (double).

BREMEN-HORN   Map 10

Landhaus Louisenthal   *Telephone:* (0421) 23.67.16
Leher Heerstrasse 105

'We found this hotel in the suburbs of Bremen outstanding in value and comfort. The building and grounds were beautiful, and the bedrooms had solid comfortable furnishings, plus shower and toilets; the whole place was spotless. At present it is a *hotel garni* (no main meals served), but our breakfast was a generous continental one, more like the Dutch than the German. They plan to open a restaurant in 1982. It was near the motorway and the hotel had a parking area as well as its own garage. Bus and tram services passed the door. The hotel is mainly a family concern, and the staff were friendly and helpful.' *(Miss M Byrne)*

Open: All year.
Rooms: 12 double, 26 single, 1 suite – all with shower and telephone.
Facilities: Salon, TV room, dining room; conference facilities. Garden. &.
Location: 6 km from centre of Bremen. Garage and car park.
Credit cards: Diners.
Terms: B & B 53 DM (single), 74 DM (double).

ERLANGEN, 8520 Bayern   Map 10

Hotel-Garni Rokokohaus   *Telephone:* (09131) 22.87.1
Theaterplatz 13

'Erlangen is a pleasant town, 20 km from Nürnberg, or 15 minutes by bus or train. It has a large university, is the headquarters of Siemens Electric and also has a fine castle and a beautiful rococo theatre. I found the *Rokokohaus* when all the better hotels in Nürnberg were full because of a trade fair. It was built over 200 years ago, and is the only building in Erlangen with a pure rococo facade. It is said that the Markgräfin Marie Caroline Sophie of Brandenburg-Culmbach used the house as a hunting lodge. It was rebuilt as a hotel 15 years ago, with charm and taste. Excellent bathrooms. There's a park in front, and a large parking lot round the corner. The Opera House-Theatre is just a few steps away (the Nürnberg Opera frequently performs in Erlangen) and many of the guest stars stay here.' *(John J Grenz)*

Open: All year.
Rooms: 12 double, 16 single, 2 suites – 7 with bath, 21 with shower, all with telephone, radio and colour TV. 6 rooms in annexe, with kitchenette. (2 rooms on ground floor.)
Facilities: Lobby, salon, breakfast room; conference facilities for 6–12 people. Courtyard. No restaurant, but plenty in neighbourhood. English spoken.

Location: In town centre; parking.
Credit cards: All major credit cards accepted.
Terms: B & B 49–72.50 DM.

GOSLAR HARZ, 3380 Niedersachsen **Map 10**

Hotel Kaiser Worth *Telephone:* (05321) 21.11.1
Markt 3 *Telex:* 095 3874

'When about to cross to the GDR, spend the vigil night not in Hanover or Helmstedt, but in this 15th-century Gothic hotel at the foot of the Harz mountains. It would be easy to spend a week, but don't linger too long, as the lead mines/works on the edge of the newer part of the town are reportedly lowering the life expectancy of the population! But this dignified, noble building on the medieval town square is one of those places that, once seen, cannot be passed by for any other hostelry in town. Large, airy rooms with firm comfortable beds, good modern bathrooms or showers, spacious lounges and corridors furnished with beautiful antiques and paintings, excellent food, either local specialities, or, if you must, international dishes, with a long and fairly distinguished cellar of German wines fairly priced, make this a marvellous place to fortify oneself for the rigours of the New Order across the man-traps and barbed wire. There is an open-air café, Gothic cellar evenings, dancing (German style), and all the delights and activities of the Harz mountains and nearby resorts to satisfy every whim. And the old town itself is a calm, walled Gothic *Stadt* of twisty alleyways, cobbled lanes, swift streams and countless beautiful buildings of every shape, size and purpose. Not cheap (rooms overlooking the square are 25% dearer) by German standards, but a haven after the expense of London or the excesses of the Rhine or Ruhr cities.' *(T J Wiseman)*

Open: All year.
Rooms: 62 – 42 with bath, all with telephone and TV.
Facilities: Salon, TV room, bar, restaurant; conference facilities.
Location: Central, in pedestrian zone; parking.
Credit cards: American Express, Diners, Euro.
Terms: B & B 47–84 DM.

HAMBURG 2000 **Map 10**

Hotel Prem *Telephone:* (040) 24.22.11
An der Alster 9 *Telex:* 2163115

The *Prem* is an elegant smallish hotel, one of the few in the medium-price range in the centre of the city. It is prettily furnished, has a particularly agreeable location looking out over the Alster, and it also has its own large and delightful garden at the back; a bonus for the motorist is that you can park outside the hotel, and the hotel has its own garage adjoining. Recommended as good value for money. *(Alan Ross, John Rowlands)*

Open: All year. Restaurant closed Sunday and holidays.
Rooms: 26 double, 23 single – 42 with bath, all with telephone, radio and TV.
Facilities: Lounge, TV room, bar, restaurant; conference facilities. Garden for fine-weather meals or drinks. English spoken.

Location: Central; garage.
Credit cards: American Express, Barclay/Visa, Diners, Euro.
Terms: B & B 66.50–149 DM; dinner, B & B 91.50–174 DM; full board 110.50–193 DM. Set meals: lunch 20 DM, dinner 22 DM. Full *alc* 35 DM. Special meals for children.

HINTERZARTEN, 7824 Baden-Württemberg   Map 10

Hotel Weisses Rössle   *Telephone:* (07652) 1411
Freiburgerstrasse 38

'There is a local slogan in this holiday resort – "The guest is our king" – and this is certainly the ambience that pervades this little place set high up in the Black Forest. One has only to leave the immediate vicinity of the town to find oneself at the start of several thousand kilometres of walks, 300 round Hinterzarten alone, all clearly colour-marked with distances, at every forest or glade intersection. Hinterzarten is only a few miles from some of the finest vineyards in southern Germany, particularly the Kaiserstuhl. The charming town of Freiburg is only 20 minutes by car – and there is an attractive 9-hole golf course on the road to Freiburg. The best time to visit the area is in the spring or autumn, or in the skiing months – omitting the high summer season when accommodation and roads are very full. In winter, road and forest walks are snow-cleared every morning so that walkers need not be housebound while skiers enjoy the slopes.

'The *Weisses Rössle* is first-class in every sense of the word. Its most important asset is the attitude of everyone from the owner-proprietor, Heinz Zimmermann, and his wife Urda, through to the attendants at the swimming pool. There are three dining rooms, two mostly used by residents, and the rooms are all extremely well-furnished. They serve a mighty German breakfast which makes lunch almost superfluous.' *(Denis Morris; also Janet Leipris, Tony Barnes)*

Open: All year.
Rooms: 29 double, 15 single, 23 suites – 43 with bath, 13 with shower, some with radio, all with telephone; TV and baby-listening on request.
Facilities: Lift, salon, TV room, games room, 3 restaurants; conference facilities; music daily except Mondays; beauty salon and hairdresser; indoor swimming pool and sauna. Terrace, garden with tennis court, volleyball, children's play area. English spoken.
Location: 29 km E of Freiburg on B31. Parking.
Credit card: Euro.
Terms: B & B 40–120 DM. Set meals: lunch/dinner 30 DM; full *alc* 40 DM. Off season reductions. Special meals for children.

LINZ AM RHEIN, 5460 Rhein   Map 10

Hotel Franz Josef   *Telephone:* (02644) 2332
Rheinstrasse 25

Linz am Rhein is a small town on the east bank of the Rhine, 28 km upriver from Bonn. It's something of a showplace, full of lovingly preserved half-timbered houses, and the fast-flowing Rhine is very much one of the attractions of the town, with its endless stream of colourful barge traffic. The *Franz Josef* is more a Gasthaus than a hotel: it's been run for more than two centuries by members of the Zimmermann family, and the present Herr Zimmermann is a chef, and a good one, with a following among the locals: not *haute cuisine*, but hearty fare at a very reasonable price. The house and its rooms have great character, and the tariff is decidedly modest. Since our original (1978) entry, many readers have written to confirm the friendly welcome of this inn. *(Heather Howliston, J Dixey, Michael and Eileen Wilkes)*

Open: All year, except June and December. Restaurant closed Tuesday.
Rooms: 3 double, 1 single.
Facilities: 2 lounges (1 with TV), dining room. English spoken.
Location: Central; parking.
Credit card: Euro.
Terms: B & B 27 DM. Set meals: lunch from 10.50 DM; dinner from 12 DM; full *alc* from 22 DM. Reduced rates and special meals for children.

MEERSBURG BODENSEE, 7758 Baden-Württemberg **Map 10**

Hotel Zum Bären *Telephone:* (07532) 6044
Marktplatz 11

'In our view, Meersburg is the prettiest town on the Bodensee (Lake Constance): romantic old castle, "new" pink baroque castle, crowded together in the Altstadt (old town) on a high bluff above the lake. The *Zum Bären*, which has been an inn since the early 17th century, is on the market square on the right when you enter the city gate from the north. This Marktplatz is one of the glories of the town, with three remarkably handsome old streets leading off it. Large comfortable rooms. Alpine furniture, beamed ceilings. We enjoyed just looking out through the lace curtains at the busy market square. Good Weinstube.' *(Jane Treat-Baum; also B W Ribbons)*

Open: March–November. Dining room closed Monday.
Rooms: 12 double, 4 single – 14 with shower, some overlooking the Marktplatz.
Facilities: Dining room, wine bar. English spoken.
Location: In town centre; parking.
Credit card: Euro.
Terms: B & B 29–42 DM. Set meals: lunch/dinner 15–20 DM; full *alc* 30 DM. (No *pension* terms.)

MUNICH, 8000 Bayern **Map 10**

Marienbad Hotel *Telephone:* (089) 59.55.85 and 59.17.03
Barerstrasse 11

'This bed and breakfast hotel is situated near the centre of the city (only a few minutes' walk away from the beautiful traffic-free shopping area), very close to the Karolinenplatz from which you must approach it (access road only) and which, with its tall metal column, is an obvious landmark. It is in a quiet situation at the back of an office block which has replaced the bombed part of a well-known pre-war hotel of the same name. The present hotel is the bedroom annexe of the old one and combines modern amenities with the size of rooms found in old buildings. The rooms are well-furnished and well-kept. There is ample parking space. The only meal provided is breakfast, but in a town like Munich with its many restaurants, this is hardly a disadvantage. The owner, Peter Conrad Grüner, and his wife Annemarie run the place and are most helpful in every way.' *(Mr and Mrs P E Roland; endorsed by N D Bain)*

Open: All year.
Rooms: 15 double, 9 single, 1 suite – 3 with bath, 17 with shower, all with telephone.
Facilities: Lift, salon with TV. Park behind hotel. English spoken.
Location: Central; approach from Karolinenplatz; parking nearby.
Terms: B & B 47–80 DM. Reduced rates for children.

MUNICH, 8000 Bayern   **Map 10**

Hotel Biederstein   *Telephone:* (089) 39.50.72
Keferstrasse 18

Readers have once again written appreciatively about Countess Harach's small hotel in the Schwabing district, about 1 km from the centre of Munich but close to the city's Englischer Garten, equivalent of Hyde Park. The building is modern (1970), but the house is full of the Countess's own antique furniture. 'A snip in the light of current big city prices,' writes one satisfied visitor. 'Our room was small but well-appointed, excellent bedside reading lamps and remarkably quiet. The staff were affable and efficient.' Another reader mentioned an additional reason for choosing the *Biederstein* – the fact that one's car can be kept in the underground garage. *(Michael Wilkes, Edward Hugo, Katie Plowden)*

Open: All year.
Rooms: 16 double, 13 single, 3 suites – all with bath and telephone, TV by arrangement.
Facilities: Lift, TV room, breakfast room; some conference facilities. Small garden. English spoken.
Location: Central; underground garage (5 DM).
Credit card: American Express.
Terms: B & B 55–74 DM. Set meals: lunch 20 DM; supper 15 DM. Reduced rates for children.

MUNICH, 8000 Bayern   **Map 10**

Hotel an der Oper   *Telephone:* (089) 22.87.11
2 Falkenturmstrasse 10   *Telex:* 522588

'Unobtrusively tucked away in a small sidestreet off the famous and beautiful Maximilianstrasse and, as its name suggests, much frequented by members of the Opera House. Don't be surprised to hear (as we did to our delight) a soprano warm up before her performance. Rooms are not large, but have every modern amenity. The hotel is very reasonably priced, but one has to book well in advance. It has, so far as I know, no public rooms apart from a smallish entrance hall with a living room corner. But it has a most excellent though expensive restaurant, *La*

Bouillabaisse.' (Katie Plowden; also – with reservations about street noises – Professor O Pick)

Open: All year.
Rooms: 55 – all with bath, telephone and radio.
Facilities: Lift, reception-cum-lounge, TV room, restaurant; conference facilities. &.
Location: Central.
Credit cards: American Express, Diners, Euro.
Terms: B & B 50–87 DM.

ROTHENBURG OB DER TAUBER, 8803 Bayern   Map 10

Hotel Adam   *Telephone:* (09861) 2364
Burggasse 29

'An excellent small hotel in this very attractive medieval walled town (see next entry). It is quiet, lovely to look at, and overlooks at the back the old city walls and public gardens. Rooms beautifully furnished with antiques. The proprietor, Hans Karl Adam, is a "character", who gives cookery lessons on German TV, and writes cookery books. Food therefore was good, but homely rather than gastronomic. The prices were reasonable.' *(A G Don)*

Open: 1 April–31 October.
Rooms: 8 double, 5 single – 3 with bath, 10 with shower and WC, all with telephone.
Facilities: Restaurant.
Location: 33 km from Ansbach.
Terms: B & B 42–58 DM. Set meals: 15–30 DM.

ROTHENBURG OB DER TAUBER, 8803 Bayern   Map 10

Hotel Eisenhut   *Telephone:* (09861) 2041
Herrngasse 3–5   *Telex:* 61367
        Reservations: In UK (01) 629 9792;
             In USA (800) 223 5652

'Romantic Road is a relatively modern touristic name for one of the oldest routes in Germany. It runs from Würzburg in the north of Bavaria to Augsburg in the south via some of the most fascinating of Germany's medieval towns. Rothenburg on the river Tauber is the most beautiful and famous of them all, a perfectly preserved and living town of tall gabled houses, old churches and cobbled streets, surrounded by the ancient city wall.

'The *Hotel Eisenhut* is very much a part of the past and present life of Rothenburg. As a hotel it is little more than a hundred years old, but the four houses which now form the hotel date back to the Middle Ages. It stands in the Herrngasse, a superb old street leading off the central market place, and over the years it has been developed as a luxury hotel in ways which enhance rather than detract from its historic character. All the 85 bedrooms have been beautifully and individually decorated. Almost all have baths. The public rooms are furnished with antiques and original paintings, and there is as much artistry in the cuisine as in the decor.

338

Considering the quality of accommodation, food and service, prices are not exorbitant. The special quality of this hotel is its personal warmth. The present owner is Frau Georg Pirner who arranges all the table decorations herself and for special occasions these include ornaments of exquisite old Meissen. The Hanover-born manager Karl Prüsse has the sensitivity of a musical conductor for the balance of clientele and staff. I enjoyed the restful atmosphere, the food and wine, but even more being made to feel such a welcome guest.' (*Penelope Turing; also Charles Oberdorf; A and B W Williams*)

Open: 1 March–10 January.
Rooms: 63 double, 19 single, 3 suites – all with telephone, radio and TV on request. 20 rooms in annexe.
Facilities: Lift, salon, TV room, 2 restaurants; conference room. Garden, terrace. English spoken. &.
Location: 33 km from Ansbach. Hotel is central; parking.
Credit cards: All major credit cards accepted.
Terms: B & B 75–125 DM. Full *alc* 55 DM. Reduced rates for children; special meals on request.

RÜDESHEIM-ASSMANNSHAUSEN, 6220 Hessen   Map 10

Hotel Krone
Rheinuferstrasse 10

Telephone: (067 22) 2036

The *Krone* has been a Rhineside inn since 1541. It was small then, and is now a substantial hotel with a famous and *soigné* restaurant. There are in fact two separate buildings facing the river, each with well-furnished rooms of varying sizes, many with balconies overlooking the well-kept gardens and the changing river scene. The hotel is well-staffed and well-served with lounges. One British publisher, returning debilitated from the Book Fair, calls it his post-Frankfurt haven. But light sleepers should be warned: there are occasional rumbles of trains passing behind the hotel, and the Rhine traffic in front is noisy too. (*Paul Langridge, Timothy Benn and others*)

Open: 15 March–15 November.
Rooms: 50 double, 32 single, 2 suites – 32 with bath, 16 with shower, all with telephone. (Some rooms on ground floor.)
Facilities: Lift, salons, TV room, bar, restaurant, large terrace/restaurant; conference facilities. Garden with swimming pool and bar. English spoken. &.
Location: 28 km from Wiesbaden; 75 km from Frankfurt airport; central; parking.
Credit cards: All major credit cards accepted.
Terms: B & B 50–100 DM. Full *alc* 45 DM.

TRENDELBURG, 3526 Hessen   Map 10

Burgotel

Telephone: (05675) 1021
Telex: 0994812

'A not-over-restored medieval castle, with great atmosphere. Most of the staff have some English and all make you most welcome. My room was large, the outlook superb, and (if you don't mind just a shower) most

339

comfortable; they even provided a chaise longue as well as a minibar. Peaceful. Good food by German standards. Good centre in delightful countryside.' *(T M Wilson)*

Open: 3 March–4 January.
Rooms: 25 – all with bath or shower, telephone and TV.
Facilities: Salon, TV room, wine bar, restaurant; conference facilities. Garden with swimming pool, tennis, riding. English spoken.
Location: 35 km N of Kassel on N83.
Credit cards: American Express, Diners.
Terms: B & B from 64 DM.

Minos Beach, Ayios Nikolaos

Greece

Claire's House   *Telephone:* Athens 322 9284
16a, Frynichou Street

'An admirable establishment. I won't describe it as an hotel; it is a *pension* run on family house lines. The rooms are absolutely clean and furnished with extreme simplicity, but large, high-ceilinged and restful. No meals are normally provided, with the exception of an excellent breakfast. The *pension* is run by Claire Anglias, a nice Englishwoman with two delightful children, and her Greek husband, Manos, who has a good command of English and is a tower of strength and helpfulness to all. The house is in the quiet part of the Plaka; within three minutes' walk you are at the foot of the Acropolis, and two minutes in the other direction you are sitting in the shade of the Royal Gardens. Each room has a shining wash-basin, and on each floor there are two or three hot showers, separate lavatory and sink in which you may wash your smalls. You are allowed to hang them out to dry on the sunny roof, where they swing happily in full view of the Acropolis on one side, and Mount Lykabettus on the other. Not perhaps to be recommended to those of inflexible habits requiring constant service and reassurance, but marvellous for anyone wanting to stay economically in the old, interesting part of Athens, with several good, cheapish tavernas close by.' *(Elsa Pomeroy)*

Open: All year.
Rooms: 22 double, 2 single, 1 suite – 8 rooms with wash-basin. 10 rooms in annexe.

Facilities: Breakfast room. Small garden for breakfast in summer.
Location: Central; opposite Hadrian's Arch turn left; parking.
Terms: B & B 450–700 drs. Reductions in low season.

ATHENS Map 15

Saint George Lykabettus Hotel   *Telephone:* Athens (01) 790 711
Kleomenous 2, Platia Dexamenis, Kolonaki   *Telex:* HEAM 214253

A de-luxe hotel in the fashionable Kolonaki section of the city, at the foot of Lykabettus Hill and close to Constitution Square. High, cool and quiet, with beautiful views. 'A lovely friendly place.' *(Hugh Leonard; also A W Gardes)*

Open: All year.
Rooms: 124 double, 21 single, 5 suites – all with bath, telephone, radio and tea-making facilities; TV on request. (Some rooms on ground floor.)
Facilities: Lift; residents' lounge, lounges with TV, bar, snack bar, restaurant, grill room, roof garden; nightly entertainment in restaurant; dancing on the roof. Swimming pool. &.
Location: At the foot of Lykabettus Hill; garage.
Credit cards: All major credit cards accepted.
Terms (excluding tax): Rooms 1,729–2,122 drs (single), 2,514–2,907 drs (double), 4,398–7,720 drs (suites). Set meals: breakfast 155 drs; lunch/dinner 552 drs.

AYIOS NIKOLAOS, Crete Map 15

Minos Beach   *Telephone:* (0841) 22 345
Telex: 262214

The *Minos Beach* is not for those seeking the air-conditioned comforts of an international-style luxury hotel, of which there are now several on Crete. It is a collection of bungalows set in beautiful gardens with hibiscus and geraniums, a huge swimming pool and children's play area. In the main building there are suites, several large and beautiful salons, a bar, dining room and terrace for eating out in good weather. Sadly, Ayios Nikolaos has expanded around the hotel since it was built, and the view towards the centre of the town is unattractive, but on the other side you can sit peacefully on the little sunbathing areas built on the rocks with chairs and umbrellas, you can swim in the clear water, and waterski, windsurf and sail. The bungalows are simple and vary considerably in standard. Two correspondents had to ask to be moved several times. A more satisfied customer writes: 'Breakfast is served at your own bungalow; friendly waiters seemed happy to bring a second pot of coffee. Lunch is the best meal, a beautiful and delicious cold buffet. We were there at the very beginning of the season. Possibly with not too much pressure on the facilities it was at its best. I can imagine with a full hotel having trouble finding a jetty to lie on by the sea or a spot by the pool.' Other correspondents found the waiters unfriendly and bar service slow; not everyone felt they had had value for money. More reports please.

Open: All year. Restaurant closed 11 January–28 February.
Rooms: 124 double, 2 single, 4 suites – 96 with bath, 30 with shower, all with telephone.

Facilities: 2 lounges, separate TV room, snack bar, indoor and outdoor restaurants, games room. Spacious gardens with heated swimming pool, mini-golf, tennis court. Disco 300 metres from hotel. Direct access to private rock and sand sea-bathing and all forms of water sports.
Location: 68 km from Heraklion; 800 metres from town centre; parking.
Credit cards: All major credit cards accepted.
Terms: Single rooms: half board 3,721–3,939 drs, full board 5,295–5,567 drs; double rooms: half board 6,026–7,024 drs for 2 people, full board 7,313–8,316 drs for 2 people; suites: half board 7,301–8,169 drs for 2 people, ful board 8,691–9,381 drs for 2 people. Set meals: lunch/dinner 650 drs; full *alc* 900 drs. Reduced rates for children sharing parents' room; special meals provided.

CHANIA, Crete Map 15

Hotel Doma *Telephone:* Chania (0821) 21 772
124 Venizelou Street

The *Doma* is on the coast – though there is a road between it and the sea wall, so front rooms are noisy – about 1 km from the centre of town and Chania's colourful and enchanting harbour. It's a neo-classical house of some breeding – a former British consulate skilfully converted. Balustraded stairs lead to a terrace with fragments of broken statuary. All the rooms have showers; some have balconies overlooking the sea. The public rooms have fine Cretan furniture and antiques, which help to give the *Doma*, personally managed by its owner, Irene Valirakis, something of the feel of a private home. On the top floor there is a long breakfast room which doubles as a bar in the evening. If asked, the owner will serve drinks and hot snacks there during the day.

'Although the rooms are by no means luxurious, and the hotel is showing signs of age, it mysteriously adds up to more than the sum of its parts. It stuck in my mind as few other hotels in Crete did, and I would be inclined to head straight for it if I were in Chania again. The final overriding impression is that it has not only great individuality, but also great charm, and is entirely without pretensions. The personal touches: splendid antique furniture – some with quite a story behind it – the photographs, pictures, ornaments, plants, archaeological fragments, and so on all seem genuinely integral elements of the house. You have the feeling, especially after you have met the owner, that you are visiting a tasteful but well-loved home.' *(LH)*

Open: All year.
Rooms: 26 double, 2 single, 1 suite (2 more planned) – all with shower and telephone, some with balconies overlooking the sea. (Some rooms on ground floor.)
Facilities: Lift, lounge, breakfast room-cum-snack bar, residents' suite. Terrace, garden, small beach. Laundry facilities.
Location: 20 minutes' walk from town centre on airport road overlooking sea; main beach 20 minutes' drive. No private car park, but parking space available near hotel. Buses stop directly outside.
Terms: B & B 1,040–1,125 drs (single), 1,515–1,780 drs (double), 2,454–2,905 drs (suites).

> DO IT NOW! Send us a report on the hotel you are staying in.

Hotel Castello   *Telephone:* (0661) 30 184
                                                 Telex: 0332136 Cast.Gr.

'In my opinion the *Castello* is the most attractive hotel on Corfu despite not having a pool and possibly being less lush than some of the larger and newer establishments. But what it lacks in facilities – and it is really only the pool that's missing – it more than makes up for in service, general ambience and personal care and trouble taken by the management. It is a mock-Florentine castle, formerly a summer residence of George II of Greece, and now converted into a luxury-class medium-sized hotel about 12 km from the town of Corfu. It's been a labour of love by the owners who, together with other members of the family, subsequently built a large hotel on the other side of the island (*Grand Hotel*, Glyfada). There is a large terrace with a fine view of a pine and cedar-wooded valley and the sea, an open-air restaurant for lunch and dinner, and 25 acres of park and well-tended garden. The public rooms are spacious with period furniture, rather English in feeling. There are two annexes in the grounds: they are modern, and one has a restaurant and dance floor, but both have something of the feel of the older building. There are also tennis courts in the grounds, and the hotel has a stretch of private beach about a kilometre away with aquatic sports facilities and a night club; a minibus plies regularly between hotel and beach where lunch can be taken. The "slightly fusty" air which one visitor commented on is in my view one of the attractions of the place.' *(Uli Lloyd-Pack)*

Open: March–November.
Rooms: 60 double, 12 single – 59 with bath, all with telephone. About half the rooms in 2 annexes.
Facilities: Lounges, TV room, bar, indoor and outdoor restaurants, terrace. 25 acres quiet parkland and gardens; tennis courts; 500 metres from sand and shingle beach where the hotel has a beach-restaurant, night club and all kinds of water sports – transport by minibus.
Location: 12 km from Corfu town. Garage; parking.
Credit cards: American Express, Diners.
Terms (excluding tax): Rooms 2,040–3,712 drs. Set meals: breakfast 151 drs; lunch/dinner 546 drs.

DELPHI   **Map 15**

Hotel Vouzas   *Telephone:* (0265) 923 7740/2

'A spectacularly placed hotel built into the side of the mountain just below the ruins, overlooking a deep valley circled by eagles. You enter the lobby which is on the *top* floor, and descend by elevator to your room. The *Vouzas* was once the great hotel in Delphi. Its business has been somewhat eclipsed by big modern hotels, and it may be considered a touch faded, but it is a marvellous place to stay. On a non-windy day meals are served from a wonderful open veranda off the lobby, birds filling the air. Food tends to be "continental" rather than indigenous.' *(Tim Wolf)*

Open: 1 November–15 March.
Rooms: 58 double, 1 suite.

Facilities: Restaurant; also open-air terrace for meals.
Terms (excluding tax): Rooms 920–1,265 drs (single), 1,200–1,725 drs (double).
Set meals: breakfast 113 drs; lunch/dinner 430 drs.

IOS, Cyclades   Map 15

Manganari Village Hotel   *Telephone:* (0286) 9.1215

'Two couples, one French, one German, one with money, the other an architect, discovered this rocky promontory 15 years ago and fell in love with it. First they built a house each, then houses for their friends, some of whom were persuaded to buy. The unused houses now operate as a hotel. A local family does all the cooking, maintains the boats (sometimes) – scuba-diving, compressors, water-skis, wind-surfing and a speedboat all somewhat erratically available – a cousin goes fishing and other cousins make the beds. The atmosphere can be a little cliquey: there can be a gap between owner and visitors, and the dominant group in residence may be either French, British or German, but the children, as usual, are interna-tional. Choose the time of your stay accordingly, or if you prefer to be left in peace in beautiful surroundings, book any time and trust that you will be in a minority. One of the "cousins" meets the Piraeus boat in the harbour of Ios, an hour away by caique, but be sure to cable your arrival time. There are large empty beaches within easy walking distance, a solitary taverna, no roads, goats, two shepherds and silence.' *(Ioana and Indrei Ratiu)*

Open: June–September.
Rooms: 27 double, 4 suites – all with shower.
Facilities: Restaurant, bar, patio, discotheque. Garden. 3 beaches nearby; waterskiing, sailing, etc.
Location: 10 km from Ios town.
Terms: Bungalow 1,200 drs. Set meals: breakfast 109 drs; lunch/dinner 369 drs.

LEMNOS   Map 15

Hotel Akti Myrina   *Telephone:* (0276) 22 681
Myrina Beach   *Telex:* 294173 MYRI GR

We should be glad to hear from recent visitors to this decidedly de-luxe hotel, but of the most exclusive and discreet kind. The green and unspoiled island of Lemnos is about 8 hours' flying time from London allowing for a change of planes in Athens. The hotel is in a beautiful setting overlooking a bay 1 km from the small main town. 'The concept is brilliant: 120 bungalows spread over the hillside, each unit hidden by greenery from its neighbour. The central services (pool, beach, etc.) are all within two minutes' pleasant walk. The design assures absolute privacy from one's neighbours, and most units have a little patio/garden with a view, ideal for breakfast and an evening "happy hour". Breakfast is served in one's room, lunch is from an irresistible garden buffet, and dinner in one of three intimate and cool restaurants. Over three weeks, I was aware of neither repetition nor monotony of dishes. In addition there are beach and poolside bars for snacks and drinks, and a formal outdoor speciality restaurant. There are typical beach sports and daily excursions in the hotel's caique.'

The anonymous writer of the above had serious criticisms: he thought the maintenance of the hotel very poor, and the *table d'hôte* menu no more than adequate. It's a *Relais de Campagne* hotel (the only one in Greece), but not in his view up to *Relais* standards elsewhere. But his final verdict was unquestionably favourable – confirming previous good reports: 'Whatever my likes or dislikes, *Akti Myrina* will be remembered for the huge friendliness of its staff. I have never met a more loving and caring people. After Britain's greedy but resentful service, this alone makes up for any local shortcomings.'

Open: 7 May–15 October.
Rooms: 110 double, 15 suites – 74 with bath, 51 with shower, all with telephone and fridge.
Facilities: Lounge, separate TV room, 3 dining rooms, disco-club, bridge room, library, hairdresser, boutique. Open-air taverna, evening with Greek dances, etc. 20 acres grounds; 2 tennis courts, heated swimming pool and mini-pool for children, volleyball, table tennis, pétanque, mini-golf, beach racquets. Sandy beach with safe bathing, waterskiing, etc. Sail boats, pedaloes, canoes, snorkelling equipment, etc., for hire. Daily trips round the island in the hotel's caique; weekly cruises to other islands.
Location: 2 km from Myrina Port. Parking.
Credit cards: American Express, Barclay/Visa, Diners.
Terms: B & B 1,500–2,500 drs; dinner, B & B 2,500–5,050 drs; full board 3,400–5,950 drs. Set meals: lunch/dinner 1,000 drs. 50% discount for children between 2 and 6 sharing parents' room; special meals available.

NAFPLION, Peloponnesus   **Map 15**

Hotel Helena   *Telephone:* (0752) 23 888 or 23 217
17 Sidiras Merarchias

A C-class gem. The *Helena* is spotless – shining marble floors, glistening porcelain in bathrooms, crisp sheets on comfortable beds, good view of antiquity from balcony, and best of all – the price is right. Only breakfast served. *(A W Gardes)*

Open: All year.
Rooms: 30 double – all with bath.
Location: 12 km from Argos; 70 km from Corinth.
Terms: Rooms 380 drs per person. Set meal: breakfast 90 drs.

OURANOUPOLIS, Chalkidiki   **Map 15**

Hotel Xenia   *Telephone:* (0377) 71 202

'The little fishing port of Ouranoupolis is the usual point of departure by caique for pilgrims to Mount Athos, where the privilege of a visit – for males only – is wisely restricted by the Greek Government to avoid the risk of a tourist take-over. As each wife must wait like Penelope for her husband's return from his odyssey, a comfortable hotel in such a setting, with every bedroom overlooking the sea to Sithonia, must help to console those who wait for their husband's return. The *Xenia* is one of an extensive chain owned by the Greek Government. It is unaggressively modern, excellently designed for its site and situated immediately along-side its own private sandy/shingly beach, as clean as they come of oil and rubbish, providing a superb swim in the Aegean Sea within a minute of leaving one's room. You can eat at the hotel – the chef is said to have been trained in France – or at any of the several excellent small restaurants nearby. The staff are friendly, if impersonal, and keen to be helpful according to the limitations of language. There seemed to be invariably someone around who could converse quite adequately in English.' *(Michael Rubinstein)*

Open: 16 May–26 September.
Rooms: 40 double – all with shower and telephone. 20 rooms in bungalows.
Facilities: Lounge, TV room, dining room, patio. 4 acres garden with basketball, volleyball; private sandy beach with safe bathing.
Location: 600 metres from town centre; parking. English spoken.
Credit cards: Access/Euro/Mastercard, American Express, Diners.
Terms: B & B 753–1,485 drs; dinner, B & B 1,163–1,895 drs; full board 1,573–2,305 drs. Set meals: lunch/dinner 410 drs; full *alc* 510 drs. 20% reduction for children; special meals provided.

PAROS   Map 15

Hotel Argo   *Telephone:* (0284) 2.1367

'We met a couple who had spent a week here and raved about it. The proprietor meets the boat in his car, but he won't drive you back if you don't like the place. However, we liked it so much that we stayed eight nights. The hotel (Class C) is comfortable and clean, with well-designed pine furniture. It's right on the beach, a stone's throw from the sea. Our only grumble was they had too many rules and regulations. They objected to us entertaining in our bedrooms and got very sour when we took their towels on the beach (So do most hotels – *Ed*). However, we thoroughly recommend it.' *(Len and Pam Ratoff)*

Open: All year.
Rooms: 37 double, 4 single – all with bath and telephone, many with balcony or veranda.
Facilities: Salon, bar, restaurant.
Location: In main town on Paros island.
Terms: Rooms 615 drs (single), 770 drs (double). Set meal: breakfast 89 drs.

THIRA, Island of Santorini   Map 15

Hotel Kavalari   *Telephone:* (0286) 22 455 and 22 347

The volcanic island of Santorini is of striking crescent shape. You sail into a wide bay, thought to be the crater of a volcano which erupted in Mycenean times, throwing up the spectacular cliffs of pumice and lava that surround the bay. The white-housed town of Thira is perched on the cliffs, 800 steps up from the harbour: you can ride up by mule or drive round by taxi or bus. 'The very pleasant C-class *Kavalari* is dug out of the mountain-side, so that every bedroom or small group of bedrooms is independent. Like many of these small hotels or *pensions* in the Greek islands, it only serves bed and breakfast. It is inexpensive, clean and romantic, and in the morning has the most beautiful views that I've seen since I lived in Hong Kong 25 years ago.' *(Lord Beaumont)*

Open: 7 April–31 October.
Rooms: 20 double – 6 with shower.
Facilities: Breakfast room. English spoken.
Location: In centre of Thira.
Restriction: No children under 10.
Terms: Rooms 500–1,140 drs. Set meal: breakfast 100 drs.

TOLON, Nr Nauplion   Map 15

Hotel Minoa   *Telephone:* (0752) 59 207 and 59 416
                                              Telex: 298157

Tolon is about three hours' drive south-west of Athens, and 11 km from Nauplion (Mycenae, Argos and Epidaurus all within easy reach). Once a simple coastal village, it has grown in tourist popularity over the years and now has hotels and tavernas running the length of the narrow beach strip. English visitors who don't care to be reminded of their native land while on holiday should be warned of the presence of British tour operators, and that in their train come signs for 'bacon and eggs' writ large. If you come by car, you will need to park your car in the old port and carry your suitcase. The *Hotel Minoa* is the first hotel you come across. It's a family business – mother and father and three brothers. The rooms are clean and simple, breakfast is on the beach beneath a large tent, dinners are taken in the restaurant. 'Unpretentious but adequate,' we said last year, but recent visitors felt we had been ungenerous; they found the food most enjoyable. Prices are very reasonable. If you don't care for noisy pop music from the bar – though it stops at 11 pm – we are told that the *Minoa*'s sister hotel, *The Knossos*, 60 yards away, has the same facilities without the sound. *(Margaret and Richard Hadley, Alan Palmer)*

Open: 15 March–6 November.
Rooms: 39 double, 5 single – 7 with bath, 37 with shower and WC, all with telephone and radio. (Some rooms on ground floor in annexe.)
Facilities: Lift, 2 lounges (1 with TV), bar, restaurant; dancing every night; breakfast under large beach awning. Small garden with bar. Sandy beach and safe bathing, sailing, pedalos, boating, fishing. English spoken.
Location: Near old port; parking.
Terms: B & B 540–910 drs; dinner, B & B 870–1,220 drs. Set meals: lunch/dinner 340 drs. Reduced rates for children.

Holland

Hotel Ambassade, Amsterdam

ALMEN, Gelderland   **Map 8**

De Hoofdige Boer   *Telephone:* (05751) 744
Dorpstraat 38

'An old-established family-run hotel in a small village east of Zutphen in
Eastern Holland. Very friendly proprietors with some English spoken.
Ideal for a quiet holiday, with tennis, swimming, bicycle-hire in the
village, and attractive towns and villages nearby. Modern bedrooms, fully
equipped, and comfortable lounge; and tea garden in summer. Outstanding food, the best we had in Holland, and excellent value.' *(P Snowden)*

Open: All year, except Christmas.
Rooms: 18 double, 2 single – 14 with bath, 6 with shower, 10 with telephone; TV
can be hired; baby-listening can be arranged. (2 rooms on ground floor.)
Facilities: Pub lounge with TV, TV room, dining room. Garden. 5 minutes' walk
to heated swimming pool. English spoken. &.
Location: Central, near the church; parking.
Credit card: Diners.
Terms: B & B 60–85 glds; dinner, B & B 75–100 glds. Set meal: dinner 25 glds;
full *alc* 37.50 glds. Reduced rates for children sharing parents' room; special meals
provided.

349

Hotel Ambassade   *Telephone:* (020) 262.333
Herengracht 341   *Telex:* 10158

'For those who prefer the small, cosy, family hotel, the *Ambassade* fits the bill perfectly. Very reasonable prices and perfectly situated, overlooking one of the many canals that form the spider's web of water on which the city sits, the *Ambassade* consists of four five-storey houses. One is given a key to the front door of the house which contains one's room (one per floor) which adds to the homely feel. The Rijksmuseum is ten minutes' walk, and one of the city's liveliest squares (Spui) is just round the corner. Breakfast includes an egg and Dutch Gouda cheese of course. An added attraction is a mini-Museum adjoining the Breakfast Room, containing a fine display of 18th-century antiques belonging to the proprietor. One word of warning: there are no lifts, so one keeps in trim negotiating the narrow, steep staircases!' *(Murray Sutton)*

Open: All year.
Rooms: 31 double, 3 single – 30 with bath, 2 with shower, all with telephone. 16 rooms in annexe.
Facilities: Reception area, lounge with TV, breakfast room. English spoken.
Location: Central; no special parking facilities.
Credit card: American Express.
Terms: B & B 47.50–65 glds.

Hotel de L'Europe   *Telephone:* (020) 23.48.36
Nieuwe Doelenstraat 2–4, 1012 CP   *Telex:* 12081
              Reservations: in UK telephone (01) 278 4211
                            in USA telephone (800) 223 6800

One of the older grander hotels in the city, built in 1895 on the Amstel, and centrally placed for all the sights. Front rooms can be noisy: rooms at the back or overlooking the river are to be preferred. The hotel's restaurant, the *Excelsior*, has an excellent reputation for its cooking and for an outstanding cellar. *(T Crone)*

Open: All year.
Rooms: 41 double, 37 single, 3 suites – all with bath, telephone, radio and colour TV; baby-sitting on request.
Facilities: Lift, lounge, bar, 2 restaurants; banqueting and conference facilities. English spoken.
Location: Central, opposite the Mint Tower and Flowermarket; limited private parking, public garage.
Credit cards: American Express, Barclay/Visa, Diners, Euro.
Terms: Rooms 100–180 glds. Set meals: breakfast 12.50 glds; lunch 55 glds; dinner 70 glds; full *alc* 75 glds.

> If you have difficulty in finding hotels because directions given in the Guide are inadequate, please help us to improve them.

DELDEN, Overijssel   **Map 8**

Carelshaven   *Telephone:* (05407) 1305
30 Hengelosestraat

Not far from the main road between Deventer and Hengelo, surrounded
by woods, *Carelshaven Hotel* was built in 1774 as a hostel for sailors and
later turned into a comfortable hotel and restaurant (rosetted in Michelin)
with a modern annexe. The hotel is a good base for visiting Twickel castle
with its beautiful gardens. 'I highly recommend this hotel, particularly for
travellers to Scandinavia and North Germany, being near the border. The
annexe is very quiet and comfortable; there are lovely walks and the
surroundings are beautiful. Good and attractive food and service. Lots of
charm and memories of the past. Not cheap.' *(Tan Crone)*

Open: All year, except 24 December–2 January.
Rooms: 20 double, 5 single, 22 with bath, all with telephone. Some rooms in
annexe.
Facilities: Salon, bar, restaurant; conference facilities. Garden and terrace.
Location: 2 km from the E8 motorway. Delden is reached by the A1. There is a
bus stop 100 m from the hotel and railway stations at Delden (1 km) and Hengelo
(5 km).
Credit cards: All major credit cards accepted.
Terms: B & B 57–80 glds. Set meals: lunch 27 glds; dinner 52 glds.

MAASTRICHT, Limburg   **Map 8**

Hotel Maastricht   *Telephone:* (043) 54171
De Ruiterij, 6221 EW   *Telex:* 56822
                            Reservations: in UK telephone (01) 940 9766
                                      in USA telephone (212) 247 7950

The *Hotel Maastricht* hit the headlines in March 1981 when the town
played host to an EEC summit. A conversion of 15th- and 16th-century
buildings adjoining the hotel enabled 23 luxurious suites to be made
available to Common Market leaders, against some background mutters
from local citizens complaining of money being wasted on a prestige
occasion. The suites have been named permanently after the leaders who
used them, with a guarantee to future residents that details of decoration
and furniture are unchanged. The Margaret Thatcher Room, we are told,
is in a converted 16th-century inn called appropriately the 'Weapon of
England'; the Giscard d'Estaing suite is in what used to be called the 'Old
Fish Store'. In the absence of a fresh report from Downing Street, we
repeat last year's entry:
  'Although most modern hotels have little to recommend them, this one
is an exception. Built two years ago, it is situated on the river bank
immediately opposite the old centre of a fascinating town. It is an
attractive brick building of interesting design, with almost all the rooms
and suites overlooking the Maas (Meuse). As it is on the waterfront, there
is hardly any traffic noise, and the only sounds you can hear are the
throbbing engines of the huge barges passing by the windows on the river.
There is an attractive restaurant and bar, also with river view, and a coffee
shop where enormous buffet breakfasts are served. The building also
includes a hairdresser's and boutique and exhibition area for paintings,

etc. Rooms are large, comfortable, and furnished with top-calibre modern furniture, lights and fitments. The furniture is all by Artifort, a manufacturer whose factory is in the town, and the quality and lack of compromise shows. We found it very refreshing.' *(Pat and Jeremy Temple)*

Open: All year.
Rooms: 103 double, 6 single, 25 suites – all with bath, telephone, radio and colour TV, some with balconies; baby-sitting by arrangement. 23 suites in annexe with tea-making facilities. (1 special bedroom and WC for the disabled.)
Facilities: Lifts, lobby, coffee shop, bar, restaurant; conference facilities for 10–300 people. English spoken. ♿.
Location: On the bank of the river Maas (Meuse), 5 minutes from town centre; hotel has its own car park. Coming from out of town use Kennedy Bridge.
Credit cards: All major credit cards accepted.
Terms: B & B 95–145 glds. Set meals: lunch 15 glds; dinner 65 glds; full *alc* 80 glds. Special weekend breaks. Special meals for children.

WASSENAAR, 2243 South Holland   Map 8

De Kieviet   *Telephone:* (01751) 79403
Stoeplaan 27

'An excellent restaurant with six rooms and a sizeable flowered terrace, set in the Wassenaar woods. Comfortable bedrooms with very super bathrooms. The restaurant, with a huge separate area for pre-dinner drinks etc., is much used by the diplomatic set from The Hague – of which Wassenaar is virtually a suburb – but also by local families. Expensive enough, but a lovely place to relax in after a hard day in art galleries and museums in The Hague, and with much more character than the big new hotels in the city itself.' *(Frank and Joan Harrison)*

Open: All year. Restaurant closed Monday.
Rooms: 6 double – 5 with bath, 1 with shower, all with telephone.
Facilities: Lounge, restaurant. Garden; beach 5 km.
Location: 8 km from the centre of the Hague; 2 km SW of Wassenaar.
Credit cards: American Express, Diners.
Terms: Rooms (including breakfast) (single) 100 glds, (double) 157.50 glds. Set meals: lunch from 45 glds; dinner from 69.50 glds; full *alc* 80 glds.

WELLERLOOI, 5856 Limburg   Map 8

Hostellerie de Hamert   *Telephone:* (04703) 1260
Hamert 2, rte Nijmegen-Venlo

'This is a famous restaurant, used by Germans and Belgians as well as Netherlanders, with four rooms. Situated on a big curve on the bank of the Maas, it has one room with a balcony overlooking the river. Though not on any usual tourist route from Britain (unless you are making the delightful trip following the Maas-Meuse from the delta to the source) it is indeed "worth a detour" for the excellent food and service, and the superb view of the river and its traffic from the balconied bedroom (where you can have breakfast), and from the tables by the window in the dining room (where you can watch the sun go down over the river and the flat green landscape). Not the place for an extended stay but perfect for a self-indulgent one-night stand.' *(Frank and Joan Harrison)*

Open: All year.
Rooms: 4 – most with bath.
Facilities: Restaurant.
Location: 20 km from Venlo.
Terms: Rooms (including breakfast) 95–115 glds. Set meals: 80–95 glds.

WITTEM, Nr Gulpen, Limburg   **Map 8**

Kasteel Wittem   *Telephone:* Wittem (04450) 1208
Wittemeralle 3, 6286 AA

'*Kasteel Wittem* really is a castle, with 12-feet-thick walls, ancient trees and roses in the garden; but above all, it has an exceptional cuisine: it's a gourmet's paradise. And more than that, Pieter Ritzen and his family run it like a country house and without any trace of stuffiness. When they took over the castle, they aimed at the highest standards – not only first-class food, but equally first-class comfort. Each room has its own private bathroom, which had to be gouged out of the cyclopean walls. It's the nearest to a stately home both in reception and standards that I've ever encountered in Holland. Businessmen can now fly to Limburg – a splendid stopping-off place for buying and selling in Holland and northern Germany. Situated as it is between Maastricht and Aachen, *Kasteel Wittem* is the perfect place for a weekend of peace and plenty before (or after) a tough business week. There is golf in the vicinity and plenty of other outdoor activities. Best of all, you will be cosseted like a favourite relative.' *(Valerie Ferguson)*

Recent American visitors warmly endorse the above: 'Everything was perfect. Well-decorated rooms, large bathrooms, pleasant personnel and ambience, and the best meal we had in Europe, beautifully prepared and served.' *(Marilee Thompson Duer)*

Open: All year.
Rooms: 11 double, 1 suite – all with bath and telephone; TV on request; tea-making facilities.
Facilities: Salon, restaurant; conference room. Garden. Golf, bicycling and walking.
Location: Between Maastricht (17 km) and Aachen (15 km). 1 km SW of Gulpen on Maastricht road.
Credit cards: All major credit cards accepted.
Terms: B & B 75 glds. Set meals: lunch 25 glds; dinner 65 glds; full *alc* 85 glds. Reduced rates and special meals for children.

Hotel Astoria, Budapest

Hungary

Hotel Astoria   *Telephone:* (1) 173-441
Kossuth Lajos utca 19   *Telex:* 224205

Our first hotel behind the Iron Curtain, but far from austere. It is an historic hotel, built before the First World War, with rooms as comfortable and spacious as you would expect from that more opulent age. It is in the heart of Budapest's Inner City, with the metro at your door and the Danube no more than a block away. Front rooms are noisy, so you need to ask for an interior room if you are a light sleeper. The hotel caters for package tours, mostly from 'socialist' countries, but the management separates sheep from goats; those who travel privately are given a special dining room and far better service. We are not sure in which dining room one correspondent was served 'cow soup' for beef consommé, but it was, he reports, delicious. 'For a last gasp of imperial taste in a slightly provincial manner, nowhere suits better than the *Astoria*.' *(George Herzog; also E George Maddocks)*

Open: All year.
Rooms: 150 double, 42 single – 80 with bath, all with telephone and radio.
Facilities: Hall, café, dining room, night club; music and dancing nightly except Monday.
Location: Central, near river and air terminal. Some noise in front rooms. Parking.
Credit cards: All major credit cards accepted.
Terms: B & B £7.50–19.50. Set meals: lunch/dinner £2.50. No charge for children under 6.

Hotel Flora,
Venice

Italy

Villa Athena   *Telephone:* (0922) 23.83.34
Via dei Templi

'The only hotel actually in the famous Valley of the Temples, opposite the
almost perfectly preserved temple of Concordia. Sit on the terrace with a
pre-prandial drink, and, at nine o'clock, the valley magically comes to
light when the temple is bathed in spotlights, an unforgettable experience,
drawing gasps of wonderment every time. All around is absolute peace,
disturbed only by the soft murmurings of hotel-guests or the chirping of
crickets. *Villa Athena* manages to combine the aura of a private villa with
the comfort of a small first-class hotel; rooms are gracious, some spectacular. The gardens are vast and hide a fine swimming pool. The very good
restaurant, now regrettably extended, is in a separate building, which,
like the main hotel, is painted in subdued ochre, blending in well with the
landscape, and reminiscent of the colour of the temples themselves.'
(Richard Wiersum)

Open: All year.
Rooms: 31 – 8 with bath, 23 with shower, all with telephone and air-conditioning.
Facilities: Salon, bar, restaurant. Large garden with swimming pool.
Location: Opposite the temple of Concordia; parking.
Terms: Rooms 34,500 L (single), 57,500 L (double); full board (minimum 3 days)
47,150 L per person per day.

Pensione Mariori   *Telephone:* (0462) 61.287

'A modest *pension* at a modest price in a quiet road close to the centre of
the village, well-placed for mountain walks and ski lifts. The *Mariori* has
fine panoramic views of the Sella and Marmolada mountains. It is a very
friendly house, and the cooking is excellent. The owner, Mr Watson, is
English, and a dab-hand with the cocktail shaker, but there are no
concessions to the English, not even tea. Signora Watson, who comes
from Canazei, does all the cooking herself. Canazei is an excellent centre
for skiing, within easy reach of many lifts, and one can use the Dolomite
Superski pass which covers over 300 lifts. In summer, it's a wonderful
centre for walking.' *(Fay Godwin)*

Open: 19 December–18 April, 12 June–30 September.
Rooms: 10 double, 4 single.
Facilities: Bar/lounge, dining room, terrace. Large grassy meadow surrounding
pension. Near mountains, with panoramic views; well-situated for mountain walks
and ski lifts. Ice skating rink nearby, open all year round. English spoken.
Location: Central; parking.
Terms: Rooms 7,500–9,500 L per person; B & B 10,500–12,500 L; dinner, B & B
13,500–18,000 L; full board (summer only) 15,000–20,000 L. Set meals: 7,500 L.
Reduced rates for children; special meals provided.

Fonte della Galletta   *Telephone:* (0575) 79.39.25

'Definitely not for those who want great comfort, and first-class facilities. But it should appeal to people who like going to somewhere a bit out of the ordinary, with peace and quiet, lovely views (although see below), friendly treatment – and superb and unusual food. *Fonte della Galletta* is 6 km up in the clouds (often literally) from the small village in the Appenine mountains which can boast of being the place where Michelangelo was born. Michelin gives it double knives and forks, a red rocking chair (= isolated) and claims a good view over the Tiber valley. Isolation: we hardly found the hotel at all, as the teetering signposts at spasmodic intervals along the climb up from Caprese Michelangelo seem to give up towards the top. We saw nothing of the view as it rained hard when we arrived and the clouds were sitting tight round the place. We had a friendly welcome from an elderly peasant-type woman who bustled round to warm the place up, and when we came to use them, our rooms were beautifully warm. They were small and plain, but spotlessly clean.

'One comes straight into a rustic bar through which one looks into the kitchen with a large open fire range topped by a huge copper dome. There is a large dining room and veranda. The walls are hung with a mixture of modern art, curios and framed photographs of our as-yet-unseen host receiving culinary awards (one was called the *Oscar della cucina italiana!*), often surrounded by the most enormous funghi I have ever seen. These in fact turned out to be the speciality of the house (and the district), and our dinner – served by the now arrived owner, Signor Boncompagni, a very aptly named gentleman who entertained us in very rapid Italian whilst distributing the most enormous helpings of food – consisted almost entirely of this fungus, *Boletus edulis*, in various disguises. A wonderful meal for a lover of mushrooms and funghi, accompanied by a strong but mellow local wine which our host called *nero*, not just a mere *rosso*.' *(Ian and Agathe Lewin)*

Open: All year.
Rooms: 14 double, 3 single, 3 suites – 13 with shower, all with telephone, colour TV and tea-making facilities. 6 rooms in annexe.
Facilities: Lounge, TV room, restaurant; conference facilities. Garden.
Location: 6 km W of Caprese Michelangelo; 50 km NE of Arezzo.
Credit card: Barclay/Visa.
Terms: Rooms 11,000 L per person; B & B 12,650 L; dinner, B & B 20,350 L; full board 22,000 L. Set meals: lunch 17,000 L, supper 7,000 L. Reduced rates for children; special meals provided.

ASOLO, 31011 Treviso   **Map 14**

Hotel Villa Cipriani   *Telephone:* (0423) 52.166
                                                      Telex: 411060

'Situated in the small town of Asolo with marvellous views of the surrounding hilly countryside, this beautiful villa is a small charming very comfortable hotel. No relation to *Cipriani* in Venice, it is part of the CIGA Hotel group, although, except for the company logo used on china, menus, stationery, etc., it is run very much as an independent country-house hotel. The manager is extremely pleasant, friendly and always at hand. The situation makes it convenient for visiting the villas of the Veneto, Venice, Padua and the many small interesting towns in the foothills of the Dolomites. Our room was large and comfortable with a beautiful view. The restaurant is superb (rosette in Michelin) and attracts plenty of local custom as well as residents. Prices are very reasonable and the wine list will not draw any gasps! The restaurant and the small bar open on to the terrace and garden where normally one takes breakfast in the sun. We had our after-dinner drinks in the garden in October! The staff are plentiful, friendly, efficient and quiet. One of the most pleasing and comfortable hotels we've visited in Italy.' *(Pat and Jeremy Temple; also Geoffrey Sharp; Pat Knopf)*

Open: All year. Restaurant closed Monday October–April.
Rooms: 32.
Facilities: Bar, restaurant, terrace, air-conditioning. Garden.
Location: 35 km NW of Treviso.
Credit cards: All major credit cards accepted.
Terms: Rooms 74,750–121,900 L. Set meal: breakfast 7,475 L; *alc* 21,850–34,500 L (excluding wine).

ASSISI, 06081 Perugia   **Map 14**

Hotel Umbra   *Telephone:* (075) 81.22.40
Via degli Archi 6

In the five years we have been editing the Guide, only one hotel in Assisi, the *Umbra*, has ever been recommended. It is by no means the largest or smartest hotel in the city, but it has a natural advantage, being close to the main square but in a quiet narrow side street, away from the main crush of tourists, with an attractive garden. It has also enjoyed for many years Assisi's only Michelin-starred restaurant. But a long detailed report received last year suggested some fall in standards; this correspondent doubted whether the hotel could any longer be recommended for a long stay. We were therefore particularly glad, among a number of mainly appreciative letters, to receive the report below from a long stayer:

'We endorse all the favourable comments on this hotel in the last edition. Perhaps because we were staying longer than the average visitor to Assisi, we were given what seemed to be the best bedroom at no extra cost. It had its own small balcony with superb views so that we could watch the full moon rising over Mount Subasio, while the sun set opposite it. The hotel is mercifully free of traffic noise, but still a word of warning to light sleepers: the very clamorous clock in the nearby Piazza del Commune strikes every quarter of an hour, and each time strikes the full hour plus the appropriate number of quarters. 12.45 am is quite a performance. We were not quite as impressed by the restaurant as we expected to be. The menu is much more ambitious than anywhere else we found in Assisi, but the occasional main dish was not as well-cooked as it should have been. However, we would not want to end on a critical note. It's a lovely small hotel and we would go back there like a shot.' *(Sarah and David Machin; also P D Scott, G H Cole)*

Open: All year. Restaurant closed 5–20 November.
Rooms: 21 double, 6 single – 17 with bath, 5 with shower, all with telephone and mono TV. (Some rooms on ground floor.)

Facilities: Lounge, TV room, American Bar, restaurant. Garden with terrace for meals in fine weather. English spoken. & .
Location: In town centre, near main square.
Credit cards: All major credit cards accepted.
Terms: B & B 15,000–25,200 L. Full *alc* 15,000 L.

AVIGLIANA, 10051 Torino

Map 14

Hotel Ristorante Hermitage

Telephone: (011) 93.81.50

Twenty-four km W of Turin, the small town of Avigliana lies just off the A13 on its way to the Mont Cenis pass and France. The *Hermitage* is a modern restaurant with rooms built in the Piedmontese Baroque style. 'Very comfortable well-equipped bedrooms, with a terrace commanding fine views over a lake to distant mountains. The food was excellent, the service quiet, friendly and attentive, and the proprietor himself particularly helpful.' *(Warren Bagust)*

Open: All year. Restaurant closed Tuesday.
Rooms: 7 – all with bath and telephone.
Facilities: Restaurant, terrace. Garden.
Location: 24 km W of Turin just off the A13.
Terms: Rooms 18,400–23,000 L; full board 34,500–40,250 L. Set meal: breakfast 2,300 L; *alc* 12,500–18,400 L (excluding wine).

BELLAGIO, 22021 Como

Map 14

Grand Hotel Villa Serbelloni

Telephone: (031) 95.02.16
Telex: 38330 Serbotel

One of the relatively few truly grand hotels in the book, a grandee's villa full of original frescoes and with a spectacular staircase flanked by gilt *putti* on giant candelabra. Everything is on a large scale: the public rooms, though some are now showing signs of wear and tear, are palatial, you could drive a coach and four along the marble corridors, and the bedrooms, also sometimes a bit shabby-grand, are suitable for regal *levées*. There's a private beach, heated outdoor pool and the hotel's own motor and rowing boats; its position on the lake, near the tip of the peninsula where Como forks, offers incomparable views for a room on the lake side. De-luxe hotels are often obsequious or disdainful towards their guests, depending on their rank and title. But the *Villa Serbelloni* has the reputation for combining style and informality – a tribute to the courteous but friendly personality of its Italian-born Swiss owner, Rudy Bucher, whose family has been running the hotel since before the turn of the century. *(Pat and Jeremy Temple, and others)*

Open: April–October.
Rooms: 60 double, 14 single, 11 suites – 75 with bath, 10 with shower, all with telephone; radio and TV on request.
Facilities: Lifts, palatial lounges, TV room, bridge room, writing room, games room, restaurant; conference facilities; terrace (also for meals), evening orchestra. Gardens with tennis courts and heated swimming pool with snack bar, which lead to private beach; boating and waterskiing facilities. English spoken. & .

Location: Bellagio is 30 km from Como. Hotel has parking facilities.
Terms: B & B 50,000–80,000 L; dinner, B & B 70,000–100,000 L; full board 80,000–110,000 L. Set meals: lunch 23,000 L; dinner 25,000 L; full *alc* 28,000 L. Reduced rates for children sharing parents' room; special meals provided.

BERGAMO, 24100   Map 14

Agnello d'Oro   *Telephone:* (035) 24.98.83
Via Gombito 22

'One of the great attractions of Bergamo, or of its Città Alta at least, is that it is so small that the visitor is spared the tourist's customary state of chronic exhaustion: its delights are all contained within a modest compass. The Piazza Vecchia was regarded by Frank Lloyd Wright as the most balanced and varied in the world. The ambience is perhaps the chief attraction, another is the views to the Città Bassa and beyond, a third is the art nouveau iron-work of the late 19th-century funicular terminus. But undoubtedly Bergamo's most notable feature is the Colleoni Chapel – the same Colleoni whose equestrian statue by Verrocchio is in Venice. The outside of the Chapel is an unpromising jumble, but Tiepolo frescoes, some fine monuments, ingenious marquetry and low-relief carving by Amadeo make the interior one of the most rewarding for its size in Italy.

'At Bergamo the place to stay is the 17th-century *Agnello d'Oro*. It's not very large, nor is it expensive, but you will find that the decor of the bedrooms has a personal quality which contrasts agreeably with the usual anonymity of hotel decoration. Outside a small fountain tinkles, and within you eat as you might in some particularly fortunate home. No parking in front of the hotel, but there's a spacious overnight garage close by.' *(Sam Carr)*

This entry, which appeared in the 1980 Guide, but was omitted last year for lack of feedback, is now reinstated on receipt of the following report: 'An *albergo* of character and charm, and the only one in the Città Alta. We think it essential to stay in the upper town if you go to Bergamo. It is somewhat basic, but the rooms are cheap. And the restaurant is excellent, with regional specialities such as *porcini con polenta*.' *(A G Don)*

Open: All year. Restaurant closed Monday 7–31 January.
Rooms: 16 double, 4 single – 4 with bath, 16 with shower.
Facilities: Lift, restaurant.
Location: Central; garage nearby.
Credit cards: American Express, Barclay/Visa.
Terms: B & B 18,000–21,000 L; full board 55,000 L. Full *alc* 25,000 L.

BRACCIANO, 00062 Roma   Map 14

Casina del Lago   *Telephone:* (06) 902.40.25

Bracciano, with its imposing 15th-century castle overlooking the lake that bears its name, is only 40 km north of Rome, but – unlike, say, Virginia Water – is wholly rural and unspoiled by developments. The lake itself is beautiful and unpolluted, and Bracciano makes a useful base for visiting Etruscan sites around. 'The *Casina del Lago*, 1.5 km out of Bracciano itself, is in Michelin as a "restaurant with rooms". It is certainly not luxurious, but splendidly peaceful, with a view over the lake, very good value, and serves efficiently excellent meals in its restaurant.' *(Shirley and Alan Bailey)*

Open: All year. Restaurant closed Tuesday.
Rooms: 12 – all with shower.
Facilities: Restaurant.
Location: 25 miles N of Rome on the N493. Hotel is 1.5 km NE of Bracciano. Parking.
Terms: Rooms 8,050–24,500 L; full board 19,550–20,700 L. Set meal: breakfast 2,300 L; *alc* (excluding 20% service and wine) 10,350–24,500 L.

CAPRI, Isle of, Naples   **Map 14**

Hotel Gatto Bianco   *Telephone:* (081) 83.70.446
Via Vittorio Emanuele 32

'A really excellent establishment, set in the heart of this superbly theatrical little town, like a backdrop for *L'Elisir d'Amore*, where the streets are without cars and everyone walks or delivers their goods, or baggage, on narrow electric trucks. It is in the mid-price range. The service is efficient, relaxed and friendly. The bedrooms are charmingly appointed, the beds are comfortable and everything works in the bathroom. There are also little balconies off the bedrooms where you can sit, drink and soak up more sun overlooking the red, cream and soft brown roofs of the town. Although in the centre, it is really very quiet from late night on. The excellent, deliberately limited menu offers every night a splendid opportunity to study Italian cooking at its succulent best. The house wines are delicious, and, in my view, better than the *Tiberio*, the island's most usual "good" wine, which is also on offer. The dining room itself is one of the best examples I have seen of a shady pergola romantically transformed by deft lighting and a profusion of flowers. The three brothers Esposito – Valentino, Giovanni and Pino – who run the hotel, belong to a family who have been catering on the island for four generations. Since the Fifties, they have expanded the *Gatto Bianco*, but it is still very much a personal hotel. It is also, one notices, used by the residents of Capri for their celebrations and family parties.' *(Charles Hodgson)*

Open: 1 April–31 October.
Rooms: 32 double, 12 single, 10 suites – all with bath, telephone and colour TV; many with balcony; air-conditioning for which a daily charge of about 2,000 L is made. 10 rooms in annexe.
Facilities: Lift, salon, TV room, dining room. Garden. 10 minutes by bus from sea. English spoken. ⅙.
Location: Central; parking.
Credit cards: All major credit cards accepted.
Terms: B & B 20,000–29,000 L; half board 35,000–45,000 L; full board 50,000–60,000 L. Set meals: lunch 15,000 L; dinner 16,000 L. Reduced rates for children under 7.

The terms indicate the range of prices in each hotel. Some have a low and high season, some do not. The lower price is likely to be for someone sharing a double room, and the higher price the maximum for a single occupant.

CASTELLINA IN CHIANTI, 53011 Siena   **Map 14**

Tenuta di Ricavo   *Telephone:* (0577) 74.02.21

A highly civilized and cosmopolitan *pensione* high up in the Chianti hills, 5 km from the hill village of Castellina in Chianti, 22 km from Siena and 34 km from Florence. The buildings, including a medieval manor, date from the 15th century and before. The estate – there are 310 acres of gardens and woods – was bought many years ago as a holiday home by Signora Scotoni who, after her husband's death, turned the place into a paying guest-house, converting the stone cottages, adding and rebuilding and furnishing each room differently. Signora Scotoni died in 1978, and the hotel is now owned and managed by a young Swiss couple, Herr and Frau Bleuler. Enthusiasts for *Ricavo* tend to be very enthusiastic indeed. In previous years, there had been a minority report that the Swiss–Germanic influence had been a trifle over-pervasive for some English-speakers. We have had no complaints on that score this last year, but have had many testimonials to the exceptional quality of the place. The following letter expresses eloquently the devotion which the *Ricavo* inspires in its guests:

'I wrote last year that "it was unfair to criticize anything that borders on perfection". I now amend that statement. *Ricavo* does not border on perfection, for it is indeed holiday perfection itself. This year, the food was better than ever, and the nationalities were more diversified. The Swiss–German families (about which the British holidaymaker seemed so worried) numbered just four. Naturally, we have already made our bookings for next year.' *(R S Phillips; also Gayle Hunnicutt, Shirley and Alan Bailey, Charles Baker, Arnold Horwell)*

Open: April–October.
Rooms: 25 rooms and apartments – all with bath. (2 rooms on ground floor.)
Facilities: Several salons. Extensive gardens and woodland. 2 swimming pools (1 heated); hiking, boccia. English spoken. &.
Location: 34 km from Florence, 22 km from Siena.
Terms (excluding 8% tax): Full board 45,100–58,000 L (3 nights minimum). Reduced rates for children.

CAVOLI, 57030 Elba   **Map 14**

Hotel Bahia   *Telephone:* (0565) 98.70.55

'After 20 years of holidays in the Mediterranean, I would recommend this spot to my most discerning friends and not worry. Elba is sheer delight. The tariff at the *Bahia* was almost half of what we pay in southern France, particularly in low season. Private sandy beach, crystal-clear seas, delightful outdoor clifftop restaurant, good service and good food. Cottage-style rooms, with air-conditioning, cool and quiet. Only snag is steep steps down to beach; not for aged or infirm, but most people drive down. A car is essential for touring the island. Better to hire as car ferry crossings can be tedious. Smoothest head-waiter almost anywhere we've been – but *nice*. All staff were willing and friendly.' *(D H Bennett)*

Open: April–September.
Rooms: 40 – all with bath or shower and telephone.

Facilities: Restaurant, air-conditioning. Garden, private beach.
Location: On the S coast between Marina di Campo and Marciana.
Credit cards: American Express, Diners.
Terms: Rooms 41,400 L; full board 40,250–66,700 L. Set meals: breakfast 4,600 L; lunch/dinner 20,700–23,000 L.

CERNOBBIO, 22012 Como   **Map 14**

Grand Hotel Villa d'Este   *Telephone:* (031) 511 471
                                            Telex: 380025

'In its beautiful garden setting on the shores of Lake Como, the *Grand Hotel Villa d'Este* retains its air of timeless elegance. The exquisite colouring and decor of the impressive entrance hall is carried in varying shades throughout the entire hotel. The greeting at Reception, though formal, is nonetheless welcoming and guests are all escorted to their rooms by one of the receptionists, the luggage being brought into the hotel by a separate entrance, your car being parked for you. On our recent visit, our spacious room faced the lake and had stunning views, though rooms with garden views should not be dismissed. It was tastefully furnished in delicate shades of soft yellow, gold and white, with appropriate antique pieces, and had an abundance of wardrobe space, the sitting room being divided from the bedroom by a curtained archway. The bathroom space was limited and only adequate. The standard of service throughout the hotel is still faultless; the food in the main (formal) restaurant is good. There is also the informal grill, outside on the terrace in warm weather; I have not eaten there recently, but the decor is attractive. Daytime amenities provided include outdoor and indoor swimming pools plus children's pool and sandpit, tennis courts and squash courts, putting green, windsurfing and the lovely gardens in which to wander. There is a bar catering for the swimming pool "Sporting Club" area and another on the terrace in front of the hotel by the lake. At night there is a discotheque, crammed with "trendy" young people, as well as a nightclub with "live" music for the "not quite so young". No sound from either reaches any of the bedrooms. In the bar a pianist plays gently "standards", thankfully without amplification. There is a card room and large lounge, and one mustn't forget the romantic gardens for a moonlight stroll. For us the hotel is an ideal retreat for a long weekend after a hectic business tour of Italy, and for those who appreciate elegant luxury in beautiful surroundings it is hard to beat. Needless to say, prices are commensurate with all that is provided, but worth every lira.' *(Evelyn S Stevens)*

Open: April–October.
Rooms: 180 – 174 with bath, 6 with shower, all with telephone.
Facilities: Lift, lounge, card room, 2 restaurants, grill, bars; disco and nightclub; conference facilities; games room, sauna, gym. Garden with tennis and squash courts; indoor and outdoor swimming pools; children's play area; putting green; private beach; windsurfing.
Location: On the shores of Lake Como, 5 km from Como.
Credit cards: All major credit cards accepted.
Terms: Rooms (with breakfast) 119,000–184,000 L

> All hotel prices are approximate. Italian hotel prices are more approximate than most.

COGNE, 11012 Aosta   **Map 14**

Hotel Bellevue   *Telephone:* (0165) 74022

'Situated in a quiet position in this resort and winter sports centre, facing the Gran Paradiso massive. We were enchanted with the view from our bedroom and with the comfort and excellent cooking here. It was obviously very popular with all nationalities. No English spoken, however. Menus in Italian were translated by waitresses into French! Sunday lunch was intriguing and delicious, including a succession of specialities – *polenta* amongst them. Lounges and public rooms beautifully furnished. Adequate parking provided. Owner manager takes a keen interest in standards. Pleasant wines of the Aosta region, and others were reasonable.' *(Joan A Powell)*

Open: 5 February–13 March, 5 June–13 September. Restaurant closed Wednesday.
Rooms: 41 double, 7 single, 4 suites in annexe – 34 with bath, 9 with shower, all with telephone, most with balcony; radio and TV in suites.
Facilities: Lift, TV room, lounge, reading room, restaurant. Garden. Hunting and winter sports nearby.
Location: 27 km from Aosta off the N90.
Terms: Rooms 14,500–30,000 L; full board 33,000–40,000 L. Set meals: breakfast 3,500 L; lunch 11,500 L; dinner 10,000 L. Reduced rates for children.

ERBA, 22036 Como   **Map 14**

Castello di Pomerio   *Telephone:* (031) 61.15.16
Via Como 5   *Telex:* 380463

'We recommend this hotel, 15 minutes by car from Como, but with some small reservations; probably because of its proximity to Milan (about an hour's drive) it is used extensively by business people and companies. However it is such a beautiful building and so well converted, we feel it is worth an entry. The castle has been superbly restored to show its 14th- and 15th-century origins, including some magnificent frescoes. The restaurant overlooks the huge inner courtyard, well floodlit and set with tables and chairs in warm weather. Rooms vary in size, but all have exposed beams and brickworks and antique furnishings. Most have bathroom, mini-bar, TV etc. Ours was on two levels with magnificent full-length windows. The garden has a swimming pool with its own bar, open-air dining area with barbecue and tennis courts. These are also used by the local tennis club. There are also several conference rooms in the castle so in this respect it can be less than peaceful. A pleasant bar/lounge area is popular in the evenings and often special musical events are arranged. Food is good although at times service was very erratic. Breakfast was a "serve yourself" buffet.' *(Pat and Jeremy Temple)*

Open: All year.
Rooms: 48 – 30 with bath, 18 with shower, most with telephone and radio, mini-bar and TV.
Facilities: Bar, restaurant, courtyard; conference facilities; sauna, games room. Garden, tennis court, swimming pool with bar. ₺ .

Location: Between Como and Lecco.
Credit cards: All major credit cards accepted.
Terms: Rooms 44,850–62,500 L; full board 92,000 L.

FIESOLE, 50014 Florence   Map 14

Pensione Bencista   *Telephone:* (055) 59 163
San Domenico di Fiesole

'The *Bencista* is situated some way down from the top of Fiesole, but still high enough to command a romantic view of Florence, two kilometres away. It is a beautiful villa set in its own acres of olive groves, which slope away steeply beneath it. The spacious public rooms are full of the antique furniture and old prints which graced it when it was the Simoni family home. The Simonis live here still, and they and their staff make you feel very welcome. The food at dinner was of limited choice, but superbly cooked. We took breakfast each morning on one of the terraces, with the city spread out below. Our only criticism was our rather small bedroom; but that was our fault for not booking earlier. Some of the larger rooms have their own bath. It is a short drive down into Florence, but we found it easier to catch the No. 9 bus which stops near the gate. And when we got back, tired, in the afternoon, what bliss to relax in this very civilized hotel. I would strongly recommend the *Bencista*, even if Florence was not there.' *(John Dwight)*

The above is a typical tribute to the charms of the *Bencista*. Another reader, equally enchanted with the place, adds a gloss to a point raised in a previous entry – the fact that Signora Simoni is firmly anti-noise; bells don't work, we had said, between 11 pm and 8 am, and if you stay late on the terrace drinking you must whisper. 'The hotel has my enthusiastic endorsement. It really does have an almost unique atmosphere – as anti-hotel in its Tuscan way as *Currarevagh* in Oughterard (q.v.) is in its Irish way. But without in any way wishing to denigrate the hotel – which, incidentally, offers *astonishing* value for money – I do think you rather overdo the "silence" bit. While it is quiet at night, it is impossible to sleep after seven in the morning because a) the wooden doors of bedrooms close with an echoing bang as people start to go to the bathroom; b) the maids sing cheerfully as they start the day's work outside your door! and c) endless bells seem to ring – but perhaps that really is after 8 am. But this is carping: I would not want the *Bencista* basically to change in any way.' *(A T W Liddell)*

Open: 15 March–31 October.
Rooms: 30 double, 10 single – 15 with bath, 5 with shower.
Facilities: 3 lounges, restaurant. 25 acres gardens with vine-covered terraces for meals or refreshments. English spoken.
Location: 7 km from Florence; parking.
Terms: Dinner, B & B 31,050–37,500 L; full board 40,200–48,300 L. Set meals: lunch/dinner, 20,500 L. Reduced rates for children.

> Please write and confirm an entry when it is deserved. If you think that a hotel is not as good as we say, please write and tell us.

Hotel Villa Bonelli   *Telephone:* (055) 59 513
Via F. Poeti 1

A small modern family-run hotel, with an attractive top-floor restaurant offering a panoramic view, though not (unlike other Fiesole hotels) of the Duomo. 'Why anyone who can stay at Fiesole should prefer Florence amazes us. Much better to take the No. 7 bus at 10p a trip than to try to park in the city. The *Villa Bonelli* is an excellently run and comfortable hotel. The food is good, well cooked and served and the wine entirely drinkable – and at 3,500 L [April 1981] dirt-cheap. But the hotel likes you to stay *demi-pension*, at least between March and October; in view of the fairly limited menu, satisfaction with the food would probably not outlast a week. We had four nights at the equivalent of £22 per day for two people half board – marvellous value.' *(D J I Garstin)*

Open: All year.
Rooms: 16 double, 7 single – 1 with bath, 13 with shower, all with telephone, colour TV on request, and baby-listening. (Some rooms on ground floor.)
Facilities: Lift, hall, TV, bar, roof-restaurant, terrace. English spoken.
Location: 300 metres from town centre, right turn after Piazza Mino; parking. Regular bus service to and from Florence.
Terms: B & B 20,600–22,800 L; dinner, B & B 34,800–36,400 L; full board 41,800–43,400 L. Set meals: lunch/dinner 12,000 L; full *alc* 15,000 L. Between March and October, the hotel prefers guests to be on half-board terms. Reduced rates for children; special meals provided on request.

Villa San Michele   *Telephone:* (055) 59451
Via Doccia 4

'This is such a marvellous place I am astonished that it has not already found a place in the Guide. I found it by accident, having been turned away from all other hotels in Fiesole, and I would not have missed it for worlds. It stands a bit above the *Pensione Bencista*, with the classic view of Florence less panoramic but somehow more vivid. Originally a monastery, with a facade said to have been designed by Michelangelo, it was skilfully restored and converted into a hotel after the last war. It aims at and achieves the highest international standards of luxury, combined with the repose and tranquillity of its situation. My room, discreetly lacking a number on the door, opened off an enormous *salone* on the first floor at one end of the hotel. As I did not see another soul in it, this became almost a private sitting room. The hotel has masses of space, with a long loggia (with the classic view) serving as dining room at one end and sitting room at the other, a courtyard for sitting, a writing room with an original fresco of the last supper, a bar and a smallish garden. Furnished throughout with many antiques and seemingly endless bowls of flowers, the whole atmosphere is one of unobtrusive luxury, impeccable taste and total peace and quiet. My bedroom, though small, was beautifully appointed, and fulfilled three of the criteria of the hotel of my dreams: (1) I could not hear the noise of anyone else's plumbing; (2) the windows were fitted with mesh screens and I could therefore sleep with them open without fear of

Florence's mosquitoes; (3) I could not hear any evidence of the existence of the other guests.

'The dining room is perhaps the Achilles' heel of the establishment. The food is of the international grand hotel kind, and as such passable but not outstanding. I also found the service a little lacking in polish. But I should add that, having travelled rather wearily in many parts of Italy, staying mostly in hotels which would never find a place in the Guide, my stay here was an unforgettable interlude. The hotel, I have discovered, is described and illustrated in Harold Acton's *Tuscan Villas*, where he says it is for "travellers of discrimination". That is so; but it must be added that it is also for travellers of means. My dinner, bed and breakfast cost me a stunning £73 (1980)! But it was worth it. Highly recommended to connoisseurs of atmosphere. I am saving up to go back.' *(Alex Liddell)*

Open: 15 March–30 October.
Rooms: 24 double, 7 single, 1 suite – 30 with bath, 1 with shower, all with telephone.
Facilities: 2 sitting rooms, writing room, bar, restaurant, courtyard; conference and banqueting rooms. English spoken.
Location: 5 km from Florence; parking.
Credit cards: All major credit cards accepted.
Terms: Rooms 165,000 L per person; B & B 175,000 L; dinner, B & B 225,000 L; full board 275,000 L. Set meals: breakfast 10,000 L. Reduced rates for children under 3.

FLORENCE   **Map 14**

Hotel Villa Belvedere   *Telephone:* (055) 22.25.01/2
Via Benedetto Castelli 3, 50124

'Situated on a hill, Poggio Imperiale, on the south side of Florence, the *Villa Belvedere* is owned and run by Signor and Signora Perotto, quietly and most efficiently. The whole atmosphere is cheerful and one or other of the Perottos is always on the spot to deal with any problems. The hotel lies above Florence (only about five minutes by car to the centre of the city, and the Nos 11 and 37 buses are not far off), and there is a wonderful view of the city and surrounding hills. It is not cheap, but there are many advantages. Parking in the large garden is easy and there is no extra charge. Swimming in the hotel's own pool is free, as is the use of the hard tennis court. The garden is beautifully kept, and sitting either round the pool or under the shady trees for breakfast in summer is peaceful after the noise of overcrowded Florence. There is no restaurant, but you can order excellent light meals and snacks in the bar veranda. There is colour TV in the drawing room and shelves with books in several languages – always a sign of enlightened management. The extremely nice and helpful waiter, Giuseppe, has been with the Perottos for 20 years.' *(Mr and Mrs H M Connolly)*

The above entry, which we ran last year, has been supported by a reader, but he tells us that the reference to bar snacks is misleading. In fact you can get a full 3-course meal from the bar in the evenings – 'and ours was of excellent quality, again under the proprietor's personal supervision.' *(C H Cole)* Another reader writes to say that Signora Perotto is the daughter of the late Signor Ceschi, well remembered by many regulars. She thus represents in person the family tradition which has distinguished this hotel; old clients are greeted as old friends of the family. *(Arnold Horwell)*

Open: 1 March–30 November.
Rooms: 22 double, 3 single, 2 suites – 25 with bath, 2 with shower, all with telephone, air-conditioning and central heating; some with balconies overlooking the garden.
Facilities: Lift, 3 sitting rooms, separate TV room, bar with veranda. Large garden with swimming pool, tennis court, play area for children. English spoken. &.
Location: Corner of Via Senese, near Porto Romano, 2 km from Ponte Vecchio; garage parking.
Terms: Rooms 29,000–39,000 L per person; B & B 34,000–44,000 L. 50% reduction for children under 7 sharing parents' room.

FLORENCE   Map 14

Villa Le Rondini   *Telephone:* (055) 40.00.81
Via Bolognese Vecchia 224, 50139

For those who prefer to stay outside Florence, the *Villa Rondini* high up on the Monterinaldi hill, only 5 km from the Duomo, offers an excellent alternative to the smart hotels of Fiesole, with a similar breathtaking view of the city and the Arno valley. The main house (there are three villas in all) is a superb building dating from the 16th century, furnished in High-Florentine style. There's a tennis court, a swimming pool and a large garden. The Reale family, whose home the Villa used to be, run the hotel and serve wine from their own estates. Not a place of culinary distinction, our readers feel – and an electric hot plate would be a useful investment – but a haven of peace after the bustle of the city, and exceptionally helpful staff and management.

Open: All year.
Rooms: 25 double, 4 single – 28 with bath, 1 with shower, all with telephone and baby-listening. Some rooms in annexe. (Some rooms on ground floor.)
Facilities: Salons, TV room, restaurant, bar. Large garden with tennis court, swimming pool and snack bar. English spoken. &.
Location: 5 km from town centre. From Piazza della Liberta take Via Bolognese towards Trespiano. At La Lastra take Via Bolognese Vecchia (left fork); parking.
Credit cards: American Express, Diners, Visa.
Terms: Rooms 23,000–38,500 L per person; dinner, B & B 43,500–59,000 L; full board 57,500–62,700 L. Set meals: breakfast 4,500 L; Lunch/dinner 17,500 L; full a/c 22,000 L. Reduced rates out of season. Special meals for children.

FLORENCE   Map 14

Pensione Monna Lisa   *Telephone:* (055) 29.62.13/26.30.19
Borgo Pinto 27, 50121

One relatively minor complaint apart, there has been another substantial vote of confidence for this dignified Florentine palazzo in the heart of the city, with its elegant public rooms overlooking a large formal courtyard garden. Three typical tributes: 'Highly recommended . . . A marvellous place to relax away from the bustle . . . Beautiful interior.' 'Very satisfactory . . . Wonderful location and excellent prices.' 'What a great place! Unbelievably quiet though smack in the middle of the city.' The matter of quietness raises some provisos. One reader warns about the room opening off the entrance hall – 'noisy all night'; another mentions that the courtyard on to which four-fifths of the bedrooms look, has superb acoustics and is favoured by Americans for late-night tête-à-têtes on their adventures since leaving home. A third, whose room, before he changed it, was close to the plumbing, summed up: 'If one knows which room to book, super.' An important bonus of the *Monna Lisa* is its own garage, 200 metres away. *(C H Cole, Edward Hugo, P D Scott, John Holloway, Marilee Thompson Duer)*

Open: All year.
Rooms: 20 double, 7 single, 1 suite – 24 with bath or shower, 26 with telephone.
Facilities: Several sitting rooms and reading rooms; American bar with taped music, dining room. Inner courtyard-garden shady with trees. English spoken.
Location: Central; garage.
Terms: Rooms 22,000–27,500 L per person; B & B 27,500–33,000 L.

FLORENCE

Pensione Splendor
Via San Gallo 30, 50129

Telephone: (055) 48.34.27

A small family hotel (bed and breakfast only) ten minutes from the cathedral, with a pleasant small terrace. Good breakfasts. Rooms – most quiet, but some give out on to a busy piazza – are of a decent size, and the family cheerfully produce cutlery and plates for a lunch-time picnic in rooms and wash up afterwards. Unsophisticated but good value for money. *(Sarah and David Machin)*

Open: All year, except November.
Rooms: 20 double, 10 single – 15 with bath, 6 with shower and WC, all with telephone.
Facilities: Lift, 2 sitting rooms, separate TV room, 2 breakfast rooms. Small terrace where drinks can be served.
Location: In city centre; garage nearby.
Terms: B & B 18,500–26,000 L.

FORTE DEI MARMI, 55042 Lucca

Hotel Tirreno
Viale Morin

Telephone: (0584) 83 333

Forte dei Marmi is one of the few attractive towns along the Ligurian coast, and a favourite summer resort of well-to-do families from the centre and north of Italy. It is a community of villas with large gardens, rich in trees and flowers, in a general setting of conifers; it also has ample public parks, a spacious traffic-free promenade and a long stretch of sandy beach. The *Tirreno*, with a delightful garden, is one of the few hotels that opens in the spring and doesn't close till end October – best to avoid the high season if you can. It is run by two generations of the Baralla family. One reader last year thought the food on the expensive side and rather dull on the set menu. No complaints, however, from our latest correspondent:

'I can't recommend this home from home too highly. I found the caring considerate attitude of owners and staff, for whom nothing was too much trouble, made our stay a rare luxury. We were offered a choice of several main courses each morning, which were specially and perfectly cooked for us at dinner, and it is the first hotel at which we have ever been offered pudding, cheese *and* bowls of fruit. The gardens and terraces are beautifully furnished with cushioned chairs, tables, etc., oases of peace, and the silver sands with shady umbrellas and mattresses are only a few yards away.' *(A S-M)*

Open: April–October. Restaurant closed May.
Rooms: 49 double, 10 single – all with bath or shower and telephone; TV and baby-listening on request. 20 rooms have balconies with sea views.
Facilities: 2 lounges, 2 TV rooms, dining room. Luxuriant garden set with garden furniture and umbrellas. 50 metres from fine, safe beach with bathing and boat rental.
Location: 200 m from town centre.
Terms: B & B 23,500–32,500 L. Set meals: breakfast 4,370 L; lunch/dinner 20,700 L. Reduced rates and special meals for children.

FROSINONE, 03100   Map 14

Hotel Palombella   *Telephone:* (0775) 85.17.06
Via Maria 234

'This hotel is on the outskirts of Frosinone (about 3 km from the town centre and the same distance from the autostrada) on the way to the famous Casamari Abbey. It is also a good base for excursions to the National Park of the Abruzzi, Pastena Grotto, Gaeta, Fossanova Abbey, Trisulti Abbey, etc. It is a family-run hotel, and the restaurant is well known in the area for excellent meals, most of them cooked "espresso" to order – you have to wait for them, of course. The helpings are generous and only first-class, genuine ingredients are used in the kitchen. Restaurant and bar prices are quite moderate for the quality served. The hotel rooms are large and comfortable. I stayed there with my family for five days to our entire satisfaction and I wish my fellow readers travelling in this area to share my lucky experience. The hotel although classed 2nd Category is extremely cheap. The staff are very kind and eager to assist, although they probably only speak Italian.' *(Candelovo Minissale)*

Open: All year.
Rooms: 34 – all with shower and telephone.
Facilities: Lift, bar, restaurant. Garden.
Location: 3 km from town centre; parking.
Terms: Rooms 13,800–23,000 L; full board 25,300–31,400 L. Set meals: breakfast 1,725 L; *alc* (excluding 10% service charge and wine) 9,200–12,500 L.

GIARDINI, 98035 Messina, Sicily   Map 14

Arathena Rocks   *Telephone:* (0942) 51349

'Which hotel nowadays offers its guests fresh lobster once a week on the *table d'hôte* menu, which always has a choice of excellently-cooked Italian food? Or gets local musicians and dancers in without stinging one for a supplement?

'I have now been to the *Arathena Rocks* several times and get fonder of it on every visit. The owners, Avv Arcidiacono and his fluently English-speaking wife, really have the best of both worlds: they run a hotel that is, at the same time, their home and presumably make money out of it, too. The 40-odd rooms are all individually styled and furnished in traditional Sicilian ways, which means that much of the furniture and doors are painted with local scenes; the overall result is delightful. The hotel always has an abundance of the most gorgeous fresh flowers, for which the Signora is a stickler, and of which the spacious garden at the rear has a profusion; there is a tennis-court here for the more energetic. Numerous pieces of art are scattered throughout the public rooms, proof of the owners' love of art. The swimming pool is hewn out of the lava-rocks immediately in front and though there is a small private, artificial beach there, the main shingle-beach of Naxos is some 200 yards away.

'The *Arathena Rocks* is amongst the very few hotels in the area enjoying absolute peace as it is at the end of a private road away from traffic, yet near to the centre of this bustling and now rather chaotic resort; Taormina itself is only some 2 miles away.' *(R W E Wiersum)*

Open: 29 March–October.
Rooms: 47.
Facilities: Salons, bar, restaurant; tennis court, swimming pool, private beach. Garden. English spoken.
Location: 5 km S of Taormina.
Terms: Dinner, B & B only: 39,100–44,850 L.

GUBBIO, 06024 Perugia   **Map 14**

Bosone Palace   *Telephone:* (075) 92.30.08
Via 20 Settembre 22

This wonderfully preserved and atmospheric medieval city, full of fine patrician palaces, straddling the side of a steep hill, deserves, if one can find it, a suitable modernized palace hotel to stay in. The *Bosone Palace* is the answer: formerly the Raffaeli Palace, it belonged to the Bosone family one of whom had a sonnet dedicated to him by Petrarch and received Dante. Breakfast only is served, and there's not much in the way of public rooms except for a TV salon. But the town, except when it rains, is itself an open-air lounge of some grandeur. The front rooms face one of the noble but narrow Gubbian streets and would be noisy at night; the best rooms are at the back with a stunning panoramic view over town, the plains and distant hills. Its principal bedrooms are decorated in High Renaissance style, complete with vaulted *trompe l'oeil* ceiling, coy maidens in flimsy negligées, *putti* and all, and grand Renaissance-style double beds. *(HR; also J P H Walker)*

Open: All year.
Rooms: 35 double – most with shower.
Facilities: Lift, salon with TV.
Location: 39 km from Perugia.
Credit card: Diners.
Terms: Rooms 21,700–32,000 L. Set meal: breakfast 3,400 L.

> In your own interest, do check latest tariffs with hotels when you make your bookings.

IVREA, Lago di Sirio, 10015 Torino   **Map 14**

Hotel Sirio   *Telephone:* (0125) 42.36.46
Via Lago Sirio 85

A quiet small modern hotel overlooking Lake Sirio, which offers rowing, sailing, swimming and fishing; it is 2 km from Ivrea which lies just off the autostrada from Aosta to Turin, Milan and points south. 'A very useful place for those who want to stop an hour and a half before or after the Mont Blanc tunnel,' writes one correspondent. 'The cooking is the big surprise for a hotel of this sort in Italy. Also it is situated a decent digestif-length's walk away from the town where you can go for another after-dinner expresso or a delicious ice cream before the walk back to bed.'

In fact, the hotel lost a Michelin star a couple of years ago, but its restaurant has continued to receive warm compliments from our readers. A correspondent this year writes: 'I found the *Sirio* all that your entry claims, but have to add a special laud for the standard of cuisine. I would also like to mention the overwhelming friendliness of the breakfast waitress, who not only acceded to our request to take the meal outside on the lawn, but was most actively promoting this. If one knows how often "outside meals" are frowned upon or refused, one has to be all the more grateful and pleased.' *(P G Bourne; also Geoffrey Sharp, Professor Anthony King, John Holloway)*

Open: All year.
Rooms: 28 double, 8 single, 1 suite – 14 with bath and WC, 22 with shower and WC, all with telephone, TV, tea-making facilities and baby-sitting.
Facilities: Lift, bar, TV room, breakfast room, 2 dining rooms. Terrace and garden – drinks and meals served there in good weather. English spoken. &.
Location: 2 km N of Ivrea, facing the lake. From Ivrea take Viale Monte Stella, then via Lago Sirio.
Credit card: American Express.
Terms: Rooms from 18,700 L; dinner, B & B 29,000 L; full board 36,000 L. Set meals: breakfast 2,700 L. Reduced rates and special meals for children.

MANTUA, 46100   **Map 14**

Albergo San Lorenzo   *Telephone:* (0376) 32.70.44
Piazza Concordia 14

'The nicest place to stay in this charming city. A small reception area only on the ground floor and no restaurant, but a lift whisks you up to pleasantly furnished rooms most of which have a lovely outlook on to the Piazza della Erbe and the Romanesque Church of San Lorenzo in the form of a Rotunda – the higher up you are the better. It is beautifully central and not noisy. The staff are most pleasant and obliging.' *(Geoffrey Sharp)*

Open: All year.
Rooms: 40 – 38 with bath and telephone, all with air-conditioning.
Facilities: Lift, reception area.
Location: Central; garage.
Terms: Rooms 29,900 L (single), 43,700 L (double). Set meal: breakfast 4,600 L.

Pensione Villa Anna   *Telephone:* (081) 87.82.504

'A gem. Adolfo Acampora, now dead, gave this little hotel, with only 15 rooms, to his wife, Anna, and she takes understandable pride in it and runs it as if it were her own house to which she has invited private friends, for that is the way guests are treated. Here, we are all one family. It's 5 km from Sorrento, but difficult to find. Cars cannot get down the steep little path, so package holiday-makers are blissfully absent, though the little beach tends to get crowded with locals on summer weekends. Rooms are surprisingly spacious and comfortable, all with private bathroom. There is no pool, but the small garden, with many interesting plants and flowers, seems to be all that guests want with the beach just in front. Food is simple but of the best Italian home-cooking, and it is a real pleasure to be able to eat out on the terrace after a drink in the thatched garden-bar where pizzas may also be had.' *(Richard Wiersum)*

Open: 1 April–31 October.
Rooms: 22 double, 1 single – 15 with bath, 7 with shower, all with telephone and tea-making facilities.
Facilities: Lounge with TV, bar, restaurant; weekly guitar music. Garden with table tennis, terrace; solarium; on beach; private bus to town centre, station and harbour. English spoken.
Location: 5 km W of Sorrento; parking.
Terms: B & B 17,000–33,000 L; dinner, B & B 25,500–33,000 L; full board 31,500–36,000 L. Set meals: lunch/dinner 11,000 L. Reduced rates for children under 6.

Grand Hotel Duomo   *Telephone:* (02) 8833
Via San Raffaele 1   *Telex:* 312086 Duomo 1

A big-city hotel, opposite the Duomo, that enjoys the peace of a square closed to all motor traffic. The building itself is listed as an ancient monument which means that the facade cannot be altered. The architects have made a virtue of necessity with the balconied rooms on the first floor which are 18 feet high: they have created split-level suites, with a drawing room at the first level and a bedroom and bathroom above, both enjoying the cathedral view. 'One of the few metropolitan hostelries where we dare request a room in the front. What a room it was! On a corner with four circular windows looking on to the roofs of the Gothic cathedral. The handsomely furnished room had a wall separating it from a generous sitting area with frigobar. Next door to the famous Galleria (shopping arcade) and in the other direction will be found less famous (but, in my opinion, better) boutiques selling gorgeous Italian shoes and other finds. Walking distance to La Scala and most of the art attractions that Milan has to offer.' *(Camille J Cook; also A G Don)*

Open: All year.
Rooms: 67 double, 75 single, 18 suites – 135 with bath, 25 with shower, all with telephone and radio, TV on request; some have sitting area and frigo-bar; baby-listening by arrangement.

Facilities: Lifts, reception hall, salon, bar, restaurant; conference rooms. Convention Hall. Fully air-conditioned. English spoken. ふ.
Location: Central; no private parking.
Credit cards: Access/Euro/Mastercard, Barclay/Visa.
Terms: B & B 62,500–82,500 L; dinner, B & B 85,000–115,000 L; full board 105,000–135,000 L. Set meal: breakfast 7,500 L; full *alc* 28,000 L. Special meals for children on request.

ORTA SAN GUILIO, 28016 Novara   Map 14

Hotel La Bussola

Telephone: (0322) 90 198

The popularity of the *San Rocco* (see below) is such that at certain seasons it is impossible to arrive casually and get a room. The *Bussola* makes an acceptable alternative. A modern purpose-built hotel, it is situated on the hill above Orta and has a beautiful panoramic view of the lake. The restaurant has an extensive terrace which enjoys the same view, and in addition there is a swimming pool and a separate sun terrace. Renato Tessera, the owner, took over *La Bussola* in September 1980 after twelve years in America. It is very much a family concern, run with relaxed efficiency. One couple, with a 13-month-old daughter, booked for three days, and found it so congenial that they stayed for ten. Another writes: 'If you are not fortunate enough to get a room at the front overlooking the lake, do not despair: the rooms at the back look out over an orchard to the mountains beyond, with not a single human habitation in sight. As the hotel stands well back from the road there is no traffic noise wherever one is. The ambience of the hotel is rather functional and characterless, but it is very comfortable. English and French are spoken and the food is a cut above the average. Prices are reasonable.' *(Alex Liddell; also Mrs Allen, Judith and David Jenkins)*

Open: All year.
Rooms: 17 double, 11 with bath, 6 with shower, all with telephone and baby-listening, 7 with refrigerator.
Facilities: TV room, bar, indoor and outdoor restaurants, banqueting room, night club. Large garden, swimming pool. 5 minutes' walk from the lake with possibility of swimming and all other water sports. English spoken.
Location: Central; garage and ample parking facilities.
Terms: B & B 16,000 L; dinner, B & B 31,000 L; full board 36,000 L.

ORTA SAN GIULIO, 28016 Novara   Map 14

Hotel San Rocco

Telephone: (0322) 90 191

An exceptionally agreeable hotel – formerly a 17th-century monastery, but, except for some cell-like rooms, you would hardly recognize it as such so extensive has been the modernization. It is right by the water on Lake Orta, one of the smaller and least spoiled of the Italian lakes, east of Maggiore and halfway between Domodossola and Novara. Following the retirement of the distinguished hotelier, Signor Terxi, a new regime has been under way, with Giuseppe Ruga in charge. Our reports, of which the following is typical, suggest that the Terxi tradition is being well maintained.

'Still a gem of a hotel situated in perfect tranquillity on the lakeside.

The village of Orta San Giulio, one minute's walk away, is a revelation of unspoilt sun-soaked buildings – a handful of café-bars, a few shops, churches, myriad alleyways and a quite stunning market square. The new management is excellent. Regular visitors insist there has been, if anything, an improvement. Signor Ruga is unfailingly charming and helpful, even to the extent of lending us his second car for excursions when he thought our plans for trips on foot were too ambitious; the reception ladies were also calm, smiling and friendly on all occasions. The rooms (rather small) have tiny balconies with glorious views across to the island of San Giulio – the cupboard space is perhaps minimal but this is largely because half the hanging room is taken up with a fridge, well stocked with bottles of this and that, e.g. fruit juices, Pellegrini, etc. Walls separating the bedrooms are perhaps a bit thin! The staff in the dining room made all meals a pleasure – lots of enthusiasm and a desire to please. The food itself was not outstanding, but certainly more than adequate. Vegetables and salads do not appear on the *table d'hôte*, except as a garnish, but once asked for, readily supplied at no extra charge.' (*Gina and Murray Pollinger; also Peter Marshall, SD and GM, F C Margetts, D St C Smallwood*)

Open: All year.
Rooms: 38 double, 2 single – all with bath and shower, telephone and balcony overlooking the lake; TV on request.
Facilities: Lift, hall, salon, TV room, bar with piano, dining room, 2 banqueting rooms. Garden with bar – swimming pool and sauna planned for 1982–83; boating, waterskiing, tennis and mini-golf nearby.
Location: 5 minutes from centre of town; private parking.
Credit cards: Access/Mastercard, American Express, Barclay/Visa.
Terms: B & B 25,000–41,000 L; dinner, B & B 37,000–43,000 L; full board 46,000–54,000 L. Set meals: lunch/dinner 16,000 L; full *alc* 20,000 L. Reduced rates for children under 6.

PORT' ERCOLE, 58018 Grosseto

Map 14

Il Pellicano

Telephone: (0564) 83.38.10
Telex: 500131 Pelican

'Il Pellicano is on the coast of Monte Argentario about 5 km from the small fishing village of Port' Ercole, which attracts tourists and yachting visitors, particularly on summer weekends. The coast round the hotel is rocky and wild; the road from the village follows its indentations and gives beautiful views of the sea. It is a small luxury hotel standing in lovely gardens overlooking the sea. The rooms are individually designed and the general atmosphere is of casual elegance. During the day the hotel is quiet and rather like having one's own private villa. Dinner is taken on the terrace overlooking floodlit trees and water.'

The above is part of last year's entry for *Il Pellicano*. There has been a change of management in the meantime, and the hotel is now run by a young Italian couple. The writer of the above report has been back since, and reports enthusiastically on improved standards of cleanliness, service and food. He concludes: 'Pellicano is a dream Mediterranean hotel. Rooms and public areas are furnished with the sort of sophisticated rusticity which unfortunately comes rather expensive (but perhaps not by British standards). One word of warning, however. If you go on holiday to make new friends or if you expect your hotel to provide night life until

3 am you'll hate the place. I wouldn't particularly recommend it to those travelling alone either. But if you want to rest and relax in romantically beautiful surroundings, be served by unobtrusive but very pleasant staff, and don't need to worry overmuch about the cost, then I know of few hotels better suited to provide just the right combination of relaxation and style. For anyone visiting outside the high season (15th June to 15th September) substantial discounts are given and the hotel becomes an absolute bargain.' *(David Wooff)*

Open: April–30 September.
Rooms: 28 double (16 with sea view, 12 with garden view) – all with bath and telephone. 3 luxury suites in cottages in the garden.
Facilities: Lounge, bar, restaurant, conference facilities; dinner-dance Friday nights in high season. Rocky beach with safe bathing; heated swimming pool; tennis, ping-pong, bowls, boats available; riding, sailing and water-skiing; golf 1 hour's drive; sightseeing to nearby Etruscan and Roman sites.
Restriction: No children under 14.
Credit cards: American Express, Barclay/Visa, Diners.
Location: 5 km S of Port' Ercole on the Monte Argentario coast.
Terms: Dinner, B & B 50,000–120,000 L; full board 70,000–140,000 L.

PORTOFINO, 16034   **Map 14**

Albergo Splendido   *Telephone:* (0185) 69 195
Viale Baratta 13   *Telex:* 331057 Splend

'The name *Albergo* does not seem to suit this luxurious hotel overlooking the bay around the corner from Portofino, a ten-minute walk away, although *Splendido* does. We stayed in January when it was very quiet, but no doubt it comes into its own more in the summer months, with its enormous terrace, swimming pool and tennis courts. (Portofino must be a nightmare in the summer months – even in January there was a half-mile queue of cars to get into the village!) Our room was large, pleasant, and had a small balcony. Many others, all of which look out over the bay, seemed to have larger terraces. The restaurant also has excellent views, and the menu, although not very large, was interesting and meals well cooked. All the staff were extremely friendly and helpful, and the housekeeping efficient. There are numerous walks from the hotel around the peninsula, visiting small villages inaccessible by car.' *(Pat and Jeremy Temple)*

Open: 10 March–10 January.
Rooms: 42 double, 12 single, 14 suites – 62 with bath, 5 with shower, all with telephone; colour TV in suites.
Facilities: Salon, bar with piano music, restaurant on terrace; conference facilities; sauna, solarium, beauty salon. Large grounds with gardens, swimming pool and tennis. Beach 20 minutes' walk.
Location: Right turn just before entering Portofino; garage (7,000 L per day) and car park.
Credit cards: Access/Euro/Mastercard, Barclay/Visa.
Terms: Rooms 71,500–134,000 L. Set meals: breakfast 8,000 L; lunch/dinner 36,000 L.

'Full *alc*', unless otherwise stated, means a three-course dinner with half a bottle of house wine, service and taxes included.

Hotel Caruso Belvedere   *Telephone:* (089) 85.71.11

Ravello, 20 minutes' twisting drive up into the hills from the hot screeching corniche road between Sorrento and Salerno, is an enchanting old town, full of noble palaces and two showplace gardens, with a wide cathedral piazza for nightlife. The *Caruso* is one of the distinguished older hotels of the town, on a steep street, with its rooms commanding a stunning view over the Gulf of Salerno towards Paestum. It's been much patronized by literati: names like Graham Greene and Gore Vidal are dropped. Signor Caruso is the third generation to run the hotel and his nephew now works alongside him. In summer meals are taken on a terrace, with fabulous views over the 'hot spots' of the coast. In cooler weather the marble-pillared dining room is used. The market square and the historic Villa Rufolo (whose garden is supposed to have inspired Klingsor's in *Parsifal*) are five minutes' walk away. The hotel also has a garden and there are many shady walks in the vicinity.

'The hotel is still run on lines that are out of date and old-fashioned in the best possible sense. The service is as impeccable and attentive as ever. Atmosphere and tradition allied to excellent food, spacious rooms, superb beds, sumptuous towels and snowy white linen combine to make a stay here a truly memorable experience. The only noticeable concession to modernity is the practical but rather ugly metal roof over the dining terrace. The well-remembered canvas canopy was so much more in keeping with the spirit of the place, the charm and the ambience. Despite advancing years, Signor Caruso Senior and his guiding hand are still much in evidence, and his courtesy on arrival and departure in particular was so heart-warming that one was left with the nagging anxiety that the *Belvedere* might not be quite the same without him. Why the Michelin Guide has not given this hotel the accolade of colouring it "red" is a source of amazement.' *(Peter Hacking and Hugh Wilson)*

Open: All year.
Rooms: 23 double, 3 single, 2 suites – 20 with bath, 2 with shower, all with telephone. (Some rooms on ground floor.)
Facilities: 2 lounges, TV room, bar, restaurant. Garden and terrace for summer meals, with magnificent views. English spoken.
Location: 25 km from Salerno, off the Salerno–Sorrento coast road. On Piazza S Giovanni del Toro. Hotel has garage.
Credit cards: American Express, Barclay/Visa.
Terms: B & B 19,000–29,500 L; dinner, B & B 35,000–45,000 L; full board 42,000–54,000 L. Set meals: lunch/dinner 15,000 L; full *alc* 18,000 L. Reduced rates and special meals for children.

ROME, 00187   **Map 14**

Hotel Marcella   *Telephone:* (06) 75.12.12
Via Flavia 106

'About ten minutes' walk from the Via Veneto and slightly north, this comfortable little hotel heralds itself with brown and white awnings. The reception – softly-lit with silk sofas and oil paintings and bar and breakfast rooms, simple but immaculate – leads the way by lift to the fourth and fifth floors where the bedrooms are. The other floors are offices. The rooms open off square landings, all thick-carpeted and beige-sofaed. The rooms themselves are simply furnished and decorated in terracotta white and chocolate with plenty of cupboard-space and well-fitted, if small bathrooms. Most rooms have a small balcony. Despite being on a fairly busy street, the hotel is quiet for Rome and there is a very pretty roof terrace with lovely views over three sides. Breakfast is the only meal served but the coffee and rolls are delicious and it's possible to get well-prepared egg and ham dishes. The boiled eggs were huge and brown and the waiter said they came fresh every day from a local hen-lady nearby. The bedrooms contain a fridge with a variety of drinks and a tin of biscuits.' *(Gillian Vincent)*

Open: All year.
Rooms: 55 – all with bath or shower, most with balcony.
Facilities: Lift, salon, breakfast room.
Terms: Room 40,000 L (single), 57,000 L (double). Set meals: breakfast 6,000 L.

ROME   Map 14

Hotel Napoleon   *Telephone:* (06) 73.76.46
Piazza Vittorio Emanuele 105, 00185   *Telex:* 611069

'Not in the choicest part of Rome but very colourful (just in front is probably the largest market in Rome). Despite all the busy life around it is quiet, because all the bedrooms are internal and therefore not facing either street or square. They claim to be the quietest hotel in the city. There are two comfortable lounges and a very friendly lounge-bar. There is a grill room which has a limited choice of dishes, but the food is well prepared, reasonably portioned and priced. Breakfast is offered buffet-style with cheeses, yogurt and four different types of bread. The bedrooms, although not luxurious, are comfortably furnished in traditional style and all have bath or shower.' *(Mrs Kay Ramsden)*

Open: All year. Restaurant closed Wednesday.
Rooms: 60 double, 20 single, 20 suites – 50 with bath, 50 with shower, all with telephone, radio and air-conditioning.
Facilities: 2 lounges, lounge/bar, dining room, card and TV room; conference facilities. Pianist 4 times a week. English spoken.
Location: In central east zone, close to railway station and air terminal, 10 m from subway.
Credit cards: Access, American Express.
Terms: Rooms 35,000–62,000 L. Set meals: breakfast 5,000 L; dinner, 1,500 L. 1,500 L.

We would like to be able to recommend more hotels in the budget class in Rome. Nominations especially welcome.

Hotel Raphaël
Largo Febo 2, 00186

Telephone: (06) 65.69.051
Telex: 68235

A quiet hotel, unobtrusively hidden behind creepers in a small side street not far from the Piazza Navona, which at night is one of Rome's liveliest piazzas. (*Warning:* the narrow streets behind the hotel are a noted hotbed of petty crime.) Very conveniently situated within easy walking distance of the main sights. The inside is air-conditioned and has an intimate atmosphere. It is very elegantly decorated in true Italian style, with sculptures, paintings, antiques and *objets d'art*. Bedrooms, air-conditioned, are less ornate but for the most part comfortable. The nicest thing about it is the rooftop; a tiny area squashed between the tiled roofs, chimney pots and belfries of the surrounding buildings, with a pretty garden and magnificent views. Tables, chairs and sun umbrellas are set out – a lovely spot to escape the bustle of the city. Restaurant adequate, but there are many eating places to choose from in the Piazza Navona. (*R A Hood, Peter Marris, A G Don*)

Open: All year.
Rooms: 85 – all with bath or shower, telephone and air-conditioning.
Facilities: Lift, lounge bar, small rooftop garden for refreshments.
Terms: Rooms 48,000 L (single), 73,600 L (double). Set meal: breakfast 5,000 L.

Hotel La Residenza
Via Emilia 22, 00187

Telephone: (06) 67.99.592

'This small, centrally placed residential hotel is situated within a stone's throw of the Via Veneto and is an ideal and relatively inexpensive base for the tourist. The rooms are comfortable and quiet provided you have a room at the back of the hotel. The front faces a night club which can be noisy late at night. Breakfast is served, but no other meals; but excellent inexpensive restaurants abound in the neighbourhood. The hotel management and staff offer excellent personal service.' (*Roger Schlesinger*)

Open: All year.
Rooms: 23 double, 3 single – 23 with bath, all with telephone.
Facilities: Lift, bar, reading room, breakfast room, air-conditioning; garden.
Location: Central, near the Via Veneto; parking.
Terms: B & B 36,000–44,000 L; 3,000 L charge for air-conditioning. Reduced rates for children sharing parents' room.

Hotel Sitea
via V Emanuele Orlando 90, 00185

Telephone: (06) 47.43.647
Telex: 614163 Sitea I

'The *Sitea* was very centrally located, and although unprepossessing on the outside, inside it was first-class in every way. Comfortable rooms, with maid service apparently continuously (every time we returned – from lunch, dinner, walks, whatever – someone had slipped in, hung up our clothes and straightened things). The breakfast room – the hotel has no restaurant – is truly lush, and the pastries were fine. The concierge was extremely helpful and friendly.' *(Martin and Deborah Zehr)*

Open: All year.
Rooms: 37 double, 3 single – 37 with bath, 3 with shower, all with telephone; radio and TV on request.
Facilities: Lounge, bar, TV room, breakfast room, coffee shop, roof garden. English spoken.
Location: In centre with own garage.
Credit card: American Express.
Terms: B & B 42,000–59,000 L. Snacks in coffee shop about 20,000 L. 20% reduction for children.

SAN GIMIGNANO, 53037 Siena   **Map 14**

Bel Soggiorno   *Telephone:* (0577) 94.03.75
via S. Giovanni   *Telex:* 53037

A beautiful 13th-century building a few yards inside the walls of the old town, recommended for its 'staggeringly low prices' and its memorable views over the vineyards, olive plantations, cypresses and fortified farm-houses of the Tuscan countryside. Rooms vary in size; some have large balconies. 'This *must* be retained in the Guide! Entry correct in all respects especially the staggeringly low price. The food was indeed excellent, and so was the Pescille wine.' *(B W Ribbons; also Katie Plowden, Charles Baker)*

Open: All year. Restaurant closed Monday.
Rooms: 27 double – all with bath.
Facilities: Restaurant, TV room. English spoken.
Location: 30 km from Siena; cars allowed in for loading and unloading only; large car park 400 m away.
Restriction: No children under 8.
Terms: Double rooms 24,000 L. Dinner, B & B 25,000 L per person.

SAN GIMIGNANO, 53037 Siena   **Map 14**

La Cisterna   *Telephone:* (0577) 94.03.28
Piazza della Cisterna 23

'Even a one-night stop-over at this truly classic hotel in San Gimignano, possibly the most attractive and best preserved Italian hill town, is strongly recommended – the tourist coaches and day trippers leave at about 4 pm and the discriminating visitor has the privilege to share and enjoy the life of this medieval "town of the beautiful towers". Even the cathedral, museum and palaces are uncrowded and can be enjoyed until 6 or 7 pm; and then the fun really starts – the visitor becomes part and parcel of the town life, the local inhabitants crowding the piazza and the main street (mercifully, pedestrian areas), the young passing up and down Via San Matteo, and old men sitting outside the cafés, not consuming anything except cigarettes (how do the proprietors make a living?). At dusk you may retire to the comfort of *La Cisterna*, formerly one of the

381

aristocratic palazzi of this town, and to dinner at its restaurant, *Le Terrazze*. This restaurant with its breathtaking view over the Val d'Elsa, formerly graced with a star in Michelin, still maintains a very high standard of cuisine and service, possibly the best *bistecca Fiorentina*, according to at least one of your correspondents. The room prices are remarkably low. We had a twin-bedded room with quite luxurious bathroom, with windows facing east and south, for 32,000 Lire, B & B [1981].' *(Arnold Horwell)*

Open: All year. Restaurant closed Tuesday, Christmas and 1 January–15 February.
Rooms: 41 double, 7 single – all with bath or shower, telephone and baby-listening.
Facilities: Lift, 14th-century salon, salon with TV, dining room.
Location: Central; cars allowed in for loading and unloading only; car park 400 m away. English spoken. ♿ .
Credit cards: American Express, Euro.
Terms: B & B 22,100–23,100 L; dinner, B & B 35,000–35,300 L; full board 46,000–47,600 L. Set meals: lunch/dinner 13,000 L; full *alc* 16,000 L.

SAN MARCO DI CASTELLABATE, 84071 Salerno   Map 14

Hotel Castelsandra   *Telephone:* (0974) 96.60.21

'70 km south of Salerno and 13 km beyond Agripoli, away from the hurly-burly of the Amalfi coast is the Cilento, an area of gentle hills, clear seas and a coastline still completely unspoiled. It is a marine preservation area and judging by the abundance of wild birds, including nightingales in the pinewoods, a wildlife preservation area as well. Here, perched 600 feet up the gentle lump of Monte Licosa (1,000 feet) is the *Hotel Castelsandra*. It enjoys superb views of the nearby hill town of Castellabate, with its pleasant twin ports of San Marco and Santa Maria, and, on a clear day, the whole of the Amalfi coast and Capri. The hotel nestles in a pine wood 4 km from San Marco so a car is advisable, although the hotel runs a courtesy bus to the beach. In an area as yet short of good hotels, we would certainly recommend the *Castelsandra*. The situation is positively idyllic; the public rooms are elegant and spacious and the grounds extensive and well laid-out; the large pool terrace (two heated pools) offers panoramic vistas and masses of new and comfortable poolside furniture. The hotel is superbly well-maintained and pristinely clean, not a little due to the presence of a formidable housekeeper of the old school!

'We do have a few reservations. The management appears a little vague and amateurish, needing somebody of the calibre of Sig. Rota of the *Ta' Cenc* on Gozo (q.v.) to pull it into shape. The bedrooms are a shade small for an hotel officially graded 1st class, and for some strange reason have fitted carpets instead of the superb and much more appropriate ceramic tiles for which the area is famous. However, the bathrooms are most stylish and brilliantly well-lit (especially for Italy) and all bedrooms have terraces with panoramic views. The food was well-cooked and presented, but rather unimaginative and the menu not very extensive. The wine list, however, was excellent and incredibly reasonable. Breakfasts were beyond reproach. Incidentally, we were the only British guests and some knowledge of Italian would be an asset.' *(Peter Hacking and Hugh Wilson)*

Open: June–September.
Rooms: 54 – all with telephone, TV and terrace.
Facilities: Salons, restaurant, terrace. Garden with tennis court and heated swimming pool; air-conditioning.
Location: 70 km S of Salerno, 13 km beyond Agripoli on the slopes of Monte Licosa; hotel is 4 km from San Marco. Parking.
Credit cards: All major credit cards accepted.
Terms: Rooms 27,600–48,150 L; full board 46,000–64,400 L. Set meals: breakfast 5,750 L; lunch/dinner 18,400 L.

SAN MARTINO AL CIMINO, 01030 Viterbo   Map 14

Balletti Park Hotel   *Telephone:* (0761) 29 177

'St Martino al Cimino is a village of great beauty close to Viterbo, and the *Balletti Park* is a gem. It is one of the most elegantly furnished ultra-modern hotels that I know. With Aram-type furniture in the lounges and very modern large wardrobes in the large bedrooms, it is light, airy and unfussy. It has a super swimming pool and a good restaurant. (On the other hand, if you want to eat superbly, there is, at La Quercia, 9 km distant, *Aquilanti*, a Michelin-starred restaurant and deservedly so.) Prices are very reasonable. Service is good. And there is lots to see round about: Viterbo itself; the fantastic park of the Villa Orsini at Bomarzo; Lago di Vico (unspoilt) and La Quercia. Ronciglione and Bagnaia (Villa Lante) are also worth a visit.' *(Martyn Goff)*

Thus our original entry. Martyn Goff has been back again and writes (July 1981): 'As good as ever and still excellent value. Staff still very courteous and efficient; swimming pool clean and little peopled.'

Open: All year. Restaurant closed Wednesday.
Rooms: 44 double – 12 with bath, 32 with shower, all with telephone, TV and terrace.
Facilities: Lift; hall, billiards room, bar, 2 restaurants, pizzeria, dancing room, conference and banqueting facilities; children's playroom. Large gardens where you can take refreshments; Olympic-size heated swimming pool, also children's pool; tennis.
Location: 5 km from Viterbo, 45 km from Orvieto and from sea, 70 km from Rome.
Credit card: American Express.
Terms: B & B 22,600–29,600 L; dinner, B & B 37,600–44,600; full board 48,000–59,600 L. Set meals: lunch/dinner, 15,000 L.

SANTA MARIA DEGLI ANGELI, Nr Assisi, 06088 Perugia   Map 14

Villa Elda   *Telephone:* (075) 81.90.67
via Patrono d'Italia 139

'This small hotel is 5 km from Assisi on the Perugia road, just after passing through Santa Maria degli Angeli. It's family-run and offers good service as well as delicious meals. Excellent local cheeses and wines. The hotel is in two parts – a nicely restored small "manor" house and a cleverly converted farm building, all surrounded by cool quiet Italian gardens and vineyards. There is ample parking space, a small room for watching TV, indoor and outdoor dining areas, and plenty of fresh, cool air away from the more confined parts of Assisi and Sta Maria. We found it by chance, and returned a year later by choice. While a few foreigners use the hotel, the clientele seems to be mainly Italian – usually a sign of a good place.' *(Barbara M Purvis)*

Open: March–November. Restaurant closed Friday.
Rooms: 21 double, 4 single – 23 with shower.
Facilities: Salon, TV room, restaurant. Garden with outdoor dining area.
Location: 5 km W of Assisi.
Credit cards: Bank Americard, Barclay/Visa.
Terms: Rooms 14,000–23,500 L. Full board 27,600 L. Set meal: breakfast 2,700 L; *alc* 12,000–19,000 L (excluding wine).

SIENA, 53100   **Map 14**

Palazzo Ravizza   *Telephone:* (0577) 28.04.62
Piano dei Mantellini 34

As in the past, the *Palazzo Ravizza* has had a mixed press this past year. It's a slightly run-down 17th-century palace within strolling distance of the cathedral and the famous piazza. It is the only hotel of its class and character in the old city. No one denies that it has atmosphere, but while some appreciate its wide staircases, antique furniture, high-ceilinged rooms and huge bathrooms and call it 'a really lovely place' others can only see the reverse side of the coin – dark passages, creaking armoires, votive lighting . . . On the whole, the food, apart from breakfast, isn't one of the more recommended features of the *Ravizza*, who say themselves that they offer 'Tuscan plain cooking'. *(Peter Marris)*

Open: All year.
Rooms: 21 double, 7 single, 1 apartment – 9 with bath, 4 with shower, all with telephone, TV and baby-listening.
Facilities: Lift, several sitting rooms (1 with TV), bar, restaurant. Very large garden with terrace for breakfast and refreshments. English spoken. &.
Location: 300 m from centre; parking.
Terms: B & B 22,000–24,000 L; dinner, B & B 33,000–35,000 L. Reduced rates for children.

SIENA, 53100   **Map 14**

Villa Scacciapensieri   *Telephone:* (0577) 41 442

The *Villa Scacciapensieri* (or *Sans-Souci*) is in the Tuscan countryside, 3 km outside Siena, on a neighbouring hill. It's a handsome Tuscan villa in a substantial park. There's a bus every half hour to the centre of town – a journey of 10 minutes. The food is strongly recommended: 'Continental breakfast was much better than in other similar hotels: no pulp in pre-sealed containers, but home-made raspberry jam and really good honey, several kinds of pastry, the usual Tuscan saltless bread, fresh red orange juice and very good coffee. The restaurant, very beautiful in quiet taste, has a good reputation.' The public rooms, too, in part modern, are 'beautifully furnished'. The grounds, which contain a large swimming pool with chaise-longues, are obviously a major attraction of the *Villa*, especially in the hot weather, but not everything in the garden is lovely;

briefly, it could do with some weeding. And there are other indications of things not being quite *comme il faut*: rooms in need of Hoover attention, or flowers being left in their vases after their day was over. Nevertheless, 'for anyone who loathes the sound of revving motorcycles and scooters during the night, and likes a rural setting and good food, this is the place.'
(Max and Katie Plowden; also Angela and David Stewart)

Open: March–November. Restaurant closed Wednesday.
Rooms: 21 double, 3 single – all with bath and telephone; TV and baby-listening by arrangement.
Facilities: Lounge, dining room. Outdoor dining on terrace with panoramic views over medieval Siena. Extensive landscaped grounds, with formal garden, heated swimming pool, tennis courts.
Location: 3 km from town centre; parking.
Credit cards: All major credit cards accepted.
Terms: Rooms 44,000–86,000 L; full board 63,000–92,000 L. Set meal: breakfast 5,000 L; *alc* 19,500–28,000 L (excluding wine).

SPERLONGA, 04029 Latine   Map 14

Parkhotel Fiorelle   *Telephone:* (0771) 54 092

'Roughly half way along the coast between Rome and Naples, Sperlonga is a cliff-top huddle of narrow streets and houses jutting out into the sea, bearing comparison with Portovenere for genuine charm (as against villages like Punta Ala, higher up the coast, which looks and feels fabricated). At the northern foot of the town is a good restaurant, *Laocoonta-da Rocco*. Half a mile along the seafront is the *Parkhotel Fiorelle*, set back in its own lush gardens. There's plenty of parking space, though in 1980 I had the petrol siphoned out of my unlocked tank during the night! A good sandy beach is enhanced by a first-class swimming pool between it and the hotel. Austrian-born Signora di Milli is always charming and helpful, while her Italian husband looks after the kitchens. Food is simple but good; service pleasant. But for sheer value – 20,000 L a day per person *demi-pension* [July 1981] – the place is unbeatable.'
(Martyn Goff)

Open: March–October.
Rooms: 33 – 7 with bath, 26 with shower, all with balcony.
Facilities: Salon, bar, restaurant; terrace for refreshments. Garden with swimming pool; private sandy beach nearby. English spoken.
Location: On the coast between Rome (127 km) and Naples (106 km).
Terms: Rooms 17,250–23,000 L; full board 23,000–32,200 L. Set meals: breakfast 2,300 L; lunch/dinner 9,775 L.

SYRACUSE, 9100 Sicily   Map 14

Grand Hotel   *Telephone:* (0931) 65 101
Viale Mazzini 12

'A small palazzo converted to a hotel, situated in Ortygia, the ancient harbour of Syracuse, overlooking the fishing boats, the Malta ferry, and the spot where Archimedes by his mastery of classical artillery, helped to destroy the fleet of Marcellus in 214 BC. But don't crane your neck to look around. The hideous pylons of the natural gas installations at Augusta (Sicily's boom industry) are creeping inexorably nearer and will surely soon obliterate the hotel's splendid views. We had a large, cool, white-painted front room with high ceilings and heavy shutters to keep out the dazzling white light. The service was competent, courteous and self-effacing. (A blind broke the first evening and was efficiently repaired almost immediately.) As in most Sicilian hotels that cater for locals not tourists, no food is served, though breakfast can be obtained as an extra in one of the alcoves off the main lounge. We followed local custom and had delicious stand-up breakfast snacks in local bars which are on every corner of the town. Another advantage was that one of Sicily's great fish restaurants, *Da Pippo*, was five minutes' walk away. The hotel's most serious drawback was that when the fishing fleet returned at around 3 am in the morning, a hideous din would break out for half an hour or more, accompanied, it seemed by sounds of dredgers and other incredibly noisy machines. Rooms at the back of the hotel with less attractive views, would probably be a great deal quieter.' *(Dennis and Madeleine Simms)*

Open: All year.
Rooms: 47, almost all double – 8 with bath, 15 with shower, all with telephone.
Facilities: Lift, lounge, bar. &.
Location: near harbour.
Terms: Rooms 24,000 L (single), 44,000 L (double). Set meal: breakfast 4,600 L.

TAORMINA, 98039 Messina, Sicily   **Map 14**

Villa Belvedere   *Telephone:* (0942) 23 791
Via Bagnoli Croce 79

'With the *Villa Fiorita*, which has no garden or pool, the *Villa Belvedere* is undoubtedly the nicest place to stay in in Taormina if one wants to be independent for meals. It offers B & B only, though light snacks can be obtained from the poolside bar. Breakfast is continental, but for once the bread is fresh and the coffee strong and individually made. Monsieur Pecaut comes from France, is married to a ravishing Italian girl, and his ochre-hued villa-hotel offers nicely-appointed new rooms with stupendous views over the flowered garden, the bay and Mount Etna, or more traditional and simpler ones with the same view or rooms towards the back (the latter tend to be a bit noisy). A delightful bar and lounge, library, but, above all, the beautiful gardens and pool, left my party of seasoned and experienced Sicily-travellers ecstatic. There is a lift, and rates this year [1981] worked out at £8 per person B & B. A real find!' *(RW)*

Open: 20 December–10 January, 20 March–15 November.
Rooms: 36 double, 4 single, 1 suite – 12 with bath, 26 with shower, all with telephone.
Facilities: Lift, lounge, library, lounge bar, breakfast room. Garden, heated swimming pool with bar. &.
Location: Central, near public gardens and tennis court; parking.
Credit cards: Access/Euro/Mastercard, Barclay/Visa.
Terms: B & B 23,250–26,300 L. Reduced rates for children sharing parents' room.

All hotel prices are approximate. Italian hotel prices are more approximate than most.

TAORMINA, 98039 Sicily   **Map 14**

Hotel Pensione Villa Paradiso   *Telephone:* (0942) 23 921
Via Roma 6   *Telex:* 980062 Attn HOTEL PARADISO

'La Villa Paradiso è stata sempre preferita dalla sua tradizionale clientela inglese.' A faithful client returns the compliment: 'Relaxed comfort and elegance in an atmosphere that is dignified without being stuffy. Excellent food in the charming top-floor restaurant. The staff are invariably well-spoken and efficient, remembering the little likes and dislikes of the guests, many of whom they have seen returning for years. Good furniture in the ground-floor lounge-area positively invites a post-prandial *Amara Averna* – the island's own digestif – unobtrusively served from the splendid corner-table that serves as a bar. A few guests watch television, others write letters or just read one of the books from the thoughtfully provided small library, whilst we stroll into the old town itself to enjoy a coffee on one of the many open-air terraces. An impeccable *pensione*.' *(CRW; also James Dubois)*

Open: All year, except 1 November–16 December.
Rooms: 30 double, 3 single – 28 with bath, 5 with shower, all with balcony, telephone, radio, air-conditioning and baby-listening. (Some rooms on ground floor.)
Facilities: Lift, TV room, library, bar, restaurant; facilities for small conferences; terrace with tables. Next door to public gardens with tennis courts. English spoken. &.
Location: In town centre. Superb views of Bay of Naxos and Mt Etna.
Credit cards: All major credit cards accepted.
Terms: B & B 24,000–28,000 L; dinner, B & B 35,000–48,000 L; full board 45,000–58,000 L. Set meals: lunch 14,000 L; dinner 16,000 L; full *alc* 20,000 L. Reductions of 50% for children up to 5; 25% 5–10; special meals provided.

TAORMINA, 98039 Messina, Sicily   **Map 14**

Villa Riis   *Telephone:* (0942) 24 875
Via Rizzo

'The ochre-stuccoed building quietly set back from the main street looks like an original palazzo. Further enquiries reveal that it is a clever imitation from the Fifties. Never mind, for it loses nothing of its charm for that. Mount Etna is hidden by the slope of a hill from the dining terrace, but the bay of Naxos, with its twinkling lights, is reasonable compensation. Candles on the tables enhance the feeling of romance, and the food does nothing to dispel it. One feels one is staying in a private home. Everything is quiet, intimate and discreet; the period furniture in the bedrooms and sitting room seem in keeping with the slightly older discriminating clientele who treat the staff and each other as courteously as they unhesitatingly allow themselves to be treated.' *(RW)*

Open: March–October. Restaurant closed midday.
Rooms: 28 double, 5 single, 1 suite – all with bathroom or shower, telephone, radio and colour TV. (Some rooms on ground floor.)
Facilities: Lift, lounge with TV, bar, dining room. Small garden and terrace. Funicular to beach. &.

Location: 5 minutes from town centre near Porta Catania; parking.
Credit cards: American Express, Bank Americard.
Terms: B & B 18,300–24,250 L; dinner, B & B 38,000–40,000 L.

TORCELLO, 30012 Burano   Map 14

Locanda Cipriani   *Telephone:* (041) 73 01 50

'*Locanda Cipriani* on the island of Torcello, the original settlement of the
Venetian lagoon, is best-known for its restaurant, part of everyone's day
trip to see the Byzantine cathedral and its attendant buildings: but it is also
a small hotel of singular character, and a night there when the day tourists
have returned to the city is a unique Venetian experience. The genre is
what you might call mock-simple, or perhaps *fête-champêtre*. The building is an old inn overlooking its own vegetable gardens, and in the evening
the island locals do their drinking in its front parlour or on its arbored
terrace. It is illusory, though, for everything has been subtly modernized,
and the place is run with all the graceful professionalism of its celebrated
parent, *Harry's Bar* in Venice. And after dinner, on a summer evening,
there can hardly be a pleasure of travel more innocently sensual than to
walk beneath the pergolas with somebody you love, a glass of the
excellent house wine in your hand, looking at the grand old shape of the
cathedral beyond the asparagus beds, and listening to the faint stir of the
wind off the lagoon. Winston Churchill and Ernest Hemingway were
among the guests who have relished this delight: if you want to round off
your stay in their style, for a smallish fortune you can get a motor-boat to
come out from Venice in the morning and take you direct to Marco Polo
airport, about 4 km away across the lagoon, to be whisked home over the
Alps in time for scrambled eggs, and the nine o'clock news.' *(Jan Morris)*

Open: Mid March–early November. Restaurant closed Monday.
Rooms: 6 – all with bath and air-conditioning.
Facilities: Restaurant, terrace. Garden.
Credit card: American Express.
Terms: Rooms 46,000–126,500 L. Set meal: breakfast 5,700 L; *alc* 33,000–42,500
L (excluding wine and 15% service charge).

TORRE PELLICE, 10066 Torino   Map 14

Hotel Gilly   *Telephone:* (0121) 93 24 77
Corso Jacopo Lombardini 1

A smart modern hotel in a wooded valley close to the Alps, 500 metres
above sea level. Torre Pellice is both a summer and a winter resort,
offering a wide range of appropriate facilities: cable-car for summer walks
and winter skiing, tennis courts, mini-golf, etc. 'Unreservedly recommended. Extremely comfortable beds. Acceptable modern decor. Food,
wine and service all first-class. Despite nearness to the main road, it is also
very quiet.' *(James Shorrocks)*

Open: All year, except 15 December–5 January.
Rooms: 26 double, 10 single, 4 apartments – 36 with bath, 28 with shower, all with
telephone and radio, 24 with colour TV, the rest black and white. 20 rooms in
annexe.

Facilities: Hall, various lounges, TV room, bar with piano, film shows; heated indoor swimming pool. Garden. Tennis, winter sports nearby. English spoken.
Location: 300 m from centre; parking.
Credit cards: American Express, Euro.
Terms: Rooms 35,000–50,000 L; B & B 38,000–53,000 L; dinner, B & B 50,000 L; full board (minimum 3 days) 45,000 L. Set meals: lunch 13,000 L; dinner 15,000 L; full *alc* 18,000 L. 50% reduction for children under 6; special meals on request.

TREVISO, 31100   Map 14

Le Beccherie   *Telephone:* (0422) 40 871
Piazza Ancillotto 10

'Treviso is a charming little town, 30 km north of Venice, surrounded by ramparts and intersected by canals. The hotel is situated in the heart of the town, near the Piazza dei Signori. The restaurant is on one side of the *tiny* piazza Ancillotto, and the hotel portion on the other. Our room was not particularly big, but well-equipped with shower and all the usual facilities, and very clean. Very friendly helpful reception. No English spoken, but it is remarkable how this improves one's Italian! The restaurant building is old and pleasantly cluttered inside with gastronomic diplomas, old pottery, pictures and mementoes. The dining room is filled with local families gorging themselves – always a good sign this – and we certainly had an excellent and very reasonably priced meal. Friendly and expert service. *Warning:* Treviso is a maze of narrow one-way streets, and one may have several shots at reaching the hotel before actually making it. Once there, the fight for an empty parking slot in the tiny piazza starts, in competition with the locals. One just has to sit it out. The sooner Treviso makes this a traffic-free area the better: it would definitely add to the attraction of this delightful little town.' *(Ian and Agathe Lewin)*

Open: All year, except 15–31 July.
Rooms: 21 double, 9 single – 16 with shower, all with telephone and radio.
Facilities: Bar, restaurant (opposite), air-conditioning.
Location: 30 km N of Venice; central in one-way street leading from railway station; no special parking facilities.
Terms: B & B 20,000–21,000 L. Set meals: lunch/dinner 15,000 L; full *alc* 20,000 L.

TRIESTE, 34121   Map 14

Hotel Duchi d'Aosta   *Telephone:* (040) 62 081
Piazza Unità d'Italia 2   *Telex:* 460358 Duchi I

The largest port in the Adriatic and, since it was busy in sea-trade even in pre-Roman days, rich in historical associations of many periods. The *Duchi d'Aosta* has a prime position in the city, being in the spacious central square, open to the quayside and lined with palaces and large cafés. The hotel's restaurant is called *Harry's Grill Bar*.
'The hotel is extremeley well-situated in the huge Piazza Unità d'Italia fronting the sea, where the evening stroll takes place by glittering gilded and spun sugar palaces, civic buildings and large cafés. Flagposts and ornate lamps soar up high into the sky in scale with the tall and ornate buildings. Our large bedroom overlooked the square and was beautifully

furnished; there was a well-stocked refrigerated drinks cupboard discreetly built into the wall. The walls and ceiling were painted to resemble old vellum, heavy plush curtains could block out all sound and light; there was retractable mosquito netting at the windows and spacious bedside tables held elegant lamps with Venetian glass bases. The bathroom was luxurious, richly tiled and with a tremendous battery of lights over the basin mirror. Our tiny rented Fiat was put away by the porter with as much ceremony as he would have extended to a Lamborghini. Dinner was good: light creamy soups and subtly flavoured pasta followed by large fillet steaks with a mozarella cheese stuffing and cooked in red wine, then fresh fruit salad. There was no pretentious palaver about a wine list – a large carafe was put in front of us and we were charged only for what we drank. The dining room was quietly elegant with especially pretty fluted glassware. Breakfast was of the continental variety but included some particularly delicious blood red orange juice. In all, a feeling of discreet luxury and a very good place to stop en route from Greece or Yugoslavia. It was, of course, expensive but a similar standard in England would probably cost much more. We thought it worth every penny.' *(Ray and Angela Evans)*

Open: All year. Restaurant closed Sunday.
Rooms: 52 double, 42 single, 8 suites – 51 with bath, all with shower, telephone, radio, mono TV, frigobar and baby-listening by arrangement.
Facilities: 3 lounges, *Harry's Grill Bar* with terrace restaurant overlooking main piazza and sea. Very near the sea; all types of water sports available. English spoken. &.
Location: Central; car park for 30 cars in front of hotel; garage 10 minutes away.
Credit cards: All major credit cards accepted.
Terms: B & B 44,500–79,500 L; dinner, B & B 70,500–105,500 L. Set meals: lunch/dinner 29,000 L; full *alc* 35,000 L. 20% discount for children; special meals available.

TURIN, 10132   **Map 14**

Villa Sassi   *Telephone:* (011) 89.05.56
Strada al Traforo del Pino 47

The *Villa Sassi*, a small hotel in terms of its accommodation, is a very grand place indeed by every other criterion. It has a pedigree that goes back over a thousand years, and is set in a splendid park on the outskirts of the city. 'Sheltered by a park filled with trees, many specimens that appeared to be centuries old, the *Villa Sassi* offers birds to wake you in the morning. Our bedroom was large and airy, sharing a huge terrace with several other bedrooms. The bathroom was imaginatively decorated and immaculately appointed. The public rooms are on a scale as befits a restaurant with rooms that earns four red knives and forks in Michelin as well as a star. Italians don't often appreciate their own wines, but this restaurant had the best vintages of Barolo, Fara, Malvasia and others.' *(Camille J Cook)*

We owe an apology to one disappointed guest at the *Sassi* for failing to mention in our entry last year that the restaurant is closed on Sundays. Our correspondent managed to get a decent lunch at the local trattoria, but nothing at all was open in the evening. 'I was able to appreciate the funny side,' he writes stoically, 'as I watched my little meths heater warming up a tin of Buitoni Ratatouille in that palatial room. It's a lovely hotel, but with *not quite* all the mod cons.' *(James Shorrocks)*

Open: All year, except August. Restaurant closed Sunday.
Rooms: 11 double, 1 apartment – all with bath, telephone and frigobar.
Facilities: Salons, bar, restaurant; conference and banqueting facilities; large park and flower gardens with terrace for meals or refreshments. English spoken.
Location: On outskirts of city; parking. Follow signs for Pino Traforo.
Credit cards: All major credit cards accepted.
Terms: Rooms 30,000–44,000 dinner, B & B from 70,000 L; full board from 93,000 L. Set meals: breakfast 5,500 L; lunch/dinner 27,000 L. Reduced rates and special meals for children.

VALNONTEY, 11012 Cogne, Aosta   **Map 14**

Hotel Herbetat   *Telephone:* (0165) 74 180

'A friendly small hotel, very efficiently run, and situated just inside the boundary of the Gran Paradiso National Park, with staggering views of the mountains and glaciers from its windows. The restaurant serves good Italian food with the inclusion of some local dishes such as casseroled chamois and succulent polenta. The local wines are hearty and unpretentious, and superior varieties are available. This is a superb centre for hill-walkers and climbers. Live chamois can sometimes be observed in the meadows across the valley; ibex can be seen (and smelt) on the higher slopes. The only drawback is that the place attracts Italian excursionists at the weekends, although they do not seem to invade the hotel.' *(Christopher Serpell)*

A recent visitor writes: 'This should remain in the Guide. It is an unpretentious mountain hotel, with a friendly and very helpful staff. The weekend excursionists were not all that numerous when we stayed in July. Our only criticism was that the hot water supply was very very slow and erratic. The four-course set dinners were excellent, especially the soups and the cheese board, and the bill was unbelievable! We are keen to stay there again.' *(B W Ribbons)*

Open: 1 June–end September. Restaurant closed Thursday.
Rooms: 20 double, 2 single – 10 with bath, some with balconies, all with baby-listening.
Facilities: Sitting room, bar, restaurant; large terrace; children's play area. Mountain village in a valley looking straight up to the Gran Paradiso massif (3,650 metres) and National Park with wild life and rare alpine flowers.
Location: 30 km S of Aosta, 3 km from Cogne.
Credit card: Euro.
Terms: Rooms 9,000–18,000 L. Set meals: breakfast 2,200 L; lunch/dinner 10,000–11,500 L.

VARENNA, 22050 Como   **Map 14**

Hotel du Lac   *Telephone:* (0341) 83.02.38 and 83.05.88
Via del Prestino 4

Varenna is a village on the eastern side of Lake Como, about 24 km north of Lecco. The *Hotel du Lac*, a place of simple refinement, is, as its name suggests, on the lakeside with its own landing stage for swimming or boating. 'We have stayed here twice – once by chance and the second time by booking – and are about to go for the third year running. The hotel is run by youngish owners, Signora and Signor Pellizzari, who live on the premises and see to the comfort of the guests. What we liked about it was that the rooms we had looked right out on the lake, as does the restaurant. The Pellizzaris speak English and are most helpful in every way. The hotel is an easy walk to the landing stage where all the ferries go in different directions across the lake.' *(Stuart and Helga Connolly)*

Last year's entry, quoted above, has some i's dotted by a 1981 visitor: 'Mrs P speaks English but not Mr P; both are most pleasant and helpful. The rooms have showers, only exceptionally a bath; my husband and I are both small but to use the lavatory without either flooring the towels or falling into the shower took all our physical ingenuity. The room itself was tiny, its salvation being a large terrace with magnificent views. The public rooms and terraces were spacious, clean and inviting, the situation of the hotel delightful, the food reasonable, adding up to a stay ended with reluctance and, having been shown a larger but still modest room, we plan a longer return visit next year.' *(Patricia Solomon)*

Open: All year.
Rooms: 12 double, 5 single, 2 suites – 19 with shower, 1 with radio, 1 with colour TV, all with telephone.
Facilities: 3 salons, bar, restaurant (with music or electric organ), TV room, 2 sun terraces; swimming from hotel pier. English spoken.
Location: 24 km N of Lecco.
Credit card: Barclay/Visa.
Terms: B & B 26,500–38,000 L; dinner, B & B 37,000–45,000 L; full board 45,000–54,000 L. Set meals: lunch/dinner 16,500 L; full *alc* 20,000 L. Reduced rates and special meals for children.

VENICE Map 14

Hotel Cipriani   *Telephone:* (041) 70.77.44
Giudecca 10, 30123   *Telex:* 410162 CIPRVE
          Reservations: In UK: (01) 583 3050
          In USA: (800) 233 6800

A hyper-elegant hotel near the eastern end of the Giudecca, facing the island of San Giorgio, and the hotel motor-boat is on constant call to take the guests the five-minute journey to its private landing-stage by the Piazzetta of San Marco. 'A way of life . . . like staying on one's own exclusive island,' we said last year, and that sums up both the attraction and (for some) the drawback of the *Cipriani*. It has its back to San Marco, facing across the lagoon to the Lido in the misty distance. It doesn't somehow belong to the city. On the other hand, it's the only hotel in Venice with its own grounds and swimming pool, and it's ideal in the summer as a haven from the heat and the crowds. And some Venetians hold that it offers the best food in the city.

Open: 1 March–30 November.
Rooms: 76 double, 4 single, 14 suites – all with bath, telephone, radio, and baby-listening; colour TV on request. (Some rooms on ground floor.)
Facilities: 2 restaurants (indoor and outdoor), 2 bars (one with piano), 5 function rooms, TV room. Gardens with Olympic-size swimming pool (heated and domed in winter). Lectures, cookery courses and guided tours between March and June. English spoken. ⅙.

If you are thinking of writing reports on hotels for us, do it NOW!

Location: 5 minutes by private motor boat to city centre.
Credit card: American Express.
Terms: On request.

VENICE   Map 14

Hotel Do Pozzi   *Telephone:* (041) 70.78.55
Calle Largo 22 Marzo 2373, 30124   *Telex:* 410275 Attention Do Pozzi

A small hotel, modern, clean and comfortable, 200 metres from the Piazza San Marco, and within a stone's throw of the *Gritti* (q.v.), but at a fraction of the price. It's at the end of a tiny alleyway, with a little flowery courtyard in front. Rooms, both the public and the bedrooms, mostly on the small side. Walls are hung with modern paintings. Breakfast only served, but the hotel has an arrangement with the nearby *Ristorante di Raffaele* – 'excellent both in quality of food and value' – with tables in the open overlooking a canal.

Open: All year.
Rooms: 22 double, 13 single – 9 with bath, 26 with shower, all with telephone and baby-listening.
Facilities: Lift, hall/reception, small sitting room, TV room, breakfast room; air-conditioning. Pretty courtyard garden with flowers; breakfast served there in fine weather. English spoken.
Location: Central.
Credit cards: American Express, Barclay/Visa, Euro.
Terms: B & B 25,000–46,000 L; dinner, B & B 26,000–52,000 L; full board 34,000–62,000 L. Set meals: lunch/dinner 11,000–13,000 L. 20% reduction for children under 6; special meals available. (Note: meal prices uncertain at time of going to press as restaurant management changes in 1982.)

VENICE   Map 14

Hotel Flora   *Telephone:* (041) 70.58.44
San Marco 2283a, 30124

'The hotel is a five-minute stroll or a two-minute sprint from St Mark's Square, going in the direction of the Accademia, at the end of a narrow alleyway. Two wings of an old house flank either side of a pretty courtyard garden. Bedrooms vary in size and position – the best look down on to the courtyard. Ours was small, but richly if fussily furnished. The welcome from the proprietor was very friendly. There were a great number of staff for a small hotel which added to the general feeling of being well looked after. Sitting in the garden with a long cool drink after a hot slog round Venice was extremely pleasant and rejuvenating. Breakfast was good – we chose smooth hot chocolate with a variety of rolls, some with a delicious surprise middle of marzipan. Small scale luxury.' *(Ray and Angela Evans; also Arnold Horwell)*

Open: 15 February–15 November.
Rooms: 39 double, 5 single – 30 with bath, 14 with shower, all with telephone. (2 rooms on ground floor.)
Facilities: Lift, lounge, TV room, bar, small breakfast room. Courtyard/garden where breakfast and drinks are served. English spoken. &.

Location: Central, just off the Calle Larga XXII Marzo.
Credit cards: All major credit cards accepted.
Terms: B & B 30,000–49,000 L.

Gritti Palace   *Telephone:* (041) 26 044
Campo Santa Maria del Giglio 2467, 30124   *Telex:* 410125 Gritti

The former home of Doge Andrea Gritti and now one of the great hotels of the world. Quiet understated elegance, immaculate service and extremely good food (served by candlelight on a lovely terrace overlooking the Grand Canal) are its hallmarks. But it also succeeds in combining these desiderata with natural, unobtrusive courtesy.

Open: All year.
Rooms: 73 double, 9 of which are suites, 17 single – all with bath, telephone, radio and TV.
Facilities: 3 salons, TV rooms, bar, restaurants; terrace-restaurant overlooking the Grand Canal. English spoken.
Location: On the Grand Canal, 10 minutes by boat from the Lido.
Credit cards: All major credit cards accepted.
Terms: B & B 123,700–175,450 L; full board on request. Full *alc* 80,000 L. Special meals for children.

Pensione Seguso   *Telephone:* (041) 22 340 or 86 858
Grand Canal 779, 30123 Zattere

'This modest *pensione* on the Zattere has been a popular haunt of English-speaking visitors to the city for many years past. (Signora Seguso speaks fluent English.) Its special attraction is the stunning view from the front-facing windows of the Guidecca and of Venetian craft of all sizes, including ocean liners; the side rooms have pleasing views over a small canal. It has the virtues of a high-class, old-fashioned establishment – fine old Venetian furniture, dining room with embroidered silk wall covering, friendly service, honest bourgeois fare. Opinions on the Seguso's food vary: one recent correspondent dubbed it 'particularly good', but others have preferred to stay on B & B rather than *pension* terms. (*Lesley and Christopher Lintott, Faith and David Levey, P D Scott, Peter Marris*)

Open: 1 March–30 November, except Wednesday.
Rooms: 26 double, 10 single – 10 with bath, 10 with shower, 4 with telephone, all with tea-making facilities and baby-listening.
Facilities: Lift, lounge, 2 dining rooms. Garden. English spoken.
Location: Central.
Credit card: American Express.
Terms: Dinner, B & B 32,000–40,250 L; full board 46,000–54,250 L. Set meals: lunch/dinner 14,000 L. Reduced rates for children under 5; special meals available.

If no one writes about a good hotel, it may get left out next year.
WRITE NOW.

Colombo d'Oro   *Telephone:* (045) 59.53.00
via C Cattaneo 10   *Telex:* 480872 COLOMB

This medium-sized hotel in the centre of Verona, within strolling distance of the Arena for opera-goers, continues to get good notices from our critics. 'Unusually large and well-appointed bedrooms offering oustanding value for money. Situated on a noisy side street, but double glazing and air-conditioning ensure peace and comfort. A totally safe private garage – a major plus in Italy. Staff couldn't have been more friendly and helpful.' No restaurant, but 'delicious breakfasts as late as you wish.' *(John Sidwick)*

Open: All year.
Rooms: 40 double, 20 single, 2 suites – 45 with bath, 17 with shower, all with telephone and air-conditioning.
Facilities: Bar, salon, TV room; conference room. English spoken.
Location: Central; garage in same building as hotel.
Credit cards: American Express, Barclay/Visa, Diners, Euro.
Terms: B & B 35,000–50,500 L. Special weekend rates 1 November–10 March. 40% reduction for children sharing parents' room.

De' Capuleti   *Telephone:* (045) 32 970
via del Pontiere 26

The *Hotel De' Capuleti* is round the corner from Juliet's tomb, near the river Adige and within comfortable walking distance of virtually everything. It is essentially a modest family hotel. Bedrooms are small but clean, most with private showers and toilets and tiny balconies. Choose a room at the back; Italian traffic seems noisier than that of any other European nation. There is no lounge, but a pleasant bar. Food is excellent and cheap. The staff are friendly and several speak English. *(Ian and Agathe Lewin, Anne Bolt, B W Ribbons)*

Open: All year, except 24 December–10 January.
Rooms: 29 double, 5 single, 2 suites – 25 with bath, most with balcony, all with telephone.
Facilities: Lift, bar, restaurant, breakfast room. English spoken.
Location: Central, near Juliet's Tomb; parking available in Via del Pontiere and other nearby streets.
Credit cards: American Express, Diners, Barclay/Visa.
Terms: Rooms 18,000–31,000 L. Set meals: breakfast 4,600 L.

Hotels were asked to estimate prices for 1982, but some hotels gave us only their 1981 prices. To avoid unpleasant shocks, always check tariff at time of booking.

Le Axidie Hotel   *Telephone:* (081) 87.98.181
Marina di Equa

We have had an entry since our first edition for this strongly anglophile
hotel in a tiny hamlet at sea level facing Naples and Vesuvius across the
bay, a mile or so beyond and below the bustling resort town of Vico
Equense. The bathing from the hotel's private beach is absolutely safe.
The sea is frequently polluted at Naples, but is consistently clear at the
Axidie. A constant slight breeze mitigates the torpor of Neapolitan heat.
The hotel is quiet except in July and August; the food is excellent, with the
menu changing every day, so that, if you stay a fortnight, you won't get the
same dish twice. It is designed for summer sunshine, with an outdoor
restaurant and outdoor sitting in the evening. The indoor public rooms
are no more than adequate – but rain is a rarity. Most of the bedrooms,
floored with Salerno tiles, have balconies overlooking the sea.
   What has made the hotel so consistently popular with our readers,
except in the really crowded high season when Italians predominate, is the
ebullient and welcoming personality of its owner, Fernando Savarese,
who built *Le Axidie* more than twenty years ago, shortly after he married
the prima ballerina Violetta Elvin. It is the kind of hotel which attracts
strong loyalties, and faithful guests have been happy to find the place
unchanging from year to year. But there have been some changes this past
year. Antonio, the *direretore*, has gone; there is a new, and pleasant
headwaiter (from *Capanina* in Romilly Street, Soho); and all the waiters
are new. Although the beach is still "private", it is much more crowded
than it used to be, many more huts having been put up. The hotel tries to
reserve one corner for its guests but this doesn't always work out. This
year's reports suggest that *Le Axidie* has lost something of its exclusive
character. We should be glad to hear from recent visitors.

Open: April–October.
Rooms: 28 double, 2 single, 6 suites – 15 with bath, 15 with shower, many with
balcony, all with telephone and baby-listening. 4 rooms in annexe.
Facilities: 2 salons, bar, restaurant, outdoor restaurant. 2 acres grounds with
tennis courts, swimming pool and private beach with safe bathing. English spoken.
Location: 36 km S of Naples. Leave the A3 at Castellammare and follow the
signpost for Sorrento as far as Vico Equense; 1½ km past Vico Equense, cross a
bridge and 100 m further on turn right. At the end of this road is *Le Axidie*.
Terms: B & B 25,000–51,000 L; dinner, B & B 33,000–63,000 L; full board
48,000–78,000 L. Set meals: lunch/dinner 19,000 L. Special out-of-season rates on
request. 25% reduction for children sharing parents' room; special meals available.

Leon d'Oro   *Telephone:* (0761) 31 012
via della Cava 36

'We wanted a base from which to visit the main Etruscan sites, and this
hotel was ideal for this part of Etruria – once we had sorted out the
typically medieval Italian traffic signs and found it. The rooms were
reasonably modern, with a lift, a large sitting room and pleasant service.
There was an acceptable restaurant attached, and a convenient garage for

the car (we were feeling sensitive about security at the time, but it should be recorded that the Viterbo police were wonderful! They found a stolen handbag, only slightly depleted, and telexed the Rome Embassy in almost no time at all to say the passports had been removed).' *(Shirley and Alan Bailey)*

Open: All year, except 20 December–10 January. Restaurant closed Sunday.
Rooms: 45 – all with bath or shower and telephone.
Facilities: Lift, sitting room, restaurant.
Location: Central; garage.
Credit cards: American Express, Barclay/Visa.
Terms: Rooms 10,350–23,000 L; full board 27,750–34,500 L. Set meal: breakfast 2,875 L; *alc* 12,500–20,700 L (excluding wine).

Hotel de la Moselle, Ehnen

Luxembourg

Hôtel de la Moselle

Telephone: 76022 and 76717

'A most delightful hotel overlooking the Moselle and vineyards. It is owned by the Bamberg family, who are exceedingly friendly and attentive; the restaurant on the ground floor of the hotel is called *Restaurant Bamberg*. The cooking is superb. The bedrooms, most with their own bath or shower, are beautifully appointed. There is a car park in front. We have been going to the *Moselle* since we first saw it mentioned in an Observer Time Off book in 1968. Unfortunately now not cheap, but worth every penny.' *(B W Ribbons)*

Open: 17 January–30 November, except Tuesday.
Rooms: 16 double, 3 single – 7 with bath, 6 with shower, all with telephone and radio, 3 with TV.
Facilities: Lift, sitting room with TV, dining room. Large park in front of hotel. English spoken.
Location: 22 km from Luxembourg town.
Credit cards: Access/Euro/Mastercard, Barclay/Visa.
Terms: B & B 600–950 frs; dinner, B & B approx 1,100 frs; full board 1,500–1,700 frs.

Ramla Bay Hotel, Marfa

Malta

Ramla Bay Hotel   *Telephone:* Marfa 573.521
Cable: Ramlabay-Malta
Telex: 477 Madata MW or 977 Rental MW (Attn Ramla Bay Hotel)

At the northern end of the island, *Ramla Bay* is itself peaceful and quiet, but is within easy reach by bus or car of Malta's historical attractions and energetic night-life. It is also only a mile from the ferry that runs to the two satellite islands of Comino and Gozo. It's a modern hotel, owned and run by the Hollands, an English family, and the rooms are spacious, airy and clean. It is very much a place for the sportive. It's the only hotel on Malta with its own internationally affiliated windsurfing school, with 30 sailboards of varying types, and there are also boats for sailing or waterskiing, and equipment for scuba diving. Those who prefer terra firma can trek ponies or use the hotel's tennis court, table tennis, games rooms or billards. There's a freshwater pool (heated in cool weather), a seawater lido and a safe, though rather grey sandy beach. And the hotel lays on lots of live entertainment in the evenings.

The *Ramla Bay* is a popular package hotel, and two years ago it nearly doubled its size with a 45-room Cabin extension. This substantial annexe, offering simple accommodation, is solar-powered, the first of its kind on Malta. We read with interest the notice given to new arrivals:

'Welcome to your Ecology Cabin! Your accommodation is solar heated by Hitachi (Japan) SK3 Solar Panels which provide your hot water. Your washing water is afterwards recycled through a Segoure (France) water processing plant which provides water for your Dual Flush (Britain) toilet and garden watering. Pressure taps (Britain) are designed to minimize water wastage as are the Dual Flush cisterns. Your bath and basin tap water is processed from sea water via a Reverse Osmosis Purifier (USA) and mixed with mains water. Your air conditioner/room heater is a reversible unit using the Heat Pump principle. We hope it all works.'

A regular at *Ramla Bay* writes: 'I have known the Holland family since 1969, staying always at this hotel. It is unpretentious and extremely comfortable. The welcome you get is indescribable; the food is excellent. If you want a relaxed holiday, this is the place to come.' *(Patricia de la Cloche)*

Open: All year.
Rooms: 100 double, 14 suites – all with bath, telephone and baby-listening. 45 rooms in annexe. (Some rooms on ground floor.)
Facilities: Main foyer, residents' lounge, bar lounge, TV lounge, games room, dining room. Once-weekly band, once-weekly disco/barbecue; film shows, fondue parties, bingo, Olde Tyme dancing and parlour games in winter; Maltese Evenings with folk dancers and singalongs. 10 acres grounds with swimming pool, tennis and mini-golf and children's playground. Situated on the sea front with private sandy beach, sea pool, safe bathing, water sports. &.
Location: 25 km from Valletta, at northern tip of Malta.
Credit cards: American Express, Barclay/Visa, Diners.
Terms (excluding service): B & B M£5–13; dinner, B & B M£6–16; full board M£7–17.50. Set meals: lunch M£3; dinner M£4; full *alc* from M£3.50. Reduced rates and special meals for children.

SANNAT, Gozo

Map 14

Hotel Ta' Cenc

Telephone: Gozo 55.68.19/55.68.30/55.15.20
Telex: MW479 Refinz

A small Mediterranean island, a friendly English-speaking population, prices that are roughly 20% less than at home – these features alone would recommend Gozo, three miles off Malta. The fact that it is well off the packaged tourist map, and has just one first-class hotel is an extra bonus. The *Ta' Cenc*, beautifully sited on a high promontory, is built of the local honey-coloured limestone on the low-profile principle: it's all one storey and cunningly terraced to blend into the hillside. The rooms (there are only 50) are individually designed bungalows, each with a private patio for breakfast or sun-worship, ranged round a central pool, with plenty of space between for oleanders, fig trees, cacti and the like. The pool itself offers a breath-taking view of the sea and Malta beyond, and many residents are content to brown and browse there all day. But for the more adventurous, there is plenty to see on the island – on foot, by bus or by cheap rented car. There's plenty of good rock bathing all round the island, but only one first-class sandy beach, six miles from the hotel – lovely golden sands, but not much shade. The food is not *haute cuisine*, but superior Italian cooking: a different home-made pasta at every meal, and always, among the choice of entrées, a local fresh caught fish. (Recent visitors, however, have reported a fall in standards in the restaurant: further reports welcome.) The service is friendly and efficient, without bullshit. There is a spacious lounge for sitting about in the evenings, and a modest disco, but don't expect any flashy night-life. For the retiring, there is TV in the bedroom, with an English channel.

In our entry last year, we quoted from a report which, while calling the *Ta' Cenc* 'one of the most captivating hotels in Europe' did criticize the breakfast coffee, and also mentioned that the delicious Gozitan bread didn't take kindly to toasting. In returning our questionnaire, Signor Italo Rota, who has been running the hotel with urbane panache since its opening ten years ago, assures us that since he received last year's edition he has stopped serving toasted Gozitan bread and has changed to another instant coffee. A mini-triumph for consumerism!

Open: All year.
Rooms: 38 double, 12 suites – all with bath, telephone, radio, TV, frigobar, breakfast patio and baby-listening service. Some small family bungalows in the grounds (self-contained).
Facilities: Lounge, bar, restaurant; billiards and table tennis room; piano and music bar; conference facilities. 3 acres gardens and terrace, with swimming pool, tennis courts (floodlit). Sand and rock beach 2 km (transport by private bus, mornings and afternoons); boating.
Location: 7 minutes by car from town centre; parking for 50 cars.
Credit cards: American Express, Barclay/Visa, Diners, Euro.
Terms: Dinner, B & B M£14–22; full board M£16–25. Set meals: lunch M£5.50; dinner M£6; full *alc* M£8.50. Special reduced rates for long winter stays. 50% reduction for children under 3 sharing parents' room; special meals provided.

XAGHRA, Gozo   Map 14

Corncopia Hotel   *Telephone:* Gozo 556.486
10 Gnien Imri Street

'In my limited experience of hotels, the *Cornucopia* is almost the ideal – much better than a normal *pensione*, a far cry from the mass package type of hotel, refreshingly unstuffy and nicely informal. Of course, the best thing about it is the fact that it is run by Peter and Deirdre Cope. They are the best possible hosts – friendly, well-connected on the island, and they manage to look after you without in any way intruding on your privacy. I loved the slightly shambolic, yet never inefficient, way they ran the hotel. I also loved their three cats, umpteen kittens, horses and donkeys. The hotel is in a beautiful situation and relaxingly quiet. Of course it isn't luxurious, but the rooms are quite adequate. For anyone going there I have two hints: firstly that they try and book one of the rooms on the upper floor, especially one with a balcony as the view is lovely; secondly to book a car through Peter Cope – cheaper than doing it from England. The food is good: mainly simple grilled fare made from fresh ingredients. Personally I'm all for honest food on holiday, and the Copes take advantage of what is around. It can become a fraction repetitive if you are on full or half board. I loved grilled swordfish but not every day. There is a choice of course but the menu is a little limited. That's it really. An unpretentious, pleasingly run friendly little hotel in an excellent location where you are nicely looked after. Not the lap of luxury but then it doesn't cost the earth.' *(Jonathan Powell)*

STOP PRESS. Sadly the Copes have left the Cornucopia *to open a restaurant in England. The hotel is under new management though the staff remain. Reports please.*

Open: All year, except January/February.
Rooms: 13 double, 2 family suites, 2 single or children's double with shower – 15 with bath and baby-listening. (5 rooms on ground floor.)

Facilities: Lounge/library, bar, restaurant, card and games room, table tennis. Patio and large garden with swimming pool; poolside barbecues. Hire of donkey and cart for children; 1 mile from fine sandy beach at Ramla; sailing and windsurfing.

Credit cards: American Express, Barclay/Visa, Diners.

Terms (excluding 10% service charge): B & B M£4.50–8.75; dinner, B & B M£5.50–10.28. Set meal: dinner M£4.50. Off-season rates November, December (except Christmas week) and March. Reduced rates and special meals for children.

Leikanger Fjord Hotel, Leikanger

Norway

BERGEN, N-5000   **Map 7**

Hotell Neptun   *Telephone:* (05) 23.20.15
Walckendorffsgate 8   *Telex:* 40040

Bergen, founded by King Olav Kym in 1070, is one of Norway's oldest
towns, and probably the most rewarding for the first-time visitor. The
Neptun is a well-equipped, modern hotel in a central position overlooking
the harbour and the old market. It is quiet at night, and the restaurant is
one of the city's best. *(Karen Brook-Barnett)*

Open: All year.
Rooms: 80 double, 30 single – 63 with bath, 47 with shower, all with radio and
colour TV.
Facilities: Lifts, lounge, bar, café and restaurant (both open till midnight);
conference facilities; English spoken.
Location: Central, near old market; garage parking 100 m.
Credit cards: All major credit cards accepted.
Terms: B & B 200–350 Nkr. Set meals: lunch 90 Nkr; dinner 110 Nkr; full *alc* 180
Nkr.

Hotel Brekkestranda   *Telephone:* (057) 15100 103

'A small village on the south of the Sognefjord, not far from the sea, Brekke has a church, a school, a ferry quay, three small shops and 200 inhabitants. Surrounded by little hill farms, it is 102 km and two ferry crossings from Bergen. *Hotel Brekkestranda* is a little way from the village in completely peaceful surroundings, and consists of a complex of wooden cottages with green turf-covered roofs strung along the shore of the fjord. Owner, Mrs Ingeborg Brekke, inspired her architect to design an unconventional and amusing series of buildings; even the rugs are trapezoid. As she says, "You seldom see right angles in nature." Rustic-style rooms are comfortable, with a rocking chair, a desk and electric radiator. In the private shower and WC there is underfloor heating. All rooms overlook the wide fjord, most are on the ground floor and you can step straight out of your room, cross a few yards of grass and dip your toes in the water. There is a rocky pool along the shore for children. Food we found interesting, company young and lively. Mrs Brekke, aided by her son, manages the hotel and like many of her guests, who are mostly Norwegian, enjoys speaking English.' *(Anne Bolt)*

Open: All year.
Rooms: 12 double, 11 single – all with bath or shower, and telephone. 6 additional rooms in chalets, with TV.
Facilities: Dining room, cafeteria; swimming in the fjord, sailing and fishing; nearby rock pool on shore for children. English spoken.
Location: 102 km from Bergen.
Terms: Rooms 150–210 Nkr. Set meals: breakfast 35 Nkr; lunch 60 Nkr; dinner 70 Nkr.

HANKØ, Østfold   Map 7

Hankø nye Fjordhotel   *Telephone:* (032) 32 105

'Hankø, a small island on the Oslofjord, is known as the Cowes of Norway, but it resembles the bustling Isle of Wight resort only in being Norway's most prestigious yachting centre where the royal family race and the King entertains at his modest house on the hill. It is ten minutes from the mainland by passenger ferry, there are blissfully no motor cars on the island and only two hotels: the *Seilersbro*, the Sailors' Inn, on the quay with 14 beds, and the *Hankø nye Fjordhotel* tucked into a small green valley. The *nye (new) Fjordhotel* has some 60 rooms and is comfortable rather than "luxe" but this is reflected in the reasonable price. It has tennis, dancing to live music and a splendid heated salt-water swimming pool. If you write in English you get a lucid and fairly prompt reply.' *(Anne Bolt)*

Open: 1 April–20 December.
Rooms: 67 doubles, 3 suites – 39 with balcony, all with bath or shower.
Facilities: Lift, lounge, TV room, ballroom-bar, dining room; conference rooms;

> Report forms (Freepost in the UK) will be found at the end of the Guide.

dancing to live music. Heated indoor swimming pool, gym, solarium, sauna; 4 tennis courts, yachting school, private beach, fishing. English spoken.
Location: 10 minutes from mainland; 15 km from Fredrikstad.
Terms: Rooms (including breakfast) 245–355 Nkr; full board 280–305 Nkr. Set meals: lunch/dinner 95 Nkr.

JELØY, P O Box 236, 1501 Moss   Map 7

Hotel Refsnes Gods   *Telephone:* 032/70411

'Jeløy, one of the largest of the many islands scattered along the east coast of the Oslofjord, is linked to the mainland and the small industrial town of Moss by a bridge. Businessmen in the upper echelons have built imposing houses, there are some six-storey flats and pretty bungalows, but gardens are spacious and the island is green and leafy with many fields. The climate allows both vines and maize to grow. Rooms at the *Refsnes Gods* overlook either the fjord or the large swimming pool. At the bottom of the garden is a lane leading to the seashore only a hundred yards away. Locals swim there regularly and assure me the water is unpolluted. Both bedrooms and the extensive public rooms are very elegantly furnished. The food we enjoyed: but beware – Saturdays and Sundays the dining room closes at 7 pm.' *(Mrs Maurice Yates)*

Open: All year.
Rooms: 39 double, 17 single, 6 suites – all with bath or shower.
Facilities: Lift, lounges, 2 dining rooms; banqueting rooms. Park, private bathing and boating, outdoor swimming pool with sauna; bicycles, fishing.
Location: Outside Moss on the W side of Jeløy island.
Terms: Rooms (including breakfast) 330–450 Nkr.

LEIKANGER, N-5842   Map 7

Leikanger Fjord Hotel   *Telephone:* 056/53622

'When we came to Norway we hoped to discover a dream hotel to report to you; we feel we have found it in the *Leikanger Fjord*. The hotel stands on the edge of the fjord with a magnificent view of the waters and surrounding mountains. It is not one of the really busy fjords, so the hotel is very peaceful: you can watch the occasional liner pass by, and a few ferries call at the quay by the hotel, including the catamaran to Bergen. The building itself is a pleasant mixture of old and new, with a large modern wing. The bedrooms are spacious and thoroughly comfortable. There are two good lounges and a pleasant dining room. Breakfast which is self-service is excellent. Dinner, although a set menu, is well-cooked and plentiful. The hotel has been run by the family Lie since 1920, and the owners and staff are very friendly and do all they can to make your stay a happy and memorable occasion. Language is no problem.
'The hotel offers various mini-bus excursions, rowing boats are available and there is a windsurfer for hire. The fjord must be a fisherman's paradise. It is within easy reach of the Nigard glacier, amongst other beauty spots. There is a beautiful medieval church, and the vicarage garden boasts several unusual trees including a maidenhair tree *(Gingko biloba)* also described as a live fossil, because it is the only surviving

species of the Tertiary period, also the *Sequida giganteum* thrives, believed to be the oldest in the world, 100 years old and six metres round.'
(Hugh and Elsie Pryor)

Open: All year, except Christmas and New Year.
Rooms: 35 double, 5 single, 2 suites – 25 with bath, 12 with shower.
Facilities: 2 lounges, dining room. Garden; boats, windsurfing, bicycles, fishing.
Location: On the edge of Sognefjord; 220 km NE of Bergen.
Terms: B & B 180–260 Nkr; dinner, B & B 265–345 Nkr. Set meals: lunch 75 Nkr; dinner 90 Nkr; full *alc* 160 Nkr. Special terms in May and September. Reduced rates for children.

NORDFJORDEID, N-6771 **Map 7**

Nordfjord Hotel *Telephone:* Nordfjordeid (057) 6400 605

'Nordfjordeid, a small village at the head of the Nordfjord, is about 320 km north of Bergen, and can be reached from there by express boat in about five hours, or in about eight hours by car. It's not at all touristy: a sea inlet edged with wooded cliffs and meadows and high snow-capped peaks in the distance: it's a haven of peace, with the clean, energizing air particular to the far north. The *Nordfjord Hotel*, opened in 1975, is about three minutes' walk from the water: typically Scandinavian with wide, sloping roof and lots of wood. All very northern and uncluttered. There's no wasted space in the agreeable bedrooms, all of which have private balconies (ask for one with a view down the fjord) and bathrooms with shower and heated floors. Big open reception area with coffee on a hot plate, open sandwiches and cakes available all day. Buffet breakfast of huge variety and unlimited quantities. Very pleasant service. There's a tennis court, putting course (rather lumpy) and a sauna; and in the evening, dancing in the bar to fairly subdued music.

'The manager will advise you on fishing in Lake Hornindal (claimed to be the deepest in Europe) and fix transport there and back and use of the hotel boat. Fjord fishing, too, is easily arranged. There are some good local walks. I have seldom felt so healthy anywhere.' *(Valerie Ferguson)*

Open: All year, except 20 December–5 January.
Rooms: 31 double, 22 single, 2 suites – 6 with bath, 49 with shower, all with telephone and radio; baby-listening by arrangement. (13 rooms on ground floor.)
Facilities: Lounges, TV room, bar, restaurant; dancing in the evening; some conference facilities. Sauna. Garden with putting green, children's playground and tennis court. Fjord and lake fishing arranged; sailing. English spoken. &.
Location: 320 km N of Bergen; in village; parking.
Credit cards: Access/Euro/Mastercard, Barclay/Visa.
Terms: B & B 165–250 Nkr; dinner, B & B 235–290 Nkr; full board 270–325 Nkr. Set meals: lunch 55 Nkr, dinner 90 Nkr; full *alc* 130 Nkr. Children under 3 free of charge; 50% reduction on *pension* price 4–12 years; special meals on request.

Do you know of a good hotel or country inn in the United States or Canada? Nominations please to our sibling publication, *America's Wonderful Little Hotels and Inns*, 345 East 93rd Street, 25C, New York, NY 10028.

OS, N-5200   **Map 7**

Solstrand Fjord Hotel   *Telephone:* (05) 30.00.99
                                                 Telex: 42050 fjord

'A wonderful place, 45 minutes by car from Bergen, on the coast, with panoramic views over the fjord. There is plenty to do for all the family: sea fishing in the hotel's own no-charge rowing boats, tennis courts, riding; and, if it starts to rain, there is a heated indoor pool overlooking the sea. The hotel has a new and an old part; the latter, which I found cosier, was built 90 years ago by Christian Michelsen, who later became Prime Minister. The place has been run by the same family for the past 30 years. The service was very friendly. The food was plain, but that was a minor drawback in view of all the excellent facilities. We enjoyed walks in the surrounding woodlands, and a visit to Lysekloster Monastery, where herbs that the monks brought with them in 1146 still grow.' *(Karen Brook-Barnett)*

Open: All year, except 10 days from about 20 December.
Rooms: 88 double, 28 single – 101 with bath, 15 with shower, 100 with radio, all with telephone.
Facilities: Lift, lounges, TV room, bar, restaurant; dancing 6 days a week; table-tennis. Garden with tennis and badminton court, putting green; heated indoor seawater swimming pool; steam baths and keep fit room; private rock beach, sea fishing, free rowing boats, speed-boat, waterskiing. English spoken.
Location: 31 km S of Bergen; parking.
Credit cards: Access/Euro/Mastercard, American Express, Barclay/Visa.
Terms: B & B 250–450 Nkr; dinner, B & B 305–540 Nkr; full board 350–450 Nkr. Set meals: buffet lunch 85 Nkr; dinner 90 Nkr; full *alc* 150–200 Nkr. Reduced rates for children; special meals on request.

OSLO 1   **Map 7**

Hotel Bristol   *Telephone:* (02) 41.58.40
Kristian 4des gt 7   *Telex:* 71668

'By convention, Scandinavia is hardly the homeland of the gourmet. Yet it was at the *Hotel Bristol* in Oslo that I had one of my finest gastronomic experiences. This was fresh trout prepared in sour cream; a combination of ineffable splendour I cannot wait to repeat. It occurred in the same dining room where, next morning, I had a long, long breakfast from a loaded buffet starting with several kinds of pickled herring and ending with limitless coffee. That too was an experience. To eat well in Norway one could do worse than breakfast three times a day. The dining room was dark, old-fashioned, with a little bit of plush and tinted window panes; rather like a set from an Ibsen play. In fact, the same may be said of the hotel, at least the public parts. The room I occupied was standard, international three star, but it had enough space; neat, but not gaudy. I found the dining room staff extremely efficient, forthright and friendly; rather like stewards on one of the now so sadly vanished ocean liners. There is character about the place, if somewhat muted. My only dis-appointment was the lighting in the bedrooms. Why are all hotels of whatever ilk or nationality so stingy in this respect? But that is a cavil. As befits the noble lord after whom it is named, the *Bristol* has the touch of a true hostelry. It does make the arrival in a strange place a little bit of an occasion – as it should be.' *(Roland Huntford)*

Open: All year.
Rooms: 85 double, 58 single, 5 suites – 81 with bath, 62 with shower, all with telephone, radio and TV.
Facilities: Reception, bars, restaurant, grill, TV room, night club. English spoken.
Location: In town centre; parking nearby.
Credit cards: Access/Euro/Mastercard, Amercian Express, Diners.
Terms: B & B 350–560 Nkr.

OSLO Map 7

Hotel Continental *Telephone:* (02) 41.90.60
Stortingsgaten 24/26 *Telex:* 11012

'Oslo has, more than any other European capital, preserved the traditions and atmosphere of the 19th century. The *Continental*, centrally situated opposite the National Theatre, preserves the grave dignity, courtesy and friendly warmth which visitors to Norway, who are privileged to count Norwegians as their friends and business associates, so much appreciate. This ambience is as much represented in restaurants and the famous Theatercaféen as in the size and comfort of the rooms which however lack no modern amenities. The Theatercaféen would deserve a star, if such could be awarded to an establishment of this kind – certainly not "Vienna-style" as the hotel's brochure will have it, but truly 19th-century Norwegian; many of the regular habitués seem to be Ibsen's contemporaries. A three-piece "orchestra" led by a nonagenarian pianist/composer, enhances this atmosphere. I could wax even more lyrical in remembering the breakfast's cold table.' *(Arnold Horwell)*

Open: All year.
Rooms: 127 double, 40 single, 12 suites – all with bath or shower.
Facilities: Salons, 2 bars, 3 dining rooms (1 with dancing); banqueting facilities.
Location: Central, near City Hall and National Theatre.
Terms: Rooms (including breakfast) 400–450 Nkr (single), 550–650 Nkr (double). Set meals: lunch 92 Nkr; dinner 110 Nkr.

OSLO Map 7

Savoy Hotel *Telephone:* (02) 20.26.55
Universitetsgaten 11

In the centre of the city opposite the National Gallery and close to a large national car park. 'Fine for a few nights – old-fashioned, but none the worse for that, with nice rooms and attentive staff. Adequate and good value.' *(Tony Morris)*

Open: All year, except 23 December–2 January.
Rooms: 28 double, 37 single – 11 with bath, 23 with shower.
Facilities: Lift; reception, lounges, TV room, bar, dining room, breakfast room.

Location: Central; parking nearby.
Credit cards: All major credit cards accepted.
Terms: B & B 190–280 Nkr.

SELJE, N-6740   **Map 7**

Selje Hotel   *Telephone:* (057) 561 07
                                             Telex: 42435 Selje N

'Selje is a small town on a sheltered sand-edged bay, its houses painted in ochre, white and deep red, and set in flowery gardens. It's on the southern (sheltered) side of the Stadland peninsula, Norway's westernmost point. The *Selje Hotel* is only a few years old and an astounding place to find in such an unlikely and remote spot. It stands right on the shore; sturdily made of logs and local stone, with a heated swimming pool built on to it – all glass windows so that you can enjoy the splendid view from inside even if a wild wind is raging without. It's managed by Harald and Gad Berge, who speak impeccable English, yet up to 1977 had never been visited by a British tourist. The hotel has its own cabin cruiser for deep-sea fishing, boats and tackle are for hire, and there's trout in hill pools behind Selje. Bliss for rugged outdoor types, and idyllic on calm days when the water laps gently and the sunsets are gaudy and romantic. But if the weather turns, there's plenty to do in the hotel. Mealtimes are on the early side and not very flexible – no disadvantage after a bracing day in the fresh, fresh air; mornings start with an unlimited buffet breakfast, and there's always a lavish cold table. It's fully licensed, an amenity not shared by all the surrounding places, so expect influx at weekends with much jollity.' *(Valerie Ferguson)*

Open: All year.
Rooms: 40 double – 10 with bath, 30 with shower, all with telephone and radio.
Facilities: Lounge with open fireplace, separate TV room, bar, dining room and mini-restaurant; live music and dancing six nights a week; conference and meeting facilities. Winter Garden, solarium, sauna; heated swimming pool, keep-fit room, children's playroom. Big garden. Close to a 500-metre-long beach with fine sand; deep-sea fishing; salmon and trout fishing in rivers and lakes. English spoken.
Location: Direct trains and buses in summer from Oslo; or express boat from Bergen to Maloy, 45 km by bus.
Credit cards: Access/Euro, American Express.
Terms: B & B 170–290 Nkr; full board 230–300 Nkr. Set meals: lunch 80 Nkr; dinner 100 Nkr.

UTNE, Hardanger N-5797   **Map 7**

Hotel Utne   *Telephone:* Grimo (054) 669 83

'On the Hardangerfjord – small, out of the way and very special. Its setting is splendid: the foot of a steep promontory where the Hardanger branches into two smaller fjords; high blue mountains across the water; sheer cliffs above it; a waterfall plunging down the cliff face and rushing through the village; apple orchards on each side. There are fine walks along the fjord in both directions. You can walk the quiet road or climb paths to the high pastures. The village is small and quiet. It has a folk museum, a collection of old farm buildings in the ancient (at least

411

medieval) style. There's a leisurely coming and going of steamers and ferries, from the port of Kvanndal across the fjord, from Bergen and other towns along the shores. You can drive up from the south, from the north-west, or come in by steamer or by a combination of bus and ferry.

'The *Hotel Utne*, which takes 40–50 guests, has been in the same family for over 250 years. It stands in the centre of the village, opposite the boat landing. Behind it, on the hillside, is a small modern annexe. Inside, the hotel is like a charming country home, with fine old furniture, painted wood, brass and copper. Meals are hearty and excellent. On Sundays you have a magnificent smorgasbord. Fru Aga Blokhus and her staff, wearing the Hardanger costume, look after you with grace and enthusiasm. You take afternoon tea with the hostess, either in the parlour or, in fine weather, on the terrace, with wide views of water and mountains.' *(Edward W Devlin)*

Recent reports fully confirm the above, with the following gloss: 'The hotel is a gem, but the socially retiring should be warned that all tables in the dining room are set for eight people. There is therefore a high risk of being placed at meals with other English, who, abroad, are almost universally distasteful, or persons who do not speak English at all. We were fortunate in having at our table two delightful English-speaking Dutch couples.' *(Douglas Rae; also Hugh and Elsie Pryor, Ray Hassell)*

Open: All year.
Rooms: 21 double, 5 single – 3 with bath, 10 with shower. 8 rooms in nearby annexe on the hillside. (1 room on ground floor.)
Facilities: Sitting rooms, dining room, games room; some off-season conference facilities; badminton. Garden and terrace; safe bathing in the fjord in front of the hotel; fishing, boating, cycling and good walks. English spoken.
Credit cards: Access/Euro/Mastercard, American Express.
Terms: B & B 130–175 Nkr; dinner, B & B 195–240 Nkr. Set meals: lunch 60 Nkr; dinner 70 Nkr; full *alc* 110 Nkr. Reduced rates for stays of 5 days and over, and for children.

Hotel Infante de Sagres, Oporto

Portugal

ARMAÇÃO DE PÊRA, 8365 Alcantarilha　　　　　　　　**Map 13**

Hotel do Garbe　　　　　　　　　　*Telephone:* (0082) 321 94
Av Marginal　　　　　　　　　　　　　　　*Telex:* 18285

'This four-star, family-run hotel overlooks the beach in a small coastal
village between Faro and Lagos. It is comfortable and friendly, with good
public rooms and an excellent restaurant. The bedrooms are reasonably
equipped. An elderly and particular cousin who stayed here was very
pleased with it. The hotel was well-heated in January, which can be quite
cold in the Algarve, whatever the travel agents say. When my cousin said
she might come back the following year, she was told that it would be best
to book immediately as many of the guests reserve their rooms a year
ahead, even in January.' *(D S Smith)*

Open:　All year.
Rooms:　110 double.
Facilities:　Salons, restaurant, air-conditioning; outdoor swimming pool.
Location:　Between Faro and Lagos just off the N125.
Terms:　Double rooms (including breakfast) 2,404–4,170 esc. Set meals: lunch/
dinner from 690 esc.

Portuguese prices are more approximate than most.

413

Estalagem Quinta das Torres   *Telephone:* Azeitão (19) 20.80.01

'Azeitão, consisting of two small villages about 1.5 km apart, is on the *old* Lisbon–Setubal main road. It is a good base for the Arrabida peninsula with a beautiful coastline, attractive beaches and the resorts of Sesimbra and Portinho. Palmela complete with castle is nearby. With the motorway and the 25 Abrile Bridge, Lisbon is an easy run (about 40 minutes). Azeitão itself is surrounded by vineyards and olive orchards. You approach the *Quinta* up a long overgrown drive between flowering shrubs. It is a beautiful rather shabby old house in its own grounds with a small ornamental lake against one wall. Our room was off a courtyard as pretty as a stage set, with a fountain in the middle and four fruit-laden orange trees at the corners. The quiet is only broken in the evenings by the competition between bullfrogs, nightingales and cicadas. The whole place is beautifully furnished with old family furniture, portraits, prints, etc. Lovely bowls of flowers everywhere. Our beds were four-posters and the big fireplace was laid ready for an immediate fire with stacks of logs beside it. A log fire blazed in the anteroom to the dining room. The food was delicious – original and well-cooked, and that very dicey Portuguese speciality, *bacalhau*, is here cooked deliciously. The *vinho de casa* is from the local vineyards. Breakfast started with huge glasses of fresh squeezed orange juice, hot rolls and big jars of honey.

'The place is run with a practically Irish dottiness. Half the rooms have no numbers and few of them keys. And no one speaks a word of anything but Portuguese – just louder and faster when you don't appear to understand. They have a mania for locking, barring and shuttering every door at odd times of day, and none of the keys in the large bunch one is given opens anything; to get to one's room, the courtyard, the hotel itself, one constantly has to clang one of the huge outside bells (whereupon a beaming minion rushes to let one in). An eccentric place, and a bit damp, but with a lot of charm.' *(Mrs R B Richards)*

One of the owners of the *Quinta*, Senhora de Souza, comments on the ambivalent last paragraph of our entry last year quoted above: 'We are now two old ladies and at any time the guest needs to speak with one of us, we are always here. We speak French, English and German, but the servants prefer to try to cope themselves, and do not call the Senhoras.'

Open: All year.
Rooms: 9 double, 3 single, 2 suites – 10 with bath, TV and tea-making facilities. 2 bungalows serving as annexe.
Facilities: Lounges, bar, restaurant; park with swimming pool; near sandy beaches. English spoken.
Location: 27 km from Lisbon off the N10; in village centre; parking.
Terms: Rooms with breakfast 1,500–1,600 esc; with breakfast and dinner 2,100–2,200 esc. Full *alc* 700 esc. Reduced rates for children under 8; special meals provided.

We asked hotels to estimate their 1982 tariffs some time before publication so the rates given here are not necessarily completely accurate. Please *always* check terms with hotels when making bookings.

BATALHA, 2240 Leiria   Map 13

Estalagem do Mestre Afonso Domingues   *Telephone:* (0044) 962 60

'This estalagem (inn) is just off the Lisbon–Oporto road, about halfway between Lisbon and Coimbra. It faces the spectacular Abbey of Batalha, a national monument, and is also near a number of interesting places such as Nazaré and Fatima. We have stayed there a number of times before when exploring this part of Portugal. It also is conveniently situated as a stopping place when journeying from the Algarve to north Portugal. It is one of the only two inns in Portugal classified as five-star. It is very well-appointed but is too small to be classed as a hotel so the price of its rooms is much lower. It has an excellent restaurant. The service is friendly and competent. It is very popular so one usually has to make a booking some weeks ahead.' *(LMS)*

Open: All year.
Rooms: 21 double.
Facilities: Restaurant, air-conditioning.
Location: Just off the E3 between Lisbon and Coimbra.
Terms: Double rooms (including breakfast) 800–1,100 esc.

BOM JESUS DO MONTE, 4700 Braga   Map 13

Hotel do Elevador   *Telephone:* Braga (0023) 250 11
Parque do Bom Jesus do Monte

'Few tourists seem to come to the Minho, a mistake in my opinion as this tender green *vinho verde* country is glorious to drive through and has some interesting old towns and villages. There aren't many good places to stay if you want to avoid the ugly modern hotels that sprawl along the Costa Verde, apart from the old-style Portuguese hotels at Bom Jesus, a 19th-century religious shrine on top of the mountain at Braga. Braga itself, while crowded and busy, has enough historic buildings to merit one day's sightseeing, but Bom Jesus is a gem, spectacularly designed and landscaped, with stone terraces and larger-than-life statuary, gardens and little round chapels depicting the Stations of the Cross, and at the top a church and hotels, reached either by a funicular or a winding drive through dense and dripping woods. The *Hotel do Elevador*, the best hotel, is small, comfortable, with an old-fashioned elegance and a fantastic view of mountain peaks and the valley. This is more a place for the Portuguese than for tourists so it hasn't been gussied up and spoiled. The menu, alas, is the standard hotel type but the food isn't bad. Certainly the view makes up for uninspired eating and there's a good selection of the regional wines. The hotel is unique in terms of location and ambience, and definitely shouldn't be missed if you are travelling in the north.' *(Jose Wilson; also Mr and Mrs C Billings)*

Open: All year.
Rooms: 25 double – all with bath.
Facilities: Restaurant. Garden.
Location: 50 km from Oporto.
Terms: Double rooms (including breakfast) 2,300–4,600 esc.

Palace Hotel do Buçaco   *Telephone:* (0031) 931 01
Floresta do Buçaco

'This "de luxe" hotel is fantastic, in all senses of the word. It was a
19th-century royal hunting lodge, built with extreme examples of Manuel-
ine architecture. It stands in a large park on the Buçaco ridge, which is
planted with a magnificent selection of trees, particularly "cedars of
Buçaco" *(Cupressus lusitanica)* which are world-famous. Originally, the
park was planted by the Carmelite monks, whose monastery stands beside
the hotel. Wellington spent the night in one of the monastery cells before
the battle of Buçaco, when he defeated the French attempt to capture
Lisbon and throw the English out of Portugal. Buçaco is only 20 km from
Coimbra, a lovely university city but without a good hotel. There are also
a number of interesting places in the neighbourhood so it makes a good
centre for exploring this part of Portugal.' *(DS)*

Open: All year.
Rooms: 70 double.
Facilities: Salons, restaurant. Garden, tennis court.
Location: 20 km N of Coimbra on the N234; parking.
Credit cards: American Express, Barclay/Visa, Euro.
Terms: Double rooms (including breakfast) 3,450–6,307 esc. Set meals: lunch/
dinner from 920 esc.

Estalagem Albatroz   *Telephone:* Cascais (19) 28.28.21
Rua Frederico Arouca 100–102

'This small and elegant inn is one of the places that has kept its pre-
Revolutionary character and standards. It has far and away the best
location in the area as it is right on the water (up to that point of coastline
the coastal railway runs between the beach and the main road), overlooking rocks, beaches and ocean. It is also exceptional in being a haven of
quiet in an excessively noisy summer-tourist town, yet only a few steps
away from the main Cascais shopping street. The inn is a lovely old house
with a modern wing, surrounded by gardens, and both the dining room
and the cocktail lounge are very attractively done – the cocktail lounge
extends outdoors to a circular deck, a super place to have a drink before
and after dinner. There's a respectable wine list and while the menu is not
very original the food is excellent and served by a very professional,
well-trained staff.' *(Jose Wilson)*

Open: All year.
Rooms: 16 double – all with bath.
Facilities: Lounge, bar, restaurant. Garden. Boating, sailing. Watersports, ten-
nis, golf nearby.
Location: 30 km from Lisbon.
Credit cards: All major credit cards accepted.
Terms: Double rooms (including breakfast) 1,280 esc.

In your own interest, do check latest tariffs with hotels when you
make your bookings.

ESTREMOZ, 7100 Evora   **Map 13**

Pousada de Rainha Santa Isabel   *Telephone:* Estremoz 226 18
Largo D. Dinaz – no Castelo de Estremoz

'This is probably one of the two best pousadas in Portugal. It is in a
13th-century castle, which was the chief residence of King Diniz. The
pousada is named after his wife, Isabel, who was both queen and saint.
We had a large bedroom, with private bathroom, and slept in comfortable
four-poster beds. Bed and breakfast for two cost less than £20 [May 1981].
The restaurant is very good and a three-course meal for two, with wine,
cost about £10. Estremoz is an interesting town with a busy market.
Almost opposite the entrance to the pousada there is a museum mainly
devoted to clay figurines, which are a speciality of the town. The museum
guide also has the keys to the room where Queen Isabel died, which was
subsequently converted into a charming little chapel, and to the big
church close by, which was originally a mosque.' *(DS; also Gerald Savory)*

Open: All year.
Rooms: 20 double, 3 suites – all with bath and telephone.
Facilities: Lounge, TV room, restaurant, bar; some conference facilities, air-conditioning. Garden.
Location: In town centre; parking for 40 cars.
Credit cards: Diners, Mastercard.
Terms: Double rooms (including breakfast) about 2,500 esc.

LISBON, 1100   **Map 13**

Albergaria Senhora do Monte   *Telephone:* Lisbon (19) 86.28.46,
Calçada do Monte 39   86.28.67 and 87.17.34
                                                        Cables: Senorita

'An unassuming small hotel with a family feeling, run by cordial, helpful
people. The reception-cum-TV room is a bit cramped, but the guest
rooms are pleasant – flowered wallpaper, and a nice old-fashioned
feeling. It is located in the older part of Lisbon; it feels off the tourist beat
since the area is residential – roosters crowing in the morning, lettuce in
the little backyard gardens. There's a bar but no restaurant – breakfast is
brought to your bedroom; there are several small, untouristy restaurants
at the end of the street as well as the wonderful Lisbon streetcars to
everywhere. I've saved the best till last: the hotel is almost at the top of
one of the Lisbon hills with a simply magnificent view over the city and the
river Tejo. The view, the interesting and convenient location and the
welcoming attitude of the staff make me prize the *Albergaria Senhora do
Monte* as one of the pleasantest hotels I've ever stayed in – well worth its
modest cost.' *(Lucia M Atlas)*

Open: All year.
Rooms: 18 double, 5 single, 4 suites – all with bath.
Facilities: Reception/TV room, bar.
Location: Central; parking.
Credit cards: Access/Euro/Mastercard, American Express.
Terms: B & B 700–1,400 esc. Reduced rates for children.

Hotel Tivoli Jardim   *Telephone:* (19) 53.99.71
Rua Julio Cesar Machado 9   *Telex:* 12172

Not an atmospheric old hostelry, like the *York House* below, but a
modern 8-storey block: 'We and most of our friends in the Algarve stay at
this hotel when we go to Lisbon. It is officially classified as four-star and is
situated just off the Avenida da Liberdade, the main central avenue. It
and its sister hotel, the *Tivoli* (on the Avenida) have a large car park and
garage. Being off the Avenida it is reasonably quiet. The bedrooms are
better equipped than in the standard hotel. The service and friendliness
are outstanding. The restaurant is good, though not outstanding, but it is
better to eat at a restaurant rather than a hotel in Lisbon, and there are a
number of good restaurants within ten minutes' walk. One can also go to
the excellent, but expensive, restaurant on the top floor of the *Tivoli
Hotel. (LMS)*

Open: All year.
Rooms: 119 double – all with bath, telephone, radio, air-conditioning and TV on
request.
Facilities: Main hall with bar, TV room, restaurant; 12 km to beach. 90% of staff
speak English.
Location: 10 minutes from town centre; garage and car park.
Terms: Rooms (including breakfast) 3,600 esc (single), 4,200 esc (double).

York House (Residencia Inglesia)   *Telephone:* Lisbon (19) 66.25.44
Rua des Janelas Verdes, 32-1, 2

A small two-part hotel on opposite sides of the road which contains the
National Art Museum and looks down over the cranes of the docks. A
little off the central track, but Lisbon taxis are wonderfully cheap. The
main part of the hotel, containing about 44 rooms and set back from the
road under trees round a courtyard, was an early 17th-century convent;
later it became a hospital, and then the Protestant cathedral in Lisbon.
The lower dining room was the former chapel, still complete with font and
marble plaques. Since 1935, it has been owned by a Frenchwoman and her
stepson, Lucien Donat, a well-known interior decorator and theatrical
designer. It has been the haunt of writers: Graham Greene stayed here,
and it was the home of Antonio Nobre, the Portuguese poet. In the
building there is much use of *azulejos*, traditional tiles, many placed
round window seats and along the upper dining room. There are polished
red tile floors in the rooms and huge wooden wardrobes. Along the
corridors are blue and white Arraiolos rugs. The rooms that once housed
the novitiates are still the cheapest. Across the street is the other part of
the hotel, decorated in *belle époque* French style with lots of red plush,
bric-à-brac, framed period photos and gold-plated taps in the bathrooms.
'Not only interesting and historic, but also extremely pretty and peaceful.
We had the family suite, which was of a size, comfort and elegance as
would grace the Master's lodgings at an Oxford college; ask for Room 8.
The food is simple but good and plentiful. An unusual feature is a baroque
TV set; somehow in keeping.' *(Shelley Cranshaw)*

Open: All year.
Rooms: 47 double, 10 single, 5 suites – 45 with bath, 17 with shower, some with telephone, all with mono TV and tea-making facilities. 14 rooms in annexe.
Facilities: TV room, bridge room, 2 bars (1 in annexe), restaurant. English spoken.
Location: In city centre; no special parking facilities.
Credit cards: Access/Euro, American Express, Barclay/Visa.
Terms: B & B 1,400–2,200 esc. Set meals: lunch/dinner 450 esc; full *alc* 500 esc.

MANTEIGAS, 6260 Guarda   Map 13

Hotel de Manteigas   *Telephone:* (0059) 47114/47127

A hotel recently acquired and modernized by the Government in the centre of the Serra da Estrela, the highest mountain chain in Portugal. As the hotel's own brochure enticingly puts it: 'Beautiful winter in Estrela is grand watched from this hotel, opened to anybody. Springtime leading to summer and always, the freezing water springs, which are close to the hotel. Lovely food as well as the famous mountain cheese, invite you to come and stay in Manteigas.' A correspondent writes: 'An ideal centre for exploring this interesting district. The bedrooms are simply but comfortably furnished. Some have private bathrooms which have full-sized baths, while others have a combined shower and bidet; you should specify which you want. The food and service were excellent, and meals remarkably cheap.' *(LMS)*

Open: All year.
Rooms: 54 – 6 with bath, 20 with shower, all with telephone, tea-making facilities and baby-listening. 28 rooms in annexes.
Facilities: Lifts; 2 bars, 1 with TV, salon, dining room. Large garden and swimming in natural pool in river in front of hotel. Winter sports November–May. English spoken. ḃ.
Location: 3 km from Manteigas; parking.
Credit cards: All major credit cards accepted.
Terms: B & B 1,700–1,800 pts. Set meals: lunch/dinner 350–600 pts. 50% reduction for children under 8.

MARVÃO, 7330 Portalagre   Map 13

Pousada de Santa Maria   *Telephone:* (0045) 932 01/2

'Marvão lies about 6 km north and about 600 m above the road from Abrantes and the valley of the Tagus into Spain. The village, of tiny white houses and narrow cobbled streets, is entirely inside the walls of a castle whose keep sits above the village. It is possible to walk round the ramparts in about half an hour, looking within at the roofs, gardens, chicken runs, kitchen and television sets, or without, over the Sierra de Torrico in Spain, and the valleys below in Portugal. The *Pousada*, like everything else in Marvão, is tiny. There are eight rooms, the building is of stone with tile floors, the public rooms are well-furnished, the beds comfortable, you can see to read, and the hot water is dependable. As befits, the staff is small (when we were there meals tended to be later than the advertised times) but amiable; the food was plain but good. No lunches are served, but it would be possible to buy picnic food in the village. There is absolutely no nightlife or entertainment to be had, but the view from the bar is fine, and the local wine excellent. The price was very reasonable. If you favour quiet, remoteness, walking, reading, then Marvão will do very well; children might get bored, and there are no great sights within 50 km or so. The Portuguese know their state hotels are good and use them – so make reservations.' *(Dugal Campbell; also DS)*

Open: All year.
Rooms: 8 double – all with bath and telephone.
Facilities: Lounge/bar, restaurant. Garden. Riding, shooting nearby.
Location: 22 km N of Portalagre on the N521.
Credit card: Euro.
Terms: Double rooms (including breakfast) 1,725–1,845 esc. Set meals lunch/dinner from 520 esc.

MONCHIQUE, 8550 Faro   Map 13

Estalagem Abrigo de Montanha   *Telephone:* (0082) 921 31
Corte Dereira/Estrada de Foia

'This estalagem is half way between the little hill town of Monchique (about 25 km inland from Portimão) and the peak of Foia. It is about 1,500 feet up with magnificent views over the hills and lush valleys with infinite variety of green. There is a main building and a long tier of separate apartments at the other end of a pretty garden. Wonderful mixture of flowers. It is family-owned and run – and the employed couple who are waiter/concierge and chambermaid respectively – are of a charm, intelligence, and sweet gentleness unparalleled. Good English spoken throughout (and French and German). We had a bedroom, a bathroom, a sitting room with a fireplace, and a roof garden. Prices extraordinarily reasonable. Flowers were put in our room and we were told they would have lit a fire for us had we asked. The coffee – best I have ever had outside anyone's home – was ground when one appeared in the dining room. When they found we liked the local honey, it was always on the table. We ate dinner there quite frequently – wonderfully fresh fish but the menu would become monotonous quite soon. However, they asked us once or twice if we would be in and then served some interesting local specialities. Hot water more reliable in the main hotel rooms, which are also cheaper (but smaller and lacking a balcony) than the annexe suites. *Warning:* it can be cold and wet in Monchique even when blazing on the coast.' *(Mrs R B Richards; also Joan Heyman)*

Open: All year.
Rooms: 6 double, 1 suite – all with bath and telephone. 4 rooms in annexe.
Facilities: Dining room. Garden, terrace. English spoken.
Location: About 25 km inland from Portimão. Hotel is 2 km on the road to Foia from Monchique.
Terms: B & B 500–1,000 esc; dinner, B & B 900–1,500 esc; full board 1,400–2,000 esc. Set meals: lunch/dinner 250 esc; full *alc* 280 esc. 50% reduction for children under 8.

If you have difficulty in finding hotels because directions given in the Guide are inadequate, please help us to improve them.

MURTOSA, 3878 Aveiro   **Map 13**

Pousada da Ria   *Telephone:* (0034) 483 32
Ria de Aveiro

'A modern pousada, standing on a peninsula between the sea and the
Aveiro lagoon. It has well-furnished rooms, each with a covered balcony
looking over the lagoon, so even if it is rainy, one can sit and watch the
local sailing boats going by. The hotel entrance exhibits a number of
recommendations from various gourmet clubs of different countries; they
are well-deserved. This is an ideal place for anyone wanting a restful time,
particularly if they are interested in sea birds. Its only disadvantage is that
it is 30 km from Aveiro, the nearest town of any size, by road, though it is
only about 3 km across the water.' *(D S Smith)*

Open: All year.
Rooms: 10 double, 2 suites – all with bath, telephone and balcony.
Facilities: Salon, TV room, restaurant. Garden; outdoor swimming pool. Near
river with fishing; beach 2 km (but seat a bit rough). English spoken.
Location: Take N109 N from Aveiro; then turn W towards Torreira, then fork
left to Murtosa.
Credit cards: All major credit cards accepted.
Terms: B & B (single) 1,725 esc, (double) 1,850 esc; half board (single) 2,220 esc,
(double) 3,000; full board (single) 2,845, (double) 4,100 esc. Set meals: lunch/
dinner 500–700 esc.

OLIVEIRA DO HOSPITAL, 3400 Coimbra   **Map 13**

Pousada de Santa Barbara   *Telephone:* (0037) 522 52
Povoa das Quartas

'This modern government-owned inn is on the Coimbra–Salamanca road,
about 80 km east of Coimbra, and 7 km east of the small town of Oliviera
do Hospital. It has a magnificent view of the 6,600 feet high Serra do
Estrela, the highest mountain range in Portugal, and it is a good base from
which to explore this area. The rooms are standard hotel type, with baths.
There are excellent public rooms. The service is especially friendly and
helpful and the cooking first-class. We always enjoy a visit here.' *(D S
Smith)*

Open: All year.
Rooms: 16 double – all with bath, telephone, colour TV and tea-making facilities.
Facilities: Sitting room, TV room, restaurant. Large garden with tennis and
fishing. English spoken.
Location: On the Coimbra–Salamanca road about 80 km E of Coimbra and 7 km
E of Oliviera do Hospital.
Credit cards: All major credit cards accepted.
Terms: Double room with breakfast 1,600 esc. Set meals: 450–600 esc. Reduced
rates and special meals for children.

If you have kept brochures for foreign hotels, please enclose them
with your reports.

Infante de Sagres _Telephone:_ (02) 281.01
Praça D Filipa de Lencastre 62

'A splendid old-style Anglo-Portuguese hotel, in the centre of the city, with a magnificent table and dining room, comfortable bedrooms and attentive service. Superb ports and the best Vinho Verdes outside the Tras es Montes. A poor bar, however, and very slow breakfasts and room service. But the British connection still appreciated.' _(MW)_

Open: All year.
Rooms: 83 double, 1 single, 4 suites – all with bath, telephone and radio; TV in suites.
Facilities: Lifts, 2 lounges, bar, dining room; conference room. Small garden. English spoken. ᗭ .
Location: In town centre; no private parking.
Credit cards: Access/Euro/Mastercard, American Express, Barclay/Visa, Diners.
Terms: B & B (single) 4,000 esc, (double) 4,400 esc. Full _alc_ 1,500 esc. Special rates for groups. 50% reduction for children under 8, and special meals on request. 30% weekend discount on B & B price.

PALMELA, Costa de Lisboa Map 13

Pousada do Castelo de Palmela _Telephone:_ (0065) 235.12.26

'When you lean out of the window on a spring day at Palmela, the perfumes in the air will stop you in your tracks – which is just as well as the drop from your window ledge looks to be several hundred feet. This pousada, opened in 1980, is a transformed monastery inside a 1,000-year-old castle. We had anticipated a sort of Tower of London with beds, but there was no hint of discomfort. The bed, the bath, the restaurant, the cloisters – set out with flowers, deck-chairs and umbrellas – were down-right glamorous. The castle is perched on top of a hill and you can see for miles, even sitting on the loo. The landscape is of windmills, orange groves and the distant shore. Things in the vicinity not to miss: the sound of sheep bells as the flock is brought down the castle hill in the evening; the Paradise garden at Quinta del Bacalhoa, the white crescent of beach at Portinho where the restaurant has its feet in the water; and the luxurious tearoom at Quintande las Torres where we wondered why it took 40 minutes for our tea to come only to discover they were baking our brioches. We thought the restaurant splendid. The olives on the table were to olives what the Muscatel is to the grape. We were blessed with a waiter like the nice one in "Bread and Chocolate". He coaxed our tired nine-year-old through his dinner with patience and singular success. The hotel is about 1 hour south of Lisbon by motorway and would make a delightful stopover for anyone heading for the Algarve.' _(Shelley Cranshaw)_

A reader, who has visited this pousada on several occasions since it opened in 1979, agreed with most of last year's rapturous entry quoted above, but felt that the restaurant was not up to the standard one expects from a top-grade pousada; the staff were willing but disorganized and the food only moderate. He thought Shelley Cranshaw was probably lucky in having a young son with her: the Portuguese adore children and spoil them outrageously, and the staff of any hotel will always help with one's children, however difficult they may be. However, as the government agency which supervises pousadas has high standards, he expected that this one will soon come up to standard. Another reader shared these reservations about the food which he felt let down the very high standard of service, and was also put out, *pace* the critic referred to above, to find that no baby-cots were available.

Open: All year.
Rooms: 25 double, 2 suites – all with bath, telephone and radio.
Facilities: Lift, lounge, breakfast room, bar, dining room, TV room. Large grounds with unheated swimming pool (not in service in 1981) and children's play area. Sandy beaches with safe bathing 15 km; river 7 km with fishing and sailing facilities.
Location: 7 km from Setúbal; parking for 40 cars.
Credit cards: Access/Euro, Barclay/Visa.
Terms: Rooms with breakfast 2,500–2,800 esc. Set meals: lunch/dinner 800–1,000 esc.

PRAIA DA ROCHA, 8500 Portimão   **Map 13**

Hotel Bela Vista   *Telephone:* (0082) 24055
Av Tomas Cabreira   *Telex:* 13185 TARIK P

'A famous old hotel on the cliff top of Praia da Rocha, the Algarve's Edwardian watering-place a mile out of Portimão. The *Bela Vista* is now overshadowed by large modern hotels built recently, but it is still an oasis of calm, surrounded by palm trees. The food is very good, and the service personal and friendly. Some of the bedrooms are small, but they are all well-equipped.' *(LMS)*

Open: All year.
Rooms: 27 – 24 double, 2 single, 1 suite – 22 with bath, 5 with shower, all with telephone. (1 room on ground floor.)
Facilities: Lounge, TV room, games room, bar, restaurant. Garden. English spoken. &.
Location: 2 km from town centre; parking.
Terms: Rooms (including breakfast) 780–2,760 esc (single), 1,200–4,650 esc (double); suites 1,380–4,200 esc. Off-season breaks available. Reduced rates for children.

PRAIA DO GUINCHO, 2750 Cascais   **Map 13**

Hotel Do Guincho   *Telephone:* Cascais (19) 285.04.91
                                    Telex: 12624

'About 10 minutes (9 km) from Cascais, on a beautiful, practically deserted, stretch of coastline is this dazzling white 15th-century fort that has been converted to a luxury hotel with great style and charm. The hotel has its own pool, and adjoins the main Guincho beach. There is a most impressive integration of old and new architecture – the old stone building with vaulted brick ceilings must have been newly done, but looks as if they were always there. Even the fireplace brick is laid in an interesting way, in chevron and herringbone designs. It is one of the most beautiful buildings I've ever seen. The decoration is a bit spotty – the bar and dining room are extremely well-done, but in some of the other public rooms it runs to the over-stuffed, cretonne-covered type of furniture. Still everything is pleasant and comfortable and the views are superb – a great sweep of ocean all around. The food is very good, the menu extensive with some Portuguese regional dishes such as pork and clams Alentejano and duck with rice, and there's an excellent cold table with smoked fish, turkey and pork that you can have for starters. Good wine list, impeccable service, dinner here is a delight. A most glorious and romantic retreat if you want to get away from it all and just enjoy the ocean and beach and be pampered.' *(Jose Wilson; also Angela and David Stewart)*

Open: All year.
Rooms: 36 double – all with bath and air-conditioning.
Facilities: Hall, salons, bar, dining room, inner courtyard. Garden. Casino. Golf course and beach with watersports nearby.
Location: 9 km from Cascais.
Credit cards: Diners, Euro.
Terms: Prices not available (it is a 5-star hotel).

SINTRA, 2710 Lisbon   **Map 13**

Estalagem Quinta dos Lobos   *Telephone:* (19) 293.02.01 or 293.32.32

The *Quinta dos Lobos* is an early 17th-century manor house, built by the Knights Templar from Tomar, with a 15th-century manorial annexe built by the Duke of Cadval. Both buildings have extensive grounds with stunning views – of the Atlantic coast, of the Serra of Sintra and its castle, and of the plain below. 'An absolutely delightful inn, small, intimate and charmingly decorated with great taste. The owners, who speak English, seem to be a mixed group of young people with bright ideas, and the inn was fairly recently converted from a private house. There are lovely antiques and paintings, and the place has the air of a country house. It's very comfortable, with enchanting bedrooms, bathrooms that are both modern and good-looking, and all kinds of interesting touches, such as black-painted old wrought-iron benches as seats in the bar, and huge massed arrangements of blue agapanthus in big jars.' *(Jose Wilson)*

Open: All year.
Rooms: 16 double, 2 suites – all with bath, telephone, TV and tea-making facilities. 8 rooms in annexe.
Facilities: 3 lounges (1 with TV), 2 bars, breakfast room, dining room. Terraces. Large grounds with croquet, swimming pool. 10 minutes from beach; riding, tennis and golf nearby. English spoken.
Location: 28 km from Lisbon.
Terms: B & B 1,250–1,800 esc. Reduced rates for children.

The length of an entry does not necessarily reflect the merit of a hotel. The more interesting the report or the more unusual or controversial the hotel, the longer the entry.

VIANA DO CASTELO, 4900   Map 13

Hotel Santa Luzia   *Telephone:* (0028) 221 92
Telex: 25220

For those motoring south along the coast road from Santiago and Vigo in Spain, Viana do Castelo is the first town of any size over the Portuguese border. The *Santa Luzia* is a smallish luxury hotel three miles north of the town and 1,000 feet up, which has recently undergone major refurbishing. 'Superb views of hills, sea and the estuary of the Lima; excellent food, wonderful walking through miles of pine woods and mimosa forests behind the hotel. Lovely swimming pool in the old garden. Spacious and gracious in every way.' *(Diana Hopkinson; also Mr and Mrs C Billings)*

Open: All year.
Rooms: 42 double, 6 suites – all with bath and telephone.
Facilities: Lift, lounge/TV room, cocktail bar, restaurant; terrace and gardens with unheated swimming pool, tennis; beach 7 km. English spoken. ⅊.
Location: 3 miles from town centre on top of Monte Santa Luzia.
Credit cards: All major credit cards accepted.
Terms: B & B 1,100–3,000 esc; dinner, B & B 1,800–3,700 esc; full board 2,500–4,400 esc. Set meals: lunch/dinner 770 esc; full *alc* 990 esc. Reduced rates for children (under 5 years, no charge; over 5, 50%). Special meals provided.

425

Hostal De San Marcos, León

Spain

ALARCÓN, Cuenca **Map 13**

Parador Nacional Marqués de Villena *Telephone:* (966) 33.13.50

There has been a castle overlooking Alarcón for many centuries; it was substantially rebuilt in the 14th century, later it fell into disrepair, but was to some extent restored during the Civil War. Now the remains of the original fortress have been turned into a comfortable parador, enjoying stunning views of the town, the river Júcar cutting through its deep gorge, and the rolling plains of Cuenca.

A correspondent, quoted last year, described this as his favourite parador: 'Not as big or as grand as Jaén or Cardona, but less messed about with – more original: a still defiant symbol of an independent and contumacious aristocracy in a kingdom stricken by faction. If you want bright lights, a disco, bars, somewhere to go at night – stay away. Once the sun goes down it is pretty dark in Alarcón; there is no disco, only one tiny bar and one small souvenir shop.'

The same correspondent has been back since, and has sent us this supplementary report on evenings in the *Marqués de Villena*: 'About 8.30 pm, a hundred or so people, dressed in their best, descended on the parador for a wedding reception. The amount and variety of liquor that was being consumed by this normally starkly sober race was quite amazing; perhaps the reason was that their time was limited, and they had to concentrate their enjoyment – and consumption. The last resonant traveller was despatched on his resounding way through the door at 9.40 pm and the sounds of a great scrubbing and brushing arose as we went to our dinner in the lounge where some tables had been laid for residents. The staff, who must by now have felt like lying down on those same tables and going to sleep, continued to cope and even managed to smile. It was a wonderful unabrasive affair, that wedding. But perhaps intending visitors who want peace and quiet, or have small children they want to put to bed early, might wish to note that paradors can be noisy, particularly at weekends. Still I suppose the same could be said of any popular hotel anywhere in the world. Personally, I wouldn't have missed it for a gold clock.' *(Jeff Driver)*

Open: 21 December–31 October.
Rooms: 10 double, 1 single – all with bath and telephone.
Facilities: Salon with TV, bar, restaurant, terraces. Garden surrounded by remains of old walls. 5 km from lake with sailing and fishing. English spoken.
Location: 87 km S of Cuenca just off the N111.
Credit cards: All major credit cards accepted.
Terms: B & B 1,522–2,515 pts; dinner, B & B 2,372–3,365 pts; full board 2,937–3,930 pts. Set meals: lunch/dinner 850 pts.

ALBARRACIN, Teruel   **Map 13**

Hotel Albarracin   *Telephone:* (974) 71.00.71
Calle Azagra

'Albarracin is a little jewel of a town on the edge of the Montes Universales, which to my mind is one of the most beautiful parts of Spain – a vast empty area of forest and mountains, most of which is a state-controlled hunting reserve. Approaching the town from the Cuenca side, you go through the bottom of a gorge, sheer cliffs on either side of you, by the side of a trout stream. Then, without any warning, the road just runs right into a cliff: a great soaring wall of grey rock through which there is a tunnel about 100 metres long. On the other side is Albarracin, clinging by a brick and an odd nail or two to the cliff face. The houses are built on the side of this precipice: two storeys on the street side, and six high at the back. We asked the way to the *Hotel Albarracin*, and the man pointed vertically up into the sky. It was perched on top of an overhang, about 100 feet above the road. The streets are spattered with arms emblazoned, renaissance mini-palaces, and houses with balconies where the occupants can easily shake hands with the people living opposite. The city walls are in the process of being carefully restored. The Spanish Government has declared the whole town a national monument, but it is not in the least bit tourist spoiled. As for the hotel, it is a small modern place, clean and well-furnished. There's a bit of a swimming pool but it did not seem to be much used when I was there in June. The food is quite good for Spain. It is very adequate indeed – but I go there because of its situation more than anything else.' *(Jeff Driver)*

Open: All year.
Rooms: 34 double, 2 single – all with bath, telephone and baby-listening.
Facilities: Salon, 2 restaurants; garden with swimming pool; direct access to river with bathing and fishing.
Location: 38 km from Teruel. Hotel is in centre of Albarracin; parking.
Credit cards: All major credit cards accepted.
Terms: B & B 1,288–1,765 pts; dinner, B & B 2,128–2,605 pts; full board 2,688–3,150 pts. Set meals: lunch/dinner 840 pts; full *alc* 1,150 pts. Special meals for children.

ARCOS DE LA FRONTERA, Cadiz   Map 13

Parador Nacional Casa del Corregidor   *Telephone:* (956) 70.05.00
Plaza de Espana

This elegant house formerly belonged to a famous mayor *(corregidor)* of Arcos. It was half in ruins when it was acquired by the Spanish Government, rebuilt in the style of the original and opened in 1966 as the *Parador Nacional Casa del Corregidor*. It is a fine hotel built round a typical Spanish patio. The thoughtfully furnished rooms look out on to the square or across the Quadalete river to the seemingly endless open country beyond. These latter have huge balconies and are quieter. The pleasant restaurant gives on to a large terrace. The three-course menu offers a good choice of dishes with generous helpings. The *à la carte* includes a commendable number of regional specialities. Pleasant and efficient service. Arcos itself is built on a steep hill which falls sheer away on two sides. The ascent by car to the Plaza de Espana is not for the faint-hearted – the streets are cobbled, tortuous and narrow with few places to pass an oncoming vehicle, pedestrians have no escape but to jump into an open doorway and the many scooters seem to have priority because they make most noise. But the dangers are amply rewarded on reaching this cool, pleasant hotel with its stunning views and relaxed atmosphere.' *(Geoffrey Sharp)*

Open: All year.
Rooms: 18 double, 3 single – all with bath and telephone, most with balcony.
Facilities: Lifts; salon, bar, dining room, patio, air-conditioning. ♿ .
Location: Between Jerez de la Frontera and Ronda on the N342/C344. Central; no special parking facilities.
Credit cards: American Express, Barclay/Visa, Diners.
Terms: B & B 1,550–3,210 pts; dinner B & B 2,500–4,160 pts; full board 3,125–4,785 pts. Set meals: lunch/dinner 950 pts; full *alc* 1,270 pts.

ÁVILA   Map 13

Parador Nacional Raimundo de Borgoña   *Telephone:* (918) 21.13.40
Marqués de Canales de Chozas 16

'One of the greatest attractions of Ávila are its old city walls, and the parador looks across a formal garden to these, and their towers with storks standing in their nests, to the hills beyond – a really lovely outlook. As often with paradors, the style is baronial – coats of armour, wide tiled floors, massive wooden and leather furniture. The feeling of space everywhere, particularly in bedrooms and bathrooms was very welcome after the cell-like arrangements of so many hotels, and the really civilized provision of towels and pillows made the place very comfortable. Unfortunately, we found the set dinner dull and mediocre and the service sullen.' *(Mrs R B Richards; also Charles Hodgson)*

Note: A major extension is under way; 35 new bedrooms are planned for 1982.

Open: All year.
Rooms: 61 double, 1 single – all with bath and telephone.

Facilities: Lounges, reading room, TV room, bar, 2 dining rooms. Garden.
Location: 500 m from centre; garage.
Credit cards: All major credit cards accepted.
Terms: Rooms 1,500–3,700 pts per person. Set meals: breakfast 180 pts; lunch/dinner 800 pts.

AYAMONTE, Huelva

Map 13

Parador Nacional Costa de la Luz
El Castillito

Telephone: (955) 32.07.00

'The parador at Ayamonte is placed at the furthest south-west corner of Spain, with only the river Guadiana between it and Portugal, making it perfectly placed either for a jumping-off ground for a tour of that country or, as we used it, for a turning-point in a tour of some of the loveliest country we have yet seen in Spain. The main characteristic of the *Costa de la Luz* is the wonderful air of peace and tranquillity it offers at the end of a long day's driving. Situated high above the salt marshes of the Guadiana that flood dramatically with gold light at sunset, it is a modern parador of notably beautiful design, much enhanced by the use of growing plants like wallpaper. The bedrooms turn their backs on the views, and open instead each on to its own tiny cobbled patio of complete privacy, with one splendid rose bush in it, designed to fill the room at night with perfume. It is impossible to speak highly enough of the charm and the absolute peace and quiet of this unusual arrangement. The beautiful public rooms are almost completely glass-walled and open to the spectacular views over the river and across to Portugal. There is also a charming and strangely old-fashioned small garden. If I have carried on a bit about the building and the ambience, it is because they are really striking, but, as well as these, the parador offers all the essential services at very high standard. Good food, boiling bath water and invariably pleasant and attentive service. There are paradors more publicized; paradors like Jaén more incredibly dramatic; ones more beautiful and spectacular. But looking at them for what they are, which is travellers' havens in the course of a long journey, we felt that Ayamonte offered more than most.' *(Madeleine Polland)*

Open: All year.
Rooms: 20 – all with bath and air-conditioning.
Facilities: Salons, bar, dining room. Garden with swimming pool.
Location: 60 km W of Huelva.
Credit cards: American Express, Diners.
Terms: Rooms 2,600–3,565 pts. Set meals: breakfast 200 pts; lunch/dinner 860 pts.

BAÑALBUFAR, Mallorca

Map 13

Mar I Vent
José Antonio 49

Telephone: (971) 61.00.25

A brother-and-sister run hotel in a small and peaceful fishing and farming village on the ruggedly picturesque west coast, the most scenic part of the island. There are wonderful views of the sea and cliffs from the hotel and from the swimming pool on the sun terrace below. For those who prefer the sea, there is good bathing from a tiny cove about 15 minutes' stroll by winding pathways through the terraced tomato fields. The hills behind the hotel offer exhilarating walking country. The *Mar I Vent* is one of the oldest hotels on the island, and has been in the same family for four generations. The building was originally 18th-century, and although it has been much renovated and modernized since, it still retains some of the older features, and there is antique furniture in both public and private rooms. Bedrooms are furnished in local style; some are on the small side but they are bright, airy and well cared for. There are only 15 rooms, and it's essential to book throughout the season. The best rooms are usually reserved for the regular clients.

'Of all the hotels I have seen in the Balearics,' wrote our Mallorcan inspector last year, 'this is one of the few that I would very happily return to. It thoroughly deserves its popularity: one of the best-placed hotels on the island if beaches and bright lights are not your priority.' A recent visitor does not dissent from this view, but mentions one or two drawbacks: the menu is monotonous, especially in the sweet course – only crème caramel, fruit salad or ice cream – and only rarely offers fish, despite the tantalizing glimpses of fishing boats on the sea below. Also 'the Señorita is *most* efficient, but can be a little fierce especially about taking last orders for coffee about 9 pm when the hotel is quiet. Luckily there is a friendly local bar at the back of the grocery shop 200 yards away.' *(Diana Holmes, SB)*

Open: All year, except 1 December–1 February.
Rooms: 15 double – all with bath, telephone and tea-making facilities. 5 rooms with bath and balcony in annexe.
Facilities: 3 salons (1 with TV), bar/restaurant. Terrace with swimming pool, tennis court. Sea-bathing in nearby coves; fine walks. English spoken.
Location: 24 km NW of Palma, on the edge of the village; parking.
Terms: B & B 810–1,110 pts; dinner, B & B 1,450–1,750 pts; full board 1,700–2,125 pts. Set meals: lunch/dinner 850 pts. 10% reduction for children; special meals available.

BURGOS   Map 13

Landa Palace Hotel   *Telephone:* (947) 20.63.43/44

The *Landa Palace* certainly earns a place in any anthology of grand hotels, but, as the report below indicates, is a good one as well – which is not always the case. It is 3½ km outside Burgos on the Madrid road. The main hall is an impressive tower reconstructed from a country castle. Above it is the King of Spain's suite, with gold fittings in the bathroom, Isabel II's bed, sumptuously comfortable sofas and English prints. Almost everything that can be made in marble is. Parts are like a museum: there are collections of beds and cribs from many places, wall clocks of various kinds, a teapot collection and much else besides. There is also a remarkable indoor swimming pool in a vault, surrounded by plants. You can swim out at one end to an outdoor pool surrounded by lawns.

'A shabby exterior hides this impeccable hotel, furnished with lavish originality, and having extensive public areas. Our apartment was pretty extensive too – a large sitting room, bedroom, bathroom and an enclosed sun lounge with wicker furniture – all beautifully furnished and lit. The staff are pleasant and efficient, the food particularly enjoyable. Easily the best hotel we stayed at in Spain, and ridiculously cheap by British standards, and considering the quality of the accommodation. That is what paradors ought to be like and rarely are.' *(David Wooff)*

Open: All year.
Rooms: 36 double, 3 single, 9 suites – all with bath, telephone and air-conditioning.
Facilities: Lifts, salons, separate TV room, bars, nightclub, air-conditioned restaurant; indoor swimming pool. Gardens with outdoor swimming pool; tennis, sailing and fishing nearby. English spoken. &.
Location: 1.5 km from town centre; garage.
Credit card: Euro.
Terms: Rooms 4,600–5,800 pts per person; suites from 6,400 pts. Set meals: breakfast 330 pts; lunch/dinner 1,950 pts.

CARMONA, Seville
Map 13

Parador Nacional Alcazar Del Rey Don Pedro   *Telephone:* (954) 14.10.10

'In 1976 the King and Queen of Spain formally opened this parador, and it is certainly worthy of a royal opening. It has been built inside the massive walls of the ancient Moorish alcazar on the top of a hill, from which there are marvellous views over the wide green plain of the Guadalquivir valley, with mountains in the northern horizon. Although the actual hotel is new, it has been built in the Spanish renaissance manner, with Moorish influences: pierced wooden shutters and doors in the public rooms, a patio with a fountain in the middle. The walls, whitewashed or of honey-coloured brick, are sparingly punctuated with black or brown wooden and leather furniture. There were skins (real) on the floor and a Sienese triptych (reproduction) on the wall of our bedroom. There is a sumptuous sitting room, its burnt-orange walls glowing in the soft lighting; the dining room is a cool, lofty hall. Every detail in the hotel is a delight for the eyes. Ask for rooms on the top floor if you are sensitive to footsteps overhead – they do echo rather.' *(Ralph Blumenau)*

This original entry for the *Rey Don Pedro* was warmly endorsed last year by Geoffrey Sharp, but he also stressed the sound-insulation problems – from bathroom flushings as well as from voices and footsteps. He waxed enthusiastic about the newly-opened swimming pool – a model of good taste, with natural brick and grass surrounds; arcades to protect you from the sun; white painted garden furniture and masses of colourful flowers. But he found the food lacking in character. A more recent correspondent hotly disagrees. He found the food exceptionally good, and served in the most beautiful hotel dining room he had ever seen. And everything about the parador he found quite admirable. *(Antony Vestrey)*

Open: All year.
Rooms: 47 double, 8 single – 50 with bath, 5 with shower, all with telephone, some with balcony. (Some rooms on ground floor.)
Facilities: Hall, sitting room, dining room, room for gatherings and banquets, air-conditioning. Garden with swimming pool.
Location: In town centre; parking.
Credit cards: American Express, Barclay/Visa, Diners, Euro.
Terms: Rooms 3,047–3,565 pts. Set meals: breakfast 220 pts; lunch/dinner 920 pts.

> In the case of many continental hotels, especially Spanish ones, we have adopted the local habit of quoting a price for the room whether it is occupied by one or more persons. Rates for B & B, half board, etc., are per person unless otherwise stated.

DEYÁ, Mallorca

Map 13

Hotel Es Moli
Carretera de Valdemossa s/b

Telephone: (971) 63.90.00
Telex: 69007 Smoli E

Deyá, on the western side of Mallorca and made famous by the long residence of the poet Robert Graves, has a spectacular position in the middle of a natural amphitheatre, backed by mountains and facing the sea. *Es Moli*, a modern hotel, is one of the spectators on the banks of the amphitheatre, looking across the valley to the roofs and gardens of the village and the pattern of terrace fields which surround it. Beyond, olive and citrus groves drop away towards the distant sea. Because the hotel is built into the hillside, finding your way round can be rather confusing. The swimming pool is on the fourth floor at the rear. Floating on your back, you can stare up through the palm and fig trees at the towering honey-coloured hillside. If you don't want to take the lift to the lower floors, you can stroll down through the terraced gardens at the side of the hotel. And what gardens they are! Lemon trees shade the paths. Geraniums crowd the flower beds and brilliantly flowered creepers overflow every doorway. And they invade the hotel too, in the form of skilfully arranged flowers in many of the public rooms.

The one thing which every visitor to *Es Moli* is agreed about is its exceptionally lovely position. And the internal furnishing and fittings, if not always in prime condition or to everyone's taste, are – again by general consent – far above the standard normally encountered in Spain. No complaints about the service either. Regrettably, the one flaw in what would otherwise be one of the most idyllic hotels in the Guide has been the *Es Moli's* food. Recent visitors, however, tell us that the hotel has made great efforts to improve the quality and variety of its menus. The latest report, received just as the typescript is being prepared for press, pulls out all the stops: 'A superbly run and lovely hotel in an idyllic situation, with immaculate service, amazingly consistent standards, good eating, and the indefinable quality of pleasurable ease. Only a semi-serpent could dislike this demi-Eden.' *(Robert Heller; also Graeme Carmichael, J A Skidmore, Larry De Waay)*

Open: 3 April–23 October.
Rooms: 58 double, 14 single, 1 suite – all with bath and shower, telephone, radio and air-conditioning; most with terrace (300 pts supplement).
Facilities: Lift; several lounges (1 with TV), card and reading room, dining terrace, dancing weekly. Large gardens with swimming pool, tennis court, ping pong, pétanque. Rock beach 6 km from the hotel (free transport by hotel minibus). English spoken.
Location: Palma 29 km; airport 37 km.
Terms: B & B 2,450–3,900 pts; dinner, B & B 2,750–4,200 pts; full board 3,250–4,750 pts. Set meals: 1,200 pts; full *alc* 1,700 pts. 25% reduction for children of 2–11 in parents' room; special meals available.

ENCAMP, Andorra

Map 13

Residencia Belvedere

Telephone: Andorra (78) 31263

A friendly informal guesthouse, run by an English couple, Terry and Jo Dixon, set slightly above the town of Encamp and commanding a dramatic Pyrenean valley. It caters for skiers in the winter and walkers in the summer. The position is agreeable, but as one visitor writes, 'Its real strengths are indoors: an attractive welcome from the Dixons, and superb home-made food.'

This was the entry we ran in the 1980 edition. We left it out last year, for lack of feedback. But just before the 1981 edition went to press, we received the following testimonial:

'We usually prefer "local" hotels, but we had been to Andorra before and its hotels generally leave everything to be desired! So when we spotted the *Belvedere* from the main road we turned in – and very glad indeed that we did. It was their last night before closing for a short break, but the Dixons really do welcome all guests as family even though they must have wished we'd not arrived when we did! It is rather spartan, but it does not pretend to be anything but a good "pension". The food is superb and the welcome unbeatable. It snowed all night (in April) but the bar never closed, the log fire was marvellous and we were lucky to get away next day. It is unbelievably cheap: it must be great fun for young skiers.' *(David and Angela Stewart; also George Brook)*

Open: All year, except 1 November–15 December.
Rooms: 10 double, 1 single – 1 with bath.
Facilities: Lounge with open log fire, dining room, bar. ½ acre grounds with sun terrace, lawn and terraced garden with magnificent views; paddling pool and slides for children. Convenient for chairlift to lake, and ski slopes. English spoken.
Location: ½ mile from Encamp; parking.
Terms: B & B 855–1,152 pts; dinner, B & B 1,674–2,000 pts. Reduced rates and special meals for children.

ESTEPONA, Malaga   Map 13

Hotel Santa Maria   *Telephone:* (952) 81.13.40
Apartado 2

'A delightful small hotel in the Costa del Sol set well back from the main coast road with hourly bus service. It is about 5 km from San Pedro, 12 or so from Estepona and Marbella. The very comfortable bedrooms are mostly in separate bungalows in a pretty garden which runs down to the beach. The majority of the bungalows have two double rooms, each with its own bathroom and veranda, some have triple rooms. Efficiently Spanish, and there is usually somebody at the reception desk who speaks English. There are beautiful hills just inland. The beach is mostly sandy and quite shallow. The shade on the beach is owned by the hotel which also runs a pleasant bar and fish restaurant with its own swimming pool at the end of the garden. It is a peaceful and lovely place to stay; it manages to be very Spanish *and* very efficient (which I think is often a contradiction in terms) – and also charming.' *(Phyllida Horniman)*

Open: 1 April–1 October.
Rooms: 32 double, 2 single, 3 suites – all with bath, shower, telephone and baby-listening.
Facilities: TV lounge, 2 bars, 2 restaurants, bridge room. Large garden, swimming pool. Golf and tennis nearby. English spoken.
Location: 3 km from town centre.
Credit cards: American Express, Barclay/Visa, Euro.
Terms: Rooms 1,000 pts per person; B & B 1,180 pts; dinner, B & B 1,800 pts; full board 2,500 pts. Full *alc* 800 pts.

FUENTERRABIA, Guipuzcoa   Map 13

Parador Nacional El Emperador   *Telephone:* (943) 64.21.40

Fuenterrabia, now a popular seaside resort and fishing port, dates from the 15th century and is full of steep narrow streets and ancient mansions with immense stone shields above the lintels. It is perched high above the border river with France, about halfway between St-Jean-de-Luz and San Sebastián. During the 17th-century wars with France, the parador, then a near-impregnable fortress, was triumphantly held against the French. Much of the structure has survived, but reconstruction has been pointedly faithful, even to leaving trees and greenery sprouting from walls. You live in a maze of great Gothic arches, old stone stairways, heavily beamed ceilings, polished floors, slabbed stone courtyards. There is nothing spartan about the bedrooms: they are the essence of comfort with all modern requirements. The food, as is customary in these state-run inns, is largely based on the produce of the area.

Recent visitors write: 'The building and the superb old town were worth the awful hassle of crossing the border into Spain, but the service – like so often in Spain – appears grudging. This may be due only to a complete lack of English spoken by any of the staff. The food we found very poor even by so-called local standards. But it is truly a magnificent building.' (*Angela and David Stewart*)

Open: All year.
Rooms: 16 – all with bath or shower and telephone.
Facilities: Salon, bar, dining room. Fishing, sailing, boating nearby.
Location: 23 km E of San Sebastián; hotel is in centre of Fuenterrabia; parking.
Credit cards: All major credit cards accepted.
Terms: Rooms (single) 1,400–2,000 pts, (double) 3,000–3,800 pts. Set meals: breakfast 200 pts; lunch/dinner 867 pts.

GOMERA, Canary Islands   Map 13

Parador Colombino Conde de la Gomera   *Telephone:* (922) 87.11.00

'An island off an island – always something to be greatly desired. The Canary Islands have fair weather all year round, and the sun does indeed shine warmly on the lobster-red tourists swarming through the pizzerias and souvenir shops on the south coast of Tenerife. If you have come this far, go just a bit further, an hour and a half by ferry, to the tiny island of Gomera. This is Spain, not cardboard and concrete tourist land. Not one tourist in sight, just the locals. Whom we joined in an outdoor bar on the waterfront where we drank two coffees and a water tumbler of brandy for a total of 40 pence, service included. A good beginning. Then up the hill to the cool luxury of the parador. More like a convent or an art museum than a hotel. Quiet, friendly service. A giant room with modern bath and antique furniture – and a balcony with a striking view of seaport and ocean hundreds of feet below. A cosy bar, a very complete dinner menu and surprisingly good food. Wine the best that Spain can offer which is very good indeed. Breakfast in bed in the morning, a stroll through the tropical gardens, a dip in the pool; living at its most relaxed and luxurious. A luxury well within the means of anyone familiar with London prices. We will return, happily, over and over again, whenever we are within striking distance of this warm little island.' (*Harry Harrison*)

Open: All year.
Rooms: 20 double, 1 single, 2 suites – all with bath and balcony or private terrace overlooking gardens and sea, telephone, tea-making facilities and baby-listening, 2 with TV.
Facilities: 2 salons (1 with colour TV), bar, restaurant with air-conditioning. Luxuriant gardens with swimming pool; beach, fishing and sailing nearby; also underwater swimming. English spoken. ở .
Location: 600 m from town centre; parking.
Credit cards: All major credit cards accepted.
Terms: Rooms (single) 2,750–3,000 pts, (double) 3,400–3,900 pts. Set meals: breakfast 215 pts; lunch/dinner 850 pts; full *alc* 1,200 pts. Special meals for children.

GRANADA   Map 13

Parador Nacional de San Francisco   *Telephone:* (958) 22.14.93 and
Alhambra   22.14.62

'The *Parador Nacional de San Francisco* is, for all practical purposes, a modern building on the site of the Franciscan monastery that was the temporary resting place of Ferdinand and Isabella, who chose to be buried at the site of what they considered to be their greatest triumph: the final extinction of Moslem rule in Spain. Their remains were later transferred to the Capilla Real adjoining the cathedral, which was completed under their grandson, Charles V. The site of the temporary sepulchre, with its commemorative plaque, the tower and the main entrance are preserved, but very little else. Nevertheless, the architects have done a work of great sympathy and harmony. It is also, perhaps, the fairest jewel in the parador crown, and, not unnaturally, the most expensive. Other paradors have their high, middle and low seasons: Granada has only one. It is, after all, like Agra, one of the fabled places of the world.

'A heatwave was doing Andalusia to a crisp, but walking into our room was like walking into a fridge. As one would expect at an establishment of this class, the *San Francisco is* air-conditioned – and weren't we glad of it! We also faced the Generalife, which was no more than two or three hundred yards away, and could sit and gaze at one of the sights of the world from the cool of our room whilst refreshing ourselves with the contents of the minibar.

'Now for the bad news. About 8 o'clock that evening I went to the reception desk to change a traveller's cheque. Two American ladies were asking the clerk if they could have some washing dried and ironed. To my great astonishment the reply was "No". Every parador that I have ever been in has had a list behind the door of the room, in four different languages, giving the price of washing and ironing. At so prestigious and expensive an establishment you would not expect a bit of ironing to present any problems.

'Then it was my turn. "No" was again the reply. "But in the brochure issued by the Administración Turística Española there is a symbol for currency exchange." "Yes, I know. But last week the pound dropped from 193 pesetas to 185 in a day and the cheques we changed in the morning were worth so much less by evening." I fully realize that the clerk has a duty to his employers, that their best interest must be his prime concern and that he is not in any way entitled to take chances with their money. But there must have been occasions when the exact opposite happened: someone changed a traveller's cheque in the morning and by the time it was presented its value had increased. Surely, if the Spanish Government agrees to deal in currency, it should be prepared to take the losses along with the gains.

'The following morning breakfast was served *al fresco* in the shade of the trees on the terrace overlooking the Generalife. Taking into account the American ladies' experiences and my own the night before, I should say, on the whole, "B minus" for service, "A plus" for appointments. Location? Ungradeable, I should say. Never in my life have I seen such a profusion and variety of flowers, and everywhere, the sight and sound of running water. If you were to reduce the entries in the Guide by 75%, this is one that I should insist you should keep.' *(Jeff Driver; also, but with reservations about the food, David Wooff)*

Open: All year.
Rooms: 26 – all with bath, telephone and air-conditioning.
Facilities: Salon. bar, dining room. Attractive gardens. Night life (flamenco dancing, etc.) in Granada; skiing in the Sierra Nevada 34 km SE by first-class winding road.
Location: 3 km from town centre.
Credit cards: American Express, Barclay/Visa, Diners, Mastercard.
Terms: Rooms 3,500–4,830 pts. Set meals: breakfast 220 pts; lunch/dinner 910 pts.

JAÉN   Map 13

Parador Nacional Castillo de Santa Catalina   *Telephone:* (953) 23.22.87

A newly modernized parador, a few miles outside the provincial capital of Jaén – a colossal eagle's nest of a castle perched precariously on a mountain above the town with dizzying views. Southern-facing rooms have balconies, but all have equally stunning vistas.

'I stayed in six paradors this trip, including Jaén. I found the same standard in all of them: friendly courtesy, surgical cleanliness, comfort, uniformly dependable cuisine. But Jaén represents the parador system at its best: the vision of the architect, his respect for the original structure, the harmonious, almost imperceptible blending of old and new, as well as the skill of the builders. The anteroom to the dining room has an arch springing from each of the four corners of the room to meet 60 or 70 feet above your head, and is worthy of a cathedral. The dining room itself, with its priceless tapestries, is only slightly less grand. You can easily become transported by this place, especially if, like me, you love to brood on mountain peaks. For a mountain brooder, this is the Promised Land. Oh, for a marriage of Spanish accommodation and French cuisine, and I don't think I would ever leave the place. Still, at the price I am not complaining.' *(J A Driver)*

Open: All year.
Rooms: 37 double, 6 single – all with bath and telephone, some with balconies. (11 rooms on ground floor.)
Facilities: Lift, 2 lounges, chess and card room, dining room, TV room, air-conditioning. 1,500 square metres of garden with trees and seating; swimming pool. English spoken. &.
Location: 5 km from town centre.
Credit cards: American Express, Barclay/Visa, Diners.
Terms: Rooms 2,185–2,530 pts (single), 2,700–3,570 pts (double). Set meals: breakfast 220 pts; lunch/dinner 914 pts. Special meals for children.

Hostal de San Marcos
Plaza de San Marcos 7

Telephone: (987) 23.73.00
Telex: 89809 HSM LE

Unquestionably one of the great hotels of Europe. Some of the rooms in this former monastery, though de luxe in their furnishings, are still a little cell-like, and the quality of the cooking doesn't quite match the amazing decor. But staying at *San Marcos* is likely to prove, for those with the taste for the ultra-grand, a once-in-a-lifetime experience.

'An entire book has been written about this gigantic superbly contrived luxury hotel; it has undoubtedly the finest renaissance facade in Europe, which is no less than 80 yards long or 120 if you include the great medieval church whose interior of cathedral-like size can be seen through plate glass doors from the upper gallery of the enormous patio which adjoins the hotel itself. There are three-quarters of a mile of carpeted corridors which are lined on both sides with exquisite reproductions of Spanish furniture through the ages – a museum in itself. To gain some idea of the size of the place, one of the smallest rooms, used only for breakfast, is 69 feet by 27, the smaller restaurant giving on to a summer terrace with the river Bernesga beyond is 78 feet long, while the main lounge, which has a polished marble floor on which are a multitude of Persian rugs, and the ceiling one enormous painting, is 84 feet square. There is no end to the wonders of this hotel: an arcade of shops; a museum with Roman and Visigothic carvings; a students' bar and a low-price cafeteria for the less affluent tourists. Luxurious though the place is, the bedroom prices are not exorbitant.' *(T A Layton)*

Open: All year.
Rooms: 100 double, 15 suites – all with bath, shower, telephone, radio and TV, some with balconies. (Some rooms on ground floor.)
Facilities: Lifts, salons, TV room, rooms for private functions, tea room, bar, 2 restaurants; conference rooms; children's playroom. Large garden. English spoken. &.
Location: 500 m from city centre; garages.
Credit cards: All major credit cards accepted.
Terms: Rooms 5,325–11,800 pts; B & B 3,350–3,850 pts; full board 6,300–6,800 pts. Set meals: lunch/dinner 1,800 pts; full *alc* 2,000 pts. Reduced rates and special meals for children.

MADRID

Map 13

Hotel Ritz
Plaza de la Lealtad 5, Madrid 14

Telephone: (91) 221.28.57
Telex: 43986 RITZ-E

Another legendary Spanish hotel – the only hotel, so far as we know, to have been built by a reigning monarch – Alfonso XIII in 1908.

'The overall impression is one of old-world charm. The service is outstanding. The doorman even turns the revolving doors for you. There is a man who runs the automatic lift. Everyone greets you. And the place is quiet. Though it's set just off a main thoroughfare close to the Prado, there are trees all around to deflect the sound. The wood-panelled room for two was huge. There was a little foyer and two walk-in closets. The bathroom was equally large. There were two basins, a separate toilet, a separate shower (which most old-world hotels don't do very well) and bath and even a separately mounted shaving or make-up mirror. Five people could have used the bathroom without getting in each other's way. Room service was prompt and excellent. When I ordered tea with cakes I got enough luscious pastry for two (even though it was only for me). We tried the restaurant. It didn't seem to be very popular for some reason (perhaps too expensive considering all the reasonable restaurants in Madrid). The food was all right but not outstanding. If you prefer the plastic/impersonal atmosphere of most modern hotels, I don't recommend the *Ritz*. But if you appreciate the more traditional ambience, the *Ritz* is one of the finest city hotels in Europe.' *(J Gazdak)*

Open: All year.
Rooms: 150 rooms and 25 suites – all with bath, shower and telephone; colour TV in the suites.
Facilities: Lifts, lounge, reading/TV room, restaurant; 3 banqueting rooms. Small garden. English spoken. &.
Location: In town centre; parking.
Credit cards: American Express, Barclay/Visa.
Terms: Rooms 3,900–8,500 pts per person, suites from 13,500 pts. Set meals: breakfast 500 pts; full *alc* 4,200 pts. Special meals for children.

MADRID   **Map 13**

Hotel Suecia   *Telephone:* (91) 231.69.00
Marqués de Casa Riera 4, Madrid 14   *Telex:* 22313

The medium-sized Swedish-run *Suecia* is tucked away in a small quiet side street just above the Plaza de Cibeles in the heart of Madrid: it's halfway between the Prado and the Puerto del Sol, round the corner from the Opera House, and convenient for shops and for banks. Its faithful clientele includes newspapermen and guest stars at the opera. 'The *Suecia* is a hotel for the discriminating tourist and the travelling businessman, depressed by the impersonal anonymity of the large international hotel. There is nothing flashy. The rooms are comfortable, but some are quite small; the bar doubles as a breakfast room; the basement restaurant, called *The Bellman*, famous for its smorgasbord, is excellent but pricey. But what gives the place its special flavour is the staff who treat their guests like old friends.' *(Stephen Aris; also AL, Michael Horniman)*

Open: All year. Restaurant closed Saturday night and Sunday.
Rooms: 56 double, 3 single, 5 suites – all with bath, telephone, baby-listening, air-conditioning and mini-bar, TV on request.
Facilities: Bar/breakfast room, restaurant, facilities for banquets and conferences.
Location: In town centre, just off the Calle de Alcala. Public car parks nearby.
Credit cards: All major credit cards accepted.
Terms: Rooms 3,703–5,290 pts. Set meals: breakfast 275 pts; lunch/dinner 1,400 pts.

> The terms indicate the range of prices in each hotel. Some have a low and high season, some do not. The lower price is likely to be for someone sharing a double room, and the higher price the maximum for a single occupant.

Hotel Los Monteros

Telephone: (52) 77.17.00
Telex: 77059

For those who like to take their holidays in style, a modern de luxe hotel –
in fact a complex of rooms and suites of varying sizes and grades –
surrounded by gardens, not to mention swimming pools, tennis courts, a
golf course and plenty of other sporting holiday amenities.

'This highly regarded hotel is about 5 km from Marbella towards
Málaga. The original portion, the Andalusian Pavilion, contains most of
the public rooms, and the "basic price" bedrooms – these might be
somewhat noisy as some of them face the main highway. The next section,
the Mirador, contains the duplex suites which consist of a spacious sitting
room with balcony, on one level, the bedroom and bathroom being on
another level. The third section, the Mediterraneo, has very large single-
level bedsitting rooms with spacious marble bathrooms, the entrance to
each balconied room being a wide hallway. This summer, making our first
visit to *Los Monteros*, we reserved a duplex suite. However, after a few
days, we decided we would prefer to have a room in the Mediterranean
Pavilion. A word of request at reception accomplished this in a trice.
Going straight back to our room, we found the housekeeper and two
maids waiting to pack for us and a porter to transport our things.

'A welcoming note and a bottle of sherry is placed in each room. Service
throughout the hotel, from the obligingly efficient hall porters' desk to
room service, at any time of day or night, could not be faulted. Having to
take our holiday in August, we found the Beach Club – which is walking
distance from the hotel – noisy and overcrowded, so preferred to spend
our time by the swimming pool in the gardens, keeping company with the
flamingoes, which wander from the greenery of one ornamental pool to
another; there is a small pool and play area for children too. The Golf
Club and course (closed in the summer) is the other side of the road; the
Tennis Club and courts are popular and well-patronized. There is an
indoor games room and a quiet Card Room. The *El Corzo* Grill Room,
indoors in the winter, outdoors on the terrace by the pool in summer, is
justifiably popular; there is "live" music for dancing each evening and
occasional other entertainment. The various lounges, furnished in differing styles, are virtually deserted in the summer, but doubtless popular in
winter, when the evening entertainments are also held indoors. A car is
advantageous, the hotel being some distance from Marbella. *Los Monteros* more than lived up to its reputation. The nearest we could come to any
criticism, was the blandness of the decor in all the bedrooms. They don't
take package groups, but you can book through the more up-market tour
operators.' *(Evelyn S Stevens)*

Open: All year.
Rooms: 168 – many with salon, all with bath and radio; TV and baby-listening on
request.
Facilities: Salons, library, TV room, bridge room, bar, restaurant; nightly dancing to orchestra; once a week flamenco shows. 2 saunas, indoor and outdoor
swimming pools, tennis club, golf club, squash; riding nearby. Private road to
sandy beach, safe bathing. English spoken. &.
Location: 5 km N of centre of Marbella, off the N340.
Credit cards: American Express, Barclay/Visa, Diners, Euro.
Terms: B & B 4,500–10,000 pts; dinner, B & B 5,600–12,300 pts. Set meals:
lunch/dinner 2,400 pts; full *alc* 2,700 pts. 20% reduction for children under 5;
special meals provided.

MIJAS, Nr Fuengirola, Málaga   Map 13

Hotel Mijas   *Telephone:* (952) 48.58.00/65
Urbanización Tamisa   *Telex:* 77393

'The *Hotel Mijas* offers high standards of service and comfort on a coast which is almost entirely devoted to the demands of the mass package market. Indeed, whilst most of the clientele at *Mijas* are package tourists, they obviously feel part of a superior breed – one which expects first-class service, albeit at cut-rate prices. And to a large extent this is what the hotel provides. There is an *à la carte* menu from which the cost of the set meal included in one's tour may be deducted. The pool-side services – mattresses, umbrellas, bar, etc. – are particularly good. The public areas are elegant and the bedrooms with Mediterranean tiled floors are well-equipped. The bar terrace is particularly attractive with views down to the coast – unfortunately one end of the terrace also overlooks the village rubbish tip. Sadly, the cuisine is indifferent. Sadly, because there is a genuine attempt to produce interesting dishes which fails because of poor kitchen technique. Bottled sauces and tinned vegetables abound. Our *demi-pension* rates, however, were so low that we happily chose to take a small snack from the lunchtime buffet by the pool as our daily meal (probably a safer bet, anyway, than the more ambitious evening meals) and eat out in the evening at the local restaurants providing really excellent food. (*La Hacienda* along the coast road towards Marbella has inspired cooking at fair prices; *La Fonda* in Marbella and *Los Duendes* in San Pedro are also serious restaurants and not too expensive.' *(David Wooff)*

Open: All year.
Rooms: 106 doubles, 3 suites – all with bath and shower, telephone, radio, colour TV, tea-making facilities and baby-listening. 15 rooms in annexe. (Some rooms on ground floor.)
Facilities: 3 salons, 3 bars, dining room, games and reading rooms; conference rooms; beauty salon, boutique, sauna, terrace. Gardens with 2 swimming pools (1 heated) and tennis courts. 8 km from the sea (bus) with sandy beach and safe bathing; golf courses 7 km and 12 km.
Location: 300 m from town centre; parking for 40 cars.
Credit cards: All major credit cards accepted.
Terms: B & B 1,880–2,845 pts; Dinner, B & B 3,040–3,995 pts; full board 4,195–5,150 pts. Set meals: breakfast 230–255 pts; lunch/dinner 1,155 pts; full *alc* 1,875 pts. Reduced rates for children; special meals on request.

MOJÁCAR, Almería   Map 13

Parador Nacional Reyes Católicos   *Telephone:* (951) 47.82.50

Mojácar has a magnificent position dominating the plains and the Andalusian coast. It has so far avoided the spoliation of development, and retains its maze of small Moorish alleys. The *Parador* is a mile out of the village on the Carboneras road. 'An excellent building of modern design, below the village and just above the sea. Elegant rooms, effortless service, good food and value for money. Apart from Nerja, the only possible place to stay on the Costa del Sol.' *(Antony Vestrey)*

Open: All year.
Rooms: 89 doubles, 9 singles – all with bath, telephone and tea-making facilities.
Facilities: Salon, TV room, air-conditioning. Garden, swimming pool.
Location: On the coast just off the N340.
Credit cards: All major credit cards accepted.
Terms: B & B 1,700–2,200 pts. Set meals: breakfast 220 pts; lunch/dinner 950 pts.

MONACHIL, Granada

Map 13

Parador Nacional de Sierra Nevada

Telephone: (958) 48.02.00

'A modern Alpine-type building, 2,500 metres up in a superb position facing the south-west. Elegant and uncluttered. Good food and service. A steal for the price. Probably hard to get into during the winter skiing season when it is on the snow-line, or in high summer.' *(Antony Vestrey)*

Open: All year.
Rooms: 20 double, 2 single, 10 4-bedded – 10 with bath, 22 with shower, all with telephone and mini-bar.
Facilities: Salon, TV room, dining room, terrace. Tennis and winter sports nearby.
Location: 35 km from Granada.
Credit cards: All major credit cards accepted.
Terms: Double room with breakfast 3,000–3,700 pts. Set meals: lunch/dinner 950 pts; full *alc* 1,000 pts. Special meals for children.

NERJA, Málaga

Map 13

Parador Nacional de Nerja
Playa de Burriano – Tabluzo

Telephone: (952) 52.00.50

'This pleasantly run and well-maintained parador was opened in 1965. It is situated high up on the cliffs overlooking the beach of Burriano on the eastern edge of the town of Nerja which does not intrude and has some local restaurants mostly tourist-orientated. The hotel grounds stretch to the very edge of the cliff and the splendid view is for the most part uninterrupted. It is a long low building of an unimaginative but unobtrusive design. The large rooms have generous-sized balconies overlooking the sea and the mountains, and are comfortably furnished with well-equipped bathrooms and bar-fridges. It is spotlessly clean everywhere. There is a pool surrounded by a delightful garden, mainly undulating lawn but with trees for shade and flowers for colour, where there is plenty of room and facilities for sunbathing. Alternatively a lift takes you directly to the beach below. Although open throughout the year, it is very much a hotel for the sun and the sea. The restaurant also looks over the sea, and as well as an *à la carte* offers an above-average three-course menu with very generous helpings. Excellent choice of first courses, good fish and boring sweets. Slightly impersonal service. An agreeable place for a reasonably simple and quiet summer holiday. A car whilst not essential would be helpful. There are some extraordinary caves nearby (about 2½ miles) which have a mind-boggling plethora of stalactites and stalagmites in two vast caverns.' *(Anne Waley)*

Open: All year.
Rooms: 38 double, 2 single – all with bath, shower, telephone, fridge-bar, balcony and air-conditioning.
Facilities: Salon/bar, reading room, games room, restaurant. Sunny terrace and gardens with swimming pool and 2 tennis courts; lift to sandy beach with safe bathing and motor boats; open-air café for meals or snacks.
Location: 2 km from Nerja, S of the CN 340 in the direction of Málaga.
Credit cards: American Express, Diners, Euro.
Terms: Rooms 725–1,025 pts. Set meals: breakfast 214 pts; lunch/dinner approx 870 pts.

ORIENT, Bunyola, Mallorca

Map 13

Hostal de Muntanya
Carretera Alaró-Buñyola

Telephone: Orient 61.33.80

'In the mountains away from the sea in a remote village where the school is an all-ages one-room affair set in a flower garden directly opposite the only hotel. This has 16 double rooms, a large dining room which on fiestas and Sundays is the mecca for people from the towns who rave about country-style eating. Tourists are still a rare sight for the 160 or so inhabitants and local farmers. It is ideal for an away-from-it-all holiday if what you are looking for is clean mountain air, clear skies and glorious countryside. Most nights the village goes to bed after dinner, unless some of the local characters join the hotel guests over jugs of tangy wine after they have eaten the superb dishes of *tumbet*, a tasty but meatless vegetable pot-pourri, or mutton rice *brut*, or delicious stews. Apart from the village dishes, which are the speciality of the hotel and its big attraction, there is a vast *à la carte*. There is no swimming and anyone wanting transport must hire a car in Palma before taking up residence. Paradise for those who want peace, quiet and a lazy holiday in beautiful natural surroundings.' *(Bert Horsfall)*

So ran our original entry for this remote mountain hostel. Recent visitors warmly endorse it: 'First-rate in all respects: a perfect setting and the road to Orient took us through some breathtaking scenery. The food – eaten on a terrace with a view of the countryside – was way above the usual Spanish standard, without being pretentious. Outstanding value too.' *(Brian Capstick)*

Open: All year, except 1–30 June.
Rooms: 14 double, 2 single – 1 with bath, 12 with shower.
Facilities: Salon/bar with TV, reading room, restaurant, terrace. Garden.
Location: 33 km from Palma on the southern edge of the Sierra de Alfabia; go N from Palma by the main Buñyola road, then fork NE to Orient.
Terms: B & B 663–875 pts; dinner, B & B 1,163–1,375 pts; full board 1,438–1,650 pts. Set meals: lunch/dinner 500 pts; full *alc* 700 pts. Reduced rates and special meals for children.

If you know a good hotel that is not in the Guide, tell us. WRITE NOW. Freepost (UK only) forms are at the back of the Guide.

Punta Negra   *Telephone:* (971) 68.07.62

Very popular with British visitors (you will need to book well in advance
for the high season) and deservedly so. It has a beautiful and isolated
position, 1½ km from the concrete blocks of Palma Nova on a small
promontory, 200 m from the road and surrounded on three sides by the
sea. It's mainly furnished in Spanish traditional style – tiled floors,
antiques, comfy leather armchairs and open fireplaces. The decor,
according to one correspondent who has travelled widely in the area, is
the most attractive in the Balearics. Some of the rooms are in a group of
bungalows perched on a bluff below the hotel, others are ranged round a
central courtyard facing out to sea. There are two small sandy beaches on
either side of the promontory, and a pool outside the main lounge. Don't
expect anything special or particularly regional from the restaurant,
though it is above average by Mallorcan standards. *(SB and NB)*

Open: All year.
Rooms: 45 double, 3 single, 13 suites – all with bath, shower, terrace facing sea,
telephone and baby-sitting facilities. (Some rooms on ground floor, and some in
bungalows below the hotel.)
Facilities: Lift, lounge, reading room, room for cards with TV, bar, restaurant;
dancing Tuesday and Friday. Courtyard and garden with heated swimming pool,
tennis; 2 small private sandy beaches with safe bathing; some boating. English
spoken.
Location: 11 km from Palma; 1½ km from Palma Nova.
Terms: B & B 1,925–1,988 pts; dinner, B & B 2,925–3,141 pts; full board
3,830–3,915 pts. Set meals: lunch/dinner 1,140 pts; full *alc* 1,600 pts. 8%, 10% or
15% reduction on more than 2 weeks, depending on length of stay. Reduced rates
and special meals for children.

Hotel Aigua Blava   *Telephone:* (972) 62.20.58

'Even better than your report would indicate,' writes a recent visitor to
this random but satisfying conglomeration of buildings amid trees, rocks
and lawns which have grown round a small fishing beach and harbour at
the northern end of the Costa Brava, 50 km east of Gerona. It's a highly
personal hotel, the creation 40-odd years ago of Xiquet (pronounced
Chickee) Sabater, who is half-Spanish, quarter-Japanese and quarter-
French, married to a French girl. It's the sort of place which those who
take to it, can't keep away from. The only snag: good bathing beaches are
a longish walk away, but the hotel has its own substantial pool and many
of the guests are only too happy to stay sybaritically poolside, being
served drinks by the many friendly waiters. *(Ann and Michael Lisamer,
Navin Sullivan)*

Open: 4 April–18 October.
Rooms: 67 double, 8 single, 10 suites – 78 with bath, 7 with shower, all with
telephone and tea-making facilities. (Some rooms on ground floor.)
Facilities: 2 lounges, 2 bars, separate TV room, 3 restaurants, night club with
dancing every night, beauty parlour. 16,000 metres of wooded grounds with lawns,

terraces; rock and sand beaches just below the hotel, marina. Olympic-sized swimming pool; smaller pool for children; tennis courts; volleyball, petanca; children's play area. English spoken. ♿ .
Location: Bagur 4 km.
Credit card: Barclay/Visa.
Terms: B & B 1,540–2,440 pts; dinner, B & B 2,150–3,350 pts; full board 2,500–3,700 pts. Set meals: lunch/dinner 1,200 pts; full *alc* 1,600 pts. Reduced rates and special meals for children.

SANTIAGO DE COMPOSTELA, La Coruña   Map 13

Hostal de los Reyes Católicos   *Telephone:* (981) 58.22.00
Plaza de España 1   *Telex:* 86004 HRCS E

'Recommending one of the best hotels in Spain may seem presumptuous or irrelevant, but it *is* fabulous and not, for what it is, expensive. Imagine staying at a cross between Hampton Court and All Souls', furnished with the best pieces from the Victoria and Albert Museum. If that's the sort of thing you like it will make your heart dance. It was built at the end of the 15th century by Ferdinand and Isabella (the firm behind Columbus) for pilgrims to the shrine of St James, just a step away across the square.

'The hotel has four quadrangles, all different, all exquisite, so magically lit at night it would knock your eye out. There are bedrooms of varying degrees of luxury – do you have ambitions to sleep in the Cardinal's bed? Ours was simple, charming and cosy. The service is the usual first-class stuff – everywhere, immediate and unobtrusive. English is spoken. The breakfast with hot croissants, brioches, churros and tiny shiny buns is twice as much as you can manage. I liked it better than the dinner which was good but not amazing. The dining room is an enormous gracefully vaulted crypt, but you can eat much more cheaply in the elegant cafeteria. The hotel is situated in the heart of medieval Santiago. If you tire of trooping in and out of the cloisters, one hour away by car you can walk by the ocean; best do both.' *(Shelley Cranshaw)*

A recent visitor, a woman on her own, files a minority report. She found rude staff, and was given a small cold damp room on the second floor. Rooms on the third and fourth floors, she tells us, are warmer and drier, and worth asking for when booking. More reports welcome.

Open: All year.
Rooms: 147 double, 10 single, 3 suites – all with bath or shower, telephone, radio, and TV. (Some rooms on ground floor.)
Facilities: Salon, bar, dining room, cafeteria; conference facilities. Beauty parlour, shops. Chapel Royal with occasional concerts.
Location: In town centre; parking.
Credit cards: All major credit cards accepted.
Terms: Rooms 3,737–6,095 pts; full board 6,842–7,532 pts. Set meals: breakfast 345 pts; lunch/dinner from 1,725 pts.

In the case of many continental hotels, especially Spanish ones, we have adopted the local habit of quoting a price for the room whether it is occupied by one or more persons. Rates for B & B, half board, etc., are per person unless otherwise stated.

Parador Nacional Gil Blas   *Telephone:* (942) 81.80.00
Pl. Ramón Playo 11

One of the showplace villages of Northern Spain, Santillana is full of fine
seignorial mansions and a Collegiate Church dating from the 12th and
13th centuries.

'Santillana is still an enchanting village despite the fact that souvenir
shops spread like measles across its face and a mushroom growth of
bar-restaurants is appearing. There are also many little stalls that sell the
regional speciality: a glass of milk with a kind of biscuit. Surprisingly, this
co-exists with the traditional life of the village. The sight – and traces – of
cows are ubiquitous. Walking beside a terrace of houses in the village
street we came to an open door and discovered that the occupants were
not people, but cows! There are quite a number of old and interesting
buildings, one of which, at least, is important enough for the Ministry of
Culture to be in the process of restoring. The parador is a beautiful old
building; more outgoing, less introspective than those further south. It is
not air-conditioned; I do not suppose there is the same need in this part of
Spain. Again, it has all the comforts and amenities of paradors without
leaving any special impression, but it is a handy place to end up at if you
are catching the ferry out of Santander the following day, being only some
20 miles outside the city, and is also convenient for visiting the awesome
cave paintings at Altamira a mile away.' *(Jeff Driver)*

Open: All year.
Rooms: 22 double, 2 single – most with bath, all with telephone. 21 rooms in
annexe. (Many rooms on ground floor.)
Facilities: Lift, salon with TV, bar, restaurant. ৬ .
Location: Central; garage and private parking.
Credit cards: All major credit cards accepted.
Terms: B & B 1,750–3,370 pts; dinner, B & B 2,700–4,320 pts; full board
3,325–4,945 pts. Set meals: breakfast 250 pts; lunch/dinner 950 pts; full *alc* 1,500
pts. Special meals for children.

Parador Nacional Santo Domingo de la Calzada *Telephone:* (941) 34.03.00
Pl. del Santo 3

'Santo Domingo was an 11th-century anchorite who built a bridge across
the Glera river and a causeway *(calzada)* to help pilgrims on their way to
Santiago de Compostela by the Camino Francés (French road). A town
grew up at the bridge and a hostel was built for the pilgrims. The parador
has been built around the former hostel, little of which now remains
except the facade and the main hall. It's nice – but noisy. Unlike William
of Orange, no Spaniard, to my knowledge, ever received the suffix "the
Silent": "the Noble", "the Cruel", "the Wise", "the Mad', "the Shaggy"
– certainly; but never even "the Quiet" let alone "the Silent". Flamenco
dancers can get refinements of noise merely out of their hands and heels,
not to mention their voices, that no other race can even approach. Give
him a drum or a motor-bike or some other soniferous instrument from

which he can feel challenged to wring the uttermost decibel, and you've got a happy Spaniard. When the baroque had reached its most florid exuberance the good people of Santo Domingo built themselves a campanile and put it on one side of their, quite tiny, main square; another side being taken up with part of the front of the cathedral and another, today, with the side of the parador. Added to the usual waking noises of the Plaza Mayor we found matutinal campanology just a little trying. Nevertheless, a good first stop in Spain for somebody travelling south from Santander after docking in the mid afternoon, as we did. All the usual remarks re. paradors apply.' *(Jeff Driver)*

Open: All year.
Rooms: 27 – most with bath, all with telephone.
Facilities: Lift, salon, bar, restaurant.
Location: Central; no private parking.
Credit cards: American Express, Diners, Euro.
Terms: Rooms 1,909–2,714 pts. Set meals: breakfast 200 pts; lunch/dinner 800 pts.

SEGOVIA   **Map 13**

Parador Nacional   *Telephone:* (911) 41.50.90

'A modern parador, standing on a hill overlooking the town. The panoramic view of the city from the dining room is superb, and the food served there, though expensive, is very good. The whole decor of the hotel is in keeping with its modern architecture, and thoroughly comfortable: well worth stopping here before or after seeing the old city, with its beautiful golden cathedral and the romantic Alcazar.' *(SK)*

Open: All year.
Rooms: 70 double, 5 single, 5 suites – all with bath, shower and telephone; air-conditioning throughout. (Some rooms on ground floor.)
Facilities: Salon, library, TV, bar, dining room; indoor swimming pool, sauna. Garden with outdoor swimming pool. English spoken. &.
Location: 2.5 km from Segovia; garage.
Credit cards: All major credit cards accepted.
Terms: B & B 1,780–3,330 pts; full board 3,350–4,700 pts. Set meals: lunch/dinner 925 pts; full *alc* 1,700 pts. Special meals for children.

SEVILLE   **Map 13**

Hotel Doña María   *Telephone:* (954) 22.49.90
Don Remondo 19

'An ideal place to stay as a base for visiting the sights of Seville. Just 100 metres from the entrance to the cathedral, it couldn't be more conveniently situated. The bells and clocks which strike fairly regularly all around may upset some, but they are dulcet and brief enough and a small price to pay for the elegant comforts of the rooms (some better than others), many of which look out on to a sub-tropical interior courtyard. Beware mosquitoes. The entrance lobby leads directly into a low but airy lounge off which is a small, cosy bar. The breakfast room in the basement is quite out of keeping with the rest of the hotel. The lift can be disturbing if your

447

room is too close to it, and a head porter was extremely disagreeable. But to find a small roof-top swimming pool surrounded by a terrace with a ringside view of the splendid Cathedral Plaza below (where you can park your car), and the Giralda so close you can almost reach out and touch it, is a real bonus – even if it is not too scrupulously maintained. The summer months in Seville get very hot and a plunge in the pool refreshes and revives one for the next church or museum.' *(Geoffrey Sharp)*

Open: All year.
Rooms: 46 double, 15 single, 2 suites – all with bath, telephone, radio; mono TV available on request at no charge.
Facilities: Lobby-cum-bar lounge; basement breakfast room; rooftop swimming pool with fine views. Only breakfast served.
Location: Central; no garage.
Credit cards: American Express, Barclay/Visa, Diners.
Terms: Rooms 2,600–4,000 pts. Set meals: breakfast 230 pts.

SON VIDA, Palma de Mallorca   Map 13

Racquet Club Hotel

Telephone: (971) 28.00.50
Telex: 69154 ABL

There is very much the air of a country club about this hotel – with its eight tennis courts in front of the building, a large swimming pool on the other side and the golf course right next door. And there is horse-riding close by too. Moreover, although you are only 10 minutes by car from the hustle and bustle of Palma, the hotel is surrounded by hills, with lovely views, and has the feeling of being in the country. Inside, the hotel has an intimate elegance: there's wood panelling in the reception and bar, and plenty of leather chairs and sofas in the lounge area, as well as pretty brass lamps on small tables. The bedrooms, too, are comfortable and have balconies with side screens to prevent you from looking at your neighbours or vice versa. The service is good and attentive, and the food, if not specially imaginative, is well above the island's average. In short, a thoroughly agreeable hotel in a quiet and secluded setting – ideal if you play tennis or golf. But major alterations are mooted; there's talk of more rooms and suites, a covered swimming pool and a conference room. The character of the *Racquet Club* could change dramatically. More reports welcome. *(SM)*

Open: All year.
Rooms: 46 double, 5 single – all with bath and shower, radio, air-conditioning and tea-making facilities; TV and baby-sitting on request. (25 rooms on ground floor.)
Facilities: Salon, TV room, cards room, bar, terrace-bar; some conference facilities. 8 clay tennis courts, large heated swimming pool, sauna; 18-hole golf course adjoining the hotel with special rates for guests; riding school nearby; 15 km from beach. English spoken. &.
Location: Bus service to Palma 7 km.
Terms: B & B 1,525–1,975 pts; dinner, B & B 2,325–2,775 pts; full board 3,125–3,575 pts. Set meals: lunch/dinner 950 pts; full *alc* 1,150 pts. 20% discount for children; special meals available.

Don't keep your favourite hotel to yourself. The Guide supports: it doesn't spoil.

TOLEDO   Map 13

Hotel Residencia Cardenal   *Telephone:* (925) 22.49.00
Paseo de Recaredo 24

'Altogether delightful. Small, the old residence of a cardinal, it abuts the
city walls. It is spotlessly clean, with good-sized rooms overlooking a
terraced garden which extends down to one of the city gates. It is
absolutely quiet and peaceful at all times – day and night. It has no
restaurant of its own, but adjoins one of the same name which is
independently run. The food there is very expensive, and we thought poor
value for money.' *(SK)*

Open: All year.
Rooms: 24 double, 3 single – all with bath, telephone and air-conditioning.
Facilities: Reading room, TV and games room. Garden. Restaurant next door.
English spoken.
Location: Central; parking. (By the old walls at the Puerto de Bisagra.)
Credit cards: American Express, Barclay/Visa, Diners.
Terms: B & B 1,715–2,215 pts. Full *alc* in restaurant 1,000–2,000 pts. Special
meals for children.

ÚBEDA, Jaén   Map 13

Parador Nacional Condestable Davalos   *Telephone:* (953) 75.03.45
Plaza Vázquez de Molina 1

'Úbeda has many interesting, old buildings; not least in this category is the
parador itself: a large, classical, renaissance palace right on the busy main
square that has two churches – each with umpteen bells. But the parador,
though a bit noisy, is built around an interior, square courtyard and, like
many Spanish buildings, seems to look inwards into itself and presents to
the world beyond its wall just a few blind, unseeing eyes. It is, of course,
an architectural answer to the problem of coping with the heat. Úbeda
was undergoing a heatwave whilst we were there and, as this parador is
not air-conditioned, we had to make do with such remedies as the
renaissance architects could provide, which were not very effective
against weather I had previously only experienced in India. I must say a
word about the staff, who were outstandingly pleasant and helpful. The
meal was – er, interesting. I had *gazpacho*, the regional speciality of
Andalusia, and pickled quail! The rest of the dish was pickled too: French
beans and some unknown vegetable that has me baffled yet. It was
pleasant enough on a sweltering evening. I would not choose it again but
perhaps others might like it. The usual high standard of parador accommodation: much antique furniture and suits of armour, that nearly all
paradors seem to display, with something of a specialization in old chests.'
*(Jeff Driver; also Ralph Blumenau and, with reservations about the
plumbing and dour girls in the restaurant, Antony Vestrey)*

Open: All year.
Rooms: 25 – all with bath or shower and telephone.
Facilities: Library, bar, restaurant.
Location: Úbeda is 9 km E of Baeza; 26 km E of Linares; 56 km NE of Jaén.

Credit cards: American Express, Diners, Euro.
Terms: Rooms 1,909–2,714 pts. Set meals: breakfast 200 pts; lunch/dinner 870 pts.

VIELLA, Lérida 42   Map 13

Parador Nacional del Valle de Arán   *Telephone:* (973) 64.01.00

'Perched above the Valle de Arán and a mile from the small village of Viella, this parador was built primarily for the winter skiers but its open-air pool makes it an ideal summer centre for walking and the nearby National Park. It is only about a twenty-minute drive south of the French border and the excellent and inexpensive food makes it a popular place for Frenchmen over the border to come and have Saturday and Sunday lunch. The furnishings, the marble bathrooms, the huge fireplaces which in winter blaze with logs are those of a luxury hotel. The views on three sides are stunning. Central feature of the hotel is a circular wing which houses a lower ground floor lounge with bar and a first floor lounge both having panoramic views reminiscent of an airship. The cooking is regional and one is likely to be offered mountain trout, wild rabbit, baby lamb, excellent fish and an hors d'oeuvre which runs to 15 separate dishes. The *table d'hôte* lunch and dinner in July 1981 was £4 – hence the weekend pilgrimage from north of the border. The Catalán specialities, the freshness of the food and its quality were remarkable. Our bill – this for a suite of rooms with private sitting room – including full board and all our drinks for four days was £149. Viella is a ten-minute walk below the hotel and the whole of the valley is remarkably unspoilt. No doubt in winter it presents a different picture but as a summer mountain resort it takes a lot of beating. The courtesy of the staff was outstanding.' *(Derek and Janet Cooper)*

Open: All year.
Rooms: 135 – most with bath, all with telephone.
Facilities: Lift, salon, restaurant, bar. Garden, swimming pool.
Location: 2 km from Viella; parking.
Credit cards: American Express, Diners, Euro.
Terms: Rooms 2,817–3,910 pts. Set meals: breakfast 200 pts; lunch/dinner 867 pts.

VILLAJOYOSA, Alicante   Map 13

Hotel El Montiboli   *Telephone:* (965) 89.02.50
Apartado 8

The *El Montiboli* is 3 km out of Villajoyosa on the Alicante road, and 11 km from Benidorm; but it stands on a rocky promontory over the sea: a position of privacy and calm, utterly remote from the razzmatazz of the nearby Costa Blanca resorts. It was built in 1978 in the Moorish style and has won a first prize for the best tourist building in Spain. There are a lot of sporting facilities available at the hotel – tennis, windsurfing, sailing, waterskiing, for all of which the hotel offers coaching. But if you feel like some more touristy life, a minitrain stops at the hotel hourly on the way to or from Benidorm and Alicante. 'Not a place where you expect to find a hotel with such first-class food, service and decor. The bedrooms are beautiful, with those little extra touches to make them perfect. The food is excellent.' *(John Gullidge)*

Open: All year.
Rooms: 32 double, 5 single, 12 suites – all with bath, telephone, radio, tea-making facilities and baby-listening; TV on request; all doubles have terrace overlooking the sea. (Some rooms on ground floor.)
Facilities: Lifts, 2 salons, TV room. Large garden with children's play area, 2 swimming pools (1 heated, 1 seawater); sauna, massage; tennis, windsurfing, sailing, waterskiing and deep sea fishing. English spoken.
Location: 3 km S of Villajoyosa on the road between Alicante and Benidorm.
Credit cards: All major credit cards accepted.
Terms: B & B 2,150–3,150 pts; dinner, B & B 3,600–4,600 pts; full board 4,900–5,900 pts. Set meals: lunch/dinner 1,650 pts; full *alc* 1,900 pts. Special meals for children.

YESA, Navarra   **Map 13**

Hostal de San Salvador de Leyre   *Telephone:* (948) 88.40.11

'This was the find of our holiday – it was our stopover on the way back from the Pyrenees to Santander. It is on the road to Pamplona. The setting is extraordinary. Imagine a landscape framed by red-gold mountains. The valley is filled by a turquoise-coloured lake. Perched on a hillside is a four-square monastery. It is the only building in sight and its 18th-century conventual buildings are used as a *hostal*. Benedictine monks sing their offices half a dozen times a day in the lovely church, the early kings of Navarre are buried there, and the crypt is 10th-century. The *hostal* is fitted out like a parador – quite luxurious. The food is simple and homely but the cost of our stay – about £7 per head for dinner, bed and breakfast [1980] made it excellent value. We have never been anywhere like it.' *(R Cranshaw)*

Open: 1 March–20 December.
Rooms: 22 double, 9 single, 4 suites – 26 with bath, 9 with shower, 30 with telephone, all with baby-listening.
Facilities: 2 lounges (1 with TV), dining room; facilities for parties, conferences, etc. Large grounds; 4 km from lake with beaches, waterskiing, etc. English spoken.
Location: Turn N off the road from Pamplona to Jaca at Yesa.
Credit cards: Access/Euro/Mastercard, Barclay/Visa.
Terms: B & B 825–1,050 pts; dinner, B & B 1,475–1,700 pts; full board 1,600–1,700 pts. Set meals: lunch/dinner 700 pts; full *alc* 1,200–1,400 pts. Reduced rates and special meals for children.

Åkerblads, Tällberg

Sweden

Hotel Gyllene Uttern   *Telephone:* (0390) 108.00

Gränna is in the centre of Sweden, roughly equidistant between Malmö
and Stockholm, on Lake Vättern, the second largest lake in the country.
The *Gyllene Uttern* stands imposingly on the shores of the lake. It belongs
to the Esso Motor Hotel chain, but unlike others in this ubiquitous and
well-regarded Scandinavian group – worth knowing about, incidentally,
in a country like Sweden not overly provided with hotel accommodation
in many country districts – it is in no way a characterless concrete motel
even though it has all the conveniences, colour TV and the like, that you
would expect from its ownership. It is a crenellated brick structure, built
in the 1930s in a traditional style for a Swedish baron, and became a luxury
hotel only a dozen years ago. The rooms in the main building have
considerable character, and there are also 13 individually styled cottages
on the slope down to the lake. The restaurant does a lot of outside
business; the cooking is said to be superb, with locally-caught trout a
speciality. Among its special features is a bridal suite and – unique, we
believe in the Guide – its own private wedding chapel. *(C R E Gillett)*

Open: All year.
Rooms: 41 rooms and 13 cottages – 37 rooms with bath, 16 with shower, all with
telephone, radio, colour TV and baby-listening. 42 rooms in 3 annexes. (1 room
with special facilities for the disabled.)
Facilities: Residents' lounge, TV room, lobby, chapel; conference facilities.

453

Table-tennis, sauna, fitness room. Near lake with fishing rights. English spoken. &.

Location: 2 km from Lake Vättern; 3 km from town centre; parking.
Credit cards: All major credit cards accepted.
Terms (excluding service): B & B 128–211 Skr. Set meal: breakfast 18 Skr; full *alc* 150 Skr. Reduced rates and special meals for children.

GRYTHYTTAN, 710 60 Västmanland

Map 7

Grythyttans Gästgivaregården

Telephone: (0591) 143 10

'*Grythyttans* is an inn that has arisen from the dead. Originally built in 1640 in the heart of the then flourishing iron-mining district, it fell into disuse with the arrival of the railway and slowly decayed. In 1972 the local cultural association acquired it and re-opened it. Carl Jan Granqvist, the manager they installed, proved to be an inspired choice; an art-historian by profession, he has the gift of re-creating the past. He bought up the surrounding 18th-century shops and cottages, converted them into comfortable bedrooms, filled the rooms with antique furniture and art, dressed the staff in period clothes and successfully re-created the atmosphere of a hundred and fifty years ago. In the eight years that have passed since the inn was re-opened it has become well known all over Sweden.

'Gourmet is the only possible word to describe the food, the highlights being Saturday evening dinner and Sunday lunch: many of the guests are passionately interested in what they eat. Every summer a few of the regulars are allowed to work in the restaurant, and Granqvist relates the story of the distracted leader of a conducted tour who rushed in one day asking for a doctor, quick. Granqvist took him into the kitchen, pointed to four of the cooks, and asked him what sort of specialist was required. The service is efficient, excellent and friendly, with a hostess to take personal care of all arrivals. We were left with the impression that the staff took great pride in what they were doing and regarded themselves as cultural pioneers rather than as ordinary hotel employees.

'Grythyttan is off the beaten track – 29 miles from the main road from Gothenburg and Dalarna and 40 from the Gothenburg–Stockholm road, but those who take the time to visit this peaceful corner of genuine old Sweden will not regret it.' *(Michael Stevens)*

Open: All year. Restaurant closed to non-residents Sunday evening.
Rooms: 45 double, 10 single – 50 with shower, some with TV, all with telephone, radio and baby-listening.
Facilities: Salons, TV room, restaurant, sauna. Dancing Saturday night. 2 acres grounds. 150 lakes in area; bathing and fishing. English spoken.
Location: 24 miles from Nora on Route 244. In centre of village; parking.
Credit cards: American Express, Diners, Euro/Mastercard.
Terms: Rooms 190–260 Skr; dinner, B & B 265–325 Skr; full board 335–395 Skr. Set meals: breakfast 25 Skr; lunch 60 Skr; dinner 100 Skr; full *alc* 170 Skr.

Hotels were asked to estimate prices for 1982, but some hotels gave us only their 1981 prices. To avoid unpleasant shocks, always check tariff at time of booking.

MARIEFRED, Södermanland S-150 30   **Map 7**

Gripsholms Värdshus   *Telephone:* (0159) 100 40

'Mariefred is a tiny town on the shores of Lake Mälar, 4 km from the main highway E3, 424 km from Gothenburg and 66 km from Stockholm. The inn, which was first opened in 1623 and is reputed to be the oldest in Sweden, is situated by the waterside facing the historic castle of Gripsholm. It is not a large inn – only eight bedrooms – but the atmosphere is cosy and friendly. All the rooms have h and c. Ours, though not large, was comfortably furnished and had a superb view of the castle across the water. We liked the small details: for instance, a large pin-cushion with a supply of pins, needles, buttons and press-studs which in fact proved very useful as I had lost a button on my shirt. Note-paper, too, which one finds all too seldom these days, and plenty of good reading lamps. We thought at first that there was no bathroom or shower, but later discovered that there is a bathroom, but on the ground floor while all the bedrooms (and the large dining room) are on the first floor. Other amenities are a small TV room, a sauna, a playground for the children and boats for hire. We thought the B & B was reasonable in price [£10 in 1981] and good value for the money. The wine-cellar is good, the food excellent, though definitely not cheap. Food plays an important part in the life of the inn, which is well-known for its good Swedish hors d'oeuvre. Open all the year round, the restaurant is obviously planned with the summer months in view, for there are tables for meals and lighter refreshments on verandas as well as under a roof in the garden.

'We thoroughly enjoyed our stay here. Not only the hotel, but the whole town is charming; it must be one of the most unspoilt places in Sweden. Almost all the houses (and the inn) are built of wood, beautifully looked after, and there is not an ugly building to be seen (except perhaps the new school, which is well tucked away). The castle, mid 16th-century, is well worth a visit. Two further attractions that can make a visit to Mariefred memorable are the narrow-gauge railway from the main line, 4 km away, and the steam-boat from Stockholm. The former, a genuine antique, operates on a regular timetable in summer and the steamer, daily except Mondays, gives you a good lunch on board.' *(Michael and Marit Stevens)*

Open: 1 March–22 December.
Rooms: 7.
Facilities: TV room, restaurant; sauna, children's playground, boating.
Location: On the shores of Lake Malar, 4 km from the E3.
Terms: Rooms 120–190 Skr; full board 247 Skr.

STENUNGSUND, 444 00 Bohuslän   **Map 7**

Hotel Stenungsbaden   *Telephone:* (0303) 831 00
Stenungsön   *Telex:* 21292 Stenba S

'The west coast of Sweden enjoys a comparatively mild climate, thanks to the Gulf Stream, and Stenungsund, 45 km north of Gothenburg, has a particularly attractive hotel right on the waterfront, the *Stenungsbaden*. Though large, 144 rooms, the atmosphere is caring and friendly. Unaccustomed to the Swedish law that headlights must be used, even in daylight, I left them on. The receptionist put a notice on the board which we did not see. Next day the battery was flat but the porter pushed me down the slope, I let in the clutch and the car started – he refused a tip with a sympathetic smile. The hotel is sited on a hill with beautiful views across the Hakefjord. It has a sauna, squash court, swimming pool, a fleet of twenty Maxi sailing boats and a few motor boats for rent; there is a disco and more traditional dancing to live music in the restaurant. I enjoyed the exercise track; you follow red markers for about 3 km along the shore and through the forest. As meals are not only good but copious, it's a great idea. *Stenungsbaden*, in common with 245 other hotels, accept Swedish Hotel Cheques, price £12 for bed and breakfast with private bath or shower, purchaseable in advance in the UK for use between May and September.' *(Anne Bolt)*

Open: All year.
Rooms: 100 double, 44 single – 28 with bath, 116 with shower, all with telephone, radio and TV.
Facilities: Lifts, ramps for disabled, 2 restaurants, 2 bars, disco; indoor swimming pool, sauna, squash court. Sea nearby. English spoken. & .
Location: 45 km N of Gothenburg, by Route 160.
Credit cards: All major credit cards accepted.
Terms: Rooms (including breakfast) 140–400 Skr. Set meals: lunch 48–53 Skr; dinner 78–86 Skr; full *alc* 125–150 Skr. Reduced rates and special meals for children.

STOCKHOLM, S-11456   **Map 7**

Hotel Diplomat   *Telephone:* (08) 63.58.00
Strandvägen 7 C   *Telex:* 17119 Diplhot S

'That placid bourgeois comfort, untouched by the troubles of 1914 and 1939, that pervades Stockholm is reflected in the calm of the *Hotel Diplomat*. Overlooking the harbour and standing between blocks of turn-of-the-century flats, it has an air of discretion. There is no restaurant but there is a ground-floor tea-shop – which has for many years been a rather smart Stockholm rendezvous – where breakfast and light meals are served as well, of course, as afternoon tea. The bar upstairs is tucked away in a series of small, cosy sitting rooms, well-furnished with armchairs, newspapers and magazines. The bedrooms have a solid comfort that is particularly agreeable when snow whirls in from the Baltic. The *Diplomat* is within a few minutes' walk of the city centre and just across the road is a floating restaurant, noted for its fish.' *(Tom Pocock)*

Open: All year, except 23–29 December. Café closed Sunday.
Rooms: 75 double, 51 single, 6 suites – 96 with bath, 36 with shower, all with telephone, radio, colour TV and minibar.
Facilities: Lounges, TV room, bar, teashop. Sauna; fishing and winter sports nearby. English spoken.
Location: 5 minutes' walk from centre; parking.
Credit cards: All major credit cards accepted.
Terms: B & B (single) 450–600 Skr, (double) 610–700 Skr. Children under 12 free.

We asked hotels to estimate their 1982 tariffs. Not all hotels in Part Two replied, so that prices in Part Two are more approximate in some cases than those in Part One.

TANUMSHEDE 45700 Bohuslän   Map 7

Tanums Gestgifveri   *Telephone:* (0525) 290 10

'Tanumshede, 6 km from the sea, is a rather ordinary large village, with
two supermarkets, a chemist, post office, small gift shop and tourist
information office. It is however a strategic 160 km from Gothenburg and
140 km from Oslo. *Gestgifveri* means a guest house, but the standard of
service and food is much higher than that suggests. The E6 runs a couple
of gardens' lengths away so it is a little noisy, despite double glazing, but
the 28 rooms are usually full of travelwise Swedes, Norwegians and
Nederlanders, so it is wise to book ahead. The inn has been serving
wayfarers since 1663, and Swedish owner manager Mr Steiner Öster
personally supervises the kitchen. Waitresses and reception staff speak
excellent English, Mr Öster is happier in French. Doubtless it is to his
French wife that guests owe the comfort and extremely elegant decor. It is
worth finding time to visit the Bronze Age rock carvings. There are
several sites within 5 km and a charming little museum supplying a fact
sheet in English. It is open from 10 am to 7 pm and has a friendly
cafeteria.' *(Mrs Maurice Yates)*

Open: 15 May–15 October.
Rooms: 29 – 4 with bath, 25 with shower, all with telephone and radio. (15 rooms
on ground floor.)
Facilities: Lift; lobby, 2 TV rooms, bar, pool room; small sauna with dip-pool.
Fishing and sea bathing 4–6 km; golf 20 km. English spoken. &.
Location: 160 km from Gothenburg; 140 km from Oslo. In village centre; park-
ing.
Credit cards: All major credit cards accepted.
Terms: B & B 175–210 Skr. Full *alc* 180 Skr. 50% reduction for children under 12;
children under 2 free; special meals provided.

TÄLLBERG, Dalarna 793 03   Map 7

Åkerblads   *Telephone:* (0247) 500 05

In the Book of Hotel Records, *Åkerblads* (pronounced 'Awkerblads')
must have an honoured place. The Åkerblad family have been in
continuous occupation here since the early 18th century, and the present
generation running the hotel are the 14th and 15th generation. We liked
their note in sending us the hotel tariff: 'We are not so much for flattery to
the guests, but we do take care of them and want them to feel like a
member of the family. They are so welcome to stay with us.' Tällberg is
halfway between Leksand and Rättvik, two of the best-known towns
round Lake Siljan, the heart of the holiday and tourist area in Dalarna, in
the middle of Sweden. The hotel, the oldest part of which is a 17th-century
farmhouse, has been tastefully converted into a comfortable and spacious
building in the old style. It has a fine view of the lake. The bedrooms, both
in the main building and the annexe, are pleasantly furnished, hardly any
two being alike. Good beds, running h and c in all rooms and a shower,
toilet etc., in most – a few have baths. There is a sauna and a warm
brine-bath (very luxurious) all the year round, a tennis court in summer
and an ice-rink in winter. Other winter attractions are good skiing for
everyone except really advanced slalom experts, torchlight sleigh-rides

through the woods and log fires in the evening. In summer there is good bathing and fishing in the lake, boats available, and good walking country all round.

'The hotel is owned by Christina and Arne Åkerblad. Both speak quite good English, which is not true of all the staff, and Christina in particular was a mine of information on all the old local customs and traditions, which are important in this part of the country. The food was good but plain. Dr Johnson would have said of our evening meal: "This was a good dinner, enough, to be sure; but it was not a dinner to *ask* a man to." The wine cellar was limited, but if it contained no really fine wines, it contained no really poor wines either. We thought that B & B here for 130 Swedish crowns (about £13) was good value and we liked the atmosphere of the place.' *(Michael and Marit Stevens)*

Open: All year, except 20–27 December.

Rooms: 26 double, 18 single, 3 suites – 1 with bath, 25 with shower, all with baby-listening. 21 rooms in 2 annexes. (7 rooms on ground floor.)

Facilities: Lounge, 2 TV rooms, 2 dining rooms; facilities for parties and functions. Large garden with tennis court, skating rink; bicycles; sauna, warm brine-bath, hair salon; skiing, sleigh-rides in winter; bathing, fishing, boating in summer. English spoken.

Location: 12 km from Leksand; on road between Leksand and Rättvik; parking.

Credit cards: Barclay/Visa, Euro/Mastercard, Diners.

Terms: B & B 97–149 Skr; dinner, B & B 161–200 Skr; full board 184–223 Skr. Set meals: lunch 51 Skr; dinner 62 Skr. Reduced rates and special meals for children.

Hotel du Lac, Montana

Switzerland

AROSA, 7050 Grisons **Map 11**

Hôtel Belvédère-Tanneck *Telephone:* (081) 31.13.35

'A second-class hotel of no great pretensions, but full of robust Swiss *en pension*. Helpful staff and welcoming reception – they had two English girls from the Wirral serving as waitress and chambermaid for the season. We had a very pleasant room with a balcony giving a spectacular view in a sunny morning of snow-clad peaks bathed in a pink light. Comfortable beds, radio, good bedside lighting and very well-equipped bathroom – and the best-heated garage our car has ever rested in. We would strongly recommend guests not to eat *en pension* as the dinners looked very dull (rice pudding was the sweet of the day) but to eat in the basement *stuberl* where we had a splendid *fondue bourguignonne* and the place filled up later with locals.' *(Angela and David Stewart)*

Open: June–September, December–April.
Rooms: 70 beds – some rooms with bath or shower and kitchenette, all with radio, telephone and balcony.
Facilities: Lift, restaurant.
Location: Central; parking.
Terms: Rooms (including dinner, B & B) 37–102 Sfrs (single), 75–206 Sfrs (double); full board 11 Sfrs per person added.

Hotel Krafft am Rhein   *Telephone:* (061) 26.88.77
Rheingasse 12   *Telex:* 64360

A medium-priced centrally-located modern hotel looking out on the Rhine and the Old Town. 'The perfect Swiss family-run hotel. Extremely friendly staff. But make sure you are on the Rhine side, otherwise it can be noisy.' *(Godfrey Pilkington)*

Open: All year.
Rooms: 26 double, 26 single – 20 with bath, 25 with shower, all with telephone and radio.
Facilities: Lift, sitting room, TV room, restaurant, terrace, café. English spoken.
Location: Central, on the Rhine; parking.
Credit cards: Access/Euro/Mastercard, American Express, Diners.
Terms: B & B 35–65 Sfrs; dinner, B & B 59–89 Sfrs; full board 83–113 Sfrs. Set meals: lunch/dinner 20–24 Sfrs; full *alc* 50 Sfrs. Reduced rates for children: under 6, 50%; 6–12, 30%. Special meals available.

CASTAGNOLA-LUGANO, 6976 Ticino   **Map 11**

Hotel Aniro   *Telephone:* (091) 52.50.31
Via Violetta 1

Once the retreat of a Russian Royal Duke, the *Aniro* has a magnificent position, 250 feet above the lake in a quiet cul-de-sac, 10 minutes' walk to the centre of town. Most of the rooms have balconies or a terrace overlooking the lake, and the hotel has a lift from the road. 'The meals were all set menus, but were not repeated during a fortnight's visit. The food was all first-class, as was the service and accommodation – and reasonably priced.' *(J Wilkinson)*

Open: March–November.
Rooms: 50 beds – all rooms with bath or shower, radio and telephone, most with balcony or terrace.
Facilities: Lift, reception, salon, restaurant, terrace. Garden, table-tennis, mini-golf, outdoor swimming pool.
Location: 10 minutes' walk from town centre, just off Via Cortiva; parking.
Terms: Rooms (including breakfast) 38–55 Sfrs (single), 75–109 Sfrs (double); half board 15 Sfrs per person added to room rate; full board 25 Sfrs per person added to room rate.

CHÂTEAU D'OEX, 1837 Vaud   **Map 11**

Chalet du Bon Acceuil   *Telephone:* (029) 463.20
                                         Telex: 36418 Chato Ch

Château d'Oex is a wide and sunny Alpine village on the French side of the Bernese Oberland, about 3,000 feet above Montreux. It has a long tradition of catering for British visitors throughout the year – winter sports in the winter, and golf, tennis, riding, swimming and, of course, walking in the spring and summer. *Bon Acceuil*, though it is a traditional Swiss chalet, built in 1756, helps to maintain the British connection. It is a very personal affair, run almost on house-party lines, by its English owners, Curtis and Sally Wilmot-Allistone, who have had the place for almost a quarter of a century; they are assisted by largely English-speaking staff, sometimes from the homeland and sometimes from the Antipodes. Over the years, the hotel has had mixed but never bland reports: many of the warmest letters are from regulars who clearly regard the place as a home from home. It is the very cosy Britishness of the *Bon Acceuil* that has put off other visitors, but there has also been another obvious cause of complaint – the poor (at least by Swiss standards) quality of the meals. We are glad to learn that the hotel has now acquired a new Swiss chef de cuisine – 'He is really outstanding and cost us a fortune!' writes Curtis Wilmot-Allistone proudly. First reports of the new kitchen regime are somewhat mixed. We suspect that we shall still get negative as well as positive views: the *Chalet* may not be equally *acceuillant* to all comers. But we give the last word to one loyalist: 'It is hard to pin down what makes the *Chalet* special. Certainly its owners provide a large ingredient. The building itself, an old Vaudois farmhouse, is also very comforting. But above all, to anybody used to the sameness of hotels all over the world, the *Chalet* is wonderfully relaxing and reassuring.' *(Jonathan Groves)*

Open: All year.

Rooms: 14 double, 3 single, 3 suites – 10 with bath, all with colour TV; English-speaking baby-sitters available free of charge. (Many rooms on ground floor.)

Facilities: 3 salons, separate TV room, bar/dining room, cellar-bar club with twice weekly dancing; some conference facilities. Lovely garden, also 7 acres grounds with meadows, woods, river and sun terrace; children's play park. Winter sports; also all manner of spring/summer activities: tennis, riding, fishing, golf, hang-gliding, walking. Convalescents welcome: resident nurse. English spoken. &.

Location: 1 km from town centre; parking. For Château d'Oex turn off the N12 towards Bulle.

Credit cards: All major credit cards accepted.

Terms: B & B 32–58 Sfrs; dinner, B & B 50–76 Sfrs; full board 61–87 Sfrs. Set meals: lunch 6–15 Sfrs; dinner 20–25 Sfrs; full *alc* 25–38 Sfrs. Special terms for extended stays. The *Chalet* offers part payment in the UK at an exchange rate of 5 Sfrs to the £. Reduced rates and special meals for children.

FLIMS, 7018 Flims-Waldhaus   **Map 11**

Hotel Adula   *Telephone:* (081) 39.01.61
                                      Telex: 74160 adula ch

'Flims is a favourite medium-height (1,100 m) summer and winter resort in the Grisons, within about 20 minutes' drive from Chur. Beautiful woods surround the favourite Waldhaus part, presenting many miles of easy walks for Senior Citizens (who are specially well looked after), and the more energetic find ample opportunity for varied mountain walks facilitated by an excellent network of chairlifts and cable cars, and an abundance of attractive mountain restaurants and refreshment huts. The *Adula* is quietly situated in the Waldhaus part, with many of the most attractive walks starting a short distance only from the hotel. It can be highly recommended in every respect. Although not all rooms are equally comfortable or attractive, the service is invariably perfect in attention and friendliness, and the food can only be described as superb in quality of preparation and variety. Breakfast is supported by an excellent buffet selection of *Aufschnitt*, cheeses, jams, honey and different types of bread and rolls. Instead of lunch (3 courses), vouchers are obtainable which are accepted in mountain restaurants, and dinner (4 courses, with a choice of main courses) is at least once a week of a Gala quality. The large indoor swimming pool can easily be reached from every room; it opens out (fine weather permitting) to a fine garden with occasional barbecue entertainment. There are extensive, comfortable and quiet public rooms with a separate bar, and an attractive speciality grill-restaurant and bar, the *Barga*, where a discreet pianist tinkles musical favourites, mainly of the Twenties and Thirties.' *(Arnold Horwell)*

Open: 18 December–18 October.
Rooms: 52 double, 31 single – 41 with bath, 30 with shower, all with telephone and radio. 22 rooms in annexe.
Facilities: 2 lifts, salon, TV room, bar with pianist, 2 dining rooms, dinner-dances, games room; indoor swimming pool. Garden with terrace and 3 tennis courts. English spoken.
Location: In the Waldhaus part of Flims; parking.
Credit cards: All major credit cards accepted.
Terms: (Annexe rooms are cheapest): B & B 40–95 Sfrs; dinner, B & B 65–120 Sfrs. Set meals: lunch 23–27 Sfrs; dinner 25–45 Sfrs. Reduced rates for children sharing parents' room; special meals on request.

GENEVA, 1204 **Map 11**

Hôtel L'Arbalète *Telephone:* (022) 28.41.55
3 rue de la Tour Maitresse *Telex:* 427293

A small de-luxe hotel, well-located near the lake and the best shops, recommended for the quality of its furnishings, its excellent reasonably priced restaurant and pleasant staff. One reader this year, endorsing the entry, particularly appreciated the restaurant's courtesy in cooking a Zurichoise speciality, a favourite of her husband's which was not on their menu. The only snag about the *Arbalète*, at least on a Saturday night, is the proximity to the Piccadilly Nightclub next door. Some readers may prefer the *Hôtel Les Armures* (see opposite) under the same ownership. *(Jill and John Dick)*

Open: All year.
Rooms: 32 double, 6 suites – all with bath, telephone, radio and colour TV.
Facilities: Lift, hall, bar, restaurant. English spoken.
Location: Central, but there are quiet rooms; parking.
Credit cards: American Express, Barclay/Visa, Diners, Eurocard.
Terms: B & B 90–160 Sfrs. Full *alc* 30 Sfrs.

Deadlines: nominations for the 1983 edition should reach us not later than 31 July 1982. Latest date for comments on existing entries: 31 August 1982.

GENEVA, CH 1204   **Map 11**

Hôtel Les Armures   *Telephone:* (022) 28.91.72
Rue du Puit St-Pierre   *Telex:* 421129
1 Vieille Ville

'In a city noted for grand, bland hotels with a view of the lake and tax exiles' villas on its placid shores, it is a relief to find somewhere as cosy and comfortable as the *Hôtel Les Armures*. Although it only opened at the end of 1980, it seems to have been settled in its quiet little square near the cathedral, high up in the Old Town, for several centuries. This is because it has been established in an old stone building and its restaurant, on to which it backs, is said to be the oldest in Geneva. It has only 28 rooms, but these are as comfortable as any visiting merchant banker could hope for and the staff is efficient and friendly. Standing in the maze of narrow streets of tall old houses, it is so quiet that the loudest sound on opening the window may well be the splash of the fountain sprouting over its *jardinières* of hydrangeas in the square below. There is a breakfast room off the lobby and the restaurant can be reached either through a connecting passage on the second floor or by a walk round the corner to its street entrance. It is a welcoming, jolly place to eat a solid Swiss meal or just a simple but sustaining *fondue*, or *raclette* (melted cheese with boiled potatoes, raw onions and gherkins) at the sort of modest price – around £2 – that one has not often associated with Switzerland.' *(Tom Pocock)*

Open: All year.
Rooms: 24 double, 4 single – all with bath, telephone, radio and colour TV.
Facilities: Lobby, salon, breakfast room, restaurant, *Stueberl* (rustic bar/restaurant). English spoken.
Location: Central, near St-Pierre cathedral; no special parking facilities.
Credit cards: All major credit cards accepted.
Terms: B & B 105–160 Sfrs. Full *alc* 35 Sfrs.

GUNTEN-THUNERSEE, 3654 Bern   **Map 11**

Hirschen am See   *Telephone:* (033) 51.22.44

'Gunten is a village on the north shore of Lake Thun, and although we had a car we had no need to use it due to the excellent boat and trolleybus services. The hotel is well-managed and comfortable with south-facing aspect. It has a lakeside garden and terrace; the lake steamers call at the adjacent landing-stage, but the rear rooms overlooking the lake are quiet. The managers, who speak good English, were most attentive, the food was excellently prepared and served, and the wine list was extensive. The lounge was light and well-furnished in an old-fashioned style. The bedrooms, although a trifle small, were comfortable and those we occupied had balconies where we enjoyed breakfast overlooking the lake and the Bernese Alps. There are numerous excursions to be made to the surrounding area and walks galore. No night-life when we were there. Warmly recommended.' *(John H Bell)*

Open: April–October.
Rooms: 110 beds – all rooms with bath or shower and telephone.

Facilities: Lift, lounge, 2 restaurants (one on terrace). Garden. Beach and sailing nearby. English spoken.
Location: On the N shore of Lake Thun.
Terms: Half board 70–107 Sfrs (single), 122–214 Sfrs (double); full board 10 Sfrs per person added. Reduced rates for children.

KANDERSTEG, 3718 Berner Oberland   Map 11

Hotel Blümlisalp   *Telephone:* (033) 75.12.44

The holiday resort of Kandersteg, 1,200 metres up in the Bernese Oberland, at the foot of the Blümlisalp range, has plenty to offer its visitors whatever the season. And for those who want to be hoisted higher, whether skiers or walkers, there is a wide range of chairlifts and cabin lifts. The *Blümlisalp* is a middle-sized, middle-priced middle-class family hotel, in a fine scenic position and particularly well-equipped with sporting adjuncts: an indoor swimming pool with what the hotel calls underwater massage and against-current swimming, an American Bowling alley (sound-proofed) as well as a games room with table tennis. In the summer, the hotel organises picnic parties, walking tours and botanic trips to Stresa in Italy; in the winter there are sledge-drives and skitours at night with *Glühwein*. 'All round excellence.' *(J C Nicholson Belwell)*

Open: 1 December–31 October.
Rooms: 20 double, 3 single – 8 with bath, 8 with shower, 6 with radio.
Facilities: Lift, TV room, lounge, bar, 2 restaurants. Bowling alley, heated indoor swimming pool, games room. Walking, winter sports. English spoken.
Location: 5 minutes from centre, in main street of village; parking.
Credit cards: Access/Euro/Mastercard, Barclay/Visa.
Terms: B & B 40–55 Sfrs; dinner, B & B 48–80 Sfrs; full board 60–92 Sfrs. Set meals: lunch 19 Sfrs, dinner 24 Sfrs; full *alc* 26 Sfrs. Reduced weekly rates in low season. Reduced rates for children sharing parents' room: under 6, 50%; under 12, 30%; special meals available.

KLOSTERS, 7250   Map 11

Hotel Bündnerhof   *Telephone:* (083) 414.50

'Old-fashioned family hotel. Mother/daughter/son-in-law. Extremely friendly and run with typical Swiss efficiency. Bedrooms (a *few* with private loo and shower) are well-equipped and beds lovely. Sitting area restricted – stuffy little room but there is a pub bit where the locals come to eat and drink and where Frau Anderhub holds court. Son-in-law is an excellent chef – there is no choice but the food is plentiful and well-served. Daughter supervises with eagle eye – second helpings are offered and she soon gets to know individual dislikes. It's not at all grand, but they speak English and love having English visitors. A member of our party had to be left behind in hospital where he was visited by the family and given every assistance to help him get down to the valley trail on his crutches. A warm, personal welcoming place.' *(E Newall)*

Our 1981 report (above) was endorsed by a July 1981 visitor: 'The 1981 entry is exactly right! Half *pension* at 100 frs per day was marvellous value. I hope they get more British guests as a result of the Guide. True – "not at all grand", but table linen, and so many other things, quite faultless.' *(B W Ribbons)*

Open: All year, except May.
Rooms: 13 double, 13 single – 8 of the doubles with shower and WC.
Facilities: Lift, lounge, bar, dining room, restaurant. Garden; bowling and table tennis. Close to heated summer swimming pool, mountain cable railway, ski-lift station and skating rink. English spoken. &.
Location: In town centre; private parking.
Terms: Dinner, B & B 40–75 Sfrs; full board 48–83 Sfrs. Bargain rates for mid-week, weekend or out-of-season stays.

LUCERNE, 6000   Map 11

Hotel Royal   *Telephone:* (041) 51.12.33
Rigistrasse 22

'Those with childhood memories of huge, hushed Swiss hotels, commanding vistas of mountains reflected in still lakes, are often disappointed on return. Often, they have been converted into flats, or are seedy shadows of their former selves, kept going by casinos and night clubs. For such seekers after a reassuring echo, the *Hotel Royal* is rewarding. It stands on the outskirts of the charming old town of Lucerne, overlooking what must be the most ridiculously beautiful view of lake and mountains in Switzerland. It is high above the waterside promenade so that a short but steep uphill walk is necessary to reach it. The view makes that worthwhile. The *Royal* was the last of the grand hotels of the great days of Swiss tourism to be built hereabouts – in 1910 – and, with about 80 beds, it is one of the smallest. It still has solid Edwardian calm and comfort but the cheerful ministrations of the Hofer family, who own and run it, save it from becoming museum-like. Once, Herr Hofer says, the guests were almost all English and they still make up a high proportion of his guests, although mostly in package-holiday groups and mostly over-50. The *Royal* is a quiet and unostentatious hotel for a rest, with the Hofers always ready to arrange an excursion on the lake or to the summits of Pilatus or the Rigi when activity is required.' *(Tom Pocock)*

Open: April–October.
Rooms: 80 beds – some rooms with bath or shower, all with telephone.
Facilities: Lift, bar, 2 restaurants (1 on terrace).
Location: On the outskirts of Lucerne; parking.
Terms: Rooms 35–105 Sfrs (including breakfast); half board 14 Sfrs per person added to room rates; full board 21 Sfrs per person added to room rates.

MONTANA, 3692 Valais   Map 11

Hotel du Lac   *Telephone:* (027) 41.34.14

'This hotel, which I first noticed 16 years ago, has a superb position on a shelf 4,000 feet above the north side of the Rhône valley overlooking the Valaisian Alps. It is owned and run by the Fischer family; the son now provides sophisticated comfort, informality, good food and wine at reasonable cost and a ready welcome to English guests with his total fluency in our language. There is a bar and most rooms have balconies facing south where breakfast is served on request without additional cost. Nothing seems to be too much trouble for the staff or management. Although development has made Montana less attractive it has not

465

affected the hotel, protected by a lake on its north side and only five minutes' walk from the main ski lifts. Apart from its skiing potential the hotel offers an attractive base for a summer walking holiday with lifts rising to over 10,000 feet and tennis, windsurfing and swimming readily available.' *(G C Brown)*

Open: June–October, December–May.
Rooms: 50 beds – some rooms with bath and shower, most with balcony, all with telephone, radio and TV on request.
Facilities: Bar, restaurant. Garden. Tennis, mini-golf, windsurfing; winter sports nearby. English spoken.
Location: N of Route E2 between Sion and Sierre.
Terms: Rooms (including breakfast) 23–60 Sfrs (single), 40–125 Sfrs (double); half board 19 Sfrs per person added to room rates; full board 29 Sfrs per person added to room rates.

MURTEN, 3280 Map 11

Hotel Weisses Kreuz *Telephone:* (037) 71.26.41

'Murten is a well-preserved medieval town, still with fortified towers and walls dating from the 15th century, which makes an attractive staging-post between Basel and Zürich and the French cantons. The rooms of the *Weisses Kreuz* are comfortable, with beautiful views over lake Murten and the Jura hills. It has a very good restaurant, with a splendid lakeside terrace, specialising in freshwater fish, including crayfish, Egli, Felchen and pike – about 20 ways of preparing them. The local white wine (Vully) is quite excellent. (Swiss wines are generally much underrated.)' *(Arnold Horwell)*

'Indeed excellent, not least in its service and caring for guests: the hot water supply to basin and shower in our room would not work, and my wife, insisting on her right to a hot shower at any time with the proverbial fierceness of a tigress, telephoned the reception on a Sunday evening at 10 pm. A few minutes later, she was collected by an apologetic lady receptionist and conducted through caverns measureless to man to a spacious bathroom. Next morning the hot water supply was in order and spontaneously a reduction of 10 frs was made on our bill.' *(P G Bourne)*

Open: All year, except 15 December–31 January.
Rooms: 25 double, 1 single, 3 triple – 11 with bath, 5 with shower, 19 with telephone. 20 rooms in annexe.
Facilities: Lift, salons, terrace restaurant overlooking the lake; banqueting and conference facilities.
Location: 50 metres from town centre; parking.
Terms: B & B 25–55 Sfrs; dinner, B & B 45–75 Sfrs; full board 60–90 Sfrs. Set meal: lunch 15 Sfrs; full *alc* 35 Sfrs.

Do you know of a good hotel or country inn in the United States or Canada? Nominations please to our sibling publication, *America's Wonderful Little Hotels and Inns*, 345 East 93rd Street, 25C, New York, NY 10028.

NYON, 1260 Vaud Map 11

Hôtel du Clos de Sadex *Telephone:* (022) 61.28.31

A superb patrician house on lac Léman (23 km from Geneva), formerly the home of Major and Madame Louis de Tscharner, who now run it as a hotel of great character and charm. The atmosphere of the aristocratic family whose seat it was (and is) is carefully preserved in the furnishing of the public rooms and the restaurant. Beautiful lakeside garden, with breakfast and lunch willingly served on the terrace overlooking the lake and French shoreline and mountains opposite. There is a modern annexe which blends in well. The bedrooms are large and have all the highest standards of comfort. 'A fantastic hotel in a magnificent position. The food is really first-class, and the staff and management are friendly and courteous. We fully endorse the remark quoted in your last report: "We wished we could take the hotel with us wherever we went." ' *(Hugh and Elsie Pryor; also Arnold Horwell)*

Open: 1 March–31 December.
Rooms: 18 – 12 with bath, 2 with shower, all with telephone. Some rooms in annexe. (3 rooms on ground floor.)
Facilities: Hall, salon with TV, restaurant; conference room. Gardens with terrace for meals, leading directly to the lake (the hotel has a small harbour); swimming, boating, waterskiing.
Location: 2 km from town centre; 23 km from Geneva.
Credit cards: American Express, Diners, Echo.
Terms: Rooms (including breakfast) 44–115 Sfrs (single), 79–168 Sfrs (double); half board 26 Sfrs per person added to room rates; full board 52 Sfrs added to room rates.

ST LUC, 3961 Valais Map 11

Hôtel Beausite *Telephone:* (027) 65.15.86

'The *Hôtel Beausite* stands high up in the mountain village of St Luc overlooking the highest mountains of Val d'Anniviers which includes the Matterhorn. Rarely have we seen a view comparable to this one. The hotel is ten years old and offers modern comfortable rooms; most have their own bathrooms *en suite*, also a balcony. It is a family-run hotel with a very friendly atmosphere, and good home cooking. It is situated in an excellent walking area, which is also a well-equipped skiing centre. One *very* important point is that the hotel has a good parking area, and also a large underground heated garage with electrically operated doors, something which is rarely (if ever) found, also a lift to all floors direct from the underground car park.' *(Hugh and Elsie Pryor)*

Open: All year.
Rooms: 23 double, 2 single, 2 studios – 16 with bath, 3 with shower, most with telephone and balcony; cooking facilities in studios.
Facilities: Lift, lounge, 2 bars, 2 dining rooms, disco in season, terrace; facilities for functions; tennis, winter sports.
Location: Half way between Lausanne and Milan; turn right at Sierre; underground car park.
Restriction: No children under 2.

Credit card: Euro.
Terms: B & B 30–40 Sfrs; dinner, B & B 40–50 Sfrs; full board 45–55 Sfrs. Set meals: lunch 12.50 Sfrs; dinner 15 Sfrs; full *alc* 24 Sfrs. Reduced rates for children sharing parents' room.

ST LUC, 3961 Valais   Map 11

Hôtel Bella Tola   *Telephone:* (027) 65.14.44

'St Luc is a typical Swiss mountain village facing south towards the Matterhorn, high up on the slopes of a sunny valley, two valleys west of Zermatt. To those whose French is more fluent than their German, one of its attractions is that it is (coming west) the first of the French-speaking valleys. The views are superb, and even the Swiss themselves admit that the wild flowers in early summer are better than almost anywhere else in Switzerland. The Bella Tola's cooking is supervised by the proprietor and his wife; the proprietor himself serves the wines, and helps those of his guests who do not know Swiss wines, with his advice (and he doesn't necessarily recommend the most expensive!). Unlike many continental hotels, there is an admirable lounge with (in the evenings) an open fire and also a very snug and cosy bar. At lunchtime, snacks and light dishes are served in this bar, or, in fine weather, in the garden. One of the pleasant things about the *Bella Tola* is that its guests include a representative selection from all over western Europe, so that it is never monopolized by any one nationality.' *(E M Sanders; also Judith and David Jenkins)*

Open: 1 June–30 September, 20 December–20 April.
Rooms: 42 – all with bath or shower.
Facilities: Lift, 3 salons (1 with TV), restaurant, bar. Garden.
Location: 22 km from Sierre; parking 100 yards.
Credit cards: American Express, Euro.
Terms: B & B 25–50 Sfrs; dinner, B & B 50–70 Sfrs. Set meals: lunch/dinner 20 Sfrs; full *alc* 29 Sfrs. Reduced rates and special meals for children.

TEGNA, 6652 Ticino Svizzera   Map 11

Casa Barbate   *Telephone:* (093) 81.14.30

'Tegna is a small unspoiled village in the Centovali area of the Ticino, near Locarno at the north east end of Lake Maggiore. It is an excellent centre for walking in lake, valley and mountain scenery, and with a car the scope extends to remote Alpine villages and the Italian border. The hotel, which is just off the main street of the village, is a modern one-storey building of character set in a pretty garden. It is light and spacious, and everything in it carries the stamp of the owner, Madame Jenny, who is herself Irish. The decor is restful and imaginative. The lounge has books, record-player, pictures, flowers, and the atmosphere of a private house. All the bedrooms have bathrooms and are furnished as bed-sitting rooms. Most open on to their own section of the garden, so one sunbathes in peace and seclusion. The small railway from Locarno to Domodossola passes the north side of the house, but I slept on that side and hardly heard the trains. Because there are no steps, the hotel can take guests in wheelchairs. The cooking is consistently excellent, and the service efficient and friendly.

People come back year after year. Madame Jenny likes to introduce newcomers to other guests, and often joins everyone in the lounge in the evening when the talk is general. One would miss a lot by opting out of this informal, friendly atmosphere. She is interested in helping each guest to have the holiday he or she wants – lending local maps to walkers, telling one where to look for gentians, recommending a concert in Locarno, advising on local wines. She enjoys the company of artists, writers and musicians, and the hotel attracts people with similar interests. Altogether, most unusual and delightful.' *(Miss H M Dillon)*

Thus the original report on *Casa Barbate*, written in 1977, and – uniquely – appearing in every edition since. We have only had one unfavourable report on the hotel – a reader who found the dinners disappointing, and would have liked mosquito nets on the bedroom windows. From this year's crop of endorsements, we single out one which crosses a few t's: 'One of the very nicest hotels I have ever stayed in, and Madame Jenny really is a quite exceptional proprietor. We entirely agree with the sentence about her cooking, which is imaginative without being showy: good plain cooking, but with subtle sauces and spices. Your plate is not piled high with the first helping, but a second helping is always offered for those who wish to eat as massively as some hotels assume everybody does. Also a most interesting selection of cheeses. Another point that deserves special mention (not only to praise her hotel but, by implication, to reproach all those hotels, some very high-class, who economize on lighting in the bedrooms – a couple of 40 watt bulbs is not unusual, we have found) is that *Casa Barbate* is very generously provided with various kinds of lighting in the bedrooms, as would be your own home.' *(Ralph Blumenau; also Daphne Pagnamenta, M Cookson, Charles Baker)*

Open: Mid March–31 October.
Rooms: 12 double, 3 single – 3 with shower, some with cooking facilities, all with telephone.
Facilities: Lounge, bar/restaurant, some private dining rooms; banqueting and conference facilities. Sun terrace overlooking the lake for meals. Garden with heated pool. Bathing, boating 200 m. English spoken. ቴ .
Credit card: Euro.
Terms: B & B 44–70 Sfrs; dinner, B & B 66–92 Sfrs. Set meal: dinner 22 Sfrs. Reduced rates for children.

THUN, 3600 Bernese Oberland   **Map 11**

Hotel Beau-Rivage   *Telephone:* (033) 22.22.36

'The small town of Thun is the gateway to the Bernese Oberland, at the western end of Lake Thun. It is far less crowded than Interlaken, at the other end of the lake, less touristy, more genuinely Swiss, and also offers a better view of the High Alps. What lifts the *Beau-Rivage* above all others in Thun is its marvellous position. It is an imposing old building which overlooks the river Aare as it leaves the lake. There is no road for cars on either side of the Aare, so the rooms facing south (the majority – but it is worth specifying the south side when booking: rooms facing the north are noisy and without an outlook) have a spectacular view across the river and the Alps beyond. Being large and roomy, the hotel offers that solid comfort so often absent in new hotels. The bedrooms are airy. Furnishings are not luxurious, but adequate. Downstairs, there is a large lounge with easy chairs, more English than Swiss, which leads out on to a garden terrace with tables and chairs facing the river and mountains. The hotel is run as a *garni*, i.e. no main meals provided, but there is an adjoining café serving snacks, and there are plenty of good restaurants in the town, a few minutes' walk away. And it is always a joy to come back, from the noise and bustle of town life, over the old wooden bridge with its weir to the peaceful situation of the *Beau-Rivage*, where all you hear is the water rushing across the weir. Prices are very reasonable for what is offered. The proprietors, Mr and Mrs J Wuthrich, both speak excellent English.' *(Richard Pinner; also Ralph Blumenau)*

Open: 1 May–31 October.
Rooms: 20 double, 10 single, 2 suites – 22 with bath, 2 with radio, all with telephone.
Facilities: Lift, salon, TV lounge, writing room, breakfast room, dining room, bar; games and fitness rooms; indoor swimming pool. Garden with coffee shop and sun terrace; situated on the river, with quay. English spoken. &.
Location: On the road from Thun to Interlaken via Gunten, between the town and the casino. 300 m from town centre; garage (7 Sfrs per night), free public car park for 150 cars nearby.
Credit cards: Access/Euro/Mastercard, American Express, Barclay/Visa.
Terms: B & B 27.50–65 Sfrs. Daily dish at the *Café Maxim* in the hotel: 7.50 Sfrs; full *alc* 20 Sfrs. Reduced rates for children.

VADUZ, Liechtenstein   Map 11

Hotel Real   *Telephone:* (075) 2.22.22
                                                  Telex: 77809

'The *Hotel Real* is one of several on the main street of Vaduz, and we chose it because it looked clean and prosperous, with an attractive restaurant on the first floor. Inside, we found excellent use of natural materials: creamy marble and natural carved dark elm, attractive lighting, good carpets. The entrance foyer and bar are tiled in an interesting rich red glazed tile, ideal for travellers coming in straight off the snow. The room we had was well-designed, with an enormous window opening on to a narrow balcony. The linen in both bedroom and restaurant had that particular polished crispness that bespeaks a first-class laundry. There was a large and well-fitted bathroom. But the food was the most surprising of all: we had enjoyed the food at a two-rosette Michelin restaurant the evening before, but here, unheralded and unsung, we found its equal. Not quite so much panache of presentation, but perfectly cooked fish, beautiful sauces, and the most delicious mousse of passion-fruit sweet. Not surprisingly, the restaurant was the scene of local celebratory meals, and the chef emerged to carve their *boeuf-en-croûte* himself. Not really a tourist centre, but well worth a detour on the way north or south.' *(David and Angela Stewart)*

Open: All year.
Rooms: 15 beds – some rooms with bath or shower, all with radio and telephone, some with balcony.
Facilities: Lift, bar, restaurant.
Location: Central.
Credit cards: All major credit cards accepted.
Terms: Rooms (including breakfast) 60–135 Sfrs.

ZERMATT, 3920 Valais   **Map 11**

Hotel Garni Metropol   *Telephone:* (028) 67.32.31

Hotels can inspire strong loyalties. A case in point is the smallish, unpretentious *Metropol*, run by the Taugwalder family on the banks of the fast-flowing Vispa, with its south-facing rooms offering the famous Matterhorn view. A particular attraction of the hotel is its own private garden. Officially, it is a breakfast-only place, though a wide range of snacks is available. Here is the latest despatch from one of its most devoted regulars:

'My favourite hotel. More and more hotels and holiday apartment blocks are being built in Zermatt, but the meadow in front of the *Metropol* has not been touched. It is the only central hotel with some space in front and at the side, and no other hotel has the same free view of the Matterhorn. There have been a number of improvements this year. The furniture in the lounge has been completely renewed, and new, more comfortable, armchairs have been put into the bedrooms. Breakfast has been changed to an enticing buffet. The menu available in the evenings has been enlarged. Most of the dishes are snacks (soups, omelettes, salads) but the portions are so generous that most of them would do as main courses, and if you order a few hours in advance, you can get real steaks, escalopes, etc. Several sweets are also available. Mr and Mrs Taugwalder lead an enthusiastic and most friendly and cheerful team of employees and they really lead, working hard themselves and prepared to do any job. I am not easily satisfied when it comes to hotels, but at the *Metropol* in Zermatt I cannot think of any improvement that could be made; perfection is something that does not exist where human beings are concerned, but this hotel is very close to it.' *(Richard Pinner; also S I R Cross, RE and W A C Wessely)*

Open: 20 November–10 May, 10 June–15 October; no evening snack on Mondays.
Rooms: 20 double, 4 single – 16 with bath, 4 with shower, all with telephone, radio and colour TV.
Facilities: Salon, bar, dining room, TV room. Small garden with river alongside. English spoken.
Credit cards: All major credit cards accepted.
Terms: B & B 32–68 Sfrs. Reduced rates for children.

ZERMATT, 3920 Valais   **Map 11**

Seiler Hotel Monte Rosa   *Telephone:* (028) 67.19.22
                                            Telex: 38.328 moros ch

'One hundred and forty years ago the village doctor of Zermatt opened his chalet as a tiny hotel; it had three bedrooms and accommodated about a dozen travellers a year. The visitors' book contained, among others, the name of John Ruskin who returned year after year. In 1855 Alexander Seiler of Brig, the founder of the great Seiler dynasty of hotelkeepers, took over the inn and christened it the *Monte Rosa Hotel*. Seiler was the hotelier *par excellence*: to him, no one was merely a room number; each visitor was the personal guest of himself and his staff. And that is exactly how it is today although the hotel has expanded to much larger dimensions. The *Monte Rosa* is still under the care of the Seiler family, the staff seldom changes, and they take an immense pride in their hotel. The concierge is at the station, with a smile and a handshake, to transport the luggage. The head waiter and his colleagues regard guests as friends to be cherished, if not spoilt. Every fad and dietetic whim is attended to, and remembered from year to year. The *Monte Rosa* has been repeatedly modernized without in any way destroying its past glories. There is telephone, radio and a mini-bar in each room and the old drawing room of former days is now the television room. The Whymper salon is a nostalgic reminder of the heroes of the past: the walls are covered with photos of famous mountaineers from 1855 down to the present day. One of the hotel's most pleasant features is a spacious lounge, reconstructed from the old billiards room. Here one can have tea, play bridge, entertain one's friends and enjoy the comfort of an open log fire in the winter season, and even in the summer should it turn very cold. Special events have always been a feature here: a gala dinner by candle-light in the winter and *raclette* luncheon picnics on the Riffelalp plateau 2,000 feet above the village in the summer are regular events for all guests. *Plus ça change* . . . especially in our present-day society, but the little old inn opened so long ago is still yesterday, today and forever the *Monte Rosa*.' *(Cecily Williams)*

Open: 30 June–mid October, December–May.
Rooms: 38 double, 25 single – 51 with bath, 4 with shower, all with telephone and radio.
Facilities: Lift, salon, reading room, TV room/library, restaurant. Small garden. Guests have free use of heated swimming pool at *Mont Cervin Hotel* 120 m away. English spoken.
Credit cards: All major credit cards accepted.
Terms: Dinner, B & B 68–130 Sfrs; full board 83–145 Sfrs. Set meals: lunch 24–28 Sfrs; dinner 28–32 Sfrs. Reduced rates for children; special meals on request.

ZÜRICH, 8023   **Map 11**

Hotel Eden au Lac   *Telephone:* (01) 479404
Utoquai 45   *Telex:* 52440

Not the largest, but certainly one of Zürich's grander hotels recalling old-style opulence of the heyday of Swiss tourism: the ornate Edwardian exterior, with statues and caryatids, flower-filled urns and balconies looking across the lake, can't have changed much this century, though the lakeside promenade on which it stands has become a dual carriageway and a major thoroughfare. However, all the rooms are now double-glazed and fully air-conditioned and the hotel has been making another concession to modernity recently in the shape of direct-dial telephones. 'Possesses the discreet charm of the aristocracy' was a *mot* we quoted in a previous entry. A recent guest warmly endorses the recommendation: 'A mixture of Swiss efficiency, superb courteous service with modern conveniences. Not cheap but excellent value. To indicate the service, no taxis were available when I wanted to leave, so the hall porter, without being asked, decided to take me to the station in the hotel's limousine. Just the right size of hotel, in my view, for Zürich.' *(Brian Whittaker)*

Open: All year.
Rooms: 30 double and suites, 21 single – 42 with bath, 9 with shower, all with telephone, radio, colour TV and baby-listening on request.

Facilities: Lift, reception rooms, bar, 2 French restaurants; conference facilities; sauna. 7–10 minutes' walk from town centre; overlooks Zürich lake; good walking, safe bathing. English spoken. &.
Location: Central (just E of Bellevue Platz); parking.
Credit cards: All major credit cards accepted.
Terms: B & B single room 110–160 Sfrs, double room 210–250 Sfrs. Set meals: approx. 40 Sfrs.

ZÜRICH, 8008   **Map 11**

Hotel Europe   *Telephone:* (01) 47.10.30
Dufourstrasse 4   *Telex:* 54186 europ ch

A medium-sized but emphatically de-luxe hotel, just behind the Opera House, with a guest book filled with the names of famous opera singers and musicians. It was opened 35 years ago by Herr Blank, who had himself been a musician when he was younger, and, though he is now over 70, he still keeps his eye on things. The general manager, Ernst Schoch, has also been with the hotel from the earliest days. It has all the trimmings you would expect from a hotel of this sort, plus, in many of the rooms (and all the suites) a few extra luxuries, such as electric bed controls, room safes, rheostat lighting, silent valets and humidifiers. But it is also the sort of hotel where you can expect to be welcomed by a bowl of fresh fruit in your room.

Open: All year.
Rooms: 24 double, 15 single, 3 suites – 28 with bath, 14 with shower, all with telephone, radio, air-conditioning, refrigerated mini-bars and TV on request.
Facilities: Lift, lounge, breakfast room. English spoken. &.
Location: Close to Opera House, lake and a short walk to the central shopping area. Ample parking, or garage space close by.
Credit cards: All major credit cards accepted.
Terms: B & B 80–110 Sfrs (single), 140–170 Sfrs (twin/double); suites 190–290 Sfrs for 2. Reduced rates for children sharing parents' room.

ZÜRICH, 8001   **Map 11**

Hotel Florhof   *Telephone:* (01) 47.44.70
Florhofgasse 4

'The *Florhof* is a charming anachronism: a 16th-century patrician house set in a small garden on a quiet, residential street which is also a well-ordered hotel with every mod-con. It is a few minutes from the centre of the city by tram or taxi. Without exaggeration, it's an oasis of calm in the midst of the city's bustle. The rooms are bright and airy, the decor pleasant, the arrangements efficient, and the cleanliness beyond reproach. The Schilter family who own and operate it, are cordial and as helpful as can be. Room service is prompt; the breakfast croissants are flaky. Meals in the restaurant are good, if not *cordon bleu*. There's a terrace in the garden where lunch, tea and drinks are served in fine weather. Nearby is the Kunsthaus, and the beautiful old quarter of the town; tree-lined streets, mansions, art galleries, antique shops and such like, to be strolled through and explored.' *(Helen Barnes)*

473

Open: All year.
Rooms: 23 double, 10 single – 22 with bath, 11 with shower, all with telephone and radio; TV on request.
Facilities: Lift, small salon, restaurant. Garden with terrace for lunch and light refreshments in fine weather. English spoken.
Location: In town centre; parking.
Credit cards: All major credit cards accepted.
Terms: B & B 50–90 Sfrs. Set meals: lunch 10–20 Sfrs; dinner 15–25 Sfrs; full *alc* 40 Sfrs.

ZÜRICH, 8001   Map 11

Hotel zum Storchen   *Telephone:* (01) 211.55.10
Weinplatz 2   *Telex:* 813 354

'A really civilized hotel. Most rooms, including the restaurant and the terrace, face the Limmat, and have the classic view of the cathedral and the ancient Town Hall across the river. The sides of the hotel not facing the river overlook the charming Weinplatz, with its beautiful fountain and the most elegant and charming streets of the Altstadt which have now become pedestrian precincts. All the rooms are therefore absolutely quiet. The cuisine is distinguished, of international standard with a Swiss touch. There is also a less recommendable *buvette* on the ground floor. Above all, the hotel is centrally situated, within easy walking distance of the Bahnhofstrasse and all the sights and is still a haven of comfort, peace and quietness.' *(Arnold Horwell)*

Open: All year.
Rooms: 37 double, 40 single – 55 with bath, 22 with shower, all with telephone, radio, colour TV and baby-listening by arrangement.
Facilities: Lift, bar, restaurant, terrace; conference and banqueting facilities.
Location: Central; no private parking.
Credit cards: All major credit cards accepted.
Terms: B & B 85–150 Sfrs. Full *alc* 50 Sfrs.

The Palace Hotel, Hvar

Yugoslavia

BELGRADE   Map 14

Hotel Moskva   *Telephone:* (011) 327 312
                                                   Telex: 11505 yu moskva

'A notable building right in the centre of the city, one of the few survivors
of the last war. It has been thoroughly modernized, and has the kind of
gentle attentive staff that any traveller anywhere would always appreciate. If you become a favoured client, they will give you a duplex, with a
sitting-room downstairs and sleeping quarters and bathroom up a little
staircase.' *(Hella Pick)*

Open: All year.
Rooms: 140 – all with bath or shower, most with telephone.
Facilities: Lift, bar, restaurant, air-conditioning.
Location: Central.
Terms (excluding tax): Rooms (including English breakfast) US$ 40–80; dinner,
B & B (minimum 3 days) US$ 50; full board (minimum 3 days) US$ 60.

Please write and confirm an entry when it is deserved. If you think
that a hotel is not as good as we say, please write and tell us.

Grand Hotel Toplice   *Telephone:* Bled (064) 77 222
                                                Telex: 34-588 yu toplice

'Lake Bled, as seen from the wide windows of the *Grand Hotel Toplice* presents a perfect picture postcard view: dense trees mask many of the hotels which edge its shores; from the wooded islet in the middle of the water rise the tower and tall turret of an ancient castle and chapel; and on the horizon, misty and mysterious as a well-painted scenic backdrop, rise the peaks of the Julian Alps. This area of Slovenia, just across the border from Austria, is a paradise for fishermen, hunters, painters, and wine connoisseurs; the Riesling here is fabulous. The Toplice (meaning "spa") stands right at the lake edge, and it is in the best traditions of 19th-century Hapsburg Vienna; but though it keeps its period elegance, mod-cons have been discreetly added. And you don't have to brave the cold lake water; the *Toplice* has its own covered swimming pool fed by a thermal spring and edged with columns like the Roman baths at Bath. For me, this is simply one of the finest hotels in Europe. Superb choice of food and wine. On this, my third visit, I received all the unobtrusive courtesy and attention I have come to expect.' *(George S Jonas)*

Open: All year.
Rooms: 121 single, double and suites – all with bath and telephone or shower, most with balcony overlooking the lake.
Facilities: Lift, salon and cocktail bar, elegant restaurant; conference rooms, bridge room; sauna, massage, solarium, keep-fit club; indoor heated swimming pool. Lakeside terrace and bathing beach; boats available; golf and tennis a short distance away.
Location: 55 km NW of Ljubljana, near the Austrian border.
Terms (excluding tax): Rooms US$20–35 (single), US$34–62 (double); full board US$25–55 (3 days minimum).

Hotel Orijent   *Telephone:* Cajnice 85 169

Cajnice, 'known since time immemorable as an air-bath', as the brochure puts it, is a small Turkish-style town on the river Jarjina, 860 metres in altitude, with good views of the surrounding forests and mountains, as well as the neighbourhood mosque and church. The *Orijent* is a modern wedge-styled building, with a steep roof and triangular bedrooms. 'Very pleasant staff. Good dinner, a grill with a local speciality – an apple pudding – eaten to the accompaniment of a deafening pop group. Comfortable beds. In the morning, the villagers came down on mules and donkeys, past the hotel to the local market, to the sound of girls staying in the hotel singing unaccompanied folk songs on the terrace.' *(Jim and Olga Lloyd)*

Open: All year.
Rooms: 58, mostly double, 3 suites – all with bath and telephone; TV in the suites.
Facilities: Salon, bar, restaurant. Entertainment in the high season only. Small garden with unheated swimming pool. Near river with fishing and safe bathing. Winter sports.

Location: About 104 km SE of Sarajevo, 19 km from Gorazde on the road to Pljevlja. In town centre; parking.

Terms (excluding tax): Rooms (including breakfast) US$16 (single), US$26 (double); half board US$15–18; full board US$18–21.

DUBROVNIK   Map 14

Hotel Dubravka   *Telephone:* Dubrovnik (050) 26 293
Ulica Od Puca 1

The *Dubravka* is quite spectacularly noisy from 5 am onwards. But it has a unique advantage over any other hotel in Dubrovnik, being the only one in the dramatically beautiful old city. There are no cars allowed in the old town, and extra-mural parking in the high season can be a long and tiresome business; and then you have to find a porter with a cart to lug your baggage a good half mile from the city gates. But the rewards for those who like to be at the centre of things, are considerable. To wake up to a dress circle seat at a colourful market in the old cathedral square adjoining the hotel is one such delight; to be at hand for the teeming *korzo* in the Placa is another; to inherit the quiet of the city late at night, when the daytime trippers have left the stage, is a third. Many people will feel the sacrifice of a few mundane creature comforts well worth it for the sake of an exceptional location. There is no restaurant at Dubravka, but it does have a pleasant roof terrace for snacks and drinks.

Open: 1 April–1 November.
Rooms: 17 double, 5 single – 9 with shower.
Facilities: Roof terrace for drinks and snacks; handy café below (not owned by the hotel).
Location: In the centre of the old town.
Credit cards: All major credit cards accepted.
Terms (excluding tax): Rooms US$12–21 (single), US$17–35 (double). Set meal: breakfast approx. US$2.

DUBROVNIK   Map 14

The Villa Dubrovnik   *Telephone:* Dubrovnik 22 933
                                                 Telex: 27503

Perched on a cliff on the south side of Dubrovnik, this medium-sized modern hotel has lovely views of the old walled town and harbour and also looks over to the island of Lokrum opposite. The hotel is terraced into the cliff on at least five different levels with lifts to all floors, except to the bathing rocks. Pine trees, flowers and blue awnings give a Riviera flavour. The bar and dining room both have superb views, and you can eat outdoors in fine weather. The service is excellent and the food good by Yugoslav standards. Most bedrooms face the front with small balconies, and are well furnished. There are high standards of cleanliness. The hotel has its own 'concrete' beach with rock bathing in unpolluted water; there are plenty of chairs and beach umbrellas and a bar service. There is no nightlife on the spot, but you can wander down to the city in about twenty minutes or take the hotel's own motor-boat, and it is easy to get a taxi back. Not recommended for the elderly or infirm, as there are steps up from the hotel entrance to the road above. *(Alan Ross)*

477

Open: 1 April–31 October.
Rooms: 56 – all with bath/shower and telephone, many with sea-facing balconies.
Facilities: Lifts, lounge, bar, restaurant; sub-tropical gardens; own bathing beach, mainly rock; sea-level bar service.
Location: On the S side of Dubrovnik.
Terms: Rooms US$20–60; dinner, B & B (minimum 3 days) US$15–50; full board (minimum 3 days) US$16–52.

HVAR   Map 14

The Palace Hotel   *Telephone:* (058) 74 013
                                                        Telex: 26235 Yu Hvar

'This small offshore island has been called Yugoslavia's Madeira for it has such a gentle winter climate. Pine trees offer shade in summer, olives and vines flourish. An important crop is lavendar, much of it exported to Britain as a basis for Olde English Lavendar! There is plenty to see in the several small towns: remains of a Greek colony, a neolithic cave, a church-fortress and so on . . . My favourite is Hvar Town, a picturesque port with palm-fringed quays, an old Venetian arsenal and a charming little 16th-century theatre. *The Palace* has a wide sun terrace overlooking Hvar harbour built above an arched loggia dating from 1515. Bedrooms, with bathrooms, are modest but modernized and there are only 70, a change from the usual huge Yugoslavian hotel complexes. A great delight was the winter swimming pool, with warm sea water. The food I found good, and the service amiable.' *(Anne Bolt)*

Open: All year.
Rooms: 63 double, 7 single, 6 suites – 51 with bath, 25 with shower, all with telephone.
Facilities: Lifts, 2 lounges, TV room, bar, restaurant. Sun terrace overlooking harbour with music and dancing every night during summer.
Location: Central; no special parking facilities.
Credit cards: All major credit cards accepted.
Terms (excluding tax): Rooms US$19–40 (single), US$28–68 (double); half board (minimum 3 days) US$16–47; full board (minimum 3 days) US$18–50.

ROVINJ-MONSENA   Map 14

Monsena Bungalows   *Telephone:* (052) 81 256

The last and the first: the last entry in this year's Guide and our first naturist hotel. *Monsena* is a bungalow settlement about 3 km from Rovinj, a charming old Venetian town, with a regular bus service. There are twelve types of bungalow for couples or families, and some with kitchens. 'A lovely place where you can swim and stay the whole day in the nude, get a clean modern bungalow in a quiet spacious park and pick your bathing place from at least 2 km of rocky beach. Every bungalow has a shower, loo, bedroom and small private terrace with umbrella. The larger bungalows have a kitchen, but we ate in the excellent restaurant *à la carte* – the full-board restaurant looked dreary. We paid 428 dinar a person a day for our bungalow, and that included an ample breakfast – not expensive for what was provided. English people should bring their own tea or they will die. There is a lot of entertainment provided – beach

478

parties, dancing and so forth – if you feel like it. Service is very good. Prices are higher for July and August, lowest in May and October.' *(Prof H C and Elsa Robbins Landon)*

Open: May–October.
Rooms: 220 bungalows accommodating 3–6 people – some with 1 bedroom, some with 2, some with living room and kitchen, all with shower and terrace.
Facilities: Bar, 2 restaurants; private beach.
Location: 3 km from town centre.
Terms (excluding tax): Bungalows for 2 with kitchenette US$22–92; bungalows without kitchenette US$13–26 (single), US$11–26 (double); half board (minimum 3 days) US$11–33; full board (minimum 3 days) US$14–36.

Appendix

MRS BRAND'S DREAM HOTEL
by Thea Brand

Our appendix last year, A Night at a New Hotel, *took a critic's eye look at a country hotel recently opened by a couple new to the business. This year, Thea Brand of* Beaconside House *in Monkleigh, Devon (q.v.), considers the hazards of the enterprise as they appear to someone on the* patronne's *side of the reception desk.*

It is now nearly four years since our decision to leave London and open 'our sort of hotel' in Devon was greeted by friends with reactions varying from shocked incomprehension to howls of derision. In between were the reasonable ones who were prepared to spend hours patiently trying to explain to us the disadvantages of exchanging our comfortable life in a chic London suburb for the long hours, hard work and generally debilitating life of hotel owners.

Even the hoteliers to whom we tremulously announced the reason for our frequent visits during househunting trips to Devon did their best to outline a life of drudgery coupled with debt. But we reasoned if it was so bad why were they all still at it? And so we went through with our plans blissfully unaware of the pitfalls to come.

Our great move took place in February 1978 during the worst blizzard ever recorded in the West Country. It was so cold my teeth chattered audibly on the edge of the housewarming glass of champagne. Two days after we moved in, even though we were not yet an hotel, we had our first guests – orphans of the storm who blew in to have a cup of tea and wait for the snow to stop. Ten days later, greatly to their embarrassment, they were still there – perched miserably on our unopened packing cases.

March and April were fairly chilly too with no floorboards, usually no heating but miles of expensive copper piping and cables to make life more hazardous for the unwary future proprietress as she skipped nimbly about with measure and pins having decreed new everything throughout and for the new proprietor struggling about with beds and bedding.

But inevitably all bad things also come to an end, and by May there was a sense of achievement. Some of the rooms had recognizable bathrooms and quite a few floorboards had been replaced.

There was also a sense of panic as we had advertised in the national press and actually had bookings for July and August and a whole cricket team of doctors from a London teaching hospital complete with wives scheduled for mid-June.

Needless to say the builders hadn't finished. No wonder it took around two centuries to complete a major undertaking like Westminster Abbey. Some of the rooms had live wires dangling from the walls and others had holes for basin pipes.

But we were fortunate. Our cricketers were a merry lot and made light of it all. Indeed the leader of the pack – a very distinguished senior consultant – even went so far as to say he was quite happy with the novel idea of a removeable door handle which he assumed was a security precaution and that his only complaint if he had one at all would be that he would prefer to have a spoon on his early-morning tea tray.

This attitude on his part was doubly noble as he had been allocated the grottiest room due to a misconception on my part that the only two guests not described as 'Doctor' on the booking list must be very senior and important. Thus the two best rooms were occupied by medical students.

I explained that the spoons ordered in January before we left London had not yet arrived. No problem, he assured me.

The following evening our party dined in a local hostelry and to our horror many of them returned bearing teaspoons (which had to be surreptitiously returned by our Wednesday waitress who worked there on Saturdays and was able to slip them into the dishwasher – but not of course until the replacements arrived from the suppliers). Our cricketers stayed four nights and departed apparently undeterred by the horrors they had endured and having booked to return the following year.

So far so good and still no sign of all this misery foretold by the Cassandras back in London who had seen us off with so many misgivings. We closed at once with another month to plug the holes in walls and tuck away the offending cables and plumb in the odd unconnected bath and re-open for business in time for the start of the school holidays in July. And then it was that the full magnitude of what we had undertaken hit us.

We intended to run *Beaconside* as a country-house party – an extension of our own lifestyle. It would, we thought, be the same as having friends to stay and we had always been told what good hosts we were. But of course what we had overlooked was that when one stays with friends the friendship enables one to overlook their shortcomings – or at least to be prepared to put up with them. What we had to digest was that the people arriving to stay with us at *Beaconside* didn't know us from Adam and were buying a service and quite naturally felt that they should get what they paid for. They were rather less interested in sparkling after dinner conversation than in having the dinner placed on the table before them at eight o'clock (or thereabouts!).

The truth is that we had worked so long and so hard to make *Beaconside* exactly the sort of place we ourselves would hope to find at the end of a long journey down the motorway and then winding lanes that it quite simply never occurred to us that other people wouldn't think it wonderful too and *say* so.

That first season we were frankly outraged and offended by people who failed to remark on the stunning views, the pretty bedrooms and good food (produced with unimaginable difficulty in a kitchen which consisted of an old Esso solid-fuel oven which only worked when the wind was in the west and a chopping board propped between two chair backs as the solitary work surface).

I shall never forget showing one couple up to a bedroom which had been completed literally as they arrived – cleaners and decorators bundling down the back stairs as the guests made their way up the front. I threw the door open with justifiable pride to display a breathtaking view framed by metres and metres of curtains which I had been hemming into the small hours, matching bedcover, sparkling new paint, carefully chosen carpet and prints and pretty hand painted tiles in the en suite bathroom. Glowing with achievement, I waited. But the only comment I bore back to the eagerly waiting staff upon their heroic effort to have the room finished in time was 'There's no soap in the bathroom.' Of course the guests were absolutely right that they should have had soap but why on earth was that the only thing they saw – or rather didn't see?

We have realized now that we do occasionally have people to stay who seem to enjoy things more if they are wrong. They take pleasure in finding things to complain about and extracting the maximum discomfort from their stay. The awful thing is that these people (for obvious reasons we always call them 'no soapers') always seem to be the ones for whom everything does go wrong. We can spot them on arrival now. They never return a welcoming smile – they're too busy already, eyes darting about the hall searching out a dead flower in a vase here or paw marks on the floor there. They've always had an appalling journey and of course it wasn't raining wherever it was they have just come from. (It really is quite amazing how often we find ourselves apologizing for the weather!) Happily, 'no soapers' are few and far between.

A far more recurrent problem are the guests who are such good company and so funny that we all sit round in the bar buying each other drinks until the small hours, delighted with each other's company. Then someone remembers that we have to get up in the morning and off they all go with apologies for keeping us up which we can truthfully say are quite uncalled for since we too have had a lovely evening. The euphoria usually lasts just long enough to get the debris swept into the dishwasher before we fall into bed to awake leaden what seems like ten minutes later but always turns out to be time to get up again.

We scoffed at the gloom mongers who warned us at the outset about the long hours we'd have to put in. I was convinced it couldn't possibly take all day to feed the 18 people we can accommodate. How wrong I was. An average day can go something like this.

. 7.15 The radio clock comes on. If it's the soothing tones of Brian Redhead and Today drift back to sleep again. If one of the cleaner's children has been fiddling with the radio and it's the local equivalent – Morning Sou'West – rise with a scream to kill it. Bath and wash hair (the only chance I'll get all day) and stagger into the kitchen to start breakfast. If its going to be a good day every one will have the same sort of egg. It's not. I do two fried eggs, two poached, one soft boiled and two scrambled plus all the brain-riddling combinations of sausage, mushrooms, tomato and kidney that they can think of within the first ten minutes. Then back to the frying pan followed by two scrambled eggs and – outrage here – fried bread. Before I've finished the bell on the kitchen door starts to ring. Very nice departing guests wanting to pay their bills. Hard to resist the temptation for a chat so it's getting on for ten by the time I get down to making lists and phoning my orders to suppliers. The upstairs cleaner has telephoned to say that one of her children isn't well so she won't be in. Reprogramme my morning to take over the bedrooms. The girl who does the shopping telephones to say she hopes I don't mind but she has a bad pain in her back and so she won't be in. I do mind. Reprogramme again to take on shopping. Bell on the door rings again. Two thermoil of hot water for No 1 – why on earth can't they boil the kettle in their room instead of milking the system for all they can get (service included). Thank goodness for a stalwart kitchen assistant recently culled from Winkfield who carries efficiently on as I depart down the town scattering lists like confetti.

By now it's getting on for twelve o'clock and all the shops will shut for an hour at one (providing it isn't Wednesday in which case they shut for the rest of the day) so I either have to get lucky and get round in an hour or hang about until they reopen.

In the event I make it by one and then drive to Barnstaple (12 miles) to collect the ducks which I have bought from Marks & Spencers ever since I read that John Dupays of Hunstrete House always buys his poultry at Marks because they're killed in a way that doesn't frighten them. He said that fright makes them tough but I don't like to think of them being frightened anyway.

Finally make it back with loaded car at about two. Kitchen assistant has just gone off duty so can't help unload. Haven't of course had any breakfast so munch the first of many sustaining but fattening snacks as I do it alone.

A space seller phones to ask if I will advertise. I say no but she argues for ages. In the end I tell her we can't afford it and slam the phone down.

Go out to the laundry room to find all the sheets taken off the beds in the morning still waiting to be washed. Set two loads going and am in the middle of sorting out the third when I remember the thermostat has gone on that machine. The downstairs cleaner (still here because she does the books too) comes running out to say I'm wanted on the phone. She doesn't know who it is (they won't ever ask) and I trek back to the house only to discover that it's another space seller. Cleaner/Book keeper lady very apologetic and promises to ask who is calling in future. Reminds me that the bank is getting fairly heavy and I should phone them today to say that various giro credits are on their way.

Door bell again. Arrivals to be shown to their room. Usually the girl who does the shopping does this too and makes the afternoon tea but she's not in so I do it and notice on my way up (as do they – Oh please not no soapers) that the flowers on the landing need to be re-done. Collect them on my way down and hurry because the telephone is ringing again. This time it's a frozen food company wanting to know if I require anything from them. I don't. Phone rings again as soon as I put it down. My husband to say that he had just remembered there is a meeting of the Chamber of Commerce so can I get someone in to do the bar this evening. Replace receiver firmly and go outside with dead flowers to put them on the compost heap. On the way back drop into the laundry to empty machines and reload them. Thank God it's raining so that I can use the tumbler dryer without compunction. If I had to hang this lot out on the line it would take another ten minutes.

Phone rings again. Race into the house and pick it up irritably thinking it'll be a rep of some sort only to find a charming caller wanting to book rooms. Change tune fast to be charming back. After phone call realise I've left empty flower vase in the laundry room and forgotten to pick any fresh flowers. Damn!

Door bell rings again. Afternoon tea for four in the drawing room.

Lovely people but why do you all drink so much tea. Carrying it through to them I meet the people from number 1 returning wet and cold from the walk/golf/fishing. Decency demands that I offer them tea too even though it is getting on for six. While I am getting it ready and finding the towels for the new arrivals (I knew it, they are no soapers) my kitchen assistant returns and registers resignedly that I have done absolutely nothing all afternoon so she will have to work harder than ever 'to make up'.

Finally make a start on what I should have done hours before. O lordy the meat should have gone in 15 minutes ago, and I forgot to ask my helper to chop the veg for the sauce and she's into sweets now so I daren't interrupt. I'll have to do it myself and the telephone is ringing again. A dinner booking for tonight for heavens sake. Can we manage another four?

7.30 Everything is humming along now. The washer upper has arrived and both the waitresses. Everyone is ready except for me. With pitying sighs they help me out. How can I be so disorganized. Why do I leave everything to the last minute. They don't say anything (just as well) but you can see them thinking it. Kitchen door bell again. The people from number 1 would like two extra pillows (they had two more last night what on earth are they up to up there) one of their light bulbs has gone and could they please have some ice (so that they can consume their own imported booze upstairs rather than pay our slightly above pub prices. The meanness of it and the nerve!).

The bar bell rings. O God I forgot to get anyone in. One of the waitresses volunteers. A good night – I'm lucky!

The telephone rings a couple of times. One is a straightforward booking. The other wants to go into dates and prices and won't be rung back. I do my best, telephone tucked into my neck, flicking through the diary with one hand and stirring my liaison with the other.

My husband drops in to grab a quick snack before going off to his meeting and wants to know why the tea trays haven't been removed from the drawing room. I tell him and I think he gets the message because he goes and does a quick stint in the bar and takes the wine orders before he dashes out again.

Nine o'clock and all the main courses have been served except for one couple with a baby who still haven't been able to settle it down yet. Their beef will be far from *saignant* if they don't appear soon. Lucky it didn't go in on time after all. On cue they arrive. Can they have it on a tray upstairs. Hooray their beef is still bloody and the waitresses will be able to get on and clear the dining room and relay for breakfast before they go.

9.45 I depart from the kitchen to try to do something to repair the damage of the day before presenting myself in the bar – that is if I don't fall asleep on my dressing table stool. As it is I don't actually make it to our flat because the phone rings again. My shopping girl won't be in for a week or so as she has a kidney infection. Poor girl . . . how painful . . . how will I cope.

Lots of people in the bar all very kind about the dinner and proffering drinks. Accept a glass of red wine and a cigarette (why) knowing I ought really to go to bed but after all I've been working all day and need to unwind.

Waitress pokes her head round the door. Can I come for a minute. There aren't any table cloths. Well where are they for goodness sake!

Reproachful look. In the washing machine. I forgot to go back and unload it again. Must I think of everything. Use the green ones. Don't I remember the green ones got spoiled the day the thermostat went wrong and they boiled all night and then the machine spat globules of oil all over them. Frantic sprint to the laundry room to take one lot out and put them in the tumbler dryer. If I give them maximum heat for 20 minutes and take them straight out and they put them straight on to the tables and it's a fairly dull morning they should pass muster.

Back in the kitchen remember I didn't eat dinner and polish off the remains of the Gâteau St Honoré. No wonder nothing fits.

Back to the bar. Still in full swing. More red wine. Party looks as if it might be about to break up when husband returns from his meeting and everyone settles back in again for another hour or so.

Midnight. Far too late to catch my kitchen helper to ask her to do breakfast because I'll have to shop. I must go to bed soon or I'll fall down. Ah! They're moving off at last just on one. Only another half hour or so. Just time to clear up. Put the glasses and coffee cups and so on into the machine. Plump up the cushions. Switch off the lights. Oops! Sorry! Who's that? People from no 9. Oh no! It's the no soapers and they haven't got an early morning tea tray. For heavens sake no towels, no tea tray. Who on earth did the bedrooms this morning. Oh I remember now. Please God let the chambermaid be all right in the morning. Yes here we are. I'm so sorry. Goodnight. Goodnight.

Staggering across to our own flat (completed in the middle of the season so we've had no time to move in properly). Cold and dreary with unmade bed. How could I forget? I haven't been in here again since we got up. I forgot to ring the bank too! Please God let it be better tomorrow.

Exchange Rates

These rates for buying currency are correct at time of printing but in some cases may be wildly awry at the time of publication. It is essential to check with bank or newspapers for up-to-date pound and dollar equivalents.

	£1 sterling	$1 US
Austria (Schillings)	28.50	15.30
Belgium (Belgian francs)	76.00	40.80
Denmark (kroner)	13.50	7.25
Finland (Finnish marks)	8.12	4.36
France (francs)	10.28	5.52
Germany (Deutschemarks)	4.09	2.1959
Greece (drachmae)	107.50	57.72
Holland (guilders)	4.51	2.42
Italy (lire)	2190.0	1175.8
Luxembourg (Luxembourg francs)	76.00	40.80
Malta (Maltese pounds)	0.7125	0.3825
Norway (kroner)	10.82	5.80
Portugal (escudos)	118.25	63.49
Spain, including Andorra, Balearics and Canaries (pesetas)	176.0	94.50
Sweden (kroner)	10.18	5.46
Switzerland, including Liechtenstein (Swiss francs)	3.28	1.76

Tourist Offices

National Tourist Offices will supply general information and literature on request. Among the booklets and leaflets available (many of them free) are accommodation lists, regional pamphlets, catalogues of the main sights and events, and details of sporting, travel, and other facilities. Ask for the area which particularly interests you. Within each country there are information offices in all main towns and resorts, able to supply more detailed local information, maps, itineraries, etc., and sometimes to assist visitors to find accommodation.

UNITED KINGDOM	London:	The British Tourist Authority, 64 St James's Street, London SW1
	New York:	680 Fifth Avenue, New York, NY 10019
ENGLAND	London:	*Correspondence:* English Tourist Board, 4 Grosvenor Gardens, London SW1 *Personal Callers:* London Tourist Board (1) Victoria Station next to main ticket office by Platform 15 (2) Heathrow Central underground station
WALES		Wales Tourist Board PO Box 1 Cardiff, CF1 2XN
SCOTLAND	Scotland:	*Correspondence:* Scottish Tourist Board, 23 Ravelston Terrace, Edinburgh *Personal Callers:* 5 Waverley Bridge, Edinburgh

| | London: | 5 Pall Mall East, London SW1 |
| | Belfast: | River House, 48 High Street, Belfast, BT1 2DS |

CHANNEL ISLANDS	Alderney:	Recreation and Tourism Committee, States Office, Alderney
	Guernsey:	States of Guernsey Tourist Committee, PO Box 23, St Peter Port, Guernsey
	Herm:	Herm Island Administrative Office, Herm
	Jersey:	States of Jersey Tourism Office, Weighbridge, St Helier, Jersey London Office: 118 Grand Buildings, Trafalgar Square, London WC2
	Sark:	Tourist Office, Sark.

| **NORTHERN IRELAND** | | Ulster Office, 11 Berkeley Street, London W1 |

REPUBLIC OF IRELAND	London:	Irish Tourist Board, 150 New Bond Street, London W1
	Dublin:	Baggot Street Bridge, Dublin 2
	New York:	590 Fifth Avenue, New York, NY 10036

| **AUSTRIA** | London: | Austrian National Tourist Office, 30 St George Street, London W1 |
| | New York: | 545 Fifth Avenue, New York, NY 10017 |

| **BELGIUM** | London: | Belgian National Tourist Office, 38 Dover Street, London W1 |
| | New York: | 745 Fifth Avenue, New York, NY 10022 |

| **DENMARK** | London: | Danish Tourist Board, Sceptre House, 169–173 Regent Street, London W1 |
| | New York: | 75 Rockefeller Plaza, New York, NY 10019 |

| **FINLAND** | London: | Finnish Tourist Board, 66 Haymarket, London SW1 |
| | New York: | Finland National Tourist Office, 75 Rockefeller Plaza, New York, NY 10019 |

FRANCE

London: French Government Tourist Office,
178 Piccadilly, London W1

New York: 610 Fifth Avenue,
New York, NY 10020

GERMANY

London: German National Tourist Office,
61 Conduit Street, London W1

New York: 630 Fifth Avenue,
New York, NY 10020

GREECE

London: National Tourist Organization of
Greece,
195–197 Regent Street, London W1

New York: 645 Fifth Avenue (Olympic Tower),
New York, NY 10022

HOLLAND

London: Netherlands National Tourist Office,
143 New Bond Street, London W1

New York: 576 Fifth Avenue,
New York, NY 10036

HUNGARY

London: Danube Travel,
6 Conduit Street, London W1

ITALY

London: Italian State Tourist Office,
201 Regent Street, London W1

New York: 630 Fifth Avenue,
New York, NY 10020

LUXEMBOURG

London: 36–37 Piccadilly, London W1

New York: 1 Dag Hammerkjold Plaza,
New York, NY 10017

MALTA

London: Malta Government Tourist Office,
Malta House, 24 Haymarket,
London SW1

New York: Malta Consulate,
249 East 35th Street,
New York, NY 10016

NORWAY

London: Norwegian National Tourist Office,
20 Pall Mall, London SW1

New York: 75 Rockefeller Plaza,
New York, NY 10019

PORTUGAL	London:	Portuguese National Tourist Office, 1–5 New Bond Street, London W1
	New York:	548 Fifth Avenue, New York, NY 10036
SPAIN (and BALEARICS and CANARY ISLANDS)	London:	Spanish National Tourist Office, 57–58 St James's Street, London SW1
	New York:	665 Fifth Avenue, New York, NY 10022
SWEDEN	London:	Swedish National Tourist Office, 3 Cork Street, London W1
	New York:	75 Rockefeller Plaza, New York, NY 10019
SWITZERLAND (and LIECHSTENSTEIN)	London:	Swiss National Tourist Office, Swiss Centre, 1 New Coventry Street, London W1
	New York:	Swiss Centre, 608 Fifth Avenue, New York, NY 10020
YUGOSLAVIA	London:	Yugoslav National Tourist Office, 143 Regent Street, London W1
	New York:	630 Fifth Avenue, Rockefeller Centre, Suite 210, New York, NY 10020

Alphabetical List of Hotels

Establishment	Listed under
ENGLAND	
Angel	Bury St Edmunds
Arundell Arms	Lifton
Ashwick House	Dulverton
Athenaeum	London
Bailiffscourt	Climping
Basil Street	London
Bay Tree	Burford
Beaconside House	Monkleigh
Bear	Wantage
Beechfield House	Beanacre
Bell Inn	Aston Clinton
Berribridge House	Thorverton
Blakeney	Blakeney
Blakes	London
Bowes Moor	Bowes Moor
Buckinghamshire Arms	Blickling
Buckland-Tout-Saints	Kingsbridge
Budock Vean	Budock Vean
Butts	Ryall
Castle	Taunton
Cavendish	Baslow
Château Impney	Droitwich Spa
Chewton Glen	New Milton
Clinchs'	Chichester
Close	Tetbury
Combe House	Gittisham
Connaught	London
Cottage in the Wood	Malvern Wells
Crantock	Crantock Bay
Deans Place	Alfriston
D'Isney Place	Lincoln
Downrew House	Barnstaple
Duke's	London
Eastwell Manor	Eastwell
Ebury Court	London

Elizabeth	London
Elms	Abberley
Farlam Hall	Brampton
Feathers	Ludlow
Fifehead Manor	Middle Wallop
Findon Manor	Findon
Forest Inn	Hexworthy
Foxdown Manor	Horns Cross
Gara Rock	East Portlemouth
Garden House	Cambridge
George of Stamford	Stamford
Gidleigh Park	Chagford
Granville	Brighton
Gravetye Manor	East Grinstead
Greenriggs	Underbarrow
Grosvenor	Chester
Hambleton Hall	Hambleton
Haycock	Wansford
Holcombe	Deddington
Homewood Park	Hinton Charterhouse
Hope Anchor	Rye
Hope End	Ledbury
Howtown	Ullswater
Hunstrete House	Hunstrete
Island	Tresco
Jervaulx Hall	Jervaulx
Kennel Holt	Cranbrook
Kildwick Hall	Kildwick
Kings Arms	Chipping Campden
King's Arms	Kirkby Stephen
Klymiarven	Looe
Lamorna Cove	Lamorna Cove
Langleigh	Ilfracombe
Langley House	Wiveliscombe
Leeming on Ullswater	Ullswater
Lastingham Grange	Lastingham
Little Thakeham	Storrington
Lodore Swiss	Keswick
Long House	Pilton
Lower Brook House	Blockley
Lower House Country Lodge	Hopton Castle
Lythe Hill	Haslemere
Maid's Head	Norwich
Mains Hall	Little Singleton
Maison Talbooth	Dedham
Mallory Court	Bishops Tachbrook
Malt House	Broad Campden
Malvern View	Cleeve Hill
Manor House	Brompton
Marine	Salcombe
Marlborough	Ipswich
Mary Mount	Borrowdale

494

Meudon	Mawnan Smith
Michael's Nook	Grasmere
Mill	Kingham
Millcombe House	Lundy Island
Miller Howe	Windermere
Milton Ernest Hall	Milton Ernest
Montcalm	London
Mount Royale	York
Nichols Nymet House	North Tawton
Number Sixteen	London
Old Bakehouse	Colyton
Old Bell	Malmesbury
Old Bridge	Huntingdon
Old Mill Floor	Trebarwith Strand
Old Vicarage	Witherslack
Peacock	Rowsley
Pheasant	Seavington St Mary
Pheasant Inn	Bassenthwaite
Plough	Clanfield
Plumber Manor	Sturminster Newton
Poltimore Guest House	South Zeal
Portobello	London
Priory Country House	Rushlake Green
Priory Court	Pevensey
Priory	Bath
Priory	Wareham
Quayside	Brixham
Riverside	Helford
Romans	Silchester
Rookery Hall	Worleston
Rose and Crown	Romaldkirk
Rothay Manor	Ambleside
Royal Crescent	Bath
Sandringham	London
Scale Hill	Loweswater
Seatoller	Borrowdale
Shakespeare	Stratford upon Avon
Sharrow Bay	Ullswater
Spindlewood	Wadhurst
Shipdham Place	Shipdham
Somerset House	Bath
Stratford House	Stratford upon Avon
Studley	Harrogate
Summer Lodge	Evershot
Swan	Lavenham
Swynford Paddocks	Six Mile Bottom
Tarr Steps	Hawkbridge
Teignworthy	Frenchbeer
Temple Sowerby	Temple Sowerby
Thornworthy	Chagford
Treglos	Constantine Bay
Trevaylor	Gulval

Wateredge	Ambleside
White House	Williton
White Moss	Grasmere
Whitwell Hall Country House	Whitwell on the Hill
West Porlock House	Porlock Weir
Woodhayes	Whimple
Woolverton House	Woolverton
Worsley Arms	Hovingham
Yeoldon House	Bideford

WALES

Abbey	Llanthony
Bontddu Hall	Bontddu
Crown Inn and Restaurant	Whitebrook
Gallt y Glyn	Llanberis
Glansevin	Llangadog
Gliffaes Country House	Crickhowell
Glyn Peris	Llanberis
Golden Lion	Dolgellau
Lake Vyrnwy	Llanwddyn
Meadowsweet	Llanrwst
Minffordd	Talyllyn
Plas Maenan	Llanrwst
Plas Penhelig	Aberdovey
Porth Tocyn	Abersoch
Portmeirion	Penrhyndeudraeth
Robeston House	Robeston Wathen
Three Cocks	Three Cocks
Warpool Court	St David's
Wolfscastle	Wolfscastle
Ynyshir Hall	Eglwysfach

SCOTLAND

Airds	Port Appin
Albany	Edinburgh
Ardfenaig House	Bunessan
Atholl Arms	Dunkeld
Auchen Castle	Beattock
Balcary Bay	Auchencairn
Banchory Lodge	Banchory
Baron's Craig	Rockcliffe
Beechwood Country House	Moffat
Clifton	Nairn
Creggans Inn	Strachur
Crinan	Crinan
Cringletie House	Peebles
Dunmor House	Seil
Edrachilles	Scourie
Eileen Iarmain	Sleat, Isle of Skye
Four Seasons	St Fillans
Greywalls	Gullane
Gigha	Gigha

Glenborrowdale Castle	Ardnamurchan
Heritage	Stirling
Houstoun House	Uphall
Inverlochy Castle	Fort William
Inverlounin House	Lochgoilhead
Inveroran	Bridge of Orchy
Invershin	Invershin
Isle of Eriska	Eriska
Killiecrankie	Killiecrankie
Kinloch Lodge	Isle Ornsay
Loch Melfort	Arduaine
Loch Torridon	Torridon
Log Cabin	Kirkmichael
Milton Park	Dalry
Osprey	Kingussie
Philipburn House	Selkirk
Polmaily House	Drumnadrochit
Pool House	Poolewe
Prestonfield House	Edinburgh
Riverside Inn	Canonbie
Ruffles	St Andrews
Scarista House	Harris
Skeabost House	Skeabost Bridge
Sligachan	Sligachan
Stewart	Duror
Summer Isles	Achiltibuie
Taycreggan	Lochaweside
Uig	Uig
Uig Lodge	Lewis
Woodside	Kelso

CHANNEL ISLANDS

Aval du Creux	Sark
Dixcart	Sark
L'Horizon	St Brelade
Longuevueville Manor	St Saviour
Petit Champ	Sark
White House	Herm

NORTHERN IRELAND

Dunadry Inn	Dunadry
Nutgrove	Annadorn

REPUBLIC OF IRELAND

Aghadoe Heights	Killarney
Arbutus Lodge	Cork
Ard na Greine Inn	Schull
Ballymaloe	Shanagarry
Cashel House	Cashel Bay
Cashel Palace	Cashel
Coopershill Farmhouse	Riverstown
Currarevagh	Oughterard

Glencar	Glencar
Inislounaght Country House	Marlfield
Longueville House	Mallow
Marlfield House	Gorey
Newpark	Kilkenny
Rosleague Manor	Letterfrack

AUSTRIA
Elefant	Salzburg
Elite	Vienna
Erika	Kitzbühel
Europa	Vienne
Gams	Bezau
Goldenen Hirschen	Freistadt
Insel	Faak-am-See
Kaiserin Elisabeth	Vienna
Markus Sittikus	Salzburg
Nossek	Vienna
Richard Löwenherz	Dürnstein
Sacher	Vienna
Schloss Drassburg	Drassburg
Schloss Dürnstein	Dürnstein
Schloss Freisitz Roith	Gmunden
Schloss Fuschl	Fuschl-am-See
Schwarzenberg, Im Palais	Vienna
Schwarzes-Rössl	Windischgarsten
Seewinkel	Fuschl-am-See
Senger	Heilgenblut
Suzanne	Vienna
Weisses Rössl	Steinach
Zur Traube	Lans Bei Innsbruck

BELGIUM
Amigo	Brussels
Balcon en Forêt	Rochehaut sur Semois
Château des Brides	Oostkamp
Damier	Kortrijk
Duc de Bourgogne	Bruges
Jorishof	Gent
Marquis, Le Relais du	Ittre
Moulin de Boiron, Hostellerie	Sart-Custinne
Moulin Hideux, Auberge du	Noirefontaine
Sanglier des Ardennes	Durbuy
Shamrock, Hostellerie	Ronse
Vieux Durbuy	Durbuy

DENMARK
d'Angleterre	Copenhagen
Bramming Hovedgård	Bramming
Dagmar	Ribe
Munkebjerg	Vejle
Store Kro	Fredensborg

498

FINLAND

Kalastajatorppa	Helsinki

FRANCE

L'Abbaye	St-Cyprien
L'Abbaye St Germain	Paris
Abbaye de Sainte-Croix	Salon-de-Provence
L'Abbaye Saint Michel	Tonnerre
Aigle Noir	Fontainebleau
Alain Chapel	Mionnay
Anne de Bretagne	La Plaine-sur-Mer
D'Antoine, Auberge	St-Jeannet
D'Arlatan	Arles
Arnold	Itterswiller
Balzac	Tours
Bannière de France	Laon
Baou	Ramatuelle
Bastide de Tourtour	Tourtour
Beach	Monte Carlo
Beffroi	Vaison-la-Romaine
Belle Rive	Najac
Bellevarde	Les Houches
Bonnet	Beynac et Cazenac
Bourgogne	Cluny
Brises	La Rochelle
Café des Arcades	Biot
Cagnard	Cagnes-sur-Mer
Caméo	Antibes
Cathédrale	Rouen
Centenaire	Les Eyzies-de-Tayac
Central	Pau
Centre	Les Eyzies-de-Tayac
Cep	Beaune
Chapeau Rouge	Dijon
Chataigneraie	Guidel
Château d'Arpaillargues	Arpaillargues
Château d'Artigny	Montbazon
Château de Beaulieu	Joué-les-Tours
Château de Coatguelen	Pléhédel
Château de la Corniche	Rolleboise
Château de Locguénolé	Hennebont
Château de Meyrargues	Meyrargues
Château de Montreuil	Montreuil
Château de Ponderach	Saint-Pons-de-Thomières
Château de Teildras	Cheffes
Château, Hostellerie du	Fère-en-Tardenois
Château, Hostellerie du	Chaumont-sur-Loire
Château, Hostellerie du	Châteauneuf en Auxois
Château, Hôtel du	Châteauneuf-les-Bains
Château Servin, Hostellerie du	Belfort
Chenaudière	Colroy-la-Roche
Cheval Blanc	Sept-Saulx

Cheval Rouge	Villandry
Chez Pierre	Raguenès-Plage
Claude Lutz	Meximieux
Clé d'Or	Barbizan
Clément, Grand Hotel	Ardres
Clos, Hostellerie du	Verneuil-sur-Avre
Clos Normand, Auberge du	Martin-Église
Colombe d'Or	St-Paul-de-Vence
Commerce	Bar-sur-Aube
Coteau Fleuri, Hostellerie du	Grimaud
Croix Blanche	Chaumont-sur-Tharonne
Cro-Magnon	Les-Eyzies-de-Tayac
Croquembouche	Courry
Dauphin	Honfleur
Demeure des Brousses	Montpellier
Deux-Îles	Paris
Deux Lions	Vernet-les-Bains
Deux Rocs	Seillans
Diana	Vence
Diderot	Chinon
Domaine de la Tortinière	Montbazon-en-Touraine
Druides	Quiberon
Durdent, Auberge de la	Héricourt-en-Caux
L'Écho et de l'Abbaye	La Chaise-Dieu
Écu de France	Château-Renault
L'Équipe	Molines-en-Queyras
L'Esplanade	Domme
Étrangers	Sospel
Europe	Avignon
L'Europe, Grand Hôtel de	Langres
Fifi Moulin	Serres
France	Nantua
France	Ham
France et Angleterre	La Rochelle
France et Clariond	Seillans
France et Fuchsias	St-Vaast-la-Hougue
Frères Troisgros	Roanne
Gourmet Lorrain	Nice
Grac, Grand Hôtel	Annot
Grand Saint-Michel	Chambord
Halle	Givry
L'Île Rousse	Bandol
D'Isly	Paris
Le Kern	Val-d'Isère
Lameloise	Chagny
Lancaster	Paris
Legris et Parc	Fontainebleau
Lenox	Paris
Lièvre Amoureux	St-Lattier
Lion d'Or	Valençay
Lion d'Or	Bayeux
Logis Bresche Arthur	Dol-de-Bretagne

Loire, Hostellerie de la	Blois
Lord Byron	Paris
Lou Calen	Cotignac
Madone, Auberge de la	Peillon
Manoir de Vaumadeuc	Pléven
Maquis	Porticcio
Mas de Chastelas	St-Tropez
Meijette	La Grave
Mère Blanc	Vonnas
Mère Poulard	Mont-St-Michel
Metropole	Beaulieu-sur-Mer
Meurice	Calais
Midi	Lamastre
Midi	St-Jean-du-Bruel
Mirabeau	Mirabel-aux-Baronnies
Moderne	Cluny
Moderne	Barfleur
Monts de Vaux	Poligny
Au Moulin	Flagy
Moulin du Landion	Dolancourt
Moulin de Mombreux	Lumbres
Moulin des Ruats, Hostellerie du	Avallon
Moulin des Templiers	Avallon
Nord	Dijon
Ombremont	Le Bourget-du-Lac
L'Orée du Bois	St-Benoit
Oustau de Baumanière	Les Baux-de-Provence
Parc	Murol
Parc	La Croix-Valmer
A Pastorella	Monticello
Pérouse, La	Nice
Pescalerie	Cabrerets
Petite Auberge	Tourtour
Au P'tit Quinquin	Céaux
Pinède	Aubenas
Plage	Ste-Anne-La-Palud
Pont de Brie, Auberge du	Goupillières
Port	Lechiagat
Poste, Hostellerie de la	Avallon
Poste et Champanne	Brioude
Poste et Lion d'Or	Vézelay
Prés d'Eugénie	Eugénie-les-Bains
Prieuré, Hostellerie du	Chenehutte-les-Tuffeaux
Régent	Villers-Cotterêts
Ramparts	Kaysersberg
Regalido, Auberge la	Fontvieille
Relais	Ardres
Relais Christine	Paris
Relais du Clergeon	Moye
Relais de Fompeyre	Bazas
Relais du Soleil	Chabeuil
Résidence	Narbonne

501

Résidence du Bois	Paris
Roblin	Paris
Rochecourbe Manoire	Vézac
Roches-Fleuries	Cordon
Royal Champagne	Champillon
St Antoine, Hostellerie de	Albi
St Clair	St-Étienne-les-Orgues
Sainte-Foy	Conques
Saône	Tournus
Sarthe	Châteauneuf-sur-Sarthe
Scandinavia	Paris
Scierie, Auberge de la	Aix-en-Othe
Soir, Auberge du	Brantôme
Sole e Monti	Quenza
La Solognote, Auberge	Brinon-sur-Sauldre
Table du Comtat	Séguret
Taillard	Goumois
Tavel, Auberge de	Tavel
Templiers, Auberge des	Les Bézards
Terminus	Cahors
Terrasse	Meyronne
Tour	Astaffort
Touristes	Prats-de-Mollo-la-Preste
Tribunal	Mortagne-au-Perche
Trois Mousquetaires, Hostellerie des	Air
Univers	Dieppe
Val d'Or	Mercurey
Vallée	La-Voulte-sur-Rhône
Valmarin	Saint-Servan
Verte Campagne	Trelly
Vieille Ferme	Serre-Chevalier
Vieux Fox, Auberge du	Fox-Amphoux
Vieux Moulin	St-Jacut-de-la-Mer
Vieux Pérouges, Hostellerie du	Pérouges
Vieux Puits, Auberge du	Pont-Audemer
Vieux Relais, Auberge du	Airvault
Vigneraie	Levens
Vistaëro	Roquebrune-Cap-Martin
Voile d'Or	St-Jean-Cap-Ferrat
Voyageurs	Bonifacio
Welcome	Villefranche-sur-Mer

GERMANY

Adam	Rothenburg ob der Tauber
Bamberg	Bamberg
Bären, zum	Meersburg
Bayerischer Hof	Bayreuth
Biederstein	Munich
Burg	Trendelburg
Drei Könige	Bernkastel-Kues
Eisenhut	Rothenburg ob der Tauber
Franz Josef	Linz am Rhein

Heusser	Bad Dürkheim
Kaiser Worth	Goslar
Krone	Rüdesheim-Assmannshausen
Landhaus Louisenthal	Bremen-Horn
Marienbad	Munich
Mönchs Posthotel	Bad Herrenalb
Oper, an der	Munich
Post	Aschheim
Prem	Hamburg
Rokokohaus	Erlangen
Weisses Rössle	Hinterzarten
Zoo	Berlin

GREECE

Akti Myrina	Lemnos
Argo	Paros
Castello	Dassia
Claire's House	Athens
Doma	Chania
Helena	Nafplion
Kavalari	Thira
Lido	Faliraki
Manganari Village	Ios
Minoa	Tolon
Minos Beach	Ayios Nikolaos
St George Lykabettus	Athens
Vouzas	Delphi
Xenia	Ouranoupolis

HOLLAND

Ambassade	Amsterdam
Carelshaven	Delden
Europe et Excelsior	Amsterdam
Hamert	Wellerlooi
Hoofdige Boer	Almen
Kasteel Wittem	Wittem
Kieviet	Wassenaar
Maastricht	Maastricht

HUNGARY

Astoria	Budapest

ITALY

Agnello d'Oro	Bergamo
Anna, Villa	Marina di Puolo
Arethena Rocks	Gardini
Athena, Villa	Agrigento
Axidie	Vico Equense
Bahia	Cavoli
Balletti Park	San Martino al Cimino
Beccherie	Treviso
Bellevue	Cogne

Belvedere, Villa	Florence
Belvedere, Villa	Taormina
Bencista	Fiesole
Bonelli, Villa	Fiesole
Bosone Palace	Gubbio
Bussola	Orta San Giulio
Capuleti, De'	Verona
Caruso Belvedere	Ravello
Castelsandra	San Marco di Castellabate
Cipriani	Asolo
Cipriani, Locanda	Torcello
Cipriani	Venice
Cisterna	San Gimignano
Colombo d'Oro	Verona
Duchi d'Aosta	Trieste
Duomo	Milan
Elda, Villa	Santa Maria degli Angeli
d'Este, Villa	Cernobbio
Fiorelle	Sperlonga
Flora	Venice
Fonte della Galletta	Alpe Faggeto
Gatto Bianco	Capri
Gilly	Torre Pellice
Grand	Syracuse
Gritti Palace	Venice
Herbetat	Valnontey
Hermitage	Avigliana
Lac	Varenna
Lago, Casino del	Bracciano
Leon d'Oro	Viterbo
Marcella	Rome
Mariori	Alba di Canazei
Monna Lisa	Florence
Napoleon	Rome
Palombella	Frosinone
Paradiso, Villa	Taormina
Pellicano	Port' Ercole
Pomerio	Erba
Pozzi	Venice
Raphaël	Rome
Ravizza, Palazzo	Siena
Residenza	Rome
Ricavo, Tenuta di	Castellina
Riis, Villa	Taormina
Rondini, Villa le	Florence
San Lorenzo	Mantua
San Michele, Villa	Fiesole
San Rocco	Orta San Giulio
Sassi, Villa	Turin
Scacciapensieri, Albergo Villa	Siena
Seguso	Venice
Serbelloni, Grand Hotel Villa	Bellagio

Sirio	Ivrea
Sitea	Rome
Soggiorno, Bel	San Gimignano
Splendido	Portofino
Splendor	Florence
Tirreno	Forte Dei Marmi
Umbra	Assisi

LUXEMBOURG

Moselle	Ehnen

MALTA

Cornucopia	Xaghra
Ramla Bay	Marfa
Ta'Cenc	Sannat

NORWAY

Brekkestranda	Brekke
Bristol	Oslo
Continental	Oslo
Hankø Nye Fjordhotel	Hankø
Leikanger Fjord	Leikanger
Neptun	Bergen
Nordfjord	Nordfjordeid
Refnes Gods	Jeløy
Savoy	Oslo
Selje	Selje
Solstrand Fjord	Os
Utne	Utne

PORTUGAL

Abrigo da Montanha	Monchique
Albatroz	Cascais
Bala Vista	Praia da Rocha
Buçaco	Buçaco
Castelo de Palmela	Palmela
Elevador	Bom Jesus do Monte
Garbe	Armação de Pêra
Guincho	Praia do Guincho
Infante de Sagres	Oporto
Manteigas	Manteigas
Mestre Afonso Domingues	Batalha
Quinta das Torres	Azeitão
Quinta dos Lobos	Sintra
Rainha Santa Isabel	Estremoz
Ria	Murtosa
Santa Barbara	Oliveira do Hospital
Santa Luzia	Viana do Castelo
Santa Maria	Marvão
Senhora do Monte	Lisbon
Tivoli Jardim	Lisbon
York House	Lisbon

SPAIN

Aigua Blava	Playa de Fornells
Albarracin	Albarracin
Alcazar del Rey Don Pedro, Parador	Carmona
Belvedere	Encamp
Cardenal	Toledo
Casa del Corregidor, Parador	Arcos de la Frontera
Colombino Conde de la Gomera, Parador	Gomera
Condestable Davalos, Parador	Ubeda
Costa de la Luz, Parador	Ayamonte
Doña María	Seville
El Emperador, Parador	Fuenterrabia
Gil Blas, Parador	Santillana del Mar
Landa Palace	Burgos
Moli, Es	Deyá
Los Monteros	Marbella
Los Reyes Catolicos, Hostal de	Santiago de Compostela
Mar I Vent	Bañyalbufar
Marques de Villena, Parador	Alarcón
Mijas	Mijas
Montiboli	Villajoyosa
Muntanya	Orient
Parador	Nerja
Parador	Segovia
Punta Negra	Palma Nova
Racquet Club	Son Vida
Raimundo de Borgona, Parador	Ávila
Reyes Catolicos, Parador	Mojácar
Ritz	Madrid
San Francisco, Parador	Granada
San Marcos, Hostal	León
San Salvador, Hostal	Yesa
Santa Catalina, Parador	Jaén
Santa Marta	Estepona
Santo Domingo de la Calzada, Parador	Santo Domingo de la Calzada
Sierra Nevada, Parador	Monachil
Suecia	Madrid
Valle de Aran, Parador	Viella

SWEDEN

Åkerblads	Tällberg
Diplomat	Stockholm
Esso Motor	Gränna
Gripsholms Värdhus	Mariefred
Grythyttans	Grythyttan
Stenungsbaden	Stenungsund
Tanumshede Gastgivari	Tanumshede

SWITZERLAND

Adula	Flims
Aniro	Castagnola-Lugano
Arbalète	Geneva

Armures	Geneva
Casa Barbate	Tegna
Beau-Rivage	Thun
Beausite	St Luc
Bella Tola	St Luc
Belvedere-Tanneck	Arosa
Blümlisalp	Kandersteg
Bündnerhof	Klosters
Chalet du Bon Accueil	Château-d'Oex
Clos de Sadex	Nyon
Eden au Lac	Zürich
Europe	Zürich
Florhof	Zürich
Garni Metropol	Zermatt
Hirschen am See	Gunten-Thunersee
Krafft am Rhein	Basel
Lac	Montana
Monte Rosa	Zermatt
Real	Vaduz
Royal	Lucerne
Weisses Kreuz	Murten
Zum Storchen	Zürich

YUGOSLAVIA

Dubravka	Dubrovnik
Villa Dubrovnik	Dubrovnik
Monsena	Rovinj
Moskva	Belgrade
Orijent	Cajnice
Palace	Hvar
Toplice	Bled

Maps

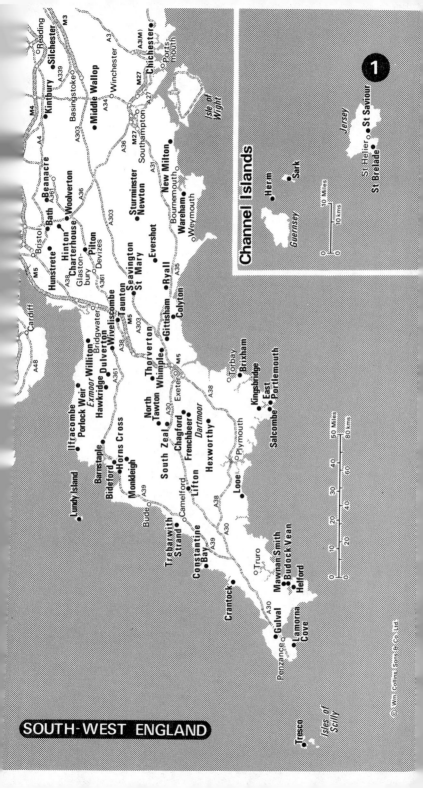

SOUTH-WEST ENGLAND

Channel Islands

1

Jersey
St Saviour
St Helier
St Brelade
Herm
Sark
Guernsey

10 Miles
10 kms

© Wm. Collins Sons & Co. Ltd.

Reading
Silchester
Kintbury
Basingstoke
Winchester
Chichester
Ports-mouth
Middle Wallop
Beanacre
Bath
Woolverton
Hinton Charterhouse
Pitton
Devizes
Hunstrete
Bristol
Glaston-bury
Cardiff
Seavington St Mary
Taunton
Ryall
Sturminster Newton
Evershot
Wareham
Weymouth
New Milton
Bournemouth
Isle of Wight
Southampton

Ilfracombe
Porlock Weir
Exmoor
Hawkridge
Dulverton
Williton
Bridgwater
Wiveliscombe
Gittisham
Colyton
Thorverton
Whimple
Exeter
Torbay
Brixham
Kingsbridge
East Portlemouth
Salcombe
Lundy Island
Barnstaple
Horns Cross
Monkleigh
Bideford
North Tawton
South Zeal
Chagford
Frenchbeer
Dartmoor
Hexworthy
Plymouth
Bude
Camelford
Lifton
Looe
Trebarwith Strand
Constantine Bay
Truro
Crantock
Mawnan Smith
Budock Vean
Helford
Gulval
Lamorna Cove
Penzance
Tresco
Isles of Scilly

Miles
kms

CENTRAL & SOUTHERN ENGLAND

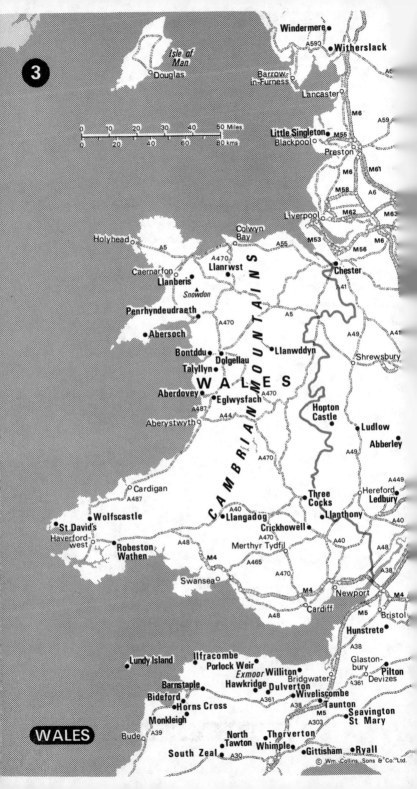

WALES

NORTHERN ENGLAND

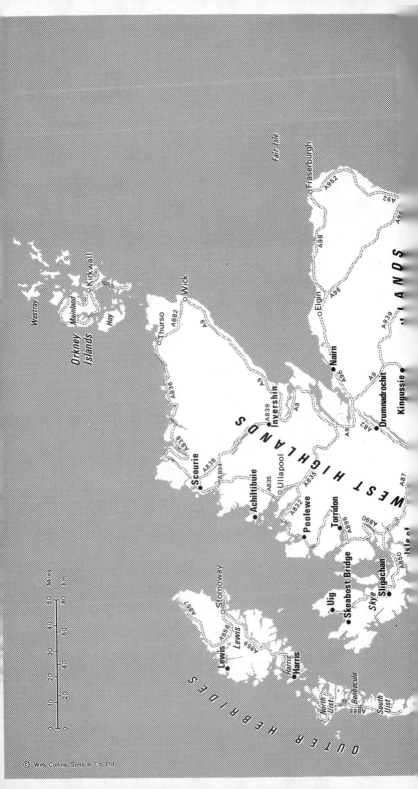

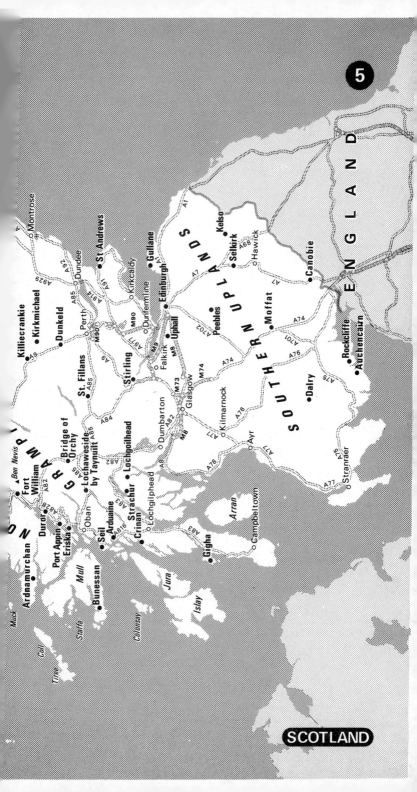

6

Coleraine

Londonderry

Larne

A26

A2

A8

N15

Donegal

Dunadry

Belfast

M1

A5

A4

Anna

N15

Sligo

Mourne Mts.

Riverstown

N17

N4

N2

N1

Castlebar

N5

N3

N59

N5

N4

Letterfrack

Oughterard

N17

Athlone

N6

N4

Dublin

Cashel Bay

N59

Galway

N6

N11

Ballyvaughan

Wicklow

N7

Wicklow Mts.

N7

N9

Gorey

N18

N8

N11

Limerick

Kilkenny

Cashel

Wexford

N24

Clonmel

N25

N21

Marlfield

N20

N8

N24

Waterford

N9

Tralee

Mallow

N25

Killarney

Glencar

N22

Cork

N71

Shanagarry

N71

Clonakilty

Schull

0   20   40   60   Miles
0   20   40   60   80   km

IRELAND

© Wm. Collins, Sons & Co. Ltd.

SOUTHERN SCANDINAVIA

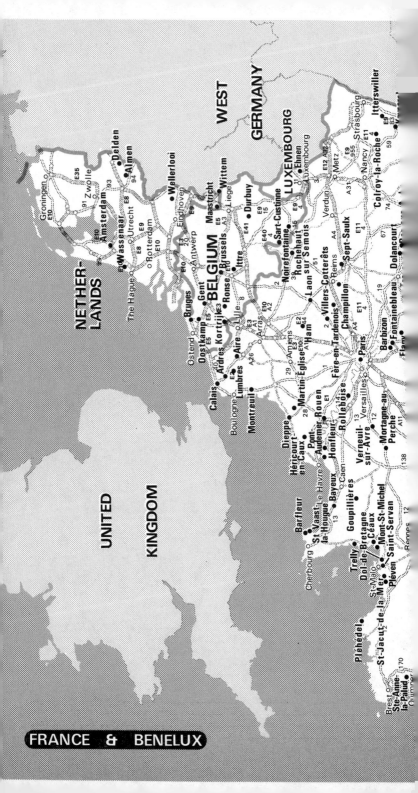

FRANCE & BENELUX

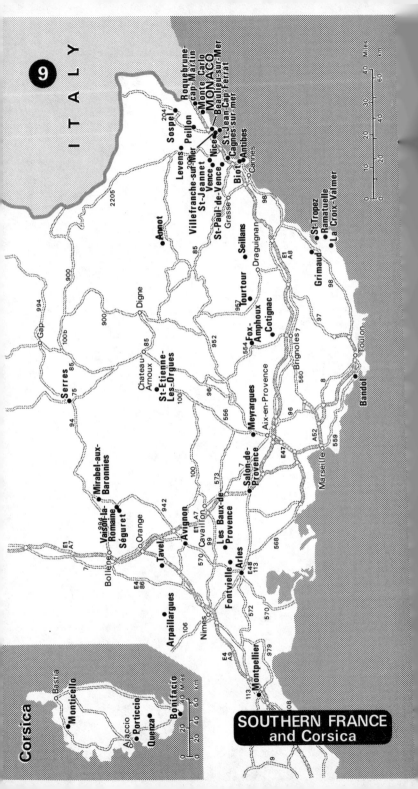

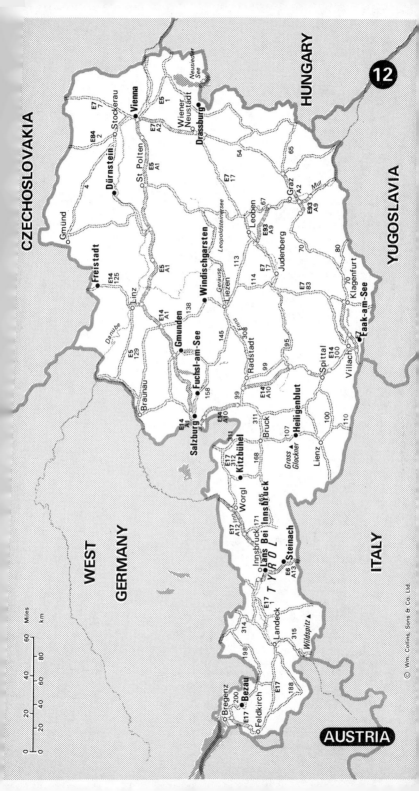

SPAIN & PORTUGAL

HUNGARY, ITALY & YUGOSLAVIA

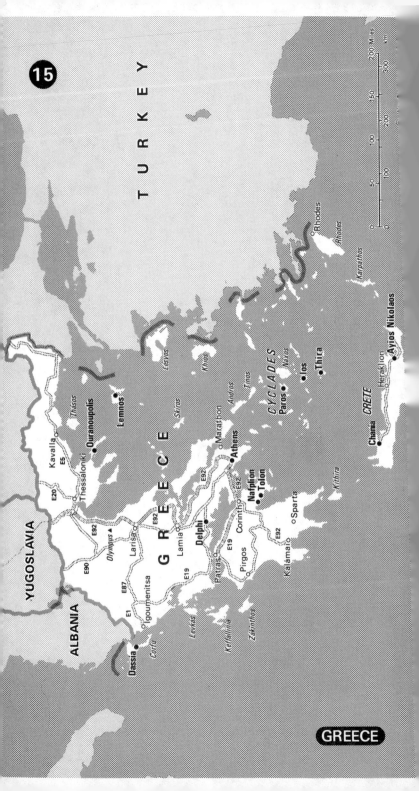

GREECE

Hotel Reports

The report forms on the following pages may be used to endorse or
blackball an existing entry or to nominate a hotel that you feel deserves
inclusion in next year's Guide. Either way, there is no need to restrict
yourself to the space available. All nominations (each on a separate piece
of paper, please) should include your name and address, the name and
location of the hotel, when you stayed there and for how long. Please
nominate only hotels you have visited in the past 18 months unless you are
sure from friends that standards have not fallen off since your stay. And
please be as specific as possible, and critical where appropriate, about the
character of the building, the public rooms, the sleeping accommodation,
the meals, the service, the night-life, the grounds. We should be glad if
you would give some impression of the location and country as well as of
the hotel itself, particularly in less familiar regions.

You should not feel embarrassed about writing at length. More than
anything else, we want the Guide to convey the special flavour of its
hotels; so the more time and trouble you can take in providing those small
details which will help to make a description come alive, the more
valuable to others will be the final published result.

There is no need to bother with prices or with routine information
about number of rooms and facilities. We obtain such details direct from
the hotels selected. What we are anxious to get from readers is information that is not accessible elsewhere, and we should be grateful, in the case
of foreign hotels, to be sent brochures if you have them available.

These report forms may also be used, if you wish, to recommend good
hotels in North America to our equivalent publication in the States,
America's Wonderful Little Hotels and Inns. They should be sent adequately stamped (no Freepost to the States), not to *The Good Hotel
Guide*, but to Barbara Crossette, Apt. 25C, 345 East 93rd Street, New
York, NY 10028, USA. And if you know of good hotels in the Caribbean,
please write to Barbara Crossette about them as well.

To: *The Good Hotel Guide,* Freepost, London W11 4BR
NOTE: No stamps needed in UK, but letters posted outside the UK should be addressed to 61 Clarendon Road, London W11 4JE and stamped normally.

Name of Hotel _____

Address _____

_____

Date of most recent visit _____ Duration of visit _____
☐ New recommendation ☐ Comment on existing entry
Report:

**(Continue overleaf if you
wish or use separate sheet)**

Signed _____

Name and address (Capitals please) _____

_____

NOTE: Unless asked not to, we shall assume that we may publish your name if you are recommending a new hotel or supporting an existing entry, and, in appropriate cases, that we may share your report with the *Good Food Guide*.

To: *The Good Hotel Guide,* Freepost, London W11 4BR
NOTE: No stamps needed in UK, but letters posted outside the UK should be addressed to 61 Clarendon Road, London W11 4JE and stamped normally.

Name of Hotel _____

Address _____

_____

Date of most recent visit _____ Duration of visit _____
☐ New recommendation   ☐ Comment on existing entry
Report:

(Continue overleaf if you wish or use separate sheet)
Signed _____

Name and address (Capitals please) _____

_____

NOTE: Unless asked not to, we shall assume that we may publish your name if you are recommending a new hotel or supporting an existing entry, and, in appropriate cases, that we may share your report with the *Good Food Guide.*

To: *The Good Hotel Guide,* Freepost, London W11 4BR
NOTE: No stamps needed in UK, but letters posted outside the UK should be addressed to 61 Clarendon Road, London W11 4JE and stamped normally.

Name of Hotel _____

Address _____

_____

Date of most recent visit _____ Duration of visit _____
☐ New recommendation   ☐ Comment on existing entry
Report:

**(Continue overleaf if you
wish or use separate sheet)**

Signed _____

Name and address (Capitals please) _____

_____

NOTE: Unless asked not to, we shall assume that we may publish your name if you are recommending a new hotel or supporting an existing entry, and, in appropriate cases, that we may share your report with the *Good Food Guide.*

HOTEL REPORTS

To: *The Good Hotel Guide,* Freepost, London W11 4BR
NOTE: No stamps needed in UK, but letters posted outside the UK should
be addressed to 61 Clarendon Road, London W11 4JE and stamped
normally.

Name of Hotel _____

Address _____

_____

Date of most recent visit _____ Duration of visit _____
☐ New recommendation ☐ Comment on existing entry
Report:

**(Continue overleaf if you
wish or use separate sheet)**
Signed _____

Name and address (Capitals please) _____

_____

NOTE: Unless asked not to, we shall assume that we may publish your
name if you are recommending a new hotel or supporting an existing
entry, and, in appropriate cases, that we may share your report with the
Good Food Guide.

To: *The Good Hotel Guide,* Freepost, London W11 4BR
NOTE: No stamps needed in UK, but letters posted outside the UK should be addressed to 61 Clarendon Road, London W11 4JE and stamped normally.

Name of Hotel _____

Address _____

_____

Date of most recent visit _____ Duration of visit _____
☐ New recommendation ☐ Comment on existing entry
Report:

**(Continue overleaf if you
wish or use separate sheet)**

Signed _____

Name and address (Capitals please) _____

_____ _____

NOTE: Unless asked not to, we shall assume that we may publish your name if you are recommending a new hotel or supporting an existing entry, and, in appropriate cases, that we may share your report with the *Good Food Guide.*

To: *The Good Hotel Guide,* Freepost, London W11 4BR
NOTE: No stamps needed in UK, but letters posted outside the UK should be addressed to 61 Clarendon Road, London W11 4JE and stamped normally.

Name of Hotel _____

Address _____

_____

Date of most recent visit _____ Duration of visit _____
☐ New recommendation ☐ Comment on existing entry
Report:

(Continue overleaf if you wish or use separate sheet)

Signed _____

Name and address (Capitals please) _____

NOTE: Unless asked not to, we shall assume that we may publish your name if you are recommending a new hotel or supporting an existing entry, and, in appropriate cases, that we may share your report with the *Good Food Guide.*

To: *The Good Hotel Guide,* Freepost, London W11 4BR
NOTE: No stamps needed in UK, but letters posted outside the UK should be addressed to 61 Clarendon Road, London W11 4JE and stamped normally.

Name of Hotel _____

Address _____

_____

Date of most recent visit _____ Duration of visit _____
☐ New recommendation   ☐ Comment on existing entry
Report:

(Continue overleaf if you wish or use separate sheet)

Signed _____

Name and address (Capitals please) _____

_____

NOTE: Unless asked not to, we shall assume that we may publish your name if you are recommending a new hotel or supporting an existing entry, and, in appropriate cases, that we may share your report with the *Good Food Guide.*

To: *The Good Hotel Guide,* Freepost, London W11 4BR
NOTE: No stamps needed in UK, but letters posted outside the UK should be addressed to 61 Clarendon Road, London W11 4JE and stamped normally.

Name of Hotel _____

Address _____

_____

Date of most recent visit _____ Duration of visit _____
☐ New recommendation ☐ Comment on existing entry
Report:

(Continue overleaf if you wish or use separate sheet)

Signed _____

Name and address (Capitals please) _____

_____

NOTE: Unless asked not to, we shall assume that we may publish your name if you are recommending a new hotel or supporting an existing entry, and, in appropriate cases, that we may share your report with the *Good Food Guide.*

To: *The Good Hotel Guide,* Freepost, London W11 4BR
NOTE: No stamps needed in UK, but letters posted outside the UK should be addressed to 61 Clarendon Road, London W11 4JE and stamped normally.

Name of Hotel _____

Address _____

_____

Date of most recent visit _____ Duration of visit _____
☐ New recommendation   ☐ Comment on existing entry
Report:

**(Continue overleaf if you
wish or use separate sheet)**
Signed _____

Name and address (Capitals please) _____

_____

NOTE: Unless asked not to, we shall assume that we may publish your name if you are recommending a new hotel or supporting an existing entry, and, in appropriate cases, that we may share your report with the *Good Food Guide.*

To: *The Good Hotel Guide,* Freepost, London W11 4BR
NOTE: No stamps needed in UK, but letters posted outside the UK should be addressed to 61 Clarendon Road, London W11 4JE and stamped normally.

Name of Hotel _____

Address _____

_____

Date of most recent visit _____ Duration of visit _____
☐ New recommendation   ☐ Comment on existing entry
Report:

**(Continue overleaf if you
wish or use separate sheet)**

Signed _____

Name and address (Capitals please) _____

_____

NOTE: Unless asked not to, we shall assume that we may publish your name if you are recommending a new hotel or supporting an existing entry, and, in appropriate cases, that we may share your report with the *Good Food Guide*.

HOTEL REPORTS

To: *The Good Hotel Guide,* Freepost, London W11 4BR
NOTE: No stamps needed in UK, but letters posted outside the UK should be addressed to 61 Clarendon Road, London W11 4JE and stamped normally.

Name of Hotel _____

Address _____

_____

Date of most recent visit _____ Duration of visit _____
☐ New recommendation   ☐ Comment on existing entry
Report:

(Continue overleaf if you wish or use separate sheet)

Signed _____

Name and address (Capitals please) _____

_____

NOTE: Unless asked not to, we shall assume that we may publish your name if you are recommending a new hotel or supporting an existing entry, and, in appropriate cases, that we may share your report with the *Good Food Guide*.

To: *The Good Hotel Guide,* Freepost, London W11 4BR
NOTE: No stamps needed in UK, but letters posted outside the UK should be addressed to 61 Clarendon Road, London W11 4JE and stamped normally.

Name of Hotel _____

Address _____

_____

Date of most recent visit _____ Duration of visit _____
☐ New recommendation ☐ Comment on existing entry
Report:

(Continue overleaf if you wish or use separate sheet)

Signed _____

Name and address (Capitals please) _____

_____

NOTE: Unless asked not to, we shall assume that we may publish your name if you are recommending a new hotel or supporting an existing entry, and, in appropriate cases, that we may share your report with the *Good Food Guide.*

To: *The Good Hotel Guide,* Freepost, London W11 4BR

NOTE: No stamps needed in UK, but letters posted outside the UK should be addressed to 61 Clarendon Road, London W11 4JE and stamped normally.

Name of Hotel _____

Address _____

_____

Date of most recent visit _____ Duration of visit _____

☐ New recommendation   ☐ Comment on existing entry

Report:

(Continue overleaf if you wish or use separate sheet)

Signed _____

Name and address (Capitals please) _____

_____

NOTE: Unless asked not to, we shall assume that we may publish your name if you are recommending a new hotel or supporting an existing entry, and, in appropriate cases, that we may share your report with the *Good Food Guide.*

HOTEL REPORTS

To: *The Good Hotel Guide,* Freepost, London W11 4BR
NOTE: No stamps needed in UK, but letters posted outside the UK should be addressed to 61 Clarendon Road, London W11 4JE and stamped normally.

Name of Hotel _____

Address _____

_____

Date of most recent visit _____ Duration of visit _____
☐ New recommendation   ☐ Comment on existing entry
Report:

(Continue overleaf if you wish or use separate sheet)

Signed _____

Name and address (Capitals please) _____

_____

NOTE: Unless asked not to, we shall assume that we may publish your name if you are recommending a new hotel or supporting an existing entry, and, in appropriate cases, that we may share your report with the *Good Food Guide*.